Europe in figures

Eurostat yearbook 2011

More information on the European Union is available on the Internet (http://europa.eu).

Cataloguing data can be found at the end of this publication.

Luxembourg: Publications Office of the European Union, 2011

ISBN 978-92-79-18414-7

ISSN 1681-4789

doi:10.2785/12017

Cat. No KS-CD-11-001-EN-C

Theme: General and regional statistics
Collection: Statistical books

Printed in Belgium

PRINTED ON ELEMENTAL CHLORINE-FREE BLEACHED PAPER (ECF)

Foreword

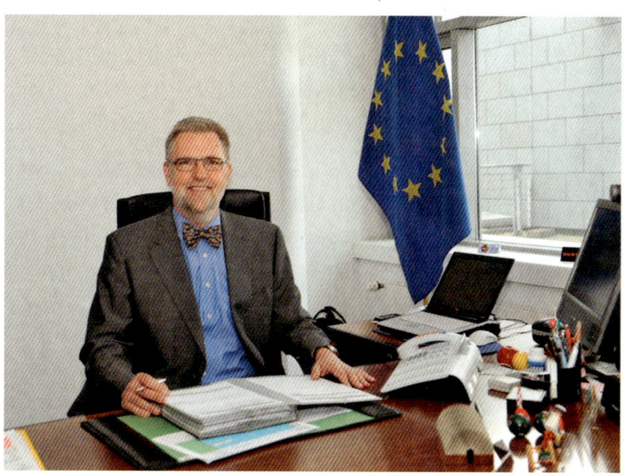

Our yearbook *Europe in figures* provides you with a selection of the most important and interesting statistics on Europe. Drawing from the huge amount of data available at Eurostat, we aim to give an insight into the European economy, society and environment - for example, how the population of the European Union is changing, how the economy is performing in comparison with the USA or Japan, or how living conditions vary between Member States. I hope that you will find information of interest both for your work and for your daily life.

In 2011, for the first time, you can find the content of this book updated online in *Statistics Explained*. As usual, the latest and most complete versions of all the data can be downloaded from the Eurostat website.

Eurostat is the statistical office of the European Union. Working together with national statistical authorities in the European Statistical System, we produce official statistics which meet the highest possible standards of quality.

I wish you an enjoyable reading experience!

Walter Radermacher

Director-General, Eurostat – Chief Statistician of the European Union

Abstract

Europe in figures – Eurostat yearbook 2011 – presents a comprehensive selection of statistical data on Europe. The yearbook may be viewed as an introduction to European statistics and provides guidance to the vast range of data freely available from the Eurostat website at: http://ec.europa.eu/eurostat.

Most data cover the period 1999-2009 for the European Union and some indicators are provided for other countries, such as members of EFTA, candidate countries to the European Union, Japan or the United States (subject to availability). With more than 420 statistical tables, figures and maps, the yearbook treats the following areas: economy and finance; population; health; education and training; the labour market; living conditions and social protection; industry, trade and services; agriculture, forestry and fisheries; international trade; transport; the environment; energy; and science and technology.

Editor-in-chief

Jukka Piirto

Eurostat, Unit D4 - Dissemination

Editors

Annika Johansson, Veronika Lang

Eurostat, Unit D4 - Dissemination

Contact details

Eurostat

Bâtiment Joseph Bech

5, rue Alphonse Weicker

2721 Luxembourg

E-mail: estat-user-support@ec.europa.eu

Production

This publication was produced by Informa sàrl

For more information please consult

Internet: http://ec.europa.eu/eurostat

Data extracted

September to December 2010 (unless otherwise noted)

Acknowledgements

The editor-in-chief and the editorial team of the Eurostat yearbook would like to thank all those who were involved in its preparation. The yearbook could only be published thanks to the support of the following colleagues:

Eurostat, the statistical office of the European Union

Directorate C: National and European accounts

C2 National accounts – production: Daniela Comini, Christine Gerstberger, Andreas Krüger, Olaf Nowak

C3 Statistics for excessive deficit procedure I: Rasa Jurkonienė

C4 Statistics for excessive deficit procedure II: John Verrinder

C5 Government and sector accounts; financial indicators: Isabel Gancedo Vallina, Boryana Milusheva, Peter Parlasca, Irena Tvarijonavičiūtė, Laura Wahrig, Ismael Ahamdanech Zarco

Directorate D: External cooperation, communication and key indicators

D4 Dissemination: Marc Debusschere, Isabelle Fiasse, Diana Ivan, Ulrich Wieland

D5 Key indicators for European policies: Viktoria Bolla, Rosa Ruggeri Cannata, Graham Lock, Iliyana Savova, Vincent Tronet

Directorate E: Sectoral and regional statistics

E1 Farms, agro-environment and rural development: Ludivine Baudouin, Catherine Coyette, Carla Martins, Anne Miek Kremer

E2 Agriculture and fisheries: Marco Artico, Steffie Bos, Fausto Cardoso, Giovanni Dore, Matthew Elliott, Henri-François Fank, Annabelle Jansen, Jean-Claude Jeanty, Werner Kerschenbauer, Garry Mahon, Pol Marquer, Angelo Milella, Iulia Pop, Henri Risch, Herta Schenk, Sorina Carmen Vâju, Franco Zampogna

E3 Environmental and forestry statistics: David Duquesnes, Manon Elsen, Jürgen Förster, Christian Freudenberger, Christian Heidorn, Jean Klein, Csaba Mózes, Hartmut Schrör, Marilise Wolf-Crowther

E5 Energy: Antigone Gikas, John Görten

E6 Transport: Luciano De Angelis, Jonas Noreland

E7 Environmental accounts and climate change: Velina Pendolovska, Cristina Popescu, Stela Stamatova

Directorate F: Social and information society statistics

F1 Population: Monica Marcu, Fabio Sartori

F2 Labour market: Verónica Álvarez González, Luis Biedma, Simone Casali, Beate Czech, Arturo de la Fuente Nuño, Sabine Gagel, Daniele Giovannola, Hannah Kiiver, Ingo Kuhnert, Hubertus Vreeswijk

F3 Living conditions and social protection: Petrica Badea, Paulina Hojny, Anna Rybkowska

F4 Education, science and culture: Ilcho Bechev, Marta Beck-Domżalska, Sadiq Kwesi Boateng, Silvia Crintea, Bernard Felix, Dominique Groenez, Ángeles Hermosa-López, Sylvain Jouhette, Lene Mejer, Sergiu Pârvan, Reni Petkova, Fernando Reis, Veijo Ritola, Paolo Turchetti

F5 Health and food safety; crime: Hartmut Buchow, Marta Carvalhido da Silva, Elodie Cayotte, Albane Gourdol, Dorota Kawiorska, Bart De Norre, Jean-Marc Pascal Schaefer, Cynthia Tavares, Geoffrey Thomas

F6 Information society; tourism: Christophe Demunter, Chryssanthi Dimitrakopoulou, Konstantinos Giannakouris, Anna Lööf, Peter Pospíšil, Petronela Reinecke, Heidi Seybert, Maria Smihily, Albrecht Wirthmann

Directorate G: Business statistics

G2 Structural business statistics: Aleksandra Stawińska, Brian Williams

G3 Short-term statistics: Ulrich Eidmann

G4 International transactions: Luis Antonio de la Fuente, Gilberto Gambini, Franca Faes-Cannito

G6 Price statistics; purchasing power parities: Jarko Pasanen, Tatiana Mrlianová, Paul Konijn, Lars Svennebye

European Free Trade Association (EFTA)

Directorate-General for Translation of the European Commission

Publications Office of the European Union

Contents

Introduction

The Eurostat yearbook

Europe in figures – Eurostat yearbook 2011 provides users of official statistics with an overview of the wealth of information that is available on Eurostat's website and within its online databases. It belongs to a set of general compendium publications and, of these, it provides the most extensive set of analyses and detailed data. Europe in figures has been conceived as a publication that provides a balanced set of indicators, with a broad cross-section of information.

Structure of the publication

Europe in figures is divided into an introduction, 13 main chapters and a set of annexes. The main chapters contain data and / or background information relating to a very wide range of Eurostat data. Each subchapter starts with a commentary on the main findings, some details regarding data sources, followed by background information and policy relevance. The core of each subchapter is a set of tables and graphs that have been selected to show the wide variety of data available for that particular topic; often these include information on how important benchmark indicators have developed during recent years within the European Union (EU), the euro area (EA) and the Member States. Users will find a great deal more information when consulting the Eurostat website, which contains subject-specific publications and online databases. The publication closes with a set of annexes that contain details of classifications, a list of statistical symbols, abbreviations and acronyms, and a subject index.

Files on the Eurostat website

The Eurostat website has a dedicated section for the yearbook, which contains the PDF version of the publication as well as all tables and graphs in MS Excel format. The PDF version of the publication allows direct access through a set of hyper-links to all of the data tables and databases that were used in the production of this publication, see: http://epp.eurostat.ec.europa.eu/portal/page/portal/publications/eurostat_yearbook_2011.

Data extraction, coverage and presentation

The statistical data presented in the yearbook were extracted between September and December 2010 and represent data availability at that time. The accompanying text was drafted between October and December 2010.

Due to its complex nature, data collection, data processing and the subsequent release of information either online or in publications often means that a significant amount of time may elapse between the collection of data and its publication / release; this can vary from a few weeks in the case of short-term monthly indicators to several years for complex, ad-hoc surveys. There is a release calendar, which provides details of the schedule for releasing euro-indicators (a collection of the most important monthly and quarterly indicators), available at: http://epp.eurostat.ec.europa.eu/portal/page/portal/release_calendars/news_releases. For other data sets, the metadata provided on the Eurostat website gives information relating to the frequency of surveys and the time that may elapse before data is published / released.

The Eurostat website is constantly being updated, therefore it is likely that fresher data will have become available since the data was extracted for the production of this publication. It is possible to access the latest version of each data set through hyper-links that are provided as part of the source under each table and graph in the PDF version of the publication.

This publication usually presents information for the EU-27 (the 27 Member States of the EU), the euro area (based on 16 members), as well as the individual Member States. The order of the Member States used in the yearbook generally follows their order of protocol; in other words, the alphabetical order of the countries' names in their respective original languages; in some figures the data are ranked according to the values of a particular indicator.

The EU-27 and euro area (EA-16) aggregates are normally only provided when information for all of the countries is available, or if an estimate has been made for missing information. Any partial totals that are created are systematically footnoted. Time-series for these geographical aggregates are based on a consistent set of countries for the whole of the time period (unless otherwise indicated). In other words, although the EU only had 25 Member States since early 2004 and has only had 27 Member States since the start of 2007, the time-series for EU-27 refer to a sum or an average for all 27 countries for the whole of the period presented, as if all 27 Member States had been part of the EU in earlier periods. In a similar vein, the data for the euro area are consistently presented for the 16 members (as of December 2010), despite the later accessions of Greece, Slovenia, Cyprus and Malta, and Slovakia to the euro area. At the time of writing (late 2010), Estonia had yet to join the euro area. As the data for this publication had already been extracted and the accompanying text had already been drafted before the accession of Estonia to the euro area (1 January 2011), Estonia is excluded from the euro area aggregates presented. Unless otherwise stated, the data for the euro area covers the 16 Member States that shared the euro as a common currency as of December 2010 (Belgium, Germany, Greece, Spain, France, Ireland, Italy, Cyprus, Luxembourg, Malta, the Netherlands, Austria, Portugal, Slovenia, Slovakia and Finland).

When available, information is also presented for EFTA countries (including Iceland that is also a candidate country) and the candidate countries of Croatia, the former Yugoslav Republic of Macedonia [1] and Turkey, as well as for Japan and the United States. Note Montenegro also became a candidate country in mid-December 2010 (but has not been included in this edition). In the event that data for any of these non-member countries does not exist, then these have been excluded from tables and graphs; however, the full set of 27 Member States is maintained

(1) The name of the former Yugoslav Republic of Macedonia is shown in tables as FYR of Macedonia – this does not prejudge in any way the definitive nomenclature for this country, which is to be agreed following the conclusion of negotiations currently taking place on this subject at the United Nations.

in tables, with footnotes being added in graphs for those Member States for which information is missing.

In the event that a reference year is not available for a particular country, then efforts have been made to fill tables and graphs with previous reference years (these exceptions are footnoted); generally, an effort has been made to go back two reference periods.

Eurostat online databases contain a large amount of metadata that provides information on the status of particular values or data series. In order to improve readability, the majority of this has been omitted when constructing the tables and graphs. The following symbols are used, where necessary:

Italic	value is a forecast, provisional or an estimate and is therefore likely to change
:	not available, confidential or unreliable value
–	not applicable or zero by default
0	less than half the final digit shown and greater than real zero

Breaks in series are indicated in the footnotes provided under each table and graph.

Eurostat – the statistical office of the European Union

Eurostat is the statistical office of the European Union, situated in Luxembourg. Its task is to provide the EU with statistics at a European level that enable comparisons between countries and regions. Eurostat's mission is '*to provide the European Union with a high-quality statistical information service*'.

As one of the Directorate-Generals of the European Commission, Eurostat is headed by a Director-General. Under him are seven Directors responsible for different areas of activity (Directorates as of December 2010):

- Cooperation in the European statistical system; resources;
- Quality, methodology and information systems;
- National and European accounts;
- External cooperation, communication and key indicators;
- Sectoral and regional statistics;
- Social and information society statistics;
- Business statistics.

In 2011, Eurostat had around 900 posts; of these some 75 % were civil servants or temporary agents, while contract agents and seconded national experts represented 20 % of the staff, leaving 5 % with other types of contract. Eurostat's executed budget was EUR 79 million in 2010 (excluding costs of statutory staff and administrative expenses) of which EUR 51 million was used for the implementation of the Community statistical programme 2008-2012, almost EUR 7 million was used for the implementation of the modernisation of European enterprise and trade statistics (MEETS), while EUR 21 million was sub-delegated to Eurostat by other Directorates-General.

Since the creation of a European statistical body in 1952, there has always been a realisation that the planning and implementation of European policies must be based on reliable and comparable statistics. As a result, the European statistical system (ESS) was built-up gradually to provide comparable statistics for the EU. For this purpose, Eurostat does not work alone, as the ESS comprises Eurostat and the statistical offices, ministries, agencies and central banks that collect official statistics in the Member States.

Regulation (EC) No 223/2009 [2] of the European Parliament and of the Council of 11 March 2009 on European statistics established a new legal framework for the development, production and dissemination of European statistics. The Regulation states that European statistics shall be developed in conformity with the statistical principles set out in Article 285(2) of the Amsterdam Treaty, namely, that: '*the production of Community statistics shall conform to impartiality, reliability, objectivity, scientific independence, cost-effectiveness and statistical confidentiality; it shall not entail excessive burdens on economic operators*'.

Article 7 of the Regulation establishes the European statistical system committee (ESSC), which is at the heart of the ESS, stating the Committee '*shall provide professional guidance to the ESS for developing, producing and disseminating European statistics*'. The ESSC is chaired by the European Commission (Eurostat) and composed of representatives from the national statistical institutes of the Member States. The national statistical institutes of EEA-EFTA countries participate as observers, as may representatives of other European / international bodies, for example, the ECB or the OECD.

To meet the challenges associated with the adoption of the Regulation, Eurostat aims:

- to provide other European institutions and the governments of the Member States with the information needed to implement, monitor and evaluate Community policies;
- to disseminate statistics to the European public and enterprises and to all economic and social agents involved in decision-making;
- to implement a set of standards, methods and organisational structures which allow comparable, reliable and relevant statistics to be produced throughout the Community, in line with the principles of the European statistics code of practice;
- to improve the functioning of European statistical system (ESS), to support the Member States, and to assist in the development of statistical systems on international level.

Eurostat and its partners in the ESS aim to provide high-quality, impartial, reliable and comparable statistical data. Indeed, access to reliable and high-quality statistics and Eurostat's obligation for trustworthiness is enshrined in law. European statistics should be provided to all types of users on the basis of equal opportunities, such that public administrations, researchers, trade unions, students, businesses and political parties, among others, can access data freely and easily. Access to the most recent statistics, as well as an expanding archive

(2) For more information: http://eur-lex.europa.eu/LexUriServ/LexUriServ.do?uri=OJ:L:2009:087:0164:0173:en:PDF.

of information, is guaranteed through free access to Eurostat databases on its website.

The data collected, harmonised and reported upon by Eurostat have been agreed through a well-defined political process at the European level in which the Member States are deeply involved. Most surveys and data collection exercises are based on European regulations or directives that are legally binding. In order to be able to produce comparable statistics between countries there needs to be a common '*statistical language*'. This language has to embrace concepts, methods and definitions, as well as technical standards and infrastructures, often referred to by statisticians as harmonisation. Indeed, this is one of Eurostat's key roles - leading and organising this standardisation process.

In order to provide a guarantee of the professional independence of the implementation of the European statistics code of practice, the European statistical governance advisory board (ESGAB) was set up; it is composed of seven independent members and met for the first time in March 2009.

The European statistical advisory committee (ESAC) is composed of 24 members representing users, respondents and other stakeholders of European statistics (including the scientific community, social partners and civil society), as well as institutional users (the European Council and the European Parliament). This committee is entrusted with ensuring that user requirements as well as the response burden on information providers and producers are taken into account when developing statistical programmes.

A practical guide to accessing European statistics

The simplest way of accessing Eurostat's broad range of statistical information is through the Eurostat website (http://ec.europa.eu/eurostat). Eurostat provides users with free access to its databases and all of its publications in PDF format via the Internet. The website is updated twice per day and gives access to the latest and most comprehensive statistical information available on the EU, its Member States, EFTA countries, and candidate countries.

For full access to all of the services available through Eurostat's website, it is recommended that users should take a few minutes to register from the homepage. Registration is free of charge and allows access to:

- tailor-made e-mail alerts providing information on new publications or statistics as soon as they are online;
- enhanced functionalities of the databases (for example, user are able to save data queries and make bulk downloads).

The information on Eurostat's website under the heading of 'Statistics' is structured according to a set of 'themes', which may be accessed from the 'Statistics' tab that is consistently present near the top of each webpage; it provides links to:

- EU policy indicators (see the end of this introduction for more details);
- general and regional statistics;
- economy and finance;
- population and social conditions;
- industry, trade and services;
- agriculture and fisheries;
- external trade;
- transport;
- environment and energy;
- science and technology.

For each of these themes, the user is presented with a range of different sub-topics – for example, within the population and social conditions theme there are sub-topics for: population; health; education and training; the labour market; income, social inclusion and living conditions; social protection; household budget surveys; crime and criminal justice; and culture. These sub-topics are presented as hyper-links that take the user to a dedicated section on the subject, with information generally presented for data (main tables and databases), publications, legislation, methodology and other background information.

Access to data

Data navigation tree

The majority of Eurostat's statistics may be accessed from the data navigation tree, at: http://epp.eurostat.ec.europa.eu/portal/page/portal/statistics/search_database; alternatively, there is an icon at the right-hand end of the top menu bar on each webpage that can be used to switch to the data navigation tree.

The data navigation tree is based on the statistical themes presented above and is collapsible and expandable. It has three main branches:

Database by themes which contains the full range of public data available on the Eurostat website. These data are presented in multi-dimensional tables with selection features that allow tailor-made presentations and extractions. The interface for databases is called the Data Explorer (icon) and this provides an intuitive way to select and organise information. Data can be downloaded (icon) from the Data Explorer in various formats (XLS, TXT, HTML, PC AXIS, SPSS and TSV).

Tables by themes which offers a selection of the most important Eurostat data in a user-friendly way. All data are presented in simple two- or three-dimensional tables, generally with European aggregates and data for the Member States on the y-axis and time on the x-axis. Tables can be viewed using an interface called TGM – tables, graphs and maps (icon) – where data can be visualised as graphs or maps in addition to a standard, tabular presentation. Data can be downloaded (icon) from TGM in various formats (XLS, HTML, XML and TSV).

Tables on EU policy which also provide access to pre-defined tables; these have particular relevance for tracking the progress being made by the EU as a whole and by the Member States in relation to some of the most important policy areas. This section of the website covers indicators in relation to short-term indicators, structural indicators, sustainable development indicators, globalisation indicators, employment and social policy indicators, and EU 2020 indicators. The tools for viewing and extracting data are the same as those described above for tables by themes.

The data navigation tree also has two special branches, where new items or recently updated items (from all databases and tables) can be displayed according to a set of user preferences (criteria set by the user).

Eurostat online data code(s) – easy access to the freshest data

Eurostat online data codes, such as tps00001 and nama_gdp_c (³), allow the reader to easily access the most recent data on Eurostat's website. In this yearbook these online data codes are given as part of the source below each table and figure.

In the PDF version of this publication, the reader is led directly to the freshest data when clicking on the hyper-links for Eurostat online data codes. Readers of the paper version can access the freshest data by typing a standardised hyper-link into a web browser, http://ec.europa.eu/eurostat/product?code=<data_code>&mode=view, where <data_code> is to be replaced by the online data code in question. The data is presented either in the TGM or the Data Explorer interface.

Online data codes can also be fed into the 'Search' function on Eurostat's website, which is found in the upper-right corner of the Eurostat homepage, at http://ec.europa.eu/eurostat.

The results from such a search present related dataset(s) and possibly publication(s) and metadata. By clicking on these hyper-links users are taken to product page(s) (⁴), which provide some background information about each dataset / publication or set of metadata. For example, it is possible to move directly to the data from the data product page by clicking the TGM or Data Explorer icons presented under the 'View table' sub-heading.

Note that the data on the Eurostat's website is frequently updated.

Note also that the description above presents the situation as of December 2010.

Policy indicators

Aside from the main tables and databases, there exists a group of policy indicators that may be accessed from the 'Statistics' tab, covering:

- Europe 2020 indicators;
- euro-indicators / Principal European Economic Indicators (PEEIs);
- sustainable development indicators;
- employment, social policy and equality indicators;
- globalisation indicators.

More details on each of these are provided at the end of this introduction.

Statistics Explained

Statistics Explained is part of the Eurostat website – it provides easy access to Eurostat's statistical information. It can be accessed via a link on the right-hand side of Eurostat's homepage, or directly at: http://epp.eurostat.ec.europa.eu/statistics_explained.

(³) There are two types of online data codes:
- Tables (accessed using the TGM interface) have 8-character codes, which consist of 3 or 5 letters – the first of which is 't' – followed by 5 or 3 digits, e.g. tps00001 and tsdph220.
- Databases (accessed using the Data Explorer interface) have codes that use an underscore '_' within the syntax of the code, e.g. nama_gdp_c and proj_10c2150p.

(⁴) The product page can also be accessed by using a hyper-link, for example, http://ec.europa.eu/eurostat/product?code=<data_code>, where <data_code> is to be replaced by the online data code in question.

Statistics Explained is a wiki-based system, with an approach somewhat similar to Wikipedia, that presents statistical topics in an easy to understand way. Together, the articles make up an encyclopaedia of European statistics, which is completed by a statistical glossary that clarifies the terms used. In addition, there are numerous links provided to the latest data and metadata, as well as further information, making Statistics Explained a portal for regular and occasional users alike.

In December 2010, Statistics Explained contained more than 1 000 articles and glossary items; its content and user-friendliness will be expanded regularly. Users may find articles using a set of navigational features in the left-hand menu; on the top-right menu bar of Statistics Explained it is possible to find options that make it possible, among others, to print, forward, cite, blog or share content easily.

Statistics Explained is not only a tool for presenting statistical analyses, it can also be used to produce analyses. The Eurostat Yearbook was created using Statistics Explained as a common platform, such that its content could already be consulted in Statistics Explained some time before it was published on paper.

Country profiles interface

The **country profiles interface** offers the possibility to visualise major statistical indicators, of different countries and / or EU aggregates, in a user-friendly map-based presentation. The interface can be accessed via the following link: http://epp.eurostat.ec.europa.eu/guip/introAction.do?.

Publications

Eurostat produces a variety of publications, which all are available on the Eurostat website in PDF format, free of charge. As with the 'Statistics' tab that is available at all times for accessing data, there is a 'Publications' tab that is always accessible near the top of each webpage for accessing material in PDF format.

There are a variety of different types of publication, ranging from news releases to more in-depth analyses in the form of statistical books.

Eurostat's publications programme consists of several collections:

News releases provide recent information on the euro-indicators and on social, economic, regional, agricultural or environmental topics;

Statistical books are larger publications with statistical analysis and data;

Pocketbooks are free-of-charge publications aiming to give users a set of basic figures on a specific topic;

Statistics in focus are short publications providing the most recent statistical data and complementary statistical analysis;

Methodologies & Working papers are technical publications for statistical experts working in a particular field;

Compact guides are leaflets offering basic figures and guidance on how to obtain more information from the Eurostat website.

Some Eurostat publications, including this publication in English, are also printed; these can be ordered from the website of the EU bookshop (http://bookshop.europa.eu).

There it is also possible to download Eurostat publications in PDF format, free-of-charge, as on the Eurostat website. The bookshop is managed by the Publications Office of the European Union (http://publications.europa.eu).

Reference metadata

The ESMS (Euro SDMX Metadata Structure) is a format based on the Statistical Data and Metadata eXchange (SDMX) Content Oriented Guidelines, which were adopted in January 2009 by seven international organisations at a worldwide level. The ESMS uses a subset of 21 cross domain concepts (plus sub-concepts) and is the new standard for reference metadata in the ESS. It puts emphasis on quality-related information (containing concepts such as accuracy, comparability, coherence and timeliness).

Reference metadata may be accessed either from the heading 'Metadata' which appears in the left-hand menu after selecting the 'Statistics' tab, or directly from the data navigation tree, where the following icon is used to signify its availability.

User support

Eurostat and the other members of the ESS have set up a system of user support centres – European Statistical Data Support (ESDS). These exist for nearly all of the EU's official languages, as well as for the EFTA and candidate countries; there are also plans to extend the user support service to cover those languages spoken in the Western Balkans.

In order to offer the best possible and personalised support, requests should, whenever possible, be addressed to the relevant language support centre. The mission of each centre is to provide free of charge additional help and guidance to users who are having difficulty in finding the statistical data they require. The list and addresses of all support centres can be reached via the User support-TAB on Eurostat's homepage.

Specific requests can be addressed to this network, via the Eurostat website at: http://epp.eurostat.ec.europa.eu/portal/page/portal/help/user_support (requires a user log-in).

Eurostat's service for journalists

Statistics make news and they are essential to many stories, features and in-depth analyses. Printed media, as well as radio and TV, use Eurostat data intensively. Eurostat's press office puts out user-friendly news releases on a key selection of data covering the EU, the euro area, the Member States and their partners. All Eurostat news releases are available free of charge on the Eurostat website at 11 a.m. (C.E.T.) on the day they are released. Just over 200 news releases were published in 2010, of which approximately three quarters were based on monthly or quarterly euro-indicators; other releases covered major international events and important Eurostat publications.

Eurostat's press centre helps professional journalists find data on all kinds of topics. Journalists can contact media support for further information on news releases and other data (tel. (352) 4301-33408; e-mail: eurostat-mediasupport@ec.europa.eu).

Linking statistics to European policies

Effective economic and political decision-making depends on the regular supply of reliable information. Statistics are one of the principle sources of such information, providing quantitative support to the development and implementation of policies. Statistics are also a powerful tool for communicating with the general public.

Information needs for policy purposes require constant interaction between policymakers and statisticians: the former formulate their needs for data, and the latter attempt to adapt the statistical production system so as to fulfil those needs. In this fashion, new policies lead to improvements in statistical production, both in terms of enhancing the quality of existing indicators and of creating new ones.

Whereas politicians ask for highly aggregated indicators which provide a synthetic and clear picture of the different phenomena they are interested in, statisticians tend to deal with detailed data. Statisticians therefore have to filter and aggregate basic data in order to increase data readability and extract signals (in other words indicators).

Over recent years, a number of policies have substantially influenced Eurostat's priorities and activities:

- economic and monetary union (EMU) and the creation of the euro area (1999);
- the Lisbon strategy (2000, revised in 2005), including the open method of coordination on social inclusion and social protection;
- the EU's sustainable development strategy, EU SDS (2001, renewed in 2006);
- the Europe 2020 strategy (2010), the successor to the Lisbon strategy.

Economic and monetary union and the setting-up of the European Central Bank (ECB) required a broad range of infra-annual short-term statistics to measure economic and monetary developments within the euro area and to assist in the implementation of a common monetary policy. Effective monetary policy depends on timely, reliable and comprehensive economic statistics giving an overview of the economic situation. Such data are also needed for the assessment of the business cycle.

Europeans place a high value on their quality of life, including aspects such as a clean environment, social protection, prosperity and equity. In recent years the European Council has focused on a number of key areas intended to shape the future social, economic and environmental development of the EU. While Europe 2020 is the EU's strategy for smart, sustainable and inclusive growth for the next decade, the sustainable development strategy is concerned with improving the quality of life and well-being, both for current and future generations, through seeking a balance between economic development, social cohesion and protection of the environment.

Eurostat has responded to politicians needs in these areas by developing five sets of 'EU policy indicators' that may be accessed through dedicated sections on the Eurostat website either directly from the homepage or from the 'Statistics' tab that appears near the top of every

webpage. These five sets of data may be summarised as:

- **Europe 2020 indicators**, which are the headline indicators for the Europe 2020 strategy. This strategy has five EU headline targets which are currently measured by eight headline indicators. Europe 2020 indicators are available on the Eurostat website at: http://epp.eurostat.ec.europa.eu/portal/page/portal/europe_2020_indicators/headline_indicators.
- **euro-indicators**, of which the Principal European Economic Indicators (PEEIs) are the core, for monetary policy purposes; this is a collection of monthly and quarterly data, useful to evaluate the economic situation within the euro area and the EU. Euro-indicators are available on the Eurostat website at: http://ec.europa.eu/eurostat/euroindicators.
- **sustainable development indicators**, for the EU's sustainable development strategy extend across a wide range of issues affecting the quality of life, in particular looking at ways to reconcile economic development, social cohesion and the protection of the environment. Sustainable development indicators are available on the Eurostat website at: http://ec.europa.eu/eurostat/sustainabledevelopment.
- **employment, social policy and equality indicators**, for monitoring and reporting in relation to employment, social policy and equality. These indicators are designed to address a range of different issues, such as employment guidelines, the open method of coordination on social inclusion and social protection, the education and training programme, i2010 (the European information society for growth and employment) and (gender) equality. Employment, social policy and equality indicators are available on the Eurostat website at: http://epp.eurostat.ec.europa.eu/portal/page/portal/employment_social_policy_equality/introduction.
- **globalisation indicators** comprise a portfolio of 25 indicators, grouped into five categories, that measure different aspects of globalisation. The main focus is to show the EU's relations with the rest of the world and, wherever possible, the situation within the EU to allow both the extent of internal EU integration and the extent of its globalisation to be grasped. Globalisation indicators are available on the Eurostat website at: http://epp.eurostat.ec.europa.eu/portal/page/portal/globalisation/indicators.

Europe 2020 indicators

The Europe 2020 strategy is the EU's new strategy to develop as a smarter, knowledge based, greener economy, delivering high levels of employment, productivity and social cohesion; it is the successor to the Lisbon strategy.

In March 2010 the European Council agreed on the key areas of the strategy where action is needed: knowledge and innovation, a more sustainable economy, high employment and social inclusion. The Council also agreed on ambitious objectives – on employment, innovation, education, social inclusion and climate / energy – to be reached by 2020. To measure progress in meeting these objectives five headline targets have been agreed for the whole EU – this limited set of targets is being translated into national targets for each EU country, reflecting the specific situation of each economy.

Statistics are an integral part of the Europe 2020 strategy. The headline indicators measure the progress made by the EU and the Member States towards achieving the headline targets of the strategy.

Employment:

- 75 % of the population aged 20-64 should be employed.

R&D / innovation:

- 3 % of the EU's GDP (public and private combined) should be invested in R & D.

Climate change / energy:

- greenhouse gas emissions should be reduced by at least 20 % compared to 1990;
- the share of renewable energy sources in final energy consumption should increase to 20 %;
- there should be a 20 % increase in energy efficiency.

Education:

- the share of early school leavers from education and training should be under 10 %;
- at least 40 % of 30-34–year-olds should have completed tertiary (or equivalent) education.

Poverty / social exclusion:

- at least 20 million people should be lifted from being in or at risk of poverty or social exclusion.

The targets cover the main areas where efforts are rapidly needed. The statistical data collected will help to measure the progress achieved in implementing the strategy for the EU to become a smart, sustainable and inclusive economy. As part of the process, Member States draw up national reform programmes which set out in detail the actions they will take under the new strategy, with a particular emphasis on efforts to meet their national targets. The European Council will assess every year the overall progress achieved both at an EU and at a national level in implementing the strategy.

Euro-indicators / PEEIs

Since October 2001 the euro-indicators / PEEIs web pages have been a reference point for all users of official statistics dealing with short-term data. They were initially conceived as an independent website, available in parallel to the Eurostat website; however, since October 2004, they have been integrated with the remaining content. It is possible to access euro-indicators / PEEIs data from the 'Statistics' tab visible in the menu near the top of the screen on each webpage, or directly via the euro-indicators / PEEIs dedicated section at: http://ec.europa.eu/eurostat/euroindicators. It is also possible to e-mail the euro-indicators / PEEIs team at: ESTAT-EUROINDICATORS@ec.europa.eu.

Euro-indicators / PEEIs aim to supply business-cycle analysts, policymakers, media, researchers, students, and other interested users with a comprehensive, well structured and high quality set of information which is useful for their daily activities. The core of euro-indicators / PEEIs comprises a set of statistical indicators giving an accurate and as timely as possible overview of the economic evolution of the euro area, the EU, and the individual Member States. The euro-indicators / PEEIs dedicated section contains the following additional products and services intended to assist in the understanding and analysis of data:

- selected Principal European Economic Indicators (PEEIs);
- background;
- news releases;
- status reports on information requirements in the European monetary union (EMU);
- data;
- publications;
- information relating to seminars / conferences.

Data

The data presented in euro-indicators / PEEIs are built around a set of the most relevant statistics, called Principal European Economic Indicators (PEEIs), a list of which can be found in the European Commission's Communication (2002) 661 (5). They are presented in three main parts:

- a selected Principal European Economic Indicators webpage (containing a set of 22 most relevant and timely short-term economic indicators for the euro area and the EU) directly accessible on the euro-indicators / PEEIs homepage;
- short-term indicators (included as the first branch of the 'Tables on EU policy' section of the data navigation tree);
- European and national short-term statistics database (included as the first branch of the 'Database by themes' section of the data navigation tree – under the heading of 'General and regional statistics' – as European and national short term indicators (euroind).

(5) For more information: http://eur-lex.europa.eu/LexUriServ/LexUriServ.do?uri=COM:2002:0661:FIN:EN:PDF.

European Union *
Euro Area **

Print

	Release date latest	next	Unit	Reference period					
				2009q2	2009q3	2009q4	2010q1	2010q2	2010q3
GDP in volume	02/12/2010	07/01/2011	% (Q/Q-1)	-0.3	0.3	0.3	0.4	1.0	0.5
			% (Q/Q-4)	-5.6	-4.0	-1.9	0.8	2.5	2.2
Private final consumption in volume	02/12/2010	07/01/2011	% (Q/Q-1)	-0.1	-0.2	0.4	0.3	0.3	0.3
			% (Q/Q-4)	-2.2	-1.8	-0.6	0.3	0.8	1.0
Investments in volume	02/12/2010	07/01/2011	% (Q/Q-1)	-2.9	-0.9	-1.3	-0.5	2.1	0.2
			% (Q/Q-4)	-14.2	-12.1	-9.8	-5.2	0.4	1.2
				2010m6	2010m7	2010m8	2010m9	2010m10	2010m11
External trade balance	17/12/2010	14/01/2011	mio euro	-14539.8	-12291.8	-14249.3	-11689.6	-7688.8	(:)
				2009q2	2009q3	2009q4	2010q1	2010q2	2010q3
Current account- Total	10/12/2010	21/01/2011	mio euro	-42121	-19285	-10018	-31787	-37122	-25521
				2010m6	2010m7	2010m8	2010m9	2010m10	2010m11
Inflation (HICP all items)	16/12/2010	14/01/2011	% (M/M-1)	0.0	-0.2	0.2	0.2	0.3	0.2
			% (M/M-12)	1.9	2.1	2.0	2.2	2.3	2.3
				2010m6	2010m7	2010m8	2010m9	2010m10	2010m11
Unemployment rate - Total	30/11/2010	07/01/2011	%	9.6	9.6	9.5	9.6	9.6	(:)
Unemployment rate - 15-24 years	30/11/2010	07/01/2011	%	20.5	20.4	20.3	20.4	20.4	(:)
Unemployment rate - above 24 years	30/11/2010	07/01/2011	%	8.3	8.3	8.3	8.3	8.3	(:)
				2009q2	2009q3	2009q4	2010q1	2010q2	2010q3
Labour Cost Index	16/12/2010	16/03/2011	% (Q/Q-1)	1.5	0.4	0.5	-0.1	0.7	0.2
			% (Q/Q-4)	3.6	2.8	2.2	2.1	1.5	1.2
Employment	15/12/2010	15/03/2011	% (Q/Q-1)	-0.7	-0.5	-0.2	-0.1	0.1	0.0
			% (Q/Q-4)	-1.9	-2.1	-2.0	-1.5	-0.6	-0.2

Both the main tables for short-term indicators and the Euroind database are divided into the following eight domains:

- balance of payments;
- business and consumer surveys;
- consumer prices;
- external trade;
- industry, commerce and services;
- labour market;
- monetary and financial indicators;
- national accounts.

Publications and working papers

The main publication in this domain is called 'Eurostatistics'. It is a monthly release that presents a synthetic picture of the economic situation together with detailed statistical analysis of the latest economic events for the euro area, the EU, and the Member States. This monthly review gives a synthetic picture of the recent macroeconomic situation. It is based on PEEIs, which are complemented

by some business cycle indicators. The latest issue of 'Eurostatistics' is accessible from the homepage of the euro-indicators / PEEIs dedicated section. Previous issues are also accessible – by selecting the 'publications' entry in the left-hand menu of the euro-indicators / PEEIs dedicated section and then clicking on the link to 'Official publications'. Under the same heading of 'publications', users may also access a collection of 'selected readings' and 'working papers', containing both methodological and empirical studies on statistical improvements and analyses of European data.

Quality reports

Since 2001, the Euroind database has been subject to monthly quality monitoring. The results of this assessment are presented in a detailed online publication called 'State of affairs', also accessible from the 'publications' link in the left-hand menu of the euro-indicators / PEEIs dedicated section. A synthesis of this monthly assessment is presented in another publication, entitled the 'Monitoring report', accessible from the same location.

Sustainable development indicators

The EU sustainable development strategy (EU SDS), adopted by the European Council in Gothenburg in June 2001, and renewed in June 2006, aims to continuously improve quality of life, both for current and for future generations, through reconciling economic development, social cohesion and protection of the environment. A set of sustainable development indicators (SDIs) has been developed to monitor progress in the implementation of the strategy. The indicators are organised under ten themes (and sub-themes) that reflect different political priorities (see first column of Table 2).

In order to facilitate communication, the set of indicators has been built as a three-level pyramid.

Table 1: Framework for sustainable development indicators

Indicator level	Hierarchical framework	Indicator types
Level 1	Lead objectives	11 headline indicators are at the top of the pyramid. They are intended to monitor the 'overall objectives' of the strategy. They are well-known indicators with a high communication value. They are robust and available for most EU Member States for a period of at least five years.
Level 2	SDS priority objectives	The second level of the pyramid consists of ca. 30 indicators related to the operational objectives of the strategy. They are the lead indicators in their respective subthemes. They are robust and available for most EU Member States for a period of at least three years.
Level 3	Actions/explanatory variables	The third level consists of ca. 80 indicators related to actions outlined in the strategy or to other issues which are useful to analyse progress towards the SDS objectives. Breakdowns of level-1 or -2 indicators are usually also found at level 3.
Contextual indicators	Background	Contextual indicators are part of the SDI set, but they either do not monitor directly any of the strategy's objectives or they are not policy responsive. Generally they are difficult to interpret in a normative way. However, they provide valuable background information on issues having direct relevance for sustainable development policies and are useful for the analysis.

This distinction between the three levels of indicators reflects the structure of the renewed strategy (overall lead objectives, operational priority objectives, and actions / explanatory variables) and also responds to different kinds of user needs. The three levels of the pyramid are complemented with contextual indicators, which do not monitor directly the strategy's objectives, but provide valuable background information for analysis. The SDI data set also describes indicators which are not yet fully developed but which will, in the future, be necessary to get a more complete picture of progress, differentiating between indicators that are expected to become available within some years, with sufficient quality ('indicators under development'), and those to be developed in the longer term ('indicators to be developed').

The table below presents the situation as regards the progress made with respect to the headline indicators, as presented within the 2009 edition of the Eurostat's monitoring report for the EU's sustainable development strategy (the weather symbols reflect in most cases the progress towards the EU objectives or targets between 2000 and 2007-2008). A new edition of this report should be available in the summer of 2011.

Table 2: Headline sustainable development indicators and progress being made within the EU

SDI theme	Headline indicator	EU-27 evaluation of change (since 2000)
Socioeconomic development	Growth of GDP per capita	
Climate change and energy	Greenhouse gas emissions (1)	
	Consumption of renewables	
Sustainable transport	Energy consumption of transport relative to GDP	
Sustainable consumption and production	Resource productivity	
Natural resources	Abundance of common birds (2)	
	Conservation of fish stocks (3)	
Public health	Healthy life years (4)	
Social inclusion	Risk of poverty (4)	
Demographic changes	Employment rate of older workers	
Global partnership	Official development assistance (5)	
Good governance	[No headline indicator]	:

Clearly favourable change / on target path

Moderately unfavourable change / far from target path

No or moderately favourable change / close to target path

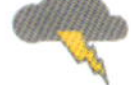

Clearly unfavourable change / moving away from target path

(1) EU-15.
(2) Based on 19 Member States.
(3) In north east Atlantic.
(4) EU-25, from 2005.
(5) From 2005.

Source: Eurostat

More information regarding sustainable development indicators may be found on the Eurostat website: http://ec.europa.eu/eurostat/sustainabledevelopment, or by contacting: estat-sdi@ec.europa.eu. There is also a comprehensive publication on the subject, 'Sustainable development in the European Union: 2009 monitoring report of the EU Sustainable Development Strategy', available at: http://ec.europa.eu/eurostat/product?code=KS-78-09-865&mode=view.

Employment, social policy and equality indicators

This collection of indicators covers various aspects of employment and social policy, as well as equality issues. The indicators are used to monitor and report upon progress being made as regards EU policies relating to:

- employment;
- social inclusion and social protection;
- education and training;
- information society;
- gender equality.

European Employment Strategy

Since the launch of the European Employment Strategy (EES) in 1997 indicators have been used for the assessment of Member States' progress on implementing the employment guidelines that have been developed under the EES, and that are proposed by the European Commission and approved by the European Council. The guidelines were most recently revised in 2010 as part of the Europe 2020 strategy.

Most of the indicators for monitoring and analysis of the employment guidelines are provided by Eurostat. However, for the time-being the coherent presentation of these indicators is under development. For more information on the list of indicators as well as the EES, please refer to the Directorate-General for Employment, Social Affairs and Inclusion website, at: http://ec.europa.eu/social/main.jsp?catId=101&langId=en.

Open method of coordination on social inclusion and social protection

The Lisbon strategy also gave rise to the open method of coordination (OMC) that provides a framework for political coordination (without legal constraints) in relation to social inclusion and social protection issues; this framework continues under the Europe 2020 strategy. The OMC is a flexible and decentralised method, which involves:

- agreeing on common objectives which set out high-level, shared goals to underpin the entire process;
- agreeing to a set of common indicators which show how progress towards these goals can be measured;
- preparing national strategic reports, in which Member States set out how they will plan policies over an agreed period to meet the common objectives;
- evaluating these strategies jointly through the European Commission and the Member States.

The indicators can be accessed directly from the Eurostat website, through the left-hand menu of the dedicated section covering employment, social policy and equality indicators, that may be found by clicking on the 'Statistics' tab near the top of the screen on each webpage. The indicators are currently divided into four strands, covering:

- overarching indicators;
- indicators of the social inclusion strand;
- indicators of the pension strand;
- indicators of the health and long term care strand.

Common indicators allow a comparison of best practices to be made and also measure progress being made towards common objectives. For more information about the open method of coordination on social inclusion and social protection, please refer to the Directorate-General for Employment, Social Affairs and Inclusion website, at: http://ec.europa.eu/social/main.jsp?catId=753&langId=en.

Education and training

To ensure their contribution to the Lisbon strategy, the ministers of education from the various Member States adopted in 2001 a report on the future objectives of education and training systems agreeing for the first time on shared objectives to be achieved by 2010. A year later, a ten-year work programme was endorsed (Education and training 2010).

As with the indicators above relating to social inclusion and social protection, these indicators are also implemented through the open method of coordination, using similar procedures to set objectives, exchange good practices, and finally to measure progress that is being made. On 25 May 2007 the Council adopted conclusions on a coherent framework of 16 core indicators for monitoring progress towards the Lisbon objectives in education and training. Indicators and methodology are available on the Eurostat website as part of the dedicated section covering employment, social policy and equality indicators.

The programme was subsequently extended to cover the period through to 2020. The long-term strategic objectives of EU education and training policies are:

- making lifelong learning and mobility a reality;
- improving the quality and efficiency of education and training;
- promoting equity, social cohesion and active citizenship;
- enhancing creativity and innovation, including entrepreneurship, at all levels of education and training.

Five new benchmark goals have already been defined for 2020, by which time:

- an average of at least 15 % of adults should participate in lifelong learning;
- the share of low-achieving 15-years olds in reading, mathematics and science should be less than 15 %;
- the share of 30-34 year olds with tertiary educational attainment should be at least 40 %;
- the share of early leavers from education and training should be less than 10 %;

- at least 95 % of children between four years of age and the age for starting compulsory primary education should participate in early childhood education.

For more information on these programmes, please refer to Directorate-General for Education and Culture website, at: http://ec.europa.eu/education/lifelong-learning-policy/doc28_en.htm.

European Information Society for growth and employment

The penultimate heading within this section covers the information society. The eEurope action plan was launched under the Lisbon strategy and included a set of benchmarking indicators on Internet and broadband take-up, as well as the use of online services. Within the context of the renewed Lisbon agenda, a strategic framework for a European information society for growth and employment (i2010) was launched. This in turn has been succeeded in 2010 by the Digital Agenda for Europe, which was launched as part of the Europe 2020 Strategy.

The benchmarking framework for measuring progress in relation to the i2010 programme was set up and approved in April 2006; it contained a set of core indicators and provides for flexible modules on specific issues to be defined each year. On 9 November 2009 a new benchmarking initiative was endorsed, providing the conceptual framework for the collection of statistics and the development of a list of core indicators through to 2015. For more information, please refer to: http://ec.europa.eu/information_society/eeurope/i2010/docs/benchmarking/benchmarking_digital_europe_2011-2015.pdf.

Annual Community surveys on ICT usage in households and by individuals are a major source of information for monitoring many of the aims of the i2010 strategy and the Digital Agenda. The data presented on Eurostat's website as part of the dedicated section covering employment and social policy indicators and referring to i2010 indicators is divided into four main themes:

- developments of broadband;
- advanced services;
- inclusion;
- public services.

For more information on the Digital Agenda, please refer to the Directorate-General for Information Society website, at: http://ec.europa.eu/information_society/digital-agenda/index_en.htm.

Gender equality

This final heading is a recent addition, covering gender equality indicators which show the situation of men and women in the EU in a variety of different areas, with statistics presented for education, the labour market, earnings, social inclusion, childcare and health. These indicators help to assess the current state of gender equality which is a fundamental objective of the EU. The indicators available on the dedicated section present just a selection of Eurostat's data which may be disaggregated according to a gender breakdown. The indicators selected have their basis in a range of policy documents covering this area, including the strategy

for equality between women and men (2010-2015), the women's charter 2010, or the roadmap for equality between women and men (2006-2010).

Equality between women and men is only one of many different types of equality which are covered by EU policy measures. The Lisbon Treaty proposes taking action to combat discrimination based on gender, race or ethnic origin, religion or belief, disability, age and sexual orientation. In some of these areas, it is difficult to gauge from statistics how far equality has been achieved, but for others information is being developed. Eurostat therefore intends to expand its collection of data in this area in order to cover these different forms of equality as and when suitable indicators may be published.

Globalisation indicators

Globalisation means the increasing interdependence and inter-linkages between nations, the increasing mobility of people, the growing flow of products, ideas and raw materials. The process of globalisation, as understood here, therefore involves social, cultural and environmental elements and goes beyond the issue of economic integration which is often the focus of globalisation indicators.

The EU has long been aware of the opportunities created by globalisation, in addition to the growing intensity of the challenges it presents. It is in this context that the Europe 2020 strategy, adopted by the European Council in 2010, aims to exploit over the next decade the potential of globalisation to boost growth and employment in the EU.

Complementary to this strategy, Europe's concerns to fulfil its international obligations to reduce poverty worldwide, and to promote global sustainable development, are addressed in the EU's sustainable development strategy; aid, international trade and investment are important tools in this respect.

While globalisation is a challenge for the EU as well as for many countries around the world, it is also a challenge for official statistics. A number of international and European initiatives concluded that current statistical measures need to be supplemented in order to better reflect the changing, globalising world. There is a strong policy and public demand for official statistics to measure globalisation. Even though not all dimensions of globalisation can be easily quantified, it is important that these phenomena are better understood with the help of proper statistical measures.

Eurostat's globalisation indicator set

The indicators can be accessed directly from the Eurostat website, through the left-hand menu of the dedicated section covering globalisation indicators, that may be found by clicking on the 'Statistics' tab near the top of the screen on each webpage. There is currently a portfolio of 25 indicators, split between five different categories that measure various aspects of globalisation. The main focus is to show the EU's relations with the rest of the world and, wherever possible, the situation within the EU to allow both the extent of internal EU integration and the extent of its globalisation to be grasped.

◉ Main dimension ○ Detailed view Print

	UNIT	BREAKDOWN	REFERENCE PERIOD				
PERSONS			2005	2006	2007	2008	2009
Non-nationals among residents	% of population	Extra EU	(:)	(:)	3.80	3.90	4.00
Non-nationals in the labour force	% of total labour force	Extra EU	3.60	3.60	3.90	4.10	(:)
Nights spent by non-EU residents inside the EU	Nights per 1000 population	Extra EU	427	459	458	456	(:)
Number of tourism nights spent abroad by residents	Nights per 1000 population	Extra EU	(:)	(:)	(:)	(:)	(:)
International air transport of passengers	per 1000 population	Extra EU	(:)	(:)	547	567	(:)
TECHNOLOGY			2005	2006	2007	2008	2009
High tech exports	% of total exports	Extra EU	18.740	16.645	15.965	15.363	(:)
High tech imports	% of total imports	Extra EU	19.461	16.831	16.174	14.713	(:)
Gross domestic expenditure on R&D (GERD)	% of GDP	-	1.82	1.85	1.85	1.92	2.01
GOODS AND SERVICES			2005	2006	2007	2008	2009
Exports of goods	% of GDP	Extra EU	(:)	(:)	(:)	(:)	(:)
Imports of goods	% of GDP	Extra EU	(:)	(:)	(:)	(:)	(:)
Exports of services	% of GDP	Extra EU	(:)	(:)	(:)	(:)	(:)
Imports of services	% of GDP	Extra EU	(:)	(:)	(:)	(:)	(:)
Intra-EU trade in goods	% of total external trade in goods	Intra EU	66	66	66	65	65
Energy dependency	% of net imports in gross inland consumption	Total	52.6	53.8	53.1	54.8	(:)
Growth of maritime transport	Growth on previous year	Total	(:)	3.1	3.4	2.8	(:)
Growth of air freight transport	Growth on previous year	Total	(:)	(:)	(:)	3.00	(:)
GLOBAL RESPONSIBILTY			2005	2006	2007	2008	2009
CO2 emissions per inhabitant in the EU and in developing countries	Tons	-	8.6	8.6	8.4	8.2	(:)
Official Development Assistance	% of gross national income	-	0.41	0.41	0.37	0.40	0.42

The selected indicators make use of data which already exist, but casting them in the light of globalisation and allowing them to be seen from a new angle. The 25 indicators which have been selected are far from exhaustive, and they do not yet cover all aspects of globalisation. The globalisation indicator set may develop further in the future. For example, Eurostat is currently working on a programme to modernise business and trade statistics and is running a project to study how to best quantify non-economic elements of globalisation.

Globalisation indicators are available on the Eurostat website at: http://epp.eurostat.ec.europa.eu/portal/page/portal/globalisation/indicators.

$700.83
$673.68
$316.40
284.48
Wool
Sateen

1

Economy and finance

Indicators from various areas, such as national accounts, government finance, exchange rates and interest rates, consumer prices, and the balance of payments support analysis of the economic situation used in the design, implementation and monitoring of European Union (EU) policies.

The EU is active in a wide range of policy areas, but economic policies have traditionally played a dominant role. Starting from a rather narrow focus on introducing common policies for coal and steel, atomic energy and agriculture as well as the creation of a customs union over 50 years ago, European economic policies progressively extended their scope to a multitude of domains.

Since 1993, the European single market has enhanced the possibilities for people, goods, services and money to move around the EU as freely as within a single country. The start of economic and monetary union (EMU) in 1999 has given economic and market integration further stimulus. The euro has become a symbol for Europe, and the number of countries that have adopted the single currency has increased from an original 11 to 16 countries by 2010.

Fostering economic and social progress, with constant improvements in living and working conditions, has also been a key objective of European policies. The strongest global financial and economic crisis since the 1930s reversed much of the economic progress made since the 2000 Lisbon strategy was adopted. In the aftermath of this crisis, in March 2010, the European Commission launched the Europe 2020 strategy for smart, sustainable and inclusive growth. Its declared objective is to overcome the effects of the crisis and prepare the EU's economy for the next decade; the integrated economic and employment guidelines have been revised within the context of this new strategy. Among the ten guidelines one aims to address macro-economic imbalances, and the other aims to reduce imbalances in the euro area. A third guideline concerns the specific issue of ensuring the quality and the sustainability of public finances (see Subchapter 1.2 on government finance statistics).

Following actions to stabilise the financial system and the economy, the recent crisis has also prompted substantial reforms of EU macro-economic, budgetary and structural surveillance. A key new element is the introduction of a European semester starting in January 2011. It will cover fiscal discipline, macro-economic stability and policies to foster growth, aligning processes under the stability and growth pact and the Europe 2020 strategy, while retaining their legal specificities. European economic statistics will play an important role in this process.

1.1 National accounts – GDP

National accounts are the source for a multitude of well-known economic indicators which are presented in this subchapter. Gross domestic product (GDP) is the most frequently used measure for the overall size of an economy, while derived indicators such as GDP per capita – for example, in euro or adjusted for differences in price levels – are widely used for a comparison of living standards, or to monitor the process of convergence across the European Union (EU).

Moreover, the development of specific GDP components and related indicators, such as those for economic output, imports and exports, domestic (private and public) consumption or investments, as well as data on the distribution of income and savings, can give valuable insights into the driving forces in an economy and thus be the basis for the design, monitoring and evaluation of specific EU policies. Economic developments in production, income generation and (re)distribution, consumption and investment may be better understood when analysed by institutional sector. In particular, sector accounts provide several key indicators for households and non-financial corporations, like the household saving rate and business profit share.

Main statistical findings

Developments in GDP

As a result of the global financial and economic crisis, the EU-27's GDP fell from EUR 12 495 000 million in 2008 to EUR 11 791 000 million in 2009. The euro area accounted for 76.0 % of this total, while the sum of the five largest EU economies (Germany, France, the United Kingdom, Italy and Spain) was 71.6 %. However, cross-country comparisons should be made with caution as notably exchange rate fluctuations may significantly influence the development of nominal GDP figures. To evaluate standards of living, it is therefore more appropriate to use GDP per capita in purchasing power standards (PPS), in other words adjusted for the size of an economy in terms of population and also for differences in price levels across countries. The average GDP per capita within the EU-27 in 2009 was PPS 23 600. The relative position of individual countries can be expressed through a comparison with this average (see Table 1.1), with the EU-27 value set to equal 100. The highest value among EU Member States was recorded for Luxembourg, where GDP per capita in PPS was more than 2.6 times the EU-27 average in 2009 (which is partly explained by the importance of cross-border workers from Belgium, France and Germany). On the other hand, GDP per capita was less than half the EU-27 average in Romania, Bulgaria (both 2008) and Latvia.

Although PPS figures should, in principle, be used for cross-country comparisons in a single year rather than over time, comparing 1999 to 2009 figures suggests that some convergence in living standards took place between the EU Member States over the past ten years, even though notably the Baltic countries suffered a significant set back in relation to the financial and economic crisis. While all Member States that joined the EU in 2004 or 2007 remained below the EU-27 average in 2009, as did Portugal and Greece, all except Malta moved closer to the EU-27 average over the last ten years. Whereas Luxembourg, Spain and Ireland moved further ahead of the EU-27 average over the ten years to 2009, and Portugal further behind, the other EU-15 Member States moved closer to the EU-27 average.

The pattern of real growth in GDP has varied significantly across the EU: the average annual growth rates of the EU-27 and the euro area between 2000 and 2009 were 1.5 % and 1.4 % respectively. The three Baltic countries averaged 4.8 % real growth per annum despite double-digit decreases in 2009. Bulgaria and Slovakia (4.7 %) and Romania (4.6 %) also recorded annual average growth around three times the EU-27 average. With the exceptions of Hungary and Malta, the economies of all other Member States that joined the EU in 2004 or 2007 grew by an average between 3 % and 4 % per annum during the period 2000 to 2009, as did Ireland, Greece and Luxembourg. The lowest rates of change within the EU during this period were recorded in Italy, Germany, Portugal and Denmark, all averaging growth of less than 1 % per annum (see Table 1.2).

Following a general upturn of the business cycle between 2003 and 2007, the impact of the financial and economic crisis resulted in a severe slowdown and recession in most countries. In 2008 real GDP growth in the EU-27 and the euro area slowed to 0.5 % and in 2009 the rate of change turned negative as GDP contracted by 4.2 % in the EU-27 and by 4.1 % in the euro area. Seven of the EU Member States recorded a negative rate of change for GDP in 2008 and by 2009 there was a contraction in all of the Member Stares except Poland. The decline in real GDP in 2009 was particularly strong in Latvia (-18.0 %), Lithuania (-14.7 %) and Estonia (-13.9 %).

Main GDP aggregates

Looking at GDP from the output side, the analysis reveals some shifts in the economic structure of the EU-27 economy over the last ten years. The comparison of 1999 and 2009 figures shows that the proportion of gross value added accounted for by agriculture and industry was falling, as was the proportion from trade, transport and communication services. In contrast, the proportion of GDP from construction, business activities and financial services as well as other services rose. This structural change is, at least in part, a result of phenomena such as technological change, developments in relative prices, and globalisation, often resulting in manufacturing activities being moved to lower labour-cost regions, both within and outside the EU. However, the decline of industry's share of gross value added within the EU-27 from 20.1 % in 2008 to 17.9 % in 2009 mainly reflected the impact of the financial and economic crisis.

Among the six activities presented in Table 1.3 the three largest were all service activities and together contributed close to three quarters (74.1 %) of the EU-27's total gross value added in 2009. Business activities and financial services accounted for 29.2 % of the EU-27's gross value added, followed by other services (largely made-up of public administrations, education and health services, as well as other community, social and personal service activities (24.0 %)) and trade, transport and communication services (20.9 %). The smallest contributions came from agriculture, hunting, forestry and fishing (1.7 %) and construction (6.3 %). The relative importance of services was particularly high in Luxembourg, France, Cyprus, Greece, Malta, the United Kingdom, Belgium, Denmark and Latvia, as services accounted for more than three quarters of total value added in each of these countries.

An analysis of labour productivity per person employed over the same ten-year period shows increases for all activities. The highest growth rate of productivity was registered in construction (40 %) and the lowest for agriculture, hunting, forestry and fishing (16 %). To eliminate the effects of inflation, labour productivity per person can also be calculated using constant price output figures. Labour productivity in those Member States that joined the EU in 2004 or 2007 converged towards the EU-27 average. Notably, labour productivity per person employed in Romania increased from 23 % to 47 % of the EU-27 average between 1999 and 2009; Estonia, Slovakia, Lithuania, Bulgaria and Latvia also recorded substantial progress towards the EU-27 average.

Turning to an analysis of the development of GDP components from the expenditure side it can be noted that final consumption expenditure across the EU-27 rose by 19.2 % in volume (constant price) terms between 1999 and 2009. This was slightly higher than the growth in GDP during the same period (16.3 %), while overall growth in gross capital formation was just 3.0 % due to a sharp fall in 2009.

In current prices, consumption expenditure by households and non-profit institutions serving households dropped 4.2 % compared with 2008, and represented 57.9 % of the EU-27's GDP in 2009. General government expenditure in the EU-27 rose between 2008 and 2009 by 1.6 % to account for a 22.2 % share of total

GDP in 2009, while gross fixed capital formation dropped by 14.5 % to record an 18.9 % share of GDP. The external balance of goods and services represented 1.0 % of the EU-27's GDP in 2009.

There was a wide variation in the overall investment intensity (public and private combined) that may, in part, reflect the different stages of economic development as well as growth dynamics among Member States over recent years. The vast majority of investment was made by the private sector: in 2009 private investment accounted for 18.4 % of the EU-27's GDP, whereas the equivalent figure for public sector investment was 2.9 %. Public investment exceeded 5 % of GDP in 2009 in the Czech Republic, Romania and Poland, while private investment rose to over 20 % of GDP in Slovakia, Cyprus (2008 data), Romania and Austria.

Gross fixed capital formation (total investment) in 2009 as a share of GDP was 19.1 % in the EU-27 and 19.6 % in the euro area. In 2009 it was highest in Romania, Bulgaria, Spain, Slovenia and Slovakia where it was around one quarter of GDP, while it was lowest in the United Kingdom, Malta and Ireland where it was around 15 % of GDP.

An analysis of GDP within the EU-27 from the income side shows that the distribution between the production factors of income resulting from the production process was dominated by the compensation of employees, which was 49.9 % of GDP in 2009, an increased share compared with 2008. The share of gross operating surplus and mixed income fell in 2009 to 38.7 % of GDP while the share of taxes on production and imports less subsidies decreased to 11.4 %.

Household consumption

The consumption expenditure of households accounted for at least half of GDP in the majority of Member States in 2009; this share was highest in Cyprus (77.4 %, 2008) and also exceeded 75 % in Greece (76.8 %) as well as the former Yugoslav Republic of Macedonia (81.2 %) and Turkey (75.1 %). In contrast, it was below 40 % in Luxembourg (36.9 %, 2008); nevertheless, average household consumption expenditure per capita was, by far, highest in Luxembourg (PPS 25 600, 2008).

A little over one fifth (22.2 %) of total household consumption expenditure in the EU-27 in 2008 was devoted to housing, water, electricity, gas and other housing fuels. Transport expenditure (13.4 %) and expenditure on food and non-alcoholic beverages (12.9 %) together accounted for a little more than a quarter of the total – see Figure 1.12.

National savings

Gross national saving as a proportion of national disposable income averaged 18.5 % in the euro area (of 13 countries) in 2009, and among the EU Member States reached its highest in Latvia (26.3 %) and lowest in Greece (2.6 %). Compared with 1999, there was a decline for the euro area and most of its members. The most substantial decreases (in percentage point terms) were in Ireland, Portugal, Greece, Finland and Cyprus where savings as a proportion of disposable income fell by 7 percentage points or more, while the largest increases were recorded in Latvia and Romania where the proportion increased by 12 points and 9 points respectively.

Sector accounts

Table 1.7 shows the household saving rate in 2009 was almost 2 percentage points higher in the euro area (15.3 %) than in the EU-27 (13.4 %). This gap is mainly explained by the relatively low saving rates of Poland (3.7 %) and the United Kingdom (6.3 %). Among the Member States within the euro area household saving rates were within a relatively narrow range and were generally high, with only Slovakia, Cyprus, Portugal and Finland reporting rates below the EU-27 average. Nevertheless, the EU-27 household saving rate increased in 2009 by 2.3 percentage points, which was more twice the increase recorded within the euro area (1.1 points); the largest increases in savings were observed in Estonia (9.9 points) and Lithuania (8.8 points).

In 2009, the household investment rate was 8.3 % in the EU-27. This rate ranged from 7.1 % in Portugal to just over 10 % in Belgium and Finland, with the Netherlands (12.2 %) and Cyprus (12.3 %) above this range, and Latvia (5.8 %), the United Kingdom, Lithuania and Sweden (all 5.0 %) below this range. The household investment rate fell by 1.3 points in the EU-27 in 2009, compared with the year before; it dropped in each of the Member States (for which data are available) except for the Czech Republic (+0.5 percentage points). Ireland experienced by far the largest fall, down 8.8 points, followed by Spain (-3.6 points).

In 2009, the household debt-to-income ratio varied considerably between Member States. While it was close to or below 50 % in Slovenia, Lithuania, Poland, the Czech Republic and Slovakia, it almost reached 200 % in Ireland and was even higher in the Netherlands and Denmark (rates of 200 % suggest that it would take two years of disposable income for households to repay their debt). A comparatively high debt-to-income ratio was recorded in several north western European Member States. In contrast, in central and eastern Europe, the debt-to-income ratio was comparatively low with household debt never greater than annual disposable income (Estonia had the highest ratio with 97.2 %). It should be borne in mind that high household debt may to some extent mirror high levels of financial assets, as shown in the analysis of the household net financial wealth-to-income ratio. It may also mirror the ownership of non-financial assets such as dwellings or be impacted by national provisions that foster borrowing (for example, the deduction of interest from taxes). Overall, the household debt-to-income ratio increased in 2009 in most EU Member States, the exceptions being the United Kingdom, Spain and Lithuania. Denmark, which already had the largest debt-to-income ratio in 2008, experienced the highest annual increase in 2009, as the ratio increased by 12.4 percentage points.

Like the debt-to-income ratio, the household net financial wealth-to-income ratio differed considerably between Member States. Belgium recorded a ratio of 328.0 %, the highest among the Member States in 2009, and high values were also observed in the Netherlands and Italy, as well as in Switzerland. Latvia and Slovakia had remarkably low net financial assets-to-income ratios, as did Norway.

Figure 1.17 shows that in 2009, the business investment rate was at 20.5 % in the EU-27. The three highest rates among the Member States were recorded in Slovakia, Austria and Slovenia, while the lowest rate was in Ireland (12.3 %). The business investment rates of the five largest EU-27 economies diverged quite significantly: in Spain and Italy the rates were clearly above the EU-27 average, while in the United Kingdom and Germany they were clearly below the average; only the French rate was close to the overall average for the EU-27. The business investment rate fell in all EU Member States in 2009 compared with 2008; however it increased by 1.4 percentage points in Norway. Overall the rate fell by 2.5 percentage points in the EU-27, with particularly large reductions in the Baltic Member States (7 points or more) - see Table 1.8.

The profit share of non-financial corporations was 36.5 % in the EU-27 in 2009. The lowest shares were recorded in Sweden, France, Denmark and Slovenia, while the highest shares were posted in Malta and Ireland, as well as in Norway. Profit shares fell in the EU-27 by 1.6 percentage points between 2008 and 2009. Slovakia and Finland experienced the largest reductions in their profit shares, along with Norway. Latvia recorded the highest percentage point increase between 2008 and 2009, up by 5.4 points, while Spain was the only one of the five largest EU economies to record an increase (up 1.2 points).

Data sources and availability

The European system of national and regional accounts (ESA) provides the methodology for national accounts in the EU. The current version, ESA95, was fully consistent with worldwide guidelines for national accounts, the 1993 SNA. Following international agreement on an updated version of the SNA in 2008, a respective update of the ESA is, at the time of writing, close to finalisation.

GDP and main components

The main aggregates of national accounts are compiled from institutional units, namely non-financial or financial corporations, general government, households, and non-profit institutions serving households (NPISH).

Data within the national accounts domain encompasses information on GDP components, employment, final consumption aggregates and savings. Many of these variables are calculated on an annual and on a quarterly basis.

GDP is the central measure of national accounts, which summarises the economic position of a country (or region). It can be calculated using different approaches: the output approach; the expenditure approach; and the income approach.

An analysis of GDP per capita removes the influence of the absolute size of the population, making comparisons between different countries easier. GDP per capita is a broad economic indicator of living standards. GDP data in national currencies can be converted into purchasing power standards (PPS) using purchasing power parities (PPPs) that reflect the purchasing power of each currency, rather than using market exchange rates; in this way differences in price levels between countries are eliminated. The volume index of GDP per capita in PPS is expressed in relation to the EU-27 average (set to equal 100). If the index of a country is higher/lower than 100, this country's level of GDP per head is above/below the EU-27 average; this index is intended for cross-country comparisons rather than temporal comparisons.

The calculation of the annual growth rate of GDP at constant prices, in other words the change of GDP in volume terms, is intended to allow comparisons of the dynamics of economic development both over time and between economies of different sizes, irrespective of price levels.

Complementary data

Economic output can also be analysed by activity: at the most aggregated level of analysis six NACE Rev. 1.1 headings are identified: agriculture, hunting and fishing; industry; construction; trade, transport and communication services; business activities and financial services; and other services. An analysis of output over time can be facilitated by using a volume measure of output – in other words, by deflating the value of output to remove the impact of price changes; each activity is deflated individually to reflect the changes in the prices of its associated products.

A further set of national accounts data is used within the context of competitiveness analyses, namely indicators relating to the productivity of the workforce, such as labour productivity measures. Productivity measures expressed in PPS are particularly useful for cross-country comparisons. GDP in PPS per person employed is intended to give an overall impression of the productivity of national economies. It should be kept in mind, though, that this measure depends on the structure of total employment and may, for instance, be lowered by a shift from full-time to part-time work. GDP in PPS per hour worked gives a clearer picture of productivity as the incidence of part-time employment varies greatly between countries and activities. The data are presented in the form of an index in relation to the EU average: if the index rises above 100, then labour productivity is above the EU average.

Data on consumption expenditure may be broken down according to the classification of individual consumption according to purpose (COICOP), which identifies 12 different headings at its most aggregated level. Annual information on household expenditure is available from national accounts compiled through a macro-economic approach. An alternative source for analysing household expenditure is the household budget survey (HBS): this information is obtained by asking households to keep a diary of their purchases and is much more detailed in its coverage of goods and services as well as the types of socio-economic breakdown that are made available. HBS is only carried out and published every five years – the latest reference year currently available is 2005.

Household saving is the main domestic source of funds to finance capital investment. The system of accounts provides for both disposable income and saving to be shown on a gross basis, in other words, with both aggregates including the consumption of fixed capital.

Sector accounts

Sector accounts group together economic subjects with similar behaviour into institutional sectors, such as: households, non-financial corporations, financial corporations and government. Grouping economic subjects in this way greatly helps to understand the functioning of the economy. The behaviour of households and non-financial corporations is particularly relevant in this respect.

The households sector covers individuals or groups of individuals acting as consumers and entrepreneurs provided, in the latter case, that their activities as market producers are not carried out by separate entities. For the purpose of the analysis within this subchapter, this sector has been merged with the relatively small sector of non-profit institutions serving households (for example, associations and charities).

Non-financial corporations cover enterprises whose principal activity is the production of goods and non-financial services to be sold on the market. It includes incorporated enterprises, but also unincorporated enterprises as long as they keep a complete set of accounts and have an economic and financial behaviour which is similar to that of corporations. Small businesses (such as sole traders and entrepreneurs operating on their own) are recorded under the households sector.

Sector accounts record, in principle, every transaction between economic subjects during a certain period and can also be used to show the opening and closing stocks of financial assets and liabilities in financial balance sheets. These transactions are grouped into various categories that have a distinct economic meaning, such as the compensation of employees (comprising wages and salaries, before taxes and social contributions are deducted, and social contributions paid by employers).

In turn, these categories of transactions are shown in a sequence of accounts, each of which covers a specific economic process. This ranges from production, income generation and income (re)distribution, through the use of income, for consumption and saving, and investment, as shown in the capital account, to financial transactions such as borrowing and lending. Each non-financial transaction is recorded as an increase in the resources of a certain sector and an increase in the uses of another sector. For instance, the resources side of the interest transaction category records the amounts of interest receivable by different sectors of the economy, whereas the uses side shows interest payable. For each type of transaction, total resources of all sectors and the rest of the world equal total uses. Each account leads to a meaningful balancing item, the value of which equals total resources minus total uses. Typically, such balancing items, such as GDP or net saving, are important economic indicators; they are carried over to the next account.

The analysis in this subchapter focuses on a selection of indicators from the wealth of sector accounts data. Households' behaviour is described through indicators covering saving and investment rate, as well as debt-to-income and net financial wealth-to-income ratios. The analysis on non-financial corporations is based on the business investment rate and business profit share.

Context

European institutions, governments, central banks as well as other economic and social bodies in the public and private sectors need a set of comparable and reliable statistics on which to base their decisions.

National accounts can be used for various types of analysis and evaluation. The use of internationally accepted concepts and definitions permits an analysis of different economies, such as the interdependencies between the economies of the EU Member States, or a comparison between the EU and non-member countries.

Business cycle and macro-economic policy analysis

One of the main uses of national accounts data relates to the need to support European economic policy decisions and the achievement of economic and monetary union (EMU) objectives with high-quality short-term statistics that allow the monitoring of macro-economic developments and the derivation of macro-economic policy advice. For instance, one of the most basic and long-standing uses of national accounts is to quantify the rate of growth of an economy, in simple terms the growth of GDP. Core national accounts figures are notably used to develop and monitor macro-economic policies, while detailed national accounts data can also be used to develop sectoral or industrial policies, particularly through an analysis of input-output tables.

Since the beginning of the EMU in 1999, the European Central Bank (ECB) has been one of the main users of national accounts. The ECB's strategy for assessing the risks to price stability is based on two analytical perspectives, referred to as the 'two pillars': economic analysis and monetary analysis. A large number of monetary and financial indicators are thus evaluated in relation to other relevant data that allow the combination of monetary, financial and economic analysis, for example, key national accounts aggregates and sector accounts. In this way monetary and financial indicators can be analysed within the context of the rest of the economy.

The Directorate-General for Economic and Financial Affairs produces the European Commission's macro-economic forecasts twice a year, in the spring and autumn. These forecasts cover all EU Member States in order to derive forecasts for the euro area and the EU-27, but they also include outlooks for candidate countries, as well as some non-member countries.

The analysis of public finances through national accounts is another well established use of these statistics. Within the EU a specific application was developed in relation to the convergence criteria for EMU, two of which refer directly to public finances. These criteria have been defined in terms of national accounts figures, namely, government deficit and government debt relative to GDP. See Subchapter 1.2 on government finance statistics for more information.

Regional, structural and sectoral policies

As well as business cycle and macro-economic policy analysis, there are other policy-related uses of European national and regional accounts data, notably concerning regional, structural and sectoral issues.

The allocation of expenditure for the structural funds is partly based on regional accounts. Furthermore, regional statistics are used for ex-post assessment of the results of regional and cohesion policy.

Encouraging more growth and more jobs is a strategic priority for both the EU and the Member States, and is part of the Europe 2020 strategy. In support of these strategic priorities, common policies are implemented across all sectors of the EU economy while the Member States implement their own national structural reforms. To ensure that this is as beneficial as possible, and to prepare for the challenges that lie ahead, the European Commission analyses these policies.

The European Commission conducts economic analysis contributing to the development of the common agricultural policy (CAP) by analysing the efficiency of its various support mechanisms and developing a long-term perspective. This includes research, analysis and impact assessments on topics related to agriculture and the rural economy in the EU and non-member countries, in part using the economic accounts for agriculture.

Target setting, benchmarking and contributions

Policies within the EU are increasingly setting medium or long-term targets, whether binding or not. For some of these, the level of GDP is used as a benchmark denominator, for example, setting a target for expenditure on research and development at a level of 3 % of GDP.

National accounts are also used to determine EU resources, with the basic rules laid down in a Council Decision. The overall amount of own resources needed to finance the EU budget is determined by total expenditure less other revenue, and the maximum size of the own resources are linked to the gross national income of the EU.

As well as being used to determine budgetary contributions within the EU, national accounts data are also used to determine contributions to other international organisations, such as the United Nations (UN). Contributions to the UN budget are based on gross national income along with a variety of adjustments and limits.

Analysts and forecasters

National accounts are also widely used by analysts and researchers to examine the economic situation and developments. Financial institutions' interest in national accounts may range from a broad analysis of the economy to specific information concerning savings, investment or debt among households, non-financial corporations or other institutional sectors. Social partners, such as representatives of businesses (for example, trade associations) or representatives of workers (for example, trade unions), also have an interest in national accounts for the purpose of analysing developments that affect industrial relations. Among other uses, researchers and analysts use national accounts for business cycle analysis and analysing long-term economic cycles and relating these to economic, political or technological developments.

Figure 1.1: GDP per capita at current market prices, 2009
(EU-27=100)

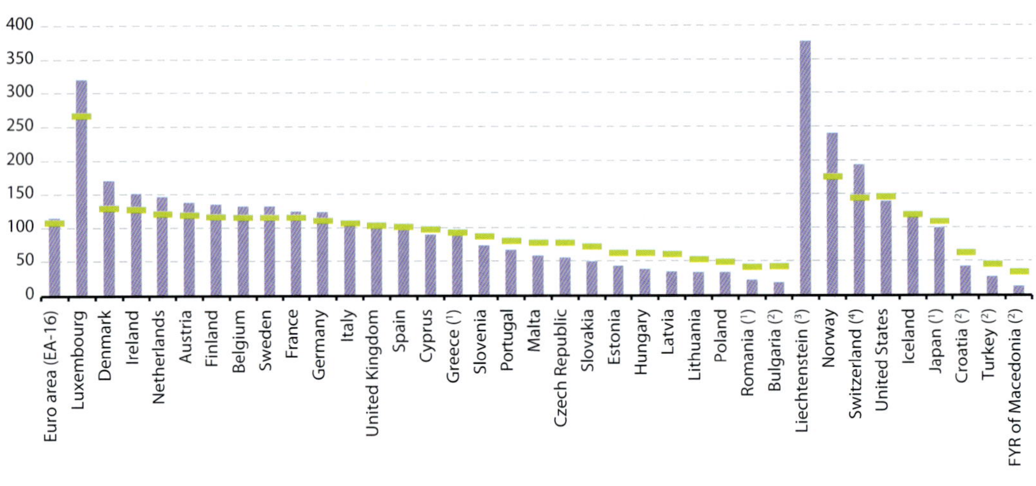

(1) 2007.
(2) 2008.
(3) 2008. PPS, not available.
(4) Provisional.

Source: Eurostat (nama_gdp_c and tec00001)

Figure 1.2: GDP at current market prices
(EUR 1 000 million)

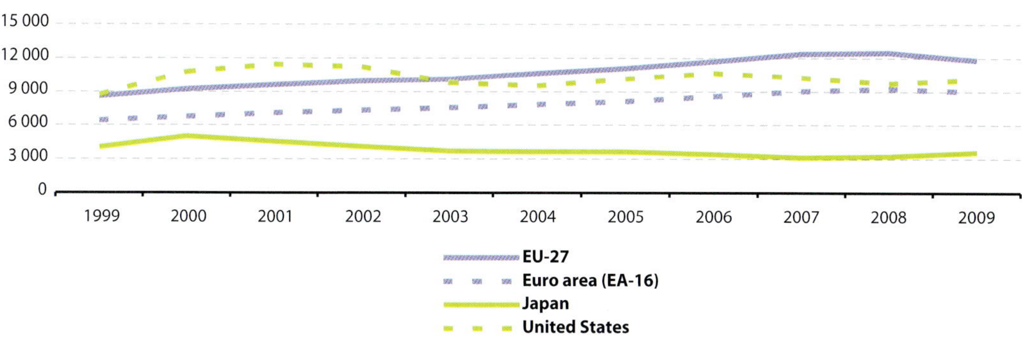

Source: Eurostat (tec00001)

Figure 1.3: Real GDP growth
(% change compared with the previous year)

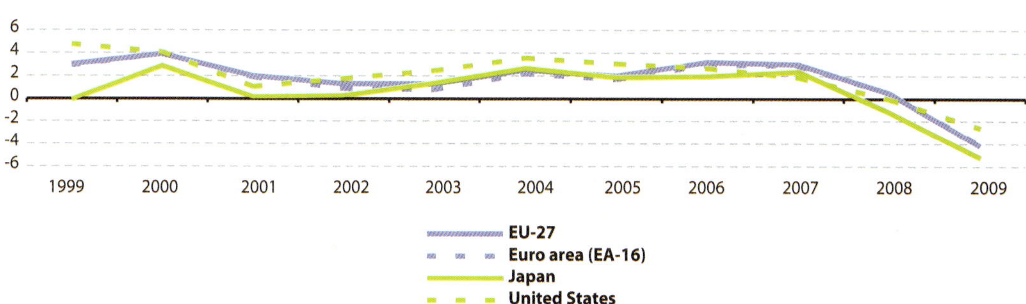

Source: Eurostat (tsieb020)

Table 1.1: GDP at current market prices

	GDP						GDP per capita			
	(EUR 1 000 million)			(PPS 1 000 million)			(PPS, EU-27=100)			(EUR)
	1999	2008	2009	1999	2008	2009	1999	2008	2009	2009 (1)
EU-27	8 589	12 495	11 791	8 589	12 495	11 791	100	100	100	23 600
Euro area (EA-16)	6 445	9 252	8 963	6 283	8 906	8 396	113	108	108	27 200
Belgium	239	345	339	224	309	294	123	115	116	31 400
Bulgaria	12	35	35	*40*	82	76	*27*	43	:	4 700
Czech Republic	56	148	137	*127*	210	199	*69*	80	81	13 100
Denmark	163	233	223	124	165	153	131	120	118	40 400
Germany	2 012	2 481	2 397	1 786	2 366	2 233	122	115	116	29 300
Estonia	5	16	14	*10*	23	20	*42*	68	63	10 300
Ireland	90	180	160	84	149	135	126	134	128	35 700
Greece	132	*236*	*233*	160	*262*	*247*	83	*93*	*93*	*20 700*
Spain	580	1 088	1 054	685	1 173	1 127	96	103	104	22 900
France	1 368	1 949	1 907	1 233	1 734	1 633	115	108	107	29 600
Italy	1 127	1 568	1 521	1 192	1 527	1 445	117	102	102	25 200
Cyprus	9	17	17	*11*	19	18	*87*	96	98	21 200
Latvia	7	23	19	*15*	32	26	*36*	57	49	8 200
Lithuania	10	32	27	*24*	52	42	*39*	62	53	8 000
Luxembourg	20	39	38	18	34	31	237	277	267	75 700
Hungary	46	106	93	100	162	149	55	64	63	9 300
Malta	4	6	6	6	8	8	81	77	78	13 900
Netherlands	386	596	572	368	552	508	131	134	130	34 600
Austria	198	283	274	187	259	241	131	124	*122*	*32 800*
Poland	157	362	310	*331*	539	547	*49*	56	61	8 100
Portugal	118	172	168	147	209	196	81	79	78	15 800
Romania	34	140	116	105	259	229	26	42	:	*5 800*
Slovenia	21	37	35	*28*	46	42	*81*	91	87	17 300
Slovakia	19	65	63	49	98	91	50	72	72	*11 700*
Finland	122	185	171	105	156	139	115	117	111	32 100
Sweden	243	334	293	199	284	265	126	122	120	31 300
United Kingdom	1 410	1 815	1 563	1 231	1 785	1 693	118	116	116	25 300
Iceland	8	10	9	7	10	9	139	121	120	27 200
Liechtenstein	2	3	3	:	:	:	:	:	:	:
Norway	149	306	273	115	226	200	145	189	176	56 500
Switzerland	252	343	354	186	271	262	*146*	*141*	*144*	*45 800*
Croatia	22	47	45	*39*	69	66	49	63	:	10 800
FYR of Macedonia	3	7	:	10	17	:	27	34	:	*3 300*
Turkey	234	499	440	*448*	811	781	*40*	*46*	:	7 000
Japan	4 102	3 313	3 639	2 657	3 369	3 112	118	109	:	*25 000*
United States	8 776	9 770	10 123	8 093	11 216	10 614	163	147	146	32 900

(1) Bulgaria, Croatia, the former Yugoslav Republic of Macedonia and Turkey, 2008; Romania and Japan, 2007.

Source: Eurostat (tec00001 and nama_gdp_c), Switzerland: Secrétariat d'Etat à l'économie, Japan: Economic and Social Research Institute, United States: Bureau of Economic Analysis

Table 1.2: Real GDP growth
(% change compared with the previous year; average 2000-2009)

	2000	2001	2002	2003	2004	2005	2006	2007	2008	2009	2000-09
EU-27	3.9	2.0	1.2	1.3	2.5	2.0	3.2	3.0	0.5	-4.2	1.5
Euro area (EA-16)	3.9	1.9	0.9	0.8	2.2	1.7	3.0	2.8	0.5	-4.1	1.4
Belgium	3.7	0.8	1.4	0.8	3.2	1.7	2.7	2.9	1.0	-2.8	1.5
Bulgaria	5.7	4.2	4.7	5.5	6.7	6.4	6.5	6.4	6.2	-4.9	4.7
Czech Republic	3.6	2.5	1.9	3.6	4.5	6.3	6.8	6.1	2.5	-4.1	3.4
Denmark	3.5	0.7	0.5	0.4	2.3	2.4	3.4	1.7	-0.9	-4.7	0.9
Germany	3.2	1.2	0.0	-0.2	1.2	0.8	3.4	2.7	1.0	-4.7	0.9
Estonia	10.0	7.5	7.9	7.6	7.2	9.4	10.6	6.9	-5.1	-13.9	4.8
Ireland	9.7	5.7	6.5	4.4	4.6	6.0	5.3	5.6	-3.5	-7.6	3.7
Greece	4.5	4.2	3.4	5.9	4.4	2.3	4.5	4.3	1.3	-2.3	3.3
Spain	5.0	3.6	2.7	3.1	3.3	3.6	4.0	3.6	0.9	-3.7	2.6
France	3.9	1.9	1.0	1.1	2.5	1.9	2.2	2.4	0.2	-2.6	1.5
Italy	3.7	1.8	0.5	0.0	1.5	0.7	2.0	1.5	-1.3	-5.0	0.5
Cyprus	5.0	4.0	2.1	1.9	4.2	3.9	4.1	5.1	3.6	-1.7	3.2
Latvia	6.9	8.0	6.5	7.2	8.7	10.6	12.2	10.0	-4.2	-18.0	4.8
Lithuania	3.3	6.7	6.9	10.2	7.4	7.8	7.8	9.8	2.9	-14.7	4.8
Luxembourg	8.4	2.5	4.1	1.5	4.4	5.4	5.0	6.6	1.4	-3.7	3.6
Hungary	4.9	3.8	4.1	4.0	4.5	3.2	3.6	0.8	0.8	-6.7	2.3
Malta (1)	:	-1.6	2.6	-0.3	0.9	4.0	3.6	3.7	2.6	-2.1	1.5
Netherlands	3.9	1.9	0.1	0.3	2.2	2.0	3.4	3.9	1.9	-3.9	1.6
Austria	3.7	0.5	1.6	0.8	2.5	2.5	3.6	3.7	2.2	-3.9	1.7
Poland	4.3	1.2	1.4	3.9	5.3	3.6	6.2	6.8	5.1	1.7	4.0
Portugal	3.9	2.0	0.7	-0.9	1.6	0.8	1.4	2.4	0.0	-2.6	0.9
Romania	2.4	5.7	5.1	5.2	8.5	4.2	7.9	6.3	7.3	-7.1	4.6
Slovenia	4.4	2.8	4.0	2.8	4.3	4.5	5.9	6.9	3.7	-8.1	3.1
Slovakia	1.4	3.5	4.6	4.8	5.0	6.7	8.5	10.6	6.2	-4.7	4.7
Finland	5.3	2.3	1.8	2.0	4.1	2.9	4.4	5.3	0.9	-8.0	2.1
Sweden	4.5	1.3	2.5	2.3	4.2	3.2	4.3	3.3	-0.4	-5.1	2.0
United Kingdom	3.9	2.5	2.1	2.8	3.0	2.2	2.8	2.7	-0.1	-5.0	1.7
Iceland	4.3	3.9	0.1	2.4	7.7	7.5	4.6	6.0	1.0	-6.8	3.1
Norway	3.3	2.0	1.5	1.0	3.9	2.7	2.3	2.7	0.8	-1.4	1.9
Switzerland	3.6	1.2	0.4	-0.2	2.5	2.6	3.6	3.6	1.9	-1.9	1.7
Croatia	3.0	3.8	5.4	5.0	4.2	4.2	4.7	5.5	2.4	-5.8	3.2
FYR of Macedonia	4.5	-4.5	0.9	2.8	4.1	4.1	4.0	5.9	4.9	-0.7	2.6
Turkey	6.8	-5.7	6.6	4.9	9.4	8.4	6.9	4.7	0.4	-4.5	3.8
Japan	2.9	0.2	0.3	1.4	2.7	1.9	2.0	2.4	-1.2	-5.2	0.7
United States	4.1	1.1	1.8	2.5	3.6	3.1	2.7	1.9	0.0	-2.6	1.8

(1) Average growth 2001-2009.

Source: Eurostat (nama_gdp_k), Switzerland: Secrétariat d'Etat à l'économie,
Japan: Economic and Social Research Institute, United States: Bureau of Economic Analysis

Table 1.3: Gross value added at basic prices
(% share of total gross value added)

	Agriculture, hunting, forestry & fishing		Industry		Construction		Trade, transport & communi-cation services		Business activities & financial services		Other services	
	1999	2009	1999	2009	1999	2009	1999	2009	1999	2009	1999	2009
EU-27	2.5	1.7	22.5	17.9	5.6	6.3	21.6	20.9	25.7	29.2	22.3	24.0
Euro area (EA-16)	2.6	1.6	22.3	17.8	5.7	6.3	21.1	20.7	25.9	29.3	22.4	24.2
Belgium	1.3	0.7	22.1	16.3	5.0	5.4	21.7	21.7	27.1	30.5	22.8	25.4
Bulgaria	15.9	5.6	20.1	21.4	5.0	8.9	22.2	25.4	19.8	23.0	17.0	15.7
Czech Republic	3.9	2.2	31.8	30.3	7.0	7.4	24.6	24.2	16.4	18.3	16.4	17.5
Denmark	2.4	1.1	20.4	17.4	5.6	4.9	22.3	19.5	21.8	27.4	27.5	29.8
Germany	1.2	0.8	24.8	22.2	5.5	4.3	17.8	17.5	28.0	31.1	22.7	24.1
Estonia	4.4	2.6	21.3	19.5	5.6	7.0	28.1	25.4	22.5	24.8	18.0	20.8
Ireland	3.6	1.4	35.8	23.9	6.6	8.5	17.8	17.5	20.0	28.7	16.2	20.0
Greece (1)	6.6	*3.2*	13.9	*13.3*	7.0	*4.6*	30.1	*33.1*	20.6	*20.1*	21.7	*25.7*
Spain	4.5	2.6	21.3	15.3	7.9	10.8	26.6	24.6	18.8	23.6	21.0	23.0
France	3.0	1.7	18.0	12.4	5.1	6.4	19.2	19.0	29.5	33.7	25.2	26.7
Italy	3.0	1.8	23.8	18.8	4.9	6.3	23.9	22.2	24.1	28.8	20.3	22.1
Cyprus	4.0	2.1	12.4	9.6	7.2	9.0	30.5	25.9	23.8	28.1	22.1	25.3
Latvia	3.9	3.1	18.3	14.0	6.4	6.6	31.4	28.0	17.9	26.1	22.0	22.2
Lithuania	7.3	4.2	22.5	20.4	7.6	6.3	27.6	32.0	12.1	16.3	23.0	20.8
Luxembourg	0.8	0.3	12.9	8.2	6.1	5.8	22.0	19.9	41.6	49.0	16.6	16.9
Hungary	5.8	3.0	26.7	24.9	4.6	4.8	21.3	21.2	19.5	23.6	22.2	22.5
Malta	2.7	1.8	22.4	16.0	3.8	3.4	32.9	23.3	16.9	24.3	21.3	31.2
Netherlands	2.7	1.7	19.0	17.9	5.5	6.0	23.2	20.3	27.4	28.2	22.3	25.9
Austria	2.1	1.5	23.0	21.8	7.8	7.3	24.4	23.5	21.1	23.7	21.5	22.1
Poland	5.2	3.6	24.6	23.0	8.2	7.5	27.0	27.1	16.9	20.2	18.1	18.6
Portugal	3.9	2.3	21.4	16.8	7.4	6.1	25.2	25.7	20.5	23.6	21.7	25.5
Romania	14.4	7.0	27.9	26.4	5.4	10.9	24.6	23.6	15.4	16.8	12.3	15.4
Slovenia	3.4	2.4	29.0	23.2	7.2	7.9	20.6	22.0	20.0	23.3	19.8	21.2
Slovakia	4.8	2.6	29.7	25.5	5.6	8.8	27.1	24.3	16.4	21.9	16.4	16.9
Finland	3.5	2.7	28.0	21.2	6.1	7.0	20.9	19.5	20.1	25.0	21.5	24.7
Sweden	2.3	1.7	24.5	19.7	4.3	5.4	19.1	20.0	24.6	25.0	25.2	28.2
United Kingdom	1.1	0.8	22.3	14.9	5.1	5.9	22.9	20.4	27.0	34.1	21.5	23.9
Iceland (2)	9.7	6.3	17.9	17.7	8.0	9.3	22.1	18.4	18.5	25.5	23.8	22.8
Norway	2.4	1.2	30.0	35.2	4.7	5.3	21.3	16.3	18.4	19.5	23.2	22.5
Switzerland	1.6	1.2	22.5	21.2	5.4	5.6	21.8	22.0	23.0	23.5	25.7	26.5
Croatia (2)	9.1	6.4	23.1	20.2	5.3	8.3	22.9	25.2	18.2	22.9	21.4	16.9
FYR of Macedonia (2)	12.9	11.6	26.5	24.1	6.1	5.7	24.3	25.0	9.7	16.0	20.5	17.7
Turkey	10.7	9.1	25.4	20.9	5.6	4.2	26.8	29.4	20.6	23.9	10.9	12.4
Japan	1.4	:	24.5	:	7.2	:	:	:	18.4	:	28.5	:
United States	1.2	:	19.6	:	4.7	:	20.0	:	31.2	:	23.2	:

(1) 2000 instead of 1999.
(2) 2008 instead of 2009.

Source: Eurostat (tec00003, tec00004, tec00005, tec00006, tec00007 and tec00008)

Figure 1.4: Gross value added, EU-27

(2000=100)

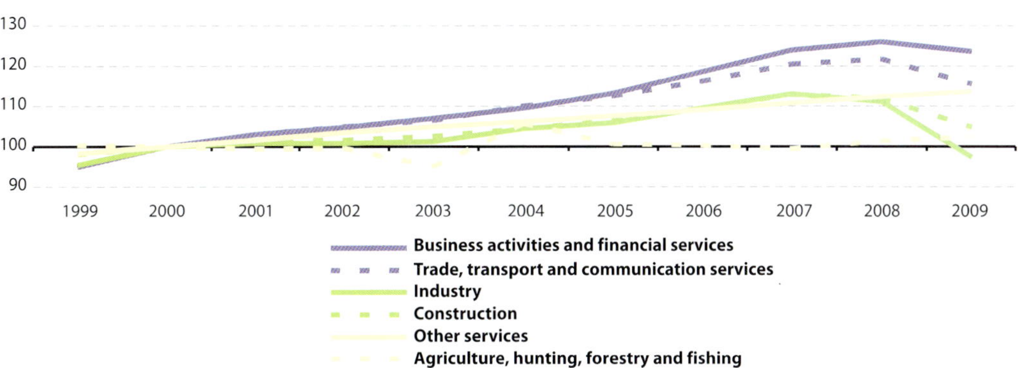

Source: Eurostat (nama_nace06_k)

Figure 1.5: Labour productivity, EU-27

(EUR 1 000 per person employed)

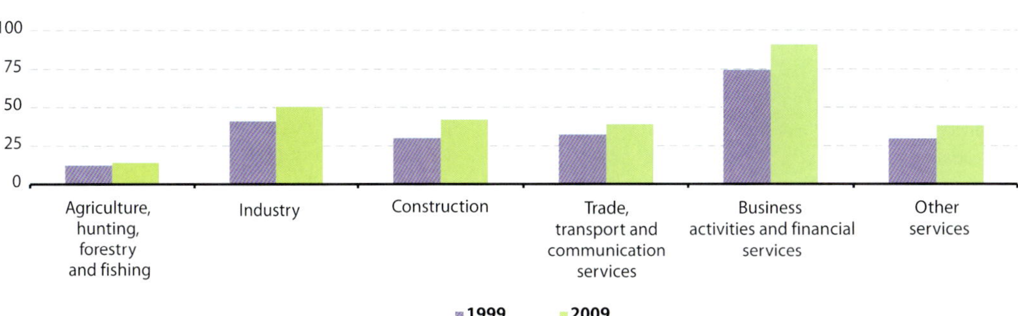

Source: Eurostat (nama_nace06_c and nama_nace06_e)

Table 1.4: Labour productivity (based on PPS)

	Per person employed (EU-27=100)						Per hour worked (EU-15=100)					
	1999	2001	2003	2005	2007	2009	1999	2001	2003	2005	2007	2009
EU-27	100	100	100	100	100	100	:	86	87	87	87	88
Euro area (EA-16)	114	112	111	110	110	109	:	100	99	99	100	100
Belgium	134	134	135	130	127	125	*124*	*124*	*125*	*121*	*119*	*117*
Bulgaria	29	32	35	36	37	39	26	28	31	32	33	34
Czech Republic	62	63	67	69	71	72	44	47	50	51	54	55
Denmark	109	108	106	107	103	101	104	101	100	100	97	96
Germany	112	107	109	109	108	105	110	107	110	112	111	109
Estonia	43	48	55	61	66	65	:	36	40	44	48	51
Ireland	125	128	136	134	137	132	94	97	105	104	108	106
Greece	*91*	*97*	101	98	*98*	*98*	:	67	70	*69*	*68*	*74*
Spain	106	103	104	101	103	111	89	87	89	89	93	98
France	125	125	122	122	121	121	113	116	116	115	114	:
Italy	128	125	115	111	110	110	100	100	92	89	89	90
Cyprus	83	87	82	83	86	89	64	65	63	66	68	70
Latvia	38	42	44	48	51	50	:	28	30	33	36	37
Lithuania	40	47	52	54	59	56	34	38	42	43	46	44
Luxembourg	176	162	167	169	179	168	:	:	154	159	168	:
Hungary	57	62	66	68	68	70	41	45	49	50	50	52
Malta	:	90	90	91	89	88	*70*	*80*	*72*	*70*	*69*	*70*
Netherlands	112	113	111	114	114	111	114	116	115	120	121	117
Austria	120	115	118	115	114	112	103	98	100	99	100	99
Poland (¹)	54	56	60	61	62	65	:	39	42	43	44	:
Portugal	72	70	71	72	73	74	:	53	53	55	55	56
Romania	23	26	31	36	43	47	19	20	25	28	34	37
Slovenia	77	76	79	84	84	82	:	:	:	72	74	:
Slovakia	57	61	63	69	76	79	46	49	55	57	63	68
Finland	113	112	109	111	113	107	94	95	93	94	97	93
Sweden	114	109	111	111	114	112	101	98	103	102	104	101
United Kingdom	109	112	113	112	110	110	*93*	*95*	*98*	*98*	*97*	*97*
Iceland	108	104	101	105	*97*	*101*	:	:	:	:	:	:
Norway	120	137	135	153	150	145	120	140	141	157	155	150
Switzerland	111	107	105	104	*109*	*109*	96	95	94	91	97	:
Croatia	63	67	69	70	*74*	*78*	:	:	:	:	:	:
FYR of Macedonia	47	46	48	54	58	*58*	:	:	:	:	:	:
Turkey	49	*49*	*50*	*58*	*62*	*63*	:	:	:	:	:	:
Japan	97	98	99	99	98	*93*	:	:	:	:	:	:
United States	143	140	142	144	139	*141*	*113*	*113*	*116*	*119*	*116*	*118*

(¹) 2005, break in series.

Source: Eurostat (tsieb030 and tsieb040), OECD

Figure 1.6: Consumption expenditure and gross capital formation at constant prices, EU-27
(2000=100)

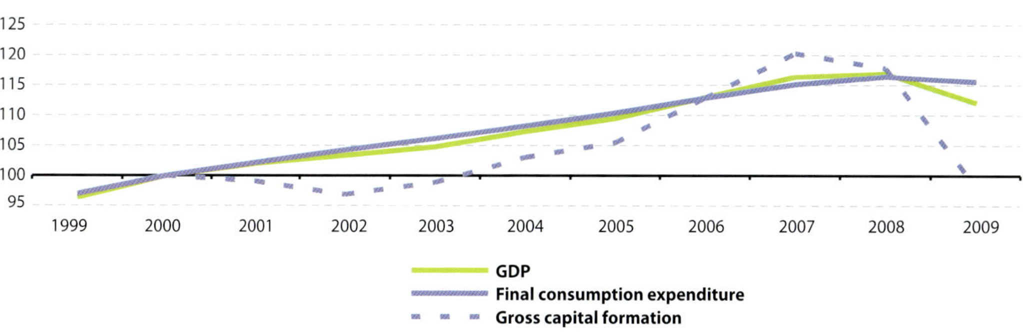

Source: Eurostat (nama_gdp_k)

Figure 1.7: Expenditure components of GDP, EU-27
(EUR 1 000 million)

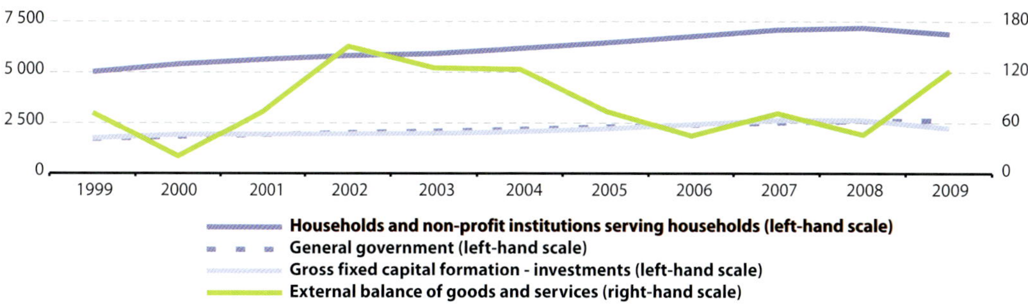

Source: Eurostat (tec00009, tec00010, tec00011 and tec00110)

Figure 1.8: Expenditure components of GDP, EU-27, 2009
(% share of GDP)

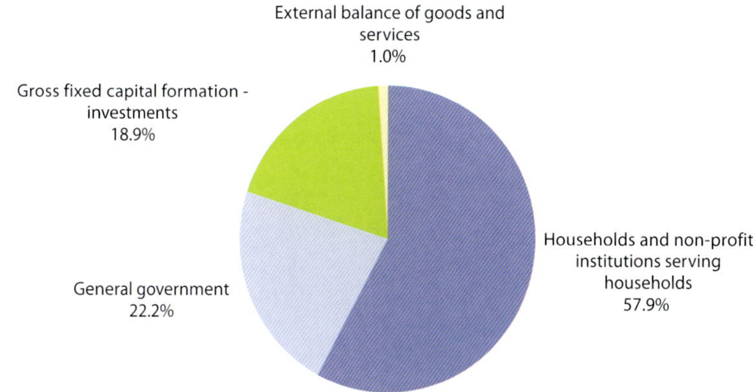

Source: Eurostat (tec00009, tec00011, tec00010 and tec00110)

Table 1.5: Investment
(% share of GDP)

	Total investment			Public investment			Business investment		
	1999	2004	2009	1999	2004	2009	1999	2004	2009
EU-27 (1)	20.4	19.6	19.1	2.3	2.4	2.9	18.1	17.2	18.4
Euro area (EA-16) (1)	21.0	20.3	19.6	2.5	2.5	2.8	18.5	17.8	19.1
Belgium	20.7	19.8	21.3	2.0	1.6	1.8	18.8	18.2	19.5
Bulgaria	15.0	20.4	24.4	3.9	2.9	4.8	11.2	17.5	19.7
Czech Republic	27.0	25.8	22.4	3.3	4.8	5.4	23.8	21.0	17.1
Denmark	19.8	19.3	18.4	1.7	1.9	2.0	18.1	17.4	16.4
Germany	21.3	17.5	17.6	1.9	1.4	1.7	19.4	16.1	16.0
Estonia	24.6	30.9	21.6	4.2	3.8	4.9	20.4	27.1	16.8
Ireland	23.1	24.4	16.0	3.1	3.5	4.5	20.0	20.9	11.3
Greece (2)	21.6	*22.0*	*17.2*	3.1	3.5	2.9	17.9	*18.5*	*14.3*
Spain	24.6	28.0	24.0	3.3	3.4	4.4	21.2	24.7	19.6
France	18.8	19.3	20.6	2.9	3.1	3.3	15.8	16.2	17.2
Italy	19.6	20.5	18.9	2.4	2.4	2.4	17.3	18.1	16.5
Cyprus (1)	17.6	19.0	20.4	2.5	4.0	4.1	13.4	12.1	20.4
Latvia	23.0	27.5	21.5	1.5	3.1	3.9	21.5	24.4	17.5
Lithuania	21.9	22.3	17.0	2.6	3.4	3.9	19.3	18.8	13.1
Luxembourg	23.5	21.5	17.5	4.3	4.3	3.6	19.2	17.3	13.9
Hungary	23.0	22.5	20.0	2.9	3.5	2.7	20.2	19.0	17.3
Malta (1)	22.2	19.2	14.8	4.5	3.9	2.2	11.8	10.2	11.3
Netherlands	22.9	18.8	19.0	3.0	3.2	4.0	19.9	15.6	15.1
Austria	23.5	22.0	21.1	1.7	1.1	1.1	21.7	20.8	20.0
Poland	24.4	18.1	21.0	3.5	3.4	5.3	20.9	14.7	15.7
Portugal	27.3	23.3	19.5	4.1	3.1	2.4	23.4	20.3	17.1
Romania	17.6	21.8	25.6	1.6	3.0	5.4	16.0	18.7	20.2
Slovenia	26.6	24.9	23.9	3.4	3.5	4.9	22.4	21.5	19.1
Slovakia	29.5	24.0	23.6	2.9	2.4	2.3	27.5	22.2	21.3
Finland	19.6	19.3	19.5	2.7	2.8	2.8	16.9	16.5	16.7
Sweden	17.5	17.0	17.9	3.1	2.9	3.6	14.4	14.1	14.3
United Kingdom	17.4	16.7	14.7	1.3	1.8	2.7	16.1	14.9	12.1
Iceland	21.8	23.5	13.9	4.7	3.9	3.9	17.1	19.7	10.0
Norway	21.9	18.0	21.4	3.4	2.9	3.6	18.5	15.1	17.8
Switzerland (3)	22.2	20.8	20.2	2.6	2.4	1.9	19.6	18.4	19.3
Croatia	20.1	25.5	*25.5*	:	:	:	:	:	:
FYR of Macedonia	16.6	17.8	*19.5*	:	:	:	:	:	:
Turkey	18.9	20.3	16.9	:	:	:	:	:	:

(1) 2008 instead of 2009 for business investment.
(2) 2000 instead of 1999 for total and business investment.
(3) 2008 instead of 2009 for public and business investment.

Source: Eurostat (nama_gdp_c, tsdec210, tec00022 and tsier140)

Figure 1.9: Gross fixed capital formation, 2009
(% share of GDP)

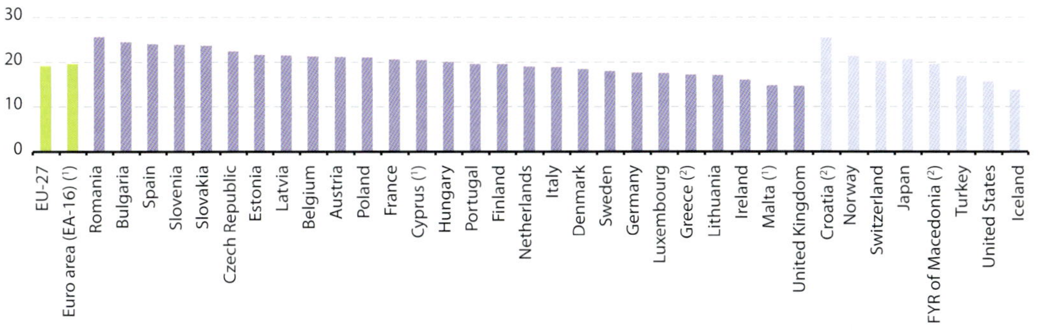

(¹) Provisional.
(²) Forecast.

Source: Eurostat (tec00011)

Figure 1.10: Distribution of income, EU-27
(2000=100)

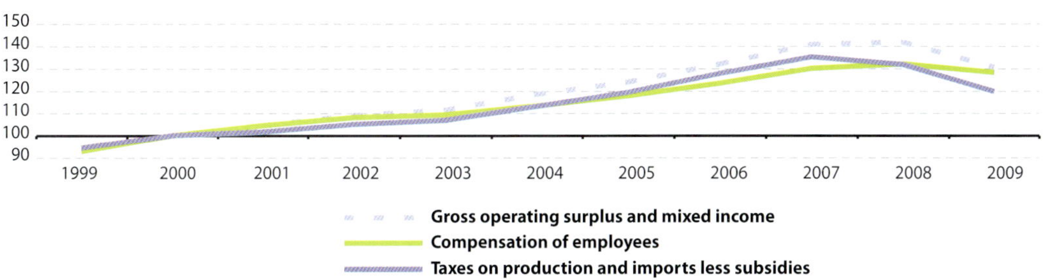

Source: Eurostat (tec00016, tec00015 and tec00013)

Figure 1.11: Distribution of income, 2009
(% share of GDP)

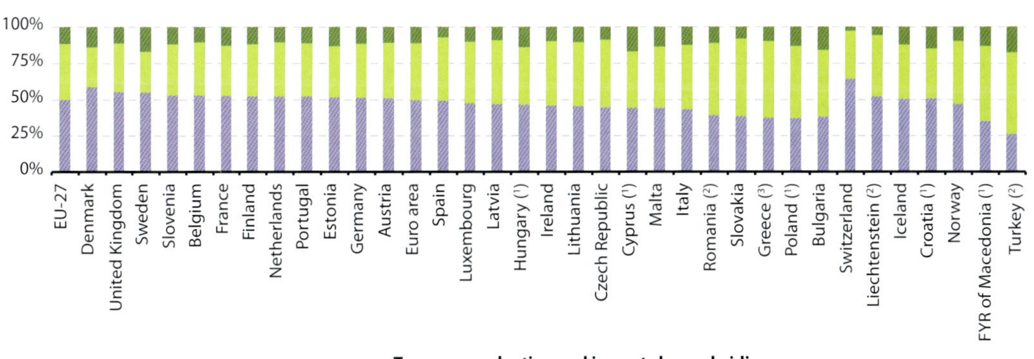

(¹) 2008.
(²) 2007.
(³) Provisional.

Source: Eurostat (tec00016, tec00015 and tec00013)

Table 1.6: Consumption expenditure of households
(domestic concept)

	As a proportion of GDP (%)			Per capita (PPS)		
	1999	2004	2009	1999	2004	2009
Belgium (1)	51.5	50.0	50.3	11 300	13 100	14 500
Bulgaria (2)	72.5	70.5	70.1	3 600	5 300	6 300
Czech Republic (1)	54.7	51.5	51.0	6 800	8 400	10 300
Denmark	48.6	47.5	48.4	11 300	12 900	13 400
Germany	55.4	55.8	55.8	12 000	14 100	15 200
Estonia	62.0	59.3	52.9	4 700	7 400	7 800
Ireland (1)	47.1	43.7	47.0	10 600	13 400	15 800
Greece (3)	75.7	*73.6*	*76.8*	12 100	*14 900*	*16 800*
Spain (1)	63.0	60.4	59.2	10 800	13 200	15 200
France	55.0	55.9	57.3	11 200	13 300	14 500
Italy	60.8	59.4	60.4	12 700	13 700	14 500
Cyprus (1)	81.1	75.6	77.4	12 600	14 800	18 600
Latvia (1)	61.0	61.2	61.1	3 900	6 100	8 700
Lithuania (4)	66.6	65.8	63.7	4 600	7 200	9 400
Luxembourg (1)	46.9	44.3	36.9	19 800	24 300	25 600
Hungary (1)	56.4	54.3	53.8	5 500	7 500	8 700
Malta	80.7	76.7	69.7	11 600	12 800	12 800
Netherlands	49.7	48.3	44.9	11 600	13 500	13 800
Austria (4)	55.5	55.9	53.9	13 000	15 300	16 600
Poland (1)	63.1	64.0	61.2	5 500	7 000	8 700
Portugal (2)	62.2	62.8	63.9	9 000	10 500	11 900
Romania	71.0	68.1	61.2	3 300	5 000	6 800
Slovenia (5)	59.3	56.8	58.0	8 500	10 600	12 000
Slovakia (1)	56.1	56.5	55.9	5 000	7 000	10 100
Finland	48.3	49.2	52.2	9 900	12 400	13 600
Sweden (1)	47.4	46.4	47.8	10 700	12 700	13 600
United Kingdom	62.1	61.3	62.0	13 000	16 400	17 000
Iceland	55.3	52.6	48.7	13 700	14 900	13 800
Norway	45.5	42.1	39.4	11 700	15 000	16 400
Switzerland (1)	59.5	58.7	55.6	*15 500*	*17 200*	*19 700*
FYR of Macedonia (1)	72.1	80.0	81.2	3 400	4 600	6 800
Turkey (6)	71.7	75.8	75.1	5 100	6 500	8 400

(1) 2008 instead of 2009.
(2) 2006 instead of 2009.
(3) 2000 instead of 1999.
(4) 2007 instead of 2009.
(5) Per capita, 2007 instead of 2009.
(6) Per capita, 2008 instead of 2009.

Source: Eurostat (nama_fcs_c)

Figure 1.12: Consumption expenditure of households, EU-27, 2008
(% of total household consumption expenditure)

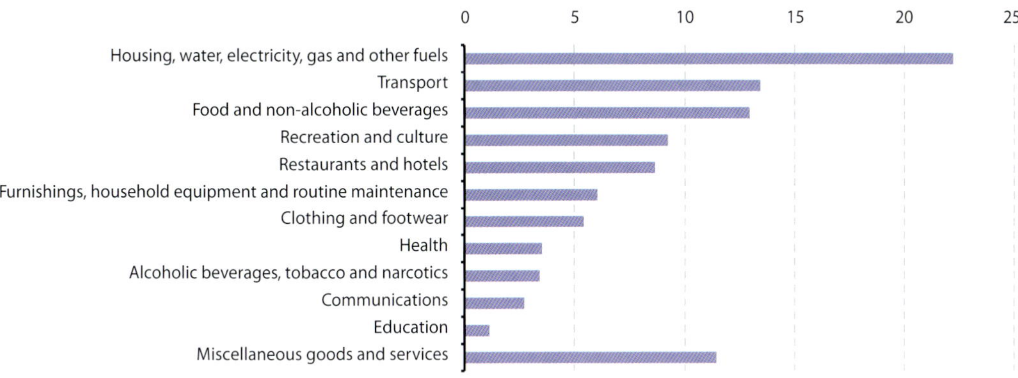

Source: Eurostat (nama_co2_c)

Figure 1.13: Gross national savings (1)
(% of gross national disposable income)

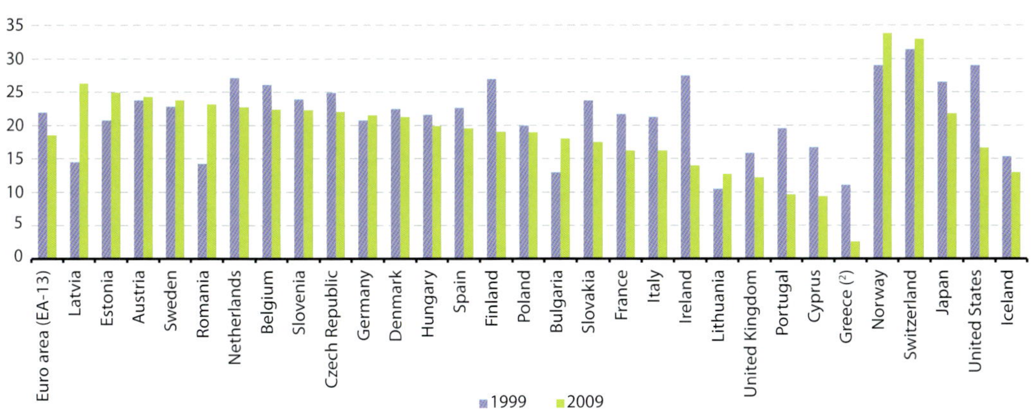

(1) EU-27, Luxembourg and Malta, not available.
(2) 2000 instead of 1999.

Source: Eurostat (nama_inc_c)

Table 1.7: Key ratios of sector accounts, households, 2009 (1)

	Saving rate (2)	Investment rate (2)	Debt-to-income ratio (3)	Net financial wealth-to-income ratio (4)	Saving rate	Investment rate	Debt-to-income ratio	Net financial wealth-to-income ratio
	(%)				Change from 2008 (percentage points)			
EU-27	13.4	8.3	:	:	2.3	-1.3	:	:
Euro area (EA-16)	15.3	9.1	96.3	:	1.1	-1.3	1.8	:
Belgium	18.3	10.1	83.6	328.0	1.3	-0.8	4.6	39.9
Bulgaria	:	:	:	:	:	:	:	:
Czech Republic	8.9	9.6	50.0	81.6	-1.1	0.5	:	:
Denmark	7.9	9.7	272.7	147.5	2.7	-1.4	12.4	25.4
Germany	17.2	8.8	89.2	184.2	-0.4	-0.3	0.6	15.0
Estonia	13.3	7.7	97.2	112.2	9.9	-3.1	6.2	12.5
Ireland	16.3	7.7	199.3	109.3	6.9	-8.8	2.0	28.9
Greece	:	:	:	:	:	:	:	:
Spain	18.1	9.2	124.6	110.5	4.7	-3.6	-2.6	8.6
France	16.0	9.3	77.2	189.3	0.9	-1.0	1.6	14.8
Italy	14.0	8.6	56.8	237.5	-0.7	-0.9	:	:
Cyprus	9.1	12.3	:	:	2.6	-2.9	:	:
Latvia	9.4	5.8	69.8	1.4	4.4	-1.9	:	:
Lithuania	6.6	5.0	45.4	53.3	8.8	-1.2	-0.1	-0.1
Luxembourg	:	:	:	:	:	:	:	:
Hungary	10.9	8.3	62.7	110.7	2.5	-0.5	1.2	21.9
Malta	:	:	:	:	:	:	:	:
Netherlands	13.4	12.2	241.3	289.2	1.3	-2.0	11.2	49.1
Austria	16.0	7.7	87.3	179.4	-0.5	-0.1	0.4	14.6
Poland	3.7	8.4	49.3	51.3	:	:	:	:
Portugal	11.0	7.1	129.3	169.3	3.2	-0.8	2.5	6.7
Romania	:	:	:	:	:	:	:	:
Slovenia	15.9	7.9	44.2	109.6	0.4	-2.5	2.7	:
Slovakia	8.1	8.0	50.9	18.1	1.6	-0.5	4.7	-0.7
Finland	11.5	10.3	100.3	94.4	3.6	-2.1	2.4	11.2
Sweden	15.6	5.0	140.8	177.0	1.6	-1.1	7.1	49.1
United Kingdom	6.3	5.0	149.0	188.5	4.2	-2.1	-4.2	:
Norway	12.4	8.3	:	20.1	3.3	-2.3	:	:
Switzerland	17.0	6.7	168.4	312.9	:	:	:	:

(1) Including non-profit institutions serving households.
(2) Poland and Switzerland, 2008.
(3) Czech Republic, Italy, Latvia, Poland and Switzerland, 2008.
(4) Czech Republic, Italy, Latvia, Poland, Slovenia, United Kingdom, Norway and Switzerland, 2008.

Source: Eurostat (nasa_ki and nasa_f_bs)

Figure 1.14: Household saving rate (gross), 2009 (1)

(%)

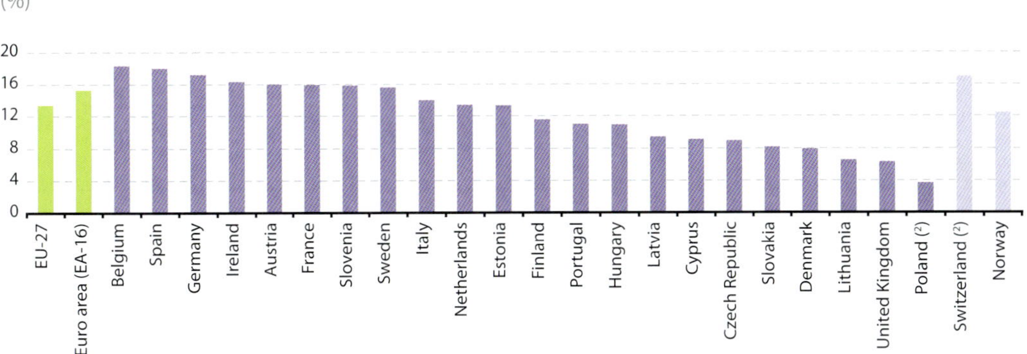

(1) Bulgaria, Greece, Luxembourg, Malta and Romania, not available.
(2) 2008.

Source: Eurostat (nasa_ki)

Figure 1.15: Household investment rate (gross), 2009 (1)

(%)

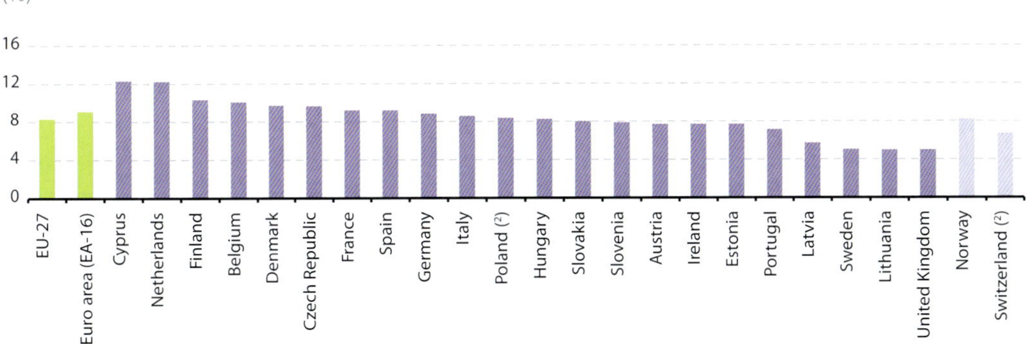

(1) Bulgaria, Greece, Luxembourg, Malta and Romania, not available.
(2) 2008.

Source: Eurostat (nasa_ki)

Figure 1.16: Household debt-to-income ratio (gross), 2009 (¹)
(%)

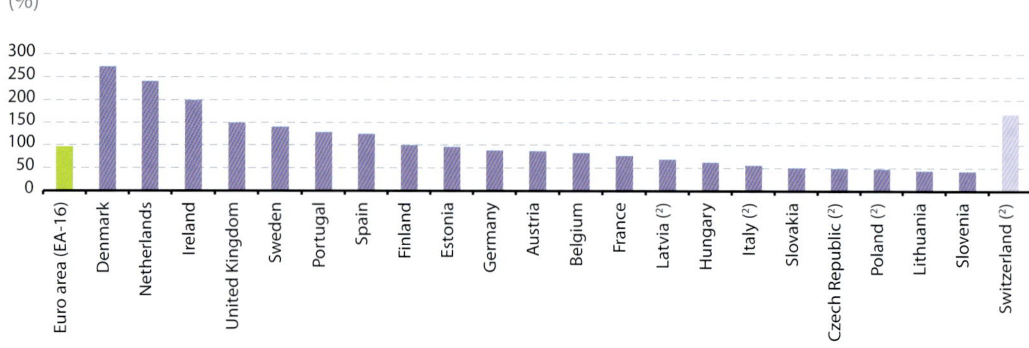

(¹) EU-27, Bulgaria, Greece, Cyprus, Luxembourg, Malta and Romania, not available.
(²) 2008.

Source: Eurostat (nasa_ki)

Figure 1.17: Investment rate (gross) of non-financial corporations, 2009 (¹)
(%)

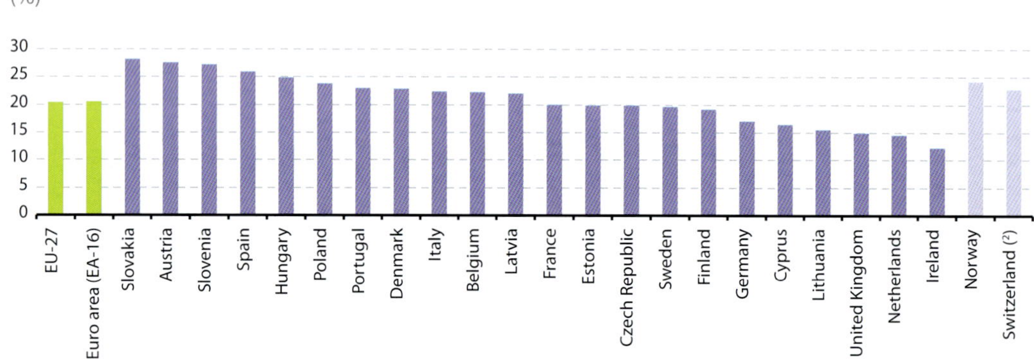

(¹) Bulgaria, Greece, Luxembourg, Malta and Romania, not available.
(²) 2008.

Source: Eurostat (nasa_ki)

Table 1.8: Key ratios of sector accounts, non-financial corporations, 2009

	Investment rate	Profit share	Investment rate	Profit share
	(%)		Change from 2008 (percentage points)	
EU-27	20.5	36.5	-2.5	-1.6
Euro area (EA-16)	20.6	37.0	-2.4	-1.8
Belgium	22.4	35.6	-1.0	-2.5
Bulgaria	:	:	:	:
Czech Republic	19.9	46.4	-3.3	1.4
Denmark	22.9	30.5	-2.9	-3.2
Germany	17.1	38.4	-2.1	-2.7
Estonia	19.9	38.3	-7.2	-1.8
Ireland	12.3	51.5	-3.3	1.1
Greece	:	:	:	:
Spain	26.0	36.6	-6.5	1.2
France	20.1	29.8	-1.0	-1.8
Italy	22.4	40.3	-2.4	-1.8
Cyprus	16.6	42.8	-3.3	-0.2
Latvia	22.1	47.5	-10.1	5.4
Lithuania	15.6	49.5	-10.9	-0.9
Luxembourg	:	42.0	:	-4.8
Hungary	25.0	42.4	-0.5	0.9
Malta	:	53.1	:	-2.4
Netherlands	14.6	37.7	-1.4	-3.3
Austria	27.7	39.8	-1.5	-2.8
Poland	23.8	49.5	-4.2	4.6
Portugal	23.0	33.2	-5.0	-2.1
Romania	:	:	:	:
Slovenia	27.3	31.0	-5.8	-3.1
Slovakia	28.2	48.9	-7.6	-6.0
Finland	19.2	37.3	-1.9	-5.5
Sweden	19.7	29.5	-3.1	-3.6
United Kingdom	15.0	32.8	-2.0	-2.3
Norway	24.4	52.1	1.4	-5.6
Switzerland (1)	23.0	35.6	:	:

(1) 2008.

Source: Eurostat (nasa_ki)

1.2 Government finances

This subchapter examines how key government finance indicators have evolved in the European Union (EU) and the euro area. Specifically, it considers public (general government) deficits, general government gross debt, total revenue and expenditure of general government, as well as total taxes and social contributions, which are the main sources of government revenue.

These statistics are crucial indicators for determining the health of a Member State's economy and under the terms of the EU's stability and growth pact, Member States have pledged to keep deficit and debt below certain limits: a Member State's government deficit may not exceed 3 % of its gross domestic product (GDP), while its debt may not exceed 60 % of GDP. If a Member State does not respect these limits, the so-called excessive deficit procedure is triggered. This entails several steps – including the possibility of sanctions – to encourage the Member State concerned to take measures to rectify the situation. The same deficit and debt limits are also criteria for economic and monetary union (EMU) and hence for joining the euro. Furthermore, the latest revision of the integrated economic and employment guidelines (revised as part of the Europe 2020 strategy for smart, sustainable and inclusive growth) includes a guideline to ensure the quality and the sustainability of public finances.

Main statistical findings

In 2009, the government deficit and government debt of both the EU-27 and the euro area (EA-16) increased considerably – reflecting the effects of the financial and economic crisis.

Government deficit

In the EU-27 the government deficit to GDP ratio increased from 2.3 % in 2008 to 6.8 % in 2009, and in the euro area it increased from 2.0 % to 6.3 %. Deficit ratios were greater than the target reference value of -3 % of GDP in 21 of the Member States in 2009, up from 11 Member States in 2008, while Hungary and Greece had a government deficit exceeding the -3 % threshold for the whole of the reporting period 2006 to 2009. The largest government deficits (as a percentage of GDP) in 2009 were recorded by Greece (-15.4 %), Ireland (-14.4 %), the United Kingdom (-11.4 %), Spain (-11.1 %), Latvia (-10.2 %), Portugal (-9.3 %), Lithuania (-9.2 %) and Romania (-8.6 %).

Two Member States, namely Estonia and Malta, recorded lower government deficit to GDP ratios in 2009 than they had in 2008. There were eight Member States that registered a government surplus in 2008; among these, Sweden, Luxembourg, Finland and Denmark each recorded deficits in 2009 that were smaller than -3 %, Germany recorded a deficit of -3.0 %, while Bulgaria, the Netherlands and Cyprus each recorded deficits that were larger than the -3 % threshold (see Figure 1.18). The remaining 17 Member States all recorded larger deficits in 2009 than in 2008, and some of these deficits increased considerably – for example, between 2008 and 2009 the deficit ratios of Ireland, Spain, Portugal, the United Kingdom and Latvia all increased by 6 percentage points or more.

Government debt

In the EU-27 the government debt-to-GDP ratio increased from 61.8 % at the end of 2008 to 74.0 % at the end of 2009, and in the euro area from 69.8 % to 79.2 %. At the end of 2009, the lowest ratios of government debt to GDP were recorded in Estonia (7.2 %), Luxembourg (14.5 %), Bulgaria (14.7 %), Romania (23.9 %), and Lithuania (29.5 %) – see Figure 1.19.

In 2009, government debt-to-GDP ratios increased for all 27 EU Member States when compared with 2008. The highest increases of debt ratios from 2008 to 2009 were observed in Ireland (up 21.2 percentage points), Latvia (17.0 points), the United Kingdom (16.1 points), Greece (16.5 points), Lithuania (13.9 points), Spain (13.4 points) and Slovenia (12.9 points). A total of 18 Member States reported a debt ratio below 60 % of GDP in 2008, a number which fell to 15 Member States in 2009 as the United Kingdom, Ireland and the Netherlands saw their debt ratio pass the 60 % threshold.

Government revenue and expenditure

The importance of the general government sector in the economy may be measured in terms of total general government revenue and expenditure as a percentage of GDP. In the EU-27, total government revenue in 2009 amounted to 44.0 % of GDP (down from 44.6 % of GDP in 2008), and expenditure to 50.8 % of GDP (up from 46.9 % of GDP in 2008) – see Figure 1.20. The level of general government expenditure and revenue varies considerably between the Member States (see Figure 1.21). In 2009, the countries with the highest levels of combined government expenditure and revenue as a proportion of GDP, of more than 100 %, were Denmark, Finland, Sweden, France, Belgium and Austria. Five Member States reported relatively low combined ratios of under 80 %: Romania, Slovakia, Bulgaria, Latvia and Lithuania. For 2009, the effects of the financial and economic crisis are reflected clearly in the numbers presented above. They show a reduction in nominal GDP experienced in many Member States, a sharp fall in government revenues in absolute terms (from 2008 to 2009 total general government revenue fell by nearly 7 % in absolute terms), as well as some counter-cyclical policies (in absolute terms government spending increased by around 2 % in the EU-27 from 2008 to 2009).

Across the EU, the main components of total general government revenue are taxes and social contributions (see Figure 1.22). In 2009, taxes made up 50.2 % of total revenue in the EU-27 (55.2 % in the euro area), while social contributions amounted to 28.7 % of total revenue (35.5 % in the euro area). Looking at each Member State (see Figure 1.23), the relative importance of the categories in which EU governments collect revenue varies widely between countries. For example, taxes made up less than 40 % of government revenue in Greece and Slovakia in 2009, but more than 80 % of government revenue in Denmark.

Turning to total general government expenditure, the largest proportion of EU-27 expenditure in 2009 concerned the redistribution of income in the form of social transfers in cash or in kind (see Figure 1.24). Social transfers made up 42.9 % of total expenditure in the EU-27 (46.2 % in the euro area). Compensation of employees accounted for 22.1 % of government expenditure (21.3 % in the euro area). Property income paid – of which by far the largest part is made up of interest payments – accounted for 5.2 % of government expenditure in the EU-27 (5.6 % in the euro area), a share which rose to over 8 % in Greece, Hungary and Italy (see Figure 1.25).

General government expenditure can be analysed in more detail using the classification of the functions of government (COFOG). Social protection measures accounted for the highest proportion of government expenditure in 2008 in all of the Member States. Their share ranged from slightly more than 20 % of GDP in Denmark, France, Sweden, Greece and Finland to just under 10 % in Latvia, Slovakia and Cyprus, while the EU-27 average was 18.2 % of GDP. As total government expenditure made up 46.9 % of GDP in 2008 in the EU-27, social protection measures accounted for nearly 40 % of total expenditure. The next COFOG functions, in order of their relative importance, for the EU-27 as a whole were health (6.9 % of GDP), general public services (6.3 %) and education (5.2 %). Spending on economic affairs in the EU-27 was close to 4 % of GDP, while less than 2 % of GDP was devoted to defence, public order and safety, environmental protection, housing and community affairs, recreation, and religion and culture (see Figure 1.26).

The main types of government revenue are taxes on income and wealth, taxes on production and imports, and social contributions. In 2009 total receipts from these taxes and social contributions in the EU-27 amounted to 39.3 % of GDP (down from 39.8 % in 2008). Looking more closely at the structure of revenues within the EU-27 it is possible to observe a relative increase in receipts from social contributions in 2009, while the two other main headings, taxes on income and wealth and taxes on production, decreased (see Figure 1.27).

While the ratio of taxes on income and wealth to GDP decreased in the EU-27 during the period up to 2003, the situation was reversed between 2004 and 2007, as taxes on income and wealth relative to GDP increased from 12.4 % to 13.4 %, before dropping back to 13.1 % in 2008 and to 12.3 % in 2009. Taxes on production and imports relative to GDP grew steadily from 13.1 % in 2001 to 13.5 % in 2007 (with a stable period between 2006 and 2007), before also dropping back to just above and below 13 % in 2008 and 2009, respectively. In contrast, social contributions had fallen from 13.9 % of GDP in 2003 to 13.4 % in 2007, before picking up to 13.6 % in 2008 and 14.1 % in 2009.

However, there was considerable variation in the structure of tax revenue across the Member States (see Figure 1.28). As may be expected, those countries that reported relatively high levels of expenditure tended to be those that also raised more taxes (as a proportion of GDP). For example, the highest return from these taxes and social contributions was 48.6 % of GDP recorded in Denmark, with Sweden recording the next highest share (46.7 %), while the proportion of GDP accounted for by such revenue was below 30 % in six of the Member States: Latvia, Romania, Bulgaria, Slovakia, Ireland and Lithuania.

In 2009 the value of public procurement which is openly advertised reached 12.2 % of GDP in Bulgaria, more than three times as high as the 3.6 % average for the EU-27 (see Figure 1.29). None of the Member States that joined the EU in 2004 or 2007 recorded ratios below the EU-27 average in 2009. Among the EU-15 Member States, the United Kingdom and Finland recorded the highest ratio of openly advertised public procurement to GDP, while Germany and Luxembourg reported the lowest.

In response to the recent financial and economic crisis, total state aid in the EU-27 rose from 0.5 % of GDP in 2007 to 2.2 % in 2008, although this average masks significant disparities between Member States (see Figure 1.30).

Data sources and availability

Member States are required to provide the European Commission with their government deficit and debt statistics before 1 April and 1 October of each year under the terms of the excessive deficit procedure. In addition, Eurostat collects more detailed data on government finances in the framework of the ESA transmission programme the programme under which Member States submit national accounts data. The main aggregates of general government are provided by the Member States to Eurostat twice a year, whereas statistics on the functions of government (COFOG) are transmitted within one year after the end of the reference period.

The data presented in this subchapter correspond to the main revenue and expenditure items of the general government sector, which are compiled on a national accounts (ESA95) basis. The difference between total revenue and total expenditure – including capital expenditure (in particular, gross fixed capital formation) – equals net lending/net borrowing of general government, which is also the balancing item of the government non-financial accounts.

Delineation of general government

The general government sector includes all institutional units whose output is intended for individual and collective consumption and mainly financed by compulsory payments made by units belonging to other sectors, and/or all institutional units principally engaged in the redistribution of national income and wealth. The general government sector is subdivided into four subsectors: central government, state government, local government, and social security funds.

Definition of main indicators

The public balance is defined as general government net borrowing/net lending reported for the excessive deficit procedure and is expressed in relation to GDP. According to the protocol on the excessive deficit procedure, government debt is the gross debt outstanding at the end of the year of the general government sector measured at nominal (face) value and consolidated.

The main revenue of general government consists of taxes, social contributions, sales and property income. It is defined in ESA95 by reference to a list of categories: market output, output for own final use, payments for the other non-market output, taxes on production and imports, other subsidies on production, receivable property income, current taxes on income, wealth, etc., social contributions, other current transfers and capital transfers.

The main expenditure items consist of the compensation of civil servants, social benefits, interest on the public debt, subsidies, and gross fixed capital formation. Total general government expenditure is defined in ESA95 by reference to a list of categories: intermediate consumption, gross capital formation, compensation of employees, other taxes on production, subsidies, payable property income, current taxes on income, wealth, social benefits, some social transfers, other current transfers, some adjustments, capital transfers, and transactions on non-produced assets.

Taxes and social contributions correspond to revenues which are levied (in cash or in kind) by central, state and local governments, and social security funds. These levies (generally referred to as taxes) are organised into three main areas, covered by the following headings:

- taxes on income and wealth, including all compulsory payments levied periodically by general government on the income and wealth of enterprises and households;
- taxes on production and imports, including all compulsory payments levied by general government with respect to the production and importation of goods and services, the employment of labour, the ownership or use of land, buildings or other assets used in production;
- social contributions, including all employers' and employees' social contributions, as well as imputed social contributions that represent the counterpart to social benefits paid directly by employers.

Data on public procurement are based on information contained in the calls for competition and contract award notices submitted for publication in the Official Journal of the European Communities (the S series). The numerator is the value of public procurement, which is openly advertised. For each of the sectors – works, supplies and services – the number of calls for competition published is multiplied by an average based, in general, on all the prices provided in the contract award notices published in the Official Journal during the relevant year. The value of public procurement is then expressed relative to GDP.

State aid is made up of sectoral state aid (given to specific activities, such as agriculture, fisheries, manufacturing, mining, services), ad-hoc state aid (given to individual enterprises, for example, for rescue or restructuring), and state aid for cross-cutting (horizontal) objectives, such as research and development, safeguarding the environment, support to small and medium-sized enterprises, employment creation or training, including aid for regional development. The first two of these (sectoral and ad-hoc state aid) are considered potentially more distortive to competition.

Context

The disciplines of the stability and growth pact (SGP) are intended keep economic developments in the EU, and the euro area countries in particular, broadly synchronised and prevent Member States from taking policy measures which would unduly benefit their own economies at the expense of others. There are two key principles to the SGP: namely, that the deficit (planned or actual) must not exceed 3 % of GDP and that the debt-to-GDP ratio should not be more than 60 %.

Under the rules on budgetary discipline within the pact, the only exceptions foreseen are for cases where the excess over the reference value is only exceptional or temporary, or where the ratios have declined substantially and continuously.

A revision in March 2005, based on the first five years of experience, left these principles unchanged, but introduced greater flexibility in exceeding the deficit threshold in hard economic times or to finance investment in structural improvements. It also gave Member States a longer period to reverse their excessive deficits – although, if they do not bring their economies back into line, corrective measures, or even fines, may still be imposed.

Each year, Member States provide the European Commission with detailed information on their economic policies and the state of their public finances. Euro area countries provide this information in the context of the stability programmes, while other Member States do so in the form of convergence programmes. The European Commission assesses whether the policies are in line with agreed economic, social and environmental objectives and may choose to issue a warning if it believes a deficit is becoming abnormally high.

Figure 1.18: Public balance ([1])
(net borrowing or lending of consolidated general government sector, % of GDP)

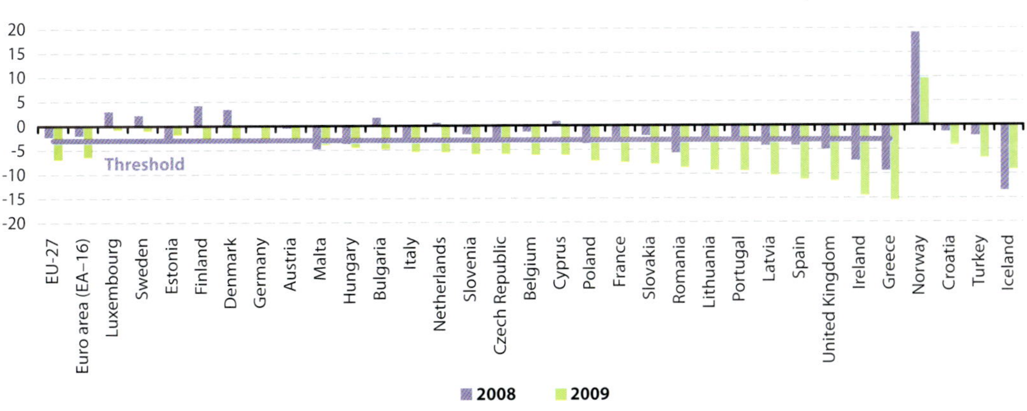

([1]) Data extracted on 29.11.2010.

Source: Eurostat (tsieb080)

Table 1.9: Public balance and general government debt (¹)

	Public balance (net borrowing/lending of consolidated general government sector, % of GDP)				General government debt (general government consolidated gross debt, % of GDP)			
	2006	2007	2008	2009	2006	2007	2008	2009
EU-27	-1.5	-0.9	-2.3	-6.8	61.5	58.8	61.8	74.0
Euro area (EA-16)	-1.4	-0.6	-2.0	-6.3	68.5	66.2	69.8	79.2
Belgium	0.2	-0.3	-1.3	-6.0	88.1	84.2	89.6	96.2
Bulgaria	1.9	1.1	1.7	-4.7	21.6	17.2	13.7	14.7
Czech Republic	-2.6	-0.7	-2.7	-5.8	29.4	29.0	30.0	35.3
Denmark	5.2	4.8	3.4	-2.7	32.1	27.4	34.2	41.4
Germany	-1.6	0.3	0.1	-3.0	67.6	64.9	66.3	73.4
Estonia	2.4	2.5	-2.8	-1.7	4.4	3.7	4.6	7.2
Ireland	2.9	0.0	-7.3	-14.4	24.8	25.0	44.3	65.5
Greece	-5.7	-6.4	-9.4	-15.4	106.1	105.0	110.3	126.8
Spain	2.0	1.9	-4.2	-11.1	39.6	36.1	39.8	53.2
France	-2.3	-2.7	-3.3	-7.5	63.7	63.8	67.5	78.1
Italy	-3.4	-1.5	-2.7	-5.3	106.6	103.6	106.3	116.0
Cyprus	-1.2	3.4	0.9	-6.0	64.6	58.3	48.3	58.0
Latvia	-0.5	-0.3	-4.2	-10.2	10.7	9.0	19.7	36.7
Lithuania	-0.4	-1.0	-3.3	-9.2	18.0	16.9	15.6	29.5
Luxembourg	1.4	3.7	3.0	-0.7	6.7	6.7	13.6	14.5
Hungary	-9.3	-5.0	-3.7	-4.4	65.7	66.1	72.3	78.4
Malta	-2.7	-2.3	-4.8	-3.8	63.4	61.7	63.1	68.6
Netherlands	0.5	0.2	0.6	-5.4	47.4	45.3	58.2	60.8
Austria	-1.5	-0.4	-0.5	-3.5	62.1	59.3	62.5	67.5
Poland	-3.6	-1.9	-3.7	-7.2	47.7	45.0	47.1	50.9
Portugal	-4.1	-2.8	-2.9	-9.3	63.9	62.7	65.3	76.1
Romania	-2.2	-2.6	-5.7	-8.6	12.4	12.6	13.4	23.9
Slovenia	-1.3	0.0	-1.8	-5.8	26.7	23.4	22.5	35.4
Slovakia	-3.2	-1.8	-2.1	-7.9	30.5	29.6	27.8	35.4
Finland	4.0	5.2	4.2	-2.5	39.7	35.2	34.1	43.8
Sweden	2.3	3.6	2.2	-0.9	45.0	40.0	38.2	41.9
United Kingdom	-2.7	-2.7	-5.0	-11.4	43.4	44.5	52.1	68.2
Iceland	6.3	5.4	-13.5	-9.1	27.9	29.1	57.4	:
Norway	18.5	17.7	19.1	9.7	55.3	52.4	49.9	43.7
Croatia	-3.0	-2.5	-1.4	-4.1	35.5	32.9	28.9	35.3
Turkey	0.8	-1.0	-2.2	-6.7	46.1	39.4	39.5	45.4

(¹) Data extracted on 29.11.2010.

Source: Eurostat (tsieb080 and tsieb090)

Figure 1.19: General government debt (¹)
(general government consolidated gross debt, % of GDP)

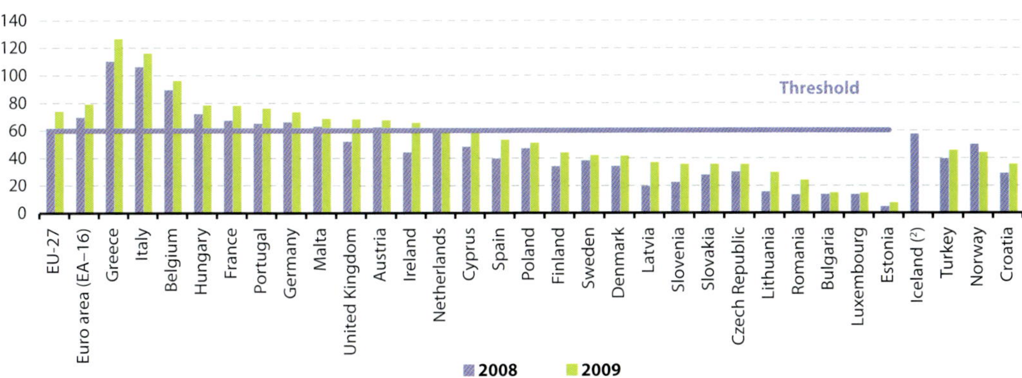

(¹) Data extracted on 29.11.2010.
(²) 2009, not available.

Source: Eurostat (tsieb090)

Figure 1.20: Development of total expenditure and total revenue (¹)
(% of GDP)

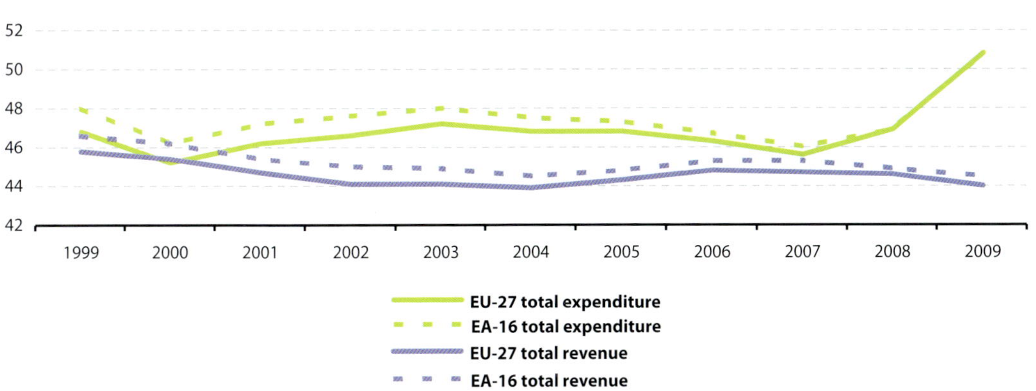

(¹) Data extracted on 09.02.2011.

Source: Eurostat (gov_a_main)

Figure 1.21: Government revenue and expenditure, 2009 (¹)
(% of GDP)

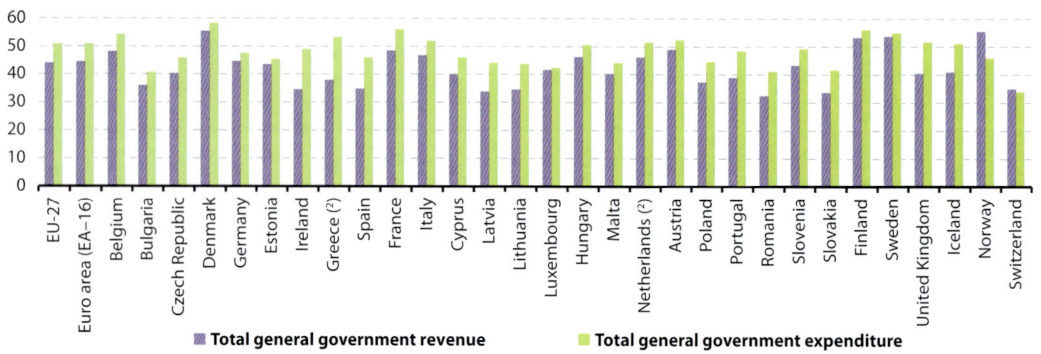

(¹) Countries ranked on the average of revenue and expenditure; data extracted on 18.01.2011.
(²) Provisional.

Source: Eurostat (tec00021 and tec00023)

Figure 1.22: Composition of total revenue, 2009 (¹)
(%)

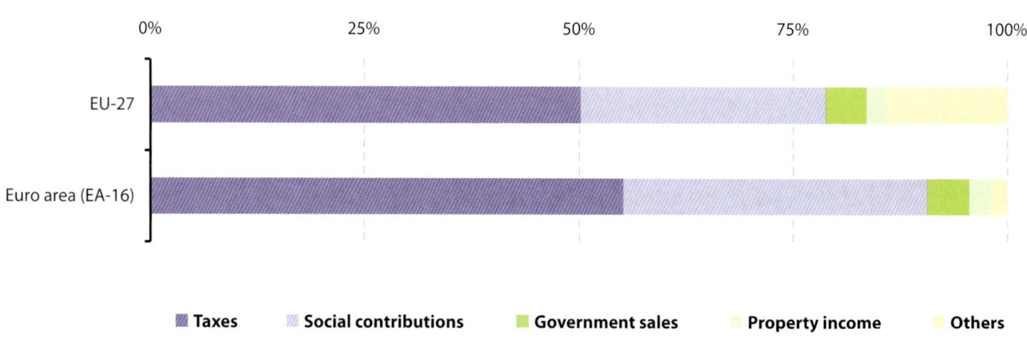

(¹) Data extracted on 09.02.2011.

Source: Eurostat (gov_a_main)

Figure 1.23: Main components of government revenue, 2009
(%)

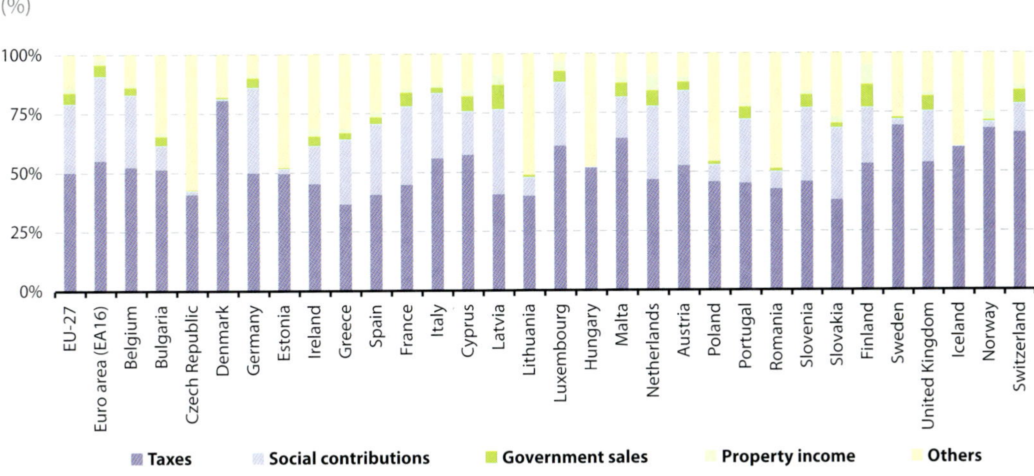

Source: Eurostat (gov_a_main)

Figure 1.24: Composition of total expenditure, 2009
(%)

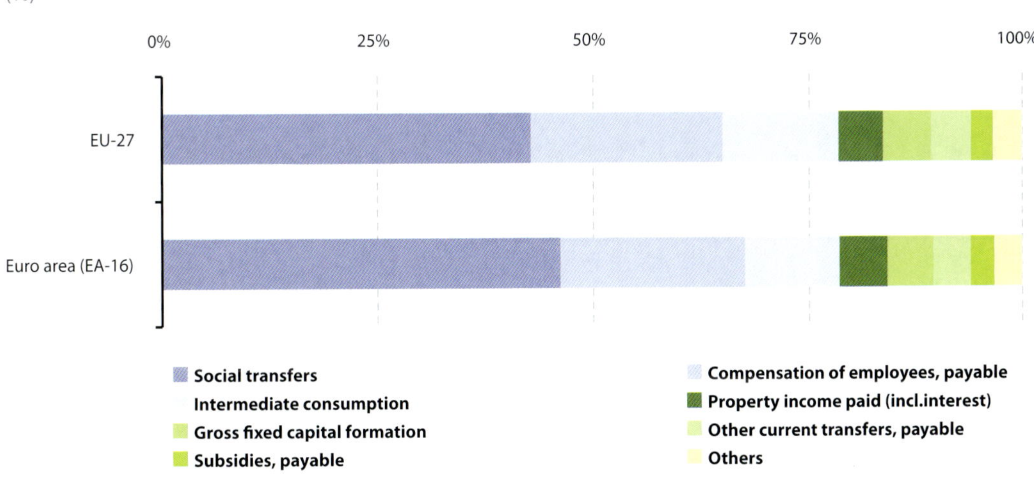

Source: Eurostat (gov_a_main)

Figure 1.25: Main components of government expenditure, 2009
(%)

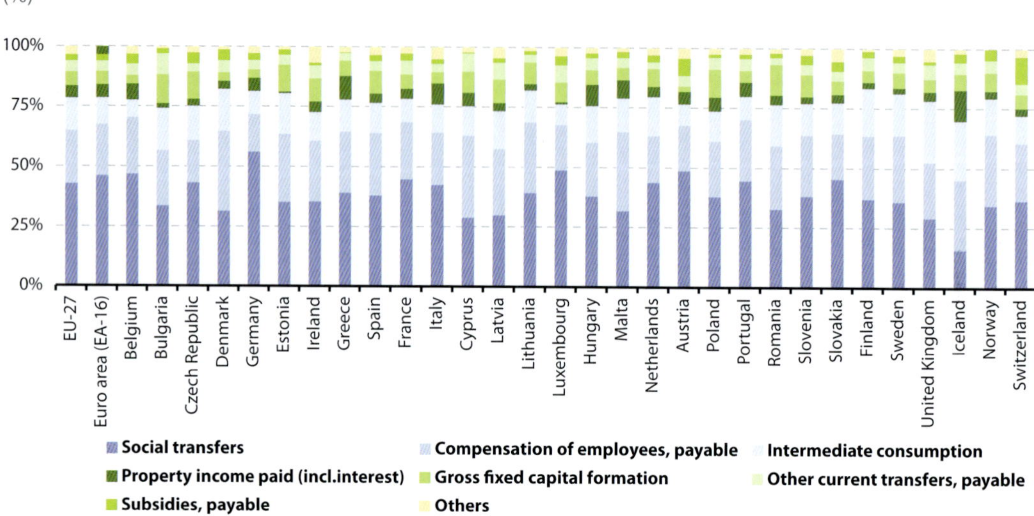

Source: Eurostat (gov_a_main)

Figure 1.26: General government expenditure by COFOG function, 2008 (1)
(% of GDP)

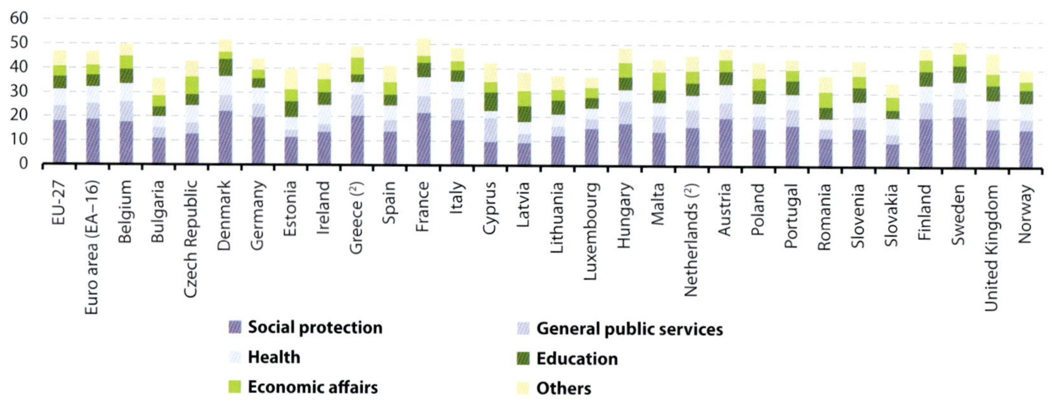

(1) COFOG: classification of the functions of government; data extracted on 29.11.2010.
(2) Provisional.

Source: Eurostat (gov_a_exp)

Figure 1.27: Taxes and social contributions, EU-27 (1)
(% of GDP)

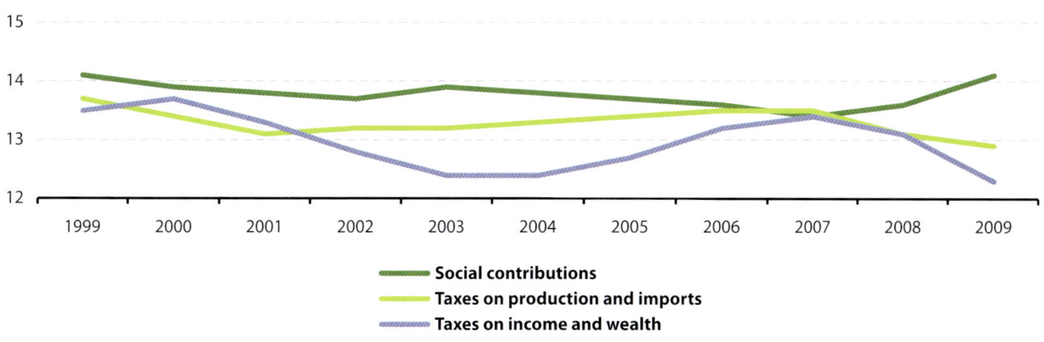

(1) Data extracted on 29.11.2010.

Source: Eurostat (tec00019, tec00020 and tec00018)

Figure 1.28: Taxes and social contributions, 2009 (1)
(% of GDP)

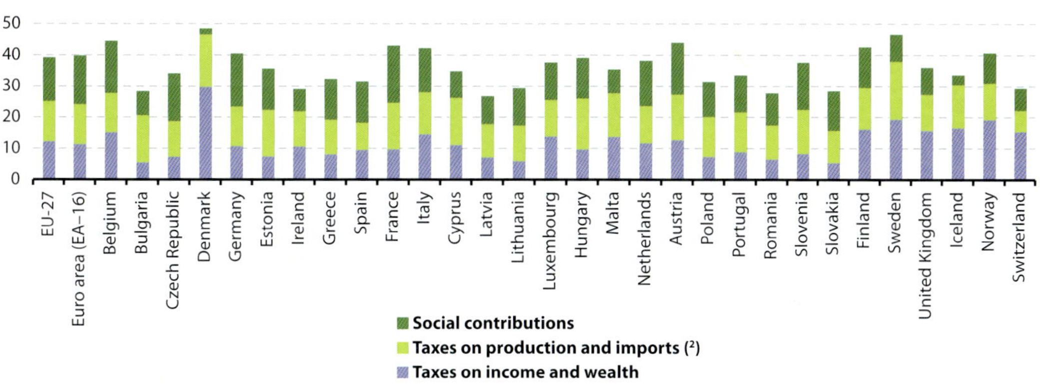

(1) Data extracted on 29.11.2010.
(2) Denmark, includes taxes on production and imports paid to the institutions of the European Union.

Source: Eurostat (tec00019, tec00020 and tec00018)

Figure 1.29: Public procurement (1)
(value of public procurement which is openly advertised, as % of GDP)

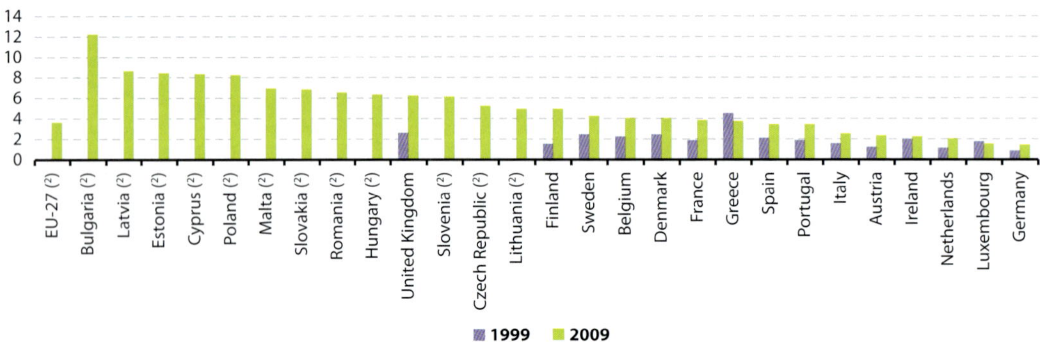

(1) Data extracted on 09.02.2011.
(2) 1999, not available.

Source: Eurostat (tsier090), Commission services

Figure 1.30: State aid, 2008
(% of GDP)

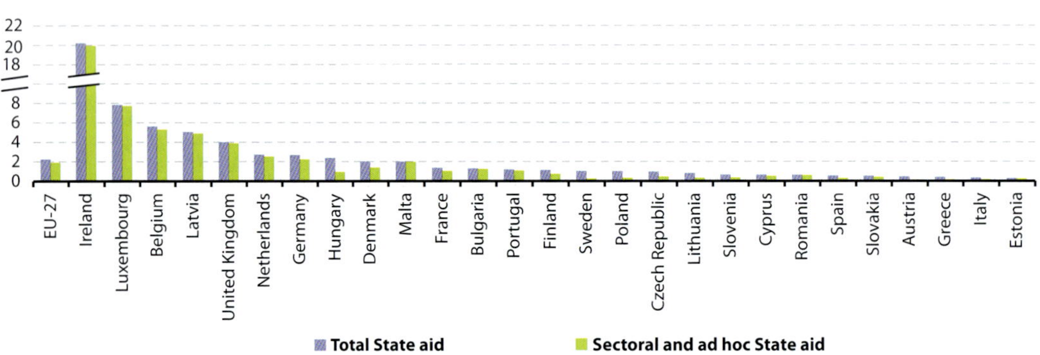

Source: Eurostat (tsier100), Commission services

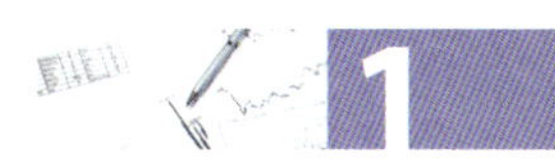

1.3 Exchange rates and interest rates

This subchapter presents an analysis of exchange rates and interest rates based on data from September 2010; as these indicators change quite frequently, the latest data can be consulted in the Eurostat main tables (exchange rates and interest rates) and data base (exchange rates and interest rates). The analysis considers the evolution of exchange rates across the European Union (EU), as well as exchange rate fluctuations between the euro, the Japanese yen, the Swiss franc and the United States dollar (all of which are important reserve currencies).

The second half of the subchapter examines interest rates - in other words, the cost of borrowing and/or lending money. At the macro-economic level, key interest rates are generally set by central banks, as a primary tool for monetary policy with the goal of maintaining price stability and controlling inflation.

Main statistical findings

It is important to note that practically all of Eurostat's data presented in monetary terms (including statistics for those Member States that are not part of the euro area and data for non-member countries) have been converted from national currencies to euro (EUR - see currency codes). When making comparisons across different countries for indicators denominated in euro terms, it is necessary to bear in mind the possible effect of currency fluctuations, in particular when analysing time series.

The index of annual average exchange rates presented in Figure 1.31 starts in 2000, during the second half of which the euro was at historically low levels against many currencies. There was a marked appreciation in the value of the euro compared with the Japanese yen during the period from 2000 to 2007, while a similar pattern was observed against the United States dollar from 2001 to 2008. In contrast, there was considerably less variation in exchange rates between the euro and the Swiss franc; no more than +/-6 % between 2000 and 2009.

A more detailed analysis - using average daily exchange rates - shows that the euro reached a relative high against the Swiss franc on 12 October 2007 (EUR 1=CHF 1.6803). In the summer of 2008 the euro rose to its most recent relative highs against the currencies of the United States and Japan, peaking against the dollar on 15 July 2008 (EUR 1=USD 1.599) and against the yen only eight days later (EUR 1=JPY 169.75).

Since these relative peaks, the value of the euro has generally depreciated. On 1 October 2010 (as this subchapter was in the process of being drafted), the latest exchange rates available showed that one euro was worth CHF 1.3423, or JPY 114.26, or USD 1.3726. A comparison between the relative highs of 2007/2008 and the latest euro exchange rates shows that the value of the euro depreciated against the yen by almost one third (32.7 %), while the value of the euro against the Swiss franc fell by 20.1 %, and the corresponding reduction against the United States dollar was 14.2 %.

Table 1.10 shows the evolution of exchange rates between the euro and a broader range of currencies. Between 2000 and 2010, the euro appreciated strongly against the Turkish lira, and also against the Icelandic krona (particularly from 2008 onwards following the collapse of several Icelandic banks). The euro also appreciated against the currencies of Latvia, Romania, Sweden and the United Kingdom. In contrast, the national currencies of the Czech Republic (among the Member States), and Switzerland and Croatia (among non-member countries) appreciated against the euro during the period 2000 to 2010. Note that some non-euro area members have fixed their exchange rates against the euro, as part of the exchange rate mechanism (ERM II) in preparation for joining the euro area.

Table 1.11 shows interest rates and yields. Note that between the three reference periods shown in the table it is possible that there was a considerable fluctuation in interest rates. Despite this, the overall pattern was that of declining interest rates over the last decade, such that interest rates often stood at historically low levels by 2009. Interest rates fell at a rapid rate during the second half of 2008 and into 2009, as the effects of the financial and economic crisis were felt. Nevertheless, interest rates in Bulgaria, Latvia, Lithuania, Hungary and Romania remained relatively high.

Data sources and availability

Exchange rates

Eurostat publishes a number of different data sets concerning exchange rates. Three main databases can be distinguished, with statistics on:

- bilateral exchange rates between currencies, including some special conversion factors for countries that have adopted the euro;
- fluctuations in the exchange rate mechanism (ERM and ERM II) of the EU;
- effective exchange rate indices.

Bilateral exchange rates are available with reference to the euro, although before 1999 they were given in relation to the European currency unit (ECU). The ECU ceased to exist on 1 January 1999 when it was replaced by the euro at an exchange rate of 1:1. From that date, the currencies of the euro area became subdivisions of the euro at irrevocably fixed rates of conversion.

Daily exchange rates are available from 1974 onwards against a large number of currencies. These daily values are used to construct monthly and annual averages, which are based on business day rates; alternatively, month-end and year-end rates are also published.

Interest rates

Interest rates provide information on the cost or price of borrowing, or the gain from lending; traditionally, interest rates are expressed in annual percentage terms, although the period for lending/borrowing can be anything from overnight to a period of many years. Different types of interest rates are distinguished either by the period of lending/borrowing involved, or by the parties involved in the transaction (business, consumers, governments or interbank operations).

Long-term interest rates are one of the convergence criteria for European economic and monetary union (EMU). In order to comply, Member States need to demonstrate an average nominal long-term interest rate that does not exceed by more than 2 percentage points that of, at most, the three best-performing Member States. Long-term interest rates are based upon central government bond yields (or comparable securities), taking into account differences in national definitions, on the secondary market, gross of tax, with a residual maturity of around ten years.

Eurostat also publishes a number of short-term interest rates, with different maturities (overnight, 1 to 12 months). Other interest rates that are published include retail bank interest rates which are lending and deposit rates for commercial banks (non-harmonised and historical series), and harmonised monetary financial institutions (MFI) interest rates.

A yield curve, also known as term structure of interest rates, represents the relationship between market remuneration (interest) rates and the remaining time to maturity of debt securities.

Context

Interest rates, inflation rates and exchange rates are highly linked: the interaction between these economic phenomena is often complicated by a range of additional factors such as levels of government debt, the sentiment of financial markets, terms of trade, political stability, and overall economic performance. Central banks seek to exert influence over both inflation and exchange rates, through controlling monetary policy – their main tool for this purpose is the setting of key interest rates.

An exchange rate is the price or value of one currency in relation to another. Those countries with relatively stable and low inflation rates tend to display an appreciation in their currencies, as their purchasing power increases relative to other currencies, whereas higher inflation typically leads to a depreciation of the local currency. When the value of one currency appreciates against another, then that country's exports become more expensive and its imports become cheaper.

The exchange rate mechanism (ERM II) was set up on 1 January 1999, with the goal of ensuring that exchange rate fluctuations between the euro and other EU currencies did not disrupt economic stability within the single market, and to help non-euro area countries prepare themselves for participation in the euro area. The convergence criteria (Maastricht criteria) on exchange rate stability requires participation in ERM II, with exchange rates of non-euro area Member States fixed against the euro such that these may only fluctuate by 15 % above or below an agreed central rate. If necessary, the currencies are supported by intervention (buying or selling) to keep the exchange rate against the euro within the agreed fluctuation band; such intervention is coordinated by the European Central Bank (ECB) and the central bank of the non-euro area Member State. The general council of the ECB monitors the operation of ERM II and ensures coordination of monetary and exchange rate policies, as well as administering the intervention mechanisms with the central banks of the Member States.

All economic and monetary union participants are eligible to adopt the euro. Aside from demonstrating two years of exchange rate stability (via membership of ERM II), those Member States wishing to join the euro area also need to adhere to a number of additional criteria relating to interest rates, budget deficits, inflation rates, and debt-to-GDP ratios.

Through using a common currency, the countries of the euro area have removed exchange rates and, therefore, hope to benefit from the elimination of currency exchange costs, lower transaction costs and the promotion of trade and investment resulting from the scale of the euro area market. Furthermore, the use of a single currency increases price transparency for consumers across the euro area.

From 1 January 2002, around 7 800 million notes and 40 400 million coins entered circulation across the euro area, as 12 Member States – Belgium, Germany, Ireland, Greece, Spain, France, Italy, Luxembourg, the Netherlands, Austria, Portugal and Finland – adopted the euro as their common currency. Slovenia subsequently joined the euro area at the start of 2007, and was followed by Cyprus and Malta on 1 January 2008, Slovakia on 1 January 2009 and Estonia on 1 January 2011, bringing the total number of countries using the euro as their common currency to 17.

In joining the euro each Member States has agreed to allow the ECB to act as an independent authority responsible for maintaining price stability through the implementation of monetary policy. As of 1999, the ECB started to set benchmark interest rates and manage the euro area's foreign exchange reserves. The ECB has defined price stability as a year-on-year increase in the harmonized index of consumer prices (HICP) for the euro area below, but close to, 2 % over the medium term (see Subchapter 1.4 on consumer prices – inflation and comparative price levels). Monetary policy decisions are taken by the ECB's governing council which meets every month to analyse and assess economic and monetary developments and the risks to price stability and thereafter to decide upon the appropriate level of key interest rates.

Figure 1.31: Exchange rates against the euro (1)

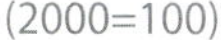
(2000=100)

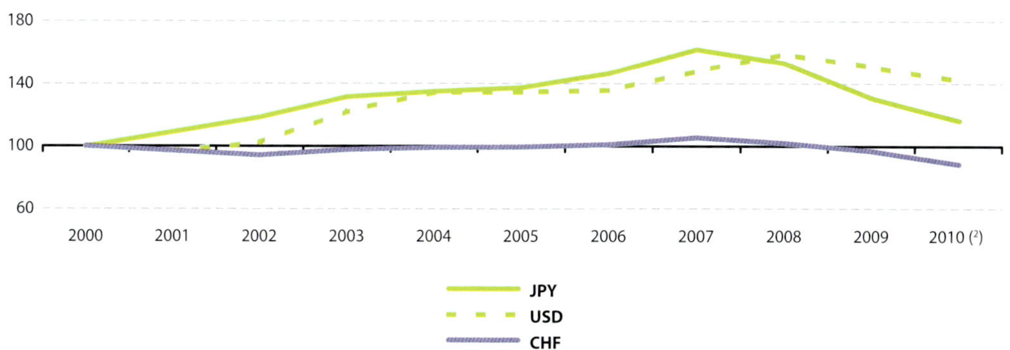

(1) CHF, Swiss franc; JPY, Japanese Yen; USD, United States Dollar; a reduction in the value of the index shows an appreciation in the value of the foreign currency and a depreciation in the value of the euro.
(2) Forecasts.

Source: Eurostat (tec00033), ECB

Table 1.10: Exchange rates against the euro (1)
(1 EUR=… national currency)

	2000	2001	2002	2003	2004	2005	2006	2007	2008	2009	2010 (2)
Bulgaria	1.9522	1.9482	1.9492	1.9490	1.9533	1.9558	1.9558	1.9558	1.9558	1.9558	1.9558
Czech Republic	35.599	34.068	30.804	31.846	31.891	29.782	28.342	27.766	24.946	26.435	25.262
Denmark	7.4538	7.4521	7.4305	7.4307	7.4399	7.4518	7.4591	7.4506	7.4560	7.4462	7.4454
Estonia	15.647	15.647	15.647	15.647	15.647	15.647	15.647	15.647	15.647	15.647	15.647
Latvia	0.5592	0.5601	0.5810	0.6407	0.6652	0.6962	0.6962	0.7001	0.7027	0.7057	0.7086
Lithuania	3.6952	3.5823	3.4594	3.4527	3.4529	3.4528	3.4528	3.4528	3.4528	3.4528	3.4528
Hungary	260.04	256.59	242.96	253.62	251.66	248.05	264.26	251.35	251.51	280.33	276.95
Poland	4.0082	3.6721	3.8574	4.3996	4.5268	4.0230	3.8959	3.7837	3.5121	4.3276	3.9922
Romania	1.9922	2.6004	3.1270	3.7551	4.0510	3.6209	3.5258	3.3353	3.6826	4.2399	4.2048
Sweden	8.4452	9.2551	9.1611	9.1242	9.1243	9.2822	9.2544	9.2501	9.6152	10.6191	9.5486
United Kingdom	0.60948	0.62187	0.62883	0.69199	0.67866	0.68380	0.68173	0.68434	0.79628	0.89094	0.85324
Iceland	72.58	87.42	86.18	86.65	87.14	78.23	87.76	87.63	143.83	172.67	161.82
Norway	8.1129	8.0484	7.5086	8.0033	8.3697	8.0092	8.0472	8.0165	8.2237	8.7278	7.9717
Switzerland	1.5579	1.5105	1.4670	1.5212	1.5438	1.5483	1.5729	1.6427	1.5874	1.5100	1.3786
Croatia	7.6432	7.4820	7.4130	7.5688	7.4967	7.4008	7.3247	7.3376	7.2239	7.3400	7.2688
Turkey	0.5748	1.1024	1.4397	1.6949	1.7771	1.6771	1.8090	1.7865	1.9064	2.1631	1.9882
Japan	99.47	108.68	118.06	130.97	134.44	136.85	146.02	161.25	152.45	130.34	115.98
United States	0.9236	0.8956	0.9456	1.1312	1.2439	1.2441	1.2556	1.3705	1.4708	1.3948	1.3137

(1) The euro replaced the ecu on 1 January 1999; on 1 January 2002, it also replaced the notes and coins of 12 Community currencies with the introduction of the euro to the euro area (EA-12) members; on 1 January 2007, the euro came into circulation in Slovenia; on 1 January 2008, the euro came into circulation in Cyprus and Malta; on 1 January 2009, the euro came into circulation in Slovakia.
(2) Forecasts.

Source: Eurostat (tec00033 and ert_bil_eur_a), ECB

Table 1.11: Interest rates
(%)

	EMU convergence criterion bond yields (Maastricht criterion) (¹)			Short-term interest rates: three-month interbank rates (annual average)		
	1999	2004	2009	1999	2004	2009
EU-27	:	4.38	4.13	:	2.86	1.56
Euro area (²)	4.66	4.12	3.82	2.96	2.11	1.22
Belgium	4.75	4.15	3.90	-	-	-
Bulgaria	:	5.36	7.22	5.88	3.74	5.72
Czech Republic	:	4.82	4.84	6.85	2.36	2.19
Denmark	4.91	4.30	3.59	3.44	2.20	2.49
Germany	4.49	4.04	3.22	-	-	-
Estonia	:	:	:	7.81	2.50	5.92
Ireland	4.71	4.08	5.23	-	-	-
Greece	6.30	4.26	5.17	10.09	-	-
Spain	4.73	4.10	3.98	-	-	-
France	4.61	4.10	3.65	-	-	-
Italy	4.73	4.26	4.31	-	-	-
Cyprus	:	5.80	4.60	6.25	4.74	-
Latvia	:	4.86	12.36	8.44	4.23	13.09
Lithuania	:	4.50	14.00	13.89	2.68	7.07
Luxembourg	4.66	2.84	4.23	-	:	:
Hungary	:	8.19	9.12	15.07	11.53	9.14
Malta	:	4.69	4.54	5.15	2.94	-
Netherlands	4.63	4.10	3.69	-	-	-
Austria	4.68	4.13	3.94	-	-	-
Poland	:	6.90	6.12	14.73	6.20	4.42
Portugal	4.78	4.14	4.21	-	-	-
Romania	:	:	9.69	79.63	19.14	11.34
Slovenia	:	4.68	4.38	8.64	4.66	-
Slovakia	:	5.03	4.71	15.67	4.68	-
Finland	4.72	4.11	3.74	-	-	-
Sweden	4.98	4.42	3.25	3.33	2.31	0.92
United Kingdom	5.01	4.93	3.36	5.55	4.64	1.21
Turkey	-	-	-	96.99	23.84	:
Japan	-	-	-	0.22	0.05	0.47
United States	-	-	-	5.41	1.62	0.69

(¹) The indicator for Luxembourg is based on a basket of long-term bonds, which have an average residual maturity close to ten years; the bonds are issued by a private credit institution.
(²) EA-11, 1999; EA-12, 2004; EA-16, 2009.

Source: Eurostat (tec00097 and tec00035), ECB, national central banks

Table 1.12: Euro yield curve (¹)
(%)

	2005	2006	2007	2008	2009
1 year until maturity	2.21	3.22	3.99	3.61	0.91
2 years until maturity	2.37	3.37	4.04	3.59	1.51
3 years until maturity	2.53	3.43	4.05	3.65	2.00
4 years until maturity	2.69	3.48	4.06	3.74	2.41
5 years until maturity	2.84	3.53	4.08	3.83	2.75
6 years until maturity	2.98	3.58	4.11	3.93	3.03
7 years until maturity	3.11	3.63	4.14	4.02	3.28
8 years until maturity	3.22	3.68	4.17	4.10	3.49
9 years until maturity	3.32	3.72	4.20	4.18	3.67
10 years until maturity	3.40	3.76	4.23	4.25	3.82
11 years until maturity	3.48	3.79	4.26	4.31	3.95
12 years until maturity	3.54	3.82	4.28	4.36	4.06
13 years until maturity	3.60	3.85	4.30	4.41	4.15
14 years until maturity	3.65	3.88	4.32	4.45	4.22
15 years until maturity	3.69	3.90	4.34	4.48	4.28
16 years until maturity	3.73	3.92	4.36	4.52	4.33
17 years until maturity	3.77	3.93	4.37	4.54	4.37
18 years until maturity	3.80	3.95	4.39	4.57	4.40
19 years until maturity	3.82	3.96	4.40	4.59	4.42
20 years until maturity	3.85	3.98	4.41	4.61	4.43
21 years until maturity	3.87	3.99	4.42	4.63	4.43
22 years until maturity	3.89	4.00	4.43	4.64	4.43
23 years until maturity	3.91	4.01	4.44	4.66	4.43
24 years until maturity	3.93	4.02	4.45	4.67	4.42
25 years until maturity	3.94	4.03	4.46	4.68	4.40
26 years until maturity	3.96	4.03	4.46	4.69	4.39
27 years until maturity	3.97	4.04	4.47	4.70	4.37
28 years until maturity	3.98	4.05	4.47	4.70	4.35
29 years until maturity	3.99	4.05	4.48	4.71	4.32
30 years until maturity	4.01	4.06	4.49	4.72	4.30

(¹) Zero-coupon yield curve spot rate for AAA rated euro area central government bonds; EA-12, 2005 and 2006; EA-13, 2007; EA-15, 2008; EA-16, 2009.

Source: Eurostat (irt_euryld_a)

1.4 Consumer prices - inflation and comparative price levels

An increase in the level of prices of goods and services in an economy is called inflation; this indicator is usually measured through consumer price indices (CPIs) or retail price indices (RPIs). Within the European Union (EU) a specific consumer price index for the purpose of tracing price developments has been developed and is called the harmonised index of consumer prices (HICP).

If there is inflation within an economy, then the purchasing power of money falls as consumers are no longer able to purchase the same amount of goods and services (for the same amount of money). In contrast, if prices fall, then they should be able to purchase more goods and services; this is often referred to as deflation. No change in prices (or relatively low rates of inflation) are often referred to as a period of price stability.

A comparison of prices between countries depends not only on movements in price levels, but also on changes in exchange rates – together, these two forces impact on the price and cost competitiveness of individual Member States.

Main statistical findings

Compared with historical trends, consumer price indices rose only at a moderate pace during the last two decades. The EU (moving aggregate based upon EU membership) inflation rate decreased during the 1990s, reaching 1.2 % by 1999, after which the pace of price increases settled at around 2 % per annum during the period 2000 to 2007.

In 2008, an annual average inflation rate of 3.7 % was recorded for the EU. This sharp rise in price inflation can be largely explained by rapid increases in energy and food prices between the autumn of 2007 and the autumn of 2008. Indeed, consumer prices for food recorded historically high inflation rates in 2008 with prices rising on average by 6.4 % in the EU; the increase may be particularly associated with steep price rises for dairy products, oils and fats.

In 2009, annual inflation for the EU was 1.0 % – on the back of decreasing food prices between the summers of 2008 and 2009. Energy prices fell from December 2008 until November 2009, with their biggest reduction in July 2009 (-10.4 %, on the basis of a comparison with July 2008).

In August 2010, the latest information available at the time of writing, there was some evidence of a modest expansion in the pace at which prices were rising. The overall EU inflation rate was nevertheless relatively stable, rising from 1.5 % in February 2010 (compared with the same month of the previous year) to 2.0 % by August 2010.

Comparative price levels of private household consumption vary considerably across the EU Member States. In 2009, they ranged from 53 in Bulgaria to 145 in Denmark (EU-27=100). Over the ten years from 1999 to 2009, several of the Member States that joined the EU in 2004 or 2007 recorded substantial changes in their comparative price levels (Bulgaria, the Czech Republic, Estonia, Latvia, Lithuania, Hungary, Romania and Slovakia). During this ten-year period, there was a convergence of price levels within the EU-27 as a whole; the coefficient of variation of comparative price levels declined from 35.6 % in 1999 to 24.3 % by 2008 (rising slightly in 2009 to 25.1 %). Although price levels were more homogeneous across the euro area than the EU-27 (with a coefficient of variation of 14.8 % in 2009), the pace at which prices were converging was less pronounced in the euro area when analysing the development of the coefficient of variation of price level indices (PLIs) from 1999 to 2009.

Data sources and availability

Inflation

The harmonised index of consumer prices (HICP) is constructed to measure, over time, the change in prices of consumer goods and services that are acquired by households. These indices cover practically every good and service that may be purchased by households in the form of final monetary consumption expenditure; owner-occupied housing is, however, not yet included. Goods and services are classified according to the international classification of individual consumption by purpose, adapted to the compilation of the harmonised indices of consumer prices (COICOP/HICP). At its most disaggregated level, Eurostat publishes around 100 sub-indices, which can be aggregated to broad categories of goods and services. The inflation rate is one such example – it equates to the all-items harmonised index of consumer prices.

The indices are calculated according to a common approach with a single set of definitions, providing comparable measures of consumer price inflation across countries, as well as for different country groupings such as the EU, the euro area, or the European Economic Area (EEA). There are three key HICP aggregate indices: the Monetary Union Index of Consumer Prices (MUICP) covering the euro area countries, the European index of consumer prices (EICP) covering all EU Member States, and the European Economic Area index of consumer prices, which includes the EU Member States as well as Iceland and Norway. Note that these aggregates reflect changes over time in their country composition through the use of a chain index formula – for example, the MUICP includes Slovenia only from 2007 onwards, Cyprus and Malta only from 2008 onwards, and Slovakia only from 2009 onwards.

Harmonised indices of consumer prices are presented with a common reference year (currently 2005=100). Normally the indices are used to calculate percentage changes that show price increases/decreases. Although the rates of change shown in the tables and figures for this subchapter are annual averages, the basic indices are compiled on a monthly basis and are published at this frequency by Eurostat. Harmonised indices of consumer prices are published some 14 to 16 days after the end of the reporting month. The majority of the data is available with series starting in the mid-1990s.

Comparative price levels

Comparative price levels across EU Member States are price level indices (PLIs) expressed as relative to the average price level of the EU-27. If the price level index of a given Member State is above 100, then prices in that country are, on average, higher than the EU average. On the other hand, a price level index below 100 shows that prices are, on average lower than the EU-27 average.

Purchasing power parities (PPPs) estimate price level differences across countries; they are aggregated price ratios calculated from price comparisons of a large number of goods and services. Purchasing power parities are used to calculate price level indices, the latter are calculated as the ratio of purchasing power parities to exchange rates.

Price level indices may be constructed for a number of expenditure aggregates based on the expenditure classification of national accounts. The differences in price levels of consumer goods and services should be analysed on the basis of household final consumption expenditure (HFCE); Eurostat publishes detailed information on price level indices for more than 30 different groups of goods and services.

Price level indices may also be used as a starting point for analysing price convergence. For this purpose, the coefficient of variation of price level indices across any number of countries (for example, the EU Member States) is calculated. A decreasing coefficient over time indicates that price levels are converging. Eurostat publishes an annual estimate of price convergence based on the temporal development of the coefficient of variation.

Context

Harmonised indices of consumer prices are, among other things, used for the purposes of monetary policy and assessing inflation convergence as required in the Treaty on the functioning of the European Union. In particular, they are used for measuring inflation in the euro area; the primary objective of the European Central Bank's (ECB) monetary policy is to maintain price stability. The ECB has defined price stability as a year-on-year increase in the harmonised index of consumer prices for the euro area of below, but close to 2 % over the medium-term.

Figure 1.32: HICP all-items, development of the annual average inflation rates
(%)

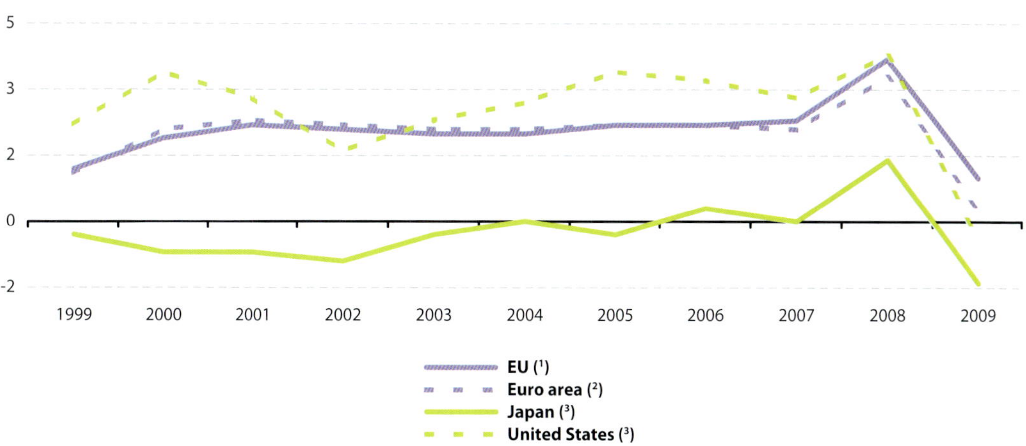

(¹) The data refer to the official EU aggregate, its country coverage changes in line with the addition of new EU Member States and integrates them using a chain index formula.
(²) The data refer to the official euro area aggregate, its country coverage changes in line with the addition of new EA Member States and integrates them using a chain index formula.
(³) National CPI: not strictly comparable with the HICP.

Source: Eurostat (prc_hicp_aind)

Table 1.13: HICP all-items, annual average inflation rates
(%)

	1999	2000	2001	2002	2003	2004	2005	2006	2007	2008	2009
EU (¹)	1.2	1.9	2.2	2.1	2.0	2.0	2.2	2.2	2.3	3.7	1.0
Euro area (²)	1.1	2.1	2.3	2.2	2.1	2.1	2.2	2.2	2.1	3.3	0.3
Belgium	1.1	2.7	2.4	1.6	1.5	1.9	2.5	2.3	1.8	4.5	0.0
Bulgaria	2.6	10.3	7.4	5.8	2.3	6.1	6.0	7.4	7.6	12.0	2.5
Czech Republic	1.8	3.9	4.5	1.4	-0.1	2.6	1.6	2.1	3.0	6.3	0.6
Denmark	2.1	2.7	2.3	2.4	2.0	0.9	1.7	1.9	1.7	3.6	1.1
Germany	0.6	1.4	1.9	1.4	1.0	1.8	1.9	1.8	2.3	2.8	0.2
Estonia	3.1	3.9	5.6	3.6	1.4	3.0	4.1	4.4	6.7	10.6	0.2
Ireland	2.5	5.3	4.0	4.7	4.0	2.3	2.2	2.7	2.9	3.1	-1.7
Greece	2.1	2.9	3.7	3.9	3.4	3.0	3.5	3.3	3.0	4.2	1.3
Spain	2.2	3.5	2.8	3.6	3.1	3.1	3.4	3.6	2.8	4.1	-0.2
France	0.6	1.8	1.8	1.9	2.2	2.3	1.9	1.9	1.6	3.2	0.1
Italy	1.7	2.6	2.3	2.6	2.8	2.3	2.2	2.2	2.0	3.5	0.8
Cyprus	1.1	4.9	2.0	2.8	4.0	1.9	2.0	2.2	2.2	4.4	0.2
Latvia	2.1	2.6	2.5	2.0	2.9	6.2	6.9	6.6	10.1	15.3	3.3
Lithuania	1.5	1.1	1.6	0.3	-1.1	1.2	2.7	3.8	5.8	11.1	4.2
Luxembourg	1.0	3.8	2.4	2.1	2.5	3.2	3.8	3.0	2.7	4.1	0.0
Hungary	10.0	10.0	9.1	5.2	4.7	6.8	3.5	4.0	7.9	6.0	4.0
Malta	2.3	3.0	2.5	2.6	1.9	2.7	2.5	2.6	0.7	4.7	1.8
Netherlands	2.0	2.3	5.1	3.9	2.2	1.4	1.5	1.7	1.6	2.2	1.0
Austria	0.5	2.0	2.3	1.7	1.3	2.0	2.1	1.7	2.2	3.2	0.4
Poland	7.2	10.1	5.3	1.9	0.7	3.6	2.2	1.3	2.6	4.2	4.0
Portugal	2.2	2.8	4.4	3.7	3.3	2.5	2.1	3.0	2.4	2.7	-0.9
Romania	45.8	45.7	34.5	22.5	15.3	11.9	9.1	6.6	4.9	7.9	5.6
Slovenia	6.1	8.9	8.6	7.5	5.7	3.7	2.5	2.5	3.8	5.5	0.9
Slovakia	10.4	12.2	7.2	3.5	8.4	7.5	2.8	4.3	1.9	3.9	0.9
Finland	1.3	2.9	2.7	2.0	1.3	0.1	0.8	1.3	1.6	3.9	1.6
Sweden	0.5	1.3	2.7	1.9	2.3	1.0	0.8	1.5	1.7	3.3	1.9
United Kingdom	1.3	0.8	1.2	1.3	1.4	1.3	2.1	2.3	2.3	3.6	2.2
Iceland	2.1	4.4	6.6	5.3	1.4	2.3	1.4	4.6	3.6	12.8	16.3
Norway	2.1	3.0	2.7	0.8	2.0	0.6	1.5	2.5	0.7	3.4	2.3
Switzerland	:	:	:	:	:	:	:	1.0	0.8	2.3	-0.7
Croatia	3.7	4.5	4.3	2.5	2.4	2.1	3.0	3.3	2.7	5.8	2.2
Turkey	61.4	53.2	56.8	47.0	25.3	10.1	8.1	9.3	8.8	10.4	6.3
Japan (³)	-0.3	-0.7	-0.7	-0.9	-0.3	0.0	-0.3	0.3	0.0	1.4	-1.4
United States (³)	2.2	3.4	2.8	1.6	2.3	2.7	3.4	3.2	2.8	3.8	-0.4

(¹) The data refer to the official EU aggregate, its country coverage changes in line with the addition of new EU Member States and integrates them using a chain index formula.

(²) The data refer to the official euro area aggregate, its country coverage changes in line with the addition of new EA Member States and integrates them using a chain index formula.

(³) National CPI: not strictly comparable with the HICP.

Source: Eurostat (prc_hicp_aind)

Figure 1.33: HICP main headings, annual average inflation rates, EU-27, 2009
(%)

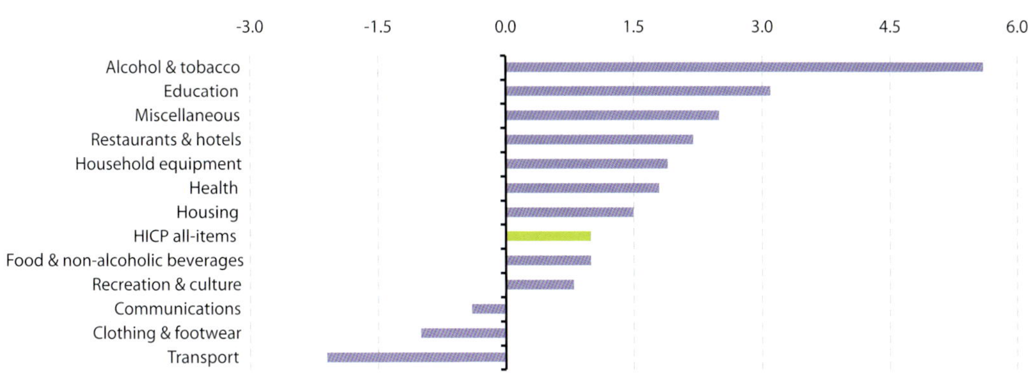

Source: Eurostat (prc_hicp_aind)

Figure 1.34: Price convergence between EU Member States
(%, coefficient of variation of comparative price levels of final consumption by private households including indirect taxes)

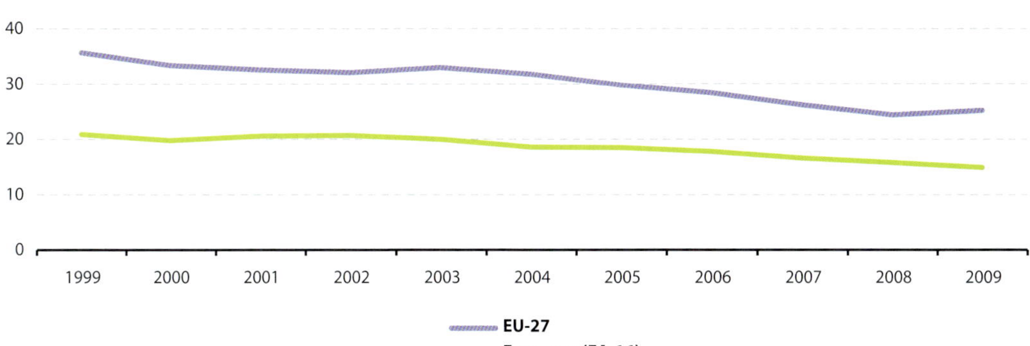

Source: Eurostat (tsier020)

Table 1.14: Comparative price levels ([1])
(final consumption by private households including indirect taxes, EU-27=100)

	1999	2000	2001	2002	2003	2004	2005	2006	2007	2008	2009
EU-27	100	100	100	100	100	100	100	100	100	100	100
Euro area (EA-16)	102	100	101	101	103	103	102	102	102	104	107
Belgium	107	102	103	102	107	107	106	108	108	111	114
Bulgaria	38	39	41	41	41	42	43	45	46	50	53
Czech Republic	46	48	50	57	55	55	58	61	62	73	71
Denmark	131	130	135	134	141	140	140	138	137	141	145
Germany	107	107	107	107	106	105	103	103	102	104	106
Estonia	57	57	61	61	62	63	65	69	73	78	75
Ireland	112	115	119	125	126	126	123	125	125	128	125
Greece	88	85	82	80	86	88	88	89	91	94	97
Spain	86	85	85	85	88	91	91	92	93	95	97
France	109	106	104	104	110	110	108	109	108	111	114
Italy	98	98	100	103	104	105	105	104	103	106	107
Cyprus	87	88	89	89	91	91	90	90	88	91	91
Latvia	52	59	59	57	54	56	57	61	67	73	75
Lithuania	47	53	54	54	52	54	55	57	60	65	68
Luxembourg	103	101	104	102	103	103	112	111	115	119	121
Hungary	47	49	53	57	58	62	63	61	67	68	66
Malta	71	73	75	75	72	73	73	75	76	79	81
Netherlands	103	100	103	103	108	106	105	104	102	104	109
Austria	105	102	105	103	103	103	103	102	102	105	108
Poland	52	58	65	61	54	53	61	62	62	69	59
Portugal	83	83	84	86	86	87	85	85	86	87	89
Romania	38	43	42	43	43	43	54	58	64	61	58
Slovenia	74	73	74	74	76	76	76	77	79	82	86
Slovakia	41	44	43	45	51	55	55	58	63	70	74
Finland	122	121	125	124	127	124	124	123	120	124	126
Sweden	126	128	120	122	124	121	119	119	116	115	107
United Kingdom	116	120	117	117	108	109	110	111	113	100	93
Iceland	127	144	128	135	139	138	153	145	149	117	102
Norway	134	138	142	151	142	135	141	140	138	139	137
Switzerland	140	143	146	147	144	141	138	135	125	131	138
Croatia	:	:	:	:	65	67	69	73	72	76	76
FYR of Macedonia	:	:	:	:	44	44	43	45	44	47	46
Turkey	56	63	48	52	57	59	67	66	72	71	67
Japan	173	198	178	156	137	130	120	110	97	103	120
United States	106	121	126	120	101	93	93	93	85	82	89

([1]) Break in series in 2005 for all countries except for Japan and the United States.

Source: Eurostat (tsier010)

1.5 Balance of payments - current account

The balance of payments records all economic transactions between resident and non-resident entities during a given period. This subchapter presents data on the current and financial accounts of the balance of payments for the European Union (EU) and its Member States. The analysis is based on data from September 2010, but the latest data can be consulted in the Eurostat main tables and data base.

The current account balance determines the exposure of an economy to the rest of the world, whereas the capital and financial account explains how it is financed. A separate Subchapter (1.6) on foreign direct investment provides more information on one component of the financial account and Subchapter 9.2 on international trade in services provides more information on one component of the current account.

Main statistical findings

The current account deficit of the EU-27 was EUR 131 800 million in 2009 (see Figure 1.35), corresponding to 1.1 % of gross domestic product (GDP), close to half the level of the deficit in 2008 when it had equalled about 2.0 %. The overall deficit for 2009 comprised deficits in the current account for goods (-0.7 % of GDP), for current transfers (-0.5 %), and for the income account (-0.4 %), alongside a positive balance for services (0.5 %).

There were a total of 15 Member States that reported current account deficits in 2009 (see Table 1.15): the largest of these (relative to GDP) were in Greece (-11.4 %) and Portugal (-10.3 %); Latvia (9.5 %) and Sweden (7.4 %) reported the largest current account surpluses. Ireland, Slovakia Germany, Italy and Romania were the only Member States to report a deficit for services in 2009, while Luxembourg (47.8 % of GDP), Cyprus (24.4 %) and Malta (15.6 %) reported relatively large surpluses. A total of 15 Member States reported a deficit for goods – most notably Cyprus (-25.0 % of GDP), while Ireland reported the largest surplus (20.3 % of GDP).

The EU-27's current account deficit with China was EUR 113 900 million in 2009, three and a half times as large as the next largest deficits, which were with Russia and Japan. A current account surplus was recorded with Switzerland (EUR 34 800 million), about one fifth larger than that with the United States (see Figure 1.36).

Three types of investment (foreign direct investment (FDI), portfolio and other) make-up the financial account, along with financial derivatives and official reserve assets. A positive value for the financial account indicates that inward investment flows (inward FDI and investment liabilities) exceed outward investment flows (outward FDI and investment assets). This was the case for the euro area in 2009, where the financial account was equivalent to 0.5 % of GDP.

The EU-27 was a net direct investor vis-à-vis the rest of the world in 2009. Inward flows of FDI represented 1.8 % of GDP, while outward flows of FDI represented 2.4 % of GDP, making it the main form of outward investment from the EU-27 in 2009. Luxembourg recorded the highest levels of both inward and outward FDI (in relation to GDP) with the rest of the world. Slovenia recorded the only notable disinvestment in inward FDI, while several countries recorded a disinvestment for outward FDI, notably Hungary and Belgium (see Table 1.17).

The EU-27 recorded investment in portfolio investment assets (outward investment) equivalent to 1.5 % of GDP in 2009. EU-27 portfolio investment liabilities (inward investment) were valued at 5.3 % of GDP, close to three times the level of inward FDI. Six of the Member States recorded disinvestment for portfolio assets, with the United Kingdom recording relatively large flows (6.1 % of GDP). The largest investments in portfolio assets were recorded in Luxembourg (home to a large fund management activity), Cyprus and Malta. Disinvestment in portfolio liabilities was also relatively uncommon, and only Estonia and Hungary reported negative flows in excess of 1 % of GDP. Again Luxembourg reported the largest positive flows relative to GDP, followed by Portugal and France.

For other assets and liabilities (such as currency and deposits) the EU-27 recorded a net disinvestment in 2009 both in assets and liabilities, in other words a reduction in outward loans and also a repatriation of inward deposits. Disinvestment in other assets was equivalent to 3.0 % of the EU-27's GDP in 2009, with the largest disinvestments in assets (in relative terms) recorded in Luxembourg and Malta. Inward disinvestment of liabilities was equivalent to 5.3 % of GDP in the EU-27. Again the largest disinvestments in relative terms were recorded in Luxembourg, followed at some distance by Ireland, Belgium and Malta. In contrast to the overall EU situation of net disinvestments, a small number of Member States recorded net investment flows in other assets and liabilities, most notably Cyprus which recorded the largest (relative to GDP) outward investment in other assets and by far the largest inward investments in liabilities.

Data sources and availability

The main methodological references used for the production of balance of payment statistics is the fifth balance of payments manual (BPM5) of the International Monetary Fund (IMF). The sixth edition of this manual (BPM6) was finalised in December 2008 with implementation planned in 2014. The transmission of balance of payments data to Eurostat is covered by Regulation 184/2005 on Community statistics concerning balance of payments, international trade in services and foreign direct investment (consolidated version 09.05.2006).

Current account

The current account of the balance of payments provides information not only on international trade in goods (generally the largest category), but also on international transactions in services, income and current transfers. For all these transactions, the balance of payments registers the value of credits (exports) and debits (imports). A negative balance – a current account deficit –

shows that a country is spending abroad more than it is earning from transactions with other economies, and is therefore a net debtor towards the rest of the world.

The current account gauges a country's economic position in the world, covering all transactions that occur between resident and non-resident entities. More specifically, the four main components of the current account are defined as follows:

Trade in goods covers general merchandise, goods for processing, repairs on goods, goods procured in ports by carriers, and non-monetary gold. Exports and imports of goods are recorded on a so-called fob/fob basis – in other words, at market value at the customs frontiers of exporting economies, including charges for insurance and transport services up to the frontier of the exporting country.

Trade in services consists of the following items: transport services performed by EU residents for non-EU residents, or vice versa, involving the carriage of passengers, the movement of goods, rentals of carriers with crew and related supporting and auxiliary services; travel, which includes primarily the goods and services EU travellers acquire from non-EU residents, or vice versa; and other services, which include communication services, construction services, insurance services, financial services, computer and information services, royalties and licence fees, other business services (which comprise merchanting and other trade-related services, operational leasing services and miscellaneous business, professional and technical services), personal, cultural and recreational services, and government services not included elsewhere.

Income covers two types of transactions: compensation of employees paid to non-resident workers or received from non-resident employers, and investment income accrued on external financial assets and liabilities.

Current transfers include general government current transfers, for example transfers related to international cooperation between governments, payments of current taxes on income and wealth, and other current transfers, such as workers' remittances, insurance premiums (less service charges), and claims on non-life insurance companies.

Under the balance of payment conventions, transactions which represent an inflow of real resources, an increase in assets, or a decrease in liabilities (such as exports of goods) are recorded as credits, and transactions representing an outflow of real resources, a decrease in assets or an increase in liabilities (such as imports of goods) are recorded as debits. Net is the balance (credits minus debits) of all transactions with each partner.

Financial account

The financial account of the balance of payments covers all transactions associated with changes of ownership in the foreign financial assets and liabilities of an economy. The financial account is broken down into five basic components: direct investment, portfolio investment, financial derivatives, other investment, and official reserve assets. Direct investment implies that a resident investor in one economy has a lasting interest in, and a degree of influence over the management of, a business enterprise resident in another economy. Direct investment is classified primarily on a directional basis: resident direct investment abroad and non-resident direct investment in the reporting economy. Within this classification three main components are distinguished: equity capital, reinvested earnings, and other capital; these are discussed in detail in the Subchapter (1.6) on foreign direct investment.

Portfolio investment records the transactions in negotiable securities with the exception of the transactions which fall within the definition of direct investment or reserve assets. Several components are identified: equity securities, bonds and notes, money market instruments.

Financial derivatives are financial instruments that are linked to, and whose value is contingent to, a specific financial instrument, indicator or commodity, and through which specific financial risks can be traded in financial markets in their own right. Transactions in financial derivatives are treated as separate transactions, rather than integral parts of the value of underlying transactions to which they may be linked.

Reserve assets are foreign financial assets available to, and controlled by, monetary authorities; they are used for financing and regulating payments imbalances or for other purposes.

Other investment is a residual category, which is not recorded under the other headings of the financial account (direct investment, portfolio investment, financial derivatives or reserve assets). It also encompasses the offsetting entries for accrued income on instruments classified under other investment. Four types of instruments are identified: currency and deposits (in general, the most significant item), trade credits, loans, other assets and liabilities.

Context

The EU is a major player in the global economy for international trade in goods and services, as well as foreign investment. Balance of payments statistics give a complete picture of all external transactions of the EU and its individual Member States. They may be used as a tool to study the international exposure of different parts of the EU's economy, indicating its comparative advantages and disadvantages with the rest of the world. Note that additional information from the balance of payments is provided in Subchapters 1.6 and 9.2 on foreign direct investment and international trade in services.

Figure 1.35: Current account transactions, EU-27 (1)
(EUR 1 000 million)

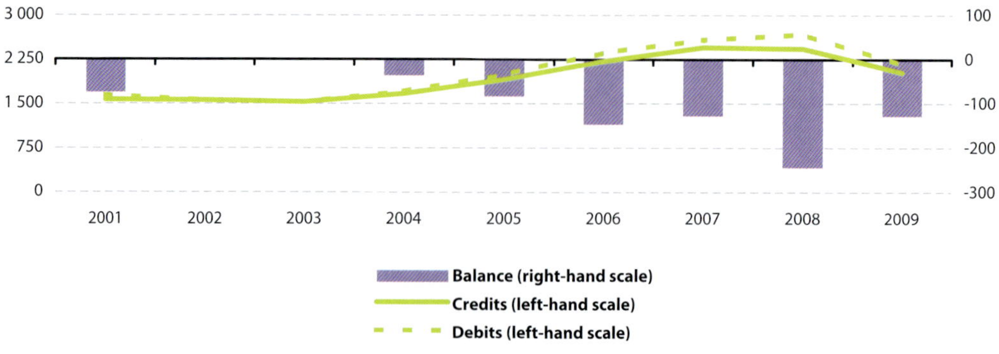

(1) EU-25, 2001-2003.
Source: Eurostat (tec00038)

Table 1.15: Current account balance for EU Member States with the rest of the world
(EUR 1 000 million)

	2004	2005	2006	2007	2008	2009
EU-27 (¹)	-36.0	-82.9	-146.2	-127.2	-243.3	-131.8
Euro area (EA-16) (²)	61.7	11.7	-10.2	13.5	-153.8	-55.9
Belgium	19.1	7.9	6.3	7.3	-10.1	1.0
Bulgaria	-1.3	-2.7	-4.6	-7.8	-8.2	-3.2
Czech Republic	-4.7	-1.3	-2.7	-4.1	-1.0	-1.5
Denmark	5.9	9.0	6.5	3.4	5.1	9.0
Germany	102.8	114.6	150.1	185.1	167.0	119.1
Estonia	-1.1	-1.1	-2.2	-2.8	-1.5	0.6
Ireland	-0.9	-5.7	-6.3	-10.1	-10.2	-4.9
Greece	-10.7	-14.7	-23.7	-32.6	-34.8	-26.6
Spain	-44.2	-66.9	-88.3	-105.3	-106.0	-58.3
France	10.0	-10.9	-9.2	-18.9	-37.1	-36.8
Italy	-13.0	-23.6	-38.3	-37.7	-53.6	-48.2
Cyprus	-0.6	-0.8	-1.0	-1.9	-3.0	-1.4
Latvia	-1.4	-1.6	-3.6	-4.7	-3.0	1.8
Lithuania	-1.4	-1.5	-2.6	-4.1	-3.8	1.0
Luxembourg	3.3	3.3	3.5	3.6	2.1	2.1
Hungary	-6.8	-6.4	-6.5	-6.6	-7.4	0.2
Malta	-0.3	-0.4	-0.5	-0.3	-0.3	-0.2
Netherlands	36.9	37.3	50.4	49.3	28.5	28.9
Austria	4.8	4.9	7.1	9.6	:	:
Poland	-8.2	-3.0	-7.4	-14.7	-18.3	-5.0
Portugal	-12.4	-15.9	-17.2	-17.1	-21.7	-17.3
Romania	-5.1	-6.9	-10.2	-16.8	-16.2	-5.2
Slovenia	-0.7	-0.5	-0.8	-1.6	-2.5	-0.5
Slovakia	-1.2	-3.2	-3.6	-2.9	-4.3	-2.0
Finland	10.0	5.7	7.6	7.6	5.8	2.3
Sweden	21.1	20.4	26.5	27.8	31.3	21.6
United Kingdom	-36.9	-48.0	-64.4	-55.3	-27.2	-17.6
Iceland	-1.1	-2.2	-3.3	-2.4	-2.3	-0.3
Norway	28.3	39.7	46.2	40.1	57.3	38.2
Croatia	-1.5	-2.0	-2.7	-3.2	-4.4	-2.5
Turkey	-11.5	-17.8	-25.6	-27.9	-28.1	-9.9
Japan	138.5	133.3	136.0	154.0	105.1	:
United States	-507.5	-604.6	-639.5	-531.5	-479.6	:

(¹) EU vis-à-vis extra-EU.
(²) Euro area vis-à-vis extra euro area.

Source: Eurostat (bop_q_eu, bop_q_euro and bop_q_c)

Table 1.16: Current account, balance by components, 2009 (1)
(% of GDP)

	Current account	Goods	Services	Income	Current transfers
EU-27	-1.1	-0.7	0.5	-0.4	-0.5
Euro area (EA-16)	-0.6	0.5	0.3	-0.4	-1.0
Belgium	0.3	0.8	0.1	1.3	-2.0
Bulgaria	-9.1	-11.7	4.4	-4.5	2.7
Czech Republic	-1.1	5.0	0.7	-6.4	-0.4
Denmark	4.0	2.2	1.3	2.5	-1.9
Germany	5.0	5.6	-0.7	1.4	-1.3
Estonia	4.6	-3.8	9.5	-2.9	1.7
Ireland	-3.0	20.3	-5.3	-17.5	-0.6
Greece	-11.4	-13.2	5.4	-4.2	0.6
Spain	-5.5	-4.3	2.4	-2.9	-0.8
France	-1.9	-2.3	0.6	1.2	-1.4
Italy	-3.2	0.1	-0.7	-1.8	-0.8
Cyprus	-8.3	-25.0	24.4	-6.5	-1.2
Latvia	9.5	-6.6	6.3	6.5	3.4
Lithuania	3.8	-2.9	2.2	0.4	4.1
Luxembourg	5.7	-8.0	47.8	-31.4	-2.7
Hungary	0.3	4.3	1.6	-6.0	0.3
Malta	-4.1	-13.6	15.6	-6.1	-0.1
Netherlands	5.1	6.1	1.0	-1.0	-1.0
Austria (2)	3.5	0.5	4.1	-0.6	-0.5
Poland	-1.6	-1.0	1.1	-3.3	1.5
Portugal	-10.3	-10.4	3.6	-4.7	1.3
Romania	-4.5	-5.9	-0.3	-1.8	3.5
Slovenia	-1.5	-2.0	3.2	-2.2	-0.4
Slovakia	-3.2	1.9	-2.0	-2.0	-1.1
Finland	1.3	2.1	0.9	-0.7	-1.0
Sweden	7.4	3.3	3.6	1.8	-1.2
United Kingdom	-1.1	-5.9	3.2	2.6	-1.1
Iceland	-3.5	5.9	2.5	-11.3	-0.6
Norway	14.0	14.6	0.1	0.6	-1.2
Croatia	-5.4	-16.3	12.5	-3.9	2.3
Turkey	-2.3	-4.0	2.6	-1.3	0.4
Japan (3)	3.2	0.8	-0.4	3.1	-0.3
United States (3)	-4.9	-5.8	1.0	0.8	-0.9

(1) EU-27, extra EU-27 flows; euro area, extra EA-16 flows; Member States and other countries, flows with the rest of the world.
(2) 2007.
(3) 2008.

Source: Eurostat (bop_q_eu, bop_q_euro, bop_q_c and tec00001)

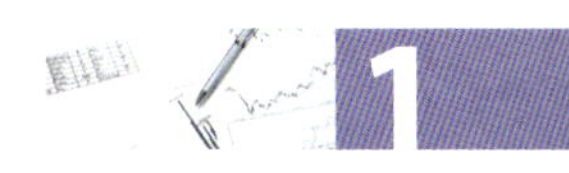

Figure 1.36: Current account balance with selected partners, EU-27, 2009
(EUR 1 000 million)

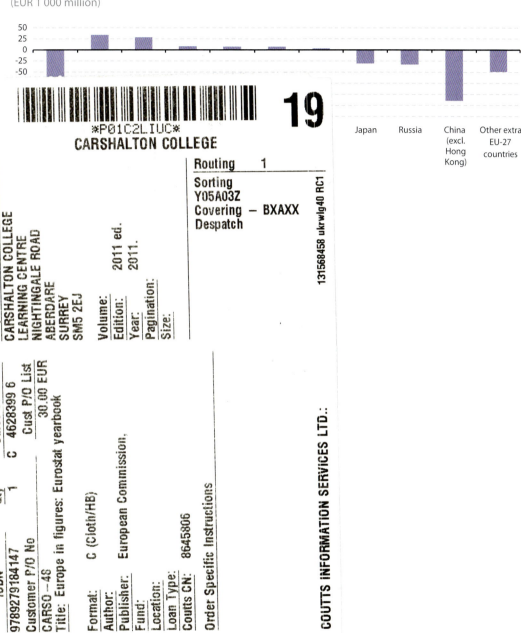

50
25
0
-25
-50

Japan
Russia
China (excl. Hong Kong)
Other extra EU-27 countries

Table 1.17: Selected items of the financial account balance, 2009 (1)
(% of GDP)

	Financial account	Outward foreign direct investment	Inward foreign direct investment	Portfolio investment, assets	Portfolio investment, liabilities	Other investment, assets	Other investment, liabilities
EU-27	:	-2.4	1.8	-1.5	5.3	3.0	-5.3
Euro area (EA-16)	0.5	-3.2	2.4	-0.8	4.2	5.5	-8.1
Belgium	-1.4	4.0	7.0	1.8	4.1	24.6	-43.1
Bulgaria	8.1	0.3	9.2	-1.7	0.0	-1.3	-0.2
Czech Republic	1.0	-0.7	1.4	0.5	2.6	0.6	-1.6
Denmark	-1.8	-5.1	2.6	-6.1	12.6	11.3	-7.7
Germany	-5.7	-1.9	1.1	-3.0	-0.8	4.1	-6.3
Estonia	-6.6	-8.0	8.8	-3.5	-6.9	6.9	-4.1
Ireland	-2.1	-10.8	11.1	6.1	5.7	33.4	-45.7
Greece	10.6	-0.6	1.0	-1.4	13.6	-10.2	8.7
Spain	5.5	-0.6	0.5	0.1	4.7	-0.1	1.5
France	3.1	-5.6	2.3	-3.2	17.3	3.4	-11.2
Italy	1.0	-2.1	1.4	-2.4	4.0	-0.3	-0.4
Cyprus	8.0	-21.7	24.6	-67.2	0.3	-18.4	89.8
Latvia	-12.7	0.1	0.3	1.5	0.0	-5.5	-5.8
Lithuania	-7.2	-0.6	0.9	-3.1	5.7	-1.5	-9.0
Luxembourg	-4.9	-360.7	319.3	-300.7	306.1	142.0	-83.1
Hungary	-0.6	5.6	-4.4	-0.8	-2.9	-0.8	8.1
Malta	2.7	-1.4	10.6	-32.7	-0.5	64.3	-36.4
Netherlands	-1.8	-3.1	4.0	-10.6	9.2	17.4	-20.8
Austria	-4.2	-18.8	16.8	-4.9	13.3	-14.0	4.4
Poland	4.9	-0.7	2.7	-0.1	3.7	1.3	1.7
Portugal	9.2	-0.6	1.2	-9.8	17.7	0.1	0.4
Romania	5.2	-0.1	3.9	-0.2	0.6	-2.3	4.3
Slovenia	0.6	-0.3	-1.2	0.2	12.9	-0.8	-10.6
Slovakia	5.6	-0.5	-0.1	-3.0	1.6	-4.8	11.1
Finland	8.0	-1.1	1.1	-12.3	12.0	-2.7	9.7
Sweden	-9.2	-7.5	2.7	-4.6	14.4	3.6	-13.5
United Kingdom	0.4	-2.1	1.1	-11.1	13.5	23.6	-26.2
Iceland	-10.1	-7.7	-1.4	3.3	-89.3	1.7	89.9
Norway	-16.4	-9.1	1.8	-1.8	1.4	9.4	-23.4
Croatia	6.9	-2.0	4.6	-1.7	2.1	1.5	4.4
Turkey	1.4	-0.3	1.3	-0.4	0.5	1.2	-0.9
Japan	-4.2	-2.8	0.5	-4.0	-2.5	3.3	1.3
United States	3.5	-2.3	2.2	0.9	3.6	1.5	-2.2

(1) EU-27, extra EU-27 flows; euro area, extra EA-16 flows; Member States and other countries, flows with the rest of the world; note that according to the balance of payments sign convention, increases in assets and decreases in liabilities are shown with a negative sign, whereas decreases in assets and increases in liabilities are shown as positive.

Source: Eurostat (bop_q_eu, bop_q_euro, bop_q_c and tec00001)

1.6 Foreign direct investment

Foreign direct investment (FDI) is the category of international investment made by an entity resident in one economy (direct investor) to acquire a lasting interest in an enterprise operating in another economy (direct investment enterprise). The lasting interest is deemed to exist if the direct investor acquires at least 10 % of the voting power of the direct investment enterprise. FDI is a component of the balance of payments showing all financial transactions between one country or area – such as the European Union (EU) – and all other countries. This subchapter discusses the developments for FDI in the EU, examining inward and outward flows, the origin and destination of these flows, important investment activities, as well as stocks of FDI at the end of the year.

Main statistical findings

Effects of the financial and economic crisis

Flows of FDI (new investments made during the reference period) fluctuate considerably from one year to the next, partly as a function of economic fortunes. FDI flows generally increase during times of rapid economic growth, while disinvestment is more likely during periods of recession as businesses focus on core activities in their domestic market.

FDI flows from the EU-27 to countries outside of the EU (extra-EU) reached a record level in 2007 (EUR 530 738 million), mainly as a result of major cross-border mergers and acquisitions and reinvestment of earnings. However, the EU-27's FDI flows were severely affected by the global financial and economic crisis. In 2008, reinvested earnings paid to extra-EU investors dropped by 50 % and these continued to decline in 2009. Equity capital, mainly mergers and acquisitions activity, showed a similar trend dropping by one third in 2008 and continuing to fall in 2009. As a result, total EU-27 outward FDI flows fell 34 % in 2008 and by a further 24 % in 2009, down to EUR 263 335 million (see Table 1.37).

Inward flows of FDI to the EU-27 (from other non-member countries) also peaked in 2007 and fell even more sharply than outward flows in 2008, down 52 %. However, inward flows returned to an upward path in 2009, increasing by 12 % to reach EUR 221 734 million.

Being influenced by particularly large mergers and acquisitions, FDI flows can fluctuate considerably from one year to another – although the main players among EU Member States generally remain the same from one year to the next. The latest data for 2009 is presented in Tables 1 and 2).

Foreign direct investment by partner

FDI flows between developed economies were the first to be affected by the financial and economic crisis. The United States was the leading investment partner for the EU-27 in 2007 (EUR 183 547 million), and the drop in incoming FDI flows was significant in 2008, as FDI inward flows from the United States to the EU-27 fell to EUR 50 458 million. However, preliminary data for 2009 shows that there was at least a partial recovery 2009 as flows of FDI from the United States to the EU-27 almost doubled with respect to 2008 to reach EUR 96 847 million. EU-27 outward investment flows to the United States saw a more moderate rate of decline in 2008 (from EUR 168 891 million to EUR 121 442 million), and this pattern continued in 2009, as outflows to the United States were valued at EUR 68 991 million.

EU-27 investments in many emerging economies continued to surge in 2008. The steady growth in EU-27 investment flows to Russia peaked in 2008 (EUR 25 561 million), although there was a sharp downturn in 2009 as a result of disinvestment. EU-27 investments to Africa also recorded growth in 2008, mainly due to a significant amount of FDI outflows to Egypt (EUR 9 808 million), which largely originated from French businesses. Total investment in Asia also continued to grow in 2008. However, EU-27 outflows to Japan fell by 43 % in 2008, and this pattern continued in 2009, such that EU-27 investments to Japan were worth EUR 126 million. There was a relatively minor degree of fluctuation in FDI outflows to China and India. Preliminary figures for 2009 show a slight increase in outflows to China (from EUR 4 734 million to EUR 5 290 million).

In 2008, inflows of FDI from outside the EU-27 were worth less than half of what they had been a year before. The drop would have been even more significant without a major inflow from Arabian Gulf countries to Luxembourg.

Average outward flows of FDI during the period 2006 to 2008 show that the United Kingdom was the main investor in countries outside the EU, followed by Luxembourg (see Figure 1.38). The main investment partners of the United Kingdom were the United States and Canada, followed by Australia and Switzerland. After peaking in 2007, the United Kingdom recorded a drastic drop in outflows of FDI to all of these partner countries, except Australia. Luxembourg's high share may be explained by the activities of special purpose entities (SPEs). In some other EU-27 Member States, especially the Netherlands and Hungary, SPEs likewise play an important role. However, the national data for these countries presented in this subchapter exclude SPEs. The fact that Luxembourg's main partners are the United States, Switzerland and offshore financial centres shows how important the financial sector is in Luxembourg.

Change in foreign direct investment positions (stocks)

The annual growth rate of both EU-27 outward and inward positions (stocks) slowed down in 2008 compared with the previous three years. In 2007, annual growth in outward stocks was 13.2 % and in inward positions 16.0 %, whereas in 2008 FDI outward and inward stocks increased only by 4.7 % and 3.2 % respectively (see Table 1.21).

One third (EUR 1 058 052 million) of total EU outward positions of FDI were held in the United States at the end of 2008. EU-27 stocks of FDI held in the United States were mainly concentrated in the service sector (69.0 % at the end of 2007), in particular in financial intermediation and business activities. In the manufacturing sector, the main stock of EU-27 FDI was concentrated within the manufacture of chemicals and chemical products in the United States. At the end of 2008, the United Kingdom was the main holder of FDI stocks in the United States, with 23.8 % of the EU-27 total (EUR 251 624 million).

Switzerland was the second most important destination of EU stocks (13.9 % of extra-EU stocks at the end of 2008), financial intermediation being the main activity sector. EU-27 stocks held in Russia have been growing significantly in recent years, up to EUR 91 955 million at the end of 2008. The service sector accounted for 55.3 % of all EU-27 stocks held in Russia (at the end of 2007), but there was major investment in the extraction of petroleum and gas. Among the Asian countries, the main EU-27 positions were in Singapore, Hong Kong and Japan. The fastest growth in the region was recorded for China and India, but these countries did not feature in the top ten main investment destinations, with stocks of EUR 47 285 million and EUR 19 362 million respectively in 2008.

The United States had the major share of the EU-27 inward positions (43 % and EUR 1 046 157 million at the end of 2008). The service sector was the major investment activity for the United States in the EU, covering almost 80 % of total inward investments from the United States at the end of 2007. The stock held in the EU-27 by Switzerland at the end of 2008 was EUR 306 199 million, which was slightly less than at the end of 2007. Japan's stocks of FDI invested in the EU-27 declined to EUR 116 927 million at the end of 2008, and the stock held by Canada remained stable at EUR 105 054 million. Finally, Brazil almost tripled its stocks in the EU-27 during the period 2006 to 2008.

Foreign direct investment by activity

The structure of EU-27 FDI stocks by activity is shown in Table 1.22. Services represented the biggest share (70 %) of the EU-27's total positions abroad in 2007. More than half of the stocks in services were concentrated within financial intermediation, which registered an annual increase of 18.6 % between the end of 2006 and the end of 2007.

For inward positions, services accounted for the highest share of stocks held in the EU-27 at the end of 2007 (80.4 % of the total), with financial intermediation again contributing the largest share. Among the sectors presented in Table 1.22, the EU-27's stocks of FDI vis-à-vis the rest of the world in 2007 only reported a deficit for textile and wood manufacturing, trade and repairs, and real estate and business services.

Income and rates of return

The financial and economic crisis also reduced income from investments abroad. EU-27 investment income dropped sharply in 2008 to EUR 195 915 million from a record high of EUR 261 390 million in 2007 (see Figure 1.39). In particular, income received from EU-27 investments in the United States declined from EUR 70 465 million in 2007 to EUR 36 743 million in 2008. EU-27 income paid to extra-EU investors recorded a modest decline of 7.5 % in 2008, to EUR 126 274 million.

Data sources and methodology

FDI statistics in the EU are collected according to Regulation (EC) No 184/2005 of the European Parliament and of the Council on Community statistics concerning balance of payments, international trade in services and foreign direct investment.

The methodological framework used is that of the OECD's benchmark definition of foreign direct investment third edition, a detailed operational definition fully consistent with the IMF balance of payments manual, fifth edition.

Annual EU foreign direct investment statistics give a detailed presentation of FDI flows and stocks, showing which Member States invest in which partner countries and in which sectors. Eurostat collects FDI statistics for quarterly and annual flows, as well as for stocks at the end of the year. FDI stocks (assets and liabilities) are part of the international investment position of an economy at the end of the year.

Through outward FDI flows, an investor country builds up FDI assets abroad (outward FDI stocks). Correspondingly, inward FDI flows cumulate into liabilities towards foreign investors (inward FDI stocks). However, changes in FDI stocks differ from FDI flows because of the impact of revaluation (changes in prices and, for outward stocks, exchange rates) and other adjustments such as catastrophic losses, cancellation of loans, reclassification of existing assets or liabilities.

FDI flows are components of the financial account of the balance of payments, while FDI assets and liabilities are components of the international investment position. FDI income consists of the income accruing to the direct investor from its affiliates abroad. Income earned from outward FDI is recorded among credits in the current account of the balance of payments, while income paid to foreign owners of inward FDI stocks is recorded among debits.

FDI flows and positions are recorded according to the immediate host/investing country criterion. The economic activity for both flows abroad and flows in the reporting economy are classified according to the economic activity of the resident enterprise; the same applies to FDI positions.

FDI flows are new investments made during the reference period, whereas FDI stocks provide information on the position, in terms of value, of all previous investments at the end of the reference period. The intensity of FDI can be measured by averaging the value of inward and outward flows during a particular reference period and expressing this in relation to GDP.

The sign convention adopted for the data shown in this subchapter, for both flows and stocks, is that investment is always recorded with a positive sign, and a disinvestment with a negative sign.

European aggregates (such as EU-27) include special purpose entities (SPEs), which are a particular class of enterprises (often empty shells or holding companies) not included in all countries' national statistics. Therefore, these aggregates are not simply the addition of national figures.

Context

In a world of increasing globalisation, where political, economic and technological barriers are rapidly disappearing, the ability of a country to participate in global activity is an important indicator of its performance and competitiveness.

In order to remain competitive, modern-day business relationships extend well beyond the traditional foreign exchange of goods and services, as witnessed by the increasing reliance of enterprises on mergers, partnerships, joint ventures, licensing agreements, and other forms of business co-operation.

FDI may be seen as an alternative economic strategy, adopted by those enterprises that invest to establish a new plant/office, or alternatively, purchase existing assets of a foreign enterprise. These enterprises seek to complement or substitute external trade, by producing (and often selling) goods and services in countries other than where the enterprise was first established.

There are two kinds of FDI, namely the creation of productive assets by foreigners or the purchase of existing assets by foreigners (acquisitions, mergers, takeovers, etc.). FDI differs from portfolio investments because it is made with the purpose of having control or an effective voice in management and a lasting interest in the enterprise. Direct investment not only includes the initial acquisition of equity capital, but also subsequent capital transactions between the foreign investor and domestic and affiliated enterprises.

Conventional trade is less important for services than for goods. While trade in services has been growing, the share of services in total intra-EU trade has changed little during the last decade. However, FDI is expanding more rapidly for services than for goods, increasing at a more rapid pace than conventional trade in services. As a result, the share of services in total FDI flows and positions has increased substantially, with services within the EU-27 becoming increasingly international.

Table 1.18: FDI outward flows by main partner, 2009 (1)
(EUR 1 000 million)

	Extra EU-27	United States	Canada	Switz-erland	Russia	Japan	China	Hong Kong	India	Brazil	Offshore financial centres
EU-27 (2)	263.3	69	2.8	44.8	-1.0	0.1	5.3	3.4	3.2	6.9	60.3
Belgium	13	4.5	4.2	-0.5	2.0	1.1	0.3	0.4	0.1	0.6	-0.3
Bulgaria	0.1	-	-	-	-	-	-	-	-	-	-
Czech Republic	0.5	-	-	-	-	-	-	-	-	-	-
Denmark	4.4	1.8	0.1	0.2	-0.3		0.1	0.1	0.1	0.1	1.4
Germany	8.3	2.7	-0.1	1.1	0.1	-0.3	2.5	0.5	0.6	0.4	-2.5
Estonia	-0.1	-	-	-	-	-	-	-	-	-	-
Ireland	4.5	1.1	-	-0.2	-	-0.1	-	-	-	-	3.2
Greece	0.2	-	-	-	-	-	-	0.1	-	-	0.1
Spain	7.6	1.2	-	1.1	-	-	0.2	0.1	0.1	1.2	0.6
France	26.4	3.3	0.3	7.2	0.8	0.4	1.3	1.1	0.4	3.8	0.6
Italy	1.5	1.1	-	0.2	0.1	-	0.1	-	0.1	-0.9	-
Cyprus	2.2	0.1	-	0.1	0.4	-	-	-	0.1	-	1.2
Latvia	-0.1	-	-	-0.1	-	-	-	-	-	-	-
Lithuania	-	-	-	-	-	-	-	-	-	-	-
Luxembourg	111.8	26.1	-0.3	42.7	-	-	0.1	0.2	-	1.5	39.9
Hungary (3)	0.9	-	-	0.6	-0.1	-	-	-	-	-	0.2
Malta	-	-	-	-	-	-	-	-	-	-	-
Netherlands (3)	20.3	-4.2	0.6	12.7	0.5	-1.7	-0.2	-0.2	-	-0.2	8.9
Austria	2.7	0.3	-0.5	-0.3	-	-	0.2	-	0.1	-	1
Poland	1	-	-	-	0.4	-	-	-	0.1	-	0.1
Portugal	-0.7	0.1	-	-	-	-	-	-	-	0.4	-0.5
Romania	-	-	-	-	-	-	-	-	-	-	-
Slovenia	0.5	-	-	-	-	-	-	-	-	-	-
Slovakia	0.1	-	-	-	-	-	-	-	-	-	-
Finland	0.2	-1.3	-0.1	1.8	-0.4	-	0.5	-	0.2	-	-0.2
Sweden	5.3	0.6	0.2	1.3	1.3	-0.1	0.3	-0.1	0.1	0.4	-
United Kingdom	30.6	-0.4	-2.1	:	:	0.6	0.1	1.6	1	1.1	-8.3

(1) Minus sign stands for disinvestment; "-" indicates less than EUR 50 million.
(2) Takes into account confidential data, estimates for Member States missing data and data for special purpose entities (SPEs) that in some cases are additionally collected by Eurostat and the ECB from Member States not including SPEs foreign direct investment in national data (see footnote 3).
(3) Excluding SPEs.

Source: Eurostat (bop_q_eu and bop_q_c)

Table 1.19: FDI inward flows by main partner, 2009 (1)
(EUR 1 000 million)

	Extra EU-27	United States	Canada	Switz-erland	Russia	Japan	China	Hong Kong	India	Brazil	Offshore financial centres
EU-27 (2)	221.7	96.8	11.4	31.7	3.1	-2.3	0.3	-0.2	0.4	2.8	39.8
Belgium	2.3	-1.7	-0.5	3.7	0.1	-4.1	0.1	0.3	-0.2	-0.2	-0.2
Bulgaria	0.5	-	-	0.1	0.1	-	-	-	-	-	0.1
Czech Republic	0.8	0.5	-	-	-	-	-	-	-	-	0.1
Denmark	1.4	1.4	-	0.2	0.1	-	-	-	-	-0.1	-0.1
Germany	7.1	2.3	-0.1	2.4	-1.6	-0.1	0.1	-	-	-0.1	-0.5
Estonia	-	-	-	-	-	-	-	-	-	-	-
Ireland	0.9	-11.8	0.7	1.9	-	1.4	-0.3	0.2	-	-	7.6
Greece	0.3	0.1	-	0.1	-	-	-	-	-	-	-
Spain	5.3	-1.7	-0.2	1.7	0.4	-	-	-	-	-	0.2
France	10.4	-1.4	0.9	2.9	0.2	0.8	0.2	0.2	-	-0.1	1.7
Italy	3.0	0.7	-	1.0	0.9	0.1	-	-	-	-	0.2
Cyprus	2.3	0.1	-	-	1.6	-	-	-	-	-	0.5
Latvia	0.5	-	-	-	-	-	-	-	-	-	0.1
Lithuania	0.2	0.1	-	-	-	-	-	-	-	-	-
Luxembourg	87.7	70.0	8.5	0.7	-0.4	0.2	-	0.5	-	0.2	5.8
Hungary (3)	4.9	0.6	0.1	0.7	0.8	-	-	-	-	0.1	2.8
Malta	0.4	-	-	-	-	-	-	-	-	-	-
Netherlands (3)	2.7	-7.8	2.2	4.9	0.0	0.5	-0.1	-0.1	-	-0.1	0.6
Austria	3.2	1.7	-	0.2	0.4	-	0.1	-	-	-	0.7
Poland	1.4	0.9	-	0.1	-	0.2	-0.2	0.1	-	-0.1	0.3
Portugal	0.7	0.1	-0.2	0.1	-	-	-	-	-	0.2	0.2
Romania	0.6	-	0.1	0.2	-	-	-	-	-	-	0.2
Slovenia	-	-	-	-0.1	0.1	-	-	-	-	-	-
Slovakia	0.6	-	-	-	-	-	-	-	-	0.1	-
Finland	-0.4	-0.7	-	-	0.1	-	-	-	-	-	-0.1
Sweden	-2.0	-3.0	-0.2	-0.3	:	-0.2	:	:	-	:	-0.7
United Kingdom	34.0	27.3	-0.2	1.3	:	-4.1	:	:	:	-	7.7

(1) Minus sign stands for disinvestment; "-" indicates less than EUR 50 million.
(2) Takes into account confidential data, estimates for Member States missing data and data for special purpose entities (SPEs) that in some cases are additionally collected by Eurostat and the ECB from Member States not including SPEs foreign direct investment in national data (see footnote 3).
(3) Excluding SPEs.

Source: Eurostat (bop_q_eu and bop_q_c)

Figure 1.37: FDI flows and stocks, EU-27
(EUR 1 000 million)

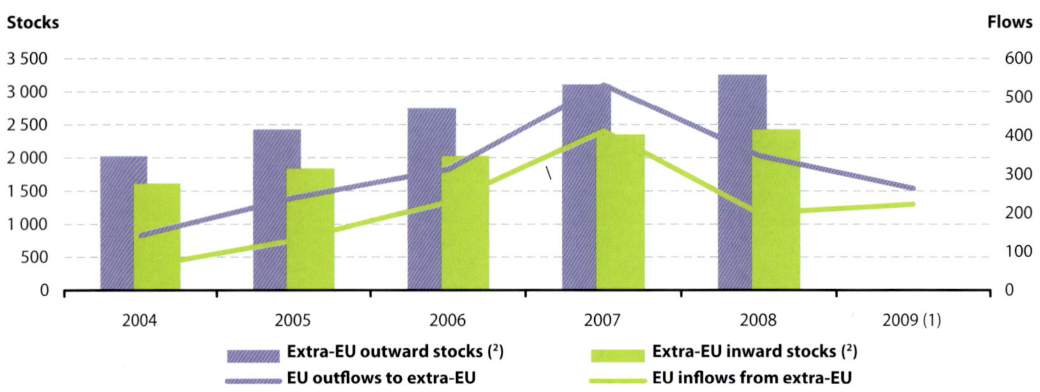

(1) Provisional.
(2) 2009, not available.

Source: Eurostat (bop_fdi_main)

Figure 1.38: FDI outward flows, 2006 to 2008 average
(% of total EU-27 outward flows)

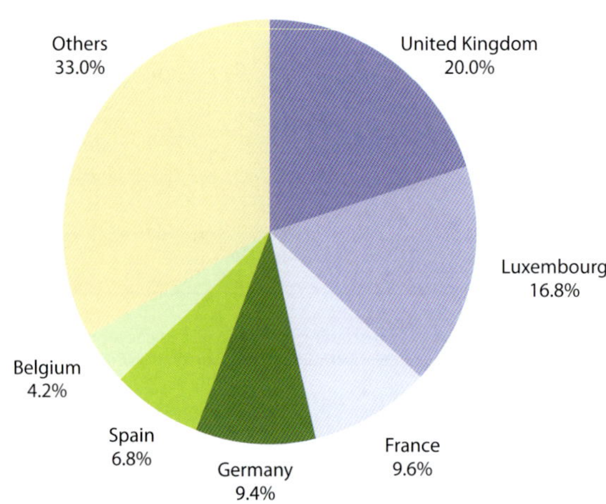

Source: Eurostat (bop_fdi_main)

Map 1.1: Outward stocks of FDI, EU-27, 2008
(EUR 1 000 million (share in extra-EU-27))

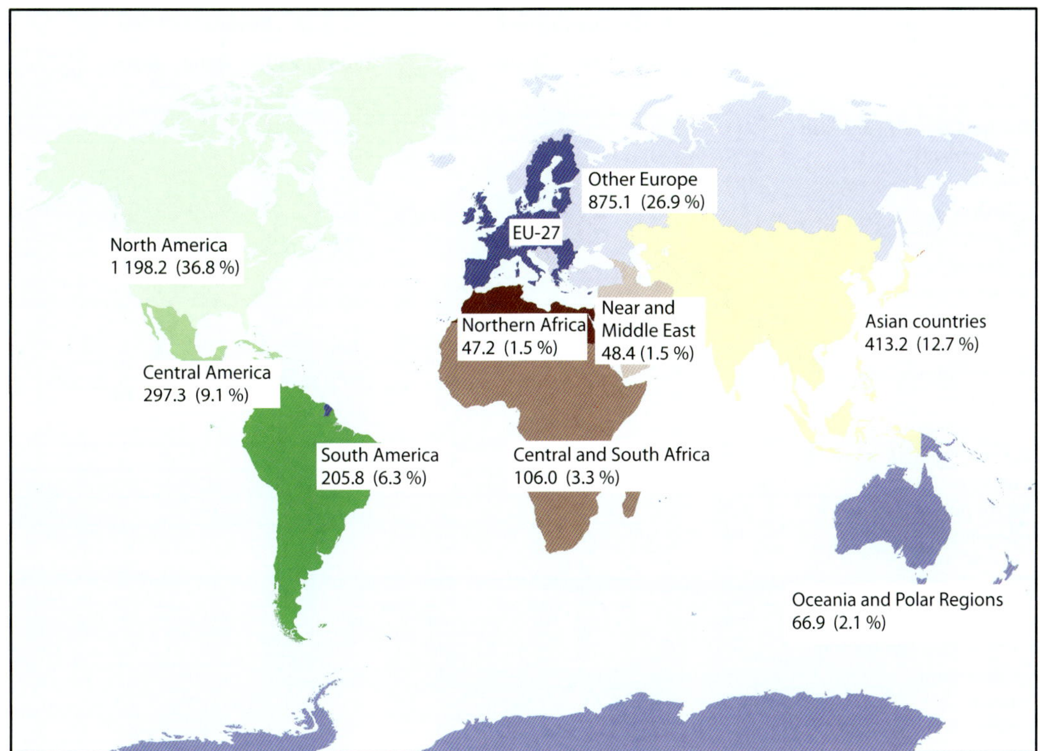

Source: Eurostat (bop_fdi_pos)

Table 1.20: Foreign direct investment, EU-27 (¹)
(EUR 1 000 million)

	Outward FDI flows					Inward FDI flows				
	2006	2007	2008	2009	Share in 2008 (%)	2006	2007	2008	2009	Share in 2008 (%)
Extra EU-27	313.0	530.7	347.7	*263.3*	100.0	229.0	411.4	198.7	*221.7*	100.0
Europe (non-EU), *of which*	74.1	130.6	103.7	:	29.8	66.4	64.0	45.8	:	23.0
Switzerland	21.9	39.9	34.0	*44.8*	9.8	24.8	29.5	10.6	*31.7*	5.4
Russia	11.3	17.2	25.6	*-1.0*	7.4	1.5	9.9	2.3	*3.1*	1.2
Croatia	4.5	2.7	2.0	:	0.6	-0.0	0.1	-0.2	:	-0.1
Turkey	12.3	15.4	6.3	:	1.8	-0.3	0.6	-0.2	:	-0.1
Ukraine	2.1	3.0	4.8	:	1.4	-0.1	0.4	0.5	:	0.2
Africa, *of which*	11.7	17.9	18.5	:	5.3	1.8	4.8	6.0	:	3.0
Egypt	2.8	2.0	9.8	:	2.8	0.1	-0.1	3.4	:	1.7
South Africa	5.1	5.1	2.7	:	0.8	0.9	1.8	0.5	:	0.2
North America, *of which*	135.8	198.7	129.3	:	37.2	85.4	190.5	65.8	:	33.1
Canada	31.0	29.8	7.8	*2.8*	2.3	11.3	6.9	15.3	*11.4*	7.7
United States	104.7	168.9	121.4	*69.0*	34.9	74.1	183.5	50.5	*96.8*	25.4
Central America, *of which*	38.5	101.5	2.1	:	0.6	33.0	75.6	-13.6	:	-
Mexico	1.7	6.5	5.7	:	1.6	0.3	0.4	0.9	:	0.5
South America, *of which*	13.0	17.6	9.6	:	2.7	2.3	27.0	13.4	:	6.7
Argentina	3.4	2.4	4.4	:	1.3	0.0	0.1	-0.3	:	-0.1
Brazil	5.4	14.3	-1.1	*6.9*	-0.3	1.5	24.7	10.7	*2.8*	5.4
Asia, *of which*	28.5	53.9	70.1	:	20.2	34.5	39.0	83.5	:	42.0
Arabian Gulf countries	2.3	4.6	18.9	:	5.4	10.1	2.3	63.2	:	31.8
China (excl. Hong Kong)	6.7	6.6	4.7	*5.3*	1.4	2.2	0.8	-0.1	*0.3*	-0.0
Hong Kong	3.5	7.3	6.2	*3.4*	1.8	-0.2	6.7	2.0	*-0.2*	1.0
Japan	-1.6	10.3	5.9	*0.1*	1.7	16.0	17.8	7.2	*-2.3*	3.6
India	2.4	4.0	3.3	*3.2*	0.9	0.5	1.0	3.7	*0.4*	1.9
Singapore	9.5	8.5	15.2	:	4.4	6.0	10.4	2.6	:	1.3
Oceania, *of which*	7.2	9.1	14.2	:	4.1	7.0	6.7	-1.3	:	-
Australia	6.7	8.6	12.8	:	3.7	6.2	6.7	-0.9	:	-0.5
Offshore financial centres	58.9	150.8	39.4	*60.3*	11.3	74.2	106.5	19.6	*39.8*	9.9

(¹) 2006-2008 annual FDI data; preliminary figures for 2009 are based on annualised quarterly data; the sum of continents does not always equal the extra-EU total because of flows that are not allocated flows.

Source: Eurostat (bop_fdi_main)

Table 1.21: Top 10 countries as extra EU-27 partners for FDI positions
(EUR 1 000 million)

	Outward				Inward			
	2006	2007	2008	Growth rate 2006-2008 (%)	2006	2007	2008	Growth rate 2006-2008 (%)
Extra EU-27	*2 746.0*	*3 108.2*	*3 252.9*	*18.5*	*2 022.7*	*2 346.1*	*2 421.4*	*19.7*
United States	949.3	992.4	1 058.1	11.5	926.1	1 041.5	1 046.2	13.0
Switzerland	364.6	404.6	453.7	24.4	282.5	312.1	306.2	8.4
Canada	114.1	141.3	139.9	22.6	105.2	105.9	105.1	-0.2
Brazil	92.4	114.4	112.5	21.8	14.6	36.2	42.1	188.3
Russia	50.5	70.4	92.0	81.9	14.6	23.6	28.4	95.0
Hong Kong	86.1	88.8	88.9	3.2	17.4	16.2	19.1	9.6
Singapore	52.5	64.2	80.9	54.0	26.8	41.1	41.1	53.2
Japan	75.7	72.2	76.1	0.5	97.9	120.8	116.9	19.4
Norway	50.2	53.2	67.1	33.8	55.6	77.9	89.0	60.2
Australia	53.6	68.2	58.7	9.5	18.8	25.2	20.7	10.0

Source: Eurostat (bop_fdi_pos)

Table 1.22: Extra EU-27 FDI stocks by economic activity, end 2007
(EUR 1 000 million)

	Outward	Inward
Total	3 108.2	2 346.1
Agriculture, hunting and fishing	1.2	1.1
Mining and quarrying	162.9	48.9
Manufacturing	642.8	336.1
Food products	72.0	51.2
Textiles and wood activities	34.1	42.0
Petroleum, chemical, rubber, plastic products	260.3	133.4
Metal and mechanical products	107.8	40.5
Machinery, computers, RTV, communication	21.1	14.1
Vehicles and other transport equipment	71.9	23.1
Electricity, gas and water	53.6	16.2
Construction	14.4	9.2
Services	2 176.8	1 885.8
Trade and repairs	124.3	143.2
Hotels and restaurants	11.5	8.9
Transport and communications	141.5	45.3
Financial Intermediation	1 387.8	1 162.1
Real estate and business services	481.5	503.6
Other services	30.1	22.7
Other sectors	56.6	48.8

Source: Eurostat (bop_fdi_pos)

Figure 1.39: FDI income and rates of return, EU-27

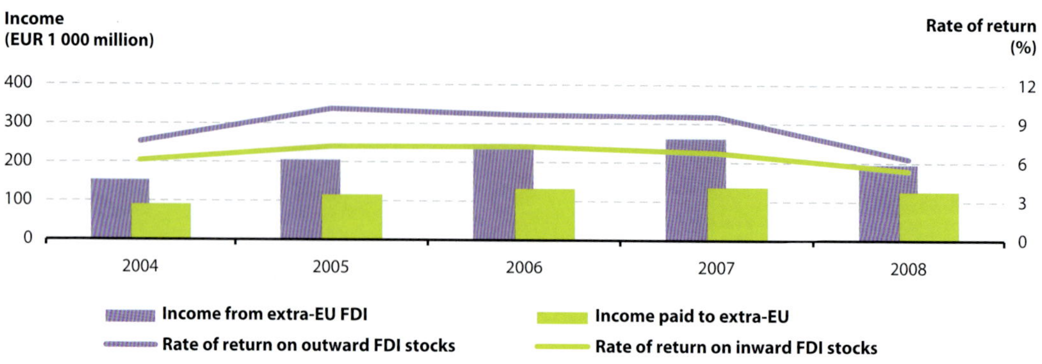

Source: Eurostat (bop_fdi_inc)

Population

2

As the population of the European Union reaches 500 million, its structure is changing. Recent demographic developments show that the EU's population is growing, while its age structure is becoming older as post-war baby-boom generations reach retirement age. Furthermore, people are living longer, as life expectancy continues to increase. On the other hand, while fertility is increasing slowly, it remains well below a level that would keep the size of the population constant in the absence of inward or outward migration. As a result, the EU will, in the coming decades, face a number of challenges associated with an ageing society which will impact on a range of areas, including labour markets, pensions and provisions for healthcare, housing, and social services.

Population change and the structure of the population are gaining importance in the political, economic, social and cultural context of demographic behaviour. Demographic trends in population growth, fertility, mortality and migration are closely followed by policymakers. EU policies, notably in social and economic fields, use demographic data for planning, and for programme monitoring and evaluation.

Eurostat provides a wide range of demographic data, including statistics on populations at national and regional level, as well as for various demographic factors (births, deaths, marriages and divorces, immigration and emigration) influencing the size, the structure and the specific characteristics of these populations. Eurostat also collects detailed information on different areas related to migration and asylum: foreign resident populations, annual flows of immigrants and emigrants, persons acquiring citizenship, monthly and quarterly information on asylum applicants and on asylum decisions, residence permits issued to non-EU nationals and persons found illegally present in EU Member States. These statistics concerning migration and asylum provide the basis for the development and monitoring of EU policy initiatives in several areas, including: the impact of migration on labour markets, the promotion of migrant integration, the development of a common asylum system, the prevention of unauthorised migration, and trafficking in human beings.

2.1 European population compared with world population

This subchapter gives an overview of the European Union's (EU's) population in relation to the rest of the world by looking at several key demographic indicators.

Main statistical findings

The world's population was approaching 7 000 million inhabitants at the beginning of 2010 and continues to grow. Asia accounted for the majority of the world's population (just over 60 %) with 4 167 million inhabitants, while Africa was the next most populous continent with 1 033 million inhabitants, or 15.0 % of the world total.

The world's population more than doubled between 1960 and 2010. The increase in global population between 1960 and 2010 can be largely attributed to growth in Asia, Africa and Latin America.

The most populous countries in the world in 2010 were China (19.6 % of world's population) and India (17.6 %), followed at some distance by the United States and Indonesia. The share of the EU-27 in the world's population was 7.3 %.

Population density within the EU-27 was 116.4 persons per km^2 in 2010, more than three times as high as in the United States, but below the values recorded for Indonesia, China, Japan, India and the Republic of Korea.

The latest United Nations (UN) population projections (world population prospects: the 2008 revision) suggest that the pace at which the world's population is expanding will slow in the coming decades; however, the total number of inhabitants is nevertheless projected to reach more than 9 000 million by 2050. According to these projections, the world's population will also be relatively older in 2050 than it is now.

Ageing societies

Ageing society represents a major demographic challenge and is linked to several issues, including, persistently low fertility rates and significant increases in life expectancy during recent decades (see Table 2.3). Improvements in the quality and availability of healthcare are likely, at least in part, to explain the latter, alongside other factors such as increased awareness of health issues, higher standards of living, or changes in workplace occupations from predominantly manual labour to tertiary activities. The average life expectancy of a new-born baby in the world was estimated at 67.6 years (for the period 2005 to 2010): the value of this indicator increased by 3.6 years compared with the period 1990 to 1995. In the EU-27, life expectancy at birth is generally higher than in most other regions of the world.

The old-age dependency ratio is used as indicator of the level of support of the old population (aged 65 years and over) by the working age population (those aged between 15 to 64 years). Both the UN's and Eurostat's population projections suggest that the population of older persons in the EU-27 will increase to such an extent that there will be fewer than two persons of working age for each person aged 65 or more by the year 2050.

Data sources and availability

The data in this subchapter is based on information from two sources: Eurostat and the UN's population division (world population prospects: the 2008 revision).

The UN is involved in several multi-national survey programmes whose results provide key information about fertility, mortality, maternal and child health. UN population data is often based on registers or estimates of mid-year population; this may be contrasted with Eurostat's data that generally reflect the situation as of 1 January in each reference year.

UN population projections are used in this subchapter to provide comparisons between EU and non-EU countries. Eurostat regularly produces population projections at a national level for the EU Member States.

Context

Europe's ageing society and its relatively static number of inhabitants may be contrasted against a rapid expansion in the world's population, driven largely by population growth in developing countries. However, the demographic challenge that the EU-27 is confronted with is by no means unique. Most developed, and also some emerging economies, will undergo changes in their demographic composition in the next four decades. Shrinking working age populations, a higher proportion of elderly persons, and increasing old age dependency rates suggest that there will be a considerable burden to provide social expenditure related to population ageing (pensions, healthcare, institutional care). The challenges associated with an ageing society are likely to be even more acute in countries such the Republic of Korea where this dependency ratio will rise rapidly and to a very high level.

Figure 2.1: World population, 2010
(% of total)

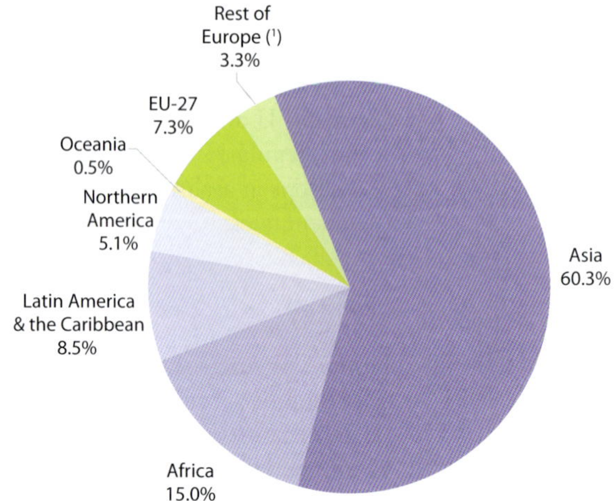

(1) Albania, Andorra, Belarus, Bosnia and Herzegovina, Croatia, Faeroe Islands, Iceland, Liechtenstein, the former Yugoslav Republic of Macedonia, Moldova, Montenegro, Norway, Russia, Serbia, Switzerland and Ukraine.

Source: United Nations, Population Division of the Department of Economic and Social Affairs

Table 2.1: World population

	1960	1965	1970	1975	1980	1985	1990	1995	2000	2005	2010
						(million)					
World	3 023	3 332	3 686	4 061	4 438	4 846	5 290	5 713	6 115	6 512	6 909
Europe (1)	604	634	656	676	693	707	721	727	727	729	733
Africa	285	322	367	419	482	556	639	726	819	921	1 033
Asia	1 694	1 886	2 125	2 379	2 623	2 890	3 179	3 448	3 698	3 937	4 167
Latin America and the Caribbean	220	252	286	323	363	402	442	482	521	557	589
Northern America	204	219	231	242	254	267	283	300	319	335	352
Oceania	16	18	20	21	23	25	27	29	31	34	36
						(% of the world population)					
Europe (1)	20.0	19.0	17.8	16.6	15.6	14.6	13.6	12.7	11.9	11.2	10.6
Africa	9.4	9.7	10.0	10.3	10.9	11.5	12.1	12.7	13.4	14.1	15.0
Asia	56.0	56.6	57.7	58.6	59.1	59.6	60.1	60.4	60.5	60.4	60.3
Latin America and the Caribbean	7.3	7.6	7.8	8.0	8.2	8.3	8.4	8.4	8.5	8.5	8.5
Northern America	6.8	6.6	6.3	6.0	5.7	5.5	5.3	5.3	5.2	5.1	5.1
Oceania	0.5	0.5	0.5	0.5	0.5	0.5	0.5	0.5	0.5	0.5	0.5

(1) EU-27, Albania, Andorra, Belarus, Bosnia and Herzegovina, Croatia, Faeroe Islands, Iceland, Liechtenstein, the former Yugoslav Republic of Macedonia, Moldova, Montenegro, Norway, Russia, Serbia, Switzerland and Ukraine.

Source: United Nations, Population Division of the Department of Economic and Social Affairs

Table 2.2: Population and population density

	Population (million)		Population density (persons per km²)	
	1960	2010	1960	2010
EU-27 (1)	402.6	501.1	93.6	116.4
Argentina	20.7	40.7	7.4	14.6
Australia	10.3	21.5	1.3	2.8
Brazil	72.7	195.4	8.5	23.0
Canada	17.9	33.9	1.8	3.7
China	645.9	1 354.1	67.3	141.1
India	448.3	1 214.5	136.4	369.4
Indonesia	93.1	232.5	48.9	125.0
Japan	93.2	127.0	246.6	337.0
Rep. of Korea	25.1	48.5	251.8	502.8
Mexico	37.9	110.6	19.4	56.5
Russia	119.9	140.4	7.0	8.6
Saudi Arabia	4.1	26.2	1.9	12.2
South Africa	17.4	50.5	14.2	41.4
Turkey	28.2	75.7	36.0	98.4
United States	186.3	317.6	19.4	34.7
World	3 023.4	6 908.7	22.0	51.0

(1) Excluding French overseas departments for 1960.

Source: Eurostat (demo_pjan and demo_r_d3area); World Population Prospects: the 2008 Revision, United Nations Population Division

Figure 2.2: Population (1)
(1960=100)

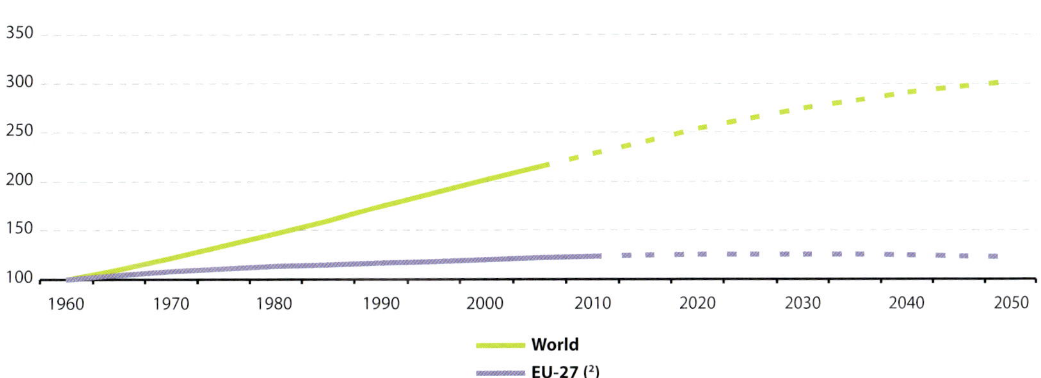

(1) Population projections (UN medium variant) are shown as a dotted line.
(2) Excluding French overseas departments up to and including 1995.

Source: Eurostat (demo_pjan); World Population Prospects: the 2008 Revision, United Nations Population Division

Table 2.3: Fertility and mortality (1)

	Total fertility rate (live births per woman)		Life expectancy at birth (years)	
	1990	2007	1990	2007
EU-27	:	1.56	:	79.2
Argentina	2.90	2.28	72.1	75.2
Australia	1.86	1.83	77.7	81.5
Brazil	2.60	1.9	67.2	72.3
Canada	1.69	1.57	77.9	80.7
China	2.01	1.77	68.8	73.0
India	3.86	2.76	58.8	63.5
Indonesia	2.90	2.19	62.8	70.7
Japan	1.48	1.27	79.5	82.7
Rep. of Korea	1.70	1.22	72.7	79.4
Mexico	3.19	2.21	71.8	76.1
Russia	1.55	1.37	66.4	66.5
Saudi Arabia	5.45	3.17	68.9	72.8
South Africa	3.34	2.55	61.3	51.6
Turkey	2.90	2.13	66.2	71.8
United States	2.03	2.09	75.7	79.2
World	3.08	2.49	64.0	67.6

(1) World and non-member countries, 1990-95 instead of 1990, 2005-2010 estimates instead of 2007.

Source: Eurostat (demo_frate and demo_mlexpec); World Population Prospects: the 2008 Revision, United Nations Population Division

Table 2.4: Old-age dependency ratio (1)
(population aged 65 years and over as % of population aged 15-64)

	1960	1970	1980	1990	2000	2010	2020	2030	2040	2050
EU-27	:	:	:	20.6	23.3	26.1	31.5	38.7	46.1	50.6
Argentina	9.0	11.2	13.5	15.3	16.2	16.6	18.6	21.0	24.1	30.2
Australia	13.8	13.3	14.8	16.8	18.8	20.7	26.9	33.6	38.0	39.9
Brazil	6.1	6.8	7.1	7.4	8.4	10.2	13.6	19.7	26.3	35.9
Canada	12.7	12.7	13.9	16.6	18.5	20.3	27.4	37.1	40.8	43.4
China	8.6	7.7	7.9	8.3	10.1	11.4	16.8	23.7	34.6	38.0
India	5.4	5.8	6.3	6.6	7.0	7.7	9.4	12.2	15.4	20.2
Indonesia	5.9	5.7	6.2	6.3	7.5	9.0	10.8	15.4	22.0	29.1
Japan	8.9	10.2	13.4	17.2	25.3	35.1	47.7	52.8	65.2	74.3
Rep. of Korea	6.7	6.1	6.2	7.2	10.2	15.2	21.7	36.1	52.0	62.9
Mexico	6.6	7.5	7.4	7.6	8.5	10.0	13.1	18.3	27.6	35.9
Russia	9.9	11.7	15.0	15.1	17.8	17.9	22.8	29.7	31.6	38.8
Saudi Arabia	6.3	6.1	5.3	4.1	4.6	4.6	6.1	9.8	15.0	19.9
South Africa	7.0	6.3	5.6	5.5	5.8	7.1	9.6	11.9	12.7	14.5
Turkey	6.4	7.9	8.3	6.8	8.2	8.8	10.8	15.1	21.4	28.7
United States	15.3	15.9	16.9	18.7	18.7	19.4	24.9	31.7	34.0	35.1
World	9.2	9.5	10.0	10.0	10.9	11.6	14.2	17.8	21.9	25.3

(1) Population projections (UN medium variant) from 2010 onwards.

Source: Eurostat (demo_pjanind); World Population Prospects: the 2008 Revision, United Nations Population Division

2.2 Population structure and ageing

The impact of demographic ageing within the European Union (EU) is likely to be of major significance in the coming decades. Consistently low birth rates and higher life expectancy will transform the shape of the EU-27's age pyramid; probably the most important change will be the marked transition towards a much older population and this trend is already becoming apparent in several Member States. As a result, the proportion of people of working age in the EU-27 is shrinking while the relative number of those retired is expanding. The share of older persons in the total population will increase significantly in the coming decades, as a greater proportion of the post-war baby boom generation reaches retirement. This will, in turn, lead to an increased burden on those of working age to provide for the social expenditure required by the ageing population.

Main statistical findings

Population structure in 2009

Young people (0 to 14 years old) made up 15.6 % of the EU-27's (excluding French overseas departments) population in 2009, while persons considered to be of working age (15 to 64 years old) accounted for 67.1 % of the population, and older persons (65 or more years old) had a 17.2 % share. Across the EU Member States (see Table 2.5), the highest share of young people was observed in Ireland (20.9 %), while the smallest share was recorded in Germany (13.6 %). The reverse situation was observed for the share of older persons, as Germany had the highest proportion (20.4 %), while Ireland had the lowest share (11.0 %).

The median age of the EU-27's (excluding French overseas departments) population was 40.6 years in 2009: this means that half of the EU-27 population is older than 40.6 years old, while half is younger. The median age of populations across the EU Member States ranged between 33.8 years in Ireland and 43.7 years in Germany (see Table 2.6).

Age dependency ratios may be used to study the level of support of the young and/or older persons by the working age population; these ratios are expressed in terms of the relative size of young and/or older populations relative to the working age population. The old age dependency ratio for the EU-27 (excluding French overseas departments) was 25.6 % in 2009. As such, there were around four persons of working age for every person aged 65 or over in the EU-27. The old age dependency ratio in the Member States ranged from 16.2 % in Ireland to 30.9 % in Germany.

The combination of young and old age dependency ratios provides the total age dependency ratio, which in 2009 was 48.9 % in the EU-27 (excluding French overseas departments), indicating that there were about two working age persons for every dependent person. The lowest total age dependency ratio was observed in Slovakia (38.0 %) and the highest in France (53.9 %).

Population pyramids (Figures 2.3 and 2.4) show the distribution of population by gender and by five-year age groups. Each bar corresponds to the share of the given gender and age group in the total (men and women combined) population. The population pyramid for the EU-27 in 2009 is narrow at the bottom and is shaped more as a rhomboid due to the baby-boom cohorts of the 1960s. The baby boom was a phenomenon characterised by high fertility rates in several European countries in the middle of the 1960s. Baby boomers currently represent an important part of the working age population and the first of these large cohorts, born over a period of 20-30 years, are now getting close to retirement (this may be observed by comparing the 2009 population pyramid with a past year, in this case 1990, see Figure 2.3).

Past and current trends of population ageing in the EU

Population ageing is a long-term trend which began several decades ago in the EU. This ageing is visible in the development of the age structure of the population and is reflected in an increasing share of older persons at the same time as a declining share of working age persons in the total population.

In the past two decades, the share of the working age population in the EU-27 increased by 0.5 percentage points, while the share of the older population increased by 3.3 percentage points; as a result, the top of the EU-27 age pyramid for 2009 became larger as compared with 1990 (see Figure 2.3). The growth in the relative share of older people may be explained by increased longevity – a pattern that has been evident for several decades as life expectancy has risen (see Subchapter 2.6 on mortality and life expectancy statistics) - it is often referred to as 'ageing at the top' of the population pyramid.

On the other hand, low levels of fertility have been maintained across the EU (see Subchapter 2.5 on fertility statistics); this has resulted in a decreasing share of young people in the total population. This process, known as 'ageing at the bottom', is visible in the population pyramids through a reduction at the base of the age pyramids, as seen between 1990 and 2009.

The development of the median age of the EU-27 (excluding French overseas departments) population also provides an illustration of population ageing. The EU median age increased from 35.2 years in 1990 to 40.6 years by 2009 (see Figure 2.6). The median age increased in all of the Member States during the past two decades, with increases higher than six years of age recorded in Slovenia, Portugal, Lithuania and Spain (see Figure 2.7).

Future trends in population ageing

Eurostat's 2008-based national population projections (EUROPOP2008) show that population ageing is likely to affect all EU Member States. The convergence scenario of these population projections is one of several possible population change scenarios that aim to provide information about the likely future size and structure of the population. According to this scenario, the EU's population will be slightly higher in 2060, while the age structure of the population will be much older than it is now; population is projected to increase by almost 5 % up to 2035, and thereafter to gradually decline by nearly 3 % through to 2060. During the same period (2008 to 2060), the median age of the EU-27 (excluding French overseas departments) population is projected to rise to 47.9 years. The population of working age is expected to decline steadily, while elderly people will likely account for an increasing share of the population – those aged 65 years or over will account for more than 30.0 % of the EU's population by 2060 (17.2 % in 2009).

Another aspect of population ageing is the progressive ageing of the older population itself, as the relative importance of the oldest people is growing at a faster pace than any other age segment of the EU's population. The share of those aged 80 years or above in the EU-27's (excluding French overseas departments) population is projected to almost triple by 2060.

As a result of the population movement between age groups, the EU's old age dependency ratio is projected to more than double from 25.6 % in 2009 to 53.5 % by 2060. The total age dependency ratio (calculated as the ratio of dependent people, young and old, over the population aged 15 to 64 years old) is projected to rise from 48.9 % in 2009 to 78.5 % by 2060.

The age pyramids for 2009 and 2060 show that the EU's population is projected to continue to age. In the coming decades, the high number of baby-boomers will swell the number of elderly people. The population pyramid shows how the baby boomer bulge is moving up while the middle and the base of the pyramid (those of working age and children) are projected to narrow considerably by 2060.

Data sources and availability

Eurostat provides information for a wide range of demographic data. Data on population includes breakdowns by several characteristics, such as age and gender. Eurostat produces population projections at a national and regional level every three years. These projections are what-if scenarios that aim to provide information about the likely future size and age structure of the population based on assumptions of future trends in fertility, life expectancy and migration; the latest projection exercise was EUROPOP2008.

Context

Eurostat's population projections are used by the European Commission to analyse the impact of ageing populations on public spending. Increased social expenditure related to population ageing, in the form of pensions, healthcare and institutional or private (health)care, is likely to result in a higher burden for working age populations.

A number of important policies, notably in social and economic fields, use demographic data for planning actions, monitoring and evaluating programmes – for example, population ageing and its likely effects on the sustainability of public finance and welfare provisions, or the economic and social impact of demographic change.

Table 2.5: Population age structure by major age groups
(%)

	0-14 years old		15-64 years old		65 years old or over	
	1990	2009	1990	2009	1990	2009
EU-27 (1)	19.5	15.6	66.7	67.1	13.7	17.2
Belgium (2)	18.1	16.9	67.1	66.1	14.8	17.1
Bulgaria	20.5	13.4	66.5	69.2	13.0	17.4
Czech Republic	21.7	14.1	65.8	71.0	12.5	14.9
Denmark	17.1	18.3	67.3	65.8	15.6	15.9
Germany	16.0	13.6	69.2	66.0	14.9	20.4
Estonia	22.3	14.9	66.1	67.9	11.6	17.1
Ireland	27.4	20.9	61.3	68.0	11.4	11.1
Greece	19.5	14.3	66.8	67.0	13.7	18.7
Spain	20.2	14.8	66.3	68.6	13.4	16.6
France (1)	20.1	18.3	65.9	65.0	13.9	16.7
Italy	16.8	14.1	68.5	65.8	14.7	20.1
Cyprus	26.0	17.1	63.1	70.1	10.8	12.7
Latvia	21.4	13.7	66.7	69.0	11.8	17.3
Lithuania	22.6	15.1	66.6	68.9	10.8	16.0
Luxembourg	17.2	18.0	69.4	68.1	13.4	14.0
Hungary	20.5	14.9	66.2	68.8	13.2	16.4
Malta	23.6	15.9	66.0	70.1	10.4	14.1
Netherlands	18.2	17.7	69.0	67.3	12.8	15.0
Austria	17.5	15.1	67.6	67.5	14.9	17.4
Poland	25.3	15.3	64.8	71.2	10.0	13.5
Portugal	20.8	15.3	66.0	67.1	13.2	17.6
Romania	23.7	15.2	66.0	69.9	10.3	14.9
Slovenia	20.9	14.0	68.5	69.6	10.6	16.4
Slovakia	25.5	15.4	64.3	72.5	10.3	12.1
Finland	19.3	16.7	67.4	66.5	13.3	16.7
Sweden	17.8	16.7	64.4	65.6	17.8	17.8
United Kingdom (2)	19.0	17.6	65.3	66.3	15.7	16.1
Iceland	25.0	20.8	64.4	67.5	10.6	11.6
Liechtenstein	19.4	16.4	70.6	70.7	10.0	12.9
Norway	18.9	19.0	64.8	66.3	16.3	14.7
Switzerland	17.0	15.3	68.4	68.1	14.6	16.6
Croatia	:	15.4	:	67.3	:	17.3
FYR of Macedonia	:	18.1	:	70.4	:	11.5
Turkey (2)	35.0	26.3	60.7	66.9	4.3	6.8

(1) Excluding French overseas departments.
(2) 2008 instead of 2009.

Source: Eurostat (demo_pjanind)

Table 2.6: Population age structure indicators, 2009

	Median age	Young age dependency ratio	Old age dependency ratio	Total age dependency ratio	Share of population aged 80 or over
	(years)		(%)		
EU-27 (1)	40.6	23.3	25.6	48.9	4.5
Belgium (2)	40.7	25.6	25.8	51.4	4.7
Bulgaria	41.1	19.4	25.2	44.6	3.7
Czech Republic	39.2	19.9	20.9	40.9	3.5
Denmark	40.3	27.8	24.1	51.9	4.1
Germany	43.7	20.6	30.9	51.5	5.0
Estonia	39.3	22.0	25.2	47.2	3.9
Ireland	33.8	30.8	16.2	47.0	2.7
Greece	41.4	21.4	27.9	49.3	4.4
Spain	39.5	21.5	24.3	45.8	4.7
France (1)	39.7	28.2	25.7	53.9	5.2
Italy	42.8	21.4	30.6	51.9	5.6
Cyprus	35.9	24.4	18.2	42.6	2.9
Latvia	39.8	19.9	25.1	44.9	3.7
Lithuania	38.9	21.9	23.2	45.1	3.5
Luxembourg	38.7	26.4	20.5	46.9	3.5
Hungary	39.6	21.6	23.8	45.4	3.8
Malta	39.0	22.6	20.1	42.7	3.2
Netherlands	40.3	26.4	22.3	48.6	3.8
Austria	41.3	22.4	25.7	48.1	4.7
Poland	37.5	21.5	18.9	40.4	3.1
Portugal	40.4	22.8	26.3	49.1	4.3
Romania	38.0	21.7	21.3	43.0	2.9
Slovenia	41.2	20.1	23.6	43.7	3.8
Slovakia	36.5	21.3	16.7	38.0	2.7
Finland	41.8	25.2	25.2	50.3	4.5
Sweden	40.7	25.4	27.1	52.5	5.3
United Kingdom (2)	39.2	26.5	24.3	50.7	4.5
Iceland	34.5	30.9	17.2	48.1	3.2
Liechtenstein	40.3	23.2	18.2	41.5	3.1
Norway	38.5	28.7	22.1	50.8	4.6
Switzerland	41.2	22.5	24.3	46.8	4.7
Croatia	41.1	22.8	25.7	48.5	3.4
FYR of Macedonia	35.5	25.7	16.3	42.0	1.7
Turkey (2)	28.2	39.3	10.2	49.5	1.2

(1) Excluding French overseas departments.
(2) 2008 instead of 2009.

Source: Eurostat (demo_pjanind)

Figure 2.3: Population pyramids, EU-27 (¹)
(% of the total population)

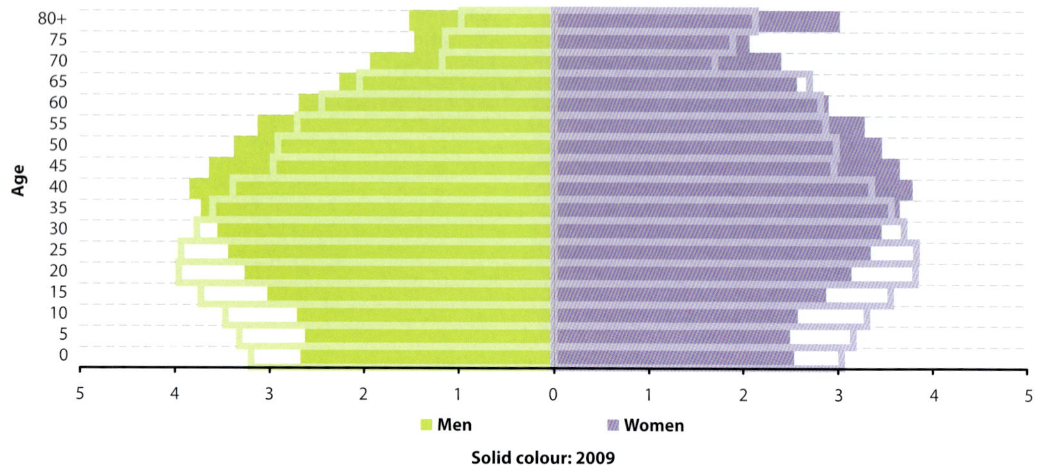

(¹) Excluding French overseas departments.

Source: Eurostat (demo_pjangroup)

Figure 2.4: Population pyramids, EU-27 (¹)
(% of the total population)

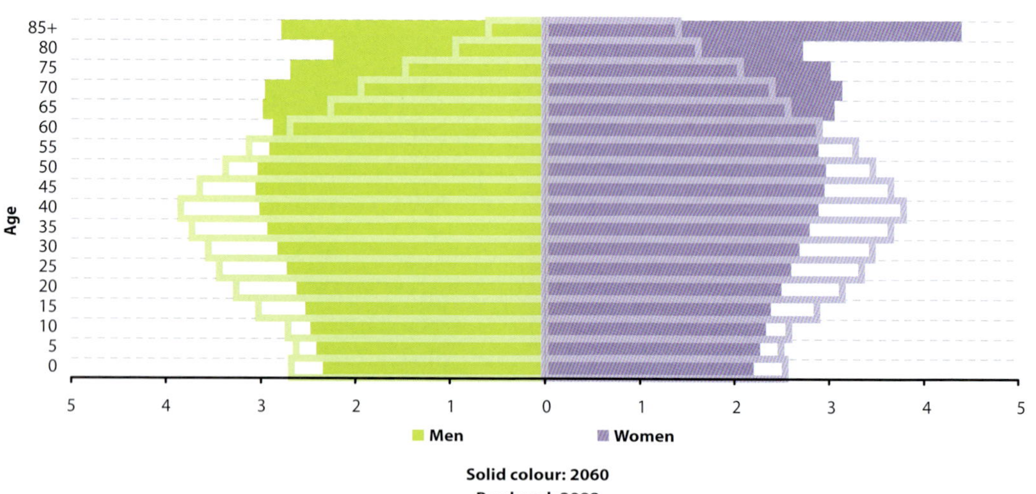

(¹) Excluding French overseas departments; 2060 data are projections (EUROPOP2008 convergence scenario).

Source: Eurostat (demo_pjangroup and proj_08c2150p)

Figure 2.5: Change in the share of the population aged 65 years or over between 1990 and 2009
(percentage point change)

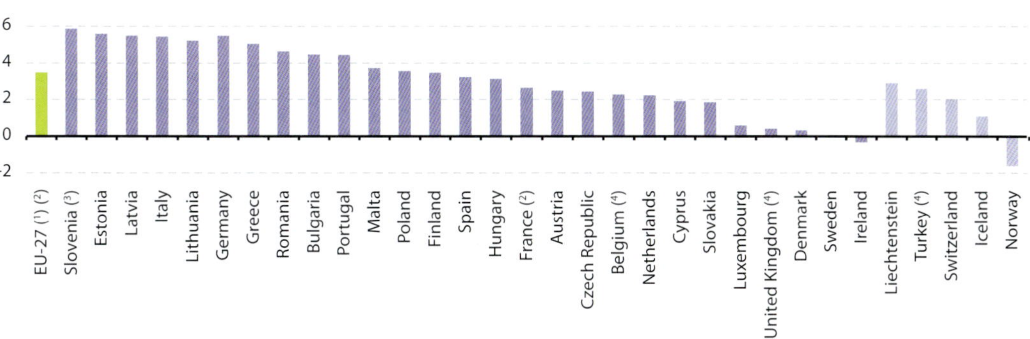

(1) Estimate.
(2) Excluding French overseas departments.
(3) Data may be affected by the change of population definition in 2008.
(4) Change between 1990 and 2008.

Source: Eurostat (demo_pjanind)

Figure 2.6: Median age of population, EU-27 (1)
(years)

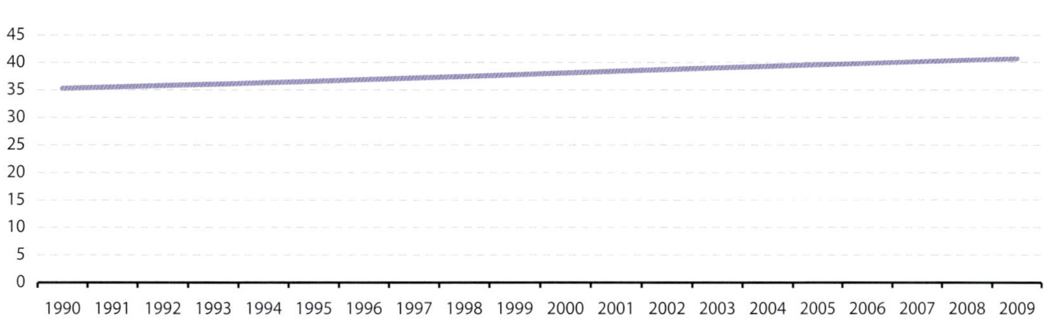

(1) Excluding French overseas departments.

Source: Eurostat (demo_pjanind)

Figure 2.7: Median age of population
(years)

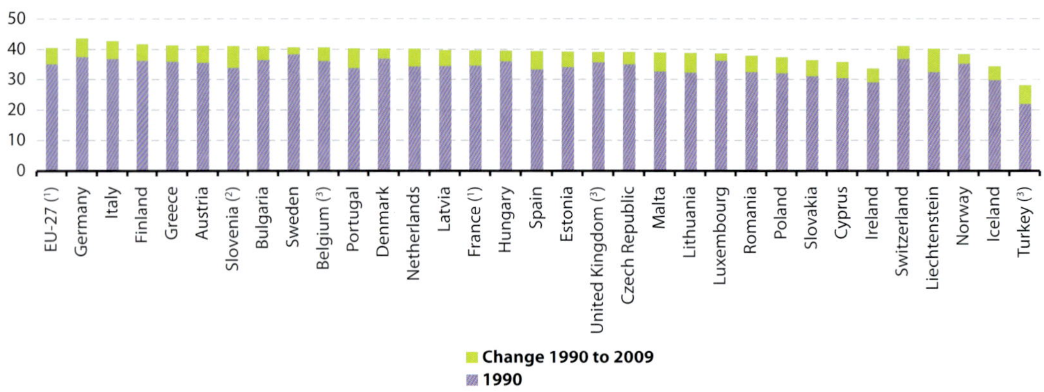

(¹) Excluding French overseas departments.
(²) Data may be affected by the change of population definition in 2008.
(³) 2008 instead of 2009.

Source: Eurostat (demo_pjanind)

Figure 2.8: Population structure by major age groups, EU-27 (¹)
(% of total population)

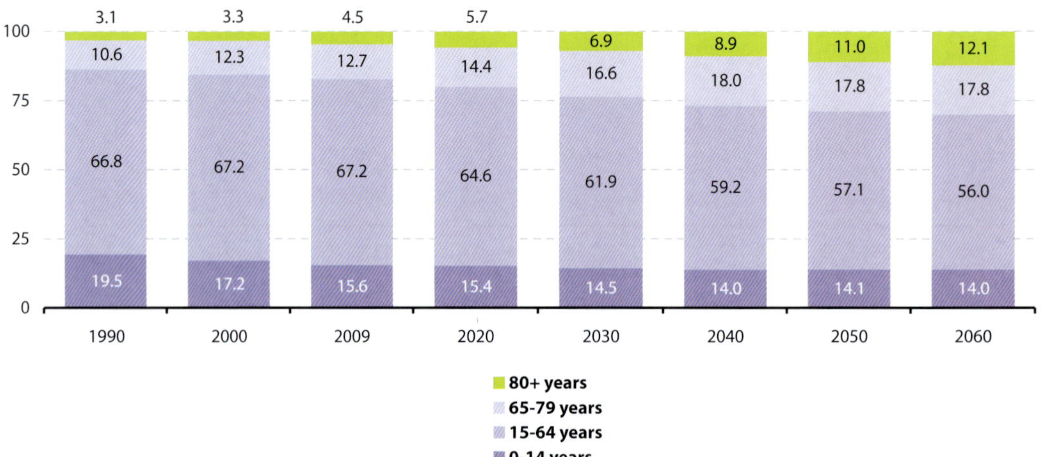

(¹) Excluding French overseas departments; 2020 to 2060 data are EUROPOP2008 convergence scenario.

Source: Eurostat (demo_pjanind and proj_08c2150p)

2.3 Population and population change

This subchapter gives an overview of the development of European Union (EU) population, detailing the two components of population change: natural population change and net migration plus statistical adjustment. More information on net migration is provided within Subchapter 2.7 on migration and migrant population statistics.

Main statistical findings

EU-27 population continues to grow

On 1 January 2010 the population of the EU-27 was estimated at 501.1 million; this was 1.4 million people more than the year before and therefore continued a pattern of uninterrupted EU-27 population growth that has been apparent since 1960. The number of inhabitants in the EU-27 grew from 402.6 million in 1960, rising by 98.5 million persons through to 2010.

Natural population growth in the EU-27 is slowly increasing in importance

The population of the EU-27 grew by 1.4 million during 2009. Just over one third (37.3 %) of this increase resulted from natural growth (defined as the difference between live births and deaths). Net migration plus statistical adjustment continued to be the main determinant of population growth in the EU-27, accounting for 62.7 % of the population increase during 2009.

The contribution of net migration plus statistical adjustment to the total population change in the EU-27 became more significant than that of natural change since 1992. The share of net migration plus statistical adjustment in total population growth peaked, in relative terms, in 2003 (95.1 %). Since this date, the contribution of net migration plus statistical adjustment decreased somewhat. Thus, the share of natural change in total population growth followed an upward trend over the most recent period (from 2004 onwards).

The relatively low contribution of natural change to total population growth is the result of two factors: net migration in the EU-27 increased considerably from the mid-1980s onwards; secondly, the number of live births fell, while the number of deaths increased.

The gap between live births and deaths in the EU-27 narrowed considerably from 1960 onwards (see Figure 2.11), almost reaching parity in 2003 before diverging again somewhat. Since the number of deaths is expected to increase as the baby-boom generation moves into retirement, and, assuming that the fertility rate continues to remain at a relatively low level, negative natural change (more deaths than births) cannot be excluded in the future. In this event, total population decline or growth is likely to depend strongly on the contribution of migration.

Population change at a national level

The number of inhabitants in EU Member States on 1 January 2010 ranged from 81.8 million in Germany to 0.4 million in Malta. Germany together with France, the United Kingdom and Italy comprised more than half (53.7 %) of the total EU-27 population in 2010.

Although the population of the EU-27 as a whole still increased in 2009, population growth was unevenly distributed across the Member States. A total of 19 Member States observed an increase in their respective populations, while the number of inhabitants fell in the Baltic Member States, south eastern parts of the EU (Bulgaria and Romania), Germany, Hungary and Malta.

Analysing the two components of population change at a national level, eight types of population change can be distinguished, separating growth from decline, and the relative weights of natural change and net migration – see Table 2.9 for the full typology. Luxembourg, Sweden, Slovenia, Belgium and the United Kingdom recorded the highest population growth rates in 2009 (more than 6 per 1 000 inhabitants), more than twice the EU-27 average of 2.7 per 1 000 inhabitants. The highest rates of natural change were registered in Ireland (10.2 per 1 000 inhabitants) and Cyprus (5.5 per 1 000 inhabitants), while the highest net migration plus adjustment was recorded in Luxembourg, followed by Sweden, Slovenia, Italy and Belgium (all above 5 per 1 000 inhabitants).

Data sources and availability

Eurostat provides information on a wide range of demographic data. The demographic balance provides an overview of the annual demographic developments in the Member States; statistics on population change are available in absolute figures and as crude rates.

Population change - or population growth - in a given year is the difference between the population size on 1 January of the given year and on 1 January of the following year. It consists of two components: natural change and net migration plus statistical adjustment.

Natural population change is the difference between the number of live births and the number of deaths. A positive natural change is also called natural increase.

Net migration is the difference between the number of immigrants and the number of emigrants. In the context of the annual demographic balance, Eurostat produces net migration figures by taking the difference between total population change and the natural change; this concept is referred to in this subchapter as 'net migration plus statistical adjustment'.

Context

Supporting policymaking and monitoring

Population change and the structure of the population are gaining importance in the political, economic, social and cultural context of demographic behaviour. In particular, this concerns recent demographic developments that focus on the working age population and the current and future evolution of the younger and older shares of the population.

A number of important policies, notably in social and economic fields, use demographic data for planning actions, monitoring and evaluating programmes. These concern, for example, population ageing and its effects on the sustainability of public finance and welfare, the evaluation of fertility as a background for family policies, the economic and social impact of demographic change, as well as any developments measured by 'per capita' indicators.

Figure 2.9: Population, EU-27 (¹)

(at 1 January, million)

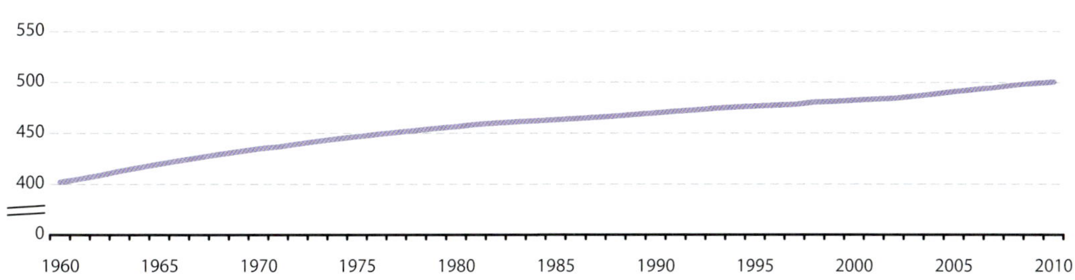

(¹) Before 1998, excluding French overseas departments; includes provisional data.

Source: Eurostat (demo_gind)

Figure 2.10: Population change by component (annual crude rates), EU-27 (¹)

(per 1 000 inhabitants)

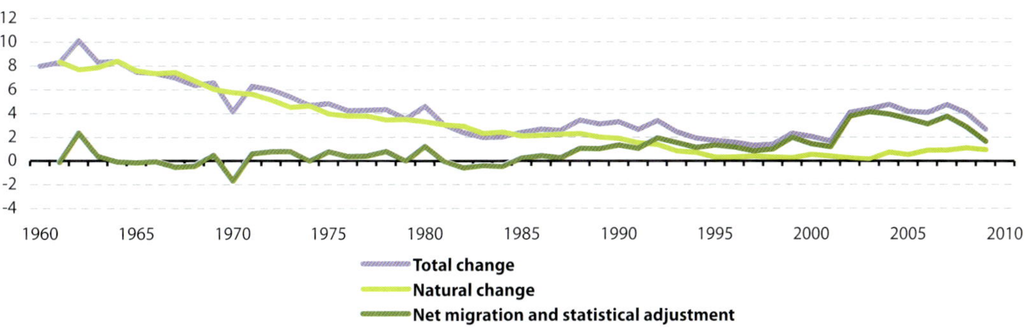

(¹) Before 1998, excluding French overseas departments; includes provisional data.

Source: Eurostat (demo_gind)

Figure 2.11: Births and deaths, EU-27 (¹)

(million)

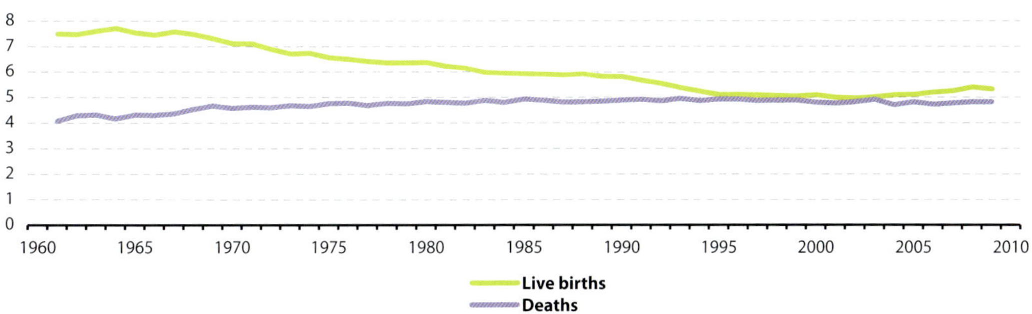

(¹) Before 1998, excluding French overseas departments; includes provisional data.

Source: Eurostat (demo_gind)

Table 2.7: Demographic balance, 2009
(1 000)

	Population 1 January 2009	Live births	Deaths	Natural change (live births - deaths)	Net migration and statistical adjustment (total change - natural change)	Total change between 1 January 2009 and 2010	Population 1 January 2010
EU-27	*499 695.2*	*5 353.1*	*4 843.9*	*509.2*	*857.2*	*1 366.4*	*501 061.5*
Belgium	*10 750.0*	*126.0*	*104.0*	*22.0*	*55.0*	*77.0*	*10 827.0*
Bulgaria	7 606.6	81.0	108.1	-27.1	-15.7	-42.8	7 563.7
Czech Republic	10 467.5	118.3	107.4	10.9	28.3	39.3	10 506.8
Denmark	5 505.5	62.8	54.9	7.9	21.3	29.2	5 534.7
Germany	82 002.4	*651.0*	*841.0*	*-190.0*	*-12.8*	*-202.8*	*81 799.6*
Estonia	1 340.4	15.8	16.1	-0.3	0.0	-0.3	1 340.1
Ireland	*4 450.0*	*74.8*	*29.2*	*45.6*	*-39.9*	*5.8*	*4 455.8*
Greece	11 260.4	*117.9*	*110.3*	*7.6*	*27.0*	*34.6*	*11 295.0*
Spain	45 828.2	*494.6*	*391.3*	*103.3*	*57.6*	160.8	45 989.0
France	*64 367.0*	*821.9*	*546.2*	*275.8*	*71.1*	*346.8*	*64 713.8*
Italy	60 045.1	*568.9*	*591.7*	*-22.8*	*318.1*	*295.3*	*60 340.3*
Cyprus	796.9	*9.7*	*5.4*	*4.4*	*-3.2*	*1.2*	*798.1*
Latvia	2 261.3	21.7	29.9	-8.2	-4.7	-12.9	2 248.4
Lithuania	3 349.9	36.7	42.0	-5.4	-15.5	-20.8	3 329.0
Luxembourg	493.5	5.6	3.7	2.0	6.6	8.6	502.1
Hungary	10 031.0	*96.5*	*130.4*	*-33.9*	*15.9*	*-18.0*	*10 013.0*
Malta	413.6	4.1	3.2	0.9	-1.6	-0.6	413.0
Netherlands	16 485.8	*184.8*	*134.2*	*50.7*	*41.2*	*91.8*	*16 577.6*
Austria	8 355.3	76.3	77.4	-1.0	21.1	20.0	8 375.3
Poland	38 135.9	417.6	384.9	32.6	-1.2	31.5	38 167.3
Portugal	*10 627.3*	*99.5*	*104.4*	*-4.9*	*15.4*	*10.5*	*10 637.7*
Romania	21 498.6	222.4	257.2	-34.8	-1.6	-36.4	21 462.2
Slovenia	2 032.4	*21.6*	*18.7*	*2.9*	*11.7*	14.6	2 047.0
Slovakia	5 412.3	61.2	52.9	8.3	4.4	12.7	5 424.9
Finland	5 326.3	60.4	49.9	10.5	14.6	25.1	5 351.4
Sweden	9 256.3	111.8	90.1	21.7	62.6	84.3	9 340.7
United Kingdom	*61 596.0*	*790.2*	*559.6*	*230.6*	*181.5*	*412.1*	*62 008.1*
Iceland	319.4	*5.0*	*2.0*	*3.0*	*-4.8*	-1.7	317.6
Liechtenstein	35.6	*0.4*	*0.2*	*0.2*	*0.1*	*0.3*	*35.9*
Norway	4 799.3	61.8	41.4	20.4	38.6	58.9	4 858.2
Switzerland	7 701.9	*78.2*	*62.6*	*15.6*	*65.6*	*81.2*	*7 783.0*
Croatia	4 435.1	44.6	52.4	-7.8	-1.5	-9.3	4 425.7
FYR of Macedonia	2 048.6	*23.7*	*19.1*	*4.6*	*-0.5*	*4.1*	*2 052.7*
Turkey	71 517.1	*1 270.0*	*461.0*	*809.0*	235.2	1 044.2	72 561.3

Source: Eurostat (demo_gind)

Table 2.8: Crude rates of population change
(per 1 000 inhabitants)

	Total change			Natural change			Net migration and statistical adjustment		
	2000	2008	2009	2000	2008	2009	2000	2008	2009
EU-27	2.1	4.1	*2.7*	0.6	1.2	*1.0*	1.5	2.9	*1.7*
Belgium	2.4	7.8	*7.1*	1.0	2.2	*2.0*	1.4	5.6	*5.1*
Bulgaria	-5.1	-4.4	-5.6	-5.1	-4.3	-3.6	0.0	-0.1	-2.1
Czech Republic	-1.1	8.3	3.7	-1.8	1.4	1.0	0.6	6.9	2.7
Denmark	3.6	5.4	5.3	1.7	1.9	1.4	1.9	3.5	3.9
Germany	1.2	-2.6	*-2.5*	-0.9	-2.0	*-2.3*	2.0	-0.7	*-0.2*
Estonia	-3.7	-0.4	-0.2	-3.9	-0.5	-0.2	0.2	0.1	0.0
Ireland	14.5	11.0	*1.3*	6.1	10.6	*10.2*	8.4	0.4	*-9.0*
Greece	2.5	4.1	*3.1*	-0.2	0.9	*0.7*	2.7	3.2	*2.4*
Spain	10.6	12.0	3.5	0.9	2.8	*2.2*	9.7	9.2	*1.3*
France	7.1	6.0	*5.4*	4.4	4.5	*4.3*	2.7	1.5	*1.1*
Italy	0.7	7.1	*4.9*	-0.2	-0.1	*-0.4*	0.9	7.3	*5.3*
Cyprus	10.2	9.6	*1.5*	4.5	5.1	*5.5*	5.7	4.5	*-4.0*
Latvia	-7.4	-4.2	-5.7	-5.0	-3.1	-3.6	-2.3	-1.1	-2.1
Lithuania	-7.2	-4.9	-6.2	-1.4	-2.6	-1.6	-5.8	-2.3	-4.6
Luxembourg	12.4	19.9	17.2	4.5	4.1	4.0	7.9	15.8	13.2
Hungary	-2.1	-1.4	*-1.8*	-3.7	-3.1	*-3.4*	1.6	1.6	*1.6*
Malta	6.1	8.1	*-1.6*	3.8	2.1	2.2	2.3	5.9	-3.8
Netherlands	7.7	4.9	*5.6*	4.2	3.0	*3.1*	3.6	1.9	*2.5*
Austria	2.3	4.4	2.4	0.2	0.3	-0.1	2.2	4.1	2.5
Poland	-10.4	0.5	0.8	0.3	0.9	0.9	-10.7	-0.4	-0.0
Portugal	6.0	0.9	*1.0*	1.4	0.0	-0.5	4.6	0.9	*1.4*
Romania	-1.1	-1.4	-1.7	-0.9	-1.5	-1.6	-0.2	0.1	-0.1
Slovenia (1)	1.2	10.9	7.2	-0.2	1.7	*1.4*	1.4	9.2	*5.8*
Slovakia (1)	-3.7	2.1	2.3	0.5	0.8	1.5	-4.1	1.3	0.8
Finland	1.9	4.9	4.7	1.4	2.0	2.0	0.5	2.9	2.7
Sweden	2.4	8.0	9.1	-0.3	1.9	2.3	2.7	6.0	6.7
United Kingdom	3.6	6.8	*6.7*	1.2	3.5	*3.7*	2.4	3.3	*2.9*
Iceland	15.3	12.3	-5.5	8.8	9.0	*9.5*	6.5	3.3	*-15.0*
Liechtenstein	13.4	6.6	*8.8*	5.5	4.1	*4.9*	7.8	2.5	*3.9*
Norway	5.6	13.0	12.2	3.4	3.9	4.2	2.2	9.1	8.0
Switzerland	5.5	14.2	*10.5*	2.2	2.0	*2.0*	3.3	12.1	*8.5*
Croatia	-13.2	-0.3	-2.1	-1.5	-1.9	-1.8	-11.7	1.6	-0.3
FYR of Macedonia	4.7	1.7	*2.0*	5.9	1.9	*2.3*	-1.2	-0.3	*-0.2*
Turkey	14.9	13.1	14.5	14.1	11.4	11.2	0.9	1.7	3.3

(1) Break in series, 2008.

Source: Eurostat (demo_gind)

Table 2.9: Contribution of natural change and net migration (and statistical adjustment) to population change, 2009

Demographic drivers	Member States
Growth due to:	
Only natural change	Ireland, Cyprus, Poland
Mostly natural change	Spain, France, Netherlands, Slovakia, United Kingdom
Mostly net migration (and adjustment)	Belgium, Czech Republic, Denmark, Greece, Luxembourg, Slovenia, Finland, Sweden
Only net migration (and adjustment)	Italy, Austria, Portugal
Decline due to:	
Only natural change	Estonia, Hungary
Mostly natural change	Bulgaria, Germany, Latvia, Romania
Mostly net migration (and adjustment)	Lithuania
Only net migration (and adjustment)	Malta

Source: Eurostat (demo_gind)

2.4 Marriage and divorce

In this subchapter, the trends in family formation and dissolution are analysed through marriage and divorce indicators. Marriage, as recognised by the law of each country, has long been considered to mark the formation of a family. Recent demographic data show that the number of marriages per 1 000 inhabitants is decreasing and the number of divorces is increasing, while more children are born to un-married women.

Main statistical findings

Fewer marriages, more divorces

The number of marriages that took place in the EU-27 in 2007 was 2.4 million, while around 1.2 million divorces were recorded in the same year. The crude marriage rate, in other words the number of marriages per 1 000 inhabitants, was 4.9, and the crude divorce rate was 2.1.

The crude marriage rate in the EU-27 declined from 7.9 per 1 000 inhabitants in 1970 to 4.9 in 2007, an overall reduction of 38 %. Over the same period, marriages became less stable, as reflected by the increase in the crude divorce rate from 0.9 per 1 000 inhabitants in 1970 to 2.1 in 2007. When considering the increase in the divorce rate it should be noted that national laws did not allow divorce in several countries until recent decades; thus, the increased number of divorces in the EU-27 may be, in part, due to divorces occurring in Member States where divorce was not previously possible.

Table 2.10 shows that in 2009 the crude marriage rate was highest in Cyprus (7.7 per 1 000 inhabitants) and Poland (6.6); the lowest crude marriage rates were reported by Slovenia (3.2) and Bulgaria (3.4).

The lowest crude divorce rates were recorded in Ireland (0.8 per 1 000 inhabitants in 2007) and Italy (0.9 in 2008). A number of other southern Member States also recorded relatively low crude divorce rates, including Slovenia (1.1) and Greece (1.2). The highest crude divorce rates were recorded in Belgium (3.0 per 1 000 inhabitants in 2009), ahead of Lithuania and the Czech Republic (both with 2.8) - see Table 2.11.

A rise in births outside marriage

The proportion of live births outside marriage continued to increase across the EU-27, reflecting a change in the pattern of traditional family formation, where parenthood followed marriage. Children born outside of marriage may be born to a couple in a non-marital relationship (for example, cohabiting couples) or to a single mother.

In the EU-27 some 37.4 % of children were born outside marriage in 2009, while the corresponding figure for 1990 was 17.4 %. The share of extramarital births has been on the rise in recent years in almost every Member State. Indeed, extramarital births accounted for the majority of live births in 2009 in Estonia, Sweden, Bulgaria, France and Slovenia. Greece (6.6 %) and Cyprus (11.7 %) were less affected by this trend (see Table 2.12).

Data sources and availability

Eurostat compiles information on a wide range of demographic data, including data on the number of marriages by gender and previous marital status and the number of divorces. Data on the number of live births according to the mother's marital status are used for the calculation of the share of births outside marriage.

Context

Family is a shifting concept: what it means to be a member of a family and the expectations people have of family relationships vary with time and space, making it difficult to find a universally agreed and applied definition. Legal alternatives to marriage, like registered partnership, have become more widespread and national legislation has evolved to confer more rights to unmarried couples. Alongside these new legal forms, other forms of non-marital relationships have appeared, making it more difficult for statisticians to collect data that can be compared across countries.

Due to differences in the timing and formal recognition of changing patterns of family formation and dissolution, these concepts have become more difficult to operationalise. Analysts of demographic statistics therefore have access to relatively few complete and reliable datasets with which to make comparisons over time and between and within countries.

Figure 2.12: Crude marriage and divorce rates, EU-27
(per 1 000 inhabitants)

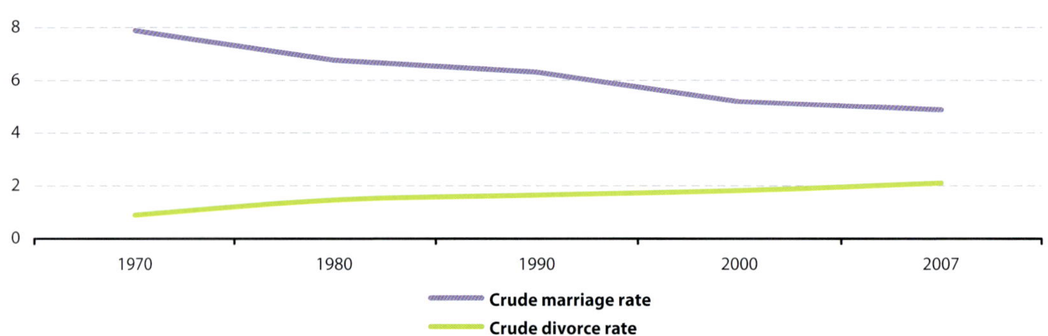

Source: Eurostat (demo_nind and demo_ndivind)

Table 2.10: Crude marriage rate
(per 1 000 inhabitants)

	1960	1970	1980	1990	2000	2009
EU-27 (1)	:	7.9	6.8	6.3	5.2	4.9
Belgium	7.1	7.6	6.7	6.5	4.4	4.0
Bulgaria	8.8	8.6	7.9	6.9	4.3	3.4
Czech Republic	7.7	9.2	7.6	8.8	5.4	4.6
Denmark	7.8	7.4	5.2	6.1	7.2	6.0
Germany	9.5	7.4	6.3	6.5	5.1	4.6
Estonia	10.0	9.1	8.8	7.5	4.0	4.0
Ireland (2)	5.5	7.0	6.4	5.1	5.0	5.2
Greece	7.0	7.7	6.5	5.8	4.5	5.2
Spain	7.8	7.3	5.9	5.7	5.4	3.8
France (3)	7.0	7.8	6.2	5.1	5.0	3.9
Italy	7.7	7.3	5.7	5.6	5.0	4.0
Cyprus (4)	:	8.6	7.6	9.7	13.4	7.9
Latvia	11.0	10.2	9.8	8.9	3.9	4.4
Lithuania	10.1	9.5	9.2	9.8	4.8	6.2
Luxembourg	7.1	6.4	5.9	6.1	4.9	3.5
Hungary	8.9	9.3	7.5	6.4	4.7	3.7
Malta	6.0	7.9	8.8	7.1	6.7	5.7
Netherlands	7.7	9.5	6.4	6.5	5.5	4.4
Austria	8.3	7.1	6.2	5.9	4.9	4.2
Poland	8.2	8.6	8.6	6.7	5.5	6.6
Portugal	7.8	9.4	7.4	7.2	6.2	3.8
Romania	10.7	7.2	8.2	8.3	6.1	6.3
Slovenia	8.8	8.3	6.5	4.3	3.6	3.2
Slovakia	7.9	7.9	7.9	7.6	4.8	4.9
Finland	7.4	8.8	6.1	5.0	5.1	5.6
Sweden	6.7	5.4	4.5	4.7	4.5	5.1
United Kingdom (2)	7.5	8.5	7.4	6.6	5.2	4.4
Iceland	7.5	7.8	5.7	4.5	6.3	4.7
Liechtenstein	5.7	5.9	7.1	5.6	7.2	4.3
Norway	6.6	7.6	5.4	5.2	5.0	5.0
Switzerland	7.8	7.6	5.7	6.9	5.5	5.4
Croatia	8.9	8.5	7.2	5.8	4.9	5.1
FYR of Macedonia	8.6	9.0	8.5	8.3	7.0	7.3
Turkey	:	:	8.2	:	:	8.2

(1) Excluding French overseas departments for 1970 to 1990; 2007 instead of 2009.
(2) 2007 instead of 2009.
(3) Excluding French overseas departments.
(4) Up to and including 2002, data refer to total marriages contracted in the country, including marriages between non-residents; from 2003 onwards, data refer to marriages in which at least one spouse was resident in the country.

Source: Eurostat (demo_nind)

Table 2.11: Crude divorce rate ([1])
(per 1 000 inhabitants)

	1960	1970	1980	1990	2000	2009
EU-27 ([2])	:	0.9	1.5	1.6	1.8	2.1
Belgium	0.5	0.7	1.5	2.0	2.6	3.0
Bulgaria	:	1.2	1.5	1.3	1.3	1.5
Czech Republic	1.4	2.2	2.6	3.1	2.9	2.8
Denmark	1.5	1.9	2.7	2.7	2.7	2.7
Germany	1.0	1.3	1.8	1.9	2.4	2.3
Estonia	2.1	3.2	4.1	3.7	3.1	2.4
Ireland ([3])	-	-	-	-	0.7	0.8
Greece ([4])	0.3	0.4	0.7	0.6	1.0	1.2
Spain	-	-	-	0.6	0.9	2.1
France ([5])	0.7	0.8	1.5	1.9	1.9	2.1
Italy ([4])	-	-	0.2	0.5	0.7	0.9
Cyprus	:	0.2	0.3	0.6	1.7	2.2
Latvia	2.4	4.6	5.0	4.1	2.6	2.3
Lithuania	0.9	2.2	3.2	3.4	3.1	2.8
Luxembourg	0.5	0.6	1.6	2.0	2.4	2.1
Hungary	1.7	2.2	2.6	2.4	2.3	2.4
Malta	-	-	-	-	-	-
Netherlands	0.5	0.8	1.8	1.9	2.2	1.9
Austria	1.1	1.4	1.8	2.1	2.4	2.2
Poland	0.5	1.1	1.1	1.1	1.1	1.7
Portugal	0.1	0.1	0.6	0.9	1.9	2.5
Romania	2.0	0.4	1.5	1.4	1.4	1.5
Slovenia	1.0	1.1	1.2	0.9	1.1	1.1
Slovakia	0.6	0.8	1.3	1.7	1.7	2.3
Finland	0.8	1.3	2.0	2.6	2.7	2.5
Sweden	1.2	1.6	2.4	2.3	2.4	2.4
United Kingdom ([4])	:	1.1	2.6	2.7	2.6	2.2
Iceland	0.7	1.2	1.9	1.9	1.9	1.7
Liechtenstein	:	:	:	:	3.9	2.7
Norway	0.7	0.9	1.6	2.4	2.2	2.1
Switzerland	0.9	1.0	1.7	2.0	1.5	2.5
Croatia	1.2	1.2	1.2	1.1	1.0	1.1
FYR of Macedonia	0.7	0.3	0.5	0.4	0.7	0.6
Turkey	:	:	:	:	:	1.6

([1]) Divorce was not possible by law in Italy until 1970; in Spain until 1981, in Ireland until 1995; divorce is not possible by law in Malta.
([2]) Excluding French overseas departments for 1970 to 1990; 2007 instead of 2009.
([3]) 2007 instead of 2009.
([4]) 2008 instead of 2009.
([5]) Excluding French overseas departments; 2008 instead of 2009.

Source: Eurostat (demo_ndivind)

Table 2.12: Live births outside marriage, as share of total live births
(%)

	1960	1970	1980	1990	2000	2009
EU-27 (1)	:	:	:	17.4	27.4	37.4
Belgium	2.1	2.8	4.1	11.6	28.0	45.7
Bulgaria	8.0	8.5	10.9	12.4	38.4	53.4
Czech Republic	4.9	5.4	5.6	8.6	21.8	38.8
Denmark	7.8	11.0	33.2	46.4	44.6	46.8
Germany	7.6	7.2	11.9	15.3	23.4	32.7
Estonia	:	:	:	27.2	54.5	59.2
Ireland	1.6	2.7	5.9	14.6	31.5	33.3
Greece	1.2	1.1	1.5	2.2	4.0	6.6
Spain	2.3	1.4	3.9	9.6	17.7	31.4
France (2)	6.1	6.9	11.4	30.1	42.6	52.9
Italy	2.4	2.2	4.3	6.5	9.7	23.5
Cyprus	:	0.2	0.6	0.7	2.3	11.7
Latvia	11.9	11.4	12.5	16.9	40.3	43.5
Lithuania	:	3.7	6.3	7.0	22.6	27.9
Luxembourg	3.2	4.0	6.0	12.8	21.9	32.1
Hungary	5.5	5.4	7.1	13.1	29.0	40.8
Malta	0.7	1.5	1.1	1.8	10.6	27.4
Netherlands	1.4	2.1	4.1	11.4	24.9	43.3
Austria	13.0	12.8	17.8	23.6	31.3	39.3
Poland	:	5.0	4.8	6.2	12.1	20.2
Portugal	9.5	7.3	9.2	14.7	22.2	38.1
Romania	:	:	:	:	25.5	28.0
Slovenia	9.1	8.5	13.1	24.5	37.1	53.6
Slovakia	4.7	6.2	5.7	7.6	18.3	31.6
Finland	4.0	5.8	13.1	25.2	39.2	40.9
Sweden	11.3	18.6	39.7	47.0	55.3	54.4
United Kingdom	5.2	8.0	11.5	27.9	39.5	46.3
Iceland	25.3	29.9	39.7	55.2	65.2	64.4
Liechtenstein	3.7	4.5	5.3	6.9	15.7	18.5
Norway	3.7	6.9	14.5	38.6	49.6	55.1
Switzerland	3.8	3.8	4.7	6.1	10.7	17.9
Croatia	7.4	5.4	5.1	7.0	9.0	12.9
FYR of Macedonia	5.1	6.2	6.1	7.1	9.8	12.2

(1) Excluding French overseas departments and Romania for 1990.
(2) Excluding French overseas departments.

Source: Eurostat (demo_find)

Figure 2.13: Live births outside marriage, as share of total live births, 2009
(% of total live births)

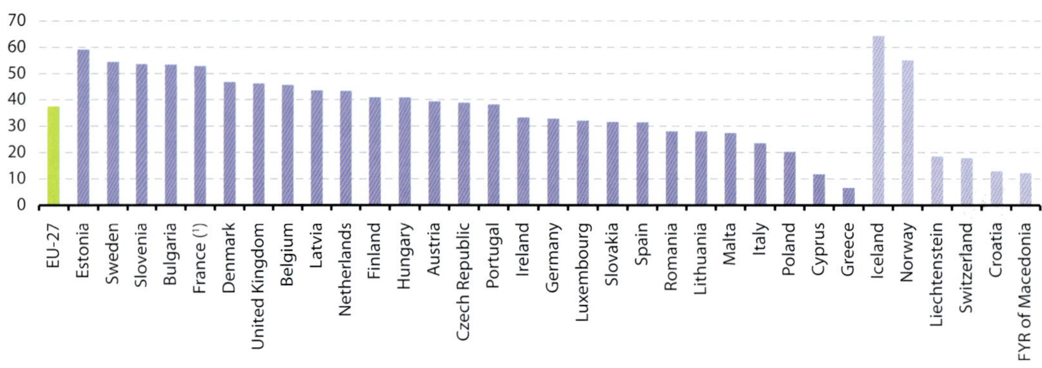

(1) Excluding French overseas departments.

Source: Eurostat (demo_find)

2.5 Fertility

This subchapter looks at the development over time of the number of births and fertility in the European Union (EU). Fertility has been steadily declining since the mid-1960s in the countries that form today the EU-27, but in recent years the total fertility rate at the EU level showed a slight recovery.

Main statistical findings

From the 1960s up to the beginning of the 21st century, the number of live births in the EU-27 declined sharply from 7.5 million to around 5.0 million in 2002. Since then there has been a modest rebound in the number of live births, as 5.4 million children were born in the EU-27 in 2008.

In recent decades Europeans have generally been having fewer children, and this can partly explain the slowdown in the EU-27's population growth (see Subchapter 2.3 on population and population change statistics). A total fertility rate of around 2.1 live births per woman is considered to be the replacement level: in other words, the average number of live births per woman required to keep the population size constant if there were no inward or outward migration. The total fertility rate in the EU-27 declined to a level well below this replacement level in recent decades, falling to 1.47 live births per woman in 2003. A slight recovery in the fertility rate was subsequently observed in most of the Member States, such that the EU-27 average had increased to 1.56 live births per woman by 2008.

The slight increase in the total fertility rate observed in recent years may, in part, be attributed to a catching-up process following a general pattern of postponing the decision to have children. When women give birth later in life, the total fertility rate first indicates a decrease in fertility, followed later by a recovery.

Total fertility rates across EU-27 Member States converged during the last few decades. In 1980, the gap between the highest (3.2 in Ireland) and the lowest (1.5 in Luxembourg) fertility rates was 1.7 live births per woman. By 1990 this difference had decreased to 1.1 live births per woman, and by 2008 it had narrowed further to 0.8. In 2008, Ireland still had the highest fertility rate, with an average of 2.1 live births per woman in 2008, while the lowest fertility rate was recorded in Slovakia with 1.3 live births per woman.

Data sources and availability

Eurostat compiles information for a large range of demographic data, including statistics on the number of live births by gender, by the mother's age and according to marital status, as well as by the rank of the child (first, second, third child and so on). A series of fertility indicators are produced and disseminated based on the information collected, such as the total fertility rate and fertility rates according to the mother's age, the mean age of women at childbirth, the crude birth rate and the share of births outside marriage.

Context

A number of important policies, notably in social and economic fields, use demographic data for planning actions, monitoring and evaluating programmes. These concern, for example, the evaluation of fertility as a background for family policymaking.

The EU's social policy does not include a specific strand for family issues. Policymaking in this area remains the exclusive responsibility of Member States, reflecting different family structures, historical developments, social attitudes and traditions from one Member State to another. There are, however, a number of common demographic themes apparent across the whole of the EU, one of them being the reduction in the number of births.

Figure 2.14: Number of live births, EU-27 (1)
(million)

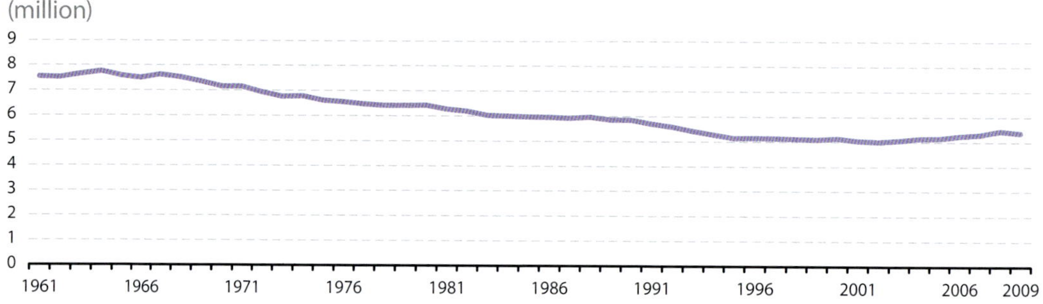

(1) Excluding French overseas departments before 1998.

Source: Eurostat (demo_gind)

Table 2.13: Total fertility rate
(live births per woman)

	1960	1970	1980	1990	2000	2003	2008
EU-27 (1)	:	:	:	:	:	1.47	*1.56*
Belgium (1)	2.54	2.25	1.68	1.62	1.67	1.66	1.82
Bulgaria	2.31	2.17	2.05	1.82	1.26	1.23	1.48
Czech Republic	2.09	1.92	2.08	1.90	1.14	1.18	1.50
Denmark	2.57	1.95	1.55	1.67	1.77	1.76	1.89
Germany	:	:	:	:	1.38	1.34	1.38
Estonia	:	:	:	2.05	1.38	1.37	1.65
Ireland	3.78	3.85	3.21	2.11	1.89	1.96	2.10
Greece	2.23	2.40	2.23	1.40	1.26	1.28	1.51
Spain	:	:	2.20	1.36	1.23	1.31	1.46
France (2)	2.73	2.47	1.95	1.78	1.87	1.87	1.99
Italy	2.37	2.38	1.64	1.33	1.26	1.29	1.41
Cyprus	:	:	:	2.41	1.64	1.50	1.46
Latvia	:	:	:	:	:	1.29	1.44
Lithuania	:	2.40	1.99	2.03	1.39	1.26	1.47
Luxembourg	2.29	1.97	1.50	1.60	1.76	1.62	1.61
Hungary	2.02	1.98	1.91	1.87	1.32	1.27	1.35
Malta	:	:	1.99	2.04	1.70	1.48	1.44
Netherlands	3.12	2.57	1.60	1.62	1.72	1.75	1.77
Austria	2.69	2.29	1.65	1.46	1.36	1.38	1.41
Poland	:	:	:	2.06	1.35	1.22	1.39
Portugal	3.16	3.01	2.25	1.56	1.55	1.44	1.37
Romania	:	:	2.43	1.83	1.31	1.27	1.35
Slovenia	:	:	:	1.46	1.26	1.20	1.53
Slovakia	3.04	2.41	2.32	2.09	1.30	1.20	1.32
Finland	2.72	1.83	1.63	1.78	1.73	1.76	1.85
Sweden	:	1.92	1.68	2.13	1.54	1.71	1.91
United Kingdom (1)	:	:	1.90	1.83	1.64	1.71	1.90
Iceland	:	2.81	2.48	2.30	2.08	1.99	2.15
Liechtenstein	:	:	:	:	1.57	1.36	1.43
Norway	:	2.50	1.72	1.93	1.85	1.80	1.96
Switzerland	2.44	2.10	1.55	1.58	1.50	1.39	1.48
Croatia	:	:	:	:	:	1.32	1.46
FYR of Macedonia	:	:	:	:	1.88	1.77	1.47
Turkey	:	:	:	:	:	:	2.10

(1) 2007 instead of 2008.
(2) Excluding French overseas departments.

Source: Eurostat (demo_frate)

Table 2.14: Fertility indicators, EU-27

	2002	2003	2004	2005	2006	2007
Total fertility rate	*1.45*	1.47	1.50	1.51	1.54	*1.56*
Mean age of women at childbirth	:	29.3	29.4	29.5	29.6	29.7

Source: Eurostat (demo_find)

2.6 Mortality and life expectancy

This subchapter looks at recent statistics in relation to mortality in the European Union (EU). Life expectancy at birth has risen rapidly in the last century due to a number of important factors, including reductions in infant mortality, rising living standards, improved lifestyles and better education, as well as advances in healthcare and medicine.

Main statistical findings

Life expectancy is increasing

The most commonly used indicator for analysing mortality is that of life expectancy at birth. Improvements in living standards and to health systems across Europe have led to a continuous increase in life expectancy at birth. In the EU-27 life expectancy at birth increased over the last 50 years by about ten years. Even in the last five years for which data are available (2002 to 2007) it gained 1.5 years (Figure 2.16). As a result, life expectancy in the EU-27 is generally higher than in most other regions of the world. Based on EU-27 observations for 2007, a new born male is expected to live, on average, to 76.1 years old, while a new born female is expected to live to 82.2 years old (Table 2.15).

Significant differences in life expectancy at birth are nevertheless observed between the EU Member States. Looking at the extremes of the ranges, a woman is expected to live 77.0 years in Bulgaria and 84.9 years in France, a range of 7.9 years. A man can be expected to live 66.3 years in Lithuania and 79.2 years in Sweden, a range of 12.9 years.

The gender gap is shrinking

With a gender gap of about six years of life in 2007, women generally live longer than men in the EU-27, but the gap between male and female life expectancies varies substantially between Member States. In 2008, the largest difference between the genders was found in Lithuania (11.3 years) and the smallest in the Netherlands (4.0 years) – see Figure 2.17.

Infant mortality

Improvements in life expectancy at birth are achieved through reductions in the probability of dying. One of the most significant changes in recent decades has been a reduction in infant mortality rates. During the 15 years from 1993 to 2008 the infant mortality rate in the EU-27 fell by a half. The reductions in infant mortality were more significant in the eastern Member States which had previously recorded higher levels of infant mortality. The lowest infant mortality rate within the EU-27 in 2008 occurred in Luxembourg (1.8 deaths per 1 000 live births). However, relatively high levels of infant mortality were recorded in Romania (11.0 ‰) and Bulgaria (8.6 ‰).

Data sources and availability

Eurostat provides information on a wide range of demographic data, including statistics on the number of deaths by age, year of birth, gender and educational attainment, as well as information on infant mortality and late foetal deaths. A series of fertility indicators are produced and published, which may be used to derive a range of information on subjects such as life expectancy by age and gender, or crude death rates.

Context

The gradual increase in life expectancy is one of the contributing factors to the ageing of the EU-27's population – alongside the low levels of fertility sustained for decades (see Subchapters 2.2 and 2.5 on population structure and ageing and fertility statistics).

Figure 2.15: Number of deaths, EU-27 (1)
(million)

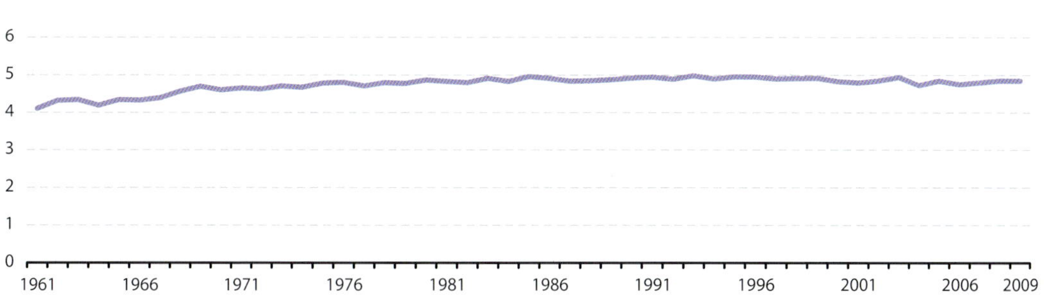

(1) Excluding French overseas departments before 1998.

Source: Eurostat (demo_gind)

Figure 2.16: Life expectancy at birth, EU-27
(years)

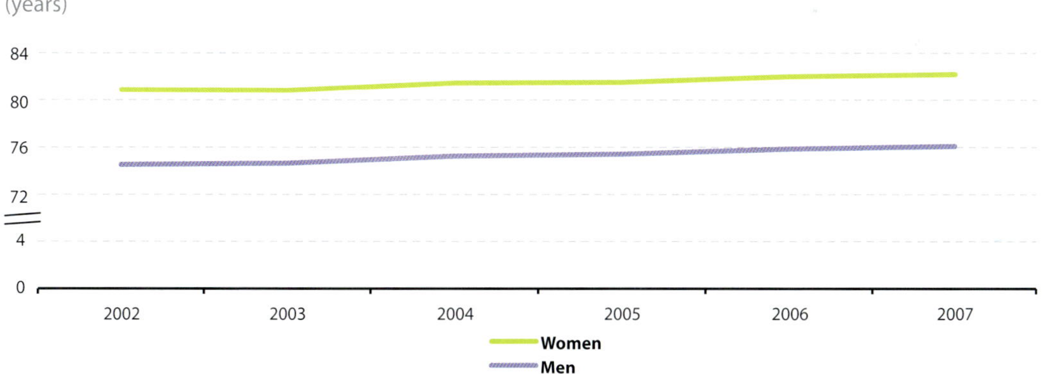

Source: Eurostat (demo_mlexpec)

Table 2.15: Life expectancy at birth
(years)

	Total		Men		Women	
	1993	2008	1993	2008	1993	2008
EU-27 (1)	:	79.2	:	76.1	:	82.2
Belgium (1)	76.5	79.9	73.0	77.1	79.9	82.6
Bulgaria	71.2	73.3	67.6	69.8	75.1	77.0
Czech Republic	72.9	77.3	69.3	74.1	76.5	80.5
Denmark	75.2	78.8	72.6	76.5	77.8	81.0
Germany	76.2	80.2	72.8	77.6	79.4	82.7
Estonia	68.1	74.3	62.3	68.7	74.0	79.5
Ireland	75.3	79.9	72.5	77.5	78.1	82.3
Greece	77.4	80.0	75.0	77.7	79.8	82.3
Spain	77.7	81.2	74.1	78.0	81.4	84.3
France (2)	77.5	81.5	73.4	77.9	81.7	84.9
Italy (1)	77.8	81.6	74.6	78.7	81.0	84.2
Cyprus	77.2	80.8	74.7	78.5	79.8	83.1
Latvia	:	72.5	:	67.0	:	77.8
Lithuania	69.0	72.0	63.1	66.3	75.0	77.6
Luxembourg	76.0	80.7	72.2	78.1	79.6	83.1
Hungary	69.2	74.2	64.7	70.0	74.0	78.3
Malta	:	79.7	:	77.1	:	82.3
Netherlands	77.1	80.5	74.0	78.4	80.1	82.5
Austria	76.3	80.6	72.8	77.8	79.5	83.3
Poland	71.5	75.6	67.2	71.3	75.9	80.0
Portugal	74.6	79.4	71.0	76.2	78.1	82.4
Romania	69.5	73.4	65.9	69.7	73.4	77.2
Slovenia	73.6	79.1	69.4	75.5	77.6	82.6
Slovakia	72.0	74.9	67.8	70.8	76.3	79.0
Finland	75.9	79.9	72.1	76.5	79.5	83.3
Sweden	78.2	81.3	75.5	79.2	80.9	83.3
United Kingdom (1)	76.2	79.8	73.5	77.7	78.9	81.9
Iceland	79.0	81.6	77.1	80.0	80.9	83.3
Liechtenstein	:	82.8	:	80.0	:	85.4
Norway	77.2	80.8	74.2	78.4	80.3	83.2
Switzerland	78.4	82.3	75.0	79.8	81.7	84.6
Croatia	:	76.1	:	72.4	:	79.7
FYR of Macedonia	:	74.4	:	72.4	:	76.5

(1) 2007 instead of 2008.
(2) Excluding French overseas departments.

Source: Eurostat (demo_mlexpec)

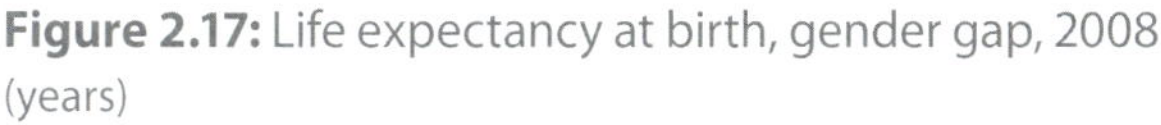

Figure 2.17: Life expectancy at birth, gender gap, 2008
(years)

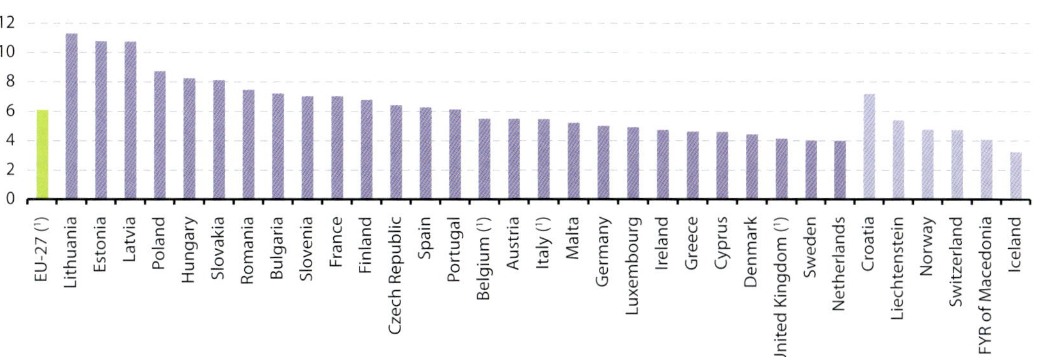

(¹) 2007.

Source: Eurostat (demo_mlexpec)

Table 2.16: Life expectancy at age 65
(years)

	Total		Men		Women	
	1993	2008	1993	2008	1993	2008
EU-27 (1)	:	18.9	:	17.0	:	20.5
Belgium (1)	16.9	19.3	14.5	17.3	18.9	21.0
Bulgaria	14.2	15.3	12.9	13.5	15.5	16.7
Czech Republic	14.5	17.3	12.6	15.3	16.0	18.8
Denmark	15.9	18.2	14.0	16.6	17.6	19.5
Germany	16.8	19.3	14.5	17.5	18.3	20.7
Estonia	14.2	16.8	11.7	13.6	15.7	18.9
Ireland	15.2	18.9	13.4	17.2	17.0	20.4
Greece	17.1	18.9	15.9	17.8	18.1	19.8
Spain	18.1	20.1	15.9	18.0	19.8	21.9
France (2)	18.5	21.0	16.0	18.5	20.6	23.1
Italy (1)	17.7	20.1	15.6	18.0	19.5	21.8
Cyprus	16.9	19.2	15.7	17.9	18.0	20.4
Latvia	:	16.0	:	13.0	:	17.9
Lithuania	15.1	16.2	12.6	13.4	16.6	18.1
Luxembourg	16.8	19.4	14.2	17.4	18.7	21.0
Hungary	14.0	16.4	11.9	13.9	15.7	18.1
Malta	:	18.7	:	17.0	:	20.1
Netherlands	16.8	19.2	14.4	17.4	18.9	20.7
Austria	17.0	19.6	14.7	17.7	18.4	21.1
Poland	14.6	17.2	12.5	14.8	16.2	19.1
Portugal	16.0	18.7	14.2	16.9	17.5	20.3
Romania	14.1	15.7	12.8	14.0	15.2	17.2
Slovenia	15.5	18.8	13.2	16.4	17.1	20.5
Slovakia	14.5	16.1	12.4	13.8	16.2	17.8
Finland	16.4	19.6	14.1	17.5	18.0	21.3
Sweden	17.5	19.6	15.6	18.0	19.3	20.9
United Kingdom (1)	16.2	19.0	14.2	17.5	17.9	20.2
Iceland	18.0	19.6	16.8	18.4	19.1	20.6
Liechtenstein	:	20.6	:	18.5	:	22.2
Norway	16.9	19.4	14.8	17.6	18.8	21.0
Switzerland	18.3	20.7	15.9	18.9	20.3	22.3
Croatia	:	16.4	:	14.3	:	18.0
FYR of Macedonia	:	14.6	:	13.6	:	15.6

(1) 2007 instead of 2008.
(2) Excluding French overseas departments.

Source: Eurostat (demo_mlexpec)

Figure 2.18: Life expectancy at age 65, 2008
(years)

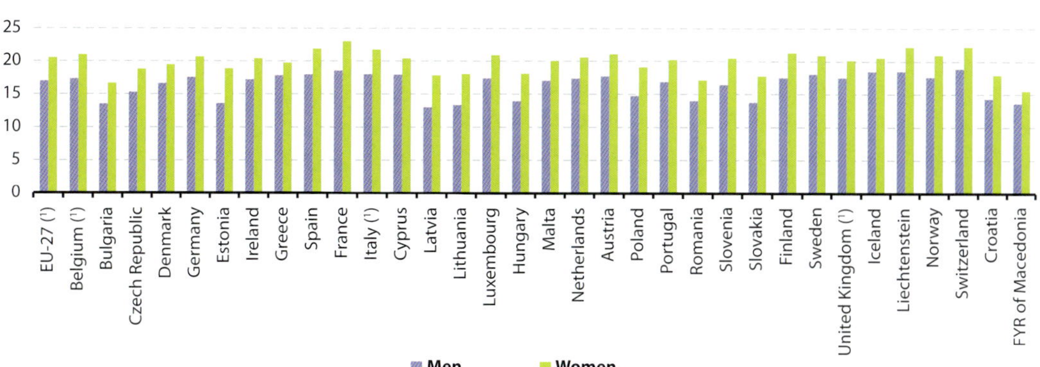

(¹) 2007.

Source: Eurostat (demo_mlexpec)

Figure 2.19: Infant mortality
(deaths per 1000 live births)

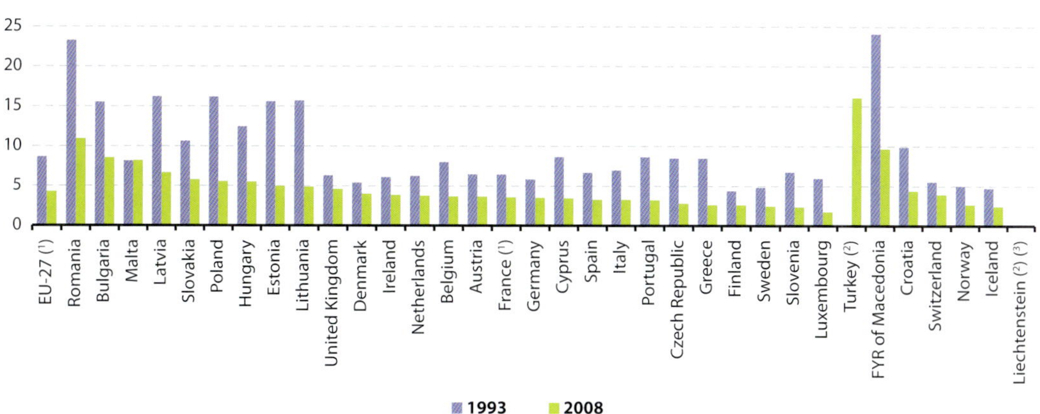

(¹) Excluding French overseas departments.
(²) 1993, not available.
(³) Infant mortality was zero in 2008: no infant death occurred among the 350 live births.

Source: Eurostat (demo_minfind)

2.7 Migration and migrant population

This subchapter presents European Union (EU) statistics on international migration, population stocks of national and foreign (non-national) citizens, and the acquisition of citizenship. Migration is influenced by a combination of economic, political and social factors, either in a migrant's country of origin (push factors) or in the country of destination (pull factors); the relative economic prosperity and political stability of the EU are thought to exert a considerable pull effect on immigrants.

In destination countries, international migration may be used as a tool to solve specific labour market shortages. At the same time though, international migration alone will almost certainly not reverse the ongoing trend of population ageing experienced in many parts of the EU.

Main statistical findings

Migration flows

During 2008 about 3.8 million people immigrated into one of the EU Member States (see Figure 2.20) and at least 2.3 million emigrants are reported to have left one of the EU Member States. Compared with 2007, immigration to EU Member States is estimated to have decreased by 6 % and emigration to have increased by 13 %. It should be noted that these figures do not represent the migration flows to/from the EU as a whole, since they also include international flows within the EU - between different Member States. Just over half of the total immigrants to EU Members States, in other words 1.8 million people, were previously residing outside the EU.

The country that reported the largest number of immigrants in 2008 was Spain (726 000), followed by Germany (682 000), the United Kingdom (590 000) and Italy (535 000). Two thirds of the total number of immigrants into the EU-27 were recorded immigrating into one of these four Member States (see Table 2.17).

Germany reported the highest number of emigrants in 2008 (738 000, resulting in negative net migration), followed by the United Kingdom with 427 000 and Spain with 266 000. There was also an important level of emigration as regards persons leaving Romania and Poland. Most EU Member States reported more immigration than emigration in 2008, but in Germany, Poland, Romania, Bulgaria and the three Baltic Member States emigrants outnumbered immigrants.

Relative to the size of the resident population (see Figure 2.21), the country that recorded the highest number of immigrants in 2008 was Luxembourg with 36 immigrants per 1 000 inhabitants, followed by Malta with 22 and Cyprus with 18 immigrants per 1 000 inhabitants. Immigration was also high in the EFTA countries, far exceeding the EU Member States' average of 7.6 immigrants per 1 000 inhabitants. Luxembourg also reported the highest rate of emigration in 2008, with 20.6 emigrants per 1 000 inhabitants. Overall, the highest rate of emigration among the countries reporting in 2008 was in Iceland, where almost 29 residents per 1 000 inhabitants left the country.

Not only foreigners immigrate to a particular Member State, but also nationals - both those returning 'home' and citizens born abroad who are immigrating for the first time. Some 600 000 immigrants, or 16 % of all immigrants into the EU Member States in 2008 were nationals.

In 2008 the share of nationals among immigrants differed from one Member State to another. The EU Member States reporting the highest shares in 2008 were Poland (75 %), Lithuania (68 %) and Estonia (48 %). In contrast, the Czech Republic, Spain, Hungary, Luxembourg, Italy, Slovakia, Cyprus and Slovenia reported very low shares, with nationals making up under 10 % of immigrants.

The share of non-nationals among immigrants to EU Member States in 2008 was 84 %. More than half of them (56 %) were citizens of non-EU countries and the rest (44 %) were citizens of other EU Member States.

Regarding the gender distribution of immigrants, there was a slight prevalence of men over women for the EU as a whole (51 % versus 49 % respectively). Only a few Member States, namely Cyprus, Italy, Spain, France and Ireland, reported more women than men among immigrants.

Immigrants to EU Member States in 2008 were on average much younger than the population of their country of destination. On 1 January 2009 the median age of the EU population was 40.6 years. The median age of immigrants in 2008 ranged from 24.8 years (in Portugal) to 37.5 years (in Greece).

Non-national population

The total number of non-nationals, in other words people who are not citizens of their country of residence, living on the territory of the EU Member States on 1 January 2009 was 31.8 million, representing 6.4 % of the EU-27's population (see Table 2.18). One year earlier, on 1 January 2008, the number of non-nationals was 30.8 million, or 6.2 % of the total population. More than one third (a total of 11.9 million persons) of all non-nationals living in the EU-27 on 1 January 2009 were citizens of a different EU Member State from the one where they were living.

In absolute terms, the largest numbers of non-nationals living in the EU on 1 January 2009 were in Germany (7.2 million persons), Spain (5.7 million), the United Kingdom (4.2 million), Italy (3.9 million) and France (3.7 million). Non-nationals in these five Member States collectively represented 77.6 % of the total number of non-nationals living in the EU-27, compared with a 62.8 % share for the same five Member States within the entire EU-27 population. In relative terms, the EU Member State with the highest share of non-nationals was Luxembourg, where non-nationals accounted for 43.5 % of the population at the beginning of 2009. The vast majority (86.3 %) of non-nationals living in Luxembourg were citizens of other EU Member States. In 2009, a high proportion of non-nationals (10 % or more of the resident population) was also observed in Latvia, Cyprus, Estonia, Spain and Austria. In contrast, the share of non-national was less than 1 % in Poland, Romania and Bulgaria.

In most Member States the majority of non-nationals are citizens of a non-member country. At the beginning of 2009 citizens of other EU Member States represented the majority of non-nationals only in Luxembourg, Ireland, Belgium (2008 data), Slovakia, Cyprus and Hungary. In the case of Latvia and Estonia, the proportion of citizens from non-member countries is particularly large due to the high number of so called recognised non-citizens; these are mainly former Soviet Union citizens, who are permanently resident in these countries but have not acquired Latvian/Estonian citizenship or any other citizenship.

Looking at the distribution by continent of origin of citizens from non-member countries living in EU Member States, the largest proportion (38.1 %) were citizens of a European country outside of the EU-27 (see Figure 2.24), a total of 7.2 million people; among these more than half were citizens of Turkey, Albania or Ukraine. The second biggest group was from Africa (24.6 %), followed by Asia (19.8 %), the Americas (16.6 %) and Oceania (0.9 %). More than half of the citizens of African countries that were living in the EU were from North Africa, often from Morocco or Algeria. Many Asian non-nationals living in the EU came from south or east Asia, in particular from India or China. Citizens of Ecuador, Brazil and Colombia made up the largest share of non-nationals from the Americas living in the EU.

Nationals of non-member countries living in the EU can also be differentiated according to the level of development of their country of citizenship, based on the human development index (HDI) calculated by the United Nations (UN) under the UN Development Programme (see Figure 2.25). Among the population of nationals of non-member countries living in the EU in 2009, 47.7 % had citizenship of a high HDI country, with Turkey, Albania and Russia accounting for almost half of these. As such, nationals of high-HDI non-member countries represented the largest proportion of all nationals of non-member countries living in the EU, whereas an analysis of the population distribution in the rest of the world (outside of the EU) shows that the medium-HDI group was the largest. A slightly smaller share (44.4 %) of nationals of non-member countries living in the EU were citizens of a medium-HDI country, one fifth of whom were citizens of Morocco, with nationals of China and Ukraine the next largest groups. The remaining 7.9 % of nationals of non-member countries living in the EU were from low-HDI countries, 30 % of whom had Nigerian or Iraqi citizenship. The citizenship structure of the population of non-nationals living in the EU varies greatly between Member States; it is influenced by factors such as labour migration, historical links between origin and destination countries, and established networks in destination countries.

Across the EU as a whole, Turkish citizens made up the biggest group of non-nationals (see Figure 2.26). This group comprised 2.4 million people in 2009, or 7.5 % of all non-nationals living in the EU. The second biggest group was Romanians living in another EU Member State (6.2 % of the non-national population), followed by Moroccans. The group of non-nationals with the most significant increase over the period 2001 to 2009 was Romanians, whose number living in other Member States increased more than sixfold over the period considered (from 0.3 million in 2001 to 2.0 million people by 2009). The number of Polish and Chinese citizens also increased significantly during this period, and citizens from both of these countries figured among the ten largest non-national groups in 2009.

An analysis of the age structure of the resident population shows that, for the EU-27 as a whole, the non-national population was overall younger than the national population. The distribution by age of non-nationals shows, with respect to nationals, a greater representation of adults aged between 20 and 46 for men and between 19 and 47 for women, a feature that is quite evident when looking at the corresponding population pyramids (see Figure 2.27). In 2009 the median age of the EU-27 population was 40.6 years, while the median age of non-nationals living in the EU was 34.3 years (36.9 for citizens of other EU Member States and 33.0 for nationals from non-member countries).

Acquisition of citizenship

The number of people acquiring the citizenship of an EU-27 Member State was almost 700 000 in 2008 (see Figure 2.28). The total number of acquisitions of citizenship declined for the second consecutive year in 2008 having risen for eight years (the time-series for this indicator begins in 1998). The decline of 1.6 % in 2008 was smaller than that recorded for 2007 (3.9 %). There was a considerable decrease in the acquisition of citizenship in the United Kingdom and Germany in 2008, a combined fall of 53 700 (see Table 2.19). The largest increases were recorded in Greece, Spain, Italy, Romania and France. Some Member States, particularly Greece, Portugal and Romania, saw a high increase in the number of citizenships granted, mostly due to changes and simplifications introduced in their respective nationality laws. The highest number of acquisitions in 2008 was recorded in France, the first time since 2004 that more people gained French citizenship than citizenship of the United Kingdom. These two Member States, along with Germany and Spain accounted for 64.0 % of the total number of persons acquiring citizenship of an EU Member State in 2008. Sweden and Luxembourg were the EU Member States which granted the highest number of citizenships per inhabitant. Looking at the ratio between the number of citizenships granted by each Member State and the respective size of the resident population of non-nationals, the countries with the highest ratios were Sweden, Portugal and Poland, with 50 or more citizenship acquisitions per 1 000 non-nationals in 2008: the EU-27 average was 22 acquisitions per 1 000 non-nationals (see Figure 2.29).

For the EU as a whole, more than 90 % of those who acquired citizenship of a Member State in 2008 were previously citizens of non-member countries; this was the case in nearly all of the Member States. However, in Hungary and Luxembourg the majority of new citizenships granted were to citizens of another EU Member State: in the case of Hungary this mainly concerned persons of Romanian citizenship. As in previous years, the largest groups that acquired citizenship of an EU Member State in 2008 were citizens of Morocco (64 000, corresponding to 9 % of all citizenships granted) and Turkey (50 000, or 7 %). Compared with 2007, the number of Moroccans acquiring citizenship in the EU rose by 7 %, while the number of Turkish people acquiring citizenship fell by 10 %. The largest share of Moroccans acquired their new citizenship in France

(45 %), Italy (14 %) and Spain (13 %). The largest share of Turkish people acquired their new citizenship in Germany (49 %) or in France (21 %).

Data sources and availability

Eurostat produces statistics on a range of issues related to international migration flows, population stocks and the acquisition of citizenship. Data are collected on an annual basis and are supplied to Eurostat by the national statistical authorities of the Member States.

Since 2008 the collection of data has been based on Regulation 862/2007. This defines a core set of statistics on international migration flows, foreign (non-national) population stocks, the acquisition of citizenship, asylum and measures against illegal entry and stay. Although Member States are able to continue to use any appropriate data according to national availability and practice, the statistics collected under the Regulation must be based on common definitions and concepts. Most Member States base their statistics on administrative data sources such as population registers, registers of foreigners/non-nationals, registers of residence permits, registers of work permits, or databases on the issuing of residence permits. Some countries use sample surveys or estimation methods to produce migration statistics. The data on the acquisition of citizenship are normally produced from administrative systems. The implementation of the Regulation is expected to result in increased availability and comparability of migration and citizenship statistics.

Previously statistics on migration flows, population stocks and the acquisition of citizenship were sent to Eurostat on a voluntary basis, as part of a joint migration data collection organised by Eurostat in cooperation with a series of international organisations, for example the United Nations Statistical Division (UNSD), the United Nations Economic Commission for Europe (UNECE) and the International Labour Organization (ILO). The recent changes in methodology, definitions and data sources used to produce migration and citizenship statistics may result, for some Member States, in a lack of comparability over time for their respective series.

There are problems with measuring emigration; in particular, it is more difficult to measure people leaving a country than those arriving. An analysis comparing 2008 immigration and emigration data from the EU Member States (mirror statistics) confirmed that this was true in many countries. As a result, this subchapter focuses mainly on immigration data.

Context

Migration policies within the EU are increasingly concerned with attracting a particular migrant profile, often in an attempt to alleviate specific skills shortages. Selection can be carried out on the basis of language proficiency, work experience, education and age. Alternatively, employers can make the selection so that migrants already have a job upon their arrival.

Besides policies to encourage labour recruitment, immigration policy is often focused on two areas: preventing unauthorised migration and the illegal employment of migrants who are not permitted to work, and promoting the integration of immigrants into society. In the EU, significant resources have been mobilised to fight people smuggling and trafficking networks.

Some of the most important legal texts adopted in the area of immigration include:

- Directive 2003/86/EC on the right to family reunification;
- Directive 2003/109/EC on a long-term resident status for non-member nationals;
- Directive 2004/114/EC on the admission of students;
- Directive 2005/71/EC for the facilitation of the admission of researchers into the EU;
- Directive 2008/115/EC for returning illegally staying third-country nationals;
- Directive 2009/50/EC concerning the admission of highly skilled migrants.

Within the European Commission, the Directorate-General for Home Affairs is responsible for immigration policy. In 2005, the European Commission relaunched the debate on the need for a common set of rules for the admission of economic migrants with a Green paper COM(2004) 811 on an EU approach to managing economic migration which led to the adoption of a policy plan on legal migration (COM(2005) 669) at the end of 2005. In July 2006, the European Commission adopted a Communication COM(2006) 402 on policy priorities in the fight against illegal immigration of third-country nationals, which aims to strike a balance between security and an individuals' basic rights during all stages of the illegal immigration process. Later that year, in September, the European Commission presented its third annual report COM(2007) 512 on migration and integration. A European Commission Communication COM(2008) 611 issued in October 2008 emphasised the importance of migration as an aspect of external and development policy. The Stockholm programme, adopted by Member State governments in December 2009, sets a framework and series of principles for the ongoing development of European policies on justice and home affairs for the period 2010 to 2014: migration-related issues are a central part of this programme.

Figure 2.20: Total immigration, EU-27 (million)

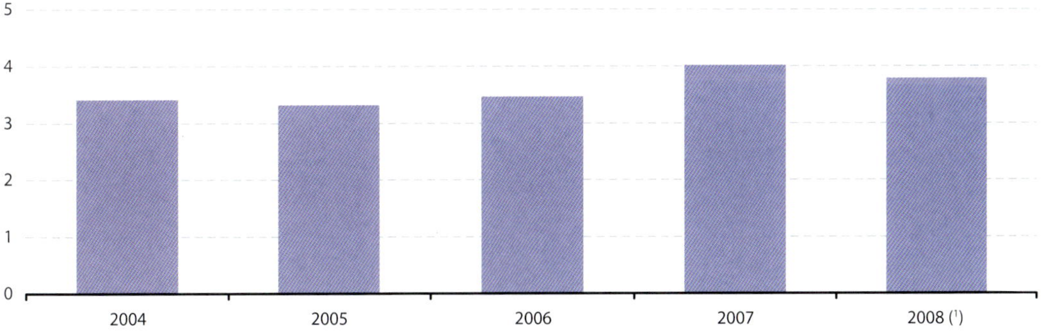

(1) Data for 2008 not fully comparable with data for previous years due to changes in methodology, sources and definitions.

Source: Eurostat (migr_imm1ctz)

Table 2.17: Immigration by main citizenship group, 2008

	Total immigrants	Nationals		Non-nationals					
				Total		Citizens of other EU Member States		Citizens of non-member countries	
	(1 000)	(1 000)	(%)	(1 000)	(%)	(1 000)	(%)	(1 000)	(%)
EU-27	*3 800.0*	*600.0*	*15.8*	*3 200.0*	*84.2*	*1 400.0*	*36.8*	*1 800.0*	*47.4*
Belgium	*150.8*	:	:	:	:	:	:	:	:
Bulgaria	1.2	1.1	92.9	0.1	7.0	0.0	0.1	0.1	7.0
Czech Republic	77.8	1.7	2.1	76.2	97.9	17.6	22.7	58.5	75.2
Denmark	57.4	19.9	34.6	37.5	65.4	20.0	34.8	17.5	30.5
Germany	682.1	108.3	15.9	573.8	84.1	335.9	49.2	237.9	34.9
Estonia	3.7	1.7	47.5	1.9	52.5	1.0	27.0	0.9	25.6
Ireland	63.9	17.9	27.9	45.6	71.4	32.1	50.3	13.5	21.1
Greece	:	:	:	74.7	:	25.7	:	49.0	:
Spain	726.0	33.8	4.7	692.2	95.3	193.3	26.6	498.9	68.7
France	216.9	64.1	29.5	152.9	70.5	63.9	29.5	89.0	41.0
Italy	534.7	38.2	7.1	496.5	92.9	212.9	39.8	283.7	53.1
Cyprus	14.1	1.1	7.8	9.8	69.7	6.5	46.0	3.4	23.8
Latvia	3.5	0.9	27.1	2.5	72.9	1.6	46.0	0.9	26.9
Lithuania	9.3	6.3	68.2	3.0	31.8	0.4	4.0	2.6	27.8
Luxembourg	17.8	1.0	5.4	16.7	94.2	13.9	78.3	2.8	15.9
Hungary	37.5	2.0	5.3	35.5	94.7	17.7	47.1	17.9	47.7
Malta	9.0	1.2	13.0	7.8	86.9	4.5	49.8	3.3	37.1
Netherlands	143.5	40.2	28.0	94.3	65.7	55.4	38.6	38.9	27.1
Austria	110.1	15.3	13.9	94.4	85.7	55.3	50.3	39.1	35.5
Poland	47.9	35.9	75.0	12.0	25.0	3.1	6.4	8.9	18.6
Portugal	29.7	9.6	32.3	20.1	67.7	4.1	13.7	16.1	54.0
Romania	:	:	:	10.0	:	:	:	:	:
Slovenia	30.7	2.6	8.6	28.0	91.1	2.1	6.7	25.9	84.4
Slovakia	17.8	1.4	7.6	16.5	92.4	8.5	47.8	7.9	44.6
Finland	29.1	9.2	31.6	19.7	67.6	7.3	25.2	12.3	42.4
Sweden	101.2	17.9	17.6	83.0	82.0	30.4	30.0	52.6	52.0
United Kingdom	590.2	85.1	14.4	505.2	85.6	197.7	33.5	307.4	52.1
Iceland	10.3	2.8	27.4	7.5	72.6	6.4	62.2	1.1	10.4
Norway	58.1	6.4	11.1	51.7	88.9	32.2	55.4	19.5	33.5
Switzerland	184.3	22.7	12.3	161.6	87.7	113.6	61.6	48.0	26.0
Croatia	14.5	12.5	86.1	2.0	13.9	0.5	3.7	1.5	10.2
FYR of Macedonia	1.1	0.2	20.8	0.8	79.1	0.1	12.0	0.7	67.1
Turkey	:	:	:	19.7	:	6.0	:	13.7	:

Source: Eurostat (migr_imm1ctz)

Figure 2.21: Immigrants, 2008 (1)
(per 1 000 inhabitants)

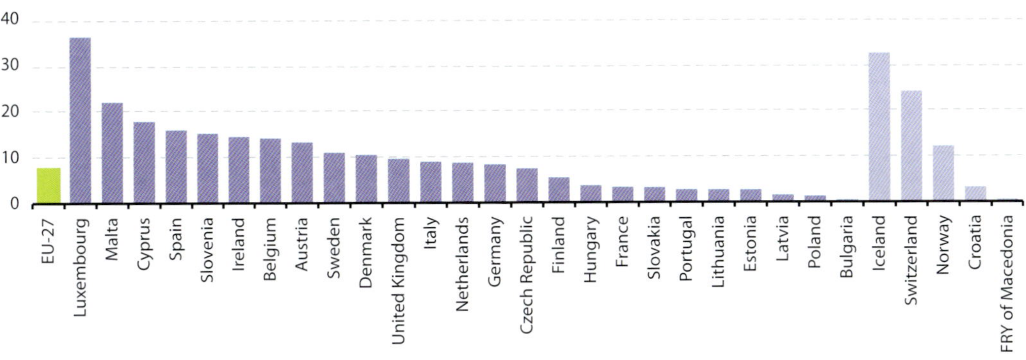

(1) Data for the number of inhabitants refers to 1 January 2009; Greece and Romania, not available.

Source: Eurostat (migr_imm1ctz and migr_pop1ctz)

Table 2.18: Total population and resident non-national population by group of citizenship, 2009

	Total population	Non-nationals					
		Total		Citizens of other EU Member States		Citizens of non-member countries	
	(1 000)	(1 000)	(%)	(1 000)	(%)	(1 000)	(%)
EU-27	*499 432.2*	*31 779.9*	*6.4*	*11 937.2*	*2.4*	*19 842.7*	*4.0*
Belgium	*10 750.0*	:	:	:	:	:	:
Bulgaria	7 606.6	23.8	0.3	3.5	0.1	20.3	0.3
Czech Republic	10 467.5	407.5	3.9	145.8	1.4	261.7	2.5
Denmark	5 511.5	320.0	5.8	108.7	2.0	211.4	3.8
Germany	82 002.4	7 185.9	8.8	2 530.7	3.1	4 655.2	5.7
Estonia	1 340.4	214.4	16.0	9.6	0.7	204.8	15.3
Ireland	4 450.0	441.1	9.9	364.8	8.2	76.2	1.7
Greece	11 260.4	929.5	8.3	161.6	1.4	767.9	6.8
Spain	45 828.2	5 651.0	12.3	2 274.2	5.0	3 376.8	7.4
France	64 366.9	3 737.5	5.8	1 302.4	2.0	2 435.2	3.8
Italy	60 045.1	3 891.3	6.5	1 131.8	1.9	2 759.5	4.6
Cyprus	796.9	128.2	16.1	78.2	9.8	50.0	6.3
Latvia	2 261.3	404.0	17.9	9.4	0.4	394.6	17.5
Lithuania	3 349.9	41.5	1.2	2.5	0.1	39.0	1.2
Luxembourg	493.5	214.8	43.5	185.4	37.6	29.5	6.0
Hungary	10 031.0	186.4	1.9	109.8	1.1	76.6	0.8
Malta	413.6	18.1	4.4	8.2	2.0	9.9	2.4
Netherlands	16 485.8	637.1	3.9	290.4	1.8	346.7	2.1
Austria	8 355.3	864.4	10.3	317.0	3.8	547.4	6.6
Poland	*37 867.9*	*35.9*	*0.1*	*10.3*	*0.0*	*25.6*	*0.1*
Portugal	10 627.3	443.1	4.2	84.7	0.8	358.4	3.4
Romania	21 498.6	31.4	0.1	6.0	0.0	25.3	0.1
Slovenia	2 032.4	70.6	3.5	4.2	0.2	66.4	3.3
Slovakia	5 412.3	52.5	1.0	32.7	0.6	19.8	0.4
Finland	5 326.3	142.3	2.7	51.9	1.0	90.4	1.7
Sweden	9 256.3	547.7	5.9	255.6	2.8	292.1	3.2
United Kingdom	61 595.1	4 184.0	6.8	1 793.2	2.9	2 390.8	3.9
Iceland	319.4	24.4	7.6	19.4	6.1	5.0	1.6
Norway	4 799.3	302.9	6.3	165.4	3.4	137.6	2.9
Switzerland	7 701.9	1 669.7	21.7	1 033.4	13.4	636.3	8.3
Croatia	4 435.1	:	:	:	:	:	:
FYR of Macedonia	2 048.6	:	:	:	:	:	:
Turkey	71 517.1	103.8	0.1	45.3	0.1	58.4	0.1

Source: Eurostat (migr_pop1ctz)

Figure 2.22: Share of nationals and non-nationals among immigrants, 2008 (1)
(%)

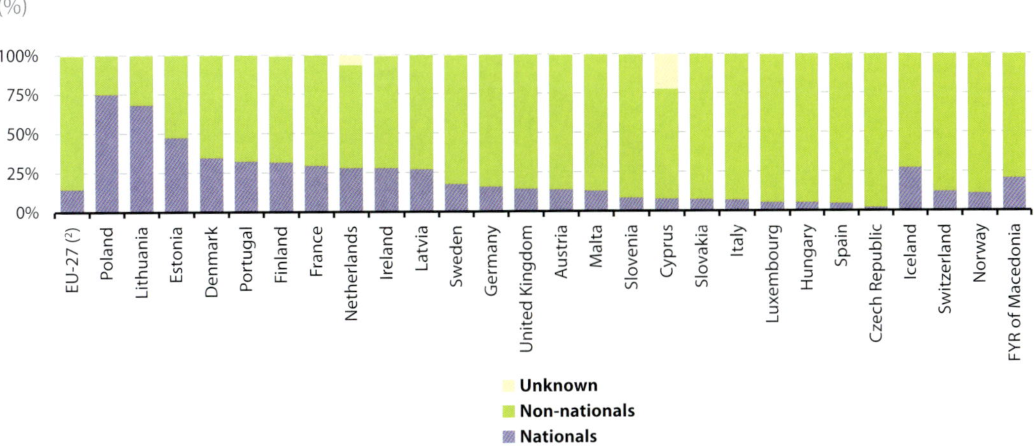

(1) Belgium, Greece and Romania, not available; Bulgaria, unreliable.
(2) Estimate.

Source: Eurostat (migr_imm1ctz)

Figure 2.23: Share of non-nationals in the resident population, 2009
(%)

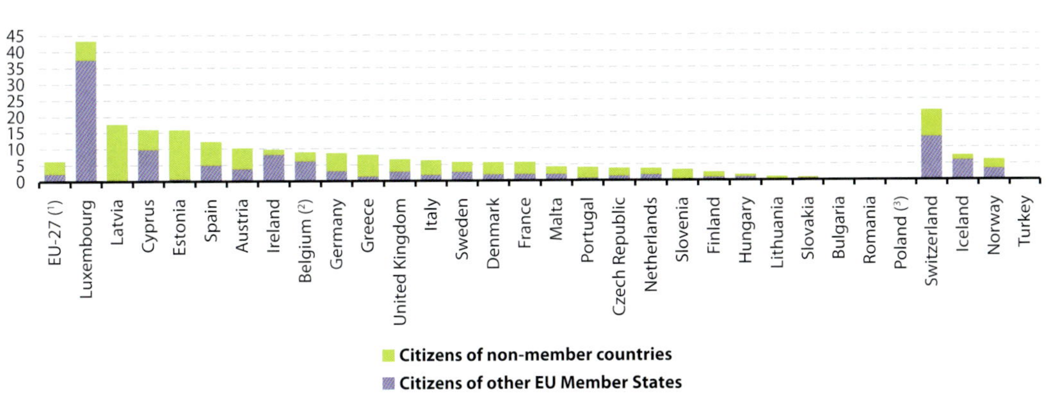

(1) Estimate.
(2) 2008.
(3) Provisional.

Source: Eurostat (migr_pop1ctz)

Figure 2.24: Citizens of non-member countries in the EU-27, 2009
(%)

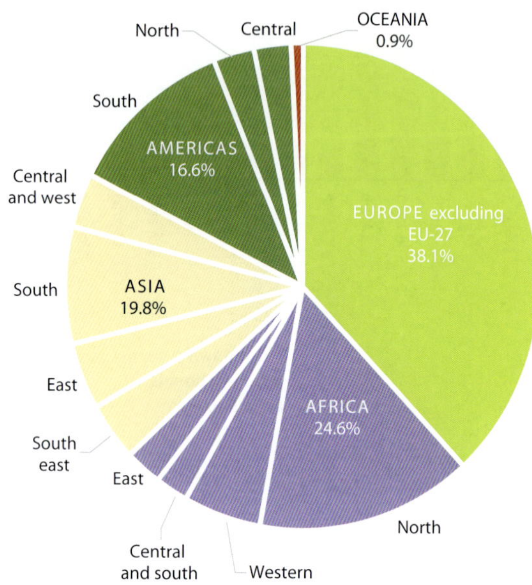

Source: Eurostat (migr_pop1ctz)

Figure 2.25: Non-nationals analysed by level of human development index (HDI), 2009
(%)

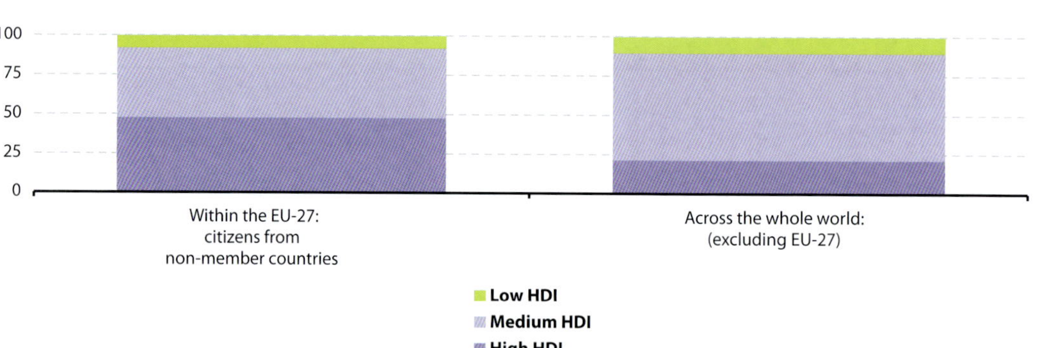

Source: Eurostat (migr_pop1ctz), UN 2009 mid-year population estimates

Figure 2.26: Main countries of origin of non-nationals, EU-27, 2009
(million)

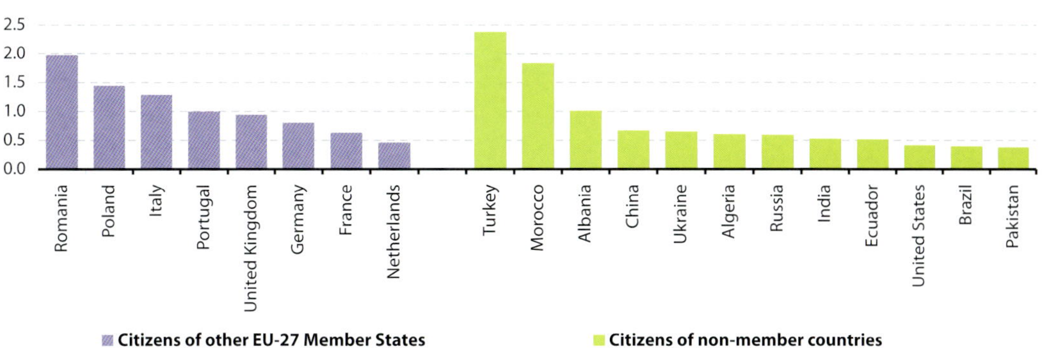

Source: Eurostat (migr_pop1ctz)

Figure 2.27: Age structure of the national and non-national populations, EU, 2009 (1)
(%)

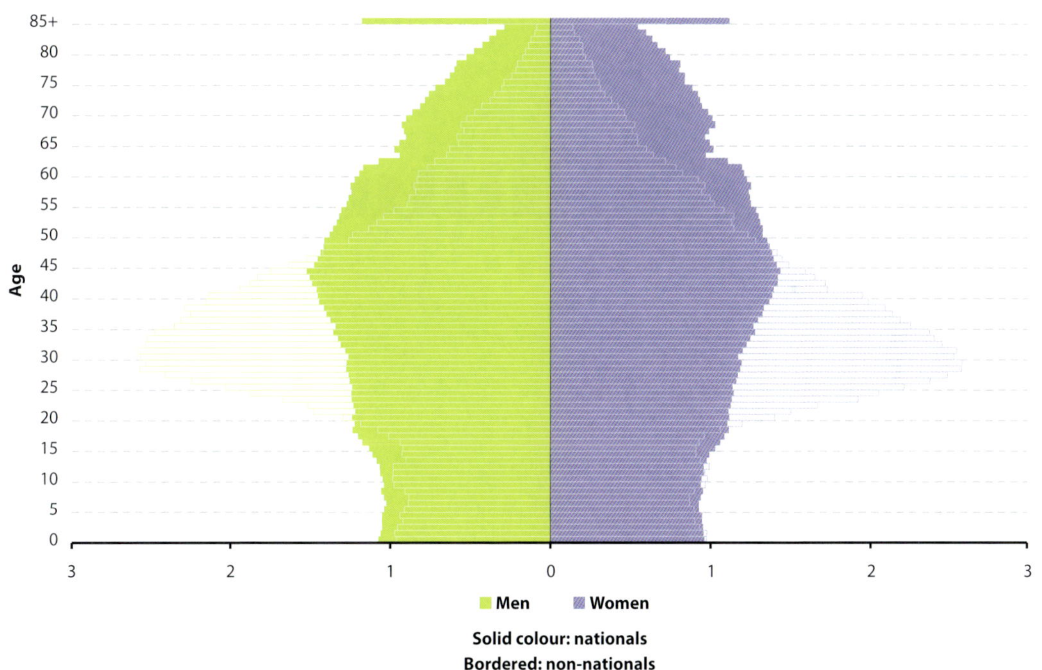

(1) Excluding Belgium, Cyprus and Romania.

Source: Eurostat (migr_pop2ctz)

Figure 2.28: Number of persons having acquired citizenship of an EU Member State, EU-27 (1 000)

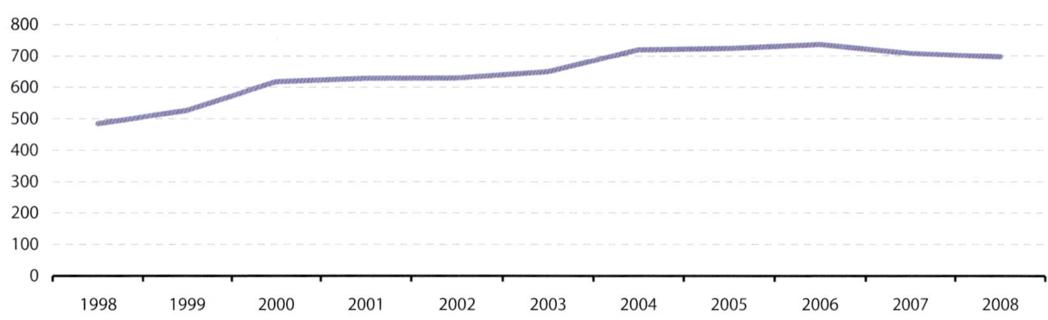

Source: Eurostat (migr_acq)

Figure 2.29: Number of persons having acquired citizenship, 2008 (¹) (per 1 000 non-nationals)

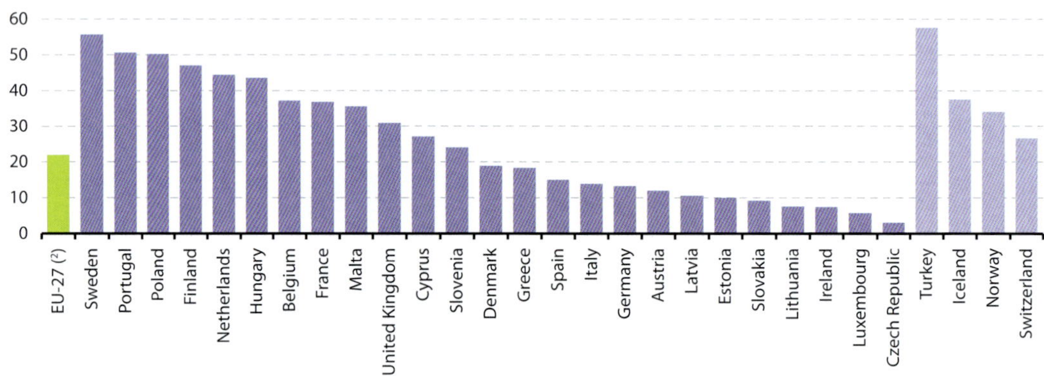

(¹) Data for the number of inhabitants refers to 1 January 2009; Belgium, 2007 and number of inhabitants refers to 1 January 2008; Bulgaria and Romania not shown for reasons of comparability.
(²) Estimate.

Source: Eurostat (migr_acq, migr_pop1ctz)

Table 2.19: Number of persons having acquired citizenship
(1 000)

	1998	1999	2000	2001	2002	2003	2004	2005	2006	2007	2008
EU-27	*483.0*	*525.3*	*616.1*	*627.0*	*628.2*	*648.2*	*718.9*	*723.5*	*735.9*	*707.1*	*696.1*
Belgium	:	24.2	:	62.2	46.4	33.7	34.8	31.5	31.9	36.1	:
Bulgaria	:	:	:	:	3.5	4.4	5.8	5.9	6.7	6.0	7.1
Czech Republic	:	7.3	:	:	3.3	2.2	5.0	2.6	2.3	2.4	1.2
Denmark	10.3	12.4	18.8	11.9	17.3	6.6	15.0	10.2	8.0	3.6	6.0
Germany	106.8	143.1	186.7	180.3	154.5	140.7	127.2	117.2	124.6	113.0	94.5
Estonia	10.0	4.5	3.4	3.1	4.1	3.7	6.5	7.1	4.8	4.2	2.1
Ireland	1.5	1.4	1.1	2.8	:	4.0	3.8	4.1	5.8	4.6	3.2
Greece	0.8	:	:	:	:	1.9	1.4	1.7	2.0	3.9	16.9
Spain	12.6	16.4	16.7	16.7	21.8	26.5	38.2	42.9	62.4	71.9	84.2
France	81.4	94.0	:	:	92.6	139.9	168.8	154.8	147.9	132.0	137.3
Italy	:	:	:	:	:	13.4	19.1	28.7	35.3	45.5	53.7
Cyprus	:	0.1	0.3	:	0.1	0.2	4.5	4.0	2.9	2.8	3.5
Latvia	:	12.9	13.5	9.9	9.4	10.0	17.2	20.1	19.0	8.3	4.2
Lithuania	0.6	0.6	0.5	0.5	0.5	0.5	0.6	0.4	0.5	0.4	0.3
Luxembourg	0.6	0.5	0.7	0.5	0.8	0.8	0.8	1.0	1.1	1.2	1.2
Hungary	6.2	6.1	5.4	8.6	3.4	5.3	5.4	9.9	6.1	8.4	8.1
Malta	:	:	:	:	:	:	:	:	0.5	0.6	0.6
Netherlands	59.2	62.1	50.0	46.7	45.3	28.8	26.2	28.5	29.1	30.7	28.2
Austria	17.8	:	24.3	31.7	36.0	44.7	41.6	34.9	25.7	14.0	10.3
Poland	:	:	:	1.1	1.2	1.7	1.9	2.9	1.1	1.5	1.8
Portugal	0.5	1.2	1.6	2.2	2.7	2.4	2.9	3.0	4.4	:	22.4
Romania	:	0.2	:	0.4	0.2	0.1	0.3	0.8	0.0	0.0	5.6
Slovenia	3.3	2.3	2.1	1.3	2.8	3.3	3.3	2.7	3.2	1.6	1.7
Slovakia	:	:	:	2.9	3.5	3.5	4.0	1.4	1.1	1.5	0.5
Finland	4.0	4.7	3.0	2.7	3.0	4.5	6.9	5.7	4.4	4.8	6.7
Sweden	46.5	37.8	43.5	36.4	37.8	33.2	28.9	39.6	51.2	33.6	30.5
United Kingdom	53.9	54.9	82.2	89.8	120.1	130.5	148.3	161.8	154.0	164.5	129.3
Iceland	0.4	0.3	0.3	0.4	0.4	:	:	:	:	0.6	0.9
Norway	9.2	8.0	9.5	10.8	9.0	7.9	8.2	12.7	12.0	14.9	10.3
Switzerland	21.3	20.4	28.7	27.6	36.5	35.4	35.7	38.4	46.7	43.9	44.4
Croatia	:	:	:	:	:	12.7	8.9	:	12.3	13.2	7.6
FYR of Macedonia	:	:	2.0	1.7	1.9	:	2.6	2.7	2.1	1.7	1.1
Turkey	:	:	:	:	:	24.8	8.2	6.9	5.1	4.4	6.0

Source: Eurostat (migr_acq)

10 A F D Z E 0,3

15 M C T H 0,2

30 N X V 0,

Health

3

Health is an important priority for Europeans, who expect to be protected against illness and disease – at home, in the workplace and when travelling. Health issues cut across a range of topics – including consumer protection (food safety issues), workplace safety, environmental or social policies – and thus have a considerable impact on the Europe 2020 strategy of the European Union (EU). The policy areas covered within this theme are under the remit of the Directorate-General for Health and Consumers and of the Directorate-General for Employment, Social Affairs and Inclusion.

The competence for the organisation and delivery of health services and healthcare is largely held by the Member States, while the EU complements the Member States' health policies through launching actions such as those in relation to cross-border health threats and patient mobility. Gathering and assessing accurate, detailed information on health issues is vital for the EU to effectively design policies and target future actions. A first programme for Community action in the field of public health covered the period 2003 to 2008.

On 23 October 2007 the European Commission adopted a new strategy 'Together for health: a strategic approach for the EU 2008-2013'. In order to bring about the changes identified within this new strategy, the second programme of Community action in the field of health came into force from 1 January 2008. It put in place an overarching, strategic framework for policy developments relating to health in the coming years; it has four main principles and three strategic themes for improving health in the EU. The principles include:

- taking a value-driven approach;
- recognising the links between health and economic prosperity;
- integrating health in all policies;
- strengthening the EU's voice in global health issues.

The strategic themes include:

- fostering good health in an ageing Europe;
- protecting citizens from health threats;
- looking to develop dynamic health systems and new technologies.

The programme is valued at EUR 321.5 million and will be implemented by means of annual work plans which will set out priority areas and funding criteria.

Set up at the Lisbon European Council of March 2000, the Open method of coordination (OMC) on social protection and social inclusion provides a framework of political coordination without legal constraints. Member States agree to identify and promote their most effective policies in the fields of social protection and social inclusion with the aim of learning from each others' experiences. The health and long-term care strand of the OMC is structured according to three objectives:

- access to care and inequalities in outcomes;
- quality of care;
- long-term sustainability of systems.

Concerning health and safety at work, the EC Treaty states that 'the Community shall support and complement the activities of the Member States in the improvement in particular of the working environment to protect workers' health and safety.' In 2007 the Council adopted Resolution 2007/C 145/01 of 25 June 2007 on a new Community strategy on health and safety at work (2007-2012). Actions in the field of health and safety at work are supported by the PROGRESS programme (2007-2013). In December 2008 the European Parliament and the Council adopted Regulation 1338/2008 on Community statistics on public health and health and safety at work.

3.1 Healthy life years

Healthy life years, the number of years that a person is expected to continue to live in a healthy condition, is an important measure of the relative health of populations in the European Union (EU). Eurostat calculates this indicator for two ages (at birth and at the age of 65), with the indicator being presented separately for males and females.

Whether extra years of life gained through increased longevity are spent in good or bad health is a crucial question. Since life expectancy at birth is not able to fully answer this question, indicators of health expectancies, such as healthy life years (also called disability-free life expectancy) have been developed. These focus on the quality of life spent in a healthy state, rather than the quantity of life – as measured by life expectancy. The calculation of the healthy life years indicator is based on a self-perceived question which aims to measure the extent of any limitations because of a health prob-

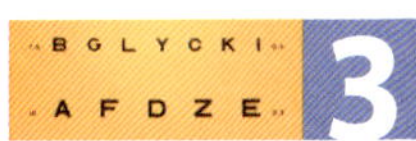

lem that may have affected respondents as regards activities they usually do (for at least six months).

Main statistical findings

In 2008 the number of healthy life years at birth in the EU-27 reached 60.8 years for men and 61.9 years for women; this represented 79.9 % and 75.3 % of total life expectancy at birth for men and women. For survivors at the age of 65, the number of remaining healthy life years was 8.2 years for men and 8.3 years for women. These figures can be contrasted with the life expectancy of those who survive to the age of 65 – close to 15 years for men and 20 years for women.

Life expectancy for women in the EU-27 was, on average, six years longer than that for men in 2008. However, most of these additional years tend to be lived with activity limitations. Indeed, the gender gap was considerably smaller in terms of healthy life years – less than two years difference in favour of women – than for overall life expectancy.

Men tend to spend a greater proportion of their shorter life expectancy free of activity limitation. Across the EU Member States, life expectancy at birth in 2008 ranged between 66.3 years and 79.2 years (12.9 years difference) for men and between 77.0 years and 84.9 years (7.9 years difference) for women. The corresponding healthy life years values ranged from 51.5 years to 69.2 years (17.7 years difference) for men and from 52.3 years to 71.9 years (19.6 years difference) for women. Differences between Member States therefore occur more in terms of the quality (health wise) of life, rather than the number of years of life expectancy. In six of the Member States (Denmark, Spain, Luxembourg, the Netherlands, Portugal and Sweden), men (at birth) could expect to live longer than women without disability, and this was also the case in Iceland and Norway. In Estonia, Lithuania and Poland the gender gap in healthy life years at birth was more than four years in favour of women.

Life expectancy was rather stable between 2007 and 2008. However, the number of healthy life years decreased both for men and women during the same period. The reduction in the number of healthy life years at birth between 2007 and 2008 was particularly noticeable in Bulgaria, Denmark, Germany, the Netherlands and Slovakia for both men and women; relatively large falls were also noted in Greece, Austria and Slovenia among women. This reduction in the number of healthy life years was generally more apparent at age 65 than at birth.

Data sources and availability

The indicator for healthy life years is calculated using mortality statistics and data on self-perceived disability. Mortality data comes from Eurostat's demographic database, while self-perceived disability data comes from a minimum European health module that is integrated within the survey on EU statistics on income and living conditions (EU-SILC). The EU-SILC question is: *For at least the past six months, to what extent have you been limited because of a health problem in activities people usually do? Would you say you have been: strongly limited? / limited? / not limited at all?*

Context

Life expectancy at birth remains one of the most frequently quoted indicators of health status and economic development. Life expectancy at birth has risen rapidly in the last century due to a number of important factors, including reductions in infant mortality, rising living standards, improved lifestyles and better education, as well as advances in healthcare and medicine. While most people are aware that successive generations are living longer, less is known about the health of the EU's ageing population.

The health status of a population is difficult to measure because it is hard to define among individuals, populations, cultures, or even across time periods. As a result, the demographic measure of life expectancy has often been used as a measure of a nation's health status because it is based on a simple and easy to understand characteristic – namely, that of death.

Indicators on healthy life years introduce the concept of the quality of life, by focusing on those years that may be enjoyed by individuals free from the limitations of illness or disability. Chronic disease, frailty, mental disorders and physical disability tend to become more prevalent in older age, and may result in a lower quality of life for those who suffer from such conditions, while the burden of these conditions may also impact on healthcare and pension provisions.

Healthy life years also monitor health as a productive or economic factor. An increase in healthy life years is one of the main goals for EU health policy, given that this would not only improve the situation of individuals (as good health and a long life are fundamental objectives of human activity) but would also lead to lower public healthcare expenditure. If healthy life years increase more rapidly than life expectancy, then not only are people living longer, but they are also living a greater proportion of their lives free from health problems. Any loss in health will, nonetheless, have significant effects. These will include an altered pattern of resource allocation within the healthcare system, as well as wider ranging effects on consumption and production throughout the economy.

Figure 3.1: Healthy life years at birth, females
(years)

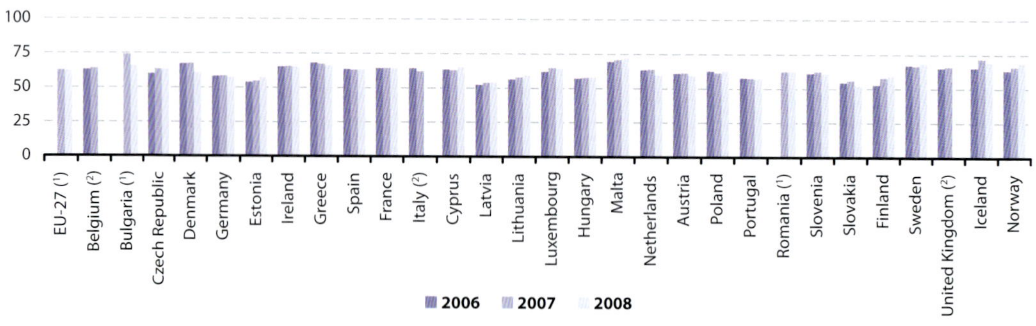

(1) 2006, not available.
(2) 2008, not available.

Source: Eurostat (hlth_hlye)

Figure 3.2: Healthy life years at birth, males
(years)

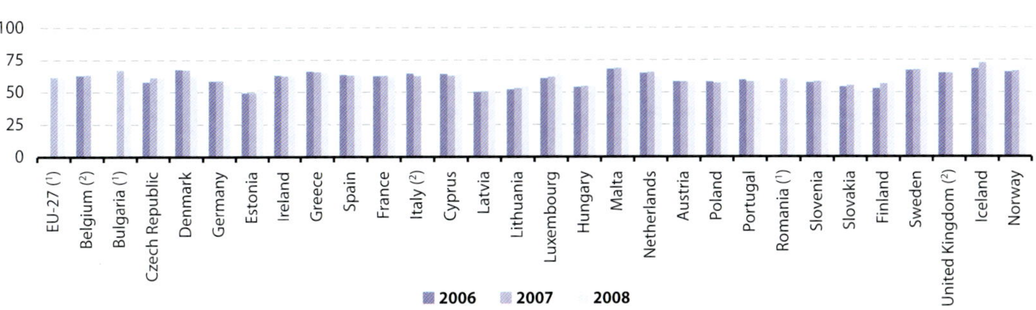

(¹) 2006, not available.
(²) 2008, not available.

Source: Eurostat (hlth_hlye)

Figure 3.3: Healthy life years at age 65, females
(years)

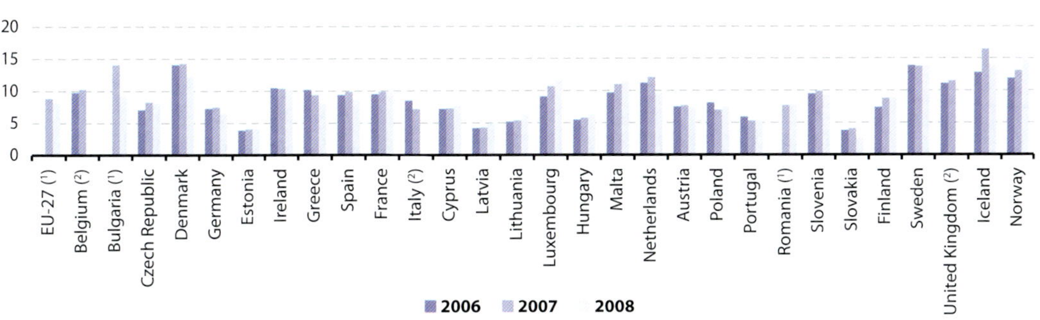

(¹) 2006, not available.
(²) 2008, not available.

Source: Eurostat (hlth_hlye)

Figure 3.4: Healthy life years at age 65, males
(years)

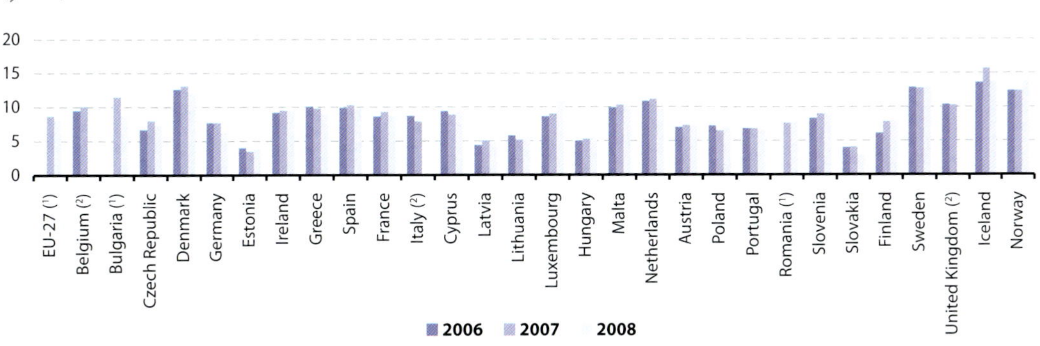

(¹) 2006, not available.
(²) 2008, not available.

Source: Eurostat (hlth_hlye)

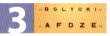

3.2 Causes of death

This subchapter gives an overview of recent statistics on causes of death in the European Union (EU). By relating all deaths in the population to an underlying cause of death, the risks associated with death from a range of specific diseases and other causes can be assessed, and these figures can be further broken down by age, gender, nationality and region (NUTS level 2), using standardised death rates.

Statistics on causes of death are important to evaluate the state of health and healthcare in the EU. They suggest which preventive and medical-curative measures and which investments in research might increase the life expectancy of the population. As these statistics are among the oldest medical statistics available, they provide an excellent view on developments over time and on differences between Member States.

Main statistical findings

The latest information available for 2008 (1) shows that diseases of the circulatory system and cancer were, by far, the leading causes of death in Europe. Between 2000 and 2008 there was a marked reduction in EU-27 death rates resulting from ischaemic heart disease and from transport accidents (each falling overall by about 30 %), while there was a reduction of almost 10 % in EU-27 death rates for cancer during the same period (see Figure 3.5).

Diseases of the circulatory system

Diseases of the circulatory system include those related to high blood pressure, cholesterol, diabetes, and smoking; although, the most common cause of death was ischaemic heart disease. The Member States with the highest death rates from ischaemic heart disease – for men and women – were the Baltic Member States, Slovakia and Hungary, while France, Portugal, the Netherlands and Spain had the lowest rates.

Cancer

Cancer was a major cause of death in each of the EU Member States, but Hungary, Denmark (2006 data), Poland, Slovenia, Slovakia and the Czech Republic were most affected by this group of diseases. The most common forms of cancer in the EU-27 in 2008 included malignant neoplasms of the larynx, trachea, bronchus and lung, colon, breast, and those that the International classification of diseases (ICD) classifies as 'stated or presumed to be primary, of lymphoid, hematopoietic and related tissue'.

Analysing the figures by gender, men outnumbered women in relation to the number of deaths from cancer. Data for cancer of the larynx, trachea, bronchi and lung showed some marked differences between Member States in 2008: for men Hungary reported the highest death rate from these cancers among the EU Member States, followed by Poland, the Baltic Member States and Belgium (2005 data); Hungary also reported a high rate for women, just behind the rate reported for Denmark (2006 data). Mortality figures for this type of cancer are generally rising for women while decreasing for men.

(1) Italy, Luxembourg, Malta, Sweden, the United Kingdom and Switzerland, 2007; Denmark, 2006; Belgium, 2005.

Breast cancer as a cause of death among women had similar values across the EU Member States, standing out slightly in Denmark and Ireland, while Spain recorded the lowest rates – see Table 3.1.

Respiratory diseases

The highest death rates from respiratory diseases in 2008 were recorded in the United Kingdom (2007 data), Belgium (2005 data), Ireland, Portugal and Denmark (2006 data). After cancer and circulatory diseases, this was the third most common cause of death in the EU-27. Within this group of diseases, chronic lower respiratory diseases were the most common cause of mortality followed by pneumonia. Respiratory diseases are age-related with the vast majority of deaths from these diseases are recorded among those aged 65 or more.

External causes of death

This category includes deaths resulting from intentional self-harm (suicide) and transport accidents. Although suicide is not a major cause of death and the data for some Member States may suffer from underreporting, it is often considered as an important indicator to be addressed by society. The lowest suicide rates in 2008 were recorded in Greece, Cyprus and Spain, and relatively low rates were also recorded in Italy, Malta and the United Kingdom (2007 data). In 2008, the death rate from suicide in Lithuania was approximately three times the EU-27 average, and relatively high rates (around double the EU-27 average) were also recorded in Hungary and Latvia. Among women, relatively high suicide rates were recorded in Luxembourg (2007 data), Belgium (2005 data), Finland and France.

Although transport accidents occur on a daily basis, the number of deaths caused by transport accidents are fewer than, for example, the number of suicides. Lithuania, Romania and Latvia were the Member States with the highest death rates resulting from transport accidents, while Malta (2007 data) and the Netherlands reported the lowest rates.

Gender

Death rates were higher for men than for women for all of the main causes of death, with death rates up to four to five times higher than those recorded for women for drug dependence and alcohol abuse. The death rates for AIDS/HIV and for suicide and intentional self-harm were three to four times higher for men than for women. Death rates for ischaemic heart diseases were about twice as high for men (120 per 100 000 inhabitants in 2008) as for women (61 per 100 000 inhabitants) in the EU-27, as reflected in Figure 3.9. There was a higher incidence of death from heart disease than from cancer for both genders in the Baltic Member States, Slovakia and Romania, while in Finland there were more deaths from heart disease than from cancer among the male population.

Age

For persons below 65 years of age the leading causes of mortality were somewhat different in terms of their relative importance (see Table 3.2). Cancer was the leading cause of death within this age group, followed by diseases of the circulatory system, external causes of mortality and morbidity, and diseases of the digestive system. However, unlike for those aged 65 years or more, diseases of the respiratory system did not figure among the four most prevalent causes of mortality.

Data sources and availability

Eurostat began collecting and disseminating mortality data in 1994, broken down by:

- a shortlist of 65 causes of death based on the International classification of diseases (ICD), developed and maintained by the World Health Organization (WHO);
- gender;
- age;
- geographical region (NUTS level 2).

Annual data are provided in absolute numbers, as crude death rates and as standardised death rates. Since most causes of death vary significantly by age and sex, the use of standardised death rates improves comparability over time and between countries as death rates can be measured independently of the age structure of populations.

Statistics on the cause of death are based on two pillars: medical information contained on death certificates, which may be used as a basis for the ascertaining the cause of death; and the coding of causes of death following the WHO-ICD system.

The validity and reliability of statistics on the cause of death rely on the quality of the data by the certifying physician. Inaccuracies may result for several reasons, including:

- errors can occur with the issue of the death certificate;
- the medical diagnosis;
- the selection of the main cause of death;
- the coding of the cause of death.

Sometimes there is ambiguity in the cause of death of a person. Besides the illness leading directly to death, the medical data on the death certificate should also contain a causal chain linked to the suffering of the deceased. Other substantial health conditions may be indicated, which did not have a link to the illness leading directly to death, but may have unfavourably affected the course of a disease and thus contributed to the fatal outcome. Indeed, there is sometimes criticism that the coding of only one illness as a cause of death appears more and more unrealistic in view of the increasing life expectancy and associated changes in morbidity. For the majority of the deceased of 65 years and older the selection of just one out of a number of possible causes of death may be somewhat misleading. For this reason, some of the EU Member States have started to consider multiple-cause coding. Eurostat has supported Member States in their efforts of developing a joint automated coding system called IRIS for the improvement and better comparability of the causes of death data in Europe.

Context

Statistics on causes of death play a key role in the general information system relating to the state of health in the European Union (EU). All deaths in the population are identified by the underlying cause of death, in other words 'the

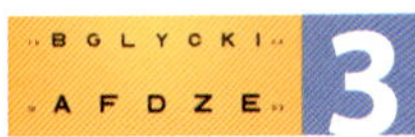

disease or injury which initiated the train of morbid events leading directly to death, or the circumstances of the accident or violence which produced the fatal injury' (a definition adopted by the World Health Assembly). The data presented in this subchapter provide information on the risks associated with death from a range of specific diseases and other causes; a breakdown by age, gender, nationality and region (NUTS level 2) of the deceased is also available.

Statistics on causes of death provide indications as to which preventive and medical-curative measures as well as investments in research have the potential to increase the life expectancy of the population. These are some of the oldest medical statistics available, and therefore can be used to look at developments over time and differences in the number of deaths between Member States. Standardised death rates may be used as a starting point for targeted epidemiological research. As there is a general lack of comprehensive European morbidity statistics, data on causes of death are often used as a tool for evaluating health systems in the EU and may also be employed for evidence-based health policy.

Figure 3.5: Causes of death - standardised death rate per 100 000 inhabitants, males, EU-27 (1)
(2000=100)

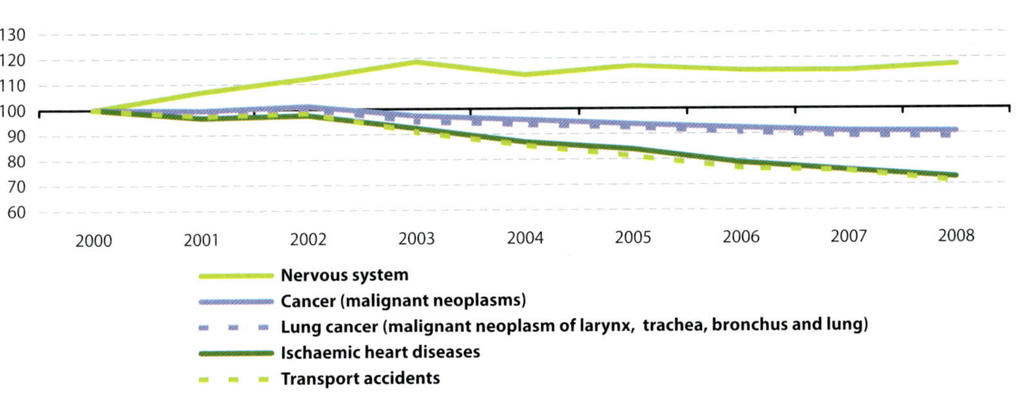

(1) Provisional.

Source: Eurostat (hlth_cd_asdr)

Table 3.1: Causes of death - standardised death rate, 2008 (1)
(per 100 000 inhabitants)

	Total							Females	
	Cancer (2)	Lung cancer (3)	Colo-rectal cancer	Circula-tory disease	Heart disease (4)	Respira-tory diseases	Transport accidents	Breast cancer	Uterus cancer
EU-27	173.0	39.6	19.3	227.2	84.1	44.7	8.3	23.7	7.4
Belgium	174.5	46.3	18.4	198.2	67.5	68.9	10.6	29.4	6.2
Bulgaria	171.6	38.9	22.7	611.3	126.0	41.7	13.3	23.3	13.1
Czech Republic	201.0	42.0	27.9	355.8	176.2	40.2	10.3	21.2	9.7
Denmark	208.0	53.9	26.2	193.7	71.6	60.6	5.8	31.1	7.0
Germany	162.6	35.0	18.8	223.2	86.4	37.7	5.4	24.6	5.6
Estonia	190.3	40.4	19.7	451.4	224.4	26.5	11.4	22.6	13.4
Ireland	176.7	37.7	20.6	190.7	102.3	64.8	6.2	31.1	7.8
Greece	157.2	40.8	12.4	258.9	67.3	53.5	14.1	21.7	4.9
Spain	154.6	36.5	19.8	151.4	47.4	52.8	7.2	18.2	5.7
France	166.0	36.6	16.7	124.7	33.8	27.3	6.9	24.1	6.4
Italy	163.7	35.9	17.6	179.1	62.0	29.6	9.2	23.6	5.4
Cyprus	121.6	22.0	9.4	208.6	73.9	36.3	11.6	22.8	7.1
Latvia	191.9	38.0	20.0	505.9	263.5	25.0	15.9	24.7	13.7
Lithuania	195.0	37.0	21.2	520.1	321.3	39.5	16.8	25.1	15.4
Luxembourg	167.7	44.4	20.5	210.8	63.8	43.4	8.7	20.5	7.3
Hungary	241.7	70.0	33.7	428.6	216.9	43.4	11.7	26.6	10.5
Malta	155.0	25.7	21.4	231.5	119.9	52.2	3.6	27.9	10.2
Netherlands	184.4	47.2	21.2	159.3	46.8	53.4	4.1	29.0	5.5
Austria	161.6	33.2	17.2	212.7	97.4	28.6	7.4	21.8	6.2
Poland	204.6	54.5	22.1	356.4	102.2	40.0	14.6	21.2	12.1
Portugal	155.6	25.5	22.4	184.9	44.4	62.0	9.1	19.8	7.7
Romania	179.7	41.5	18.8	557.9	194.1	49.5	16.6	21.6	17.8
Slovenia	201.9	43.2	26.2	234.9	67.4	36.4	11.5	27.4	8.8
Slovakia	201.7	38.6	30.3	465.0	280.5	49.9	13.3	22.1	13.3
Finland	137.0	26.0	13.3	224.0	128.8	22.3	6.9	19.8	5.0
Sweden	149.1	25.9	17.5	200.9	93.0	30.8	5.0	20.0	6.3
United Kingdom	178.1	41.1	17.8	188.7	93.0	73.7	5.3	26.8	5.9
Iceland	159.2	39.3	11.4	173.7	93.7	43.4	4.9	27.3	5.2
Norway	160.5	35.0	22.5	167.2	69.6	49.9	6.0	18.7	6.7
Switzerland	146.1	30.4	15.1	161.2	66.1	27.2	5.0	22.1	5.1
Croatia	212.6	49.4	28.6	402.7	157.1	33.7	15.0	25.8	9.8
FYR of Macedonia	170.0	41.7	18.1	573.9	92.2	37.8	6.0	23.9	13.4

(1) Italy, Luxembourg, Malta, Sweden, the United Kingdom and Switzerland, 2007; Denmark, 2006; Belgium, 2005.
(2) Malignant neoplasms.
(3) Malignant neoplasm of larynx, trachea, bronchus and lung.
(4) Ischaemic heart diseases.

Source: Eurostat (hlth_cd_asdr)

Figure 3.6: Causes of death - standardised death rate per 100 000 inhabitants, females, EU-27 (¹)
(2000=100)

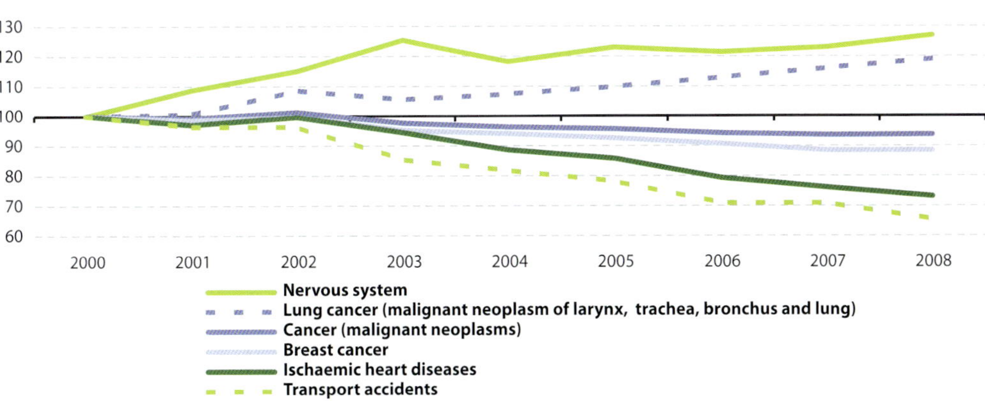

(¹) Provisional.

Source: Eurostat (hlth_cd_asdr)

Figure 3.7: Causes of death - standardised death rate, EU-27, 2008 (¹)
(per 100 000 inhabitants)

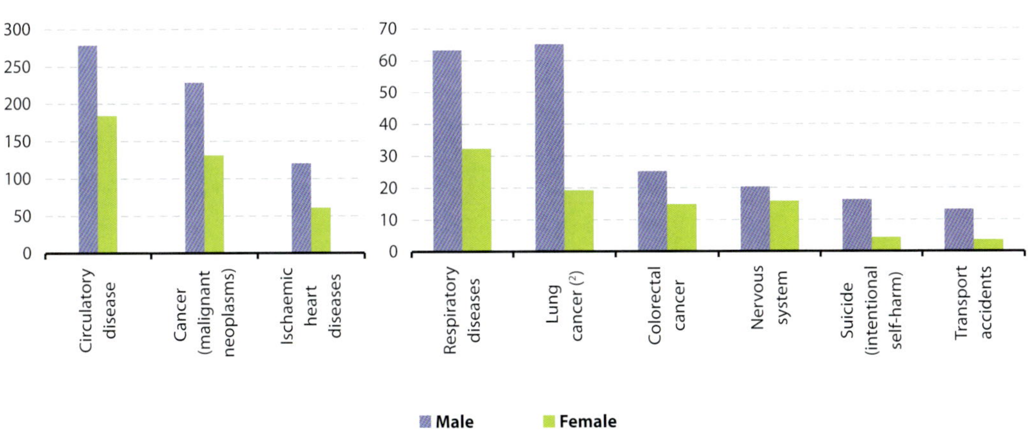

(¹) Provisional; note the differences in the scales employed between the two parts of the figure; the figure is ranked on the average of male and female.
(²) Malignant neoplasms of the larynx, trachea, bronchus and lung.

Source: Eurostat (hlth_cd_asdr)

Figure 3.8: Deaths from ischaemic heart diseases - standardised death rate, 2008 (1)
(per 100 000 inhabitants)

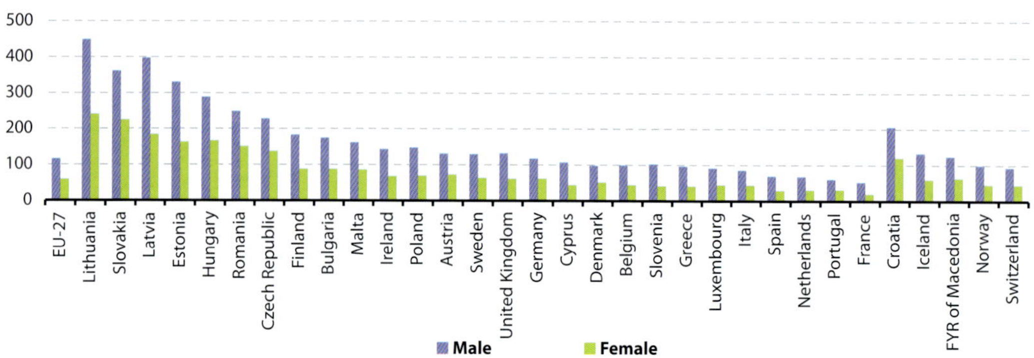

(1) EU-27, provisional; the figure is ranked on the average of male and female; Italy, Luxembourg, Malta, Sweden, the United Kingdom and Switzerland, 2007; Denmark, 2006; Belgium, 2005.

Source: Eurostat (tps00119)

Figure 3.9: Deaths from suicide - standardised death rate, 2008 (1)
(per 100 000 inhabitants)

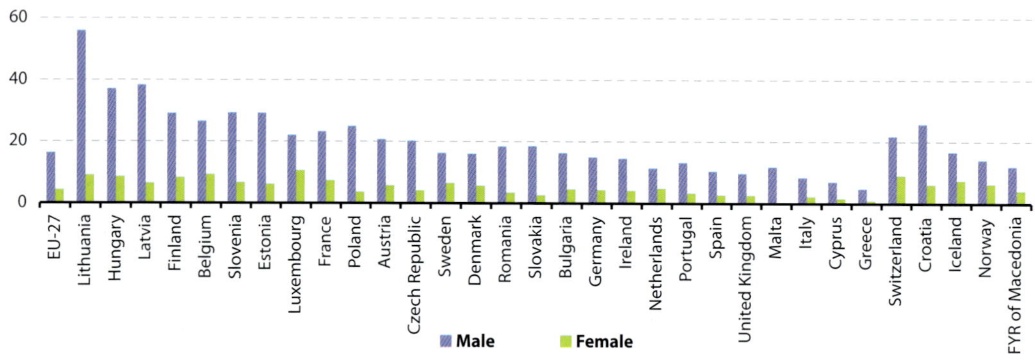

(1) EU-27, provisional; the figure is ranked on the average of male and female; Italy, Luxembourg, Malta, Sweden, the United Kingdom and Switzerland, 2007; Denmark, 2006; Belgium, 2005.

Source: Eurostat (tps00122)

Table 3.2: Causes of death - standardised death rate, 2008 (1)
(per 100 000 inhabitants aged less than 65)

	Total							Females	
	Cancer (2)	Lung cancer (3)	Colo-rectal cancer	Circula-tory disease	Heart disease (4)	Suicide (5)	Transport accidents	Breast cancer	Uterus cancer
EU-27	73.9	19.2	6.4	46.8	20.4	9.2	8.0	13.8	4.3
Belgium	73.5	21.8	5.7	37.6	16.5	16.5	10.4	17.7	3.0
Bulgaria	95.1	25.5	9.1	143.1	38.1	8.1	13.0	15.3	9.8
Czech Republic	85.1	20.3	9.4	64.0	31.1	10.8	9.7	10.6	5.4
Denmark	77.6	21.1	7.2	35.3	13.4	8.8	5.4	15.8	3.0
Germany	67.5	17.0	5.9	38.0	17.2	8.2	5.2	13.5	3.0
Estonia	83.2	18.4	5.3	114.0	46.5	16.0	10.9	14.7	8.5
Ireland	65.6	13.9	6.8	34.5	20.5	9.7	5.7	18.9	4.8
Greece	61.5	19.4	3.6	46.6	28.0	2.6	13.5	11.0	2.5
Spain	67.5	18.9	6.7	28.6	12.4	5.6	6.8	11.5	3.0
France	75.0	20.7	5.4	25.6	8.9	13.5	6.8	14.3	3.3
Italy	63.0	14.3	5.8	27.1	11.6	4.5	8.9	13.7	2.7
Cyprus	44.3	9.2	3.0	40.9	25.3	4.6	10.1	13.6	3.4
Latvia	95.6	21.3	7.5	157.0	77.4	19.4	15.6	17.1	9.2
Lithuania	97.5	19.8	7.5	135.1	73.8	30.0	16.4	17.3	10.8
Luxembourg	60.8	17.8	8.2	31.3	15.2	15.3	8.6	11.7	3.8
Hungary	130.7	45.6	13.2	108.8	53.6	18.9	10.9	15.2	7.4
Malta	58.1	10.5	6.7	34.1	18.9	5.7	3.0	19.1	6.1
Netherlands	72.2	19.3	6.6	29.0	10.9	7.7	3.6	17.4	2.9
Austria	65.2	17.0	5.3	30.5	16.5	10.5	6.7	11.5	3.3
Poland	94.3	28.2	7.7	85.9	29.5	13.6	13.7	13.3	7.7
Portugal	69.0	13.8	7.7	29.2	10.5	6.0	8.3	12.1	4.3
Romania	100.3	25.9	7.7	118.4	51.0	9.8	15.7	13.6	13.9
Slovenia	83.7	22.4	8.6	40.5	19.6	15.3	11.4	14.4	4.7
Slovakia	93.4	19.9	11.2	90.4	46.6	9.6	12.7	12.0	7.2
Finland	51.6	9.9	4.6	47.1	24.2	18.4	6.2	11.0	2.0
Sweden	52.0	10.0	5.2	30.4	17.0	10.9	4.8	10.7	2.7
United Kingdom	66.1	14.3	5.9	40.0	23.0	6.1	5.1	15.4	3.3
Iceland	48.4	11.4	3.0	24.8	14.9	12.2	3.5	14.5	1.5
Norway	57.2	13.4	7.0	26.6	13.5	10.2	5.7	10.2	3.1
Switzerland	57.4	14.2	5.1	23.9	11.7	12.4	4.5	11.6	2.2
Croatia	97.1	27.4	9.8	72.9	32.5	12.2	14.7	13.6	5.1
FYR of Macedonia	83.5	23.7	7.1	98.8	32.7	5.4	4.9	14.4	9.2

(1) EU-27, provisional; Italy, Luxembourg, Malta, Sweden, the United Kingdom and Switzerland, 2007; Denmark, 2006; Belgium, 2005.
(2) Malignant neoplasms.
(3) Malignant neoplasm of larynx, trachea, bronchus and lung.
(4) Ischaemic heart diseases.
(5) Suicide and intentional self-harm.

Source: Eurostat (hlth_cd_asdr)

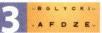

Figure 3.10: Causes of death - standardised death rate per 100 000 inhabitants aged less than 65, EU-27 (1)
(2000=100)

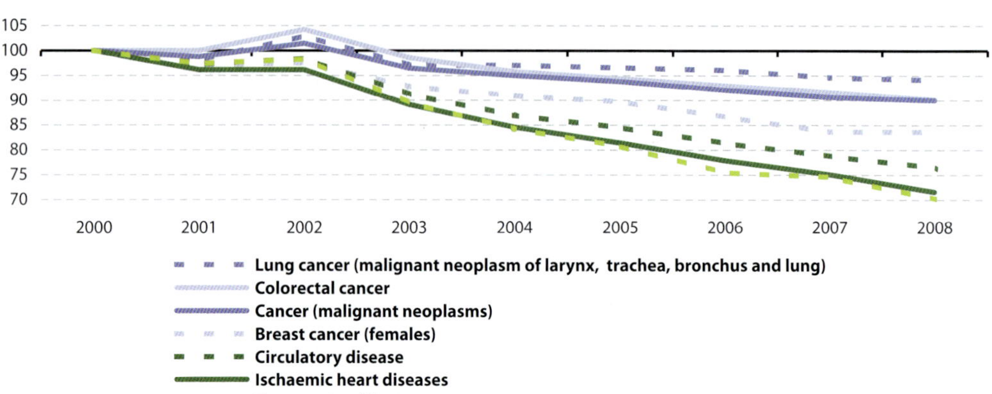

(1) Provisional.

Source: Eurostat (hlth_cd_asdr)

3.3 Healthcare

This subchapter presents key statistics on monetary and non-monetary aspects of healthcare in the European Union (EU) and its Member States. The state of health of individuals and of the population in general is influenced by genetic and environmental factors, cultural and socio-economical conditions, as well as the healthcare services that are available. Healthcare systems are organised and financed in different ways across the EU Member States, but most Europeans would agree that universal access to good healthcare, at an affordable cost to both individuals and society at large, is a basic need.

Monetary and non-monetary statistics may be used to evaluate how a country's healthcare system responds to this basic need, through measuring financial, human and technical resources within the healthcare sector and the allocation of these resources between healthcare activities (for example, preventive and curative care), groups of healthcare providers (for example, hospitals and ambulatory centres), or healthcare professionals (for example, medical and paramedical staff). Combining these data with information on technical and managerial choices that are made in relation to healthcare provision (for example, the use of inpatient or outpatient care, or the average length of stays in hospital), it is possible to assess and measure the performance of healthcare systems.

Main statistical findings

Healthcare expenditure

Total current healthcare expenditure (both in relative and absolute terms) varied significantly among the EU Member States in 2008 (2). As shown in Figure 3.11 the share of current healthcare expenditure exceeded 10 % of gross domestic product (GDP) in Germany and France (2007 data), which represented almost twice the share recorded in Romania, Cyprus and Estonia (below 6 % of GDP). The disparity was even bigger when comparing the level of healthcare spending per inhabitant, which varied from PPS 635 in Romania to more than PPS 4 280 in Luxembourg. Notwithstanding the differences in organising and financing healthcare systems, these comparisons suggest that individuals living in those Member States with a higher average level of income per capita generally spend more on purchasing healthcare goods and services.

Public and private healthcare expenditure by financing agent

The mix of public and private funding reflects specific arrangements in healthcare financing systems across the EU Member States. Table 3.3 provides a breakdown of healthcare expenditure into public and private units that incur health expenditure. In 2008, public funding dominated the healthcare sector in the majority of EU Member States, the main exception being Cyprus, where public funding accounted for a 42 % share of total funding. Among the remaining Member States for which data are available, the share of public funding in current healthcare spending ranged from 56 % in Bulgaria to more than 80 % in Romania, the Netherlands, the Czech Republic, Sweden, Luxembourg and Denmark.

(2) Belgium, Denmark, France, the Netherlands, Austria and Finland, 2007; Latvia, Portugal and Slovakia, 2006.

Public financing of healthcare is conducted through a variety of funding paths. For example, social security accounted for three quarters or more of overall spending on healthcare in the Czech Republic and the Netherlands (77 %) in 2008. In contrast, Denmark and Sweden reported that government financing accounted for more than four fifths of their total current expenditure on healthcare.

Private expenditure on healthcare is often used as an indicator to measure the accessibility of healthcare systems. The major source of private funding in 2008 was direct household payments, referred to as 'out-of-pocket' expenditure, which in the Netherlands and France represented less than 7 % of current healthcare expenditure, a share that rose to over 40 % of overall spending on healthcare in Bulgaria, and to half of all healthcare expenditure in Cyprus. Private insurance generally represented a small share of healthcare financing among the Member States for which data are available; its relative share only exceeded 10 % in Slovenia and France.

Healthcare expenditure by function

The functional patterns of healthcare expenditure presented in Table 3.4 show that in 2008 curative and rehabilitative services incurred more that 50 % of current healthcare expenditure in the majority of EU Member States, the exceptions being Slovakia, Romania and Hungary.

Medical goods delivered to outpatients was the second largest function, with average spending accounting for around one quarter of total current healthcare expenditure – although with a significant degree of variation, from 13 % in Luxembourg and Denmark up to more than one third of the total in Slovakia, Bulgaria and Hungary.

Services related to long-term nursing care accounted for less than 10 % of current healthcare expenditure in more than half of the Member States, but reached almost 20 % in Luxembourg and just over 21 % in Denmark. It should be noted that the relatively low share reported for many Member States could well be due to the main burden of long-term nursing care residing with family members with no payment being made for providing these services. In addition, limitations within the data compilation exercise also make it difficult to separate medical and social components of expenditure on long-term nursing care, leading to an inevitable impact on cross-country comparisons.

The proportion of current healthcare expenditure incurred by ancillary services such as laboratory testing or the transportation of patients varies significantly among EU Member States, ranging from 2.4 % in Belgium to 10 % in Estonia. Similarly, expenditure related to prevention and public health programmes exhibits large discrepancies between Member States. In both cases the figures are likely to provide an under-estimate of the true values, as it is likely that some of the expenditure is attributed to medical treatment and as such may be recorded under the heading of curative care. Expenditure on healthcare administration and health insurance was generally lower in those Member States with centralised social security systems or those Member States where private insurance plays a relatively restricted role, ranging from

less than 1.5 % of total current healthcare expenditure in Bulgaria, Portugal, Denmark, Hungary and Sweden, through to 7 % and more of expenditure in France and Belgium. In general, the expenditure associated with collective services reported under preventive programmes and the administration of healthcare systems did not surpass 10 % of overall current healthcare expenditure except in the Netherlands and Belgium.

Healthcare expenditure by provider

The breakdown of current healthcare expenditure by provider is shown in Table 3.5. Hospitals generally accounted for the highest share of expenditure, ranging from 27 % in Slovakia to more than 46 % in Denmark, Estonia, and Sweden. The second most important category was that of ambulatory care providers, its share ranging from just over 16 % of total healthcare expenditure in Romania and Bulgaria to more than 30 % of the total in Germany, Finland, Cyprus and Portugal. The share of various retail establishments and other providers of medical goods varied considerably more - around threefold - from 11 % in Luxembourg and 13 % in Denmark, through a middle band of Member States where the share was between 16 % and 27 %, to 30 % or more of total healthcare provision in Lithuania, Hungary, Bulgaria and Slovakia. However, it should be borne in mind that healthcare providers classified under the same group do not necessarily perform the same set of activities. Hospitals, for example, may, in addition to inpatient services, offer outpatient, ancillary or other type of services.

Non-expenditure data on healthcare

High demand for healthcare staff in some Member States may result in qualified resources moving from other countries. One of the key indicators for measuring healthcare staff is the total number of physicians (head count), expressed per 100 000 inhabitants. In this context, Eurostat gives preference to the concept of practising physicians (although data are not available for six Member States - being replaced by the number of professionally active physicians for Greece, France and Italy, and by the number of licensed physicians for Ireland, the Netherlands and Portugal) – see Table 3.6.

In 2008 the highest number of practising physicians per 100 000 inhabitants was recorded in Austria (458.1) followed by Lithuania (370.6) among the EU Member States, while Norway (398.1) recorded a ratio between these two figures. Between 1998 and 2008 the number of physicians per 100 000 inhabitants increased in the majority of EU Member States, although reductions were recorded in Lithuania and Poland. Nevertheless, the reduction of practising physicians in Poland may be explained by several breaks in the data series - for example, from 2004 the Polish data excludes private practices (thought to account for about 2 000 physicians).

The number of hospital beds per 100 000 inhabitants in 2008 ranged among those Member States for which data are available from 325 in Spain to 820 in Germany, with Turkey (244) below the Spanish level. During the ten years between 1998 and 2008, the number of hospital beds per 100 000 inhabitants fell in every

Member State, except Malta (where the main general hospital was reconstructed). The largest reductions in the availability of hospital beds were recorded in the three Baltic Member States and in Bulgaria. The reduction in hospital bed numbers may reflect, among others, economic constraints, increased efficiency through the use of technical resources (for example, imaging equipment), a general shift from inpatient to outpatient operations, and shorter periods spent in hospital following an operation.

A closer look at the availability of hospital beds, broken down for curative care beds and psychiatric beds (see Table 3.7) shows a reduction in bed numbers between 1998 and 2008 in each of the Member States for which data are available, except for the number of curative care beds in Greece. The EU-27 averaged 379 curative care beds and 64 psychiatric care beds per 100 000 inhabitants in 2008.

In terms of healthcare activity, diseases of the circulatory system often accounted for the highest number of hospital discharges in 2008 – see Table 3.8. One third of the Member States for which data are available reported in excess of 3 000 discharges per 100 000 inhabitants for diseases of the circulatory system. The average length of a hospital stay was generally highest among those patients suffering from cancer or problems relating to the circulatory system (see Table 3.9).

Data sources and availability

Eurostat, the Organisation for Economic Co-operation and Development (OECD) and the World Health Organization (WHO) have established a common framework for a joint healthcare data collection. Following this framework, EU Member States submit their data to Eurostat on the basis of a gentlemen's agreement. The data collected relates to:

- healthcare expenditure following the methodology of the system of health accounts (SHA);
- statistics on human and physical resources in healthcare – supplemented by additional Eurostat data on hospital activities (discharges and procedures).

Healthcare expenditure

Healthcare data on expenditure are based on various surveys and administrative (register-based) data sources, as well as estimations made within the Member States, reflecting country-specific ways of organising healthcare and different reporting system for the collection of statistics pertaining to healthcare.

Total current healthcare expenditure quantifies the economic resources of both the public and private sectors dedicated to healthcare, with the exception of those related to capital investment. It reflects current expenditure of resident units on final consumption of goods and services directed at improving the health status of individuals and of the population.

The SHA provides a framework for interrelated classifications and tables relating to the international reporting of healthcare expenditure and its financing. The set of core SHA tables addresses three basic questions: i) who finances healthcare goods and services; ii) which healthcare providers deliver them, and; iii) what kinds of healthcare goods and services are consumed. Consequently, the SHA is organised around a tri-dimensional system for the recording of health expenditure, by means of the international classification for health accounts (ICHA), defining:

- healthcare expenditure by financing agents (ICHA-HF) - which provides a breakdown of public and private units that directly pay providers for their provision of healthcare goods and services;
- healthcare expenditure by provider (ICHA-HP) - which classifies units contributing to the provision of healthcare goods and services such as hospitals, various outpatients settings, diagnosis centres or retailers of medical goods;
- healthcare expenditure by function (ICHA-HC) - which details the split in healthcare expenditure following the purpose of healthcare activities - such as, health promotion, curing illnesses, rehabilitation or long-term care.

Data coverage is close to 100 % for the first-digit level of each of the three core classifications, but ranges between 75 % and 85 % at the second-digit level. However, it is possible that despite relatively high rates of coverage, there may be departures from the standard classifications. Expenditure reported under some of these ICHA categories may be under or overestimated and it is recommended to refer to specific country metadata before analysing the data.

Non-expenditure data on healthcare

Non-expenditure healthcare data are mainly based on administrative national sources. However, a few countries compile this information from surveys. As a consequence, the information collected is not always comparable. Information on the non-expenditure component of healthcare can be divided into two broad groups of data:

- resource-related healthcare data on human, physical and technical resources, including staff (such as physicians, dentists, nursing and caring professionals, pharmacists and physiotherapists) and hospital beds;
- output-related data that focuses on hospital patients and their treatment(s), in particular for inpatients.

Hospitals are defined according to the classification of healthcare providers within the SHA; all public and private hospitals should be covered.

Data on healthcare staff, in the form of human resources available for providing healthcare services, are provided irrespective of the sector of employment (in other words, regardless of whether the personnel are independent, employed by a hospital, or any other healthcare provider). Three main concepts are used for health professionals: practising, professionally active and licensed. Practising physicians provide services directly to patients; professionally active physicians include those who practise as well as those working in administration and research with their medical education being a pre-requisite for the job they carry out; physicians licensed to practice are those entitled to work as physicians plus, for example, those who are retired.

Hospital bed numbers provide information on healthcare capacities, in other words on the maximum number of patients who can be treated by hospitals. Hospital beds (occupied or unoccupied) are those which are regularly maintained and staffed and immediately available for the care of admitted patients. This indicator should ideally cover beds in all hospitals, including general hospitals, mental health and substance abuse hospitals, and other specialty hospitals. The statistics should include public as well as private sector establishments – although some Member States provide data only for the public sector – for example, Denmark (psychiatric beds), Ireland (total and curative beds), Cyprus (curative and psychiatric beds) and the United Kingdom. Curative care (or acute care) beds are those that are available for curative care; these form a subgroup of total hospital beds.

Output-related indicators focus on hospital patients and cover the interaction between patients and healthcare systems, namely in the form of the treatment they receive. Data are available for a range of indicators including hospital discharges of inpatients and day cases by age, gender, and selected (groups of) diseases; the average length of stay of inpatients; or the medical procedures performed in hospitals. The number of hospital discharges is the most commonly used measure of the utilisation of hospital services. Discharges, rather than admissions, are used because hospital abstracts for inpatient care are based on information gathered at the time of discharge.

Context

Health outcomes across the EU are strikingly different according to where you live, your ethnicity, gender and socio-economic status. The EU promotes the coordination of national healthcare policies through an open method of coordination which places particular emphasis on the access to, and the quality and sustainability of healthcare. Some of the main objectives include: shorter waiting times; universal insurance coverage; affordable care; more patient-centred care and a higher use of outpatients; greater use of evidence-based medicine, effective prevention programmes, generic medicines, and simplified administrative procedures; and strengthening health promotion and disease prevention.

In the current economic climate, access to healthcare, the introduction of technological progress and greater patient choice is increasingly being considered against a background of financial sustainability. Many of the challenges facing governments across the EU are outlined in the European Commission's White paper, titled 'Together for health: a strategic approach for the EU 2008-2013' (COM(2007) 360).

Figure 3.11: Current healthcare expenditure, 2008 (1)

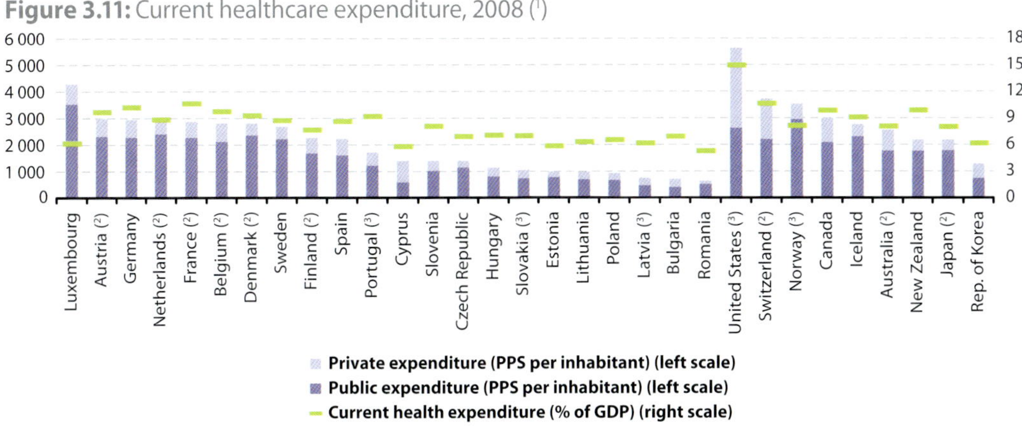

(1) Countries are ranked on the current health expenditure (PPS per inhabitant); Ireland, Greece, Italy, Malta and the United Kingdom, not available.
(2) 2007.
(3) 2006.

Source: Eurostat (hlth_sha_hf)

Figure 3.12: Number of hospital beds, EU-27
(per 100 000 inhabitants)

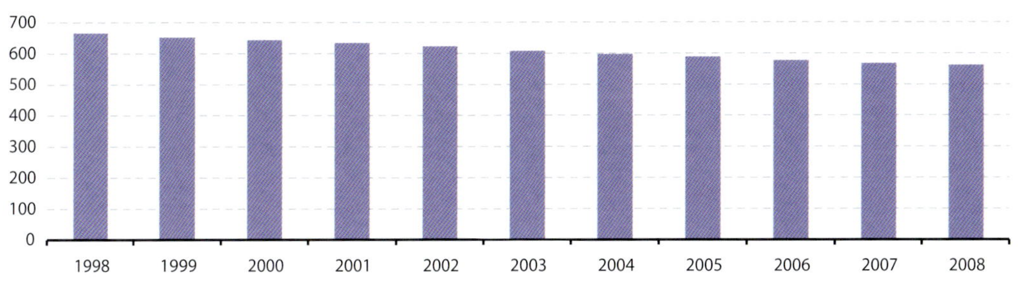

Source: Eurostat (tps00046)

Table 3.3: Healthcare expenditure by financing agent, 2008
(% of current health expenditure)

	General government excluding social security funds	Social security funds	Private insurance enterprises (including private social insurance)	Private household out-of-pocket expenditure	Non-profit institutions serving households	Corporations (other than health insurance)	Rest of the world
Belgium (¹)	12.4	62.8	5.6	19.0	0.3	0.0	0.0
Bulgaria	17.7	38.5	0.5	42.6	0.4	0.3	0.0
Czech Republic	5.0	77.1	0.2	16.1	1.2	0.4	0.0
Denmark (¹)	83.8	0.0	1.7	14.4	0.1	0.0	0.0
Germany	7.1	70.2	9.7	12.3	0.4	0.4	0.0
Estonia	10.8	67.6	0.3	20.5	0.0	0.8	0.1
Ireland	:	:	:	:	:	:	:
Greece	:	:	:	:	:	:	:
Spain	67.3	4.8	5.8	21.5	0.6	0.0	0.0
France (¹)	5.3	73.5	13.5	6.9	0.1	0.7	0.0
Italy	:	:	:	:	:	:	:
Cyprus	42.0	0.1	5.7	50.2	2.0	0.0	0.0
Latvia (²)	61.5	0.0	2.6	35.6	0.3	0.0	0.0
Lithuania	10.0	61.4	0.5	28.0	0.0	0.1	0.0
Luxembourg	8.5	73.9	3.5	13.7	0.4	0.0	0.0
Hungary	10.0	60.8	2.2	24.5	1.7	0.9	0.0
Malta	:	:	:	:	:	:	:
Netherlands (¹)	5.4	76.7	6.2	6.0	3.2	2.5	0.0
Austria (¹)	30.5	47.0	4.8	16.3	1.3	0.1	0.0
Poland	7.6	64.5	0.6	24.0	1.1	2.1	0.0
Portugal (²)	70.3	0.9	4.3	23.9	0.3	0.2	0.0
Romania	10.9	70.5	0.1	18.2	0.1	0.2	0.0
Slovenia	1.7	70.9	13.8	12.7	0.0	0.8	0.0
Slovakia (²)	6.4	63.6	0.0	26.6	0.8	2.6	0.0
Finland (¹)	59.0	15.4	2.2	20.0	1.2	2.1	0.0
Sweden	82.3	0.0	0.2	16.5	0.2	0.8	0.0
United Kingdom	:	:	:	:	:	:	:
Iceland	54.9	28.3	0.0	15.3	1.4	0.0	0.0
Norway (²)	69.8	13.6	0.0	16.5	0.0	0.2	0.0
Switzerland (¹)	16.2	42.9	9.2	30.7	1.0	0.0	0.0
Australia (¹)	69.2	0.0	8.3	19.1	0.0	3.4	0.0
Canada	68.1	1.5	13.5	15.5	0.0	1.5	0.0
Japan (¹)	15.1	66.5	2.5	14.8	0.0	1.0	0.0
Rep. of Korea	12.2	45.1	4.6	37.2	0.7	0.2	0.0
New Zealand	70.4	10.1	4.8	13.9	0.9	0.0	0.0
United States (²)	*46.4*	:	*36.8*	*13.1*	*3.5*	*0.3*	*0.0*

(¹) 2007.
(²) 2006.

Source: Eurostat (hlth_sha_hf)

Table 3.4: Healthcare expenditure by function, 2008
(% of current health expenditure)

	Services of curative & rehab-ilitative care	Services of long-term nursing care	Ancillary services to health-care	Medical goods dispensed to out-patients	Preven-tion & public health services	Health admin-istration & health insurance	Not specified by kind
Belgium (1)	50.5	17.0	2.4	17.6	4.1	8.5	0.0
Bulgaria	53.6	0.1	3.6	36.8	4.3	1.0	0.6
Czech Republic	58.5	3.4	5.6	24.6	2.7	3.5	1.7
Denmark (1)	58.1	21.4	4.7	13.2	1.5	1.2	0.0
Germany	53.3	12.3	4.7	20.5	3.7	5.4	0.0
Estonia	55.8	4.2	10.1	24.9	2.8	2.3	0.0
Ireland	:	:	:	:	:	:	:
Greece	:	:	:	:	:	:	:
Spain	56.4	9.2	5.3	23.5	2.4	3.3	0.0
France (1)	53.7	10.8	5.2	21.2	2.0	7.1	0.0
Italy	:	:	:	:	:	:	:
Cyprus	59.3	2.5	9.5	23.9	0.7	4.2	0.0
Latvia (2)	52.9	3.5	8.4	26.0	3.1	6.1	0.0
Lithuania	53.4	7.4	5.6	29.9	1.4	2.3	0.0
Luxembourg	58.3	19.9	5.9	12.5	1.9	1.7	0.0
Hungary	48.9	4.0	4.5	36.5	4.0	1.3	1.0
Malta	:	:	:	:	:	:	:
Netherlands (1)	53.8	13.4	4.9	17.2	5.1	5.6	0.0
Austria (1)	60.0	13.2	3.1	18.1	1.8	3.7	0.0
Poland	57.7	5.6	5.9	26.9	2.4	1.7	0.0
Portugal (2)	62.3	1.4	8.5	24.7	1.9	1.2	0.0
Romania	47.5	12.4	4.7	26.6	6.0	2.8	0.1
Slovenia	57.5	8.6	3.0	23.0	3.9	4.0	0.0
Slovakia (2)	44.7	0.4	7.3	39.1	4.5	4.1	0.0
Finland (1)	59.0	12.1	3.0	17.8	5.8	2.3	0.0
Sweden	64.4	7.9	4.9	16.9	3.6	1.4	0.9
United Kingdom	:	:	:	:	:	:	:
Iceland	59.4	19.0	2.3	16.0	1.6	1.8	0.0
Norway (2)	50.5	26.4	6.4	13.9	2.0	0.8	0.0
Switzerland (1)	57.7	19.4	3.3	12.3	2.3	5.0	0.0
Australia (1)	70.3	0.3	6.0	18.4	2.1	2.8	0.0
Canada	46.4	14.8	6.3	20.9	7.1	3.8	0.6
Japan (1)	57.9	15.1	0.7	21.5	2.4	2.4	0.0
Rep. of Korea	63.5	3.1	0.3	27.3	2.5	3.3	0.0
New Zealand	57.0	14.2	4.7	10.9	6.1	7.2	0.0
United States (2)	*69.0*	*6.4*	*0.0*	*14.0*	*3.2*	*7.4*	*0.0*

(1) 2007.
(2) 2006.

Source: Eurostat (hlth_sha_hc)

Table 3.5: Healthcare expenditure by provider, 2008
(% of current health expenditure)

	Hospitals	Nursing & residential care facilities	Ambulatory health-care	Retail sale & medical goods	Admin. of public health pro-grammes	General health admin. & insurance	Other (rest of economy)	Rest of the world
Belgium (1)	29.9	11.1	29.8	16.6	4.3	7.9	0.4	0.0
Bulgaria	41.0	0.8	16.7	36.9	1.8	1.0	1.7	0.0
Czech Republic	43.7	1.1	24.3	20.6	0.2	3.7	0.7	0.2
Denmark (1)	46.2	12.4	26.2	13.2	0.2	1.5	0.1	0.2
Germany	29.4	7.8	30.8	21.8	0.8	5.9	3.1	0.5
Estonia	46.5	2.7	21.0	24.9	2.5	2.3	0.0	0.2
Ireland	:	:	:	:	:	:	:	:
Greece	:	:	:	:	:	:	:	:
Spain	39.9	5.4	28.8	21.5	1.0	3.3	0.3	0.0
France (1)	35.5	6.8	27.4	21.9	0.5	7.1	0.8	0.0
Italy	:	:	:	:	:	:	:	:
Cyprus	41.9	2.5	33.4	18.8	0.2	1.9	0.0	1.2
Latvia (2)	41.2	2.8	26.7	24.6	1.4	3.2	0.1	0.0
Lithuania	37.1	1.5	22.8	29.9	0.9	2.5	5.4	0.1
Luxembourg	32.9	15.7	26.2	11.2	0.4	1.4	2.8	9.5
Hungary	33.1	3.5	21.1	36.5	2.7	1.2	1.8	0.2
Malta	:	:	:	:	:	:	:	:
Netherlands (1)	36.9	12.0	24.0	16.4	1.6	5.6	2.6	1.0
Austria (1)	38.8	7.6	24.3	18.1	0.7	4.0	6.4	0.2
Poland	34.5	1.3	29.6	26.5	1.7	1.7	4.8	0.1
Portugal (2)	37.2	1.8	33.7	24.7	0.0	1.2	1.3	0.2
Romania	39.1	2.1	16.3	26.6	1.4	1.7	12.8	0.1
Slovenia	41.6	5.3	24.6	22.4	0.6	4.1	1.2	0.2
Slovakia (2)	27.1	0.0	24.7	39.1	1.9	4.1	3.1	0.2
Finland (1)	35.9	8.5	31.5	18.3	1.4	1.3	3.1	0.0
Sweden	46.9	3.0	20.6	16.8	1.0	1.7	9.8	0.2
United Kingdom	:	:	:	:	:	:	:	:
Iceland	40.6	11.5	27.8	16.0	1.6	1.8	0.0	0.8
Norway (2)	38.2	17.4	27.3	13.6	1.6	0.0	1.9	0.1
Switzerland (1)	35.1	17.2	32.1	9.1	0.0	6.5	0.0	0.0
Australia (1)	39.9	0.0	37.7	17.6	2.1	2.8	0.0	0.0
Canada	28.9	10.6	28.4	20.9	6.6	3.8	0.2	0.6
Japan (1)	48.0	3.1	27.7	16.4	2.4	2.4	0.0	0.0
Rep. of Korea	41.6	0.6	29.2	22.6	1.5	3.3	0.9	0.2
New Zealand	37.4	8.8	30.7	10.8	3.3	7.6	1.3	0.0
United States (2)	*33.0*	*6.4*	*36.3*	*14.0*	*3.0*	*7.4*	*0.0*	*0.0*

(1) 2007.
(2) 2006.

Source: Eurostat (hlth_sha_hp)

Table 3.6: Healthcare indicators
(per 100 000 inhabitants)

	Practising physicians (1)		Hospital beds		Hospital discharges of inpatients (excluding healthy new born babies)	
	1998 (2)	2008 (3)	1998	2008 (4)	2000 (5)	2008 (6)
EU-27	:	:	666.3	561.9	:	:
Belgium	373.1	293.2	787.5	660.1	16 252	15 741
Bulgaria	346.0	361.3	843.5	650.8	:	21 665
Czech Republic	303.1	352.7	793.7	715.8	16 799	20 624
Denmark	286.2	341.0	454.8	357.8	16 316	16 498
Germany	317.5	356.2	929.3	820.3	19 586	22 692
Estonia	322.9	335.0	761.9	571.5	:	:
Ireland	217.1	309.3	642.6	519.9	13 805	13 501
Greece	412.0	599.8	485.7	478.4	:	:
Spain	287.3	354.8	378.4	324.5	11 243	10 567
France	327.1	332.3	832.5	684.8	18 397	16 075
Italy	416.3	414.0	555.1	371.4	:	13 887
Cyprus	252.0	285.6	455.9	377.2	6 795	7 500
Latvia	275.2	298.6	965.5	638.3	:	20 290
Lithuania	373.5	370.6	910.1	685.3	9 088	21 686
Luxembourg	242.7	282.1	:	562.4	18 075	13 887
Hungary	308.6	309.3	809.7	705.0	:	19 486
Malta	:	303.9	559.8	481.9	:	9 512
Netherlands	292.5	369.4	512.3	426.3	9 088	10 953
Austria	377.2	468.2	819.0	769.2	:	27 539
Poland	233.0	216.1	:	662.1	:	13 965
Portugal	306.3	377.3	387.5	336.8	:	:
Romania	188.2	221.5	731.6	657.4	:	22 495
Slovenia	219.1	238.8	559.1	476.9	:	16 154
Slovakia	:	300.0	803.7	655.0	19 876	18 174
Finland	231.8	271.4	778.2	653.8	9 088	18 821
Sweden	297.5	356.6	:	:	15 272	14 910
United Kingdom	190.0	270.2	:	336.7	9 088	12 248
Iceland	329.7	372.0	:	585.7	17 085	15 018
Norway	272.2	398.1	392.8	354.0	15 409	17 214
Switzerland	:	385.4	664.0	524.9	9 088	16 217
Croatia	227.5	266.1	601.5	547.3	12 710	16 259
FYR of Macedonia	219.3	253.5	516.0	516.0	:	9 876
Turkey	102.9	158.2	:	243.9	:	:

(1) Greece, France, Italy, the former Yugoslav Republic of Macedonia and Turkey, professionally active physicians; Ireland, Netherlands and Portugal, licensed physicians.
(2) Romania, 1999.
(3) Spain, Latvia, Malta, Austria, Portugal, the United Kingdom and Switzerland, 2009; Denmark, Luxembourg, the Netherlands and Slovakia, 2007; Sweden and the former Yugoslav Republic of Macedonia, 2006.
(4) Latvia and Malta, 2009; Ireland and Iceland, 2007; the former Yugoslav Republic of Macedonia, 2006.
(5) The Czech Republic, the Netherlands, Finland, the United Kingdom and Switzerland, 2002; Lithuania, 2001
(6) Belgium, the Czech Republic, Denmark, Italy, Cyprus, Luxembourg, Poland and the United Kingdom, 2007; Sweden, Iceland and the former Yugoslav Republic of Macedonia, 2006.

Source: Eurostat (hlth_rs_prs, tps00046 and hlth_co_disch2t)

Table 3.7: Hospital beds
(per 100 000 inhabitants)

	Curative care beds in hospitals			Psychiatric care beds in hospitals		
	1998	2003 (1)	2008 (2)	1998	2003 (1)	2008 (3)
EU-27	471.8	416.6	379.5	80.7	71.4	63.5
Belgium	485.8	451.7	425.2	259.6	248.0	180.3
Bulgaria	:	484.3	499.8	72.8	64.4	67.3
Czech Republic	610.3	556.4	505.7	113.3	112.6	104.5
Denmark	375.9	342.5	299.2	78.9	71.4	58.7
Germany	650.5	605.5	564.7	46.1	51.0	47.5
Estonia	587.1	440.4	385.2	89.5	58.7	56.8
Ireland	285.1	282.2	267.4	150.5	109.3	79.8
Greece	380.9	382.2	396.1	104.8	88.1	82.4
Spain	292.6	265.2	250.8	53.2	49.0	41.4
France	424.0	375.9	347.6	114.1	95.3	88.8
Italy	501.7	352.9	301.0	33.1	13.6	11.0
Cyprus	400.2	398.7	351.1	55.7	32.4	26.1
Latvia	673.2	555.7	516.1	198.9	155.7	154.4
Lithuania	700.1	582.8	505.9	125.7	108.0	103.1
Luxembourg	:	505.8	436.5	:	110.1	89.3
Hungary	593.5	553.4	411.4	46.1	40.1	28.8
Malta	383.9	338.6	275.9	175.9	142.0	167.8
Netherlands	343.4	313.7	286.3	167.1	136.3	140.0
Austria	635.2	590.7	562.2	80.0	71.5	77.6
Poland	552.9	486.1	441.2	:	71.4	64.8
Portugal	318.7	299.9	276.5	68.8	65.6	59.6
Romania	525.1	452.3	451.0	88.6	76.3	80.4
Slovenia	461.6	401.3	385.4	79.8	73.7	69.5
Slovakia	588.9	509.1	486.7	92.6	89.8	80.9
Finland	259.4	228.5	191.2	109.0	98.2	84.8
Sweden	256.9	222.7	:	66.3	51.3	48.6
United Kingdom	:	310.6	270.3	:	83.1	63.7
Norway	320.6	292.0	250.9	72.2	113.3	92.0
Switzerland	442.3	386.5	336.9	119.8	107.8	101.1
Croatia	378.1	338.0	341.0	100.3	95.5	94.9
FYR of Macedonia	335.7	318.1	:	73.4	67.1	:
Turkey	:	202.1	235.4	:	5.3	6.2

(1) Luxembourg, 2004.
(2) Ireland, 2007.
(3) Sweden, 2007.

Source: Eurostat (tps00168 and tps00047)

Table 3.8: Hospital discharges of inpatients by diagnosis (ISHMT - international shortlist for hospital morbidity tabulation), 2008
(per 100 000 inhabitants)

	Neoplasms (cancers)	Diseases of the circulatory system	Diseases of the respiratory system	Diseases of the digestive system	Pregnancy, childbirth & the puerperium	Injury, poisoning & certain other consequences of external causes
Belgium (1)	1 183.9	2 068.1	1 359.1	1 649.9	1 369.7	1 634.7
Bulgaria	1 502.8	3 479.6	3 033.9	1 967.8	1 964.6	1 283.5
Czech Republic (1)	1 775.4	3 086.8	1 397.8	1 811.3	1 596.2	1 677.8
Denmark (1)	1 396.1	2 068.8	1 468.5	1 352.4	1 220.8	1 502.9
Germany	2 444.1	3 463.1	1 400.1	2 156.0	1 091.8	2 186.5
Estonia	:	3 493.6	:	1 606.0	1 918.4	1 196.0
Ireland	856.2	1 180.0	1 305.5	1 204.6	2 773.0	1 276.8
Greece	:	:	:	:	:	:
Spain	927.9	1 316.4	1 133.4	1 254.6	1 393.0	889.9
France	1 131.7	1 865.1	967.0	1 571.1	1 540.5	1 338.3
Italy (1)	1 298.4	2 329.9	1 087.2	1 325.5	1 282.1	1 215.7
Cyprus (1)	518.6	869.9	763.0	730.8	408.9	1 019.9
Latvia	1 945.6	3 782.9	1 895.1	1 824.2	1 719.1	1 944.8
Lithuania	1 682.2	4 226.4	2 116.7	1 844.1	1 659.5	1 757.2
Luxembourg	1 560.0	2 172.3	1 347.7	1 509.6	1 397.5	1 234.2
Hungary	2 368.1	3 543.9	1 524.9	1 482.6	1 510.0	1 332.6
Malta	372.2	944.7	766.0	1 002.5	986.9	913.5
Netherlands	1 039.7	1 589.5	776.1	955.3	942.2	923.8
Austria	2 896.8	3 726.9	1 637.2	2 507.9	1 300.4	2 937.5
Poland (1)	1 403.1	2 329.2	1 288.8	1 269.3	1 377.8	1 048.6
Portugal	:	:	:	:	:	:
Romania	1 842.0	3 053.2	3 026.0	2 225.3	1 838.0	1 292.3
Slovenia	1 797.9	1 942.2	1 294.5	1 415.9	1 371.3	1 505.6
Slovakia	1 580.3	2 711.9	1 460.6	1 787.6	1 571.8	1 466.2
Finland	1 731.6	2 826.6	1 426.4	1 377.0	1 295.3	1 894.0
Sweden (2)	1 376.2	2 370.6	964.4	1 174.6	1 306.2	1 421.2
United Kingdom (1)	936.3	1 275.3	1 134.0	1 144.9	1 381.5	1 208.1
Iceland (1)	1 282.8	1 547.5	900.0	1 322.3	1 970.8	1 051.4
Norway	1 677.8	2 467.7	1 439.9	1 248.1	1 550.8	1 903.7
Switzerland	1 086.0	1 743.6	884.7	1 405.4	1 204.0	1 962.7
Croatia	1 934.6	2 031.7	1 077.0	1 162.6	1 406.9	1 230.9
FYR of Macedonia (2)	849.5	1 669.5	1 494.6	1 104.9	494.5	624.9

(1) 2007.
(2) 2006.

Source: Eurostat (hlth_co_disch2)

Table 3.9: Hospital discharges of inpatients by diagnosis (ISHMT - international shortlist for hospital morbidity tabulation), average length of stay, 2008
(days)

	Neoplasms (cancers)	Diseases of the circulatory system	Diseases of the respiratory system	Diseases of the digestive system	Pregnancy, childbirth & the puerperium	Injury, poisoning & certain other consequences of external causes
Belgium (1)	9.3	8.2	8.1	5.9	4.8	8.6
Bulgaria	6.9	5.5	7.3	5.8	4.4	5.7
Czech Republic (1)	9.9	13.8	9.1	7.6	5.3	10.4
Denmark (1)	6.4	5.4	5.4	5.0	3.4	5.1
Germany	10.1	10.2	8.7	7.2	4.7	9.0
Estonia	:	10.8	:	5.3	3.0	8.8
Ireland	11.2	9.7	7.1	6.3	2.8	5.8
Greece	:	:	:	:	:	:
Spain	9.3	8.2	7.1	5.8	3.1	8.4
France	7.1	6.7	7.0	5.0	4.7	5.3
Italy (1)	9.5	9.0	8.5	6.8	3.9	8.5
Cyprus (1)	8.9	6.4	5.2	5.1	5.4	5.8
Latvia	9.3	8.6	7.7	6.2	5.2	7.9
Lithuania	9.2	8.8	7.0	6.3	4.4	7.1
Luxembourg	9.3	7.9	6.3	5.8	4.8	7.9
Hungary	6.4	8.7	7.1	6.4	5.0	7.2
Malta	5.9	6.5	4.8	4.4	3.2	5.5
Netherlands	7.5	7.0	7.2	6.2	3.4	7.0
Austria	7.6	10.8	8.4	6.8	5.5	8.8
Poland (1)	7.6	7.9	8.3	6.0	5.2	6.5
Portugal	:	:	:	:	:	:
Romania	6.8	7.9	7.1	6.5	5.0	6.2
Slovenia	7.9	8.4	6.9	6.2	4.5	7.0
Slovakia	8.7	8.1	7.9	6.1	5.6	6.4
Finland	8.7	16.3	12.5	5.6	3.6	10.5
Sweden (2)	7.9	6.5	5.6	4.9	2.9	6.2
United Kingdom (1)	8.9	10.6	7.7	6.3	2.5	8.6
Iceland (1)	7.3	6.9	6.4	4.0	2.6	6.7
Norway	6.6	4.9	6.1	4.5	3.4	4.6
Switzerland	9.7	7.8	7.4	6.2	5.0	6.7
Croatia	9.2	10.0	7.9	7.2	5.9	9.4
FYR of Macedonia (2)	10.2	7.3	7.6	5.9	3.4	8.1

(1) 2007.
(2) 2006.

Source: Eurostat (hlth_co_inpst)

3.4 Health and safety at work

A safe, healthy working environment is a crucial factor in an individual's quality of life and is also a collective concern. Member State governments across the European Union (EU) recognise the social and economic benefits of better health and safety at work. This subchapter presents a selection of statistical findings concerning health and safety in Europe; it focuses on accidents at work, work-related health problems and occupational diseases.

Main statistical findings

Accidents at work

According to the labour force survey (LFS) ad-hoc module for 2007, 3.2 % of workers aged 15 to 64 in the EU-27 had an accident at work in the 12 months prior to the survey; this corresponded to approximately 6.9 million persons. Data concerning European statistics on accidents at work (ESAW) show that 2.9 % of workers had an accident at work with more than three days of sickness absence in 2007, while a total of 5 523 workers died in fatal accidents.

The LFS data shows that accidents at work occurred more often among men, younger workers, and workers with a low educational level. Highly-skilled manual workers and workers in the construction, manufacturing, as well as agriculture, hunting and forestry sectors were more often involved in accidents at work. Approximately 70 % of the non-fatal accidents at work resulted from loss of control, a fall, or body movement under stress. Wounds and superficial injuries as well as dislocations, sprains and strains were the most common types of injury. In fatal accidents, multiple injuries were most often registered.

According to the same LFS source, 72.3 % of accidents at work resulted in sick leave of at least one day and 21.7 % resulted in sick leave of at least one month. Men reported a higher propensity to be on sick leave than women, while older workers were more likely to take sick leave of one month or more.

It is estimated that accidents at work resulted in at least 83 million calendar days of sick leave in the EU-27 in 2007; this figure excludes workers that do not think they will return to work, nor does it include workers that were still on sick leave at the time of the survey.

Work-related health problems

In the EU-27, 8.1 % of those aged 15 to 64 that worked or had previously worked reported a work-related health problem in the 12 months prior to the survey for the LFS ad-hoc module in 2007; this was equivalent to approximately 23 million persons.

Musculoskeletal problems were most often reported as the main work-related health problem (59.8 %), followed by stress, depression or anxiety (13.7 %). The occurrence of work-related health problems generally increased with age, but the rate of increase slowed down for workers aged 55 to 64 years; this may be due to unhealthy workers leaving the workforce early.

Workers with a low level of education reported work-related health problems more often than their colleagues. In particular, such workers more often identified musculoskeletal health problems as their most serious work-related health problem, whereas persons with higher levels of education most often identified stress, depression or anxiety as their main work-related health problem.

Work-related health problems were more likely to occur in agriculture, hunting and forestry, or in mining and quarrying; among women, work-related health problems were also more likely for those working in the health and social work sector. Furthermore, manual workers more often reported work-related health problems than non-manual workers.

Half (50.0 %) of all persons with a work-related health problem in the EU experienced some limitations in their ability to carry out day-to-day activities, and an additional 22.6 % experienced considerable limitations. Work-related health problems resulted in sick leave of at least one day in the past 12 months for 62.0 % of persons with a work-related health problem, and in sick leave of at least one month for 27.1 %.

It is estimated that work-related health problems resulted in at least 367 million calendar days of sick leave in the EU in 2007; this figure excludes persons that never expect to work again because of their work-related health problem.

Occupational diseases

According to European occupational diseases statistics (EODS), between 2001 and 2007, musculoskeletal diseases were the most common occupational diseases recognised by the authorities in European countries. Neurologic diseases, lung diseases, diseases of the sensory organs, and skin diseases were also frequently recorded. Men were registered more often with an occupational disease than women. Most men with an occupational disease worked in the manufacturing and construction sectors, whereas most women worked in the wholesale and retail trade sector or the health and social work sector. Approximately 25 % of recognised occupational diseases led to permanent incapacity to work.

Data sources and availability

An accident at work is a discrete occurrence during the course of work which leads to physical or mental harm. The phrase 'in the course of work' means whilst engaged in an occupational activity or during the time spent at work. This includes cases of road traffic accidents in the course of work but excludes accidents during the journey between home and the workplace.

The labour force survey (LFS) ad-hoc module in 2007 provided data on self-reported occupational accidents in the 12 months prior to the survey, irrespective of whether these accidents resulted in absence from work.

European statistics on accidents at work (ESAW) include case-by-case data on occupational accidents with more than three days of absence from work and fatal accidents. A fatal accident is defined as an accident which leads to the death of the victim within one year.

European occupational diseases statistics (EODS) contain harmonised data on occupational diseases from 2001 onwards. Some 22 Member States provide case-by-case data on occupational diseases, as recognised by national authorities. The EODS contains the number of newly recorded occupational diseases and fatal occupational diseases during the reference year. Since national compensation authorities approve the occupational origin of diseases, the concept of occupational diseases is dependent on national legislation and compensation practices.

Context

Reliable, comparable, up-to-date statistical information is vital for setting policy objectives and adopting suitable policy measures: an accurate statistical picture of health and safety at work is critical for monitoring policy and identifying preventive needs.

The main principles governing the protection of workers' health and safety are laid down in the 1989 Framework Directive 89/391/EEC, the basic objective of which is to encourage improvements in occupational health and safety. All sectors of activity, both public and private, are covered by this legislation, which establishes the principle that the employer has a duty to ensure workers' safety and health in all aspects relating to work, while the worker has an obligation to follow the employer's health and safety instructions and report potential dangers.

In this field, the policy agenda of the European Commission is set out in a Communication ((2007) 62) which details a Community strategy for 2007-2012 on health and safety at work, outlining actions to make workplaces across the EU safer and healthier. It also sets a quantitative target of a 25 % reduction in accidents at work, to be achieved through various EU and national measures.

Figure 3.13: Workers reporting one or more accidental injuries at work, EU-27, 2007 (1)
(% of male and female persons employed aged 15-64 years old)

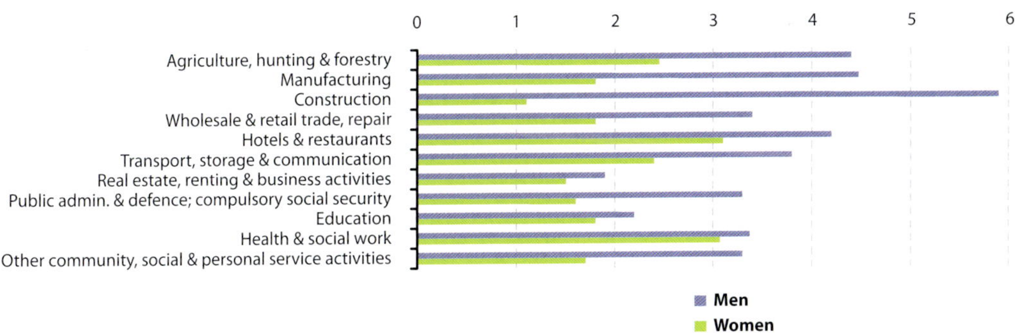

(1) At work or in the course of work in their main job during the 12 months prior to the survey.

Source: Eurostat (hsw_ac5)

Figure 3.14: Type of work-related health problem indicated as the most serious among persons with a work-related health problem, EU-27, 2007 (1)
(%)

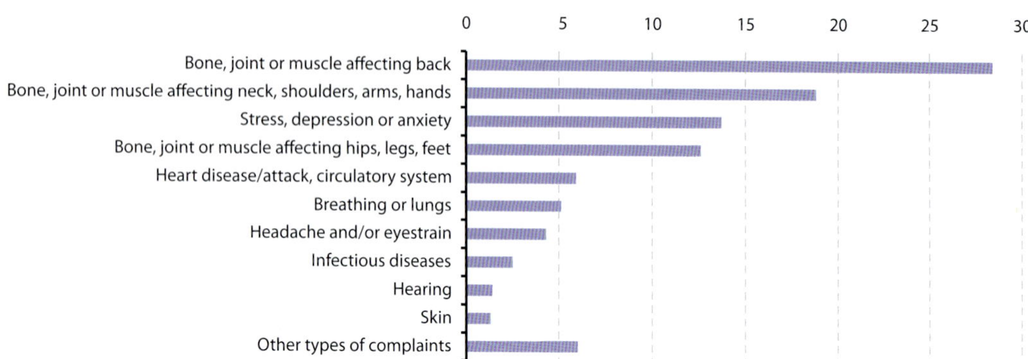

(1) Excluding France.

Source: Eurostat (hsw_pb5)

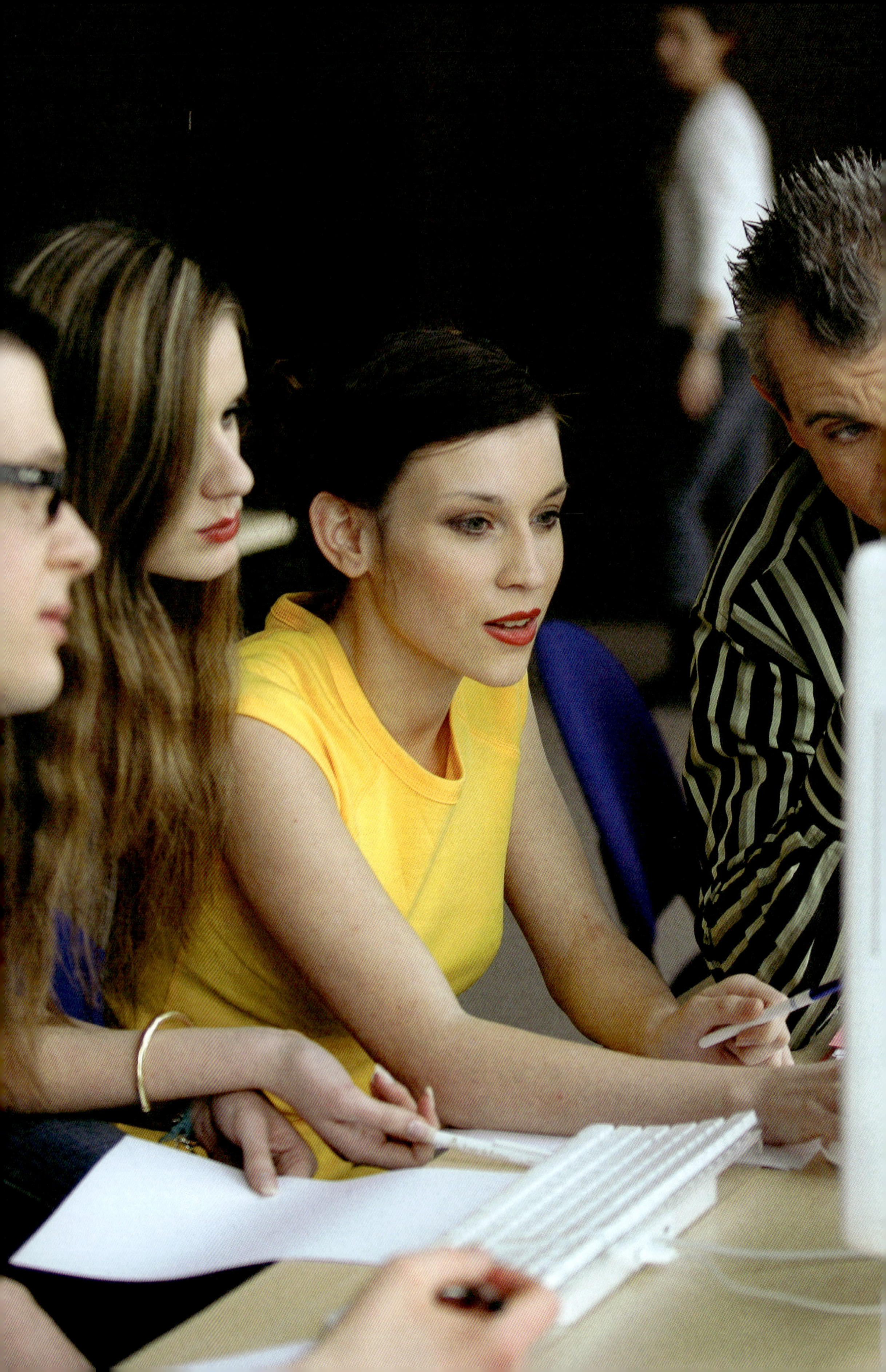

4

Education and training

Education, vocational training and more generally lifelong learning play a vital role in both an economic and social context. The opportunities which the European Union (EU) offers its citizens for living, studying and working in other countries make a major contribution to cross-cultural understanding, personal development and the realisation of the EU's full economic potential. Each year, well over a million EU citizens of all ages benefit from EU-funded educational, vocational and citizenship-building programmes.

The Treaty establishing the European Community acknowledged the importance of these areas by stating that 'the Community shall contribute to the development of quality education by encouraging cooperation between Member States and, if necessary, by supporting and supplementing their action ... The Community shall implement a vocational training policy which shall support and supplement the action of the Member States'. As such, the European Commission follows up on policy cooperation and work with the Member States, while funding programmes such as the lifelong learning programme (LLP).

Political cooperation within the EU has been strengthened through the education and training 2010 work programme which integrated previous actions in the fields of education and training. The follow-up to this programme is the strategic framework for European cooperation in education and training which was adopted by the Council in May 2009. This set a number of benchmarks to be achieved by 2020:

- at least 95 % of children between the age of four and the age for starting compulsory primary education should participate in early childhood education;
- the share of low-achieving 15-year-olds with insufficient abilities in reading, mathematics and science should be less than 15 %;

- the share of early leavers from education and training should be less than 10 %;
- the share of 30 to 34-year-olds with tertiary educational attainment should be at least 40 %;
- an average of at least 15 % of adults aged 25 to 64 should participate in lifelong learning.

The Bologna process put in motion a series of reforms to make European higher education more compatible, comparable, competitive and attractive for students. Its main objectives were: the introduction of a three-cycle degree system (bachelor, master, doctorate); quality assurance; and recognition of qualifications and periods of study. Through these objectives one of the operational goals was to remove the obstacles to student mobility across Europe, and more broadly support the mobility of students, teachers and researchers.

The Bologna process set out plans to create a European higher education area and in March 2010 the Minsters of the 47 participating countries adopted the Budapest-Vienna Declaration and officially launched the European higher education area (EHEA). The next decade will be aimed at consolidating the EHEA and making it operational.

Since 2002 national authorities and social partners from 32 European countries are taking part in the Copenhagen process to help develop vocational education and training systems. The overall aim is to encourage more individuals to make wider use of vocational learning opportunities, whether at school, in higher education, in the workplace, or through private courses. The actions and tools developed as part of the process aim to allow users to link and build on learning acquired at various times, in both formal and non-formal contexts.

The lifelong learning programme has been a flagship programme of the European Commission in the field of education and training since 2007, covering all learning opportunities from childhood to old age. Over the period 2007 to 2013, this programme has a budget of nearly EUR 7 000 million in order to support projects that foster interchange, cooperation and mobility between education and training systems within the EU. It is made up of four sub-programmes that focus on the different stages of education and training, each with quantified targets:

- Comenius for schools should involve at least 3 million pupils in joint educational activities over the period of the programme;
- Erasmus for higher education should reach a total of 3 million individual participants in student mobility actions since the action began;
- Leonardo da Vinci for vocational education and training should increase placements in enterprises to 80 000 persons per year by the end of the programme;
- Grundtvig for adult education should support the mobility of 7 000 individuals involved in adult education each year by 2013.

The measurement of progress towards these objectives within the field of education policy requires a range of comparable statistics on enrolment in education and training, numbers of graduates and teachers, language learning, student and researcher mobility, educational expenditure, as well as data on educational attainment and adult learning. Education statistics cover a range of subjects, including: expenditure, personnel, participation rates, and attainment. The standards for international statistics on education are set by three international organisations:

- the United Nations Educational, Scientific, and Cultural Organization (UNESCO) institute for statistics (UIS);
- the Organisation for Economic Co-operation and Development (OECD), and;
- the statistical office of the European Union (Eurostat).

The main source of data is a joint UNESCO/OECD/Eurostat (UOE) questionnaire on education statistics and this is the basis for the core components of the Eurostat database on education statistics; Eurostat also collects data on regional enrolments and foreign language learning. Data on educational attainment and adult learning are mainly provided by household surveys, in particular the EU labour force survey (LFS), which is complemented by an adult education survey.

4.1 School enrolment and levels of education

School helps young people acquire the basic life skills and competences necessary for their personal development. The quality of a pupil's school experience affects not only their development, but also his or her place in society, educational attainment, and employment opportunities. The quality of the education may be linked to teaching standards, which in turn are related to the demands placed upon teachers, the training they receive and the roles they are asked to fill.

With this in mind, several European Union (EU) Member States are revising their school curricula in line with the changing needs of society and the economy, as well as reflecting on how to improve teacher training and evaluation. This subchapter presents statistical data on relevant aspects of teaching and education in the EU, such as class sizes and enrolments.

Main statistical findings

The level of educational enrolment depends on a wide range of factors, such as the age structure of the population, legal requirements concerning the start and end of compulsory education, and the availability of educational resources – in particular, access to specialist tertiary education may be limited in some of the smallest Member States.

In 2008, there were about 93.1 million pupils and students enrolled in educational establishments in the EU-27. The highest share of pupils and students in the EU-27 total was accounted for by Germany, where 14.1 million pupils and students attended educational establishments in 2008; this figure was 1.4 million higher than the next largest student population in the United Kingdom, and 1.8 million higher than in France (see Table 4.1).

The proportion of students found in each level of education varied somewhat between the Member States, most notably for primary and lower secondary levels of education. This variation reflects, to some degree, the demographic structure of each population. The high proportion of pupils in primary education in Luxembourg (44.4 % in 2008), for example, reflects the lack of a developed tertiary education sector in this country. At the other end of the spectrum, Greece, Slovenia, the Baltic Member States, Romania and Poland all had relatively high proportions (more than one quarter) of their student populations within the tertiary education sector.

The figures above exclude pre-primary education – where 90.1 % of all four-year-olds in the EU-27 were in education in 2008 (see Figure 4.1). The general objectives for pre-primary education are fairly similar across countries, focusing on the development of children's independence, well-being, self-confidence, citizenship, and preparation for life and learning at school. Enrolment in pre-primary education is normally voluntary and participation rates of four-year-olds ranged from 100 % in France, to less than one child in two across Ireland and Poland. The strategic framework for European cooperation in education and training adopted in May 2009 set a benchmark to be achieved by 2020 that at least 95 % of children between the age of four and the age for starting compulsory primary education should participate in early childhood education.

More than three quarters (76.8 %) of all 18-year-olds within the EU-27 remained within the education system in 2008. However, this ratio rose to above 90 % in five Member States, while just over half of all 18-year-olds were still attending an educational establishment in Malta and the United Kingdom; the ratio was lower still in Cyprus (see Figure 4.2). These figures may reflect a number of factors, in particular the need for students to go abroad to continue their (tertiary) education, or the practise of making students re-take a whole year if their performance at the end of an academic year is deemed unsatisfactory.

School expectancy is a related indicator, as Member States with longer school expectancy generally have a higher proportion of 18-year-olds in education. Nevertheless, Ireland and Italy had a larger proportion of 18-year-olds in education than the average for the EU-27, but a length of school expectancy in line with or below the EU-27 average. Greece and Portugal had the reverse situation, with amongst the lowest proportions of 18-year-olds in education, despite longer than average school expectancy (see Figure 4.3).

Pupil/teacher ratios

Pupil/teacher ratios within primary education ranged from an average of less than 11 pupils per teacher in Lithuania, Denmark, Greece (2007), Poland, Italy, Hungary and Malta in 2008, to almost double that rate in France and the United Kingdom (both above 19 pupils per teacher). Between 2003 and 2008 there was a general reduction in the average number of pupils per teacher within primary education establishments in most of the Member States, with the most notable increases in Slovenia and Luxembourg (see Table 4.2).

In 2008 the average number of pupils per teacher was generally lower for secondary education than for primary education. Nevertheless, Italy recorded higher average numbers of pupils per teacher within upper secondary education than in primary education, as did Malta, Finland and Sweden, while Hungary and Poland recorded higher average pupil numbers in both lower and upper secondary education than in primary education.

Youth education attainment level and early leavers from education and training

Data on educational attainment show that, in 2009, just over three quarters (78.6 %) of the EU-27's population aged 20 to 24 had completed at least an upper secondary level of education, a figure that reached 81.4 % for women. However, 14.4 % of those aged 18 to 24 (16.3 % of men and 12.5 % of women) were early leavers from education and training (previously called *early school leavers*), with at most a lower secondary education. This share fell from 16.1 % five years earlier, with large reductions in percentage point terms in Cyprus, Portugal, Bulgaria, Romania and Malta (see Table 4.3). The strategic framework for European cooperation in education and training adopted a benchmark to be achieved by 2020 that the share of early leavers from education and training should be less than 10 %.

Data sources and availability

The international standard classification of education (ISCED) is the basis for international education statistics, describing different levels of education, as well as fields of education and training. The current version, ISCED 97, distinguishes seven levels of education: pre-primary education (level 0); primary education (level 1); lower secondary education (level 2); upper secondary education (level 3); post-secondary non-tertiary education (level 4); tertiary education (first stage) (level 5); tertiary education (second stage) (level 6).

The indicator for four-year-olds in education presents the percentage of four-year-olds who are enrolled in education-oriented pre-primary institutions. These institutions provide education-oriented care for young children. They must recruit staff with specialised qualifications in education. Day nurseries, playgroups and day care centres, where the staff are not required to hold a qualification in education, are not included.

The indicator for 18-year-olds who are still in any kind of school (all ISCED levels) provides an indication of the number of young people who have not abandoned their efforts to improve their skills through initial education; it includes both those who had a regular education career without any delays, as well as those who are continuing even if they had to repeat some steps in the past.

The indicator of school expectancy corresponds to how many years, on average, a child starting in school can expect to stay at school (calculated by adding the single-year enrolment rates for all ages).

Pupil-teacher ratios are calculated by dividing the number of full-time equivalent pupils and students in each level of education by the number of full-time equivalent teachers at the same level; all institutions, both public and private, are included. This ratio should not be confused with average class-size. There can be a difference between the number of hours of teaching provided by individual teachers and the number of hours of instruction prescribed for pupils; more than one teacher can be teaching in a class at the same time; or teachers for special education needs can work with small groups or on a one-to-one basis.

Youth education attainment is defined as the proportion of the population aged 20 to 24 having completed at least an upper secondary education, in other words, those with a minimum education level of ISCED levels 3a, 3b or 3c long. The denominator consists of the total population of the same age group, excluding non-response.

The indicator for early leavers from education and training is defined as the proportion of the population aged 18 to 24 with at most a lower secondary level of education (ISCED levels 1, 2 or 3c short), who are no longer in further education or training; respondents declared not having received any education or training in the four weeks preceding the survey. The denominator consists of the total population of the same age group, excluding non-response.

Context

Demographic trends in the last three decades reflect reductions in birth rates that have resulted in the structure of the EU's population ageing and the proportion of those aged under 30 decreasing in the majority of Member States. These changes can have a significant impact on human and material resources required for the sound functioning of education systems – such as average class sizes or teacher recruitment strategies.

In general, compulsory education is completed at the end of lower secondary education, although in some countries it continues into upper secondary education. On average, compulsory education lasts nine or ten years in most of the EU: lasting longest in Hungary, the Netherlands and the United Kingdom. Age is generally the sole criterion for admission to compulsory primary education, which starts at the age of five or six in most Member States, although Bulgaria, the Baltic Member States, Finland and Sweden have a compulsory starting age of seven.

Most Europeans spend significantly longer in education than the legal minimum requirement. This reflects the choice to en-

rol in higher education, as well as increased enrolment in pre-primary education and wider participation in lifelong learning initiatives, such as mature (adult) students returning to education – often in order to retrain or equip themselves for a career change.

While national curricula include broadly the same subjects across the Member States, the amount of time allocated to each subject varies considerably. In addition, there are wide-ranging differences in the freedoms that schools and teachers have: to shape the content of their classes, or to follow a strict curriculum. The most significant differences between countries tend to relate to the degree of instruction given in foreign languages, information and communication technology, artistic activities, or religious/moral instruction. In contrast, all countries allocate a considerable amount of time to teach their mother tongue and mathematics, particularly in primary education. Teaching time tends to be more evenly spread across subjects in compulsory secondary education, with an increasing emphasis given to natural and social sciences, as well as foreign languages.

As part of the lifelong learning programme the Comenius programme addresses developments in education and school policy and aims to:

- improve and increase the mobility of pupils and educational staff;
- enhance and increase partnerships between schools in different Member States, with at least three million pupils taking part in joint educational activities by 2010;
- encourage language learning, innovative ICT-based content, services and better teaching techniques and practices;
- enhance the quality and European dimension of teacher training;
- improve pedagogical approaches and school management.

Table 4.1: Pupils and students (excluding pre-primary education) (¹)

	Total (ISCED 1-6) (1 000)		Breakdown of total number of pupils and students (% of total)							
			Primary level of education (ISCED 1)		Lower secondary level of education (ISCED 2)		Upper and post-secondary non-tertiary education (ISCED 3-4)		Tertiary education (ISCED 5-6)	
	2003	2008	2003	2008	2003	2008	2003	2008	2003	2008
EU-27	97 027	93 116	29.9	30.4	24.6	23.8	:	25.3	18.3	20.4
Belgium	2 373	2 428	32.1	30.2	17.7	13.7	34.3	39.5	15.8	16.5
Bulgaria	1 274	1 142	26.1	23.0	27.3	23.2	28.4	30.6	18.1	23.2
Czech Republic	1 928	1 855	29.4	24.8	26.5	23.3	29.2	30.7	14.9	21.2
Denmark	1 069	1 152	39.3	35.6	21.0	21.4	20.9	22.9	18.9	20.0
Germany	14 525	14 065	22.7	23.0	39.0	35.6	22.3	24.9	15.4	16.0
Estonia	298	258	33.6	29.0	22.3	18.8	22.8	25.7	21.3	26.5
Ireland	1 001	1 053	44.7	46.2	17.5	16.5	19.6	20.4	18.1	16.9
Greece	1 961	2 009	33.3	31.7	17.4	17.1	20.7	19.5	28.6	31.7
Spain	7 382	7 615	33.7	36.3	26.7	25.8	14.6	14.5	24.9	23.4
France	11 884	12 265	31.9	33.7	27.6	26.4	22.0	22.2	17.8	17.6
Italy	9 266	9 510	30.0	30.1	19.8	18.5	29.5	30.2	20.6	21.2
Cyprus	146	148	43.1	38.3	22.5	22.1	21.8	22.3	12.5	17.3
Latvia	506	431	20.4	27.2	34.8	19.2	21.3	23.9	23.5	29.7
Lithuania	807	738	22.7	18.4	41.6	37.4	14.9	16.5	20.8	27.7
Luxembourg	73	80	46.8	44.4	23.1	24.5	26.0	27.3	4.2	3.8
Hungary	1 968	1 873	23.6	21.1	25.6	24.0	31.0	32.8	19.8	22.1
Malta	79	74	40.3	36.2	36.7	34.9	11.6	16.2	11.4	12.8
Netherlands	3 239	3 380	39.8	38.0	24.4	22.8	19.5	21.4	16.3	17.8
Austria	1 429	1 468	26.6	23.0	27.5	26.0	29.8	31.6	16.1	19.4
Poland	9 077	8 168	32.9	29.1	19.0	18.0	26.3	26.4	21.8	26.5
Portugal	1 962	2 109	39.9	36.7	20.1	25.0	19.6	20.5	20.4	17.9
Romania	3 915	3 904	25.3	22.2	30.8	23.7	27.4	27.1	16.4	27.1
Slovenia	408	388	21.4	25.6	22.7	17.3	31.0	27.4	24.9	29.8
Slovakia	1 104	1 059	24.5	21.2	34.5	29.3	26.7	27.8	14.3	21.7
Finland	1 193	1 251	32.9	28.6	16.3	16.2	26.3	30.5	24.5	24.7
Sweden	2 119	2 023	36.6	33.0	18.5	19.7	25.4	27.2	19.6	20.1
United Kingdom	16 043	12 671	28.0	35.2	14.6	19.3	:	27.0	14.3	18.4
Iceland	80	87	39.3	34.6	16.5	16.1	27.4	30.2	16.7	19.2
Liechtenstein	6	6	37.6	34.3	27.8	28.0	26.9	25.0	7.5	12.7
Norway	1 036	1 078	41.8	39.9	16.9	17.5	20.8	22.9	20.5	19.7
Switzerland	1 315	1 355	40.7	37.3	21.7	21.8	22.7	23.5	14.1	16.6
Croatia	725	722	26.5	25.2	29.7	28.8	27.1	26.1	16.8	19.9
FYR of Macedonia	381	385	30.6	29.9	32.2	28.2	25.2	24.8	12.0	17.0
Turkey	15 565	16 649	66.4	65.3	-	-	21.3	19.5	12.3	15.2
Japan	19 646	18 658	37.0	38.4	19.8	19.6	21.7	19.9	20.3	21.1
United States	65 738	68 041	37.8	36.3	19.7	18.9	17.2	18.0	25.3	26.8

(¹) Refer to the Internet metadata file (http://epp.eurostat.ec.europa.eu/cache/ITY_SDDS/en/educ_esms.htm).

Source: Eurostat (tps00051 and educ_enrl1tl)

Figure 4.1: Four-year-olds in education, 2008 (1)
(% of all four-year-olds)

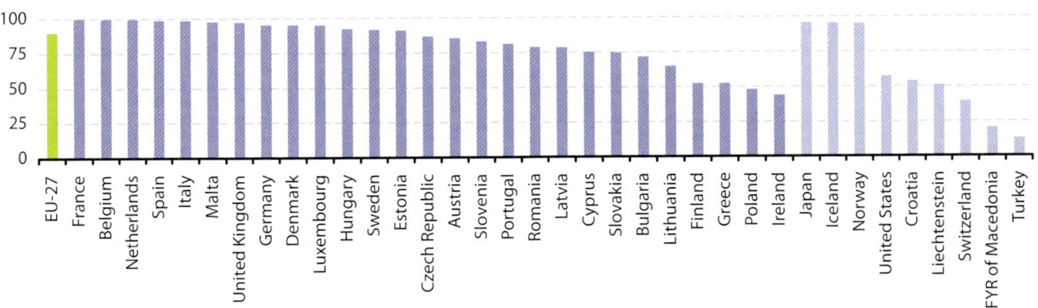

(1) Refer to the Internet metadata file (http://epp.eurostat.ec.europa.eu/cache/ITY_SDDS/en/educ_esms.htm).

Source: Eurostat (tps00053)

Figure 4.2: 18-year-olds in education, 2008 (1)
(% of all 18-year-olds)

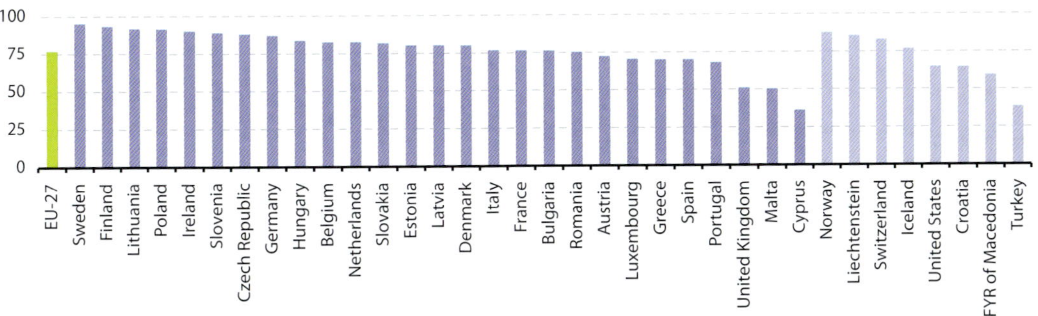

(1) Refer to the Internet metadata file (http://epp.eurostat.ec.europa.eu/cache/ITY_SDDS/en/educ_esms.htm).

Source: Eurostat (tps00060)

Figure 4.3: School expectancy, 2008 (1)
(years)

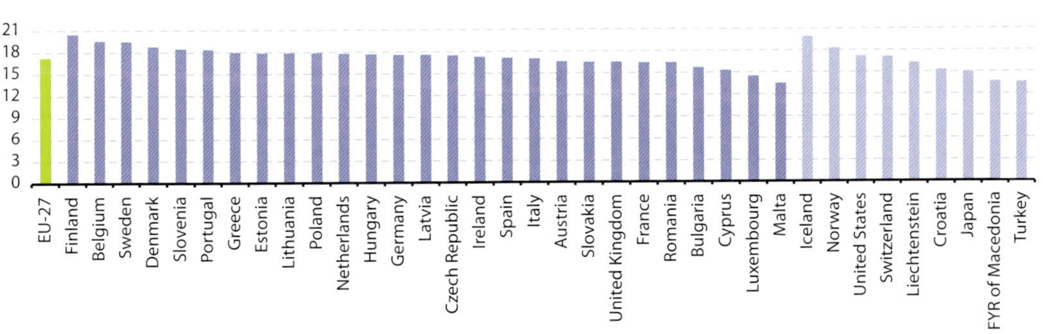

(1) School expectancy corresponds to the expected years of education over a lifetime and has been calculated adding the single-year enrolment rates for all ages.

Source: Eurostat (tps00052)

Table 4.2: Pupil-teacher ratio in primary, lower and upper secondary education (1)
(average number of pupils per teacher)

	Primary education (ISCED 1)		Lower secondary/second stage of basic education (ISCED 2)		Upper secondary education (ISCED 3)	
	2003	2008	2003	2008	2003	2008
Belgium	13.1	12.6	10.6	8.1	9.6	10.8
Bulgaria	17.2	16.1	13.3	12.0	11.9	11.5
Czech Republic	18.3	18.1	14.3	11.8	12.6	14.0
Denmark	10.8	10.1	:	:	13.4	:
Germany	18.7	18.0	15.6	15.0	13.7	14.0
Estonia	:	16.4	:	16.0	:	12.4
Ireland	18.7	17.8	13.9	:	13.9	12.9
Greece (2)	12.1	10.1	8.7	7.7	8.6	7.3
Spain	14.3	13.1	13.3	10.3	7.9	8.7
France	19.4	19.9	13.7	14.6	10.6	9.4
Italy	10.9	10.6	10.3	9.7	10.8	11.8
Cyprus	19.2	15.0	12.8	10.8	12.0	10.6
Latvia	15.9	12.8	13.1	9.2	12.2	11.9
Lithuania	12.2	9.7	9.3	7.7	:	:
Luxembourg	10.8	12.1	9.0	:	9.0	9.0
Hungary	10.6	10.6	10.6	10.9	13.2	12.3
Malta	18.4	10.6	10.0	7.1	10.1	15.3
Netherlands	16.0	15.8	:	:	15.7	15.8
Austria	14.4	12.9	10.0	9.9	10.2	10.5
Poland	11.9	10.5	12.6	12.9	13.5	12.2
Portugal	11.3	11.3	8.9	8.1	8.3	7.3
Romania	17.8	16.3	13.7	12.5	15.8	14.8
Slovenia	12.8	15.8	13.0	8.9	14.6	13.5
Slovakia	19.4	18.6	13.9	14.5	14.0	15.1
Finland	16.6	14.4	9.8	10.6	15.9	15.9
Sweden	12.3	12.2	12.1	11.4	14.1	14.7
United Kingdom	20.0	20.2	17.4	15.0	20.3	12.4
Iceland	11.3	10.0	:	:	10.7	10.6
Liechtenstein	11.3	9.1	:	8.6	:	8.6
Norway	11.7	10.8	10.4	10.1	9.2	9.9
Croatia	18.0	16.6	12.6	12.1	11.7	11.3
FYR of Macedonia	20.3	17.4	15.8	12.8	18.1	15.8
Turkey	25.9	24.4	:	:	18.0	17.0
Japan	19.9	18.8	15.7	14.7	13.5	12.3
United States	15.5	14.3	15.5	14.8	15.6	15.6

(1) Refer to the Internet metadata file (http://epp.eurostat.ec.europa.eu/cache/ITY_SDDS/en/educ_esms.htm)
(2) 2007 instead of 2008.

Source: Eurostat (tps00054 and educ_iste)

Table 4.3: Youth education attainment level and early leavers from education and training (1)
(%)

	Youth education attainment level				Early leavers from education & training			
	Total		Male	Female	Total		Male	Female
	2004	2009	2009	2009	2004	2009	2009	2009
EU-27	77.1	78.6	75.9	81.4	16.1	14.4	16.3	12.5
Euro area (EA-16)	74.0	75.6	72.3	79.0	18.0	15.9	18.3	13.5
Belgium	81.8	83.3	80.9	85.8	13.1	11.1	12.8	9.3
Bulgaria	76.1	83.7	84.8	82.5	21.4	14.7	13.7	15.8
Czech Republic	91.4	91.9	91.6	92.3	6.3	5.4	5.5	5.2
Denmark (2)	76.2	70.1	62.2	78.4	8.8	10.6	13.2	7.7
Germany (2)	72.8	73.7	71.7	75.8	12.1	11.1	11.5	10.7
Estonia (3)	80.3	82.3	78.2	86.4	13.1	13.9	18.4	9.3
Ireland	85.3	87.0	83.4	90.5	13.1	11.3	14.4	8.2
Greece	83.0	82.2	77.8	86.9	14.7	14.5	18.3	10.6
Spain (4)	61.2	59.9	53.1	67.1	32.0	31.2	37.4	24.7
France	81.8	83.6	81.3	85.9	12.8	12.3	14.3	10.3
Italy	73.4	76.3	72.8	79.9	22.3	19.2	22.0	16.3
Cyprus (4)	77.6	87.4	84.2	90.2	20.6	11.7	15.2	8.8
Latvia	79.5	80.5	76.2	84.8	14.7	13.9	17.5	10.4
Lithuania (3)	85.0	86.9	83.0	91.0	10.5	8.7	11.5	5.7
Luxembourg (2) (5)	72.5	76.8	76.1	77.6	12.7	7.7	8.9	6.6
Hungary	83.5	84.0	82.1	85.8	12.6	11.2	12.0	10.4
Malta	51.0	52.1	48.2	56.7	42.1	36.8	39.7	33.6
Netherlands	75.0	76.6	72.1	81.2	14.1	10.9	13.1	8.6
Austria	85.8	86.0	85.8	86.1	9.5	8.7	8.5	8.9
Poland	90.9	91.3	89.3	93.2	5.6	5.3	6.6	3.9
Portugal	49.6	55.5	50.0	61.3	39.4	31.2	36.1	26.1
Romania	75.3	78.3	77.8	78.9	22.4	16.6	16.1	17.2
Slovenia (6)	90.5	89.4	86.2	93.1	4.3	5.3	7.2	3.2
Slovakia	91.7	93.3	92.6	94.0	6.8	4.9	5.7	4.1
Finland	84.5	85.1	84.4	85.9	10.0	9.9	10.7	9.0
Sweden	86.0	86.4	84.9	87.9	9.2	10.7	11.9	9.5
United Kingdom (4)	77.0	79.3	77.4	81.3	12.1	15.7	17.0	14.5
Iceland	51.7	53.6	48.9	58.5	24.9	21.4	25.2	17.5
Norway (2)	95.1	69.7	64.9	74.6	4.7	17.6	21.8	13.4
Switzerland	78.7	80.2	79.4	80.9	9.5	9.2	9.1	9.3
Croatia (6)	93.5	95.1	94.6	95.8	5.4	3.9	4.2	3.7
FYR of Macedonia	:	81.9	84.3	79.5	:	16.2	14.1	18.5
Turkey	42.0	50.0	57.1	44.0	54.5	44.3	37.9	50.2

(1) Refer to the Internet metadata file (http://epp.eurostat.ec.europa.eu/cache/ITY_SDDS/en/lfsi_edu_a_esms.htm); early leavers from education and training: based on annual averages of quarterly data.
(2) Break in series between 2004 and 2009.
(3) Female early leavers from education and training: unreliable or uncertain data.
(4) Early leavers from education and training: break in series between 2004 and 2009.
(5) Male and female early leavers from education and training: unreliable or uncertain data.
(6) Early leavers from education and training: unreliable or uncertain data.

Source: Eurostat (tsiir110 and tsisc060)

4.2 Foreign language learning

Currently 23 official languages are recognised within the European Union (EU), in addition to which there are regional, minority languages, and languages spoken by migrant populations.

School is the main opportunity for the vast majority of people to learn these languages – although linguistic diversity is actively encouraged within schools, universities and adult education centres, as well as the workplace. This subchapter presents statistics on language learning at primary and secondary schools in the EU Member States.

Main statistical findings

Primary education

Within primary education, a clear majority of pupils (choose to) study English. Indeed, learning English is mandatory in several countries within secondary education institutions, and so a number of Member States have close to 100 % of pupils learning this language already in primary education, as shown in Figure 4.4. The highest shares of primary education pupils studying English were recorded in Malta (where English is a second official language), Italy, Austria, Greece and Spain, where over nine out of every ten children were studying English. The relative importance of English as a foreign language may be further magnified because pupils tend to receive more instruction in their first foreign language than they do for any subsequent languages they (choose to) study.

The central and eastern European Member States that joined the EU in 2004 and 2007 are in a particular position with regard to language teaching, as learning Russian was compulsory for many pupils in the past. This situation has changed rapidly and these days most pupils have more choice concerning the language(s) they wish to study, for example, in most countries there has also been a marked increase in the proportion of pupils learning English, often above 40 % of all students and in Bulgaria, Estonia and Lithuania over 60 %. Luxembourg is also of particular interest, insofar as there are three official languages, with most pupils receiving instruction in Luxembourgish, German and French at primary level; English is introduced at secondary school.

Secondary education

Turning to language learning in upper secondary education (as shown in Table 4.4), some 83.5 % of all EU-27 students at ISCED level 3 were studying English as a foreign language in 2007, compared with around one fifth studying French (21.8 %) or German (22.5 %).

Luxembourg and the Netherlands stood out as the countries with the highest proportion of secondary education students (at ISCED levels 2 or 3) learning three or more languages in 2007; note this indicator includes all foreign languages, not just German, English and French.

Data sources and availability

Data on the number of pupils studying foreign languages are related to the corresponding numbers of students enrolled; mentally handicapped students enrolled in special schools are excluded.

The average number of foreign languages learned per pupil is collected for different ISCED levels. The data refer to all pupils, even if teaching languages does not start in the first years of instruction for the particular ISCED level considered. This indicator is defined as the sum of language students divided by the total number of students enrolled in the educational level considered. Each student studying a foreign language is counted once for each language he or she is studying, in other words students studying more than one language are counted as many times as the number of languages studied. The educational curriculum drawn up in each country defines the languages, which are to be considered as foreign languages in that country and this definition is applied in the data collection. Regional languages are included, if they are considered as alternatives to foreign languages by the curriculum. Only foreign languages studied as compulsory subjects or as compulsory curriculum options are included. The study of languages when the subject is offered in addition to the minimum curriculum is not included. Also data on non-nationals studying their native language in special classes or those studying the language of the host country are excluded.

Context

For several decades it has been mandatory for most European children to learn at least one foreign language during their compulsory education, with the time devoted to foreign language instruction generally increasing in recent years. In 2002, the Barcelona European Council recommended that at least two foreign languages should be taught to all pupils from a very early age. This recommendation has been implemented to varying degrees, usually for compulsory secondary education, either by making it mandatory to teach a second language, or ensuring that pupils have the possibility to study a second foreign language as part of their curriculum. In September 2008 the European Commission adopted a Communication titled 'Multilingualism: an asset for Europe and a shared commitment' (COM(2008) 566 final), which was followed in November 2008 by a Council Resolution on a European strategy for multilingualism (2008/C 320/01). The Communication addressed languages in the wider context of social cohesion and prosperity and focused on actions to encourage and assist citizens in acquiring language skills. It explored issues such as:

- the role languages play in developing mutual understanding in a multicultural society;
- how language skills improve employability and ensure a competitive edge for European businesses;
- what to do to encourage European citizens to speak two languages in addition to their mother tongue;
- how the media and new technologies can serve as a bridge between speakers of different languages.

Figure 4.4: Proportion of pupils learning foreign languages in primary education, by language, 2007 (1)
(%)

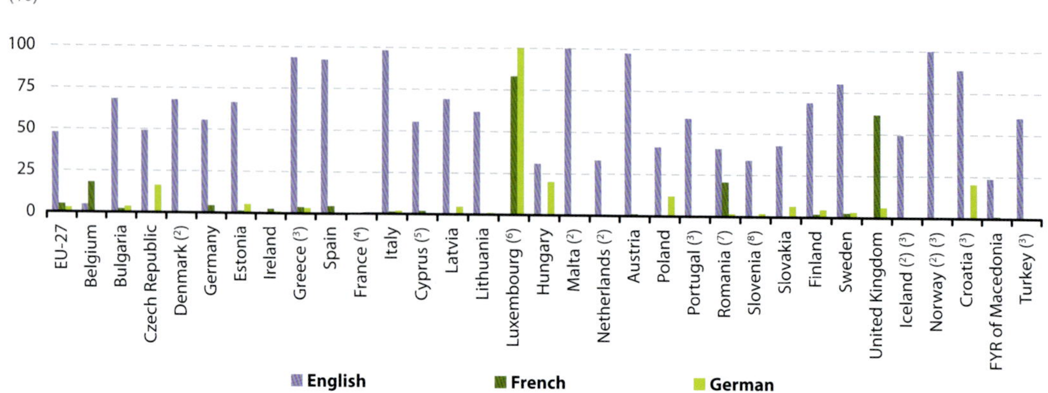

(1) Refer to the Internet metadata file (http://epp.eurostat.ec.europa.eu/cache/ITY_SDDS/en/educ_esms.htm).
(2) French and German, not available.
(3) 2006.
(4) Not available.
(5) German, not available.
(6) English, not available.
(7) German, 2006.
(8) French, not available.

Source: Eurostat (educ_ilang), Unesco, OECD

Table 4.4: Foreign languages learnt per pupil in secondary education (1)
(%)

	Proportion of students learning 3 or more languages (at ISCED level 2 or 3)		Upper secondary education (ISCED 3)					
			Pupils learning English in general programmes		Pupils learning French in general programmes		Pupils learning German in general programmes	
	2002	2007	2002	2007	2002	2007	2002	2007
EU-27	4.7	2.8	69.7	83.5	17.7	21.8	17.7	22.5
Belgium	15.2	14.5	94.1	94.1	47.7	48.1	30.1	28.5
Bulgaria	0.7	0.5	80.8	86.2	18.7	15.0	39.3	38.5
Czech Republic	:	1.0	98.9	100.0	17.3	24.5	73.5	65.8
Denmark	:	2.3	:	91.8	:	10.7	:	35.6
Germany	:	:	90.9	91.0	27.1	27.4	-	-
Estonia	28.6	18.9	91.2	95.0	4.7	6.7	45.6	41.6
Ireland	0.3	0.3	-	-	65.7	59.6	18.7	18.3
Greece (2)	-	:	95.2	94.0	10.3	8.6	2.1	2.9
Spain	0.0	0.2	95.9	95.3	27.7	27.7	1.1	1.1
France	3.4	:	99.4	99.4	-	-	30.5	21.8
Italy	3.1	2.1	85.9	95.3	27.2	20.5	8.2	7.2
Cyprus	:	:	100.0	78.5	60.4	32.2	1.0	2.4
Latvia	3.8	4.6	89.3	96.0	3.1	4.1	48.1	32.2
Lithuania	1.5	0.8	76.5	85.1	6.8	4.9	35.1	25.4
Luxembourg	60.7	61.9	96.3	96.5	96.3	96.5	96.3	96.5
Hungary	:	0.2	57.6	76.4	6.3	6.5	49.3	50.1
Malta	13.4	20.0	78.5	70.2	8.3	9.6	0.8	2.2
Netherlands (3)	20.4	56.7	99.9	100.0	22.7	70.3	23.3	86.3
Austria	2.1	2.4	96.9	96.9	42.8	54.1	-	-
Poland	:	0.7	90.6	91.2	14.1	9.8	61.5	62.7
Portugal (2)	:	:	:	50.7	:	15.1	:	1.6
Romania (4)	:	1.1	87.8	95.9	85.1	83.0	10.7	11.6
Slovenia	2.2	3.2	98.2	98.3	9.1	10.8	83.0	76.0
Slovakia	0.1	0.7	96.0	97.9	12.4	16.0	78.2	71.2
Finland	44.4	34.6	99.7	99.3	21.9	19.3	41.5	33.2
Sweden	4.5	3.3	99.8	99.9	25.8	21.1	48.9	29.6
United Kingdom	:	:	-	-	:	32.0	:	11.7
Iceland (5)	15.8	19.1	66.2	76.1	14.7	17.1	32.1	30.7
Norway (2)	:	:	:	100.0	:	20.3	:	31.3
Croatia (2)	:	1.2	:	98.3	:	3.4	:	65.6
Turkey (2)	:	:	:	67.3	:	0.7	:	6.5

(1) Refer to the Internet metadata file (http://epp.eurostat.ec.europa.eu/cache/ITY_SDDS/en/educ_esms.htm).
(2) 2006 instead of 2007.
(3) Proportion of students learning three or more languages: break in series, 2004.
(4) Pupils learning German: 2006 instead of 2007.
(5) Pupils learning English, French or German: 2006 instead of 2007.

Source: Eurostat (educ_thfrlan, tps00057, tps00058 and tps00059), Unesco, OECD

4.3 Educational expenditure

Expenditure on education may help foster economic growth, enhance productivity, contribute to people's personal and social development, and promote the reduction of social inequalities. The proportion of total financial resources devoted to education is one of the key choices made by governments in each country of the European Union (EU). In a similar vein, enterprises, students and their families also make decisions on the financial resources that they will set aside for education.

Main statistical findings

Public expenditure on education in the EU-27 in 2007 was equivalent to 5.0 % of GDP, while the expenditure of both public and private sources of funds on educational institutions amounted to 5.7 % of GDP (see Table 4.5).

The highest public spending on education was observed in Denmark (7.8 % of GDP), while Cyprus (6.9 %), Sweden (6.7 %) and Malta (6.3 %) also recorded relatively high proportions. Most Member States reported that public expenditure on education accounted for between 4 % and 6 % of their GDP, although this share was lower in Slovakia. It should also be noted that GDP growth can mask significant increases that have been made in terms of education spending over the last decade within some Member States. Furthermore, declining birth rates in many countries will result in reduced school age populations, which will have an effect on ratios such as the average expenditure per pupil (given that expenditure is held constant).

Annual expenditure on public and private educational institutions shows that an average of PPS 6 251 was spent per pupil/student in 2007 in the EU-27; this ratio was approximately six times higher in Austria than in Romania (2005).

Data sources and availability

Indicators on education expenditure cover schools, universities and other public and private institutions involved in delivering or supporting educational services. Expenditure on institutions is not limited to that made on instructional services, but also includes public and private expenditure on ancillary services for students and families, where these services are provided through educational institutions. At the tertiary level, spending on research and development can also be significant and is included, to the extent that the research is performed by educational institutions.

Total public expenditure on education includes direct public funding for educational institutions and transfers to households and enterprises. Generally, the public sector funds education either by bearing directly the current and capital expenses of educational institutions (direct expenditure for educational institutions) or by supporting students and their families with scholarships and public loans as well as by transferring public subsidies for educational activities to private enterprises or non-profit organisations (transfers to private households and enterprises). Both types of transactions together are reported as total public expenditure on education.

Expenditure on educational institutions from private sources comprises: school fees; materials (such as textbooks and teaching equipment); transport to school (if organised by the school); meals (if provided by the school); boarding fees, and; expenditure by employers on initial vocational training.

Expenditure per pupil/student in public and private institutions measures how much central, regional and local government, private households, religious institutions and enterprises spend per pupil/student. It includes expenditure for personnel, as well as other current and capital expenditure. Public schools/institutions are defined as those which are directly or indirectly administered by a public education authority. Private schools/institutions are directly or indirectly administered by a non-governmental organisation (such as a church, trade union, a private business concern or another body).

Context

Education accounts for a significant proportion of public expenditure in all of the EU Member States – the most important budget item being expenditure on staff. The cost of teaching increases significantly as a child moves through the education system, with expenditure per pupil/student considerably higher in universities than in primary schools. Although tertiary education costs more per head, the highest proportion of total education spending is devoted to secondary education systems, as these teach a larger share of the total number of pupils/students.

There is an ongoing debate in many EU Member States as to how to increase or maintain funding for education, improve efficiency and promote equity – a challenge that has become harder in the context of a very severe economic, social and financial crisis and increased public debt. Possible approaches include tuition fees, administrative or examination charges, the introduction of grants or income-contingent loans to try to stimulate enrolment rates in higher education, in particular among the less well-off members of society. Another fundraising source is partnerships between business and higher educational establishments.

Figure 4.5: Public expenditure on education, 2007 (1)
(% of GDP)

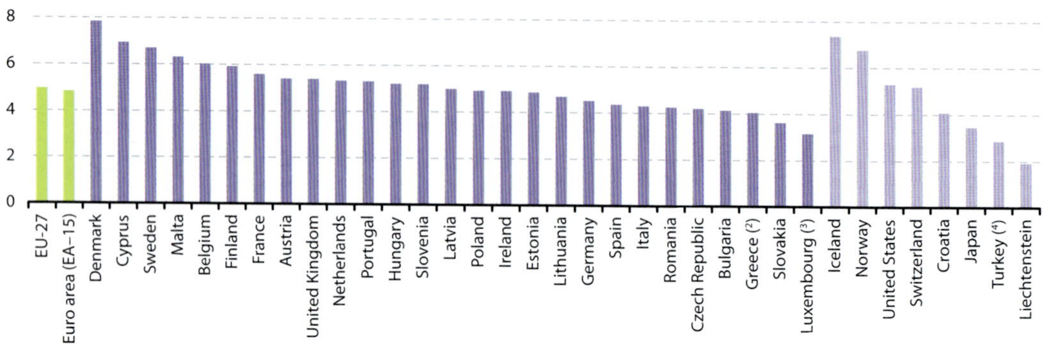

(1) Refer to the Internet metadata file (http://epp.eurostat.ec.europa.eu/cache/ITY_SDDS/en/tsiir010_esms.htm).
(2) 2005.
(3) Excludes tertiary education.
(4) 2006.

Source: Eurostat (tsiir010)

Table 4.5: Expenditure on educational institutions (1)

	Public expenditure (% of GDP)		Private expenditure (% of GDP)		Expenditure on public and private educational institutions per pupil/student (PPS for full-time equivalents)	
	2002	2007	2002	2007	2002	2007
EU-27	5.10	4.96	0.60	0.72	5 307	6 251
Euro area (EA-15)	5.00	4.83	0.58	0.56	5 798	6 709
Belgium	6.10	6.02	0.36	0.34	6 574	7 264
Bulgaria	4.03	4.13	0.69	0.62	1 575	2 290
Czech Republic	4.32	4.20	0.24	0.51	2 947	4 452
Denmark	8.44	7.83	0.28	0.53	7 379	8 595
Germany	4.70	4.50	0.87	0.69	6 058	6 752
Estonia	5.48	4.85	:	0.32	:	3 675
Ireland	4.29	4.90	0.28	0.24	4 940	7 172
Greece (2)	3.57	:	0.17	0.26	3 549	4 485
Spain	4.25	4.35	0.54	0.61	4 850	6 773
France	5.88	5.59	0.56	0.53	6 161	6 928
Italy	4.62	4.29	0.35	0.40	5 736	6 205
Cyprus	6.55	6.93	1.40	1.27	5 495	7 708
Latvia	5.71	5.00	0.82	0.56	2 267	3 666
Lithuania	5.84	4.67	:	0.45	2 012	3 174
Luxembourg (3)	3.79	3.15	:	:	:	:
Hungary (4)	5.38	5.20	0.55	0.54	:	3 995
Malta (5)	4.38	6.31	0.61	0.38	3 448	6 437
Netherlands	5.15	5.32	0.89	0.90	6 780	7 891
Austria	5.72	5.40	0.38	0.48	7 692	8 695
Poland	5.41	4.91	0.64	0.50	2 507	3 226
Portugal	5.54	5.30	0.09	0.46	4 191	5 125
Romania (6)	3.51	4.25	0.16	0.50	:	1 438
Slovenia	5.78	5.19	0.83	0.73	4 930	6 055
Slovakia	4.30	3.62	0.20	0.53	2 032	3 122
Finland	6.21	5.91	0.13	0.14	5 707	6 682
Sweden	7.43	6.69	0.17	0.16	6 743	7 907
United Kingdom	5.11	5.39	0.89	1.75	5 708	7 972
Iceland	6.79	7.36	0.57	0.77	13 162	8 172
Liechtenstein	2.96	1.92	:	:	8 470	7 788
Norway	7.58	6.76	0.26	:	8 555	9 708
Switzerland	5.75	5.18	0.61	0.55	:	:
Croatia	3.72	4.07	0.13	0.35	:	3 742
FYR of Macedonia	3.35	:	:	:	:	:
Turkey (7)	2.82	2.86	0.33	:	:	:
Japan	3.65	3.45	1.21	1.64	6 446	7 752
United States	5.58	5.29	1.90	2.58	9 335	11 785

(1) Refer to the Internet metadata file (http://epp.eurostat.ec.europa.eu/cache/ITY_SDDS/en/educ_esms.htm).
(2) 2005 instead of 2007.
(3) Excludes tertiary education.
(4) Private expenditure and expenditure per pupil/student, 2006 instead of 2007.
(5) Private expenditure and expenditure per pupil/student, break in series.
(6) Expenditure per pupil/student, 2005 instead of 2007
(7) 2006 instead of 2007.

Source: Eurostat (educ_figdp, tps00068 and tps00067), UNESCO, OECD

4.4 Tertiary education

This subchapter presents statistics on tertiary education in the European Union (EU). Tertiary education – provided by universities and other higher education institutions – is the level of education following secondary schooling. The EU-27 has around 4 000 higher education (undergraduate and postgraduate) institutions, with over 19 million students. Some European universities are among the most prestigious in the world. Higher education plays an essential role in society, creating new knowledge, transferring knowledge to students and fostering innovation.

The decade since the introduction of the Bologna process (see the introduction for the chapter on education and training) has brought about a major expansion in higher education systems, accompanied by significant reforms in degree structures and quality assurance systems. However, the financial and economic crisis has affected higher education in different ways, with some countries investing more and others making radical cutbacks in spending.

Main statistical findings

There were 19.0 million students active within tertiary education in the EU-27 in 2008 (see Table 4.6). Five Member States reported more than 2 million tertiary students in 2007, namely the United Kingdom, Germany, Poland, France and Italy; together with Spain these six countries accounted for two thirds of all EU-27 students in tertiary education. Across the EU more than one third (34.4 %) of students in tertiary education were studying social sciences, business or law, with more female than male students in this field of education, as shown in Figure 4.6. The second largest number of students by field of education was in engineering, manufacturing and construction with 14.1 % of the total, with male students accounting for three quarters of the students in this field.

In 2008, the median age of students in tertiary education ranged from 20.6 in France to 22.6 in Latvia, with the Nordic countries of Denmark, Sweden and Finland, as well as Germany and Austria above this range (see Figure 4.7). The age of students in tertiary education can be influenced by a number of factors: whether students postpone starting tertiary education either by choice (for example, by taking a break or a gap year between secondary and tertiary education) or obligation (for example, for military service); the length of the tertiary education courses studied; the extent to which mature students return to tertiary education later in life.

The strategic framework for European cooperation in education and training adopted in May 2009 sets a number of benchmarks, including one for tertiary education, namely that by 2020 the share of 30 to 34-year-olds with tertiary educational attainment should be at least 40 %. Just under one third (32.3 %) of the population aged 30 to 34 in the EU-27 had a tertiary education in 2009, rising to over one third (35.7 %) among women, and falling to 28.9 % among men. In Ireland and Denmark, the overall proportion of 30 to 34-year-olds with tertiary educational attainment was approaching 50 % and for women went beyond this threshold (see Figure 4.8); this was also the case in Norway. In contrast, less than 20 % of the population in this age range had a tertiary education in Romania, the Czech Republic, Slovakia and Italy.

Around 4.2 million students graduated from tertiary education establishments in the EU in 2008. An analysis of the number of graduates by field of education shows that 35.9 % had studied social sciences, business and law; this share was higher than the equivalent share (34.4 %) of tertiary education students still in the process of studying within this field, suggesting that less students had started this type of study in recent years, or that drop-out rates were higher in other fields. A similar situation was observed for engineering, manufacturing and construction, which made up 14.4 % of graduates from 14.1 % of the tertiary student population, as well as in the smaller field of services. The reverse situation was observed for the other fields of education shown in Figures 4.6 and 4.9, most notably for agriculture and veterinary studies, where the proportion of graduates (1.7 %) was lower than corresponding share of the current student population (1.9 %).

Within the EU, female graduates outnumbered male graduates by a ratio of approximately three to two; this ratio reached three to one in health and welfare fields of education. Male graduates outnumbered female graduates slightly in agriculture and veterinary fields, more so in science, mathematics and computing fields, and by close to three to one in engineering, manufacturing and construction fields.

Data sources and availability

The international standard classification of education (ISCED) is used to define levels of education: tertiary education includes both programmes which are largely theoretically based and designed to provide qualifications for entry to advanced research programmes and professions with high skills requirements, as well as programmes which are classified at the same level of competencies but are more occupationally oriented and lead to direct labour market access.

ISCED also classifies the fields of education, with 25 fields of education in all at the 2-digit level, which can be further refined into a 3-digit level. At the highest 1-digit level the following nine broad groups of fields of education are distinguished: general programmes; education; humanities and arts; social sciences, business and law; science; engineering, manufacturing and construction; agriculture; health and welfare; services.

Context

While the Bologna process put in motion a series of reforms to make European higher education more compatible, comparable, competitive and attractive for students, it is only one strand of a broader effort concerning higher education. The modernisation agenda of universities is supported through the implementation of the 7th EU framework programme for research and the competitiveness and innovation programme. Furthermore, to establish synergies between the Bologna process and the Copenhagen process (for enhanced European cooperation in vocational education and training), the European Commission and Member States have established a European qualifications framework for lifelong learning (EQF) – see Subchapter 4.5 on lifelong learning statistics.

At the end of 2007, agreement was reached on establishing a European institute of innovation and technology (EIT). Its aim is to bring together higher education, research and industry through the creation of 'knowledge communities', while it should contribute towards Europe's capacity for innovation.

The integrated economic and employment guidelines were revised most recently as part of the Europe 2020 strategy for smart, sustainable and inclusive growth. Guideline 9 concerns improving the performance of education and training systems at all levels and increasing participation in tertiary education.

The Erasmus programme is one of the most well-known European programmes. Around 4 000 higher education institutions take part in it and some 2.2 million students have already participated in exchanges since it started in 1987. Erasmus became part of the EU's lifelong learning programme in 2007 and was expanded to cover student placements in enterprises, university staff training and teaching for enterprise staff. The programme seeks to expand its mobility actions in the coming years, with a target of 3 million Erasmus students by 2012.

Some of the most recent policy initiatives in this area include efforts to develop links between universities and businesses. In April 2009, the European Commission presented a Communication titled 'A new partnership for the modernisation of universities: the EU forum for university-business dialogue'. The Communication includes proposals to establish a university-business forum as a European platform for dialogue, to enable and stimulate the exchange of good practice, discuss common problems, and work together on possible solutions.

Table 4.6: Students in tertiary education, 2008 (1)

	Total number of students in tertiary education (1 000)	of which, studying (%)						
		Humanities & arts	Social sciences, business & law	Science, math. & computing	Engin., manuf. & construction	Agricul. & veterinary	Health & welfare	Services
EU-27	19 040	12.6	34.4	10.3	14.1	1.9	13.0	4.0
Belgium	402	10.5	29.7	6.6	9.4	2.5	19.7	1.6
Bulgaria	265	7.8	45.0	5.0	19.5	2.4	6.5	7.9
Czech Republic	393	8.7	31.2	10.8	15.7	3.6	10.3	4.9
Denmark	231	15.3	30.4	8.2	9.8	1.5	21.5	2.2
Germany	2 245	15.2	27.5	15.2	15.8	1.5	14.4	3.0
Estonia	68	12.1	40.2	9.6	13.0	2.3	8.2	7.9
Ireland	179	15.7	29.8	12.5	12.8	1.3	15.6	5.2
Greece	638	14.1	31.4	13.6	17.0	5.8	9.2	3.6
Spain	1 781	10.4	31.7	9.9	17.7	1.9	12.3	5.8
France	2 165	15.4	36.1	12.3	13.0	1.2	15.6	3.3
Italy	2 014	13.4	35.1	7.6	15.3	2.1	13.1	2.8
Cyprus	26	10.4	49.5	9.8	7.7	0.1	6.5	7.1
Latvia	128	7.5	53.7	4.8	11.0	1.0	6.9	5.9
Lithuania	205	7.1	44.6	5.5	18.0	2.1	8.6	3.1
Luxembourg	3	12.0	37.1	16.1	8.5	0.0	1.1	1.6
Hungary	414	9.1	40.9	6.9	12.5	2.5	8.9	9.1
Malta	10	17.9	34.9	9.4	7.8	0.5	17.5	1.4
Netherlands	602	8.5	37.3	6.2	8.1	1.1	16.9	6.2
Austria	285	14.4	36.2	11.6	13.9	1.3	9.6	2.1
Poland	2 166	10.1	40.3	8.9	12.4	2.1	6.6	5.9
Portugal	377	8.7	31.9	7.5	22.3	2.1	16.6	5.8
Romania	1 057	8.5	56.0	5.6	16.5	2.2	6.4	3.2
Slovenia	115	8.1	39.3	5.9	18.2	3.3	7.6	9.6
Slovakia	230	6.5	29.3	8.4	15.0	2.6	17.6	5.6
Finland	310	14.6	22.9	10.9	24.9	2.3	14.2	5.0
Sweden	407	13.1	26.1	8.9	15.8	1.0	18.2	2.1
United Kingdom	2 330	16.8	26.5	12.9	8.2	1.0	18.2	1.6
Iceland	17	14.3	37.8	7.6	8.6	0.7	12.6	1.5
Liechtenstein	1	1.3	74.3	0.0	20.4	0.0	4.1	0.0
Norway	213	10.7	31.6	8.5	7.5	0.7	20.0	4.3
Switzerland	225	12.3	36.2	9.9	12.7	1.0	13.7	3.7
Croatia	143	9.5	41.9	7.9	15.4	3.8	7.1	9.9
FYR of Macedonia	66	12.1	39.5	10.7	12.7	2.8	9.5	4.4
Turkey	2 533	6.6	48.8	7.6	13.0	4.1	5.6	3.6
Japan	3 939	15.9	29.2	2.9	15.7	2.3	12.9	5.7
United States	18 248	15.8	29.1	9.0	7.7	0.7	15.8	6.6

(1) Refer to the Internet metadata file (http://epp.eurostat.ec.europa.eu/cache/ITY_SDDS/en/educ_esms.htm).

Source: Eurostat (tps00062 and educ_enrl5)

Figure 4.6: Students in tertiary education, by field of education and gender, EU-27, 2008 (¹)
(1 000)

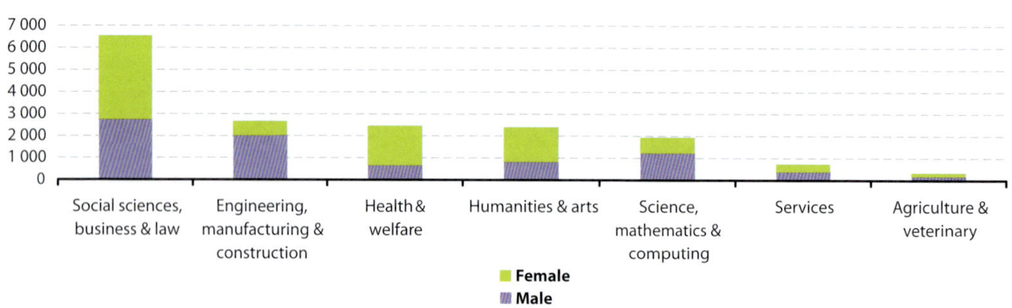

(¹) Refer to the Internet metadata file (http://epp.eurostat.ec.europa.eu/cache/ITY_SDDS/en/educ_esms.htm).

Source: Eurostat (educ_enrl5)

Figure 4.7: Median age in tertiary education, 2008 (¹)
(years)

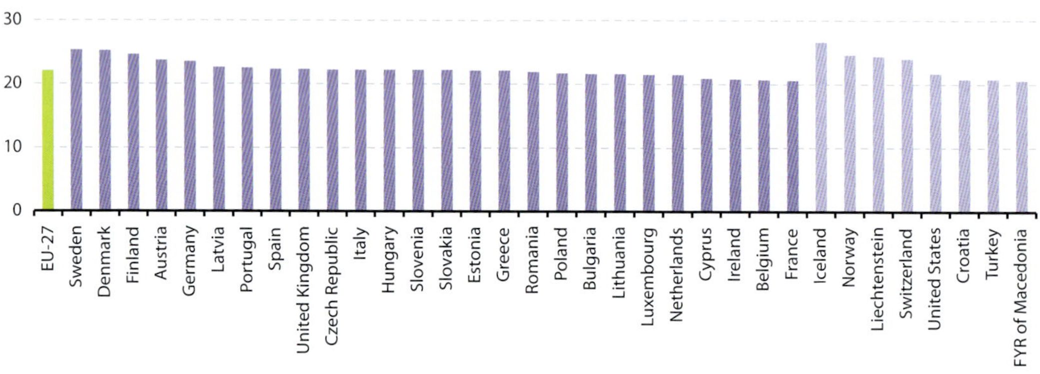

(¹) Malta, not available; refer to the Internet metadata file (http://epp.eurostat.ec.europa.eu/cache/ITY_SDDS/en/educ_esms.htm).

Source: Eurostat (tps00061)

Figure 4.8: Proportion of the population aged 30 to 34 having a tertiary educational attainment, 2009 (1)
(%)

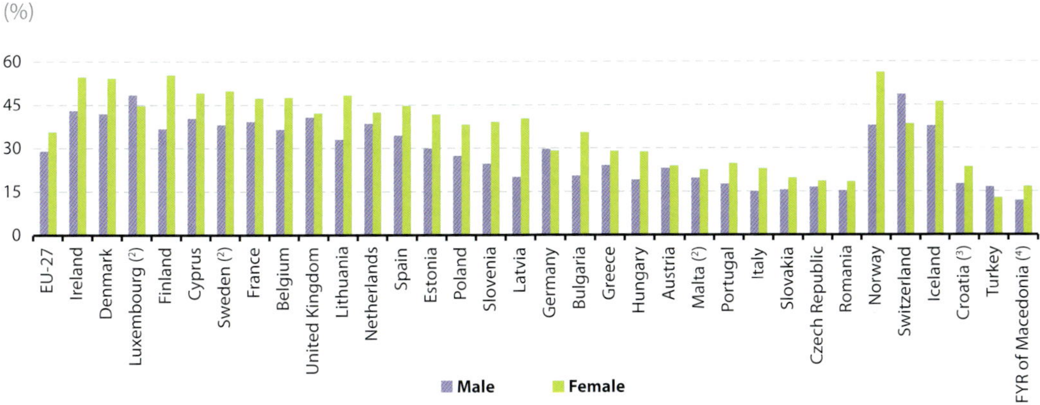

(1) Refer to the Internet metadata file (http://epp.eurostat.ec.europa.eu/cache/ITY_SDDS/en/educ_esms.htm).
(2) Provisional.
(3) Unreliable or uncertain data.
(4) Male proportion: unreliable or uncertain data.

Source: Eurostat (t2020_41)

Figure 4.9: Graduates from tertiary education, by field of education and gender, EU-27, 2008 (1)
(1 000)

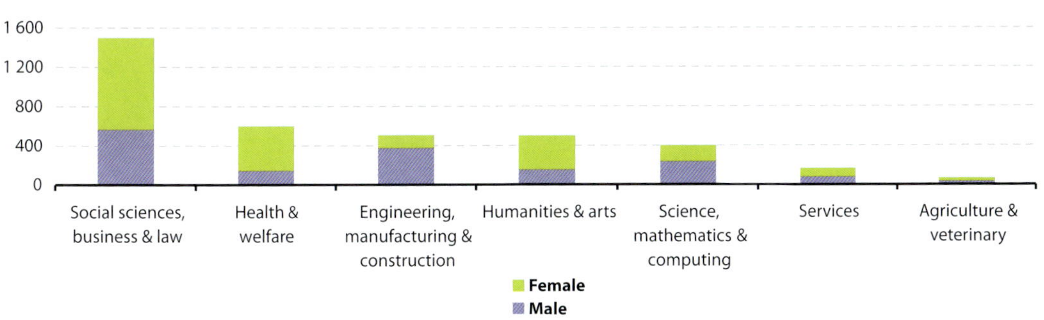

(1) Refer to the Internet metadata file (http://epp.eurostat.ec.europa.eu/cache/ITY_SDDS/en/educ_esms.htm).

Source: Eurostat (educ_grad5)

Table 4.7: Graduates from tertiary education, by field of education, 2008 ([1])

	Total number of graduates from tertiary education (1 000)	of which, studying (%)							
		Humanities & arts	Teaching & training	Social sciences, business & law	Science, math. & computing	Engin., manuf. & construction	Agricul. & veterinary	Health & welfare	Services
EU-27	4 182	12.1	9.8	35.9	9.7	12.2	1.7	14.4	4.1
Belgium	97	11.2	13.0	30.6	5.6	10.2	2.8	20.6	1.4
Bulgaria	55	6.0	6.3	52.7	3.6	14.3	1.8	6.7	8.6
Czech Republic	89	7.2	14.7	31.2	9.4	16.0	3.7	9.0	4.7
Denmark	50	13.0	7.9	31.3	7.1	12.4	2.5	22.5	3.3
Germany	467	17.3	9.2	23.4	13.1	13.2	1.7	18.2	3.4
Estonia	11	11.0	8.3	38.0	10.1	10.5	2.4	10.2	9.6
Ireland	60	21.9	7.3	32.4	13.9	10.5	0.7	11.0	2.1
Greece	67	12.9	8.1	30.0	10.9	14.0	4.1	11.6	8.4
Spain	291	9.0	13.2	27.1	9.2	16.4	1.7	15.3	7.6
France	621	10.7	1.7	41.4	10.6	15.6	1.5	14.5	4.0
Italy	236	17.2	5.4	34.9	6.8	14.8	1.8	14.8	2.9
Cyprus	4	10.0	11.4	46.4	9.4	3.2	0.2	7.5	11.7
Latvia	24	7.1	10.3	55.0	5.1	7.6	0.7	7.9	6.0
Lithuania	43	6.6	13.9	42.6	5.5	15.5	2.0	10.3	3.6
Luxembourg	0	15.1	0.0	48.2	28.7	3.8	0.0	0.0	1.8
Hungary	63	8.4	17.6	41.0	5.9	7.6	2.1	10.4	8.5
Malta	3	16.1	11.4	43.8	8.2	4.6	0.1	14.0	1.7
Netherlands	124	8.7	15.0	37.2	6.3	7.7	1.4	18.1	5.2
Austria	44	9.1	10.6	34.7	10.8	17.8	2.4	11.2	3.7
Poland	558	8.3	17.7	42.3	7.6	8.4	1.8	8.5	5.3
Portugal	84	9.9	8.8	31.3	14.2	21.0	2.5	23.0	6.7
Romania	311	10.3	3.1	58.4	6.4	10.1	1.4	7.2	3.1
Slovenia	17	5.7	8.3	49.9	4.1	13.6	2.5	7.8	8.3
Slovakia	65	6.4	17.0	31.0	7.5	13.3	2.4	17.1	5.3
Finland	60	17.1	7.9	26.1	11.7	15.1	2.3	15.1	4.8
Sweden	60	6.0	18.6	24.6	7.2	17.2	1.2	25.3	2.9
United Kingdom	676	16.2	11.2	30.1	12.7	8.6	0.9	18.2	1.3
Iceland	4	10.7	22.8	37.3	6.5	7.0	0.4	13.7	1.6
Liechtenstein	0	0.0	0.0	78.0	0.0	22.0	0.0	0.0	0.0
Norway	35	8.7	18.0	29.0	7.5	7.7	0.9	23.6	4.5
Switzerland	80	8.2	10.4	38.3	8.7	11.8	1.8	13.8	6.5
Croatia	27	10.1	6.5	38.0	9.2	13.7	3.4	8.0	11.0
FYR of Macedonia	11	13.3	13.6	34.0	8.2	9.5	1.8	10.9	8.8
Turkey	445	6.1	15.1	40.5	8.2	13.7	5.2	5.8	5.3
Japan	1 034	14.9	7.1	26.5	3.0	17.7	2.3	13.1	9.5
United States	2 782	13.1	10.8	38.0	8.4	7.0	1.1	14.8	6.8

([1]) Refer to the Internet metadata file (http://epp.eurostat.ec.europa.eu/cache/ITY_SDDS/en/educ_esms.htm).

Source: Eurostat (educ_grad5)

4.5 Lifelong learning

This subchapter provides an overview of lifelong learning statistics in the European Union (EU), on the basis of data collected by the labour force survey (LFS), supplemented by the adult education survey (AES).

Main statistical findings

The strategic framework for European cooperation in education and training adopted in May 2009 sets a number of benchmarks to be achieved by 2020, including one for lifelong learning, namely that an average of at least 15 % of adults aged 25 to 64 years old should participate in lifelong learning. In 2009, the proportion of persons aged 25 to 64 in the EU receiving some form of education or training in the four weeks preceding the labour force survey was 9.3 %; a share that was unchanged compared with the corresponding share for 2004 (see Table 4.8).

The proportion of the population who had participated in such lifelong learning activities was higher among women (10.2 % in 2009) than among men (8.5 %), and furthermore the share for women had increased compared with 2004. Denmark, Sweden, Finland and the United Kingdom stood out as they reported considerably higher proportions of their respective populations participating in lifelong learning, between one fifth and one third; in contrast, Bulgaria and Romania reported lifelong learning participation rates of less than 2 %.

In addition to the labour force survey, a pilot survey - the adult education survey (AES) - was conducted on a voluntary basis between 2005 and 2008. According to this, a majority of participants took part in non-formal education and training, while most of the education and training undertaken was job-related. Indeed, the main reason given by respondents for their participation in non-formal education and training (see Table 4.9) was to do their job better/improve their career prospects, while getting knowledge or skills relating to interesting subjects and getting useful skills/knowledge for everyday life were also common reasons. The three most commonly cited obstacles to participation in education and training among those who wanted to participate but did not do so were family responsibilities (40.2 % of those not participating), conflict with work schedules (38.7 %) and cost (31.2 %) (see Table 4.10).

Employers were the most common providers of non-formal education and training activities, providing close to two fifths of such activities, as shown in Table 4.11. Employers provided more than two thirds of non-formal education and training in Bulgaria, and half of such activities in the United Kingdom. Among the less common providers used across the EU-27 as a whole, the importance of employers' organisations and chambers of commerce was particularly high in Hungary (32.8 %) and Slovenia (20.8 %), non-commercial institutions (such as libraries) were relatively frequent providers in Finland (29.5 %) and Cyprus (15.5 %), while trade unions provided a higher than average share of non-formal education and training in Hungary (13.1 %).

Data sources and availability

Lifelong learning encompasses all purposeful learning activity, whether formal, non-formal or informal, undertaken on an ongoing basis with the aim of improving knowledge, skills and competence. The intention or aim to learn is the critical point that distinguishes these activities from non-learning activities, such as cultural activities or sports activities. The information collected relates to all subjects whether they are relevant or not for the respondent's current or possible future job.

Within the domain of lifelong learning statistics, formal education corresponds to education and training in the regular system of schools, universities, colleges and other formal educational institutions that normally constitute a continuous 'ladder' of full-time education for children and young people (up to 20 or 25 years of age). Non-formal education is defined as any organised and sustained educational activities that do not correspond to the definition of formal education. Non-formal education may or may not take place in educational institutions and cater to persons of all ages. It may cover educational programmes to impart adult literacy, basic education for out-of-school children, life skills, work skills, and general culture. Note that the statistics presented do not, therefore, cover informal learning, which corresponds to self-learning (through the use of printed material, computer-based learning/training, (Internet) web-based education, visiting libraries, etc).

The target population for lifelong learning statistics refers to all persons in private households aged between 25 and 64 years. Data are collected through the EU's labour force survey (LFS). The denominator used for the ratios devised from LFS data consists of the total population of the same age group, excluding those who did not answer the question concerning participation in education and training.

Additional information is available from an adult education survey which was carried out by EU, EFTA and candidate countries. Surveys have been carried out between 2005 and 2008 as a pilot exercise with a standard questionnaire, covering participation in education and lifelong learning activities whether formal, non-formal or informal, and included job-related activities. The survey also collects information on learning activities, self-reported skills, as well as modules on social and cultural participation. Learning includes activities with the intention to improve an individual's knowledge, skills, and competences. Intentional learning (as opposed to random learning) is defined as a deliberate search for knowledge, skills, competences, or attitudes of lasting value. Organised learning is defined as learning planned in a pattern or sequence with explicit or implicit aims.

Context

Lifelong learning can take place in a variety of environments, both inside and outside formal education and training systems. Lifelong learning implies investing in people and knowledge; promoting the acquisition of basic skills, including digital literacy and broadening opportunities for innovative, more flexible forms of learning. The aim is to provide people of all ages with equal and open access to high-quality learning opportunities, and to a variety of learning experiences.

The integrated economic and employment guidelines were revised most recently as part of the Europe 2020 strategy for smart, sustainable and inclusive growth. Guideline 8 concerns developing a skilled workforce responding to labour market needs, and promoting job quality and lifelong learning.

The Copenhagen process, established in 2002, lays out the basis for cooperation in vocational education and training (VET), with 32 European countries involved. In June 2010, the European Commission presented a ten year vision for the future of vocational education and training in a Communication titled 'A new impetus for European cooperation in vocational education and training to support the Europe 2020 strategy' (COM(2010) 296 final).

There are a number of initiatives under development to enhance the transparency, recognition and quality of competences and qualifications, facilitating the mobility of learners and workers. These include the European Qualifications Framework (EQF), Europass, the European Credit System for VET (ECVET), and the European Quality Assurance Reference Framework for VET (EQAVET). The launch of EQF aims to help employers and individuals compare qualifications across the EU's diverse education and training systems: it encourages countries to relate their national qualifications systems to the EQF so that all new qualifications issued from 2012 carry a reference to an appropriate EQF level. The EQF also represents a shift in European education as it is based on an approach which takes into account learning outcomes rather than the resources which are put into learning. In other words, it is a qualifications framework based on what learners are actually able to do at the end of a course of education, rather than where the learning took place and how long it took.

The Leonardo da Vinci programme in the field of vocational education and training is designed to encourage projects which give individuals the chance to improve their competences, knowledge and skills through a period spent abroad, as well as to encourage Europe-wide cooperation between training organisations.

The Grundtvig programme was launched in 2000 and now forms part of the lifelong learning programme. It aims to provide adults with ways of improving their knowledge and skills. It not only covers learners in adult education, but also the teachers, trainers, education staff and facilities that provide these services.

Table 4.8: Lifelong learning (1)
(% of the population aged 25 to 64 participating in education and training)

	Total		Male		Female	
	2004	2009	2004	2009	2004	2009
EU-27	9.3	*9.3*	8.7	*8.5*	10.0	*10.2*
Euro area (EA-16)	7.3	*8.1*	7.2	*7.7*	7.5	*8.5*
Belgium	8.6	6.8	8.7	6.4	8.5	7.2
Bulgaria	1.3	1.4	1.2	1.3	1.3	1.5
Czech Republic	5.8	6.8	5.5	6.5	6.0	7.0
Denmark	25.6	31.6	22.1	25.6	29.1	37.6
Germany	7.4	7.8	7.8	7.8	7.0	7.7
Estonia	6.4	10.5	5.1	7.6	7.5	13.2
Ireland	6.1	6.3	5.1	5.7	7.1	7.0
Greece	1.8	3.3	1.8	3.2	1.8	3.3
Spain (2)	4.7	10.4	4.2	9.6	5.1	11.3
France	7.1	6.0	7.0	5.6	7.1	6.4
Italy	6.3	6.0	5.9	5.6	6.7	6.4
Cyprus (2)	9.3	7.8	9.0	7.8	9.6	7.8
Latvia	8.4	5.3	5.7	3.6	10.8	6.9
Lithuania	5.9	4.5	4.2	3.6	7.4	5.4
Luxembourg (2)	9.8	13.4	9.5	13.4	10.1	13.5
Hungary	4.0	2.7	3.4	2.5	4.6	3.0
Malta	4.3	5.8	4.8	5.6	3.8	6.0
Netherlands	16.4	17.0	16.1	16.5	16.8	17.5
Austria	11.6	13.8	10.9	12.8	12.2	14.7
Poland	5.0	4.7	4.3	4.3	5.7	5.1
Portugal	4.3	6.5	4.1	6.2	4.4	6.8
Romania	1.4	1.5	1.3	1.3	1.4	1.6
Slovenia	16.2	14.6	14.8	12.9	17.6	16.4
Slovakia	4.3	2.8	3.8	2.2	4.8	3.3
Finland	22.8	22.1	19.2	18.5	26.4	25.9
Sweden (2)	:	*22.2*	:	*16.1*	:	*28.5*
United Kingdom (2)	29.0	20.1	24.9	16.8	33.1	23.3
Iceland	24.2	25.1	19.6	20.4	28.9	30.0
Norway	17.4	18.1	16.3	16.8	18.6	19.5
Switzerland	28.6	24.0	29.7	22.8	27.4	25.2
Croatia (3)	1.9	2.3	1.8	2.4	2.0	2.1
FYR of Macedonia	:	3.3	:	3.2	:	3.4
Turkey	1.1	2.3	1.5	2.4	0.8	2.1

(1) Refer to the Internet metadata file (http://epp.eurostat.ec.europa.eu/cache/ITY_SDDS/en/lfsi_edu_a_esms.htm).
(2) Break in series, 2007.
(3) 2009 male and female rates, unreliable or uncertain data.

Source: Eurostat (tsiem080)

Table 4.9: Reasons for participation in non-formal education and training, 2007 (¹)
(%)

	To get knowledge/ skills relating to interesting subjects	To get knowledge/ skills useful for everyday life	To increase possibility of getting a job/ changing job	To be obliged to participate	To be less likely to lose job	Do job better/ improve career prospects	Meet new people, for fun	Obtain qualification	Start own business	Other/ no resp.
Belgium	38.7	29.8	9.2	24.1	3.3	64.4	11.8	8.1	2.6	1.9
Bulgaria	38.5	40.0	20.8	22.1	22.0	77.3	9.2	34.3	1.8	1.2
Czech Republic	46.2	33.7	16.8	7.4	13.3	54.6	10.4	20.8	4.5	0.5
Denmark	:	:	:	:	:	:	:	:	:	:
Germany	45.9	14.3	15.6	25.0	19.9	68.0	10.5	11.6	3.8	5.4
Estonia	21.1	17.6	5.8	24.9	15.1	80.2	2.4	8.8	1.6	5.5
Ireland	:	:	:	:	:	:	:	:	:	:
Greece	76.7	52.4	25.5	18.1	16.0	74.8	20.6	48.6	7.9	4.3
Spain	66.6	50.8	28.4	11.8	12.7	68.4	11.8	25.0	4.8	5.0
France	:	:	:	:	:	:	:	:	:	:
Italy	43.9	20.9	10.9	13.8	2.5	47.6	13.3	13.5	2.6	3.9
Cyprus	64.3	38.2	8.7	16.9	2.1	53.6	14.7	13.3	1.6	4.4
Latvia	43.8	58.6	17.8	33.7	27.7	74.7	24.3	37.8	4.4	1.8
Lithuania	50.6	42.3	17.5	26.2	31.3	77.5	11.8	41.4	3.4	3.2
Luxembourg	:	:	:	:	:	:	:	:	:	:
Hungary	56.0	52.0	33.3	51.4	38.3	67.8	13.2	35.2	7.5	1.3
Malta	:	:	:	:	:	:	:	:	:	:
Netherlands	42.4	40.2	12.8	35.9	6.6	66.4	19.2	23.7	4.2	10.1
Austria	57.4	57.2	16.2	23.7	10.5	67.1	20.9	10.7	4.6	5.1
Poland	7.6	7.2	7.2	5.2	6.6	67.1	0.5	7.2	1.4	2.8
Portugal	80.5	81.6	31.8	12.2	16.0	69.9	23.7	47.4	6.6	6.2
Romania	:	:	:	:	:	:	:	:	:	:
Slovenia	12.5	21.2	1.7	13.1	1.0	54.4	1.8	2.3	0.3	2.5
Slovakia	34.6	30.2	23.1	66.1	26.5	63.1	8.8	19.2	4.6	1.8
Finland	62.1	41.1	16.1	35.3	14.3	69.1	30.0	13.5	3.7	9.4
Sweden	59.3	41.8	6.5	36.4	8.0	61.8	20.8	8.9	1.5	5.5
United Kingdom	82.0	44.8	18.1	57.7	2.8	55.0	9.7	33.9	9.3	86.1
Norway	67.9	33.2	9.6	43.1	12.7	71.8	16.0	18.3	1.5	7.2
Croatia	45.4	35.9	17.3	31.7	17.6	78.1	8.3	15.3	4.9	1.4

(¹) Multiple answers allowed; Bulgaria, the Czech Republic, Greece, Spain, Cyprus, Portugal, Finland and the United Kingdom did not interview participants taking part in guided on the job training; refer to the Internet metadata file (http://epp.eurostat.ec.europa.eu/cache/ITY_SDDS/en/trng_aes_esms.htm).

Source: Eurostat (trng_aes_142)

Table 4.10: Obstacles to participation in education and training, 2007 (1)
(%)

	Health or age	None within reachable distance	No time due to family	Did not have the pre-requis-ites	Too expen-sive, could not afford	Did not like idea of going back to school	Lack of em-ployer support	Conflict with work schedule	Other/ no resp.
EU	14.8	20.8	40.2	15.6	31.2	14.9	18.4	38.7	26.8
Belgium	21.8	13.1	38.4	9.5	17.9	4.8	14.7	33.1	10.6
Bulgaria	11.5	29.7	28.8	16.3	56.7	6.2	11.6	24.1	7.7
Czech Republic	11.9	16.1	38.5	7.8	19.7	2.1	22.5	36.8	3.6
Denmark	:	:	:	:	:	:	:	:	:
Germany	12.1	24.9	33.9	24.1	43.7	11.1	32.8	36.9	13.3
Estonia	18.2	34.5	38.8	2.9	53.1	8.5	8.8	32.6	42.6
Ireland	:	:	:	:	:	:	:	:	:
Greece	10.5	19.1	48.3	7.5	33.4	9.7	9.7	43.0	19.0
Spain	5.8	8.5	41.2	7.5	13.4	2.7	4.7	32.5	27.7
France	:	:	:	:	:	:	:	:	:
Italy	19.7	16.8	49.5	19.2	26.2	16.6	15.2	44.1	12.4
Cyprus	9.3	12.0	67.9	5.2	16.2	4.8	5.2	42.1	12.3
Latvia	11.9	24.1	40.1	11.2	50.8	11.9	29.7	36.8	11.4
Lithuania	13.2	19.6	34.3	3.2	45.6	4.9	16.2	48.4	13.5
Luxembourg	:	:	:	:	:	:	:	:	:
Hungary	12.5	32.4	37.5	13.9	42.3	18.9	39.9	53.2	15.0
Malta	:	:	:	:	:	:	:	:	:
Netherlands	23.8	13.0	29.9	4.2	25.1	13.5	20.1	17.6	22.8
Austria	6.3	22.4	42.3	7.1	34.6	2.8	16.1	39.5	15.8
Poland	9.1	31.0	29.2	9.2	61.3	17.5	20.4	31.4	11.5
Portugal	6.8	34.2	34.5	11.8	22.7	4.1	20.0	26.5	18.9
Romania	:	:	:	:	:	:	:	:	:
Slovenia	*15.5*	*30.2*	*37.7*	*7.6*	*48.5*	*7.3*	*22.3*	*55.5*	*8.8*
Slovakia	10.8	30.9	35.5	56.5	39.3	3.0	25.2	40.7	3.7
Finland	17.1	25.6	31.0	11.6	22.2	7.2	24.0	43.7	21.4
Sweden	23.7	22.0	23.0	5.8	32.5	6.9	19.1	32.4	20.5
United Kingdom	17.0	25.9	42.5	20.8	33.8	24.1	22.6	43.9	56.5
Norway	19.5	13.6	25.8	4.3	17.6	9.2	21.1	32.2	15.7
Croatia	11.0	26.7	48.7	14.9	53.8	4.2	17.1	28.8	8.6

(1) Multiple answers allowed; Denmark, Ireland, France, Luxembourg, Malta and Romania are not included in the EU average; refer to the Internet metadata file (http://epp.eurostat.ec.europa.eu/cache/ITY_SDDS/en/trng_aes_esms.htm).

Source: Eurostat (trng_aes_176)

Table 4.11: Providers of non-formal education and training activities, 2007 (1)
(%)

	Em-ployer	Non-formal educ. & train-ing instit.	Formal educ. instit.	Comm. Instit. where educ. & training is not main activity	Em-ployers' org., chamber of com-merce	Non-comm. instit. (e.g. library)	Non-profit assoc.	Individ.	Trade union	Other
EU	38.3	16.5	10.4	8.9	5.0	4.5	4.3	4.3	1.4	4.0
Belgium	41.7	7.3	15.2	8.9	2.8	7.1	7.4	5.6	0.7	0.6
Bulgaria	68.8	14.1	3.1	3.1	3.0	5.8	0.7	1.1	0.2	0.2
Czech Republic	42.9	27.9	10.7	7.6	1.8	2.1	1.5	3.2	0.6	1.1
Denmark	:	:	:	:	:	:	:	:	:	
Germany	42.4	14.7	4.8	13.8	4.8	6.2	5.3	5.8	1.1	0.5
Estonia	29.2	34.4	10.0	9.4	1.2	3.9	2.1	2.5	5.5	1.7
Ireland	:	:	:	:	:	:	:	:	:	
Greece	36.0	12.1	14.6	13.6	3.3	5.2	3.2	1.4	2.3	4.8
Spain	19.9	26.2	9.7	5.0	6.7	4.5	5.4	2.9	4.2	11.5
France	*25.4*	*2.9*	*1.9*	*6.3*	:	:	:	*1.7*	:	*60.2*
Italy	27.6	8.5	12.9	8.0	12.9	2.2	4.4	6.3	1.3	11.3
Cyprus	27.1	19.3	5.4	10.1	1.3	15.5	7.1	12.9	0.9	0.3
Latvia	42.6	21.3	13.4	6.8	2.7	1.6	2.2	2.1	0.2	5.2
Lithuania	14.5	28.7	20.8	15.0	9.2	:	1.4	8.7	0.4	:
Luxembourg	:	:	:	:	:	:	:	:	:	
Hungary	0.6	32.0	7.0	3.5	32.8	6.2	0.1	1.9	13.1	2.7
Malta	:	:	:	:	:	:	:	:	:	
Netherlands	38.6	:	38.2	:	:	:	4.7	2.1	1.9	11.8
Austria	27.7	21.8	6.7	12.4	4.6	1.4	4.9	4.5	0.3	14.2
Poland	20.8	49.9	13.1	6.1	1.7	:	2.2	3.8	0.2	2.1
Portugal	40.7	20.9	9.1	8.4	2.3	4.5	5.5	1.4	1.4	5.8
Romania	:	:	:	:	:	:	:	:	:	
Slovenia	11.8	44.6	8.7	8.0	20.8	:	3.9	1.9	0.3	:
Slovakia	40.0	28.2	17.0	7.5	2.8	:	0.7	1.8	0.1	1.1
Finland	36.0	10.1	8.8	1.1	6.7	29.5	0.8	3.0	3.0	:
Sweden	45.5	14.6	4.2	17.1	3.9	3.4	5.6	2.5	2.0	0.5
United Kingdom	50.2	8.2	11.1	:	7.0	1.8	1.9	4.3	0.1	5.4
Croatia	22.0	24.2	15.6	12.8	5.0	1.6	3.3	0.8	0.4	7.7
Turkey	26.4	27.0	7.3	3.2	2.8	25.4	3.8	3.6	0.4	:

(1) Denmark, Ireland, France, Luxembourg, Malta and Romania are not included in the EU average; refer to the Internet metadata file (http://epp.eurostat.ec.europa.eu/cache/ITY_SDDS/en/trng_aes_esms.htm).

Source: Eurostat (trng_aes_170)

5 Labour market

Labour market statistics measure the involvement of individuals, households and businesses in the labour market, where the former mainly appear offering their labour in return for remuneration while the latter act as employers. The market outcomes – for example employment, unemployment, vacant posts, wage levels, labour cost – heavily affect not only the economy, but directly the personal life of virtually every citizen. Eurostat statistics cover both the supply and the demand side as well as policy interventions on the labour market. Data is collected on short-term and structural aspects, in monetary and non-monetary terms.

Labour market statistics are at the heart of many European Union (EU) policies following the introduction of an employment chapter into the Amsterdam Treaty in 1997. The European employment strategy (EES) seeks to create more and better jobs throughout the EU. A central element of the EES under the Lisbon objectives was the employment policy guidelines as part of an integrated approach based on three pillars: macro-economic policies, micro-economic reforms and employment policies.

The financial and economic crisis has however reversed much of the progress achieved in Europe since 2000. The Europe 2020 strategy for smart, sustainable and inclusive growth put forward by the European Commission is the EU's growth strategy for the coming decade. As part of the flagship initiatives, 'An agenda for new skills and jobs' and 'Youth on the move', (youth) unemployment rates will be targeted through a range of policies, including proposals aimed at education and training institutions, or measures for the creation of a (work) environment conducive to higher activity rates and higher labour productivity. There are also initiatives aimed at improving the entry rate of young people into the labour market. To measure progress in meeting the Europe 2020 goals, five headline targets to be met by 2020 have been agreed; these are to be translated into national targets in each EU Member State, reflecting different situations and circumstances. One of these targets is that 75 % of 20 to 64 year-olds should be employed in the EU by 2020. The integrated economic and employment guidelines were also revised as part of the Europe 2020 strategy.

5.1 Employment

Labour market statistics are at the heart of many European Union (EU) policies following the introduction of an employment chapter into the Amsterdam Treaty in 1997. The employment rate, in other words the proportion of working age population in employment, is a key social indicator. This subchapter provides information on recent EU employment statistics, including an analysis based on important socio-economic dimensions: employment statistics show significant differences by gender, age and educational level attained, and there is also considerable variation across EU Member States and regions within these Member States.

Main statistical findings

Total employment rate – differences by gender, age and educational attainment level

The EU-27 employment rate for persons aged 15 to 64, as measured by the European Union labour force survey (EU LFS), decreased in 2009 to 64.6 %, down from 65.9 % in 2008. This decrease of 1.3 percentage points was the first time that the EU-27 employment rate decreased since Eurostat started to estimate this indicator; the EU-27 employment rate had stood at 61.2 % in 1998 (the first year data are available for this series).

The Lisbon European Council in 2000 set a target of 70 % for the employment rate that was to be achieved by 2010. In 2009, employment rates above 70 % were recorded in five of the Member States (the Netherlands, Denmark, Sweden, Austria and Germany). In contrast, employment rates below 60 % were recorded in Malta, Hungary, Italy, Romania, Poland and Spain.

Employment rates vary considerably not only across but also within the Member States according to regional patterns, with a relatively high dispersion (17.4 %) observed across Italy (as measured by the coefficient of variation for regions at the NUTS 2 level) in 2009. In contrast, there was relatively little divergence in employment rates across the regions of Greece, Austria, Portugal, Sweden, the Netherlands or Denmark (all below 4 %). The dispersion of regional employment across the whole of the EU-27 declined, as the coefficient of variation fell from 12.1 % to 11.8 % between 2004 and 2009.

Employment rates are generally lower among women and older workers. In

2009, the employment rate for men reached 70.7 % in the EU-27, as compared with 58.6 % for women. These values may be compared with the data for 2008, when employment rates stood at 72.8 % and 59.1 % respectively. The values recorded in 2009 exceed those of 1998 (when the series starts), considerably for women (52.0 % in 1998) and marginally for men (70.3 % in 1998). The Lisbon European Council set a target for the female employment rate of 60 % by 2010. There were 14 Member States which recorded employment rates for women above this 60 % threshold in 2009, with the ratio exceeding 70 % in Denmark, Sweden and the Netherlands.

The EU-27 employment rate for older workers (aged between 55 and 64) reached 46.0 % in 2009, compared with 45.6 % in 2008; it was considerably higher than its corresponding rate for 2001 (40.0 %). The Stockholm European Council of 2001 set a target employment rate for older workers of 50 % by 2010; in 2009 there were 11 Member States that had either reached or exceeded this rate. The highest employment rates for older workers were recorded in Sweden (70.0 %) and Estonia (60.4 %).

Employment rates vary considerably according to levels of educational attainment: for statistics on education level attainment, the age group 25 to 64 is used instead of 15 to 64. The employment rate of those aged 25 to 64 who had completed a tertiary education was 84.5 % across the EU-27 in 2009, much higher than the rate (54.7 %) for those who had attained a primary or lower secondary education. The EU-27 employment rate of persons with a medium level of educational attainment was 73.7 %.

Part-time and fixed-term contracts

The proportion of the EU-27 workforce reporting that their main job was part-time increased steadily from 15.9 % in 1998 to 18.8 % by 2009. The highest proportion of part-time workers was found in the Netherlands (48.3 % in 2009), followed by Sweden, the United Kingdom, Germany and Denmark, where part-time work accounted in each case for over a quarter (26-27 %) of those in employment. In contrast, part-time employment was relatively uncommon in Bulgaria (2.3 % of employment) and Slovakia (3.6 %).

The incidence of part-time work differs significantly between men and women. A little less than one third (31.5 %) of women employed in the EU-27 worked on a part-time basis in 2009, a much higher proportion than the corresponding figure for men (8.3 %). Three quarters (75.8 %) of all women employed in the Netherlands worked on a part-time basis in 2009, by far the highest rate among the Member States [3].

The share of employees with a contract of limited duration (fixed-term employment) was 13.4 % in the EU-27 in 2009, down from 14.0 % in 2008 and 14.5 % in 2007. More than one in four employees had a temporary contract in Spain and Poland in 2009, and the proportion was more than one in five in Portugal. Among the remaining Member States, the share of employees working on a contract of limited duration ranged from 18.0 % in the Netherlands, down to just 1.0 % in Romania. The considerable range in

[3] Anyone working fewer than 35 hours a week is considered as working part-time in the Netherlands.

the propensity to use limited duration contracts between Member States may, at least to some degree, reflect national practices, the supply and demand of labour, and the ease with which employers can hire or fire.

Data sources and availability

Source statistics

The main data source for labour market statistics is the European Union labour force survey (EU LFS); another frequently used source for employment statistics is national accounts. Both of these sources use similar employment definitions based on international standards from the International Labour Organization (ILO) and the system of national accounts, respectively. A third source for information on employment statistics is that of enterprise statistics.

The data source for all of the information presented in this subchapter is the EU LFS, except for the information on employment growth, which is based on national accounts. National accounts publish employment estimates with no age thresholds, nor socio-demographic breakdowns, which makes data more suitable for an analysis of employment as a labour input to production activities, rather than as a social phenomenon.

The EU LFS is a quarterly sample survey covering the population in private households in the EU, EFTA (except Liechtenstein) and the candidate countries. It provides annual ([4]) and quarterly results in relation to the labour participation of persons aged 15 and over. The EU LFS collects information on labour force status (all persons being either in employment, unemployed or economically inactive), employment characteristics, working time, job search among the unemployed, levels of education, recent education and training, as well as each individuals' demographic background and family composition.

The EU LFS sample size amounts to approximately 1.5 million individuals each quarter. The quarterly sampling rates vary between 0.2 % and 3.3 % in each country. Eurostat started the collection of LFS micro data in 1983 with one reference quarter per year (usually the spring). During the period from 1998 to 2005 the survey underwent a transition to a continuous quarterly survey; all 27 Member States now provide quarterly results.

Definition of employment and main employment characteristics

The economically active population (labour force) comprises employed and unemployed persons. The EU LFS defines persons in employment as those aged 15 and over, who, during the reference week, performed some work, even for just one hour per week, for pay, profit or family gain. It also includes people who were not at work but had a job or business from which they were temporarily absent, for example, because of illness, holidays, industrial disputes, education or training.

Employment can be measured in terms of the number of persons or jobs, in full-time equivalents or in hours worked. All the estimates presented use the number of persons; the information presented for employment rates is also built on

([4]) For Switzerland only spring LFS results (quarter 2) are available and used as annual estimates in the respective tables and figures.

estimates for the number of persons. Employment statistics are frequently reported as employment rates to discount the changing size of countries' populations over time and to facilitate comparisons between countries of different sizes. They are typically published for the working age population, which is generally considered to be those between 15 and 64 years old within the EU-27 Member States, although the age range of 16 to 64 is used in Italy, Spain, Sweden (only until 2001) and the United Kingdom, as well as in Iceland; this age group (15 to 64 years) is also a standard used by other international statistical organisations.

Annual employment growth gives the change, in percentage terms, from one year to another of the total number of persons employed on the economic territory of the country or the geographical area; the data source for employment growth is national accounts.

Some main employment characteristics, as defined by the EU LFS, include:

- employees are defined as those who work for a public or private employer and who receive compensation in the form of wages, salaries, payment by results, or payment in kind; non-conscript members of the armed forces are also included.
- self-employed persons work in their own business, farm or professional practice. A self-employed person is considered to be working during the reference week if she/he meets one of the following criteria: works for the purpose of earning profit; spends time on the operation of a business; or is currently establishing a business.
- a full-time/part-time distinction in the main job is declared by the respondent, except in Germany, Ireland and the Netherlands, where thresholds for usual hours worked are used.
- indicators for employed persons with a second job refer only to people with more than one job at the same time; people having changed job during the reference week are not counted as having two jobs.
- an employee is considered as having a temporary job if employer and employee agree that its end is determined by objective conditions, such as a specific date, the completion of an assignment, or the return of an employee who is temporarily replaced. Typical cases include: people in seasonal employment; people engaged by an agency or employment exchange and hired to a third party to perform a specific task (unless there is a written work contract of unlimited duration); people with specific training contracts.

The dispersion of regional (NUTS level 2) employment rates shows regional differences in employment within countries and between groups of countries. This measure is zero when employment rates across all regions are identical, and will rise as the differences between regional employment rates increase. The indicator is not applicable for several countries as these comprise only one or two NUTS level 2 regions. However, the employment rates of these countries (regions) are used to compute the indicator at a European level.

Context

Employment statistics can be used for a number of different analyses, including macro-economic (in other words, labour as a production factor),productivity or competitiveness studies. They can also be used to study a range of social and behavioural aspects related to an individual's employment situation, such as the social integration of minorities, or employment as the source of a household's income.

Employment is both a structural indicator and a short-term indicator. As a structural indicator, it may shed light on the structure of labour markets and economic systems, as measured through the balance of labour supply and demand, or the quality of employment. As a short-term indicator, employment follows the business cycle; however, it has limits in this respect, as employment is often referred to as a lagging indicator.

Employment statistics are at the heart of many EU policies. The European employment strategy (EES) was launched at the Luxembourg jobs summit in November 1997 and was revamped in 2005 to align the EU's employment strategy more closely to a set of revised Lisbon objectives. In July 2008, the European Council updated its employment policy guidelines for the period 2008 to 2010; these guidelines included the aims of achieving full employment, improving quality and productivity at work, and strengthening economic, social and territorial cohesion. In March 2010, the European Commission launched the Europe 2020 strategy for smart, sustainable and inclusive growth; this was formally adopted by the European Council in June 2010. The European Council agreed on five headline targets, the first being to raise the employment rate for women and men aged 20 to 64 years old to 75 % by 2020. Member States may set their own national targets in the light of these headline targets and will draw up national reform programmes that will include the actions they aim to undertake in order to implement the strategy. The European Commission will further develop and submit to the European Council a range of actions that it proposes to take for the EU as a whole, notably through a series of flagship initiatives. The implementation of the strategy might be achieved, at least in part, through the promotion of flexible working conditions – for example, part-time work or work from home – which are thought to stimulate labour participation. Other initiatives that may encourage more people to enter the labour market include improvements in the availability of childcare facilities, providing more opportunities for lifelong learning, or facilitating job mobility within the EU. Central to this theme is the issue of 'flexicurity': policies that simultaneously address the flexibility of labour markets, work organisation and labour relations, while taking into account the reconciliation of work and private life, employment security and social protection.

Figure 5.1: Employment rate, age group 15-64, 2009
(%)

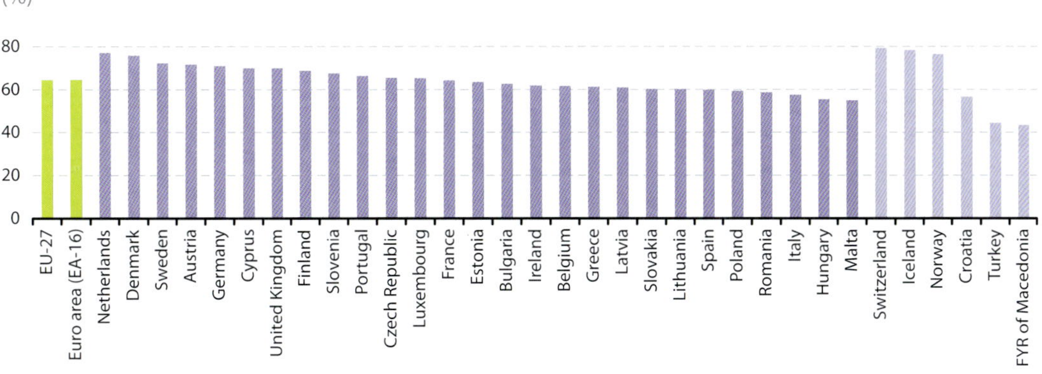

Source: Eurostat (lfsi_emp_a)

Figure 5.2: Dispersion of regional employment rates ([1])
(coefficient of variation of employment rates (of the age group 15-64) across regions
(NUTS 2 level))

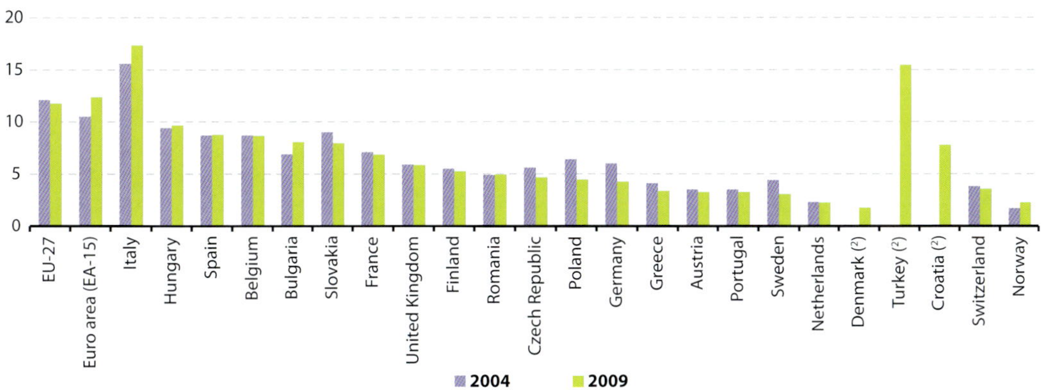

([1]) At the NUTS 2 level: Estonia, Cyprus, Latvia, Lithuania, Luxembourg and Malta are treated as one region, as was Denmark in 2004; Ireland and Slovenia have only two regions; for non-member countries statistical regions equivalent to NUTS level 2 are used.
([2]) 2004, not available.

Source: Eurostat (tsisc050)

Figure 5.3: Employment rates by gender, 2009 (1)
(%)

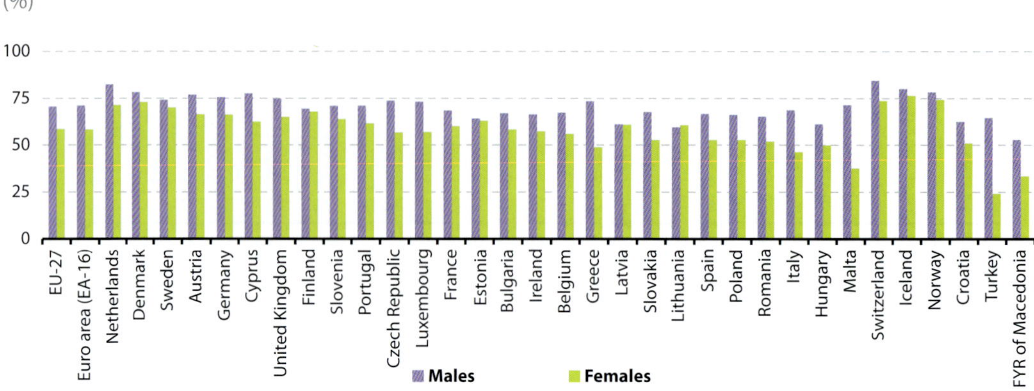

(1) The figure is ranked on the average of employment rates for males and females.

Source: Eurostat (lfsi_emp_a)

Table 5.1: Employment rate, age group 15-64
(%)

	1999	2000	2001	2002	2003	2004	2005	2006	2007	2008	2009
EU-27	61.8	62.2	62.6	62.4	62.6	63.0	63.5	64.5	65.4	65.9	64.6
Euro area (EA-16)	60.4	61.4	62.1	62.3	62.6	63.1	63.7	64.6	65.6	66.0	64.7
Belgium	59.3	60.5	59.9	59.9	59.6	60.3	61.1	61.0	62.0	62.4	61.6
Bulgaria	:	50.4	49.7	50.6	52.5	54.2	55.8	58.6	61.7	64.0	62.6
Czech Republic	65.6	65.0	65.0	65.4	64.7	64.2	64.8	65.3	66.1	66.6	65.4
Denmark	76.0	76.3	76.2	75.9	75.1	75.7	75.9	77.4	77.1	78.1	75.7
Germany (1)	65.2	65.6	65.8	65.4	65.0	65.0	66.0	67.5	69.4	70.7	70.9
Estonia	61.5	60.4	61.0	62.0	62.9	63.0	64.4	68.1	69.4	69.8	63.5
Ireland	63.3	65.2	65.8	65.5	65.5	66.3	67.6	68.7	69.2	67.6	61.8
Greece	55.9	56.5	56.3	57.5	58.7	59.4	60.1	61.0	61.4	61.9	61.2
Spain (1)	53.8	56.3	57.8	58.5	59.8	61.1	63.3	64.8	65.6	64.3	59.8
France	60.9	62.1	62.8	63.0	64.0	63.8	63.7	63.7	64.3	64.9	64.2
Italy (2)	52.7	53.7	54.8	55.5	56.1	57.6	57.6	58.4	58.7	58.7	57.5
Cyprus	:	65.7	67.8	68.6	69.2	68.9	68.5	69.6	71.0	70.9	69.9
Latvia	58.8	57.5	58.6	60.4	61.8	62.3	63.3	66.3	68.3	68.6	60.9
Lithuania	61.7	59.1	57.5	59.9	61.1	61.2	62.6	63.6	64.9	64.3	60.1
Luxembourg	61.7	62.7	63.1	63.4	62.2	62.5	63.6	63.6	64.2	63.4	65.2
Hungary	55.6	56.3	56.2	56.2	57.0	56.8	56.9	57.3	57.3	56.7	55.4
Malta	:	54.2	54.3	54.4	54.2	54.0	53.9	53.6	54.6	55.3	54.9
Netherlands	71.7	72.9	74.1	74.4	73.6	73.1	73.2	74.3	76.0	77.2	77.0
Austria (2)	68.6	68.5	68.5	68.7	68.9	67.8	68.6	70.2	71.4	72.1	71.6
Poland	57.6	55.0	53.4	51.5	51.2	51.7	52.8	54.5	57.0	59.2	59.3
Portugal	67.4	68.4	69.0	68.8	68.1	67.8	67.5	67.9	67.8	68.2	66.3
Romania (3)	63.2	63.0	62.4	57.6	57.6	57.7	57.6	58.8	58.8	59.0	58.6
Slovenia	62.2	62.8	63.8	63.4	62.6	65.3	66.0	66.6	67.8	68.6	67.5
Slovakia	58.1	56.8	56.8	56.8	57.7	57.0	57.7	59.4	60.7	62.3	60.2
Finland	66.4	67.2	68.1	68.1	67.7	67.6	68.4	69.3	70.3	71.1	68.7
Sweden (1)	71.7	73.0	74.0	73.6	72.9	72.1	72.5	73.1	74.2	74.3	72.2
United Kingdom	71.0	71.2	71.4	71.4	71.5	71.7	71.7	71.6	71.5	71.5	69.9
Iceland	:	:	:	:	83.3	82.3	83.8	84.6	85.1	83.6	78.3
Norway	:	77.5	77.2	76.8	75.5	75.1	74.8	75.4	76.8	78.0	76.4
Switzerland	78.4	78.3	79.1	78.9	77.9	77.4	77.2	77.9	78.6	79.5	79.2
Croatia	:	:	:	53.4	53.4	54.7	55.0	55.6	57.1	57.8	56.6
FYR of Macedonia	:	:	:	:	:	:	:	39.6	40.7	41.9	43.3
Turkey	:	:	:	:	:	:	:	44.6	44.6	44.9	44.3
Japan	68.9	68.9	68.8	68.2	68.4	68.7	69.3	70.0	70.7	70.7	70.0
United States	73.9	74.1	73.1	71.9	71.2	71.2	71.5	72.0	71.8	70.9	67.6

(1) Break in series in, 2005.
(2) Break in series in, 2004.
(3) Break in series in, 2002.

Source: Eurostat (lfsi_emp_a)

Table 5.2: Employment rates for selected population groups
(%)

	Males			Females			Older workers (55-64)		
	1999	2004	2009	1999	2004	2009	1999	2004	2009
EU-27	70.7	70.4	70.7	53.0	55.6	58.6	36.5	40.7	46.0
Euro area (EA-16)	70.7	71.5	71.2	50.2	54.6	58.3	33.7	38.5	45.1
Belgium	68.1	67.9	67.2	50.4	52.6	56.0	24.6	30.0	35.3
Bulgaria	:	57.9	66.9	:	50.6	58.3	:	32.5	46.1
Czech Republic	74.0	72.3	73.8	57.4	56.0	56.7	37.5	42.7	46.8
Denmark	80.8	79.7	78.3	71.1	71.6	73.1	54.5	60.3	57.5
Germany	72.8	70.8	75.6	57.4	59.2	66.2	37.8	41.8	56.2
Estonia	65.8	66.4	64.1	57.8	60.0	63.0	47.5	52.4	60.4
Ireland	74.5	75.9	66.3	52.0	56.5	57.4	43.7	49.5	51.0
Greece	71.1	73.7	73.5	41.0	45.2	48.9	39.3	39.4	42.2
Spain	69.3	73.8	66.6	38.5	48.3	52.8	35.0	41.3	44.1
France	68.0	69.5	68.5	54.0	58.3	60.1	28.8	37.8	38.9
Italy (1)	67.3	70.1	68.6	38.3	45.2	46.4	27.6	30.5	35.7
Cyprus	:	79.8	77.6	:	58.7	62.5	:	49.9	56.0
Latvia	64.1	66.4	61.0	53.9	58.5	60.9	36.6	47.9	53.2
Lithuania	64.3	64.7	59.5	59.4	57.8	60.7	40.9	47.1	51.6
Luxembourg	74.5	72.8	73.2	48.6	51.9	57.0	26.4	30.4	38.2
Hungary	62.4	63.1	61.1	49.0	50.7	49.9	19.4	31.1	32.8
Malta	:	75.1	71.5	:	32.7	37.7	:	31.5	28.1
Netherlands	80.9	80.2	82.4	62.3	65.8	71.5	36.4	45.2	55.1
Austria (1)	77.6	74.9	76.9	59.6	60.7	66.4	29.7	28.8	41.1
Poland	64.2	57.2	66.1	51.2	46.2	52.8	31.9	26.2	32.3
Portugal	75.8	74.2	71.1	59.4	61.7	61.6	50.1	50.3	49.7
Romania	69.0	63.4	65.2	57.5	52.1	52.0	49.6	36.9	42.6
Slovenia	66.5	70.0	71.0	57.7	60.5	63.8	22.0	29.0	35.6
Slovakia	64.3	63.2	67.6	52.1	50.9	52.8	22.3	26.8	39.5
Finland	69.2	69.7	69.5	63.4	65.6	67.9	39.0	50.9	55.5
Sweden	74.0	73.6	74.2	69.4	70.5	70.2	63.9	69.1	70.0
United Kingdom	77.7	77.9	74.8	64.2	65.6	65.0	49.6	56.2	57.5
Iceland	:	85.8	80.0	:	78.8	76.5	:	81.8	80.2
Norway	:	77.9	78.3	:	72.2	74.4	:	65.8	68.7
Switzerland	87.2	84.4	84.5	69.6	70.3	73.8	64.7	65.2	68.4
Croatia	:	61.8	62.4	:	47.8	51.0	:	30.1	38.4
FYR of Macedonia	:	:	52.8	:	:	33.5	:	:	34.6
Turkey	:	:	64.5	:	:	24.2	:	:	28.2
Japan	81.0	80.0	80.2	56.7	57.4	59.8	63.4	63.0	65.5
United States	80.5	77.2	72.0	67.6	65.4	63.4	57.7	59.9	60.6

(1) Break in series, 2004.

Source: Eurostat (lfsi_emp_a)

Table 5.3: Employment rate by highest level of education, age group 25-64, 2009
(%)

	Pre-primary, primary & lower secondary - ISCED levels 0-2	Upper secondary & post-secondary non-tertiary - ISCED levels 3-4	Tertiary - ISCED levels 5-6
EU-27	54.7	73.7	84.5
Euro area (EA-16)	55.2	74.8	84.1
Belgium	48.0	74.0	84.2
Bulgaria	46.4	75.4	85.8
Czech Republic	43.9	75.1	84.3
Denmark	64.6	79.7	87.4
Germany	55.3	76.2	87.1
Estonia	47.4	71.6	82.8
Ireland	50.0	69.1	82.0
Greece	59.7	68.4	82.5
Spain	54.0	70.7	81.1
France	56.2	74.8	83.6
Italy	51.2	73.1	79.2
Cyprus	64.7	78.2	86.4
Latvia	49.3	69.2	83.3
Lithuania	38.6	68.3	86.9
Luxembourg	61.6	70.2	85.1
Hungary	37.4	67.0	78.8
Malta	47.8	82.0	84.9
Netherlands	63.6	81.7	88.1
Austria	55.6	77.6	86.7
Poland	41.6	66.3	85.3
Portugal	69.0	80.1	86.7
Romania	54.7	68.5	86.0
Slovenia	53.7	74.6	88.4
Slovakia	30.3	72.0	83.2
Finland	56.8	74.8	84.4
Sweden	65.2	82.6	88.1
United Kingdom	57.8	77.4	85.3
Iceland	77.1	82.6	88.3
Norway	66.2	82.7	90.4
Switzerland	67.9	81.9	89.8
Croatia	45.9	65.6	81.8
FYR of Macedonia	33.6	58.7	74.3
Turkey	43.3	58.3	73.5

Source: Eurostat (lfsa_ergaed)

Figure 5.4: Employment rates by age group, 2009 (¹)
(%)

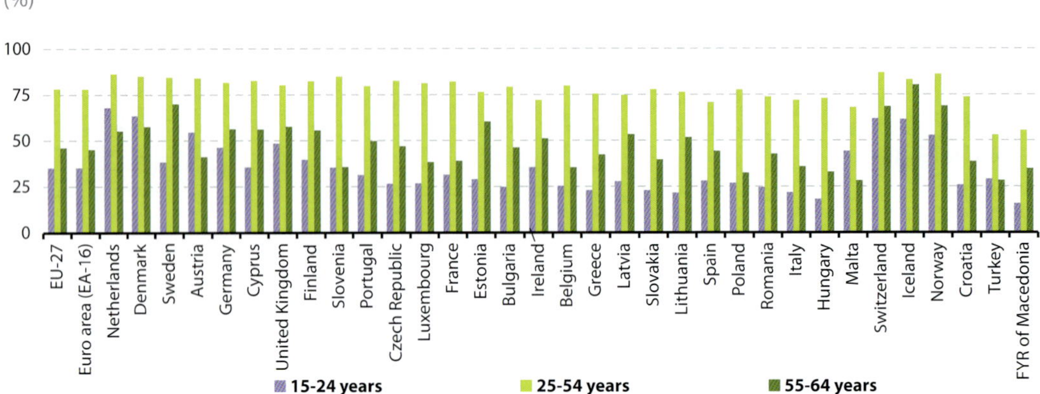

(¹) The figure is ranked on the overall employment rate.

Source: Eurostat (lfsi_emp_a)

Figure 5.5: Annual employment change
(% change compared with previous year)

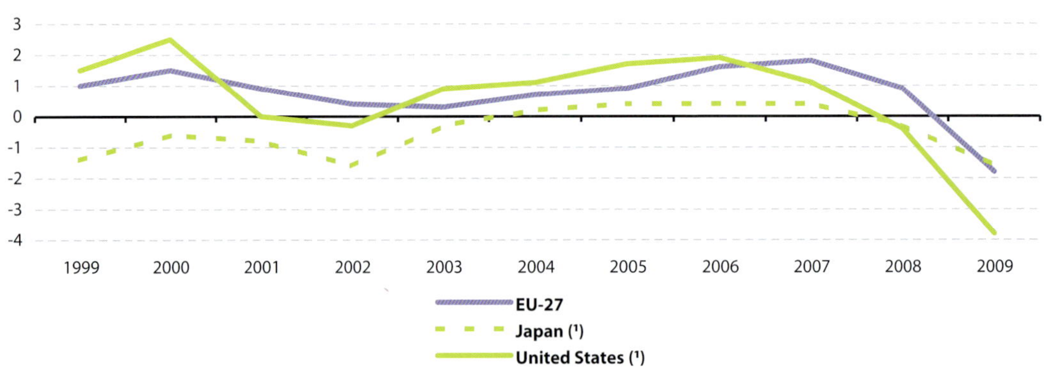

(¹) 2009, forecasts.

Source: Eurostat (lfsi_grt_a)

Table 5.4: Annual employment change
(% change compared with previous year)

	Total			Males			Females		
	1999	2004	2009	1999	2004 ([1])	2009	1999	2004 ([1])	2009
EU-27	1.0	0.7	-1.8	0.4	0.3	-2.7	1.9	1.2	-0.7
Euro area (EA-16)	1.9	0.8	-1.9	1.2	0.2	-2.9	2.8	1.6	-0.6
Belgium	1.4	0.9	-0.4	-0.2	0.8	-1.1	3.7	1.0	0.5
Bulgaria	-4.3	2.6	*-2.7*	:	2.8	-2.9	:	2.4	-2.5
Czech Republic	-3.4	0.3	-1.2	-3.7	0.3	-1.2	-3.0	0.4	-1.2
Denmark	0.8	-0.6	-3.4	0.6	-1.2	-4.5	1.1	0.1	-2.1
Germany	1.4	0.4	0.0	0.6	0.3	-0.8	2.3	0.6	0.9
Estonia	-4.4	0.0	-10.0	-5.2	-1.4	-13.6	-3.6	1.3	-6.2
Ireland	6.5	3.4	-8.2	5.4	3.2	-11.5	8.1	3.6	-3.8
Greece	*0.3*	*2.2*	*-1.2*	*-0.4*	*1.6*	*-2.1*	*1.5*	*3.2*	*0.3*
Spain	4.6	3.5	-6.6	3.4	2.3	-9.1	6.8	5.5	-3.3
France	2.0	0.1	-1.3	1.9	-0.2	-1.8	2.2	0.5	-0.7
Italy	1.1	0.4	-1.7	0.4	-1.6	-2.0	2.4	3.8	-1.2
Cyprus	1.9	3.8	-0.7	:	5.6	-1.2	:	1.5	0.0
Latvia	-1.8	1.2	-13.2	-1.4	1.0	-17.1	-2.2	1.4	-9.1
Lithuania	-2.2	0.0	-6.8	:	1.1	-11.5	:	-1.2	-2.0
Luxembourg	5.0	2.2	1.0	5.4	1.4	1.1	4.2	3.4	0.8
Hungary	2.7	-1.4	-2.8	2.5	-1.3	-3.4	3.1	-1.6	-2.1
Malta	:	-0.6	-0.5	:	0.3	-0.9	:	-2.9	0.2
Netherlands	2.6	-0.9	-1.1	1.2	-1.2	-1.8	4.5	-0.5	-0.4
Austria	1.5	1.4	-0.9	1.1	1.2	-2.2	2.0	1.7	0.7
Poland	-3.9	1.2	*0.4*	-4.8	1.7	0.0	-2.8	0.6	0.9
Portugal	1.4	-0.1	-2.6	0.6	-0.3	-3.7	2.4	0.2	-1.2
Romania	:	-1.7	-2.0	:	-2.4	-1.8	:	-0.8	-2.3
Slovenia	1.4	0.3	-1.9	:	-0.1	-2.6	:	0.8	-1.0
Slovakia	-2.5	-0.2	-2.4	-3.4	0.9	-2.3	-1.5	-1.6	-2.4
Finland	2.5	0.4	-2.8	1.6	0.5	-4.5	3.4	0.3	-1.0
Sweden	2.1	-0.7	-2.0	1.9	-0.6	-2.6	2.3	-0.8	-1.4
United Kingdom ([2])	1.3	1.0	-2.2	1.2	0.8	-3.2	1.5	1.1	-1.1
Iceland	3.7	-0.4	*-6.0*	:	0.1	-9.1	:	-1.1	-2.3
Norway	0.9	0.5	-0.4	:	0.5	-0.9	:	0.4	0.1
Croatia	-3.3	1.7	-2.5	:	1.8	-4.6	:	1.5	0.1
Turkey	2.1	3.0	*0.4*	:	:	-1.2	:	:	4.9
Japan	-1.4	0.2	*-1.6*	:	:	:	:	:	:
United States	1.5	1.1	*-3.8*	:	:	:	:	:	:

([1]) Italy and Austria, break in series.
([2]) Eurostat estimates of persons employed are based on the estimates of jobs transmitted by the United Kingdom.

Source: Eurostat (lfsi_grt_a)

Table 5.5: Persons working part-time or with a second job as a proportion of total employment
(% of total employment)

	Persons working part-time			Persons with a second job		
	1999	2004	2009	1999	2004	2009
EU-27	15.9	17.2	18.8	:	3.6	3.8
Euro area (EA-16)	15.5	17.5	20.0	:	3.0	3.4
Belgium	18.4	21.4	23.4	3.9	3.8	4.0
Bulgaria	:	2.4	2.3	:	0.9	0.6
Czech Republic	5.6	4.9	5.5	2.9	2.5	1.9
Denmark	21.6	22.2	26.0	7.0	11.4	9.3
Germany	19.0	22.3	26.1	2.5	2.7	3.7
Estonia	8.1	8.0	10.5	7.2	3.7	4.2
Ireland	16.4	16.8	21.2	1.7	2.0	2.3
Greece	5.8	4.6	6.0	4.5	2.4	3.4
Spain	8.0	8.7	12.8	1.7	2.1	2.3
France	17.1	16.8	17.3	3.3	2.9	3.4
Italy	7.9	12.7	14.3	1.4	2.1	1.5
Cyprus	6.5	8.6	8.4	:	6.8	3.9
Latvia	12.1	10.4	8.9	4.7	6.6	4.6
Lithuania	:	8.4	8.3	9.1	5.2	5.0
Luxembourg	9.8	16.4	18.2	1.3	1.5	3.2
Hungary	3.8	4.7	5.6	2.2	1.8	1.8
Malta	:	8.7	11.3	:	4.6	5.1
Netherlands	39.7	45.5	48.3	5.6	6.1	7.3
Austria	16.4	19.8	24.6	4.4	5.1	4.1
Poland	10.5	10.8	8.4	7.4	7.7	7.4
Portugal	11.0	11.3	11.6	5.6	6.3	6.5
Romania (1)	15.9	10.6	9.8	5.8	3.4	3.0
Slovenia	6.1	9.3	10.6	1.8	3.1	3.5
Slovakia	2.1	2.7	3.6	1.0	0.9	1.0
Finland	12.1	13.5	14.0	3.7	4.1	4.4
Sweden	19.7	23.6	27.0	8.9	9.3	8.2
United Kingdom	24.6	25.7	26.1	4.6	3.8	3.9
Iceland	:	:	11.3	:	11.9	9.1
Norway	:	29.2	28.6	:	7.7	8.8
Switzerland	30.3	33.0	34.6	6.1	6.4	7.4
Croatia	:	8.5	9.0	:	3.2	2.9
FYR of Macedonia	:	:	5.6	:	:	2.3
Turkey	:	:	11.3	:	:	2.7

(1) Break in series, 2002.

Source: Eurostat (tps00159, lfsa_e2gis and lfsa_egan)

Figure 5.6: Persons employed part-time, 2009
(% of total employment)

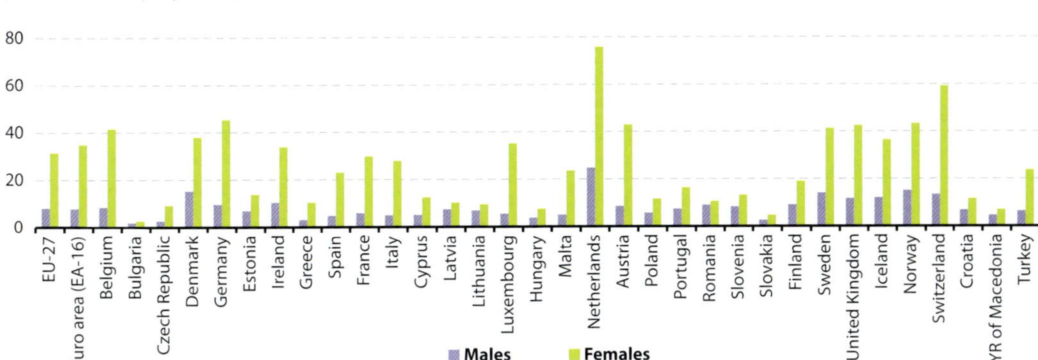

Source: Eurostat (tps00159)

Figure 5.7: Proportion of employees with a contract of limited duration, age group 15-64, 2009
(% of total employees)

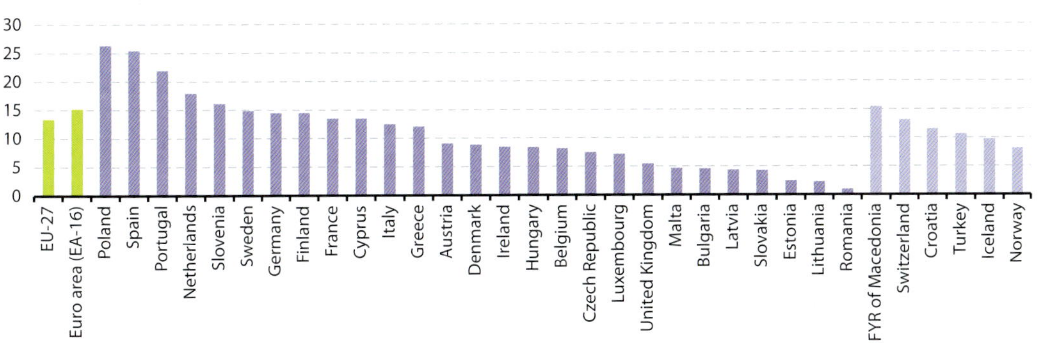

Source: Eurostat (lfsa_etpga)

5.2 Unemployment

Unemployment levels and rates move in a cyclical way, largely related to the general business cycle. However, other factors such as labour market policies and demographic changes may influence the short and long-term development of unemployment. This subchapter gives an overview of statistical information for unemployment in the European Union (EU).

Main statistical findings

Unemployment trends

In early 2000, just less than 20 million persons were unemployed in the EU-27, slightly below 9 % of the total labour force. This figure fell to around 19 million (or 8.5 %) in early 2001 before rising back to around 21 million persons by the middle of 2002, where it remained through until the middle of 2005. From mid-2005 there was a period of several years of steadily declining unemployment within the EU-27. By the first quarter of 2008, EU-27 unemployment had hit a low of 16 million persons (equivalent to a rate of 6.7 %) before rising sharply in the wake of the financial and economic crisis.

The unemployment rate in the euro area followed roughly the same trend as in the EU-27. However, between 2000 and the middle of 2004 the unemployment rate in the euro area was below that recorded in the EU-27. This pattern was subsequently reversed as unemployment declined more rapidly between 2005 and 2008 in the EU Member States outside of the euro area.

In 2000, the unemployment rate in the United States was around 4 %, considerably lower than in the EU-27. It remained much lower until early 2008, when unemployment started to increase rapidly in the United States. By mid-2009, the unemployment rate in the United States had reached the same level as in the EU-27. Unemployment rates in Japan were much lower than in the EU-27, and this was the case throughout the last ten years for which data are available.

Youth unemployment trends

Youth unemployment rates are generally much higher than unemployment rates for the whole of the population. This does not necessarily mean that the group of unemployed persons aged between 15 and 24 is large. Many young people are studying full-time and are therefore neither working, nor looking for a job, so they are not part of the labour force (which is used as the denominator for calculating the unemployment rate). However, high youth unemployment rates do reflect the difficulties faced by young people in finding jobs.

Throughout the last decade the youth unemployment rate in the EU-27 was about twice as high as the unemployment rate for the total population. The EU-27 youth unemployment rate was systematically higher than the equivalent rate in the euro area between 2000 and early 2008; since this date, these two rates have been almost identical.

Male and female unemployment trends

Historically, women have been more likely to be unemployed than men. In 2000, the unemployment rate for women in the EU-27 was around 10 %, while the rate for men was around 8 %. By the end of 2002, this gender gap had narrowed to around 1.3 percentage points and between 2002 and early 2007 the gap remained more or less constant. In recent years, most markedly since the first quarter of 2008, male and female unemployment rates in the EU-27 have converged and by the second quarter of 2009 the male unemployment rate was higher.

A detailed look at 2009

The overall unemployment rate in the EU-27 reached 8.9 % in 2009. After four consecutive years of declining unemployment, there was a steep rise in the unemployment rate, which gained 1.9 percentage points compared with 2008. The impact of the financial and economic crisis on unemployment almost wiped out the reduction experienced in the EU-27 unemployment rate between 2004 and 2008. In the United States, where the unemployment rate grew from 5.8 % to 9.3 % between 2008 and 2009, the increase in unemployment associated with the crisis was even more marked.

The unemployment rate rose in all 27 EU Member States between 2008 and 2009. The smallest increase was recorded in Germany, where the impact of the crisis was limited to a 0.2 percentage point increase, while in the three countries forming the Benelux the impact of the crisis did not have an impact of more than 1.0 percentage point. With an increase of just below 10 percentage points, Latvia recorded the largest annual increase in unemployment between 2008 and 2009, followed by the other two Baltic states of Estonia and Lithuania. Spain remained the Member State with the highest overall unemployment rate in 2009, at 18.0 %. The dispersion of unemployment across the EU-27 increased because those countries with relatively low unemployment rates in 2008 saw smaller increases, on average, than those countries with already relatively high unemployment rates.

Long-term unemployment is one of the main concerns of policymakers. Apart from its financial and social effects on personal life, long-term unemployment negatively affects social cohesion and, ultimately, may hinder economic growth. Some 3.0 % of the labour force in the EU-27 in 2009 had been unemployed for more than one year; half of these, 1.5 % of the labour force, had been unemployed for more than two years.

For the first time since the calculation of EU-27 unemployment statistics started (in 2000), the unemployment rate for women was lower than that for men in 2009. Male unemployment rates were higher than the corresponding rates for women in 14 out of 27 Member States. In the euro area, the unemployment rate for women remained higher than the corresponding rate for men. The gender gap between male and female unemployment rates varied from -6.3 percentage points in Greece to +6.9 percentage points in Ireland.

The youth unemployment rate in the EU-27 was more than double the overall unemployment rate in 2009. At 19.6 %, almost one out of every five young persons (under 25 years of age) in the labour force was not employed, but looking and available for a job. In the euro area, the youth unemployment rate was marginally lower at 19.4 %. The unemployment rate among young persons was higher than the rate among those aged between 25 and 74 in all of the Member States. In Spain (37.8 %), Latvia (33.6 %) and Lithuania (29.2 %), youth unemployment rates were particularly high. The Netherlands (6.6 %) was the only Member State with a youth unemployment rate below 10 %.

Educational qualifications would appear to help job-seekers, as unemployment rates tend to decrease the higher the level of education attained. This characteristic was noted in almost every Member State in 2009. The average unemployment rate in the EU-27 for those having attained at most a lower secondary education was 12.8 %, much higher than the rate for those that had obtained a tertiary education qualification (4.5 %); note that during periods of recession it is common for well-educated persons to accept jobs for which they would generally be considered as over-qualified.

Data sources and availability

The main source used by Eurostat for unemployment figures is the EU's labour force survey (LFS). This household survey is carried out in all of the Member States in accordance with European legislation; it provides figures at least each quarter.

Quarterly and annual unemployment figures from the LFS are published with detailed breakdowns – for example, a wider range of age groups, by nationality, or by educational attainment; there are also figures available on long-term unemployment.

There is currently no legal basis for producing and disseminating monthly unemployment data. For many countries, Eurostat calculates monthly data by using additional monthly figures from unemployment registers. The quarterly LFS results are always used as a benchmark to ensure international comparability. Few countries actually supply monthly unemployment figures directly from the LFS.

Monthly unemployment figures are published by Eurostat as rates (as a percentage of the labour force) or levels (in thousands), by gender and for two age groups (persons aged 15 to 24, and those aged 25 to 74). The figures are available as unadjusted, seasonally adjusted and trend series. There are monthly estimates for all EU-27 Member States except for Estonia, Greece, Latvia, Lithuania and Romania. Data for the EU-27 aggregate start in 2000 and for the euro area in 1995; the starting point for individual Member States varies.

Context

The unemployment rate is an important indicator with both social and economic dimensions. Rising unemployment results in a loss of income for those individuals affected, increased pressure with respect to government spending on social benefits, and a reduction in tax revenue. From an economic perspective, unemployment may be viewed as unused labour capacity.

The International Labour Organization (ILO) definition of the unemployment rate is the most widely used labour market indicator because of its international comparability and relatively timely availability. Besides the unemployment rate, indicators such as employment and job vacancies also give useful insights into labour market developments.

Time series on unemployment are used by the European Commission, other public institutions, and the media as an economic indicator; banks may use the data for business cycle analysis. Finally, the general public may also be interested in changes in unemployment.

The unemployment rate is considered to be a lagging indicator. When there is an economic downturn, it usually takes several months before the unemployment rate begins to rise. Once the economy starts to pick up again, employers usually remain cautious about hiring new staff and it may take several months before unemployment rates start to fall.

Male, youth and long-term unemployment appear to be more susceptible to cyclical economic changes than overall unemployment. Indeed, social policymakers often face the challenge of remedying these situations by designing ways to increase employment opportunities for various groups of society, those working in particular economic activities, or those living in specific regions.

Globalisation and technological progress have an ever-increasing effect on daily life, and the demand for different types of labour and skills is changing at a rapid pace. While enterprises try to improve their productivity and become more competitive and innovative, they may well seek to pass on risk to the labour force through greater flexibility – both in relation to those already in employment, as well as those searching for a new job. Within the context of the European employment strategy (EES), there are a number of measures that are designed to help encourage people to remain in work or find a new job, including: the promotion of a life-cycle approach to work, encouraging lifelong learning, improving support to those seeking a job, as well as ensuring equal opportunities. The integrated employment guidelines for 2008-2010 encouraged Member States, among others, to:

- work with renewed endeavour to build employment pathways for young people and reduce youth unemployment, in particular, through adapting education and training systems in order to raise quality, broaden supply, diversify access, ensure flexibility, respond to new occupational needs and skills requirements, and;
- take action to increase female participation and reduce gender gaps in employment, unemployment and pay, through better reconciliation of work and private life and the provision of accessible and affordable childcare facilities and care for other dependents.

The guidelines also set a number of additional benchmarks, whereby Member States were encouraged:

- to ensure that by 2010 every unemployed person is offered a job, apprenticeship, additional training or another employability measure (for young persons leaving school within four months, and for adults within no more than 12 months), and;
- to work towards 25 % of the long-term unemployed participating in training, retraining, work practice, or other employability measures by 2010.

The financial and economic crisis has however reversed much of the progress achieved in Europe since 2000. The Europe 2020 strategy sets out a vision of Europe's social market economy for the 21st century; flagship initiatives include 'an agenda for new skills and jobs' and 'youth on the move'. These are designed to lower (youth) unemployment rates through a range of policies, including proposals aimed at education and training institutions, or measures for the creation of a (work) environment conducive to higher activity rates and higher labour productivity; there are also initiatives aimed at improving the entry rate of young people into the labour market.

Table 5.6: Unemployment rate
(%)

	1999	2000	2001	2002	2003	2004	2005	2006	2007	2008	2009
EU-27	:	8.7	8.5	8.9	9.0	9.1	8.9	8.2	7.1	7.0	8.9
Euro area (EA-16)	9.3	8.4	8.0	8.4	8.8	9.0	9.0	8.3	7.5	7.5	9.4
Belgium	8.5	6.9	6.6	7.5	8.2	8.4	8.5	8.3	7.5	7.0	7.9
Bulgaria	:	16.4	19.5	18.2	13.7	12.1	10.1	9.0	6.9	5.6	6.8
Czech Republic	8.6	8.7	8.0	7.3	7.8	8.3	7.9	7.2	5.3	4.4	6.7
Denmark	5.2	4.3	4.5	4.6	5.4	5.5	4.8	3.9	3.8	3.3	6.0
Germany	8.2	7.5	7.6	8.4	9.3	9.8	10.7	9.8	8.4	7.3	7.5
Estonia	:	13.6	12.6	10.3	10.0	9.7	7.9	5.9	4.7	5.5	13.8
Ireland	5.6	4.2	3.9	4.5	4.6	4.5	4.4	4.5	4.6	6.3	11.9
Greece	12.0	11.2	10.7	10.3	9.7	10.5	9.9	8.9	8.3	7.7	9.5
Spain	12.5	11.1	10.3	11.1	11.1	10.6	9.2	8.5	8.3	11.3	18.0
France	10.4	9.0	8.3	8.6	9.0	9.3	9.3	9.2	8.4	7.8	9.5
Italy	10.9	10.1	9.1	8.6	8.4	8.0	7.7	6.8	6.1	6.7	7.8
Cyprus	:	4.9	3.8	3.6	4.1	4.7	5.3	4.6	4.0	3.6	5.3
Latvia	14.0	13.7	12.9	12.2	10.5	10.4	8.9	6.8	6.0	7.5	17.1
Lithuania	13.7	16.4	16.5	13.5	12.5	11.4	8.3	5.6	4.3	5.8	13.7
Luxembourg	2.4	2.2	1.9	2.6	3.8	5.0	4.6	4.6	4.2	4.9	5.2
Hungary	6.9	6.4	5.7	5.8	5.9	6.1	7.2	7.5	7.4	7.8	10.0
Malta	:	6.7	7.6	7.5	7.6	7.4	7.2	7.1	6.4	5.9	7.0
Netherlands	3.2	2.8	2.2	2.8	3.7	4.6	4.7	3.9	3.2	2.8	3.4
Austria	3.9	3.6	3.6	4.2	4.3	4.9	5.2	4.8	4.4	3.8	4.8
Poland	13.4	16.1	18.3	20.0	19.7	19.0	17.8	13.9	9.6	7.1	8.2
Portugal	4.5	4.0	4.1	5.1	6.4	6.7	7.7	7.8	8.1	7.7	9.6
Romania	7.1	7.3	6.8	8.6	7.0	8.1	7.2	7.3	6.4	5.8	6.9
Slovenia	7.3	6.7	6.2	6.3	6.7	6.3	6.5	6.0	4.9	4.4	5.9
Slovakia	16.4	18.8	19.3	18.7	17.6	18.2	16.3	13.4	11.1	9.5	12.0
Finland	10.2	9.8	9.1	9.1	9.0	8.8	8.4	7.7	6.9	6.4	8.2
Sweden (1)	6.7	5.6	5.8	6.0	6.6	7.4	7.6	7.0	6.1	6.2	8.3
United Kingdom	5.9	5.4	5.0	5.1	5.0	4.7	4.8	5.4	5.3	5.6	7.6
Norway	3.0	3.2	3.4	3.7	4.2	4.3	4.5	3.4	2.5	2.5	3.1
Croatia	:	:	:	14.8	14.2	13.7	12.7	11.2	9.6	8.4	9.1
Turkey	:	:	:	:	:	:	9.2	8.7	8.8	9.7	12.5
Japan	4.7	4.7	5.0	5.4	5.3	4.7	4.4	4.1	3.9	4.0	5.1
United States	4.2	4.0	4.8	5.8	6.0	5.5	5.1	4.6	4.6	5.8	9.3

(1) Break in series, 2001.

Source: Eurostat (une_rt_a)

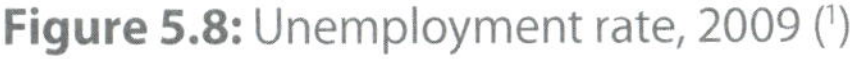

Figure 5.8: Unemployment rate, 2009 (¹)
(%)

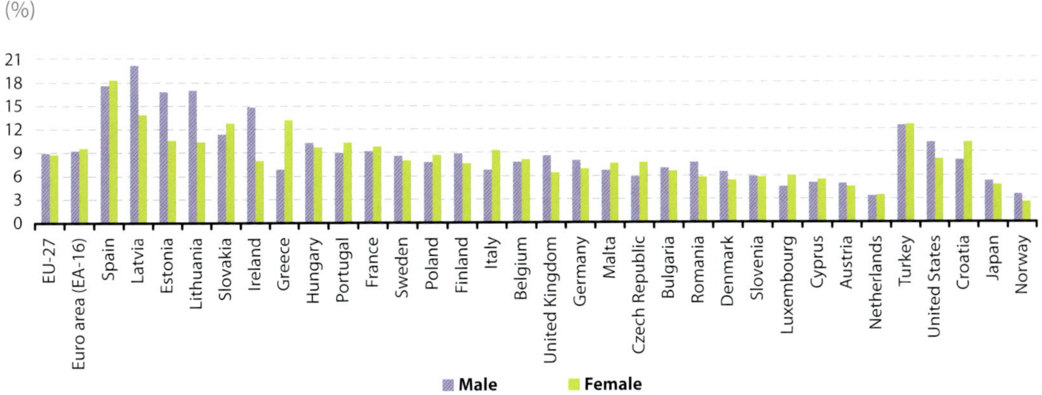

(¹) The figure is ranked on the average of male and female.

Source: Eurostat (une_rt_a)

Figure 5.9: Unemployment rate by duration, 2009
(%)

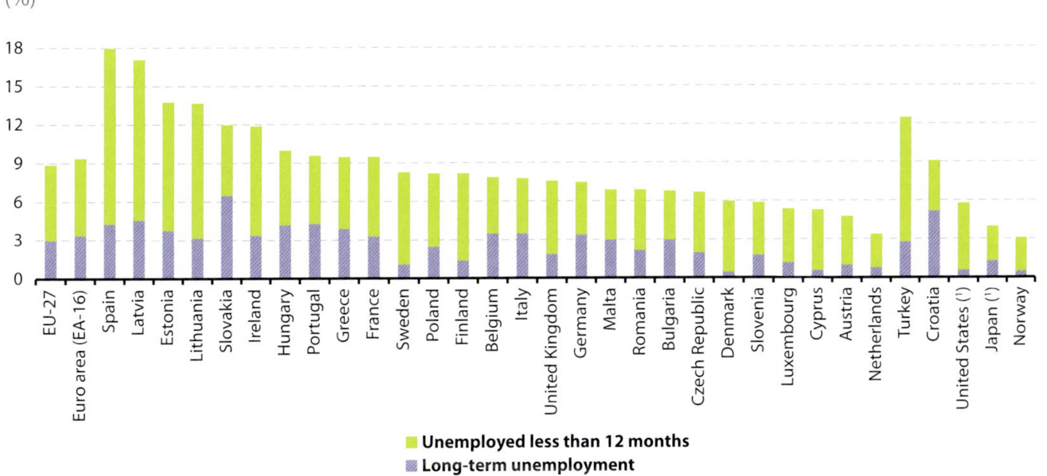

(¹) 2008.

Source: Eurostat (tsiem110 and tsisc070)

Table 5.7: Unemployment rate by gender and by age
(%)

	Male		Female		< 25 years	25-74 years
	2004	2009	2004	2009	2009	2009
EU-27	8.5	9.0	9.8	8.8	19.6	7.6
Euro area (EA-16)	8.1	9.3	10.1	9.6	19.4	8.2
Belgium	7.5	7.8	9.5	8.1	21.9	6.6
Bulgaria	12.6	7.0	11.5	6.6	16.2	6.0
Czech Republic	7.1	5.9	9.9	7.7	16.6	5.8
Denmark	5.1	6.5	6.0	5.4	11.2	5.0
Germany	10.3	8.0	9.1	6.9	10.4	7.1
Estonia	10.4	16.9	8.9	10.6	27.5	12.0
Ireland	4.8	14.9	4.0	8.0	24.4	10.1
Greece	6.6	6.9	16.2	13.2	25.8	8.3
Spain	8.0	17.7	14.3	18.4	37.8	15.9
France	8.4	9.2	10.3	9.8	23.3	7.8
Italy	6.4	6.8	10.5	9.3	25.3	6.4
Cyprus	3.6	5.2	6.0	5.5	14.0	4.4
Latvia	10.6	20.3	10.2	13.9	33.6	14.9
Lithuania	11.0	17.1	11.8	10.4	29.2	12.1
Luxembourg	3.6	4.6	6.8	6.0	16.9	4.2
Hungary	6.1	10.3	6.1	9.7	26.5	8.7
Malta	6.6	6.7	9.0	7.6	14.3	5.4
Netherlands	4.3	3.4	4.8	3.5	6.6	2.8
Austria	4.5	5.0	5.4	4.6	10.0	3.9
Poland	18.2	7.8	20.0	8.7	20.6	6.8
Portugal	5.9	9.0	7.7	10.3	20.0	8.7
Romania	9.1	7.7	6.9	5.8	20.8	5.4
Slovenia	5.9	5.9	6.9	5.8	13.6	5.1
Slovakia	17.4	11.4	19.2	12.8	27.3	10.4
Finland	8.7	8.9	8.9	7.6	21.5	6.4
Sweden	7.6	8.6	7.1	8.0	25.0	5.9
United Kingdom	5.1	8.6	4.2	6.4	19.1	5.5
Norway	4.6	3.6	3.9	2.6	8.9	2.2
Croatia	12.1	8.0	15.7	10.3	25.0	7.3
Turkey	:	12.5	:	12.6	22.7	10.3
Japan	4.9	5.3	4.4	4.8	9.1	4.7
United States	5.6	10.3	5.4	8.1	17.6	7.9

Source: Eurostat (une_rt_a)

Table 5.8: Unemployment rate, EU-27

(%)

	2001	2002	2003	2004	2005	2006	2007	2008	2009
Male	7.8	8.3	8.4	8.5	8.3	7.6	6.6	6.6	9.0
Female	9.4	9.7	9.7	9.8	9.6	8.9	7.8	7.5	8.9
Less than 25 years	17.4	18.0	18.2	18.6	18.4	17.2	15.4	15.5	19.7
Between 25 and 74 years	7.2	7.6	7.7	7.8	7.6	7.0	6.1	5.9	7.6
Long-term unemployment rate	3.9	4.0	4.1	4.2	4.0	3.7	3.1	2.6	3.0
Male	3.5	3.6	3.8	3.9	3.7	3.4	2.8	2.4	2.9
Female	4.4	4.5	4.5	4.6	4.4	4.0	3.3	2.8	3.1
Very long-term unemployment rate	2.3	2.3	2.3	2.4	2.3	2.2	1.8	1.5	1.5

Source: Eurostat (une_rt_a, lfsa_ugad and une_ltu_a)

Figure 5.10: Unemployment rate (among persons aged 25-64 years) by level of educational attainment, 2009

(%)

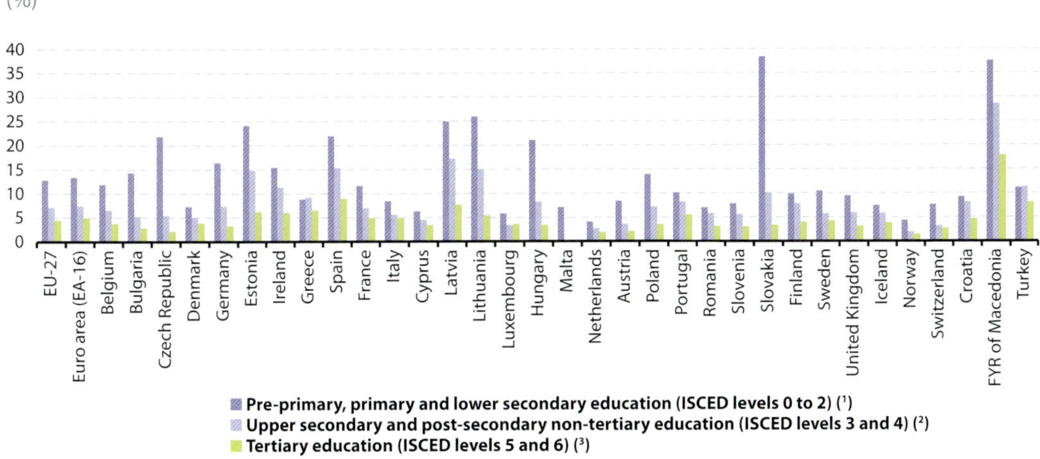

(1) Estonia, Luxembourg, Slovenia and Croatia, unreliable data.
(2) Malta, not available; Luxembourg, unreliable data.
(3) Malta, not available; Slovenia and Croatia, unreliable data.

Source: Eurostat (tps00066)

5.3 Wages and labour costs

The level and structure of wages and labour costs are important macro-economic indicators used by policymakers, employers and trade unions to assess labour market supply and demand conditions. This subchapter compares and contrasts figures on wages and labour costs in the European Union (EU), the latter being generally defined as employers' expenditure on personnel.

Main statistical findings

Gross earnings

Among EU Member States, the mean (average) gross annual earnings of full-time employees in enterprises with ten or more employees were highest in Denmark (EUR 55 001) in 2008, followed by Luxembourg, the United Kingdom (2007 data), Germany and Belgium – all above EUR 40 000 – while earnings were lowest in Romania (EUR 5 464) and Bulgaria (EUR 3 328). In 2006, median annual earnings showed a broadly similar ranking of countries (see Figure 5.11), with mean earnings higher than median earnings in all countries except Malta. The proportion of employees considered to be low wage earners in 2006 was highest in Latvia, at 30.9 %, while more than one in four employees received low wages in Lithuania, Bulgaria and Romania.

Gender pay gap

Despite some progress, there remains an important gap between the average earnings of men and women in the EU-27. Women were paid, on average, 17.5 % less than men in 2008. The smallest differences in average pay between the sexes were found in Italy, Slovenia, Belgium, Romania, Malta, Portugal and Poland (less than 10 %), the biggest in Estonia (2007 data), the Czech Republic and Austria (more than 25 %). Various effects may contribute to these gender pay gaps, such as: differences in labour force participation rates, differences in the occupations and activities that tend to be male- or female-dominated, differences in the degrees to which men and women work on a part-time basis, as well as the attitudes of personnel departments within private and public bodies towards career development and unpaid/maternity leave.

Minimum wages

In July 2010, a total of 20 of the 27 EU Member States (all except Denmark, Germany, Italy, Cyprus, Austria, Finland and Sweden) and two candidate countries (Croatia and Turkey) had national legislation setting a minimum wage by statute or by national inter-sectoral agreement.

Monthly minimum wages varied considerably in July 2010 (see Figure 5.14). The differences reflect, at least to some degree, the price levels in each economy, with the highest minimum wage being recorded in Luxembourg (EUR 1 725 per month) and the lowest in Bulgaria and Romania (EUR 123 and EUR 137 respectively).

Net earnings and tax rates

Tax wedge data for 2003 and 2008 show a slight reduction in the overall figure for the EU-27 between these two periods. Indeed, the tax wedge fell in 18 of the Member States and remained unchanged in three others. Consequently, the tax wedge only increased between these two years in six of the Member States, by 1 to 4 percentage points in Ireland, Greece, Hungary, Italy, the Netherlands and Austria.

Labour costs

Average hourly labour costs (see Figure 5.16) and the structure of labour costs (see Figure 5.17) varied widely across the Member States in 2009. The relative importance of wages and salaries in total labour costs was 66 % in Sweden and was also less than 70 % in Belgium and France (2008), while it was 85 % or more in the United Kingdom, Slovenia, Luxembourg and Malta (2008).

Data sources and availability

Gross earnings

Gross earnings are the largest part of labour costs – information is provided on average annual gross earnings. The main definitions on earnings are provided in European Commission Regulation 1738/2005 of 21 October 2005. Gross earnings cover remuneration in cash paid directly by the employer, before tax deductions and social security contributions payable by wage earners and retained by the employer. All bonuses, regardless of whether they are regularly paid, are included (13th or 14th month, holiday bonuses, profit-sharing, allowances for leave not taken, occasional commissions, etc.). The information is presented for full-time employees working in industry, construction and services (as covered by NACE Rev. 1.1 Sections C to K up to and including 2007 and by NACE Rev. 2 Sections B to N for 2008). The statistical unit is the enterprise or local unit. The population consists of all units with employees, although it is limited to enterprises with at least ten employees in most countries.

Data on median earnings are based on gross annual earnings, and represent the median earnings of full-time employees in enterprises with ten or more employees. Low wage earners are full-time employees that earn less than two thirds of the median gross annual earnings.

Gender pay gap

The gender pay gap (in its unadjusted form) is defined as the difference between average gross hourly earnings of male paid employees and female paid employees, expressed as a percentage of average gross hourly earnings of male paid employees. The methodology for the compilation of this indicator has recently changed and is now based on data collected from the structure of earnings survey (SES), rather than on non-harmonised sources (as was previously the case).

According to the new methodology the unadjusted gender pay gap indicator covers all employees (there are no restrictions for age and hours worked) of enterprises (with at least ten employees) belonging to industry, construction and services (as covered by NACE Rev. 2 Sections B to N and P to S).

Minimum wages

Minimum wage statistics published by Eurostat refer to monthly national minimum wages; data are published showing the wage on the 1 January and the 1 July of each year.

The national minimum wage is enforced by law, often after consultation with social partners, or directly by national inter-sectoral agreement (this is the case in Belgium and Greece). The national minimum wage is usually applicable for all employees, or at least for a large majority of employees in the country. Minimum wages are gross amounts, that is, before the deduction of income tax and social security contributions; such deductions vary from country to country. In some countries the basic national minimum wage is not fixed at a monthly rate but at an hourly or weekly rate. For these countries the hourly or weekly rates are converted into monthly rates according to conversion factors directly supplied by the countries:

- Ireland: hourly rate x 39 hours x 52 weeks / 12 months;
- France for data from January 1999 to January 2005: hourly rate x 39 hours x 52 weeks / 12 months; for data from July 2005: hourly rate x 35 hours x 52 weeks / 12 months;
- Malta: weekly rate x 52 weeks / 12 months;
- United Kingdom: (hourly rate x mean basic paid hours per week for full-time employees in all sectors x 52.18 weeks) / 12 months;
- United States: hourly rate x 40 hours x 52 weeks / 12 months.

In addition, when the minimum wage is paid for more than 12 months per year (as in Greece, Spain and Portugal, where it is paid for 14 months a year), data have been adjusted to take these payments into account.

Net earnings and tax rates

Net earnings are derived from gross earnings and represent the part of remuneration that employees can actually keep to spend or save. Compared with gross earnings, net earnings do not include social security contributions and taxes, but do include family allowances.

The tax rate indicators (tax wedge on labour costs, unemployment trap and low wage trap) aim to monitor work attractiveness. The tax wedge on labour costs is defined as income tax on gross wage earnings plus employee and employer social security contributions, expressed as a percentage of total labour costs. This indicator is compiled for single people without children earning 67 % of the average earnings of a worker in industry, construction and services (NACE Rev. 1.1 Sections C to K).

The unemployment trap measures the proportion of gross earnings taxed away by higher tax and social security contributions and the withdrawal of unemployment and other benefits when an unemployed person returns to employment; it is defined as the difference between gross earnings and the increase of net income when moving from unemployment to employment, expressed as a percentage of the gross earnings. This indicator is compiled for single persons without children earning 67 % of the av-

erage earnings of a worker in industry, construction or services (NACE Rev. 1.1 Sections C to K).

The low wage trap measures the proportion (as a percentage) of gross earnings which is taxed away through the combined effects of income taxes, social security contributions, and any withdrawal of benefits when gross earnings increase from 33 % to 67 % of the average earnings of a worker in industry, construction or services (NACE Rev. 1.1 Sections C to K). This indicator is compiled for single people without children and also for single-earner couples with two children between 6 and 11 years old.

Labour costs

Labour costs are defined as employer's expenditure that is related to employing personnel. They encompass employee compensation (including wages, salaries in cash and in kind, employers' social security contributions); vocational training costs; and other expenditure (such as recruitment costs, expenditure on work clothes, and employment taxes regarded as labour costs minus any subsidies received). These labour cost components and their elements are defined in Regulation 1737/2005 of 21 October 2005.

Data relate to three core indicators:

- average monthly labour costs, defined as total labour costs per month divided by the corresponding number of employees, expressed as full-time equivalent units;
- average hourly labour costs, defined as total labour costs divided by the corresponding number of hours worked;
- the structure of labour costs (wages and salaries; employers' social security contributions; other labour costs), expressed as a percentage of total labour costs.

Context

The structure and development of labour costs and earnings are important features of any labour market, reflecting labour supply from individuals and labour demand by enterprises.

Article 157(1) of the Treaty on the functioning of the European Union (TFEU) sets out the principle of equal pay for male and female workers for equal work or work of equal value, and Article 157(3) provides the legal basis for legislation on the equal treatment of men and women in employment matters. The strategy for equality between women and men (2010-2015) was adopted by the European Commission in September 2010. This builds on the experience of a roadmap that was developed for the period 2006-2010 and aims to be a comprehensive framework which will commit the European Commission to promote gender equality in all of its policies. The strategy highlights the contribution of gender equality to economic growth and sustainable development, and supports the implementation of the gender equality dimension in the Europe 2020 strategy. One of the six thematic priorities is the area of equal pay for work of equal value.

Some underlying factors that may, at least in part, explain gender pay gaps include sectoral and occupational segregation, education and training, awareness and transparency, as well as direct discrimination. Gender pay gaps also reflect other inequalities – in particular, women's disproportionate share of family responsibilities and associated difficulties of reconciling work with private life. Many women work part-time or under atypical contracts: although this permits them to remain in the labour market while managing family responsibilities, it can have a negative impact on their pay, career development, promotion prospects and pensions. The EU seeks to promote equal opportunities implying progressive elimination of the gender pay gap.

Figure 5.11: Median gross annual earnings of full-time employees, 2006 (1)
(EUR)

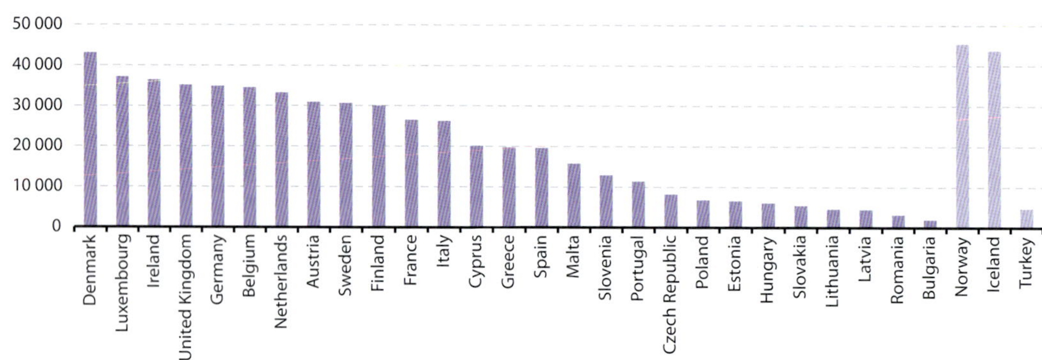

(1) Enterprises employing ten or more employees; excluding agriculture, fishing, public administration, private households and extra-territorial organizations.

Source: Eurostat (earn_ses_adeci)

Figure 5.12: Low wage earners - full-time employees earning less than two thirds of the median gross annual earnings, 2006 (1)
(% of employees)

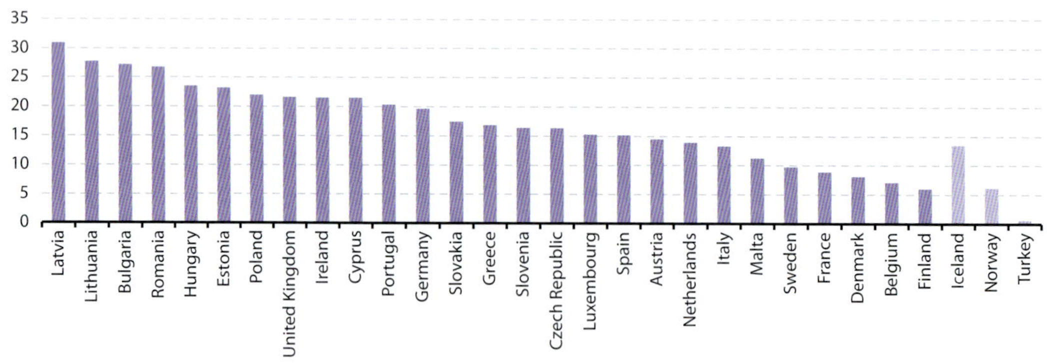

(1) Enterprises employing ten or more employees; excluding agriculture, fishing, public administration, private households and extra-territorial organizations.

Source: Eurostat (earn_ses_adeci)

Table 5.9: Earnings in the business economy (average gross annual earnings full-time employees) (1) (EUR)

	2000	2001	2002	2003	2004	2005	2006	2007	2008
EU-27	:	27 947	30 140	30 347	28 226	29 114	31 302	:	:
Belgium (2)	31 644	33 109	34 330	34 643	35 704	36 673	37 674	38 659	40 698
Bulgaria	1 430	1 514	1 588	1 678	1 784	1 978	2 195	2 626	3 328
Czech Republic	:	:	6 016	6 137	6 569	7 405	8 284	:	:
Denmark	40 962	41 661	43 577	44 692	46 122	47 529	48 307	53 165	55 001
Germany	34 400	35 200	36 400	37 200	38 100	38 700	39 364	40 200	41 400
Estonia	:	:	:	:	:	:	:	:	:
Ireland	:	:	:	:	:	40 462	:	39 858	:
Greece	14 723	15 431	16 278	16 739	:	:	:	:	25 915
Spain	17 432	17 874	18 462	19 220	19 931	20 333	21 402	21 891	25 208
France (2)	26 712	27 418	28 185	28 847	29 608	30 521	31 369	32 413	33 574
Italy	:	:	:	:	:	:	:	:	:
Cyprus	16 086	16 736	17 431	18 165	19 290	20 549	21 310	:	:
Latvia (3)	:	:	:	:	3 806	4 246	5 211	6 690	8 109
Lithuania (4)	:	:	:	:	:	:	:	:	7 398
Luxembourg	35 875	37 745	38 442	39 587	40 575	42 135	43 621	45 284	51 392
Hungary	4 173	4 898	5 846	6 447	7 119	7 798	7 866	8 952	9 805
Malta (2)	13 461	13 791	14 068	14 096	14 116	14 706	15 278	15 679	16 158
Netherlands	31 901	33 900	35 200	36 600	37 900	38 700	40 800	42 000	43 146
Austria	:	:	:	:	34 995	36 032	36 673	37 716	39 061
Poland (4)	:	7 510	:	:	6 230	6 270	8 178	:	10 787
Portugal	12 620	13 338	13 322	13 350	13 700	14 042	14 893	15 345	16 691
Romania	:	:	:	:	2 414	3 155	3 713	4 825	5 464
Slovenia (4)	:	:	:	:	:	:	:	:	15 997
Slovakia	3 583	3 837	4 582	4 945	5 706	6 374	7 040	8 400	9 677
Finland (2)	27 398	28 555	29 916	30 978	31 988	33 290	34 080	36 114	37 946
Sweden	31 621	30 467	31 164	32 177	33 344	34 027	35 084	36 871	37 597
United Kingdom	37 676	39 233	40 553	38 793	41 286	42 866	44 496	46 051	:
Iceland	37 641	34 100	:	:	:	:	:	:	:
Norway	36 202	38 604	43 750	40 883	42 152	45 560	47 221	:	52 632
Switzerland (3)	43 682	:	48 499	:	45 760	:	46 058	:	47 096
Croatia	:	:	:	8 491	9 036	9 634	:	:	:

(1) Enterprises employing ten or more employees; 2000-2007, NACE Rev. 1.1 Sections C to K; 2008, NACE Rev. 2 Sections B to N.
(2) 2008: all enterprises.
(3) 2008: NACE Rev. 1.1.
(4) 2008: full-time units.

Source: Eurostat (earn_gr_nace2, earn_gr_nace)

Figure 5.13: Gender pay gap, 2008 (1)
(% difference between average gross hourly earnings of male and female employees, as % of male gross earnings, unadjusted form)

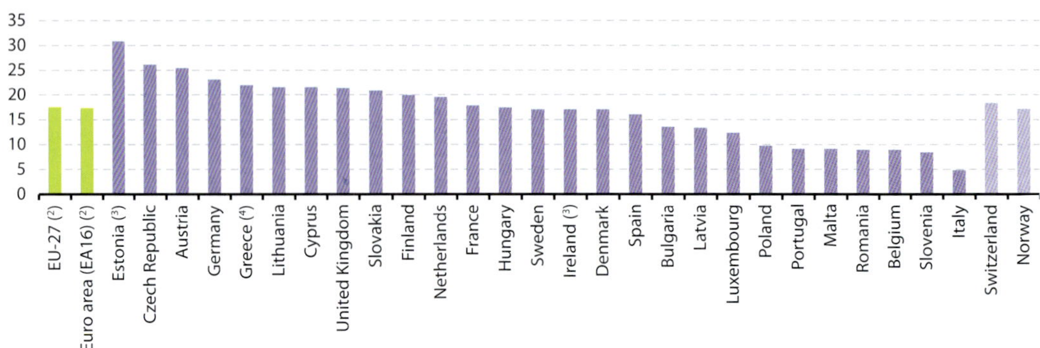

(1) Enterprises employing ten or more employees; NACE Rev. 2 Sections B to N and P to S.
(2) Provisional.
(3) 2007 data; NACE Rev. 1.1 Sections C to K and M to O.
(4) NACE Rev. 1.1 Sections C to K and M to O.

Source: Eurostat (tsiem040)

Figure 5.14: Minimum wage (1)
(EUR per month, as of 1 July 2010)

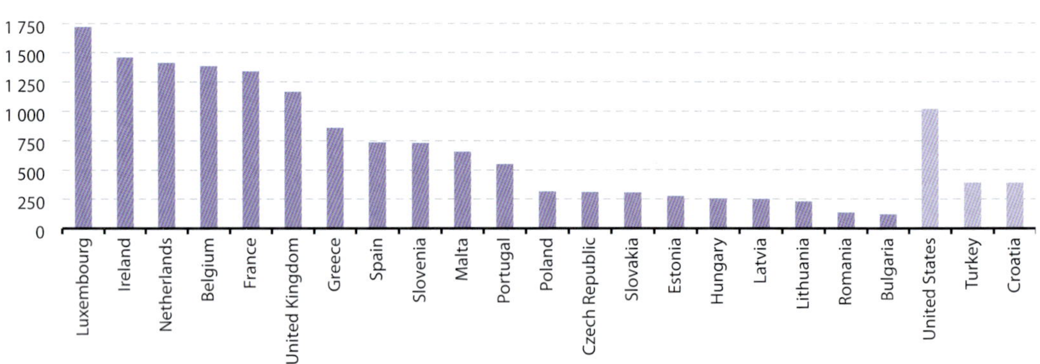

(1) Member States not shown: not applicable.

Source: Eurostat (earn_mw_cur)

Figure 5.15: Tax rate on low wage earners - tax wedge on labour cost, 2008
(%)

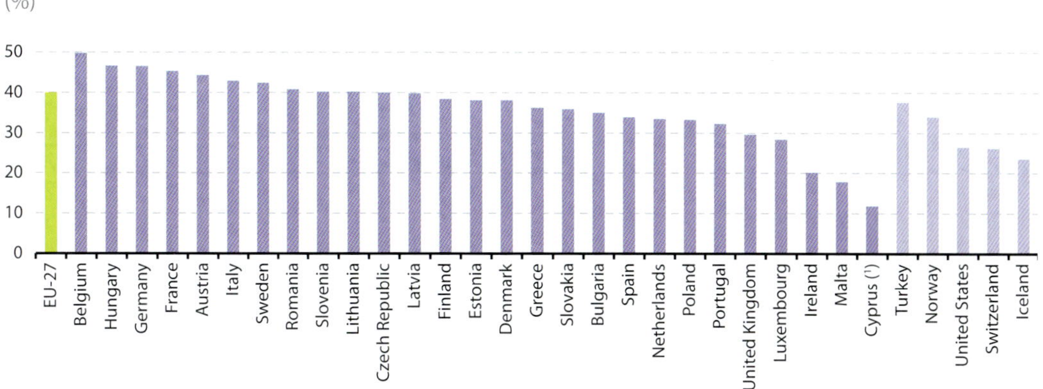

(1) 2007.

Source: Eurostat (tsiem050), OECD, Commission services

Table 5.10: Tax rate indicators on low wage earners
(%)

	Tax wedge on labour cost (¹)		Unemployment trap (²)		Low wage trap - single person without children (²)		Low wage trap - one earner couple with two children (²)	
	2003	2008	2003	2008	2003	2008	2003	2008
EU-27	41	40	74	75	48	50	61	63
Belgium	50	50	87	85	58	59	49	48
Bulgaria	36	35	75	80	20	22	46	22
Czech Republic	42	40	66	68	36	41	65	45
Denmark	40	38	91	89	84	79	106	95
Germany	49	47	75	74	53	56	68	84
Estonia	41	38	50	63	28	23	85	3
Ireland	16	20	71	74	43	50	77	88
Greece	34	36	62	61	16	24	16	18
Spain	35	34	80	80	23	21	15	14
France	45	45	79	78	37	47	59	60
Italy	42	43	59	80	29	37	-12	-5
Cyprus	19	12	54	61	-10	6	57	115
Latvia	41	40	88	85	32	32	100	50
Lithuania	41	40	56	81	36	27	86	79
Luxembourg	29	29	86	86	51	52	108	107
Hungary	45	47	66	80	37	39	53	54
Malta	17	18	60	58	17	19	11	27
Netherlands	40	34	83	82	68	84	80	116
Austria	44	44	67	68	37	41	80	65
Poland	42	33	82	75	65	62	74	53
Portugal	32	32	81	82	22	23	68	60
Romania	43	41	65	71	30	30	17	24
Slovenia	43	40	86	83	46	53	95	68
Slovakia	41	36	70	44	30	25	100	25
Finland	40	39	80	74	63	56	100	100
Sweden	47	43	87	79	59	45	96	79
United Kingdom	30	30	69	65	59	52	84	84
Iceland	24	24	71	82	41	39	72	48
Norway	35	34	75	76	39	34	88	90
Switzerland	27	26	:	:	:	:	:	:
Turkey	41	38	:	:	:	:	:	:
Japan	:	:	57	58	19	21	137	132
United States	28	27	71	71	28	28	54	51

(¹) Cyprus, 2007 instead of 2008.
(²) EU-27, Cyprus and Romania, 2007 instead of 2008.

Source: Eurostat (tsiem050, earn_nt_unemtrp and earn_nt_lowwtrp)

Figure 5.16: Average hourly labour costs in the business economy of full-time employees, 2009 (1)
(EUR)

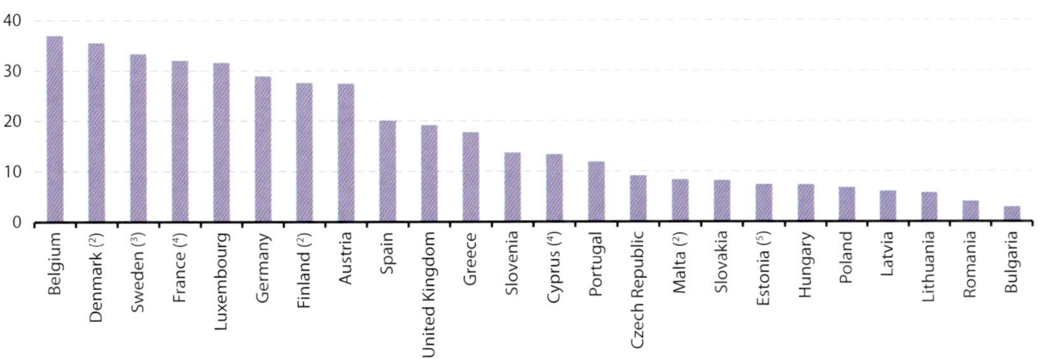

(1) Enterprises employing ten or more employees; NACE Rev. 2 Sections B to N; Ireland, Italy and Netherlands not available.
(2) 2008, NACE Rev. 2 Sections B to N.
(3) 2007, NACE Rev. 1.1 Sections C to K.
(4) 2008, NACE Rev. 1.1 Sections C to K.
(5) All enterprises.

Source: Eurostat (lc_an_costh_r2 and lc_an_costh)

Figure 5.17: Breakdown of labour costs in the business economy, 2009 (1)
(% share of total labour costs)

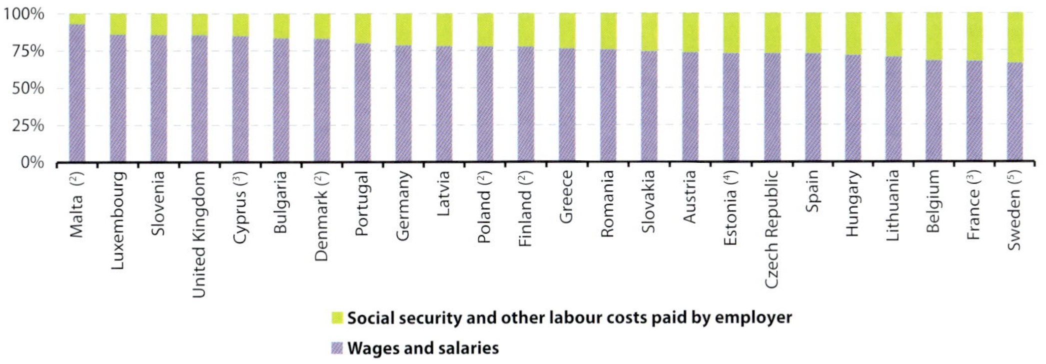

(1) Enterprises employing ten or more employees; NACE Rev. 2 Sections B to N; Ireland, Italy and Netherlands not available.
(2) 2008, NACE Rev. 2 Sections B to N.
(3) 2008, NACE Rev. 1.1 Sections C to K.
(4) All enterprises.
(5) 2007, NACE Rev. 1.1 Sections C to K.

Source: Eurostat (lc_an_struc_r2 and lc_an_struc)

5.4 Job vacancies

This subchapter gives an overview of annual job vacancy statistics in the European Union (EU), notably the job vacancy rate. Eurostat also collects quarterly job vacancy statistics.

EU policies in the area of job vacancies aim to improve the functioning of the labour market by trying to match more closely supply and demand. In order to enable job seekers to consult all vacancies publicised in each of the Member State's employment services, the European jobs and mobility portal (EURES) was set up.

Main statistical findings

There was an upward development in the job vacancy rate in the EU-27, with the rate rising during four consecutive years through to a relative peak of 2.2 % in 2007. The EU-27 job vacancy rate then fell to an historic low of 1.4 % in 2009; the time series for this indicator is available from 2003 onwards.

Among the Member States for which data are available, the job vacancy rate in 2009 was highest in Germany (2.5 %), Malta (1.8 %) and the United Kingdom (1.7 %); the rate was lowest in France and Latvia (both 0.3 %).

Data sources and availability

Data on job vacancies and occupied posts may be presented broken down by economic activity, occupation, size of enterprise and region. The national statistical authorities responsible for compiling job vacancy statistics send these statistics to Eurostat. Their data are used to compile the job vacancy rate for the EU and the euro area.

Some of the data provided by the Member States fails to match common criteria and there may be differences in the coverage of the data between countries; as a result, there are currently no EU-27 totals for the actual numbers of job vacancies or occupied posts. The EU-27 and euro area job vacancy rates are calculated on the basis of the information that is available; no estimates are made for missing or incomplete data. It is therefore not possible, at present, to present EU-27 or euro area job vacancy rates broken down by economic activity, occupation or size of enterprise.

Context

The job vacancy rate, in part, reflects the unmet demand for labour, as well as potential mismatches between the skills and availability of those who are unemployed and those sought by employers. Job vacancy statistics are used by the European Commission and the European Central Bank (ECB) to analyse and monitor the evolution of the labour market at national and European level. These statistics are also a key indicator used for an assessment of the business cycle and for a structural analysis of the economy.

Policy developments in this area have mainly focused on trying to improve the labour market by more closely matching supply and demand, through:

- modernising and strengthening labour market institutions, notably employment services;

- removing obstacles to worker mobility across Europe;
- better anticipating skill needs, labour market shortages and bottlenecks;
- managing economic migration;
- improving the adaptability of workers and enterprises so that there is a greater capacity to anticipate, trigger and absorb economic and social change.

The European jobs and mobility portal (EURES) was set-up with the aim of providing job seekers in the EU with the opportunity to consult all job vacancies publicised in each of the Member State's employment services. The website provides access to a range of job vacancies from 31 European countries (the 27 EU Member States, as well as Iceland, Liechtenstein, Norway and Switzerland). In autumn 2010, there were around one million job vacancies advertised by over 22 000 registered employers on the website, while more than 500 000 people had posted their CVs on the website.

European job days are another EU initiative in this domain and 2010 was the fourth edition of this programme of activities: during September and October 2010, a wide range of events (around 500) took place all over Europe with the aim of raising awareness about the opportunities and practicalities of living and working in another European country. The events typically include job fairs, seminars, lectures, workshops and cultural events, all aimed at improving labour mobility.

Figure 5.18: Job vacancy rate (1)
(%)

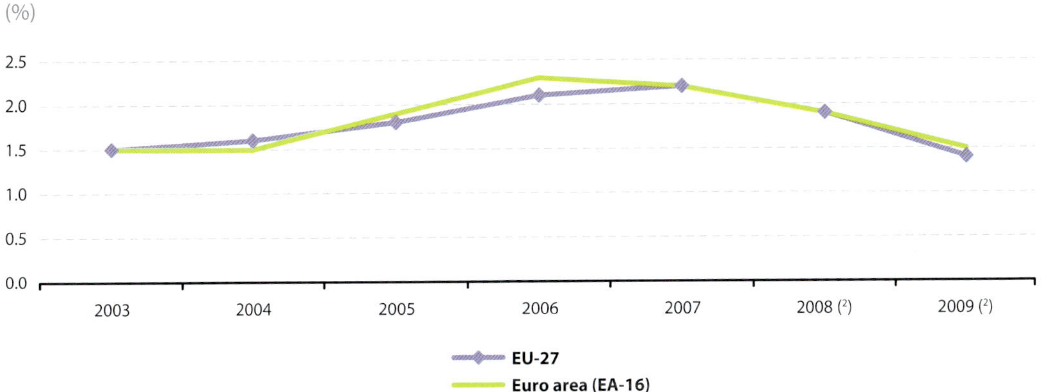

(1) Data from 2003 to 2008 cover NACE Rev. 1.1 Sections A to O; data for 2009 cover NACE Rev. 2 Sections B to S.
(2) Provisional.

Source: Eurostat (jvs_a_nace1 and jvs_a_nace2)

Figure 5.19: Job vacancy rate, 2009 (¹)
(%)

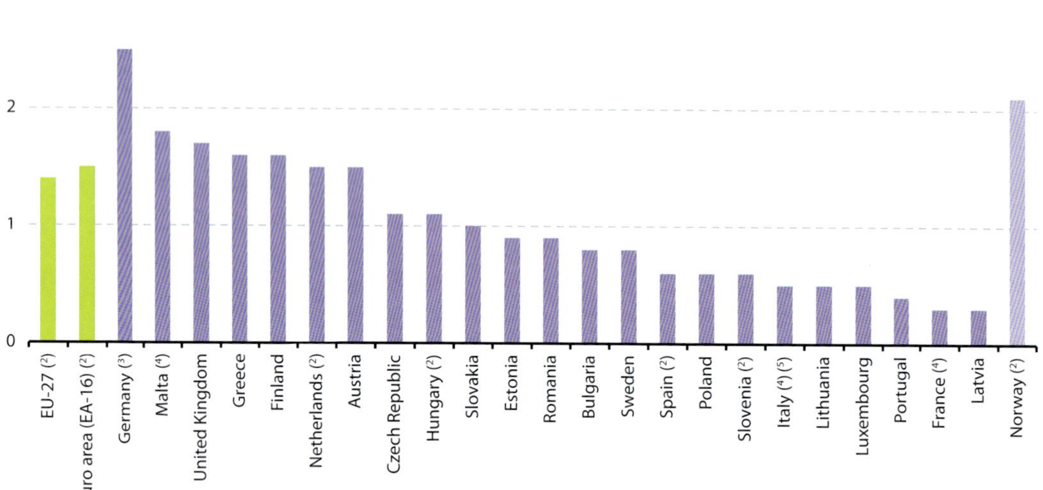

(¹) NACE Rev. 2 Sections B to S; Belgium, Denmark and Ireland, not available; Cyprus, confidential.
(²) Provisional.
(³) NACE Rev. 1.1 Sections A to O.
(⁴) Job vacancy rate for enterprises with 10 or more employees.
(⁵) NACE Rev. 2 Sections B to N.

Source: Eurostat (jvs_a_nace1, jvs_a_nace2, jvs_q_nace1 and jvs_q_nace2)

5.5 Labour market policy interventions

Labour market policy (LMP) interventions are generally targeted at providing assistance to the unemployed and other groups of people who face particular difficulties to enter the labour market. In most European Union (EU) Member States the primary target group is people registered as unemployed by national public employment services. However, policy objectives aimed at increasing participation in the labour market are increasingly focused on a broader range of persons who are not formally unemployed but are often receiving some other form of social benefit and are believed to be capable of working given the right support and opportunities. As a result, the types of intervention used, and the groups that are targeted, vary between Member States depending on national circumstances and priorities.

Main statistical findings

Across the EU-27, a total of 1.6 % of gross domestic product (GDP) was spent on LMP interventions in 2008. Approximately 60 % of this expenditure was directed to LMP supports, 28 % to LMP measures and 12 % to LMP services. However, the level of expenditure and the breakdown of both expenditure and participants between the different types of LMP intervention varied considerably between Member States, reflecting the diverse characteristics and problems within national labour markets, as well as the different political convictions of their respective governments.

Within the EU Member States, the highest level of relative expenditure on LMP interventions in 2008 was reported in Belgium (3.3 % of GDP), followed by Spain, Denmark, the Netherlands, Finland, Ireland and France, which all spent between 2.0 % and 2.5 % of their GDP on such interventions (see Figure 5.20). At the other end of the scale, ten Member States spent 0.5 % of GDP or less on these interventions: Malta, the United Kingdom, Cyprus, Latvia, Bulgaria, Slovenia, the Czech Republic, Lithuania, Estonia and Romania. Relative to GDP, Belgium spent the most on both LMP measures and LMP supports, being the only Member State to spend more than 1.0 % and more than 2.0 % of GDP respectively, while the Netherlands reported the highest relative expenditure on LMP services – at just over 0.3 % of GDP.

LMP measures (see Figure 5.21) mostly support the transition from unemployment or inactivity into employment, either: by improving employability through training or work experience; by providing incentives for employers to take on people from selected target groups; or by encouraging individuals to become self-employed. Total public expenditure on LMP measures across the EU-27 in 2008 was equivalent to 0.45 % of GDP. The largest part of this expenditure went on training (39.0 %), just less than a quarter (24.0 %) on employment incentives, while 16.1 % was accounted for by supported employment and rehabilitation (measures that promote labour market integration of people with reduced working capacity) and 13.4 % by direct job creation (which covers the provision of temporary jobs that are additional to normal market supply).

Across the EU-27 there was an average of 10.3 million people participating in LMP measures at any point during 2008. Of these, just less than 4 million received employment incentives, which mostly involve the use of public funds to provide a fixed-term subsidy to employers who take on people from selected target groups, either into a regular job or into a specially arranged placement for work experience. A further 3.2 million people were engaged in some form of labour market training (see Table 5.11).

Data sources and availability

LMP statistics cover all labour market interventions which can be described as 'public interventions in the labour market aimed at reaching its efficient functioning and correcting disequilibria and which can be distinguished from other general employment policy interventions in that they act selectively to favour particular groups in the labour market'. The scope of LMP statistics is limited to public interventions that explicitly target groups with difficulties in the labour market. This includes the unemployed, those employed but at risk of involuntary job loss, and people who are currently inactive in the labour market but would like to work.

Three types of interventions

LMP interventions are classified into three main types:

- **LMP services** refer to labour market interventions where the main activity of participants is job-search related and where participation usually does not result in a change in labour market status.
- **LMP measures** refer to labour market interventions where the main activity of participants is not job-search related and where participation usually results in a change of labour market status. In other words, a person who is unemployed typically ceases to be considered as such when participating in an LMP measure because they are temporarily in training or work and therefore not both actively seeking and immediately available for work. An activity that does not result in a change of labour market status may still be considered as a measure if the intervention fulfils the following criteria:

1. the activities undertaken are not job-search related, are supervised and constitute a full-time or significant part-time activity of participants during a significant period of time, and;
2. the aim is to improve the vocational qualifications of participants, or;
3. the intervention provides incentives to take-up or to provide employment (including self-employment).

- **LMP supports** refer to interventions that provide financial assistance, directly or indirectly, to individuals for labour market reasons, or which compensate individuals for disadvantage caused by labour market circumstances.

Additional category breakdowns

The three main types of intervention are further broken down into nine detailed categories according to the type of action:

- **LMP services**

1. Labour market services;

- **LMP measures**

2. Training;
3. Job rotation and job sharing;
4. Employment incentives;
5. Supported employment and rehabilitation;
6. Direct job creation;
7. Start-up incentives;

- **LMP supports**

8. Out-of-work income maintenance and support;
9. Early retirement.

The LMP methodology provides guidelines for the collection of data on LMP interventions: which interventions to cover; how to classify interventions by type of action; how to measure the expenditure associated with each intervention; and how to measure the number of participants in each intervention using observations of stocks and flows (entrants and exits).

Context

LMP interventions provide assistance to the unemployed and other groups facing difficulties entering the labour market. The LMP data collection was developed by the European Commission (EC) as an instrument to monitor the implementation and development of targeted employment policies across the EU in response to two agreements of the European Council in 1997. The first, held in Amsterdam in June 1997, confirmed that whilst employment policy should be a national responsibility, it was also an issue of common concern and that there should be a coordinated strategy at a European level. The second, held in November 1997 in Luxembourg – the so-called 'Jobs Summit' – launched the European employment strategy (EES) in which LMPs had a key role in relation to employability. Since that time, LMP statistics have been used to monitor both active and passive interventions in the labour market and, in particular, relevant areas of the employment guidelines as set out under the Lisbon strategy.

Within the new Europe 2020 strategy, the flexicurity approach aims to result in the provision and implementation of active LMPs while ensuring adequate benefits for those out of work. The concept of flexicurity came to the forefront of the EU's employment agenda in 2007 when the European Commission released a Communication titled 'Towards common principles of flexicurity – more and better jobs through flexibility and security' (COM 2007/359), which highlighted the idea of reconciling flexibility in the labour market with security for workers. Within this modern flexicurity approach, security refers not only to security of income (for example, through the provision of adequate unemployment benefits) but also to securing people's capacity to work by ensuring lifelong access to opportunities to develop and adapt their skills to meet new demands in the labour market. Hence, the Europe 2020 strategy specifically refers to the provision of active LMPs, which cover LMP measures and LMP services, and modern social security systems, which include LMP supports. These policies for labour market are, therefore, key instruments within the Europe 2020 strategy and a series of indicators based on LMP data continue to be used for monitoring progress.

Figure 5.20: Public expenditure on labour market policy interventions, 2008
(% of GDP)

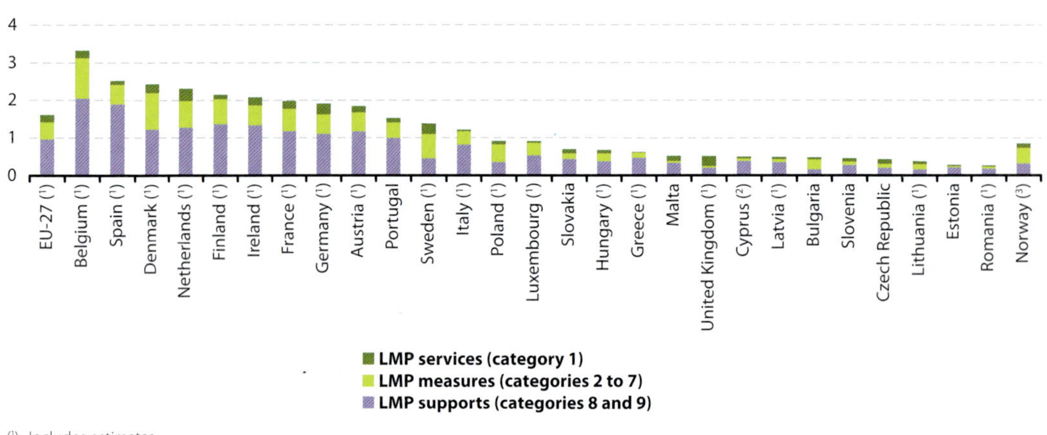

(¹) Includes estimates.
(²) Includes provisional data and estimates.
(³) Services data 2007; includes estimates.

Source: Eurostat (lmp_expsumm)

Figure 5.21: Public expenditure on labour market policy measures, EU-27, 2008 (¹)
(% of total)

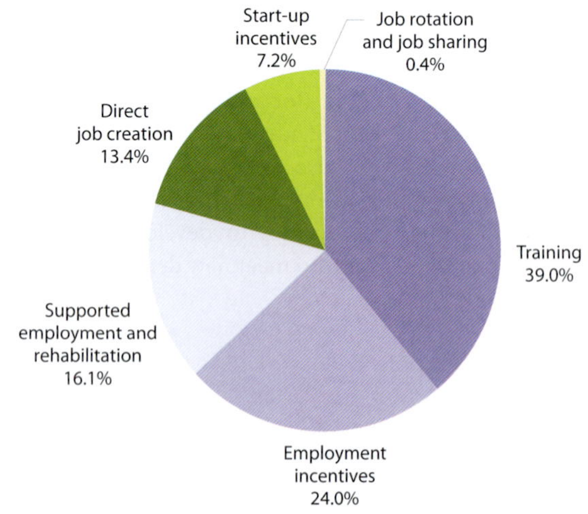

(¹) Estimates; figures do not sum to 100 % due to rounding.

Source: Eurostat (tps00077)

Table 5.11: Labour market policy measures, participants by type of action, 2008
(annual average stock in 1 000)

	Training	Job rotation & job sharing	Employment incentives	Supported employment & rehabilitation	Direct job creation	Start-up incentives
EU-27 (1)	3 181.9	122.5	3 986.1	1 220.3	983.6	772.5
Belgium (2)	109.4	-	216.3	37.7	152.1	1.3
Bulgaria (2)	8.2	-	10.6	1.4	65.8	3.9
Czech Republic	4.8	-	7.4	28.8	4.3	3.4
Denmark (2)	61.4	0.0	22.9	65.7	-	-
Germany	828.5	0.4	187.3	45.1	331.1	180.5
Estonia	1.0	-	0.0	0.0	0.0	0.2
Ireland (2)	34.5	-	4.5	3.2	24.4	4.6
Greece (2)	14.5	-	22.7	0.0	0.9	4.7
Spain (1)	199.3	93.8	1,976.8	54.5	:	392.0
France (1)	587.6	-	:	134.4	233.1	130.0
Italy (1)	799.8	20.0	612.7	-	23.2	5.1
Cyprus (1)	0.3	-	1.0	0.3	-	0.1
Latvia	1.5	-	2.3	0.0	1.6	:
Lithuania	4.1	0.3	:	4.5	2.4	0.1
Luxembourg (1)	0.8	-	12.0	0.1	0.7	-
Hungary	16.4	-	35.3	-	13.6	3.0
Malta (1)	0.4	-	0.1	-	0.0	:
Netherlands (2)	142.8	-	32.2	150.9	-	-
Austria (2)	103.9	0.2	63.3	2.0	6.8	2.6
Poland (1)	95.7	-	45.5	620.9	11.3	6.1
Portugal	50.0	-	83.1	6.1	21.1	6.1
Romania	34.6	-	39.0	-	11.9	:
Slovenia	3.4	-	0.6	-	2.3	0.8
Slovakia (2)	1.3	-	10.1	2.0	57.2	21.0
Finland (2)	45.7	7.9	13.8	8.2	11.7	4.4
Sweden	10.4	-	83.4	38.4	-	2.7
United Kingdom (1)	21.7	-	46.7	16.2	8.3	-
Norway	29.5	-	5.0	13.9	6.7	0.3

(1) Includes some values that are incomplete (participant data available for >80 % but <100 % of expenditure).
(2) Includes estimates.

Source: Eurostat (lmp_partsumm)

6

Living conditions and social protection

Eurostat data on living conditions and welfare aim to show a comprehensive picture of the social situation in the European Union (EU), covering variables related to income, housing, poverty, social exclusion and other living conditions. The demand for statistics on living conditions and welfare received a new impetus following the social chapter of the Amsterdam Treaty (1997) which became the driving force for EU social statistics. This was reinforced by successive European Councils that have kept the social dimension high on the political agenda. Moreover, 2010 was designated as the European year for combating poverty and social exclusion.

Eurostat collects and publishes a broad portfolio of social inclusion indicators employment and social policy indicators. Data covering living conditions and welfare come from three main sources:

- household budget surveys (HBS);
- EU statistics on income and living conditions (EU-SILC);
- the European system of integrated social protection statistics (ESSPROS).

Information is collected through an open method of coordination, designed to encourage national governments to provide regular data concerning social protection and social inclusion/exclusion, while focusing on combating poverty and social exclusion, reforming social welfare systems, and tackling the challenges posed by demographic change (in particular, population ageing). Social risks (such as unemployment, ill health or social exclusion) or actions that are undertaken to help meet social needs can be evaluated by studying data on social protection expenditure and receipts.

The Europe 2020 strategy for smart, sustainable and inclusive growth put forward by the European Commission provides a growth strategy for the coming decade. A European platform against poverty will be one of the seven flagship initiatives of this strategy. The goals are to:

- ensure economic, social and territorial cohesion;
- guarantee respect for the fundamental rights of people experiencing poverty and social exclusion, and enable them to live in dignity and take an active part in society;
- mobilise support to help people integrate in the communities where they live, get training and help to find a job and have access to social benefits.

To measure progress in meeting the Europe 2020 goals, five headline targets to be met by 2020 have been agreed and translated into national targets in each EU Member State, reflecting different situations and circumstances. One of these targets is that for the EU as a whole there will be at least 20 million fewer people in or at-risk-of poverty and social exclusion by 2020. The integrated economic and employment guidelines, first combined in 2008, were also revised as part of the Europe 2020 strategy. Guideline 10 concerns promoting social inclusion and combating poverty.

6.1 Living conditions

This subchapter analyses recent statistics on living conditions in the European Union (EU). Favourable living conditions depend on a wide range of factors, which may be divided into those that are income-related and those that are not. The income distribution within a country provides a picture of inequalities: on the one hand, inequalities may create incentives for people to improve their situation through work, innovation or acquiring new skills, while on the other, crime, poverty and social exclusion are often seen as being linked to such income inequalities. Non-income related factors that may influence living conditions include the quality of healthcare services, education and training opportunities, or individual's access to goods and services – aspects that affect everyday lives and well-being.

Main statistical findings

At-risk-of-poverty rate and threshold

In 2008, 16.5 % of the EU-27 population was assessed to be at-risk-of-poverty. This figure, calculated as a weighted average of national results, conceals considerable variations between countries. In five Member States, namely Latvia (25.6 %), Romania (23.4 %), Bulgaria (21.4 %), Greece (20.1 %) and Lithuania (20.0 %), one fifth or more of the population was assessed to be at-risk-of-poverty. Among the EU Member States the lowest percentages of persons at-risk-of-poverty were observed in the Czech Republic (9.0 %), the Netherlands (10.5 %) and Slovakia (10.9 %); Iceland (10.1 %) and Norway (11.3 %) also reported relatively low shares of their respective populations at-risk-of-poverty (see Figure 6.1).

The at-risk-of-poverty threshold is set at 60 % of the national median equivalised disposable income. It is often expressed in purchasing power standards (PPS) in order to take account of the differences in the cost of living across countries. It varies greatly from about PPS 2 000 in Romania and PPS 3 000 in Bulgaria to more than PPS 10 000 in eight Member States as well as Iceland and Norway, with the highest value in Luxembourg (PPS 16 000) – see Figure 6.1. In general, the at-risk-of-poverty rate is very stable from one year to the next. Between 2007 and 2008, the main exceptions to this rule were Latvia (with a sharp increase of 4.4 percentage points) and Ireland (with a reduction of 1.7 percentage points).

Different groups in society are more or less vulnerable to monetary poverty. Although in 2008 there was little difference in the at-risk-of-poverty rate (after social transfers) between men and women in the EU-27 (15.4 % compared with 17.4 % respectively), there were notable differences when the population was classified according to activity status (see Tables 6.1 and 6.2).

The unemployed are a particularly vulnerable group: a little over two fifths (44.5 %) of the unemployed were at-risk-of-poverty in the EU-27 in 2008, with the highest rates in Estonia (61.3 %), Germany (56.8 %), the United Kingdom and Bulgaria (both 55.0 %). About one in six (16.2 %) retired persons in the EU-27 were at-risk-of-poverty in 2008; rates were much higher in the Baltic Member States, Cyprus, Bulgaria and the United Kingdom. Those in employment were far less likely to be at-risk-of-poverty (8.5 % in the EU-27), although there were relatively high rates in Romania (17.5 %) and Greece (14.3 %) – see Table 6.2.

Social protection measures can be used as a means for reducing poverty and social exclusion. This may be achieved, for example, through the distribution of benefits. One way of evaluating the success of social protection measures is to compare at-risk-of-poverty indicators before and after social transfers. In 2008, social transfers reduced the at-risk-of-poverty rate among the population of the EU-27 from 25.1 % before transfers to 16.5 % after transfers, thereby lifting 34 % of those in poverty above the poverty line. In percentage terms, the impact of social benefits was lowest in Greece, Latvia, Spain, Italy, Bulgaria, Estonia, Romania and Cyprus. In contrast, half or more of those persons who were at-risk-of-poverty in Hungary, Denmark, Sweden, the Czech Republic, Ireland and Finland were removed as a result of social transfers; this was also the case in Norway (see Figure 6.2).

Income inequalities

Societies cannot combat poverty and social exclusion without analysing inequalities within society, whether they are economic in nature or social. Data on economic inequality becomes particularly important for estimating relative poverty, because the distribution of economic resources may have a direct bearing on the extent and depth of poverty (see Figure 6.3).

There were wide inequalities in the distribution of income among the population of the EU-27 in 2008: the 20 % of the population with the highest equivalised disposable income received five times as much income as the 20 % of the population with the lowest equivalised disposable income. This ratio varied considerably across the Member States, from 3.4 in the Czech Republic, Slovenia and Slovakia to more than 6.0 in Portugal and Bulgaria, reaching highs of 7.0 in Romania and 7.3 in Latvia.

There is policy interest in the inequalities felt by many different groups in society. One group of particular interest is that of the elderly, in part reflecting the growing proportion of the EU's population aged over 65 years. Pension systems can play an important role in addressing poverty amongst the elderly. In this respect, it is interesting to compare the incomes of the elderly with the rest of the population. Across the EU-27 as a whole, people aged 65 and more had a median income which in 2008 was around 85 % of the median income for the population under the age of 65. Hungary was the only Member State where the income of the elderly was at the same level as for persons under 65. In Luxembourg, Poland, France and Austria, the median income of the elderly was more than 90 % of that recorded for people under 65. In contrast, the elderly in Latvia and Cyprus had median incomes that were less than 60 % of those recorded for people under 65, with shares between 60 % and 70 % in Estonia, Bulgaria and Denmark (see Figure 6.4). These relatively low proportions may broadly reflect pension entitlements.

The depth of poverty, which helps to quantify just how poor the poor are, can be measured by the relative median at-risk-of-poverty gap. The median income of persons at-risk-of-poverty in the EU-27 was an average 21.8 % below the 60 % poverty threshold in 2008. Among the countries shown in Figure 6.5, the national at-risk-of-poverty gap was widest in Romania (32.3 %), Latvia (28.6 %) and Bulgaria (27.0 %), but also relatively wide in Lithuania (25.7 %) and Greece (24.7 %). The lowest gap among the Member States was observed in the Netherlands (4.9 %), followed by Austria (15.3 %), while there was also a relatively low gap in Iceland (15.0 %).

Material deprivation

Income-related measures of poverty need to be analysed together with other measures – such as material deprivation – in order to have a deeper understanding of poverty. The material deprivation rate provides a headcount of the number of people who cannot afford to pay for at least three from a list of nine items, while those who lack four or more items are considered to be severely deprived. About one in every six (17.3 %) members of the EU population were materially deprived in 2008, while 8.5 % suffered from severe material deprivation; there were considerable discrepancies between the Member States that joined the EU in 2007, those that joined in 2004, and the EU-15 Member States. Less than one in ten people in Luxembourg, the Nordic Member States, the Netherlands and Spain were materially deprived, whereas the proportion rose to around one third of the population in Latvia, Hungary and Poland and reached around half of the population in Romania and Bulgaria. The proportion of people severely deprived ranged from below 3 % in Spain, Denmark, the Netherlands, Sweden and Luxembourg to more than 30 % in Romania and Bulgaria (see Figure 6.6).

Persons living in households with a low work intensity

Being in employment is generally an effective way to secure oneself against the risk of poverty. People living in households with a low work intensity (people aged 0 to 59 living in households where the adults worked less than 20 % of their total work potential during the year prior to the survey) were more likely to be exposed to social exclusion. In 2008, 9.0 % of the EU-27 population lived in households with low work intensity. The highest percentages among the countries shown in Figure 6.7 were registered in Ireland (13.6 %), Hungary (12.0 %), Belgium (11.7 %) and Germany (11.6 %) while the lowest were in Sweden (5.4 %), Estonia (5.3 %), Slovakia (5.2 %), Latvia, Lithuania (both 5.1 %), Luxembourg (4.7 %) and Cyprus (4.1 %), as well as in Iceland (2.6 %).

Data sources and availability

EU statistics on income and living conditions (EU-SILC) was launched in 2003 on the basis of a gentlemen's agreement between Eurostat, six Member States (Austria, Belgium, Denmark, Greece, Ireland, Luxembourg) and Norway. It was formally launched in 2004 in 15 countries and expanded in 2005 to cover all of the then EU-25 Member States, together with Iceland and Norway. Bulgaria launched EU-SILC in 2006, while Romania, Switzerland and Turkey introduced the survey in 2007.

EU-SILC comprises both a cross-sectional dimension and a longitudinal dimension. While comparisons of standards of living between countries are frequently based on GDP per capita, such figures say little about the distribution of income within a country. In this subchapter, indicators measuring the distribution of income and relative poverty are presented.

Household disposable income is established by summing up all monetary incomes received from any source by each member of the household (including income from work, investment and social benefits) plus income received at the household level and deducting taxes and social contributions paid. In order to reflect differences in household size and composition, this total is divided by the number of 'equivalent adults' using a standard (equivalence) scale, the so-called 'modified OECD' scale, which attributes a weight of 1 to the first adult in the household, a weight of 0.5 to each subsequent member of the household aged 14 and over, and a weight of 0.3 to household members aged less than 14. The resulting figure is called equivalised disposable income and is attributed to each member of the household. For the purpose of poverty indicators, the equivalised disposable income is calculated from the total disposable income of each household divided by the equivalised household size; consequently, each person in the household is considered to have the same equivalised income.

The income reference period is a fixed 12-month period (such as the previous calendar or tax year) for all countries except the United Kingdom for which the income reference period is the current year of the survey and Ireland for which the survey is continuous and income is collected for the 12 months prior to the survey.

The at-risk-of-poverty rate is defined as the share of people with an equivalised disposable income that is below the at-risk-of-poverty threshold (expressed in purchasing power standards – PPS), set at 60 % of the national median equivalised disposable income. This rate may be expressed before or after social transfers, with the difference measuring the hypothetical impact of national social transfers in reducing poverty risk. Retirement and survivors' pensions are counted as income before transfers and not as social transfers. Various analyses of this indicator are available, for example by age, gender, activity status, household type, or education level. It should be noted that this indicator does not measure wealth but is instead a measure of low current income (in comparison with other people in the same country) which does not necessarily imply a low standard of living. The EU-27 aggregate is a population-weighted average of individual national figures. In line with decisions of the European Council, the at-risk-of-poverty rate is measured relative to the situation in each country rather than applying a common threshold to all countries.

Context

At the Laeken European Council in December 2001, European heads of state and government endorsed a first set of common statistical indicators for social exclusion and poverty that are subject to a continuing process of refinement by the indicators sub-group (ISG) of the social protection committee (SPC). These indicators are an essential element in the open method of coordination to monitor the progress of Member States in the fight against poverty and social exclusion.

EU-SILC was implemented in order to provide underlying data for these indicators. Organised under framework Regulation 1177/2003, it is now the reference source for statistics on income and living conditions and for common indicators of social inclusion in particular.

In the context of the Europe 2020 strategy, the European Council adopted in June 2010 a headline target on social inclusion. EU-SILC is the source for the three sub-indicators on which this new target is based, namely the at-risk-of-poverty rate, severe material deprivation rate and persons living in households with low work intensity.

Figure 6.1: At-risk-of-poverty rate and threshold, 2008

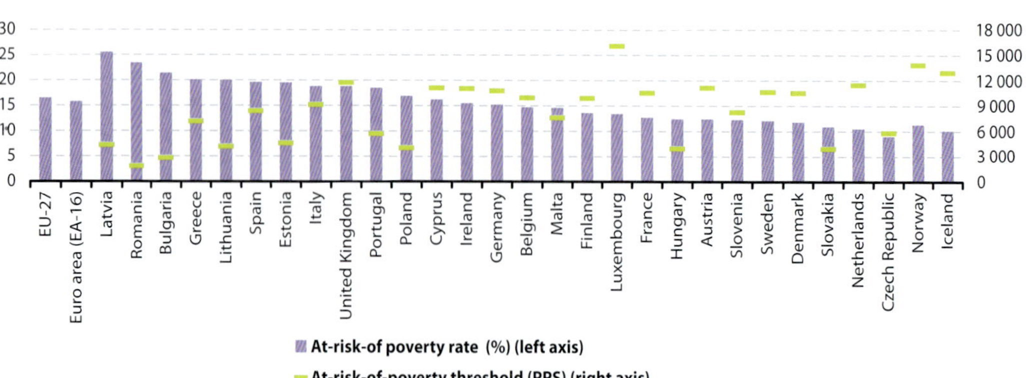

Source: Eurostat (ilc_li01 and ilc_li02)

Table 6.1: At-risk-of-poverty rate after social transfers
(%)

	Male			Female		
	2006	2007	2008	2006	2007	2008
EU-27	*15.3*	15.9	15.4	*16.9*	17.5	17.4
Euro area (EA-16)	14.5	15.1	14.8	16.4	17.1	16.8
Belgium	13.7	14.4	13.6	15.6	15.9	15.9
Bulgaria (1)	17.3	20.9	19.8	19.3	23.0	22.9
Czech Republic	8.9	8.7	8.0	10.8	10.5	10.1
Denmark	11.4	11.3	11.7	12.0	12.0	12.0
Germany	12.1	14.1	14.2	13.0	16.3	16.2
Estonia	16.3	16.7	16.5	19.9	21.7	22.0
Ireland	17.5	16.0	14.5	19.5	18.5	16.4
Greece	19.5	19.6	19.6	21.4	20.9	20.7
Spain	18.5	18.5	18.3	21.3	20.9	21.0
France (2)	12.3	12.8	11.9	14.0	13.4	13.4
Italy	18.0	18.4	17.1	21.1	21.3	20.1
Cyprus	13.5	13.5	14.0	17.7	17.4	18.3
Latvia	21.1	19.3	23.1	24.8	22.7	27.7
Lithuania	19.1	16.7	17.6	20.8	21.3	22.0
Luxembourg	13.8	12.9	12.5	14.3	14.1	14.3
Hungary	16.3	12.3	12.4	15.5	12.3	12.4
Malta	13.2	13.8	13.7	14.1	14.9	15.5
Netherlands	9.5	9.6	10.5	9.9	10.7	10.4
Austria	11.0	10.6	11.2	14.0	13.3	13.5
Poland	19.7	17.6	17.0	18.5	17.1	16.7
Portugal	17.7	17.2	17.9	19.1	19.0	19.1
Romania (3)	:	24.3	22.4	:	25.3	24.3
Slovenia	10.3	10.0	11.0	12.9	12.9	13.6
Slovakia	11.8	9.8	10.1	11.5	11.2	11.5
Finland	12.1	12.1	12.7	13.1	13.8	14.5
Sweden	12.3	10.5	11.3	12.3	10.6	13.0
United Kingdom	18.0	17.7	17.5	20.0	20.0	20.1
Iceland	9.1	8.9	9.5	10.1	11.0	10.7
Norway	10.0	10.6	9.8	12.6	14.1	12.9

(1) Break in series, 2006.
(2) Break in series, 2008.
(3) Break in series, 2007.

Source: Eurostat (ilc_li02)

Table 6.2: At-risk-of-poverty rate after social transfers by most frequent activity status, 2008 (¹)
(%)

	Total population	Persons employed	Not employed	Unemployed	Retired	Inactive population, others
EU-27	15.4	8.5	23.3	44.5	16.2	27.1
Euro area (EA-16)	14.9	8.0	22.5	43.9	14.4	26.3
Belgium	13.9	4.8	23.8	34.8	18.3	25.6
Bulgaria	20.5	7.5	34.9	55.0	31.7	23.9
Czech Republic	8.0	3.6	13.5	47.8	8.0	12.4
Denmark	12.3	5.0	22.7	33.9	16.5	30.6
Germany	14.5	7.1	22.8	56.8	15.0	22.6
Estonia	20.1	7.3	39.9	61.3	43.3	31.9
Ireland	14.6	6.5	25.1	28.3	18.0	26.6
Greece	19.4	14.3	24.5	36.8	20.3	26.0
Spain	18.7	10.6	28.6	37.4	21.3	31.1
France	11.7	6.8	16.7	39.0	8.8	24.9
Italy	17.3	8.9	24.6	41.8	14.8	28.6
Cyprus	16.8	6.4	32.5	32.0	48.1	20.0
Latvia	25.7	11.0	47.6	52.8	55.1	32.6
Lithuania	19.2	9.3	32.6	51.0	30.8	31.5
Luxembourg	11.5	9.4	14.1	52.2	4.9	15.9
Hungary	10.5	5.8	15.0	48.9	6.8	23.9
Malta	13.3	5.1	21.0	29.4	21.5	20.1
Netherlands	9.2	4.8	15.3	36.3	8.3	18.8
Austria	11.7	6.3	18.2	41.0	13.1	21.9
Poland	15.4	11.5	19.7	38.8	9.6	25.0
Portugal	17.4	11.8	24.8	34.6	20.1	28.3
Romania	20.9	17.5	24.7	42.7	19.0	31.8
Slovenia	12.3	5.1	20.2	37.6	17.9	21.6
Slovakia	9.5	5.8	14.5	43.2	9.7	15.7
Finland	13.8	5.1	25.6	43.5	21.7	29.1
Sweden	11.7	6.8	20.0	39.2	14.9	32.1
United Kingdom	17.6	8.6	32.5	55.0	29.1	35.4
Iceland	9.5	6.7	18.8	25.1	18.1	19.3
Norway	11.4	5.3	22.3	40.0	13.7	40.3

(¹) Persons aged 18 or over.

Source: Eurostat (ilc_li04)

Figure 6.2: At-risk-of-poverty rate, 2008
(%)

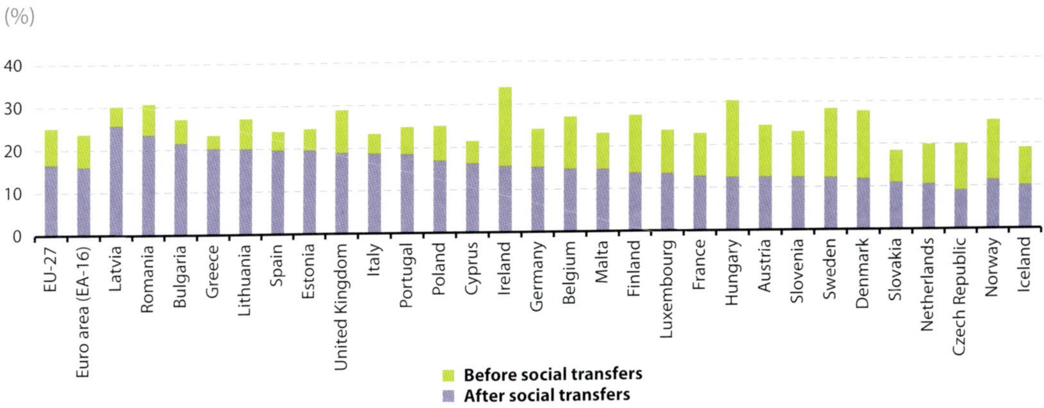

Source: Eurostat (ilc_li02 and ilc_li10)

Figure 6.3: Inequality of income distribution, 2008
(income quintile share ratio)

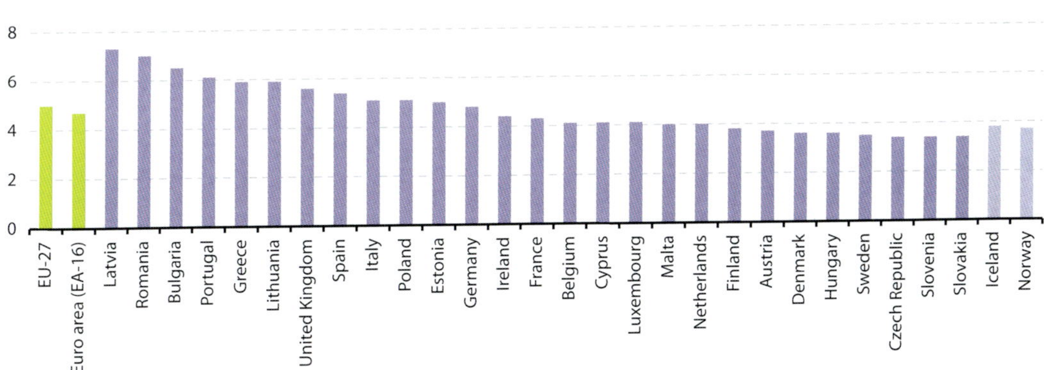

Source: Eurostat (ilc_di11)

Figure 6.4: Relative median income ratio, 2008
(ratio)

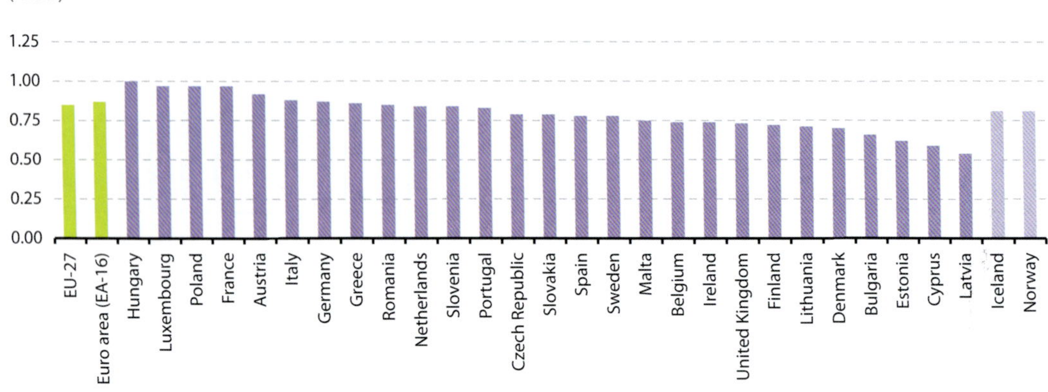

Source: Eurostat (ilc_pnp2)

Figure 6.5: Relative median at-risk-of-poverty gap, 2008
(%)

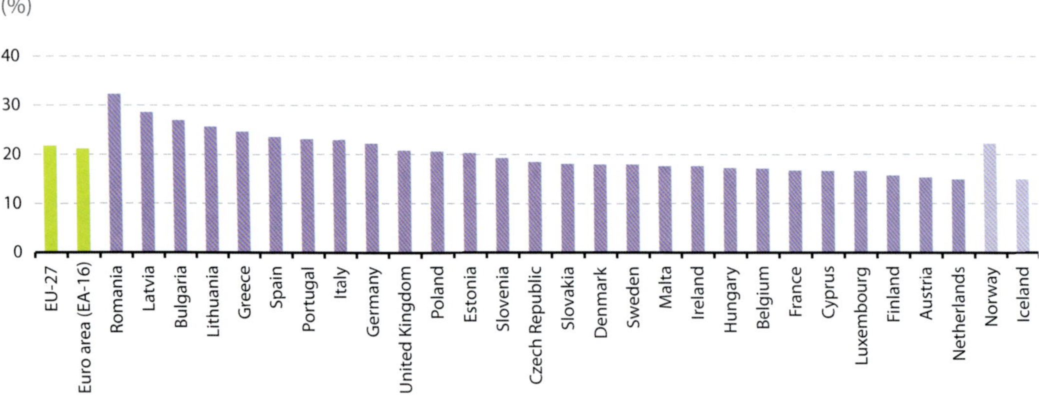

Source: Eurostat (ilc_li11)

Figure 6.6: Material deprivation rate - proportion of persons who cannot afford to pay for selected items, 2008
(%)

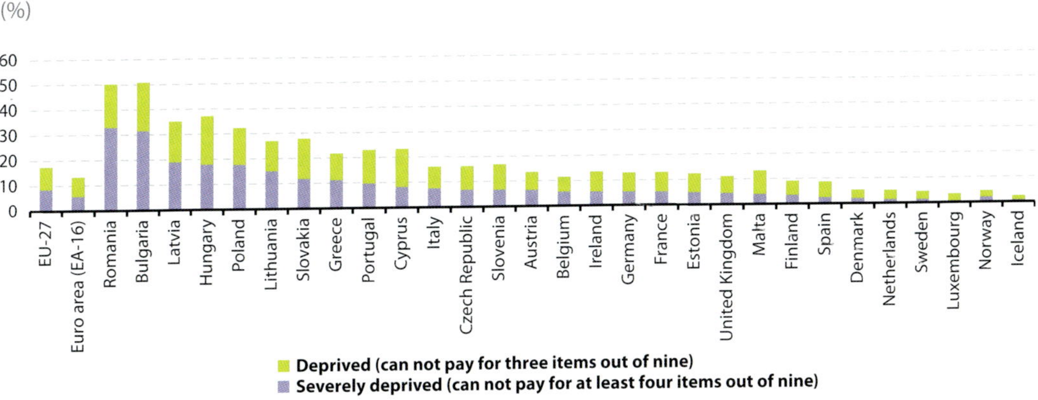

Source: Eurostat (ilc_sip8)

Figure 6.7: People living in households with very low work intensity, 2008
(%)

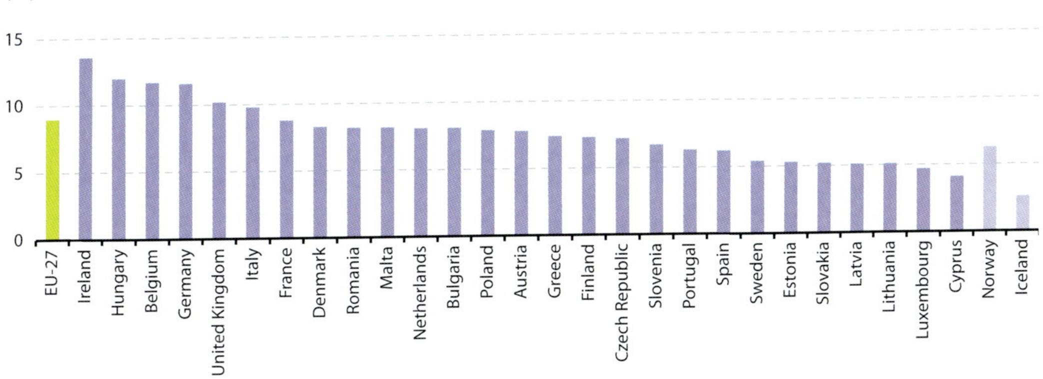

Source: Eurostat (t2020_51)

6.2 Housing

Decent housing, at an affordable price in a safe environment, is a fundamental need and right. Ensuring this need, which is likely to alleviate poverty and social exclusion, is still a significant challenge in a number of European countries. This subchapter provides information in relation to recent statistics on housing in the European Union (EU), focusing on dwelling types, tenure status (owning versus renting), housing quality and affordability.

Main statistical findings

Type of dwelling

In 2008, 41.8 % of the EU-27 population lived in flats, 34.1 % in detached houses and 22.6 % in semi-detached houses. The share of persons living in flats was highest in Latvia (66.5 %), Estonia (65.2 %) and Spain (64.4 %). The share of people living in detached houses was highest in Slovenia (68.1 %), Hungary (65.4 %), Romania (59.7 %) and Denmark (59.0 %), while the highest propensity to live in semi-detached houses was reported in the Netherlands (62.0 %), followed by the United Kingdom (60.5 %) and Ireland (55.4 %) – see Figure 6.8.

Tenure status

In 2008, just over one quarter of the EU-27 population lived in an owner-occupied home for which there was an outstanding loan or mortgage, while close to half of the population lived in an owner-occupied home without a loan or mortgage. As such, a total of nearly three quarters (73.6 %) of the population lived in owner-occupied dwellings, while 12.5 % lived in dwellings with a market price rent, and 13.9 % in reduced-rent or free accommodation.

At least half of the population lived in owner-occupied dwellings in 2008 across all of the EU Member States; the figures ranged from 57.7 % in Austria to 96.5 % in Romania. In the Netherlands (59.6 %) and Sweden (55.6 %) more than half of the population lived in owner-occupied dwellings with an outstanding loan or mortgage; this was also the case in Iceland (72.2 %) and Norway (61.5 %).

The share of persons living in rented dwellings with a market price rent in 2008 was less than 10 % in 14 of the EU Member States, as well as in Iceland. In Denmark, the Netherlands, Sweden and Austria more than one quarter of the population lived in rented dwellings with a market price rent. The share of the population living in a dwelling with a reduced price rent or occupying a dwelling free of charge was less than 20 % in all of the Member States except for Poland where this share reached 31.7 % (see Figure 6.9).

Housing quality

One of the key dimensions in assessing the quality of housing conditions is the availability of sufficient space in the dwelling. The overcrowding rate describes the share of people living in a dwelling considered as overcrowded. Based on the number of rooms available to the household, this indicator depends on the household's size, as well as its members' ages and family situation.

Some 18.2 % of the EU-27 population lived in overcrowded dwellings in 2008; the highest overcrowding rates were registered in Latvia (58.1 %), Romania (56.5 %), Poland (50.8 %) and Lithuania (49.9 %). In contrast, Cyprus (1.2 %) and the Netherlands (1.7 %) recorded the lowest rates of overcrowding.

Within the population at-risk-of-poverty (whose equivalised disposable income was below 60 % of national median equivalised disposable income) the overcrowding rate in the EU-27 was 29.3 % in 2008, 11 percentage points above the rate for the whole population. The highest overcrowding rates among the population at-risk-of-poverty were registered in Poland (67.2 %), Hungary (65.7 %) and Romania (63.3 %), while the overcrowding rate was below 5 % in Cyprus and Malta. Malta and Latvia were the only Member States where the overcrowding rate was lower among the population at-risk-of-poverty than among the population as a whole (see Figure 6.10).

In addition to overcrowding some aspects – such as the lack of a bath or a toilet, a leaking roof in the dwelling, or a dwelling considered as too dark – are taken into account to build a more complete indicator of housing quality. The severe housing deprivation rate is defined as the share of persons living in a dwelling which is considered as overcrowded, while having at the same time at least one of the housing deprivation measures. Across the EU-27 as a whole 6.6 % of the population suffered from severe housing deprivation in 2008. In Bulgaria, Hungary and Latvia between one fifth and one quarter of the population faced severe housing deprivation in 2008, rising to a high of 30.2 % in Romania. In contrast, less than 1 % of the population in the Netherlands, Finland, Cyprus, Ireland, Malta and Spain lived in conditions which could be qualified as severe housing deprivation (see Figure 6.11).

Housing affordability

Some, 12.5 % of the EU-27 population spent 40 % or more of their equivalised disposable income on housing in 2008. The proportion of the population whose housing costs exceeded 40 % of their equivalised disposable income was highest for tenants with market price rents and lowest for persons in owner-occupied dwellings without a loan or mortgage (see Table 6.3).

The EU-27 average masks significant differences between Member States: at one extreme there were a number of Member States where a relatively small proportion of the population had housing costs in excess of 40 % of their disposable income, notably Cyprus (2.0 %), Ireland (3.3 %), France (3.4 %), Estonia (3.6 %), Luxembourg (3.7 %) and Malta (3.8 %). At the other extreme, 24.7 % of the population in Germany spent more than 40 % of their equivalised disposable income on housing, well above the next highest shares recorded in Greece (22.6 %), Romania (18.9 %) and the United Kingdom (16.7 %).

Data sources and availability

The data used in this section are primarily derived from micro-data from EU statistics on income and living conditions (EU-SILC). The reference population is all private households and their current members residing in the territory of the Member State at the time of data collection; persons living in collective households and in institutions are generally excluded from the target population.

Context

Questions of social housing, homelessness or integration play an important role within the social policy agenda. The charter of fundamental rights stipulates in Article II-94 that 'in order to combat social exclusion and poverty, the Union recognises and respects the right to social and housing assistance so as to ensure a decent existence for all those who lack sufficient resources, in accordance with Community law and national laws and practices'.

However, the EU does not have any responsibilities in respect of housing; rather, national governments develop their own housing policies. Many countries face similar challenges: for example, how to renew housing stocks, how to plan and combat urban sprawl, how to promote sustainable development, how to help young and disadvantage groups to get into the housing market, or how to promote energy efficiency among house owners.

Figure 6.8: Population by dwelling type, 2008
(% of population)

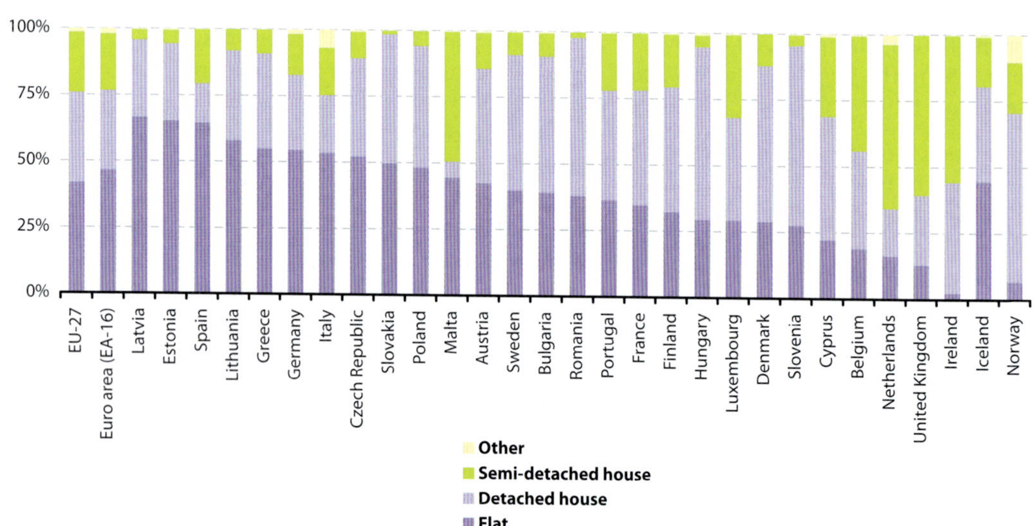

Source: Eurostat (ilc_lvho01)

Figure 6.9: Population by tenure status, 2008 (1)
(% of population)

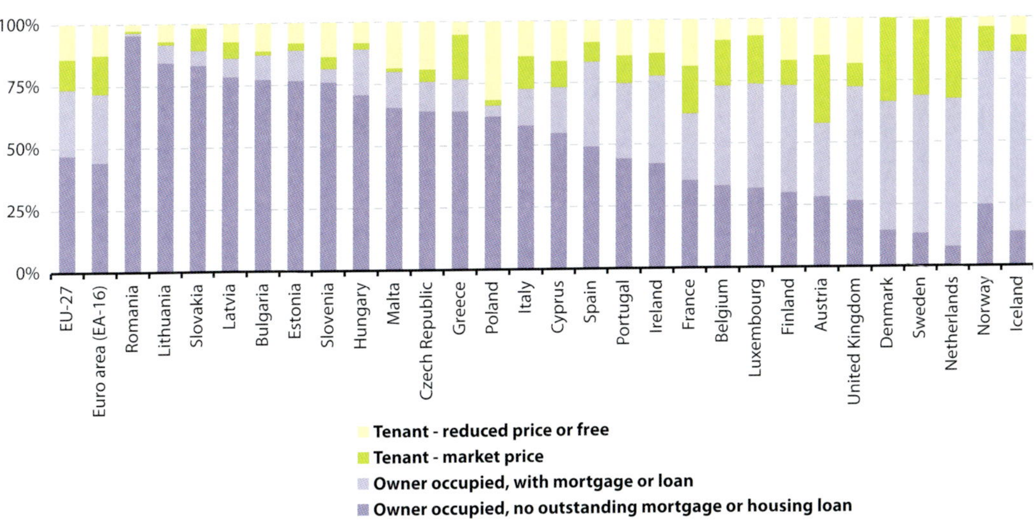

(1) Germany, not available.

Source: Eurostat (ilc_lvho02)

Figure 6.10: Overcrowding rate, 2008
(% of specified population)

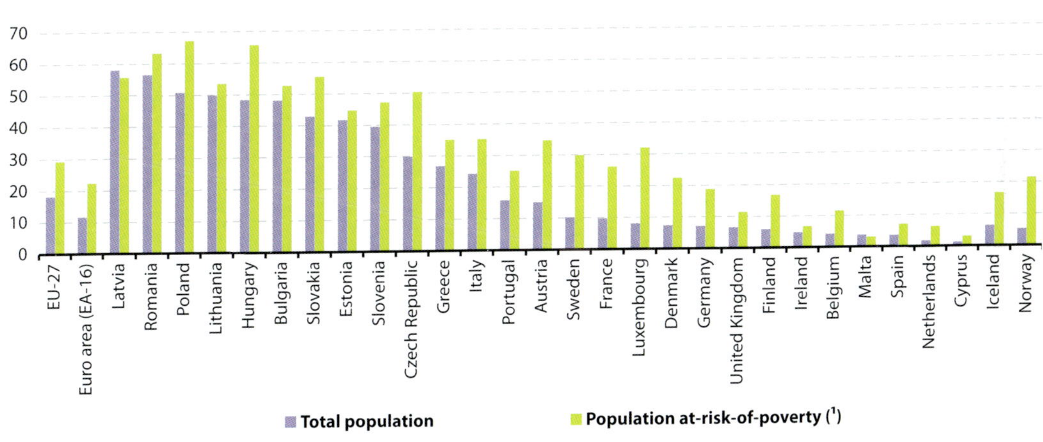

(1) Population below 60 % of median equivalised income.

Source: Eurostat (ilc_lvho05a)

Figure 6.11: Severe housing deprivation, 2008
(% of population)

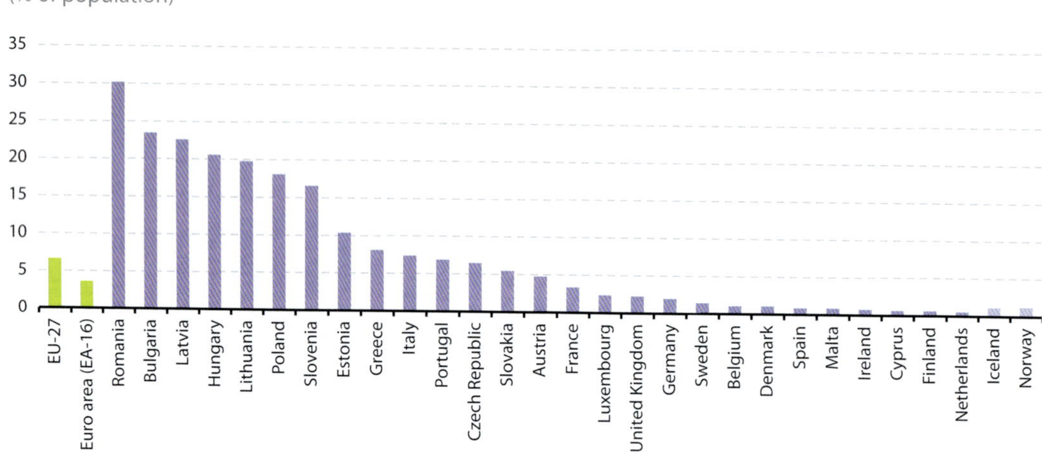

Source: Eurostat (ilc_mdho06a)

Table 6.3: Housing cost overburden rate by tenure status, 2008
(% of population)

	Total population	Owner occupied, with mortgage or loan	Owner occupied, no outstanding mortgage or housing loan	Tenant - market price	Tenant - reduced price or free
EU-27	12.5	*8.6*	*6.8*	*24.6*	*11.6*
Euro area (EA-16)	12.0	*6.9*	*3.4*	*23.0*	*6.4*
Belgium	12.5	6.5	9.5	30.5	13.8
Bulgaria	13.9	18.9	11.8	36.6	20.5
Czech Republic	12.8	28.7	9.4	25.4	11.1
Denmark	6.1	3.5	3.5	11.2	:
Germany	24.7	:	:	:	:
Estonia	3.6	6.0	2.0	25.1	7.2
Ireland	3.3	2.7	1.0	17.1	2.6
Greece	22.6	11.3	13.2	69.0	5.2
Spain	8.1	10.4	2.3	35.4	6.3
France	3.4	0.2	0.5	11.7	4.9
Italy	8.1	9.2	3.1	28.6	8.3
Cyprus	2.0	1.3	0.4	13.4	0.7
Latvia	9.3	14.0	8.0	17.4	9.9
Lithuania	4.8	5.8	4.5	8.4	7.5
Luxembourg	3.7	1.6	0.3	14.3	2.6
Hungary	11.6	18.9	7.8	48.7	16.9
Malta	3.8	7.2	2.4	31.3	3.8
Netherlands	13.8	11.2	6.1	20.7	9.3
Austria	4.7	1.6	1.4	10.4	6.8
Poland	9.7	7.3	8.8	26.6	10.6
Portugal	8.2	13.1	3.8	19.0	3.2
Romania	18.9	15.0	18.1	72.8	28.8
Slovenia	4.4	17.4	2.9	15.2	4.2
Slovakia	6.0	3.7	5.2	11.6	20.5
Finland	4.8	3.2	2.3	13.3	8.7
Sweden	8.6	2.1	8.9	19.8	26.5
United Kingdom	16.7	12.6	9.7	39.6	26.1
Iceland	10.6	11.7	5.9	14.2	4.5
Norway	11.0	11.0	4.8	30.7	5.0

Source: Eurostat (ilc_lvho07c and ilc_lvho07a)

6.3 Social protection

Social protection encompasses all interventions from public or private bodies intended to relieve households and individuals of the burden of a defined set of risks or needs, provided that there is neither a simultaneous reciprocal nor an individual arrangement involved. This subchapter analyses recent statistics on social protection in the European Union (EU).

Main statistical findings

Social protection expenditure in the EU-27 was equivalent to 26.2 % of gross domestic product (GDP) in 2007 (see Table 6.4). Among the Member States its share was highest in France (30.5 %) and Sweden (29.7 %), and was higher than 25 % in ten of the EU-15 Member States. In contrast, social protection expenditure represented less than 20 % of GDP in all of the Member States that joined the EU in 2004 or 2007 with the exceptions of Slovenia and Hungary, and was also below 20 % in Ireland (18.9 %) and Luxembourg (19.3 %).

The use of a purchasing power standard (PPS) allows a comparison of social protection expenditure per inhabitant between countries, taking account of differences in price levels. The highest level of expenditure on social protection per inhabitant in 2007 was registered for Luxembourg (PPS 13 231 per inhabitant), followed some way behind by the Netherlands, Sweden, Belgium, Austria, Denmark and France - where social protection per inhabitant was between PPS 8 200 and PPS 9 300 (see Figure 6.12). In contrast, expenditure in Latvia, Bulgaria and Romania was less than PPS 2 000 per inhabitant. These disparities between countries are partly related to different levels of wealth, but may also reflect differences in social protection systems, demographic trends, unemployment rates and other social, institutional and economic factors.

Among social protection benefits (the largest component of total expenditure), a majority of the EU-27's expenditure was directed towards old age benefits (for example, pensions) or to sickness and healthcare benefits; together these two items accounted for close to 70 % of total EU-27 benefits in 2007 (see Figure 6.13). Benefits related to family/children, disabilities, survivors and unemployment each accounted for shares of between 5 % and 8 % of total expenditure in the EU-27, while housing accounted for 2.3 %.

Expenditure on pensions across the EU-27 was equivalent to 11.8 % of GDP in 2007, ranging from 14.6 % in Italy to 5.2 % in Ireland (see Figure 6.14). Expenditure on care for the elderly accounted for 0.5 % of GDP in the same year, although Sweden reported a rate that was almost five times as high; expenditure on the elderly fell to less than 0.1 % of GDP in Greece, Estonia, Belgium, Bulgaria, Romania and Cyprus (see Figure 6.15).

Average (median) pension levels of 65 to 74 year olds were generally lower than average earnings of those aged 50 to 59 in 2008 (see Figure 6.16). This was particularly the case in Latvia,

Cyprus and Bulgaria where pensions represented around one third of the earnings among those aged 50 to 59. This aggregate replacement ratio was highest in Austria, France, Sweden and Hungary, where it was above 60 %. It should be borne in mind that relatively low ratios may reflect low coverage and/or low income replacement from statutory pension schemes and maturing pension systems, as well as incomplete careers or an under-declaration of earnings.

A breakdown of social protection receipts across the EU-27 in 2007 shows that the majority of receipts could be attributed to employers' social contributions (38.5 %) and general government contributions (38.0 %); one fifth (20.0 %) of all EU-27 receipts were funded by contributions made by protected persons (see Figure 6.17).

Data sources and availability

Data on social protection expenditure and receipts are drawn up according to the European system of integrated social protection statistics (ESSPROS) methodology; this system has been designed to allow a comparison of social protection flows between Member States. In April 2007, a legal basis was established for the provision of ESSPROS with the delivery of data to start from reference year 2006, as provided by a European Parliament and Council Regulation 458/2007; this was later supplemented by two European Commission implementing Regulations (1322/2007 and 10/2008).

Expenditure on social protection includes: social benefits, administration costs (which represent the costs charged to the scheme for its management and administration) and other expenditure (which consists of miscellaneous expenditure by social protection schemes, principally, payment of property income).

Social protection benefits are direct transfers, in cash or in kind, by social protection schemes to households and individuals to relieve them of the burden of one or more of the defined risks or needs. Social benefits are paid to households by social security funds, other government units, NPISHs (non-profit institutions serving households), employers administering unfunded social insurance schemes, insurance enterprises, or other institutional units administering privately funded social insurance schemes. Benefits are classified according to eight social protection functions (which represent a set of risks or needs):

- sickness/healthcare benefits – including paid sick leave, medical care and the provision of pharmaceutical products;
- disability benefits – including disability pensions and the provision of goods and services (other than medical care) to the disabled;
- old age benefits – including old age pensions and the provision of goods and services (other than medical care) to the elderly;
- survivors' benefits – including income maintenance and support in connection with the death of a family member, such as survivors' pensions;
- family/children benefits – including support (except healthcare) in connection with the costs of preg-

nancy, childbirth, childbearing and caring for other family members;
- unemployment benefits – including vocational training financed by public agencies;
- housing benefits – including interventions by public authorities to help households meet the cost of housing;
- social exclusion benefits not elsewhere classified – including income support, rehabilitation of alcohol and drug abusers and other miscellaneous benefits (except healthcare).

The pensions aggregate comprises part of periodic cash benefits under the disability, old age, survivors and unemployment functions. It is defined as the sum of the following social benefits: disability pension, early-retirement benefit due to reduced capacity to work, old age pension, anticipated old age pension, partial pension, survivors' pension, and early-retirement benefit for labour market reasons.

Expenditure on care for the elderly is defined as the percentage share of social protection expenditure devoted to old age care in GDP. These expenditures cover care allowance, accommodation, and assistance in carrying out daily tasks.

Pension systems can also play a key role in allowing retirees to maintain living standards they previously enjoyed in the later years of their working lives. The aggregate replacement ratio measures the difference between gross retirement benefits and gross earnings. It is defined as the median individual gross pensions of those aged 65 to 74 relative to median individual gross earnings of those aged 50 to 59, excluding other social benefits; it is expressed in percentage terms.

The schemes responsible for providing social protection are financed in different ways. Social protection receipts comprise social security contributions paid by employers and protected persons, contributions by general government, and other receipts from a variety of sources (for example, interest, dividends, rent and claims against third parties). Social contributions by employers are all costs incurred by employers to secure entitlement to social benefits for their employees, former employees and their dependants; they can be paid by resident or non-resident employers. They include all payments by employers to social protection institutions (actual contributions) and social benefits paid directly by employers to employees (imputed contributions). Social contributions made by protected persons comprise contributions paid by employees, by the self-employed and by pensioners and other persons.

Context

Social protection systems are highly developed in the EU: they are designed to protect people against the risks and needs associated with unemployment, parental responsibilities, sickness/healthcare and invalidity, the loss of a spouse or parent, old age, housing and social exclusion (not elsewhere classified). The main challenge that is likely to face social protection systems in the coming years is that of demographic change, in particular the ageing of Europe's population.

The organisation and financing of social protection systems is the responsibility of each of the Member States. The model used in each Member State is therefore somewhat different, while the EU plays a coordinating role to ensure that people who move across borders continue to receive adequate protection. This role also promotes actions among the Member States to combat poverty and social exclusion, and to reform social protection systems on the basis of policy exchanges and mutual learning. This policy is known as the social protection and social inclusion process – it underpins the Europe 2020 strategy and will play an important role as Europe seeks to become a smart, sustainable and inclusive economy.

Table 6.4: Expenditure on social protection
(% of GDP)

	1997	1998	1999	2000	2001	2002	2003	2004	2005	2006	2007
EU (¹)	27.4	27.0	26.9	26.5	26.7	27.0	27.4	27.2	27.1	26.7	26.2
Euro area (EA-16)	:	:	:	26.7	26.8	27.4	27.8	27.7	27.7	27.4	27.0
Belgium	27.4	27.1	27.0	26.5	27.3	28.0	29.0	29.2	29.6	30.2	29.5
Bulgaria	:	:	:	:	:	:	:	:	16.0	14.9	15.1
Czech Republic	18.6	18.5	19.2	19.5	19.4	20.2	20.2	19.3	19.2	18.7	18.6
Denmark	30.1	30.0	29.8	28.9	29.2	29.7	30.9	30.7	30.2	29.3	28.9
Germany	29.0	28.9	29.2	29.3	29.4	30.1	30.4	29.8	29.7	28.7	27.7
Estonia	:	:	:	13.9	13.0	12.7	12.5	13.0	12.6	12.3	12.5
Ireland	16.4	15.2	14.6	13.9	14.9	17.5	17.9	18.1	18.2	18.3	18.9
Greece	20.8	21.7	22.7	23.5	24.3	24.0	23.5	23.5	24.6	24.5	24.4
Spain	20.8	20.2	19.8	20.3	20.0	20.4	20.6	20.7	20.9	20.9	21.0
France	30.4	30.1	29.9	29.5	29.6	30.4	30.9	31.3	31.4	30.7	30.5
Italy	24.9	24.6	24.8	24.7	24.9	25.3	25.8	26.0	26.4	26.6	26.7
Cyprus	:	:	:	14.8	14.9	16.3	18.4	18.1	18.4	18.4	18.5
Latvia	15.3	16.1	17.2	15.3	14.3	13.9	13.8	12.9	12.4	12.3	11.0
Lithuania	13.7	15.1	16.3	15.8	14.7	14.0	13.5	13.3	13.1	13.2	14.3
Luxembourg	21.5	21.2	20.5	19.6	20.9	21.6	22.1	22.3	21.7	20.3	19.3
Hungary	:	:	20.3	19.6	19.2	20.3	21.2	20.6	21.9	22.4	22.3
Malta	18.0	17.9	17.8	16.9	17.8	17.8	18.3	18.8	18.6	18.2	18.1
Netherlands	28.7	27.8	27.1	26.4	26.5	27.6	28.3	28.3	27.9	28.8	28.4
Austria	28.8	28.4	29.0	28.4	28.8	29.2	29.6	29.3	28.9	28.5	28.0
Poland	:	:	:	19.7	21.0	21.1	21.0	20.1	19.7	19.4	18.1
Portugal	20.3	20.9	21.4	21.7	22.7	23.7	24.1	24.7	25.3	25.4	24.8
Romania	:	:	:	13.0	12.8	13.6	13.0	12.7	13.2	12.5	12.8
Slovenia	23.9	24.1	24.1	24.2	24.5	24.4	23.7	23.4	23.0	22.7	21.4
Slovakia	19.8	20.0	20.2	19.4	19.0	19.1	18.2	17.2	16.5	16.3	16.0
Finland	29.1	27.0	26.3	25.1	24.9	25.7	26.6	26.7	26.8	26.2	25.4
Sweden	32.2	31.4	31.0	30.1	30.8	31.6	32.6	32.0	31.5	30.7	29.7
United Kingdom	26.9	26.3	25.7	26.4	26.8	25.7	25.7	25.9	26.3	26.1	25.3
Iceland	18.5	18.3	18.8	19.2	19.4	21.2	23.0	22.6	21.6	21.2	21.5
Norway	25.1	26.9	26.9	24.4	25.4	26.0	27.2	25.9	23.8	22.6	22.8
Switzerland	27.3	27.4	27.4	27.0	27.7	28.5	29.2	29.3	29.3	28.0	27.3

(¹) EU-15 for 1997-1999; EU-25 for 2000-2004; EU-27 for 2005-2007.

Source: Eurostat (tps00098)

Figure 6.12: Expenditure on social protection per inhabitant, 2007
(PPS)

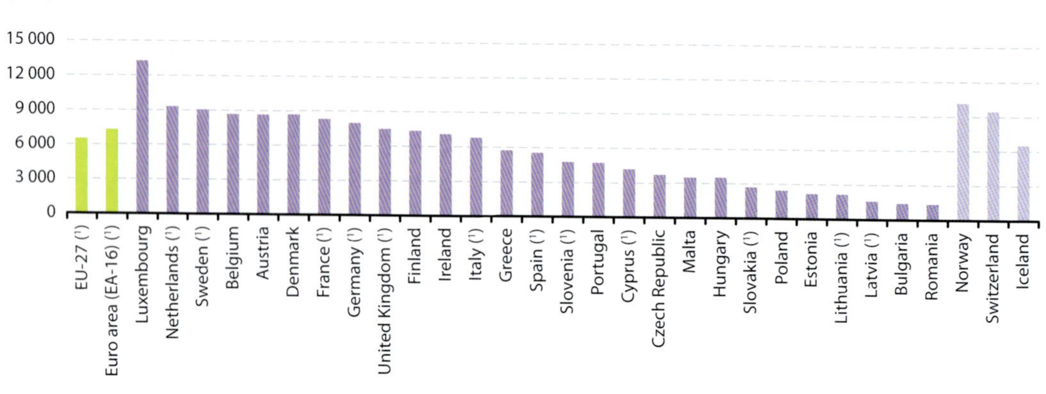

(¹) Provisional.

Source: Eurostat (tps00100)

Figure 6.13: Social benefits, EU-27, 2007 (¹)
(%, based on PPS)

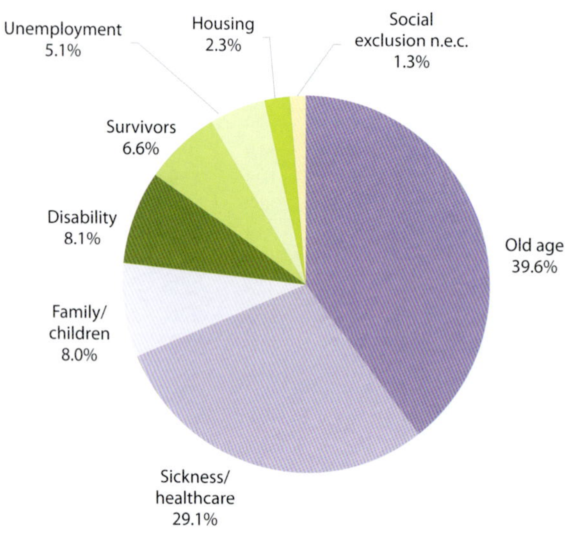

(¹) Provisional; figures do not sum to 100 % due to rounding.

Source: Eurostat (tps00107)

Figure 6.14: Expenditure on pensions, 2007
(% of GDP)

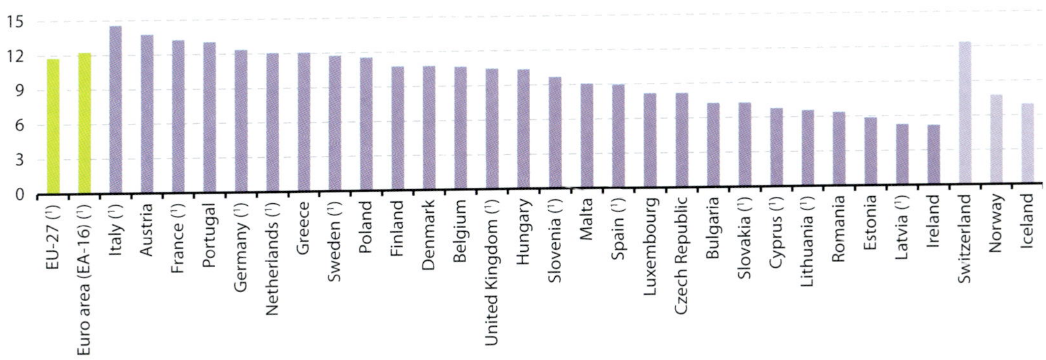

(¹) Provisional.

Source: Eurostat (tps00103)

Figure 6.15: Expenditure on care for the elderly, 2007

(% of GDP)

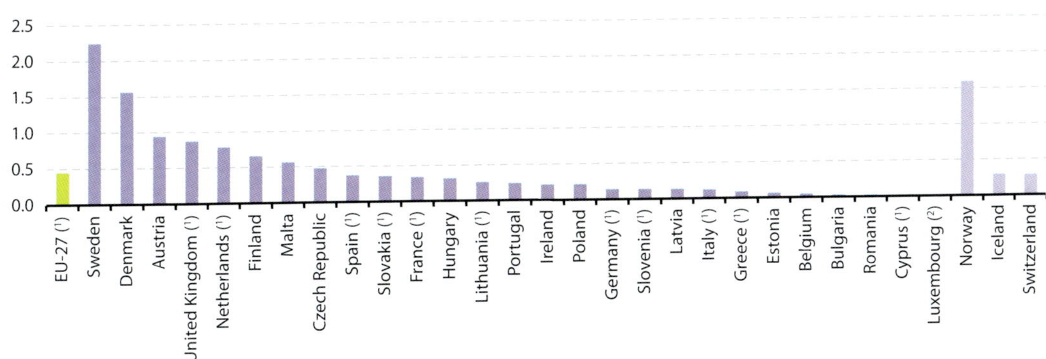

(¹) Provisional.
(²) Not available: expenditure was recorded together with similar benefits under the disability function as the split between old-age and disability was not available.

Source: Eurostat (tsdde530)

Figure 6.16: Aggregate replacement ratio, 2008 (1)
(%)

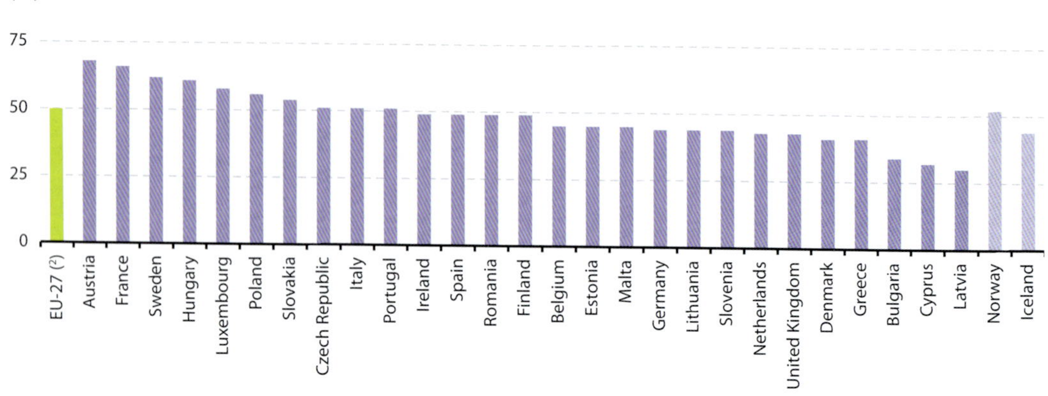

(1) The income reference period concerns the year preceding the survey year for the majority of countries.
(2) Eurostat calculation based on population-weighted averages of national data.

Source: Eurostat (ilc_pnp3)

Figure 6.17: Social protection receipts, EU-27, 2007 (1)
(% of total receipts)

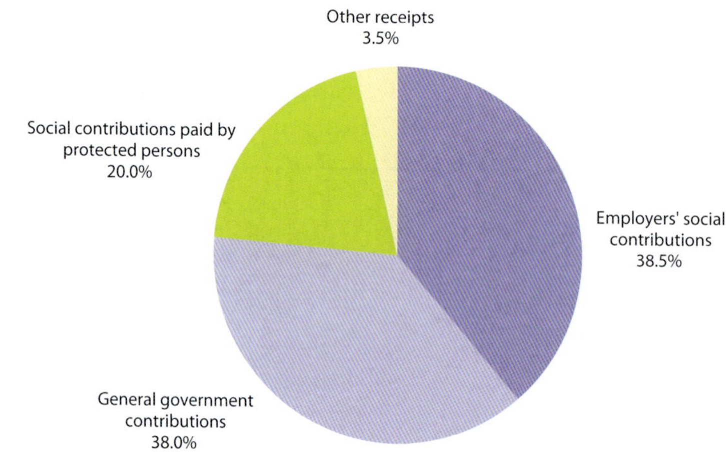

(1) Provisional.

Source: Eurostat (tps00108)

6.4 Crime

Statistics that are currently available on crime and criminal justice reflect the diversity of policing and legal systems within the European Union (EU). While the development of crime and criminal justice statistics is still in its infancy, a more comparable system is in the process of being developed.

Comparisons of crime statistics between Member States should ideally be based on trends over time, rather than direct comparisons of levels between countries, given that the data presented can be affected by a range of issues, including different levels of criminalisation, the efficiency of criminal justice systems, and police recording practices; furthermore, it is likely that a relatively high proportion of crime remains unrecorded.

Main statistical findings

There were 1.7 million police officers in the EU-27 in 2007, which marked an overall increase of nearly 6 % when compared with five years earlier (see Table 6.5). There were some quite rapid changes in the size of national police forces during the period from 1997 to 2007, with expansions of at least 20 % recorded for Italy (to 2006), Cyprus and Luxembourg (where the highest overall growth was registered, at 36.0 %). On the other hand, the size of the police force was reduced by more than a fifth in each of the Baltic Member States, and by as much as 28 % in Slovakia (again between 1997 and 2007).

There were an estimated 29 million crimes recorded by the police within the EU-27 in 2007 (see Table 6.6). From 1999, the number of recorded crimes in the EU-27 rose to a peak around 2002, but subsequently fell each year through to 2007. In recent years (from the peak in recorded crime in the EU in 2003 through to 2007), the number of recorded crimes has fallen in a number of Member States; particularly in Poland, the United Kingdom, Malta, Lithuania and the Netherlands, where recorded crime fell by more than 10 % during the period under consideration.

The EU-27 prison population rose by 1.3 % per year during the period 1997 to 2006 to reach a total of almost 600 000, which equated to 0.12 % of the EU's population; for comparison, the prison population of the United States was some 0.79 % of the total population (see Table 6.7).

When expressed in relation to total population, the Baltic Member States and Poland had more than 200 prisoners per 100 000 inhabitants. At the other end of the range, the Nordic countries of Finland, Denmark and Sweden (as well as Iceland and Norway among non-member countries), Slovenia and Ireland (2006), each reported less than 75 prisoners per 100 000 inhabitants in 2007.

Data sources and availability

Eurostat publishes statistics on crime and criminal justice systems from 1950 onwards for the total number of recorded crimes, and from 1993 onwards for a set of specific offences. In addition, the database also includes statistics for prison populations from 1987 onwards and the number of police officers from 1993 onwards. Figures for the United Kingdom are reported separately (as there are three separate jurisdictions for England and Wales, Scotland, and Northern Ireland); these have been summed together for the purpose of this subchapter.

Comparisons of crime statistics between countries may be affected by a range of factors, including:

- different legal and criminal justice systems;
- the rates at which crimes are reported to the police and recorded by them;
- differences in the timing of recording crimes (for example, when reported to the police, when a suspect is identified, etc.);
- differences in the rules by which multiple offences are counted;
- differences in the list of offences that are included in the overall crime figures.

Consequently, care should be taken when analysing the information presented.

Figures for the prison population may also be affected by a range of factors, including:

- the number of cases dealt with by the courts;
- the percentage of convicted criminals given a custodial sentence;
- the length of the sentences imposed; the size of the population on remand;
- the date at which the survey was conducted (especially where amnesties or other early release arrangements might apply).

The prison population is measured as the total number of adult and juvenile prisoners (including pre-trial detainees) as of 1 September each year. The figures include offenders held in prison administration facilities, juvenile offenders' institutions, drug addicts' institutions and psychiatric or other hospitals.

As a general rule, comparisons should be based upon trends rather than upon levels, on the assumption that the characteristics of the recording system within a country remain fairly constant over time. There are, however, a large number of breaks in time series and other methodological/definitional changes – more information is available through the dedicated section on crime and criminal justice statistics on the Eurostat website.

Context

The progressive elimination of border controls within the EU has considerably facilitated the free movement of European citizens, but may have also made it easier for criminals to operate, especially since the scope of law enforcement authorities and criminal justice systems is generally limited to the boundaries of national borders.

Since the adoption of the Amsterdam Treaty, the EU has set itself the objective of providing a common area of freedom, security and justice. This goal was further developed by the Hague programme in 2004, which outlined ten priority areas: strengthening fundamental rights and citizenship; anti-terrorist measures; defining a balanced approach to migration; developing integrated management of the EU's external borders; setting up a common asylum procedure; maximising the positive impact of immigration; striking the right balance between privacy and security while sharing information;

developing a strategic concept on tackling organised crime; ensuring a genuine European area of justice; and sharing responsibility and solidarity.

As part of the work to harmonise and develop crime and criminal justice systems, EU Member States agreed to approximate the definitions of offences and the level of sanctions for certain type of offences. Furthermore, mutual recognition of decisions taken by national judges is set to become the cornerstone of judicial cooperation in criminal matters, with a range of tools having been developed to facilitate practical cooperation across borders.

With respect to police cooperation, the EU seeks to grant law enforcement authorities in each of the Member States access to relevant information (such as DNA, fingerprint, vehicle registration or immigration databases), and to improve police cooperation within a common framework for the protection of personal data. Access to information is covered by a raft of legislation, including the Data Retention Directive (Directive 2006/24/EC of the European Parliament and of the Council), the Swedish Framework Decision (Council framework Decision 2006/960/JHA), the Prüm Decision (Council Decision 2008/615/JHA) and a Regulation of the European Parliament and of the Council (767/2008) concerning a visa information system (VIS) and the exchange of data between Member States.

Police cooperation has been encouraged through legislation such as, a Framework Decision on Joint Investigation Teams (Council framework Decision 2002/465/JHA), and a Decision on improved cooperation between special intervention units (Council Decision 2008/617/JHA), while a range of organisations/bodies have been created to aid cooperation between different law enforcement agencies, such as the European Police College (CEPOL), the European Police Office (Europol), or the European agency for the management of operational cooperation at the external borders of the Member States of the EU (Frontex). Furthermore, the EU supports a range of national and multi-national projects, through programmes such as the 'Prevention of and fight against crime' (Council Decision 2007/125/JHA).

The first steps towards a more comparable system of crime and criminal justice statistics was outlined in a European Commission Communication (COM/2006/437), titled 'Developing a comprehensive and coherent EU strategy to measure crime and criminal justice: an EU action plan 2006-2010'. In the short term, its objective was to collect national data and to assess its quality. However, the longer-term goal is for the European Commission's Directorate-General for Home Affairs, in close collaboration with Eurostat, to develop a harmonised methodology, on which the collection of EU-wide statistics should be based, allowing comparisons of the structure and trends of crime between Member States.

Particular progress has been made in the collection of statistics related to the police and in the development of a common victimisation survey. The collection of data relating to money laundering is underway, and subsequent priorities include information on the trafficking of human beings, corruption and cybercrime.

Table 6.5: Police officers

	Police officers (units)			Police officers (per 100 000 inhabitants)		
	1997	2002	2007	1997	2002	2007
EU-27 (1) (2)	:	1 611 355	1 703 982	:	339.2	352.3
Belgium	35 613	37 242	38 718	350.2	361.2	365.8
Bulgaria	:	:	:	:	:	:
Czech Republic	43 722	45 538	44 101	424.1	446.2	428.7
Denmark	9 837	10 233	10 620	186.5	190.6	195.0
Germany	229 424	247 190	250 353	279.7	299.8	304.1
Estonia	4 400	3 503	3 247	312.9	257.3	241.9
Ireland (2)	10 968	11 895	12 954	300.1	305.0	307.8
Greece	44 183	51 634	51 152	411.2	470.7	457.9
Spain	:	190 119	214 935	:	464.1	483.3
France (3)	224 693	235 116	238 478	386.6	393.9	385.9
Italy (2)	261 082	272 282	324 339	459.0	477.7	552.1
Cyprus	4 092	4 531	5 139	614.1	642.2	660.0
Latvia	11 067	10 265	8 222	452.7	437.6	360.4
Lithuania	14 559	11 678	11 173	405.8	336.0	330.1
Luxembourg	1 117	1 254	1 519	268.0	282.4	319.0
Hungary	29 532	28 996	26 334	286.7	285.0	261.6
Malta	:	1 796	1 933	:	455.1	474.0
Netherlands	31 884	36 766	35 923	204.8	228.3	219.6
Austria	26 291	27 798	26 623	330.1	344.7	321.4
Poland	100 201	99 502	98 337	259.3	260.2	257.9
Portugal	44 448	48 060	51 779	441.3	465.3	488.5
Romania	50 261	45 245	45 391	222.6	207.2	210.5
Slovenia	6 815	7 392	7 971	343.0	370.7	396.5
Slovakia	19 577	13 997	14 134	364.0	260.2	262.1
Finland	7 843	8 284	8 156	152.8	159.5	154.6
Sweden	16 783	16 149	17 866	189.8	181.3	196.0
United Kingdom	142 208	144 890	156 735	244.2	244.7	257.9
Iceland	:	678	683	:	236.6	222.0
Liechtenstein	:	79	93	:	235.6	264.4
Norway	7 404	8 221	7 453	168.6	181.7	159.2
Switzerland	14 210	15 073	16 808	200.7	207.7	223.8
Croatia	23 130	19 537	20 424	510.3	439.6	459.9
FYR of Macedonia	:	:	9 599	:	:	470.1
Turkey	304 265	370 095	329 533	479.3	537.6	472.9
Japan	226 401	233 251	:	:	:	:
United States	618 127	666 555	699 850	:	:	:

(1) Excluding French overseas departments and territories.
(2) 2006 instead of 2007.
(3) Excluding overseas departments and territories.

Source: Eurostat (crim_plce and tps00001)

Table 6.6: Crimes recorded by the police
(1 000)

	1997	1998	1999	2000	2001	2002	2003	2004	2005	2006	2007
EU-27 (¹)	:	:	:	28 614	29 613	30 677	30 864	30 254	29 840	29 660	29 172
Belgium (²)	:	:	:	1 002	959	1 008	1 001	1 005	990	1 010	1 003
Bulgaria (²)	228	159	145	149	147	147	144	142	138	136	135
Czech Republic	404	426	427	391	359	372	358	352	344	336	357
Denmark	531	499	494	504	473	492	486	474	433	425	445
Germany	6 586	6 457	6 302	6 265	6 364	6 507	6 572	6 633	6 392	6 304	6 285
Estonia (³)	41	46	52	58	58	53	54	53	53	52	50
Ireland (⁴)	91	86	81	73	87	106	103	99	102	103	:
Greece	:	386	374	369	440	441	442	406	456	464	423
Spain (⁵)	:	1 866	1 896	1 853	2 052	2 183	2 144	2 141	2 231	2 267	2 310
France (⁶)	3 493	3 566	3 568	3 772	4 062	4 114	3 975	3 825	3 776	3 726	3 589
Italy (⁷)	2 441	2 426	2 374	2 206	2 164	2 232	2 457	2 418	2 579	2 771	2 933
Cyprus (⁸)	4	4	4	4	5	5	7	8	7	8	8
Latvia (⁹)	37	37	44	50	51	49	52	62	51	62	56
Lithuania (⁸)	76	78	77	82	79	73	79	84	82	75	68
Luxembourg (¹⁰)	24	27	27	23	23	26	26	27	25	26	28
Hungary	514	601	506	451	466	421	413	419	437	426	427
Malta	:	15	16	17	16	17	18	18	19	17	15
Netherlands	1 220	1 235	1 303	1 329	1 379	1 402	1 369	1 319	1 255	1 218	1 215
Austria (¹⁰)	482	480	493	560	523	592	643	644	605	589	594
Poland	992	1 073	1 122	1 267	1 390	1 404	1 467	1 461	1 380	1 288	1 153
Portugal	322	341	363	363	372	392	417	416	392	399	400
Romania	361	399	364	354	340	312	277	232	208	233	281
Slovenia (¹¹)	37	55	62	68	75	77	77	87	84	90	88
Slovakia	92	94	94	89	93	107	112	131	124	115	111
Finland	374	383	372	386	361	365	367	354	340	325	344
Sweden	1 196	1 181	1 194	1 215	1 189	1 235	1 255	1 249	1 242	1 225	1 306
United Kingdom (¹²)	5 081	5 650	5 856	5 714	6 086	6 544	6 549	6 194	6 096	5 969	5 445
Iceland (⁵)	:	:	:	19	19	20	18	17	12	13	13
Liechtenstein	1	1	1	1	1	1	1	1	1	1	1
Norway	285	294	292	307	300	320	304	288	276	277	272
Switzerland	383	378	355	317	322	357	379	389	353	335	326
Croatia	55	56	58	68	78	78	80	85	80	81	76
FYR of Macedonia	:	:	:	20	17	18	23	23	23	22	26
Turkey (¹³)	357	357	339	340	414	459	499	533	674	987	963
Japan	1 900	2 034	2 166	2 443	2 736	2 854	2 790	2 563	2 269	2 051	:
United States	13 195	12 486	11 634	11 608	11 877	11 879	11 827	11 679	11 565	11 402	11 252

(¹) Excluding French overseas departments and territories; the figure for 2007 is calculated using data for Ireland for 2006; care should be taken in interpreting the time-series due to a large number of breaks in series.
(²) Break in series, 1999.
(³) Break in series, 2002 and 2005.
(⁴) Break in series, 1999 and 2006.
(⁵) Break in series, 2004.
(⁶) Excluding overseas departments and territories.
(⁷) Break in series, 2003.
(⁸) Break in series, 2002.
(⁹) Break in series, 2003, 2004 and 2005.
(¹⁰) Break in series, 1999 and 2001.
(¹¹) Break in series, 1999 and 2002.
(¹²) Break in series, 2001 and 2003.
(¹³) Break in series, 2004 and 2005.

Source: Eurostat (crim_gen)

Figure 6.18: Recorded crimes, EU-27, 2000-2007 (1)
(%, average annual change)

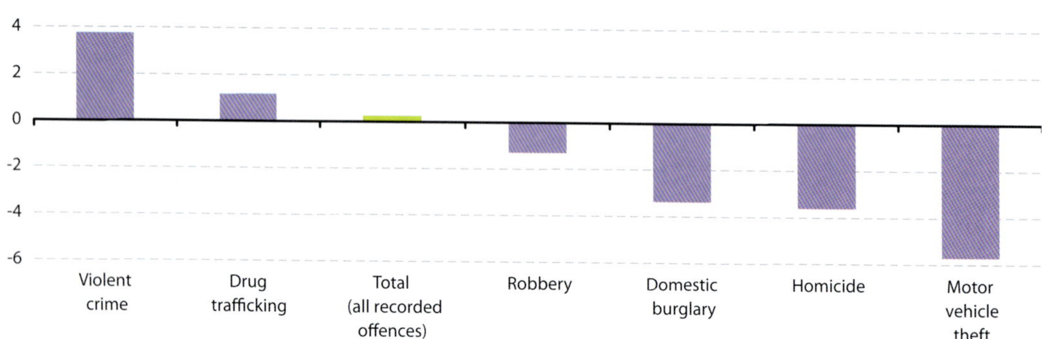

(1) EU-27 excluding French overseas departments and territories; total recorded crimes including data for Ireland for 2006 instead of 2007; drug trafficking, also excluding Malta; violent crime, also excluding Cyprus and Malta; care should be taken in interpreting the time-series due to a large number of breaks in series.

Source: Eurostat (crim_gen)

Table 6.7: Prison population

	Prison population (units)			Prison population (per 100 000 inhabitants)		
	1997	2002	2007	1997	2002	2007
EU-27 (1)(2)	535 592	588 772	599 829	111.9	121.9	122.1
Belgium	8 156	8 605	9 950	80.2	83.5	94.0
Bulgaria	11 847	9 607	10 792	142.0	121.7	140.5
Czech Republic	21 560	16 597	19 110	209.1	162.6	185.8
Denmark	3 170	3 435	3 646	60.1	64.0	66.9
Germany (3)	68 029	75 025	73 319	82.9	91.0	89.1
Estonia	4 638	4 775	3 486	329.9	350.8	259.7
Ireland (2)	2 424	3 028	3 053	66.3	77.6	72.5
Greece (2)(4)	5 577	8 284	10 280	51.9	75.5	92.4
Spain	43 453	50 537	67 100	109.9	123.4	150.9
France (5)	54 442	53 463	60 403	93.7	89.6	97.7
Italy	50 527	55 670	48 693	88.8	97.7	82.3
Cyprus	263	351	671	39.5	49.7	86.2
Latvia	12 736	8 358	6 548	520.9	356.3	287.0
Lithuania	13 205	11 345	7 770	368.0	326.4	229.6
Luxembourg	443	391	666	106.3	88.1	139.9
Hungary	13 405	17 838	14 743	130.1	175.3	146.5
Malta	254	283	382	67.9	71.7	93.7
Netherlands	11 770	13 060	14 450	75.6	81.1	88.3
Austria (3)	6 946	7 511	8 887	87.2	93.1	107.3
Poland	57 424	80 990	90 199	148.6	211.8	236.6
Portugal	14 167	13 772	11 587	140.6	133.3	109.3
Romania	45 121	48 075	29 390	199.8	220.2	136.3
Slovenia	768	1 120	1 336	38.7	56.2	66.5
Slovakia	7 656	7 849	8 235	142.3	145.9	152.7
Finland	2 836	3 469	3 370	55.3	66.8	63.9
Sweden	5 221	6 506	6 740	59.0	73.0	74.0
United Kingdom	69 554	78 828	88 590	119.4	133.1	145.8
Iceland	:	107	115	:	37.3	37.4
Liechtenstein	82	67	38	263.3	199.9	108.1
Norway	2 536	2 832	3 420	57.7	62.6	73.1
Switzerland (3)	5 428	4 937	5 715	76.7	68.0	76.1
Croatia	:	2 641	4 290	:	59.4	96.6
FYR of Macedonia (2)	965	1 291	2 090	48.5	63.3	102.5
Turkey	60 843	59 512	90 732	95.8	86.5	130.2
Japan (6)	50 091	67 354	77 932	:	:	:
United States	1 743 643	2 033 331	2 375 615	:	:	:

(1) Excluding French overseas departments and territories; care should be taken in interpreting the development over time due to a large number of breaks in series.
(2) 2006 instead of 2007.
(3) Break in series, 1997-2002.
(4) Break in series, 1997-2002 and 2002-2007.
(5) Excluding overseas departments and territories; break in series, 2002-2007.
(6) 2005 instead of 2007.

Source: Eurostat (crim_pris and tps00001)

7

Industry, trade and services

The European Commission's enterprise policies aim to create a favourable environment for business to thrive within the European Union (EU), thus creating higher productivity, economic growth, jobs and wealth. Policies are aimed at reducing administrative burden, stimulating innovation, encouraging sustainable production, and ensuring the smooth functioning of the EU's internal market.

European industry contributes to output, jobs, innovation and exports and is interrelated with service activities. Indeed, many service activities such as transport, information and communication depend on industry to produce the equipment and hardware which they use. The internal market for goods is one of the EU's most important and continuing priorities which aims to create a user-friendly environment for businesses and consumers. Creating a single market for the service sector – one of the main drivers of the EU's economy – relies largely on the opportunities available for businesses to provide and access services in the EU.

The business environment in which enterprises operate in the EU plays a significant role in their potential success through factors such as access to capital markets (in particular for venture capital), or the openness of markets. Ensuring that businesses can compete openly and fairly is also important with respect to making Europe an attractive place in which to invest and work. Creating a positive climate in which entrepreneurs and businesses can flourish is considered by many as the key to generating the growth and jobs that Europe needs. This is all the more important in a globalised economy, where some businesses have considerable leeway to select where they wish to operate. The regulatory environment in which businesses operate influences their competitiveness and their ability to grow and create jobs. The European Commission is committed to developing a better regulatory environment for businesses; one that is simple, understandable, effective and enforceable. The better regulation agenda of the Commission aims at:

- implementing a strategy to simplify existing legislation through a simplification programme;
- reducing administrative burdens by 25 % by 2012;
- placing greater emphasis on the use of impact assessments and public consultations when drafting new rules and regulations;
- monitoring the application of the Union's law.

The 21 million small and medium-sized enterprises (SMEs) in the EU in 2007 represented 99.8 % of enterprises in the non-financial business economy, and are regarded as a key driver for economic growth, innovation, employment and social integration. The European Commission aims to promote successful entrepreneurship and improve the business environment for SMEs, to allow them to realise their full potential in the global economy.

At the European Council meeting of 26 March 2010, EU leaders set out their plan for Europe 2020, a strategy to enhance the competitiveness of the EU and to create more growth and jobs. The latest revision of the integrated economic and employment guidelines (revised as part of the Europe 2020 strategy for smart, sustainable and inclusive growth) includes a guideline to improve the business and consumer environment and modernise Europe's industrial base. Additional information about the Europe 2020 strategy can be found on the Europe 2020 website. In October 2010 the European Commission presented a Communication on 'An industrial policy for the globalisation era', which provides a blueprint that puts industrial competitiveness and sustainability centre stage. The new industrial policy establishes a strategic agenda and proposes some broad cross-sectoral measures, as well as tailor-made actions for specific industries, mainly targeting the so-called 'green innovation' performance of these sectors. Furthermore, a report on Member States' competitiveness policies and performance will be published annually. A European Commission Communication titled, 'A Digital Agenda for Europe' (COM(2010) 245) outlines policies and actions aimed at maximising the benefit of the digital era to all sections of society. The agenda outlines seven priority areas for action – see Subchapter 7.6 on the information society for more detail.

7.1 Structural business statistics

This subchapter presents Eurostat's structural business statistics (SBS) describing the structure, main characteristics and performance of economic activities in the European Union (EU). The data presented in this subchapter are mainly analysed at the level of NACE sections or divisions, but readers should note that structural business statistics are available at a much more detailed level (several hundred sectors).

Structural business statistics can provide answers to questions on the wealth creation and number of jobs in different activities, the structural shift from industry to services and where this trend is most notable, country specialisations, sectoral productivity, profitability and average wages, as well as many other topics. Because they are available broken down by enterprise size-class, structural business statistics also permit a detailed analysis of small and medium-sized enterprises (SMEs), which is of particular use to EU policymakers and analysts wishing to focus on entrepreneurship and the role of SMEs. Furthermore, structural business statistics provide useful background information on which to base an interpretation of short-term statistics and the business cycle.

The knowledge-based economy and the demand for intangibles, either for consumption or investment purposes, as well as international outsourcing, has led to a major restructuring of many European economies, with a shift away from industrial activities towards services. Traditionally, structural business statistics were concentrated on industrial and construction activities, and to a lesser extent distributive trades and services. Since the early 1990s, major developments in official statistics within the EU have seen data collection efforts focus more on services.

Main statistical findings

In 2007 there were an estimated 20.9 million enterprises within the EU-27's non-financial business economy which covers industry, construction, distributive trades and non-financial services. Collectively these enterprises employed 133.8 million persons in 2007 and generated EUR 6 146 thousand million of value added in 2007.

Among the eight NACE Rev. 1.1 sections in the non-financial business economy, manufacturing was the largest in terms of employment and value added. Some 2.3 million manufacturing enterprises generated EUR 1 813 thousand million of value added in 2007, whilst providing employment for about 34.5 million persons. Distributive trades enterprises (motor trades, wholesale trade, and retail trade and repair), which represented a little under one in every three (30.4 %) enterprises within the EU-27's non-financial business economy, provided employment for 32.5 million persons and generated a further EUR 1 184 thousand million of value added. However, it should be noted that the employment data presented here are head counts and not, for example, full-time equivalents, and there may be a significant proportion of persons working part-time in some activities, notably distributive trades activities as well as hotels and restaurants. Real estate, renting and business activities had the third largest workforce, some 27.8 million persons, and the second largest value added, EUR 1 397 thousand million.

Looking in more detail, namely at the NACE Rev. 1.1 division level, a little under one in every five enterprises in the EU-27's non-financial business economy were active in the other business activities sector composed of professional, technical and administrative business activities, such as legal services, accounting, advertising, industrial cleaning, and security services (see Figure 7.1). Many of these business services have benefitted from the outsourcing phenomenon, which may explain, in part, the structural shift towards services. Retail trade and repair and construction had the next largest populations of enterprises, with none of the other activities (at this level of detail) recording a share in excess of 10 %. The same three activities had the largest shares of employment within the non-financial business economy, in each case in excess of 10 % of the total; their employment shares were lower than for the number of enterprises, indicating that these activities were all characterised by a large number of relatively small (in terms of average employment) enterprises. These three activities had even lower shares of non-financial business economy value added. Again the other business activities sector accounted for the biggest proportion, some 13.0 % of the total, but by this measure wholesale trade was the second largest activity, followed closely by construction and then retail trade and repair.

High rates of part-time work in many service sectors also help explain, in part, the considerable differences in average personnel costs within the non-financial business economy of the EU-27, as shown in Table 7.3. Average personnel costs in the EU-27's electricity, gas and water supply sector were EUR 43 000 per employee, a level that was 2.6 times that for hotels and restaurants and 1.7 times that for the distributive trades. The variation in wages and salaries was even more marked between Member States. For example, average personnel costs across the manufacturing sectors (of available Member States) ranged by a factor of 18, from a high of EUR 55 700 per employee in the Netherlands to a low of EUR 3 100 per employee in Bulgaria.

The wage adjusted labour productivity ratio, which shows the relation between average value added per person and average personnel costs, was high for many of the energy-related activities, particularly for the extraction of crude petroleum and natural gas sector (862 % in the EU-27 in 2007); it was also high for the capital intensive sector of renting (see Figure 7.3).

Structural business statistics broken down by enterprise size-class (defined in terms of the number of persons employed) show that less than one enterprise in 400 within the EU-27's non-financial business economy employed 250 or more persons (and was therefore considered as large) in 2007, but these enterprises accounted for approximately one third of employment and more than two fifths of value added. Nevertheless, small and medium-sized enterprises (SMEs), with less than 250 persons employed, generated the majority of value added and employed most (67.4 %) of the workforce in the non-financial business economy. Micro enterprises (those with less than 10 persons employed) played a particularly important role, providing employment to nearly as many persons as large enterprises.

Large enterprises were particularly dominant within the sectors of mining and quarrying, electricity, gas and water supply, and transport, storage and communication. These activities are characterised either by a relatively high minimum efficient scale of production, or by their (transmission) networks that are rarely duplicated due to the high fixed investment cost, or both. Micro and small enterprises were relatively important within the activities of construction, and hotels and restaurants. In both these sectors, enterprises with less than 50 persons employed made up more than three fifths of the value added (see Tables 7.5 and 7.6).

In general, foreign-controlled enterprises are few in number, but due to their larger than average size they have a significant economic impact; in all of the countries providing data to Eurostat, foreign-controlled enterprises accounted for less than 1 % of the total enterprise population within the non-financial business economy but usually generated more than 15 % of value added and contributed more than 10 % of total employment. The highest percentage contributions of foreign-controlled enterprises to total value added in 2007 were registered in Hungary, Slovakia, the Czech Republic and Estonia, where foreign-controlled enterprises accounted for close to 40 % or more of the value added that was generated in the non-financial business economy, as shown in Figure 7.7.

Business demography statistics are presented in Table 7.8, which shows enterprise birth, death and survival rates. Note that since most new enterprises are small, the share of newly born enterprises among the whole business enterprise population is much higher than the corresponding proportion of the workforce accounted for by these enterprises.

There are significant changes in the stock of enterprises within the business economy from one year to the next, reflecting the level of competition and entrepreneurial spirit. Among the countries providing data to Eurostat, enterprise birth rates in 2007 ranged from around 3 % in Cyprus to around 15 % in Bulgaria and Romania, with Lithuania recording an enterprise birth rate (25 %) well above this range.

Data sources and availability

Eurostat's structural business statistics (SBS) describe the structure, conduct and performance of economic activities, down to the most detailed activity level (several hundred sectors). Without this structural information, short-term data on the economic cycle would lack background and be hard to interpret.

SBS cover the 'business economy', which includes industry, construction and many services (NACE Rev. 1.1 Sections C to K); the financial services (NACE Section J) are treated separately within SBS because of their specific nature and the limited availability of most types of standard business statistics in this area. As such, the term 'non-financial business economy' is generally used in business statistics to refer to economic activities covered by Sections C to I and K of NACE Rev. 1.1 and the units that carry out those activities. SBS do not cover agriculture, forestry and fishing, nor public administration and (largely) non-market services, such as education or health.

SBS describe the business economy through the observation of units engaged in an economic activity; the unit in SBS is generally the enterprise. An enterprise carries out one or more activities, at one or more locations, and it may comprise one or more legal units. Enterprises that are active in more than one economic activity (plus the value added and turnover they generate, the people they employ, and so on) are classified under the NACE heading according to their principal activity. This is normally the one which generates the largest amount of value added.

A revised classification (NACE Rev. 2) was adopted at the end of 2006, and at the time of writing SBS is implementing NACE Rev. 2. This will allow a broader and more detailed collection of information to be compiled on services, while also updating the classification to identify better new areas of activity (such as technology-producing sectors). The first reference year for which SBS data are due to be provided according to NACE Rev. 2 is 2008. The SBS data presented in this subchapter remain based on the NACE Rev. 1.1 version of the classification.

SBS are compiled under the legal basis provided by Parliament and Council Regulation 295/2008 of 11 March 2008 and Council Regulation 58/97 of December 1996 (and later amendments) on structural business statistics, and in accordance with the definitions, breakdowns, deadlines for data delivery, and various quality aspects specified in the regulations implementing it.

The SBS data collection consists of a common module (Annex 1), including a set of basic statistics for all activities, as well as six sector-specific annexes covering a more extensive list of characteristics. The sector-specific annexes are: industry, trade, construction, insurance services, credit institutions, and pension funds. There are also two further annexes added in 2008: business services and business demography.

SBS are also available broken down by region or by enterprise size-class. In SBS, size-classes are defined by the number of persons employed, except for specific data series within retail trade activities where turnover size-classes are also used. A limited set of the standard SBS variables (for example, the number of enterprises, turnover, persons employed and value added) is available, mostly down to the three-digit (group) level of the NACE Rev. 1.1 classification, divided by size-class. The European Commission Recommendation (2003/361/EC), adopted on 6 May 2003, classifies SMEs according to their number of persons employed, annual turnover, and independence. For statistical purposes, SMEs are generally defined as those enterprises employing fewer than 250 persons. The number of size-classes available varies according to the activity under consideration. However, the main groups used in this publication for presenting the results are:

- small and medium-sized enterprises (SMEs): with 1 to 249 persons employed, further divided into;
  - micro enterprises: with less than 10 persons employed;
  - small enterprises: with 10 to 49 persons employed;
  - medium-sized enterprises: with 50 to 249 persons employed;

- large enterprises: with 250 or more persons employed.

SBS contain a comprehensive set of basic variables describing business demographics and employment characteristics, as well as monetary variables (mainly concerning operating income and expenditure, or investment). In addition, a set of derived indicators has been compiled: for example, ratios of monetary characteristics or per head values. The variables presented in this section are defined as follows.

- The **number of enterprises** is a count of those enterprises active during at least a part of the reference period; the enterprise is the smallest combination of legal units that is an organisational unit producing goods or services, and which benefits from a certain degree of autonomy in decision-making, especially for the allocation of its current resources. An enterprise carries out one or more activities at one or more locations. An enterprise may be a sole legal unit.
- **Value added** represents the difference between the value of what is produced and the intermediate consumption entering production; value adjustments (such as depreciation) are not subtracted. It can be calculated by adding to turnover the capitalised production and other operating income, adjusting for changes in stocks, and then subtracting the purchases of goods and services, as well as indirect taxes and duties. Alternatively, it can be calculated from the gross operating surplus by adding personnel costs.
- The **number of persons employed** is defined as the total number of persons who work in the observation unit (inclusive of working proprietors, partners who work regularly in the unit, and unpaid family workers). It also includes persons who work outside the unit but who belong to it and are paid by it (for example, sales representatives, delivery personnel, and repair and maintenance teams). It excludes manpower supplied to the unit by other enterprises, persons carrying out repair and maintenance work in the observation unit on behalf of other enterprises, as well as those on compulsory military service.
- **Turnover** comprises the totals invoiced by the observation unit during the reference period, which corresponds to the market sales of goods or services, supplied to third parties. Turnover also includes all other charges (transport and packaging, etc.) passed on to the customer, even if these charges are listed separately on the invoice. Turnover excludes VAT and other similar deductible taxes that are directly linked to turnover, as well as all duties and taxes on the goods or services invoiced by the unit. Price reductions, rebates and discounts, plus the value of returned packing, must be deducted from the turnover. However, price reductions, rebates and bonuses are not considered if they are conceded to clients later, for example, at the year's end.
- **Average personnel costs** (or unit labour costs) equal personnel costs divided by the number of employees (persons who are paid and

have an employment contract). Personnel costs are defined as the total remuneration, in cash or in kind, payable by an employer to an employee (regular and temporary employees, as well as home workers) in return for work done by the latter during the reference period. Personnel costs also include taxes and the employees' social security contributions that are retained by the unit, as well as the employer's compulsory and voluntary social security contributions.

- **Apparent labour productivity** is equal to the value added divided by the number of persons employed.
- The **wage adjusted labour productivity** ratio is equal to value added at factor cost divided by personnel costs – this is multiplied by the ratio of the number of (paid) employees to the number of persons employed to account for differences in the number of working proprietors and unpaid family workers; expressed as a percentage.
- The **gross operating rate** is the size of the gross operating surplus relative to turnover (which is one measure of profitability).
- The **gross operating surplus** is the surplus generated by operating activities after the labour factor input has been recompensed (it can be calculated from value added at factor cost less personnel costs).

SBS also provide information on certain special topics, such as foreign-controlled enterprises. Statistics on foreign affiliates (FATS) provide information that can be used to assess the impact of foreign-controlled enterprises on the European economy. The data may also be used to monitor the effectiveness of the internal market and the gradual integration of economies within the context of globalisation. A foreign affiliate, as defined in inward FATS statistics, is an enterprise resident in a country which is under the control of an institutional unit not resident in the same country. Control is determined according to the concept of the 'ultimate controlling institutional unit' (UCI). The UCI is the institutional unit, proceeding up a foreign affiliate's chain of control, which is not controlled by another institutional unit.

Another special topic covered by SBS is that of business demography statistics, which present data on all active enterprises, their birth, death and survival (followed up to five years after birth) and death; the information presented in this subchapter focuses on the two-year survival rate. Within the context of business demography statistics, special attention is paid to the impact of these demographic events on employment levels. Business demography variables presented in this section are defined as follows.

- An **enterprise birth** amounts to the creation of a combination of production factors, with the restriction that no other enterprises are involved in the event. Births do not include entries into the business population due to mergers, break-ups, split-offs or restructuring of a set of enterprises, nor do the statistics include entries into a sub-population that only result from a change of activity. The birth rate is the number of births relative to the stock of active enterprises.

- An **enterprise death** amounts to the dissolution of a combination of production factors, with the restriction that no other enterprises are involved in the event. An enterprise is only included in the count of deaths if it is not reactivated within two years. Equally, a reactivation within two years is not counted as a birth.
- An **enterprise survival** occurs if an enterprise is active in terms of employment and/or turnover in the year of its birth and subsequent year(s). Two types of survival can be distinguished:
  - an enterprise born in one year x is considered to have survived in the next year x+1 if it is active in terms of turnover or employment, or both, in any part of that year x+1 (survival without change);
  - an enterprise is also considered to have survived if the linked legal unit(s) have ceased to be active, but their activity has been taken over by a new legal unit, set up specifically to take over that enterprise's factors of production (survival by take-over).

Context

In October 2010 the European Commission presented a Communication on a renewed industrial policy. 'An industrial policy for the globalisation era' provides a blueprint that puts industrial competitiveness and sustainability centre stage. This initiative establishes a strategic agenda and proposes some broad cross-sectoral measures, as well as tailor-made actions for specific industries, mainly targeting the so-called 'green innovation' performance of these sectors.

The internal market remains one of the EU's most important priorities. The central principles governing the internal market for services were set out in the EC Treaty. This guarantees EU enterprises the freedom to establish themselves in other Member States and the freedom to provide services on the territory of another EU Member State other than the one in which they are established. The objective of the Services Directive 2006/123/EC of 12 December 2006, on services in the internal market, is to eliminate obstacles to trade in services, thus allowing the development of cross-border operations. It is intended to improve competitiveness, not just of service enterprises but also of European industry as a whole. In December 2006, the Directive was adopted by the European Parliament and the Council with transposition by the Member States required by the end of 2009. It is hoped that the Directive will help achieve potential economic growth and job creation. By providing for administrative simplification, it also supports the better regulation agenda.

SMEs are often referred to as the backbone of the European economy, providing a potential source for both jobs and economic growth. In June 2008 the European Commission adopted a Communication on SMEs referred to as the 'Small business act for Europe'. This aims to improve the overall approach to entrepreneurship, to irreversibly anchor the 'think small first' principle in policymaking from regulation to public service, and to promote SMEs' growth by helping them tackle the remaining problems which hamper their development. The Communication sets out ten principles which should guide the conception and implementation of policies both at EU and national level to create a level playing field for SMEs throughout the EU and improve the administrative and legal environment to allow these enterprises to release their full potential to create jobs and growth. It also put forward a specific and far reaching package of new measures including four legislative proposals which translate these principles into action both at EU and Member State level.

Figure 7.1: Breakdown of number of enterprises within the non-financial business economy, EU-27, 2007 (1)
(%)

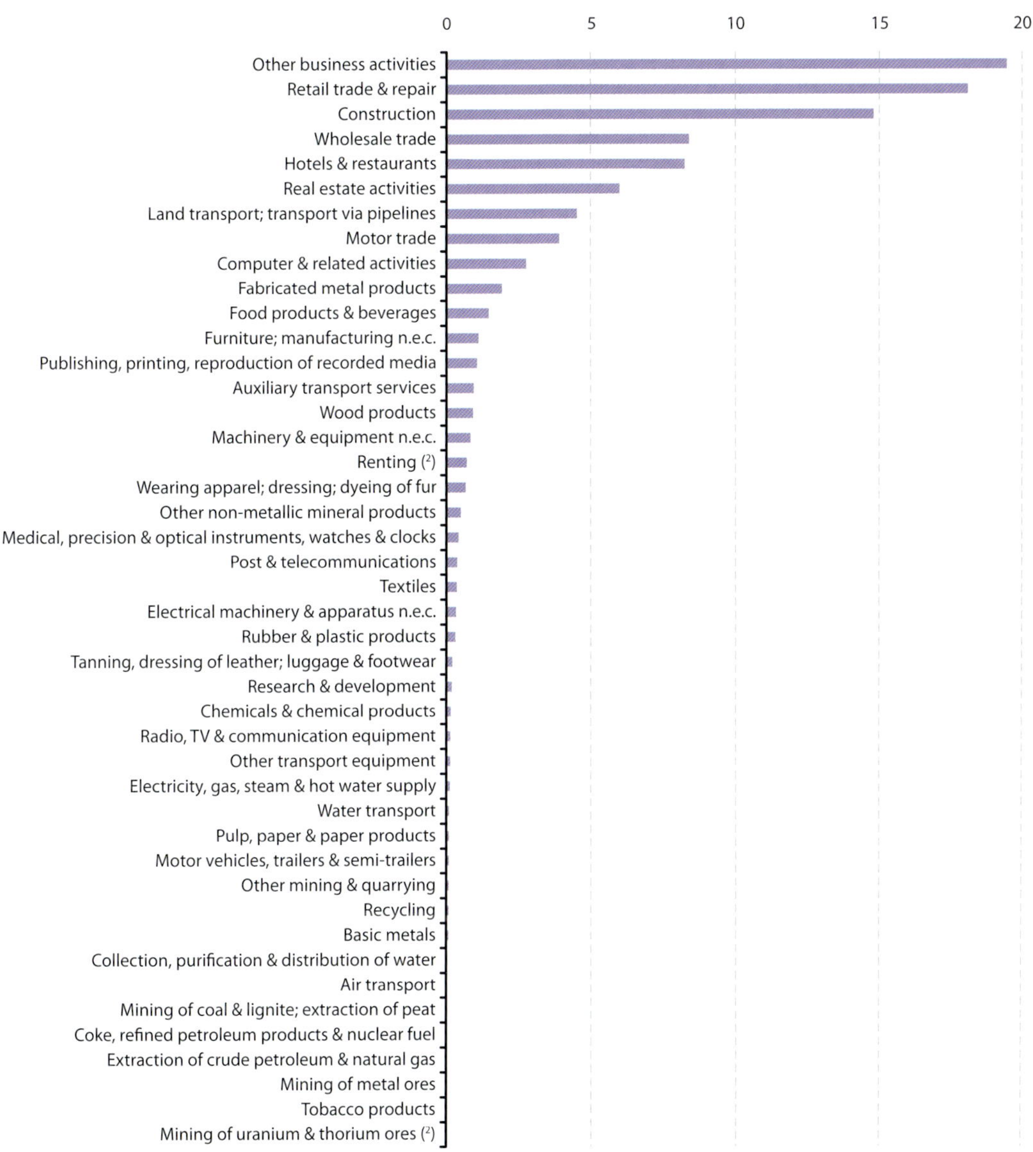

(1) The total number of enterprises in the EU-27 non-financial business economy was estimated as 20.9 million in 2007; manufacture of office machinery and computers, not available; estimates.
(2) 2006.

Source: Eurostat (ebd_all)

Table 7.1: Value added, 2007
(EUR 1 000 million)

	Mining & quarrying	Manufacturing	Elec., gas & water supply (1)	Construction	Distrib. trades	Hotels & restaur.	Trans., storage & communication	Real estate, renting & business activities
EU-27	92.49	1 812.96	*215.97*	561.99	1 183.56	195.45	687.26	1 396.60
Belgium	0.32	51.67	6.17	12.31	35.63	3.79	20.00	33.85
Bulgaria	0.60	4.73	1.10	1.75	3.04	0.40	2.22	1.71
Czech Republic	1.55	29.71	4.90	6.05	13.00	1.30	8.60	10.85
Denmark	7.16	29.23	2.54	11.08	24.09	2.54	15.35	30.55
Germany	6.47	484.55	46.83	57.97	216.15	24.96	122.47	267.09
Estonia	0.12	2.28	0.37	1.12	1.99	0.19	1.08	1.40
Ireland	1.08	36.87	2.07	7.95	18.45	3.76	8.31	16.76
Greece	1.02	16.81	2.71	6.21	24.89	3.85	9.62	10.77
Spain	2.60	136.27	17.49	101.15	113.35	26.67	62.81	114.96
France	4.40	222.65	25.88	75.77	159.99	30.19	100.28	221.83
Italy	7.44	233.47	21.32	70.71	121.24	25.49	76.49	117.52
Cyprus	0.05	1.20	0.31	1.38	1.96	1.00	1.20	*1.41*
Latvia	0.06	2.13	0.52	1.44	2.80	0.25	1.80	1.94
Lithuania	0.11	3.13	0.69	1.81	3.24	0.21	1.89	1.74
Luxembourg	0.04	3.64	0.28	1.69	2.82	0.50	2.84	5.54
Hungary	0.06	18.75	2.47	2.62	9.19	0.84	6.54	7.57
Malta	:	:	:	:	:	:	:	:
Netherlands	6.88	63.66	7.32	25.86	64.79	7.07	34.92	71.85
Austria	0.87	48.32	5.69	13.64	28.35	6.66	16.02	27.92
Poland	6.79	54.08	9.67	*12.78*	*33.54*	*1.92*	*17.22*	*23.55*
Portugal	0.69	19.78	3.84	9.46	17.01	3.36	10.12	12.54
Romania	3.02	13.81	2.61	5.26	9.67	0.75	5.94	5.30
Slovenia	0.13	7.00	0.73	1.76	3.78	0.55	1.93	2.31
Slovakia	0.25	8.48	2.71	1.16	4.46	0.21	2.39	2.79
Finland	0.43	35.99	3.42	7.99	14.40	1.93	10.23	15.49
Sweden	1.76	57.22	6.86	14.85	31.99	3.95	18.02	44.85
United Kingdom	38.59	226.92	37.33	108.06	223.17	42.84	128.07	344.04
Norway	59.10	25.30	5.03	12.01	22.26	2.80	18.89	27.69

(1) EU-27, estimate made for the purpose of this publication; Ireland, 2006.

Source: Eurostat (ebd_all)

Table 7.2: Number of persons employed, 2007
(1 000)

	Mining & quarry-ing	Manu-facturing	Elec., gas & water supply	Con-struction	Distrib. trades	Hotels & restaur.	Trans., storage & commun-ication	Real estate, renting & business activities
EU-27	702	34 541	1 590	14 788	32 542	9 545	12 212	27 831
Belgium	3	611	25	272	640	172	247	570
Bulgaria	30	669	54	221	483	122	187	195
Czech Republic	42	1 384	55	402	705	157	345	524
Denmark	3	421	16	207	470	109	188	406
Germany	84	7 244	272	1 522	4 918	1 387	2 016	4 756
Estonia	5	132	8	59	101	21	47	71
Ireland (1)	7	224	9	71	339	157	95	249
Greece	14	407	23	305	990	298	236	364
Spain	39	2 545	75	2 881	3 413	1 283	1 096	2 929
France	30	3 601	195	1 724	3 368	931	1 626	3 630
Italy	43	4 604	115	1 964	3 523	1 174	1 254	2 913
Cyprus	1	37	2	37	67	41	24	22
Latvia	3	158	14	86	191	32	84	101
Lithuania	3	259	25	139	289	42	110	116
Luxembourg	0	37	1	38	43	15	26	57
Hungary	5	774	49	243	601	128	265	525
Malta	:	:	:	:	:	:	:	:
Netherlands	8	777	25	486	1 425	366	478	1 688
Austria	6	638	31	262	625	248	243	436
Poland	183	2 704	203	*797*	*2 282*	*237*	*794*	*1 049*
Portugal	13	818	24	515	871	287	195	638
Romania	93	1 508	127	513	1 032	134	399	484
Slovenia	4	241	12	80	116	33	59	79
Slovakia	9	424	36	74	214	24	109	132
Finland	4	413	15	147	271	56	164	241
Sweden	9	806	31	298	633	139	315	640
United Kingdom	60	3 072	152	1 431	4 897	1 931	1 600	4 994
Norway	39	272	15	173	369	89	174	282

(1) Electricity, gas and water supply, 2006.

Source: Eurostat (ebd_all)

Figure 7.2: Breakdown of non-financial business economy value added and employment, EU-27, 2007 (1)
(% of non-financial business economy value added and employment)

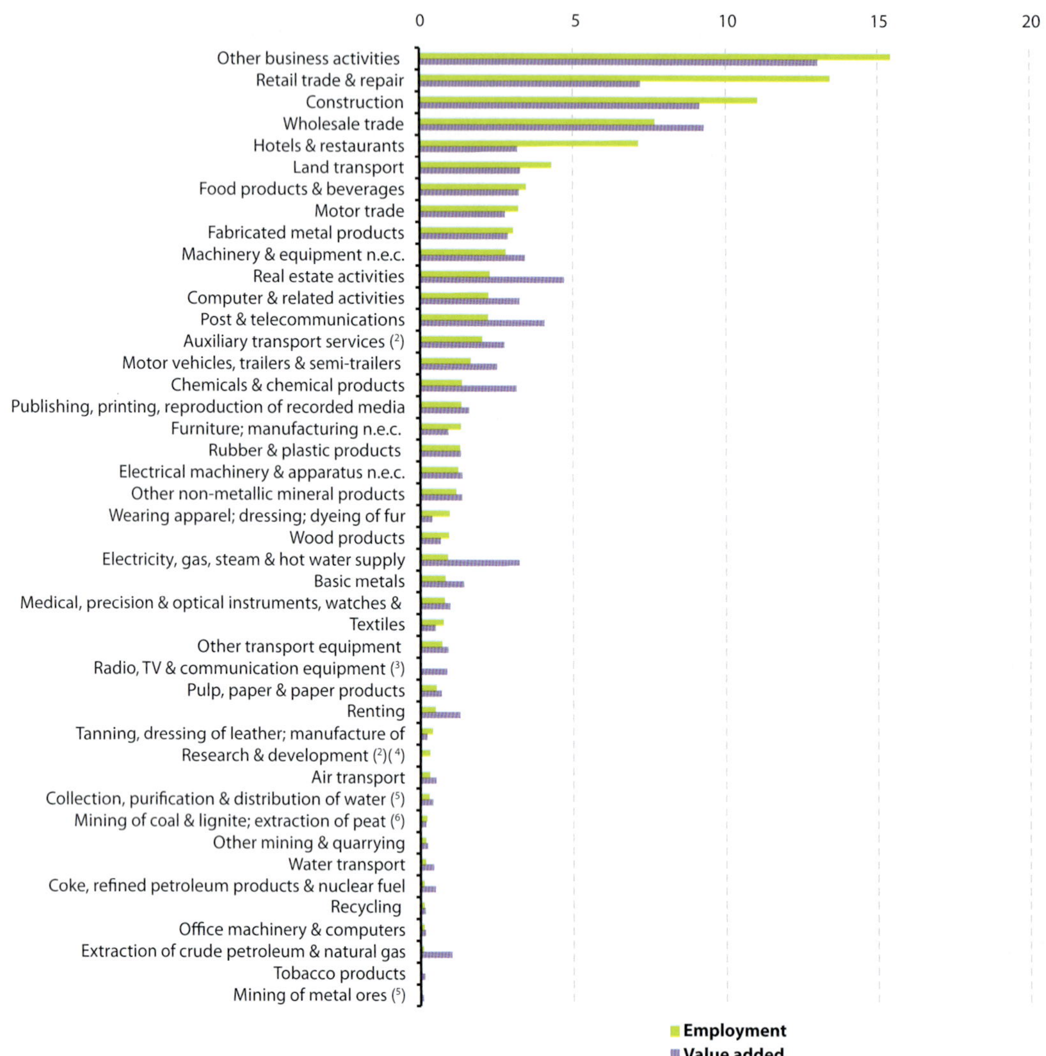

(1) Mining of uranium and thorium ores, not available; based on totals for the non-financial business economy estimated for the purpose of this publication.
(2) Employment, 2006.
(3) Employment, not available.
(4) Value added, not available.
(5) 2006.
(6) Value added, 2005.

Source: Eurostat (ebd_all)

Table 7.3: Average personnel costs, 2007
(EUR 1 000 per employee)

	Mining & quarry-ing	Manu-facturing	Elec., gas & water supply	Con-struction	Distrib. trades	Hotels & restaur.	Trans., storage & commun-ication	Real estate, renting & business activities
EU-27	33.9	34.4	*43.0*	29.2	24.7	16.2	33.6	32.2
Belgium	48.8	53.0	94.5	38.7	40.2	17.7	48.4	46.0
Bulgaria	6.4	3.1	7.1	2.8	2.6	1.9	4.6	4.1
Czech Republic	16.3	12.2	17.7	12.1	11.9	7.3	13.6	14.7
Denmark	66.1	48.2	49.9	43.0	35.8	17.4	47.2	42.1
Germany	51.3	47.4	63.5	34.2	27.0	12.5	33.2	30.8
Estonia	13.1	10.6	13.3	12.3	10.8	6.8	12.0	11.4
Ireland (1)	54.8	45.9	92.9	49.3	31.1	19.3	47.7	42.2
Greece	44.7	27.6	54.2	17.3	19.2	15.0	32.2	22.2
Spain	35.1	32.7	54.7	28.2	24.4	18.5	33.1	25.1
France	46.5	45.4	63.6	38.8	35.8	27.4	41.6	43.6
Italy	50.3	35.6	52.5	29.7	30.0	20.9	38.8	30.2
Cyprus	31.8	20.7	44.1	24.4	20.6	16.7	27.1	*24.4*
Latvia	8.1	6.8	12.6	7.3	6.3	4.5	8.2	7.7
Lithuania	10.6	7.3	10.6	8.9	6.7	4.0	7.7	7.6
Luxembourg	47.2	50.7	80.0	36.7	37.5	25.5	52.9	45.8
Hungary	14.4	12.0	19.3	8.2	9.5	6.0	14.3	11.2
Malta	:	:	:	:	:	:	:	:
Netherlands	95.9	55.7	68.1	47.5	28.0	13.3	40.8	28.0
Austria	54.9	45.6	71.7	38.5	32.5	21.6	42.3	39.4
Poland	20.2	9.6	16.0	*9.0*	*7.7*	*5.6*	*10.7*	*10.5*
Portugal	17.9	14.8	38.3	12.6	12.8	9.1	24.4	12.3
Romania	13.0	5.2	10.2	4.9	4.3	3.4	7.1	5.5
Slovenia	28.2	18.5	27.1	15.7	18.6	13.0	20.8	20.8
Slovakia	11.1	10.1	14.9	8.9	9.8	6.0	11.4	11.5
Finland	43.8	46.8	53.4	40.5	35.5	28.3	41.4	42.3
Sweden	57.8	51.6	64.9	45.1	41.3	25.9	44.8	49.8
United Kingdom	83.8	43.1	51.0	42.2	26.4	14.6	44.9	40.2
Norway	134.6	62.9	69.7	57.3	42.0	27.9	55.0	62.0

(1) Electricity, gas and water supply, 2006.

Source: Eurostat (ebd_all)

Figure 7.3: Wage adjusted labour productivity within the non-financial business economy, EU-27, 2007 (1)
(%)

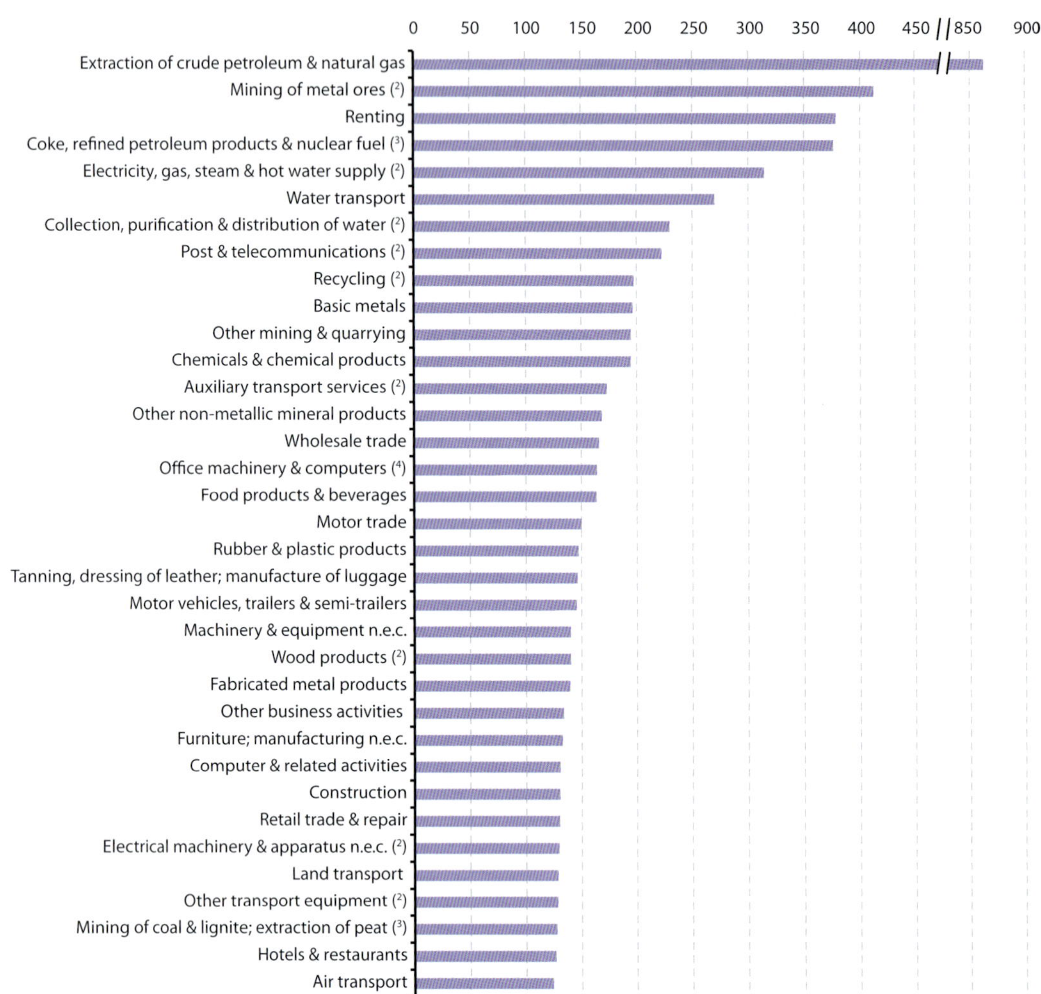

(1) Mining of uranium and thorium ores, tobacco products, textiles, wearing apparel; dressing; dyeing of fur, pulp, paper & paper products, publishing, printing, reproduction of recorded media, radio, TV & communication equipment, medical, precision & optical instruments, watches & clocks, real estate activities, research & development, not available.
(2) 2006.
(3) 2005.
(4) Estimate, 2005.

Source: Eurostat (ebd_all)

Figure 7.4: Gross operating rate within the non-financial business economy, EU-27, 2007 (1)
(%)

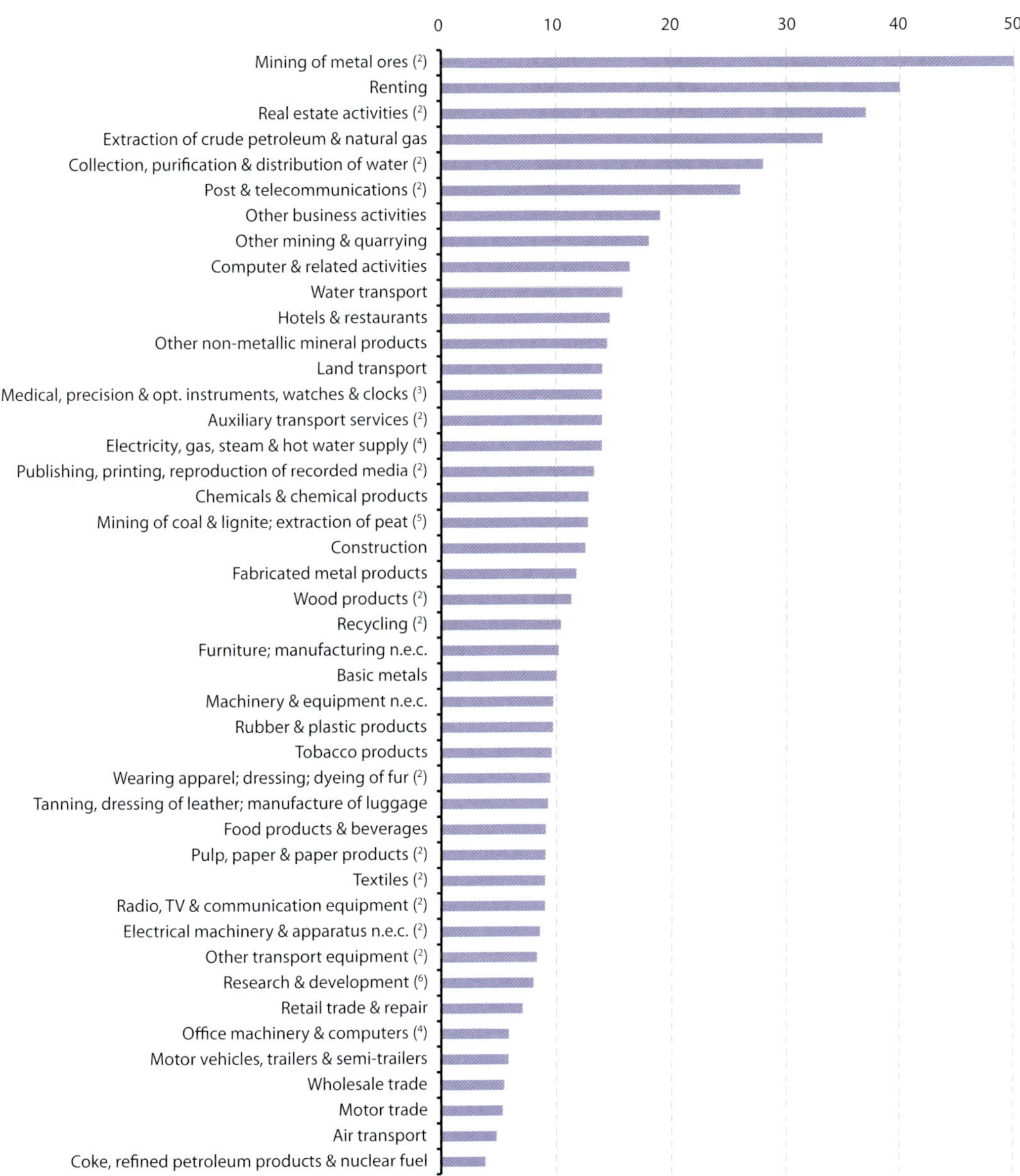

(1) Mining of uranium and thorium ores, not available.
(2) Estimate.
(3) Estimate, 2006.
(4) 2006.
(5) 2005.
(6) Estimate, 2005.

Source: Eurostat (ebd_all)

Figure 7.5: Value added breakdown by enterprise size-class, EU-27, 2007 (1)
(% of sectoral total)

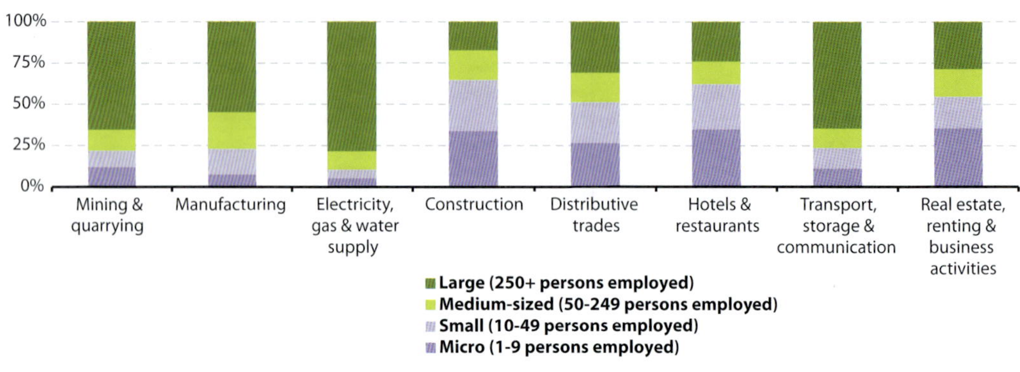

(1) Estimates, including estimates made for the purpose of this publication.

Source: Eurostat (sbs_sc_2d_mi02, sbs_sc_2d_dade02, sbs_sc_2d_el02, sbs_sc_4d_co02, sbs_sc_3ce_tr02 and sbs_sc_1b_se02)

Figure 7.6: Employment breakdown by enterprise size-class, EU-27, 2007 (1)
(% of sectoral total)

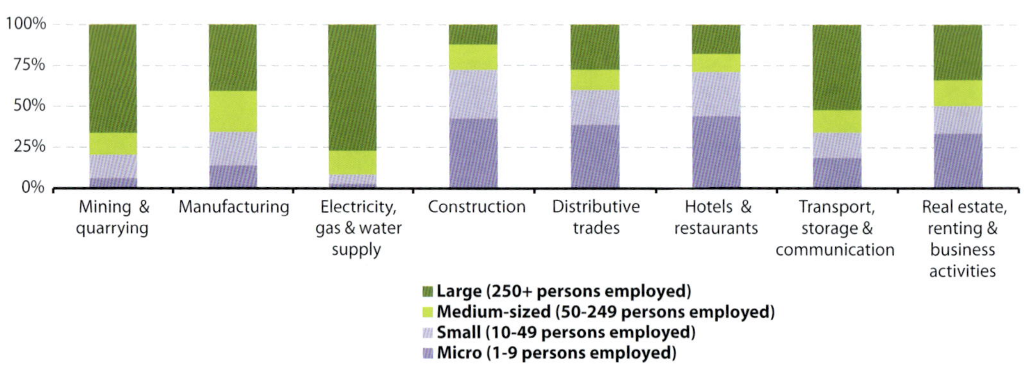

(1) Estimates.

Source: Eurostat (sbs_sc_2d_mi02, sbs_sc_2d_dade02, sbs_sc_2d_el02, sbs_sc_4d_co02, sbs_sc_3ce_tr02 and sbs_sc_1b_se02)

Table 7.4: Value added by enterprise size-class, mining and quarrying and manufacturing, 2007 (1)

	Mining & quarrying: size class share in total value added (%)				Manufacturing: size class share in total value added (%)			
	Micro	Small	Medium-sized	Large	Micro	Small	Medium-sized	Large
EU-27	*11.9*	9.7	13.0	65.4	7.5	15.4	*22.6*	*55.2*
Belgium	12.6	:	:	:	5.7	13.6	21.8	58.9
Bulgaria	0.7	5.6	8.5	85.1	4.6	14.5	29.8	51.1
Czech Republic	0.5	3.1	6.7	89.7	7.7	11.1	23.9	57.2
Denmark (2)	74.3	14.8	9.5	1.4	6.5	14.8	25.5	53.3
Germany	4.3	15.5	14.0	66.2	3.4	10.3	21.3	65.0
Estonia	3.9	21.6	:	:	6.1	21.4	43.3	29.2
Ireland	4.2	13.7	19.2	62.9	2.0	6.7	21.8	69.5
Greece	7.5	21.8	17.5	53.2	31.7	10.8	20.6	36.9
Spain	11.5	42.1	30.3	16.0	9.9	23.2	24.2	42.7
France	7.5	28.0	15.7	48.8	8.8	15.2	19.4	56.6
Italy	5.6	14.9	6.8	72.7	13.9	28.6	25.9	31.7
Cyprus	9.6	90.4	0.0	0.0	23.6	34.6	28.3	13.5
Latvia	8.8	:	40.3	:	5.4	22.0	40.8	31.8
Lithuania	7.9	12.3	79.8	0.0	3.7	14.7	33.3	48.3
Luxembourg	6.6	:	:	0.0	2.8	6.4	17.9	72.9
Hungary	:	:	:	:	4.6	9.7	18.4	67.3
Malta	:	:	:	:	:	:	:	:
Netherlands	2.2	3.0	:	:	7.5	17.9	26.1	48.5
Austria	7.8	16.8	:	:	5.9	12.4	23.7	58.0
Poland	*0.8*	*1.5*	*6.4*	*91.4*	*7.7*	*9.0*	*25.1*	*58.1*
Portugal	:	24.0	17.4	:	9.5	22.9	31.9	35.7
Romania (3)	0.6	1.3	2.4	95.7	4.2	11.4	24.9	59.5
Slovenia	4.3	:	18.1	:	10.1	13.7	25.0	51.3
Slovakia	1.7	14.2	14.6	69.6	4.1	10.4	19.5	66.0
Finland	20.6	:	:	:	5.8	11.2	18.4	64.5
Sweden	4.2	5.5	3.6	86.7	5.8	11.9	19.6	62.6
United Kingdom	9.0	5.0	12.7	73.3	7.9	13.9	22.7	55.5
Norway	56.8	0.9	11.7	30.6	8.3	17.3	25.7	48.6

(1) Micro: 1-9 persons employed; small: 10-49 persons employed; medium-sized: 50-249 persons employed; large: 250+ persons employed.
(2) Mining and quarrying, 2006.
(3) 2006.

Source: Eurostat (sbs_sc_2d_mi02 and sbs_sc_4d_co02)

Table 7.5: Value added by enterprise size-class, electricity, gas and water supply and construction, 2007 (1)

	Electricity, gas & water supply: size class share in total value added (%)				Construction: size class share in total value added (%)			
	Micro	Small	Medium-sized	Large	Micro	Small	Medium-sized	Large
EU-27 (2)	5.2	5.0	11.2	78.6	33.7	30.6	18.5	17.2
Belgium	23.1	2.7	11.1	63.1	34.2	31.4	21.5	12.9
Bulgaria	0.2	7.4	9.2	83.2	19.7	27.3	32.8	20.1
Czech Republic	0.9	13.4	11.2	74.5	34.0	23.5	20.5	22.0
Denmark	36.0	9.7	12.0	42.2	30.9	35.4	17.7	16.1
Germany	:	:	:	:	28.5	39.4	21.3	10.8
Estonia	4.9	7.6	31.5	56.0	20.9	36.6	32.3	10.2
Ireland	:	:	:	:	:	:	:	:
Greece	0.0	2.7	3.2	94.1	44.9	29.2	16.1	9.8
Spain	7.5	5.1	9.6	77.9	33.2	32.4	19.5	14.9
France	2.1	1.6	2.6	93.7	38.4	31.5	13.2	16.9
Italy	5.7	9.4	6.0	78.9	52.0	32.5	10.1	5.4
Cyprus	0.0	17.3	:	:	26.0	32.0	19.2	22.9
Latvia	3.0	3.9	4.9	88.2	13.3	30.2	39.6	16.9
Lithuania	3.5	3.8	7.8	84.9	7.4	23.7	42.9	26.0
Luxembourg	4.1	:	:	:	14.2	34.8	37.7	13.2
Hungary	4.0	6.1	22.0	67.9	29.0	31.4	21.4	18.2
Malta	:	:	:	:	:	:	:	:
Netherlands	7.1	:	:	:	27.8	29.5	20.0	22.7
Austria	13.3	5.0	12.1	69.6	21.2	33.6	21.8	23.4
Poland	*0.5*	*2.7*	*21.5*	*75.3*	*36.7*	*17.0*	*25.3*	*21.0*
Portugal	:	2.7	10.1	:	30.1	30.2	22.0	17.8
Romania	0.3	2.8	6.3	90.6	19.6	21.9	32.8	25.7
Slovenia	0.6	:	24.2	:	29.8	26.2	22.6	21.4
Slovakia	0.2	2.5	9.6	87.7	16.7	29.5	29.9	23.8
Finland	7.5	14.2	30.2	48.1	38.2	25.5	13.9	22.4
Sweden	7.6	10.7	26.3	55.5	32.5	28.4	14.2	24.9
United Kingdom	2.7	1.8	4.9	90.7	29.2	24.8	19.9	26.2
Norway	10.0	18.5	41.7	29.9	31.5	32.4	14.5	21.5

(1) Micro: 1-9 persons employed; small: 10-49 persons employed; medium-sized: 50-249 persons employed; large: 250+ persons employed.
(2) Electricity, gas and water supply, 2006.

Source: Eurostat (sbs_sc_2d_el02 and sbs_sc_4d_co02)

Table 7.6: Value added by enterprise size-class, distributive trades and transport, hotels and restaurants, 2007 ([1])

	Distributive trades: size class share in total value added (%)				Hotels & restaurants: size class share in total value added (%)			
	Micro	Small	Medium-sized	Large	Micro	Small	Medium-sized	Large
EU-27	26.5	24.4	18.2	30.9	*34.8*	*27.0*	14.1	24.1
Belgium	26.9	29.0	18.6	25.5	47.8	28.8	9.5	13.9
Bulgaria	25.7	35.0	23.7	15.7	17.9	26.1	36.5	19.5
Czech Republic	29.3	28.0	21.2	21.6	40.5	22.4	19.9	17.3
Denmark	21.4	29.3	22.5	26.9	28.8	31.4	21.0	18.9
Germany	17.6	25.4	21.1	35.9	32.3	34.2	16.9	16.5
Estonia	27.7	33.4	23.2	15.6	15.5	37.5	35.0	12.0
Ireland	16.6	37.0	23.3	23.1	17.9	33.0	36.6	12.5
Greece	40.5	29.5	16.5	13.6	43.8	30.4	16.0	9.8
Spain	33.3	24.2	16.6	25.9	39.5	26.0	16.4	18.2
France	27.4	24.7	16.4	31.5	42.7	27.7	7.8	21.8
Italy	47.4	25.7	12.1	14.8	48.4	30.0	9.1	12.6
Cyprus	34.6	30.1	25.5	9.8	33.0	22.6	29.7	14.6
Latvia	22.4	35.2	25.9	16.4	16.7	28.2	35.3	19.8
Lithuania	16.2	31.0	25.9	26.9	11.4	35.0	35.2	18.4
Luxembourg	33.5	30.1	22.9	13.6	40.5	:	9.9	:
Hungary	28.6	26.4	26.1	19.0	28.6	25.7	19.9	25.9
Malta	:	:	:	:	:	:	:	:
Netherlands	24.9	27.3	23.1	24.7	40.5	26.9	11.1	21.5
Austria	22.1	26.3	21.7	29.9	41.8	33.6	17.0	7.5
Poland	*31.8*	*19.6*	*22.8*	*25.8*	*32.8*	*17.1*	*19.5*	*30.6*
Portugal	31.7	28.5	18.2	21.5	35.6	26.8	19.6	18.0
Romania	23.8	28.7	25.0	22.5	15.1	31.8	25.7	27.4
Slovenia	28.1	27.3	21.0	23.6	31.9	23.0	20.7	24.5
Slovakia	33.0	35.9	15.7	15.4	:	37.9	38.9	:
Finland	26.5	23.5	16.7	33.3	35.1	23.4	14.3	27.1
Sweden	22.7	25.8	20.1	31.4	34.4	31.2	16.6	17.8
United Kingdom	19.6	17.4	15.9	47.1	18.8	19.0	13.8	48.4
Norway	24.9	30.6	19.0	25.5	21.1	36.2	24.2	18.5

([1]) Micro: 1-9 persons employed; small: 10-49 persons employed; medium-sized: 50-249 persons employed; large: 250+ persons employed.

Source: Eurostat (sbs_sc_3ce_tr02 and sbs_sc_1b_se02)

Table 7.7: Value added by enterprise size-class, transport, storage and communication and real estate, renting and business activities, 2007 (1)

	Transport, storage & communication: size class share in total value added (%)				Real estate, renting & business activities: size class share in total value added (%)			
	Micro	Small	Medium-sized	Large	Micro	Small	Medium-sized	Large
EU-27	11.2	12.1	12.1	64.5	35.5	*18.9*	17.0	*28.6*
Belgium	10.0	19.4	15.2	55.4	29.1	18.2	17.8	35.0
Bulgaria	8.7	10.4	11.9	68.9	46.2	27.4	15.7	10.7
Czech Republic	12.3	8.8	9.4	69.5	43.2	20.7	21.3	14.8
Denmark	14.9	15.1	15.7	54.2	38.8	21.2	16.3	23.7
Germany	9.9	14.9	14.5	60.8	36.7	19.5	19.0	24.7
Estonia	11.6	19.5	32.3	36.6	44.9	26.5	18.0	10.6
Ireland	12.0	10.8	10.0	67.2	32.0	23.5	17.8	26.7
Greece	22.5	13.4	6.7	57.4	45.1	21.8	15.4	17.8
Spain	20.4	12.9	11.4	55.2	42.5	19.2	14.4	24.0
France	6.2	9.4	9.3	75.2	32.7	18.8	15.8	32.7
Italy	12.2	12.2	10.9	64.7	53.0	17.0	10.4	19.6
Cyprus (2)	12.0	11.6	15.0	61.4	56.7	21.3	12.7	9.2
Latvia	10.0	21.5	18.7	49.8	47.1	30.1	14.9	7.9
Lithuania	7.6	21.1	23.9	47.4	40.6	27.7	22.6	9.1
Luxembourg	12.0	11.9	15.8	60.1	49.5	20.0	14.2	16.2
Hungary	10.6	11.0	12.7	65.7	42.5	22.4	19.4	15.7
Malta	:	:	:	:	:	:	:	:
Netherlands	10.8	14.1	16.9	58.2	28.3	21.6	20.3	29.9
Austria	7.6	14.0	19.4	59.0	39.0	22.2	22.2	16.7
Poland	*12.9*	*6.4*	*11.2*	*69.4*	*48.8*	*12.7*	*19.2*	*19.4*
Portugal	10.0	15.5	14.3	60.2	40.9	19.9	18.5	20.6
Romania	8.9	9.8	10.6	70.7	35.4	24.7	21.6	18.4
Slovenia	20.1	13.3	11.9	54.7	46.0	28.1	16.4	9.5
Slovakia	5.3	7.9	11.4	75.4	36.1	26.8	19.9	17.2
Finland	23.2	13.4	11.7	51.7	32.9	20.4	18.8	27.9
Sweden	16.2	14.6	14.0	55.2	35.8	19.3	17.0	27.9
United Kingdom	9.2	9.3	9.8	71.8	27.3	17.7	17.6	37.4
Norway (2)	29.1	11.1	11.0	48.8	45.5	18.6	15.8	20.0

(1) Micro: 1-9 persons employed; small: 10-49 persons employed; medium-sized: 50-249 persons employed; large: 250+ persons employed.
(2) Real estate, renting and business activities, 2006.

Source: Eurostat (sbs_sc_1b_se02)

Figure 7.7: Share of value added and employment accounted for by foreign controlled enterprises, non-financial business economy, 2007 (1)
(%)

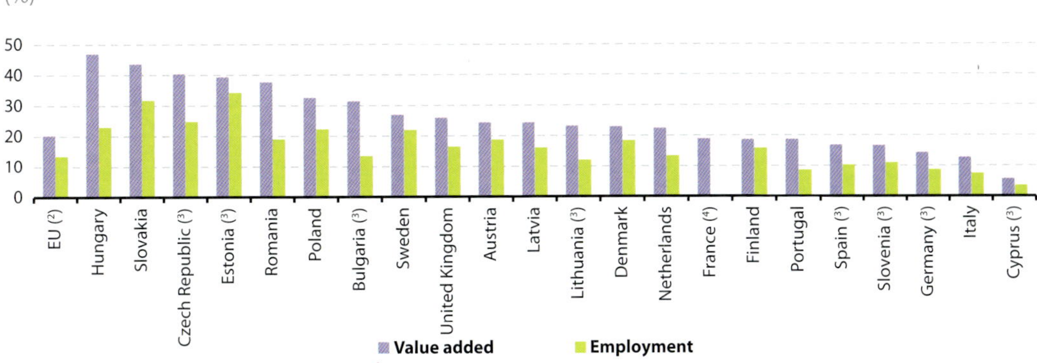

(1) Belgium, Ireland, Greece, Luxembourg and Malta, not available.
(2) Weighted average based on the latest data available for those countries shown in the graph.
(3) 2006.
(4) Value added, 2006; employment, not available.

Source: Eurostat (fats_g1a_03)

Table 7.8: Enterprise demography, business economy, 2007 (¹)

	Enterprise birth rates (% of enterprise births among active enterprises)	Enterprise death rates (% of enterprise deaths among active enterprises) (²)	Enterprise survival (% of enterprise births of year n-2 which are still active in year n) (³)
Belgium	7.0	5.2	:
Bulgaria	15.1	*9.2*	51.3
Czech Republic	9.5	*12.1*	64.9
Denmark	12.9	9.9	66.2
Germany	9.5	9.5	62.3
Estonia	13.2	7.0	77.6
Ireland	:	:	:
Greece	:	:	:
Spain	9.6	6.2	73.4
France	10.1	7.1	80.7
Italy	8.4	*7.7*	74.7
Cyprus	3.3	1.7	90.9
Latvia	11.1	4.4	71.1
Lithuania	24.7	*18.8*	55.4
Luxembourg	10.4	8.0	77.9
Hungary	9.0	*11.8*	61.6
Malta	:	:	:
Netherlands	13.3	*6.9*	65.0
Austria	7.5	6.6	78.3
Poland	:	:	:
Portugal	13.8	*15.3*	53.7
Romania	15.6	*8.7*	75.9
Slovenia	10.2	6.2	84.2
Slovakia	13.3	*14.3*	65.9
Finland	10.1	7.5	73.0
Sweden	7.4	5.8	86.2
United Kingdom	14.3	9.9	79.6
Norway	10.3	*6.7*	66.7
Switzerland	:	:	70.7

(¹) Covers the business economy (NACE Rev. 1.1 Sections C to K) excluding holdings (NACE Rev. 1.1 Class 74.15); Romania, sole proprietorships are not covered.
(²) 2006, except France, 2007.
(³) Slovenia, 2006; Switzerland, 2005.

Source: Eurostat (tsier150)

7.2 Industrial production

This subchapter examines recent statistics on industrial production in the European Union (EU). Prodcom is the name given to the system of industrial production statistics which covers mining and quarrying and manufactured products.

Main statistical findings

Prodcom covers mining and quarrying as well as manufacturing, in other words, NACE Rev. 2 Sections B and C. Prodcom statistics are based on a list of products called the Prodcom List which consists of about 4 000 headings and is revised every year. Products are detailed at an 8-digit level – only information at this level can be found in the Prodcom database, as production data for different products cannot be meaningfully aggregated. The purpose of Prodcom statistics is to report, for each product in the Prodcom List, how much has been produced in the reporting country during the reference period. This means that Prodcom statistics relate to products (not to activities) and are therefore not strictly comparable with activity-based statistics such as structural business statistics.

Prodcom information is currently requested for each heading in terms of the value of production sold during the survey period. Table 7.9 shows the level of production in the EU-27 for a selection of products. As can be seen, transport equipment products dominated the list of the most sold manufacturing products in the EU-27 in value terms in 2009, occupying the top place with a number of further products among the top 15 shown.

As well as data by value, information on the physical quantity (also referred to as volume) of production sold during the survey period is also requested. Table 7.10 shows the quantity of production for a selection of products. In certain circumstances this information can be supplemented by the physical quantity of actual production during the survey period, including therefore any production which is used (as an intermediate product) by the enterprise in the manufacture of other products.

Data sources and availability

The Prodcom List is linked to the activity classification NACE and to the classification of products by activity (CPA): the first four digits of each Prodcom code refer to a NACE class, the fifth and sixth digits relate to a CPA subcategory, and the seventh and eighth digits are specific to the Prodcom List. Most headings correspond to one or more combined nomenclature (CN) codes: some headings (mostly industrial services) do not correspond to a CN heading at all.

The production surveyed covers only the production actually carried out on the territory of the declaring country. This means that the production of subsidiaries which takes place outside an enterprise's territory is not included in the survey for that country. As a general principle, when a production process takes as an input a material that does not match the description of the product, and produces as an output something that does, then production of the product should be recorded. On the other hand, if the processing merely works on a product without changing the heading under which it is classified, it should not be recorded, since this would result in double-counting. This means that the link to turnover is tenuous, since some activity does not result in new products and should not be recorded in Prodcom.

Prodcom data are available for all of the EU Member States, Iceland, Norway and Croatia, and Eurostat produces aggregates for the EU-27 and the EU-25. Data are available during the year following the reference year, with the first release by Eurostat normally in July. As more complete and revised data becomes available updates are released on a monthly basis.

Context

The development of Prodcom dates back to 1985 when there were the first meetings of a working party on production statistics, whose objective was to harmonise the various ways industrial production statistics were collected in the Member States. Although statistics were collected on production in most countries, these covered the national situation, and national classifications were used and different survey methods applied. The basis of Prodcom is to enable these national statistics to be compared and where possible aggregated geographically to give a picture of the output of a product in the European context. This aim became more urgent with the creation of the single market in 1992, and with rapid changes occurring in Europe, the statistical system had to adapt to these changes.

Table 7.9: Production sold in value terms, selected products, EU-27, 2009

PRODCOM code	Product	Value (EUR million)	Rounding base (million) (1)
29.10.22.30	Motor vehicles with a petrol engine > 1 500 cm^3	83 753	
21.20.13.80	Other medicaments of mixed or unmixed products, p.r.s., n.e.c.	60 154	
29.10.23.30	Motor vehicles with a diesel or semi-diesel engine > 1 500 cm^3 but <= 2 500 cm^3	60 000	20 000
10.00.00.Z1	Prepared and preserved meat, meat offal or blood, including prepared meat and offal dishes	46 965	
29.32.30.90	Other parts and accessories, n.e.c., for vehicles of HS 87.01 to 87.05; parts thereof	42 000	6 000
29.10.21.00	Motor vehicles with a petrol engine <= 1 500 cm^3	36 262	
10.90.10.Z0	Preparations for animal feeds other than dog and cat food	35 618	
25.11.23.60	Other structures of iron or steel	32 667	
11.05.10.00	Beer other than non-alcoholic and low-alcohol beer, excluding alcohol duty	29 944	
10.71.11.00	Fresh bread	26 949	
29.32.20.90	Parts and accessories of bodies (including cabs), n.e.c.	24 744	
10.51.40.50	Grated, powdered, blue-veined and other non-processed cheese	24 000	3 000
30.30.50.90	Parts for all types of aircraft excluding propellers, rotors, under carriages, for civil use	21 607	
17.21.13.00	Cartons, boxes and cases, of corrugated paper or paperboard	21 213	
23.63.10.00	Ready-mixed concrete	20 742	

(1) Indicates the magnitude of the rounding employed to protect confidential cell (in the case of PRODCOM code 29.10.23.30, the confidential value lies within the range +/- EUR 20 000 million of the reported value).

Source: Eurostat, from http://epp.eurostat.ec.europa.eu/portal/page/portal/statistics/search_database go to Data Navigation Tree/ Database by themes/Industry, trade and services/Statistics on the production of manufactured goods (prom)/NACE Rev. 2 (prodcom_n2)/Prodcom Annual Sold (NACE Rev. 2.) (DS-066341)

Table 7.10: Quantity of production sold, selected products, EU-27, 2009

PRODCOM code	Product	Quantity (1 000)	Rounding base (1 000) (1)	Unit
24.10.22.10	Flat semi-finished products (slabs) (of stainless steel)	89 764		kg
23.51.12.10	Portland cement	170 710 000		kg
11.02.11.30	Champagne (important: excluding alcohol duty)	165 128		l
20.42.11.50	Perfumes	12 303		l
20.11.11.70	Oxygen	23 723 810		m^3
16.10.23.03	Coniferous wood in chips or particles	34 483 920	60	kg
12.00.11.50	Cigarettes (excluding tobacco duty)	705 113 340		p/st
27.90.52.20	Fixed electrical capacitors, tantalum or aluminium electrolytic (excluding power capacitors)	6 643 576		p/st

(1) Indicates the magnitude of the rounding employed to protect confidential cell (in the case of PRODCOM code 16.10.23.03, the confidential value lies within the range +/- 60 000 kg of the reported value).

Source: Eurostat, from http://epp.eurostat.ec.europa.eu/portal/page/portal/statistics/search_database go to Data Navigation Tree/ Database by themes/Industry, trade and services/Statistics on the production of manufactured goods (prom)/NACE Rev. 2 (prodcom_n2)/Prodcom Annual Sold (NACE Rev. 2.) (DS-066341)

7.3 Industry and construction

This subchapter examines recent statistics on the developments of both industry and construction in the European Union (EU). Short-term business statistics (STS) are provided in the form of indices that allow the rapid assessment of the economic climate within an economy. STS are presented as indices showing developments over time, and also as rates of change typically showing comparisons of a month or quarter with the preceding period, or the same period of the previous year. Unlike structural business statistics (SBS) (see Subchapter 7.1), STS do not provide information on levels such as the monetary value of output or the number of persons employed.

Main statistical findings

The EU-27's indices of industrial production and industrial output prices (based on the NACE Rev. 2 classification) show clearly the impact of the economic and financial crisis. Relatively stable growth over several years was interrupted in the second half of 2007 when the rate of increase of prices accelerated as the production index growth slowed and the month on month rate of change turned negative in February 2008. The domestic output price index peaked six months later than the production index, in July 2008. The fall in the production index lasted more than one year, returning to a positive rate of change in May 2009, while the domestic producer price index starting a run of sustained growth from May 2009 (see Figure 7.8).

The decline in the index of industrial production for the EU-27 from its relative peak in February 2008 was particularly steep, as the relative trough recorded in March 2009 was the lowest level for this index since December 1997. By contrast, although the index of industrial output prices in July 2009 was 8.0 % lower than at its relative peak a year earlier, it remained similar to the pre-economic and financial crisis level recorded in October 2007; in part, this continued to reflect the relatively high price of oil and associated energy-related and intermediate products.

The downturn was widespread within the EU, illustrated by the fact that every Member State recorded a lower index of industrial production in 2009 than in 2008, with falls ranging from -3.6 % in Poland to -25.9 % in Estonia, as shown in Table 7.11. Equally, the downturn was spread across the whole of the industrial economy: in 2009 there was growth recorded for a single industrial activity (at the NACE Rev. 2 division level) within the EU-27 as a whole, as the manufacture of pharmaceutical products and preparations rose 3.1 % compared with the year before. The downturn was so severe that, despite the output growth that most activities had experienced leading up to the crisis, average annual growth between 2004 and 2009 was negative for most activities (see Figure 7.9).

Although slightly less in magnitude, the length of the downturn in activity for construction within the EU was greater than in industry. The EU-27 index of production for construction peaked in December 2006 and fell gradually for seven months. This initial downturn was followed by a slight, temporary recovery until January 2008, after which the index fell substantially, reaching a low in January 2010, just over three years after the initial downturn. Over this period the index of production for construction fell by a total of 15.6 % in the EU-27, deteriorating to a level not seen since May 1999.

The production index for buildings is the dominant subindex of the index of production for construction, and unsurprisingly followed a similar path to the overall index for construction, although the magnitude of the contraction from the end of 2006 to the beginning of 2010 was slightly greater, totalling -18.2 % in the EU-27 (see Figure 7.10). For civil engineering the developments were less clear cut. From March to November 2008 the EU-27 index of production for civil engineering fell in a similar manner to the index for building. However, there followed renewed growth through to April 2009, perhaps reflecting increased public spending in reaction to the economic and financial crisis. Civil engineering output remained stable through much of 2009, before contracting again between November 2009 and March 2010 after which the index remained relatively unchanged.

Data sources and availability

Short-term business statistics (STS) are compiled within the scope of the STS Regulation 1165/98 of 19 May 1998 concerning short-term statistics. Despite major changes brought in by the STS Regulation, and improvements in the availability and timeliness of indicators which followed its implementation, strong demands for further development were voiced, even as the STS Regulation was being adopted. The emergence of the European Central Bank (ECB) fundamentally changed expectations as regards STS. As a result, the STS Regulation was amended by Regulation 1158/2005 on 6 July 2005.

Indicators common to industry and construction include the production index and the labour input indices concerning employment, wages and salaries and hours worked. For industry there are additional STS indicators concerning turnover, new orders and output prices, all three of which are compiled as a total and also distinguishing between domestic and non-domestic markets, with a further analysis of non-domestic markets between euro area and non-euro area markets. For construction activities there is a distinction in the production index between building and civil engineering, additional indicators are collected on building permits, as well as construction cost and price indices.

The presentation of short-term statistics may take a variety of different forms. Gross or unadjusted indices are the basic form of an index. Working-day adjustment takes into account the calendar nature of a given month in order to adjust the index. The adjustment of working days is intended to adjust for calendar effects, whatever their nature. The number of working days for a given month depends on: the timing of certain public holidays (Easter can fall in

March or in April depending on the year); the possible overlap of certain public holidays and non-working days (1 May can fall on a Sunday); whether or not a year is a leap year, and other reasons. Seasonal adjustment, or the adjustment of seasonal variations aims, after adjusting for calendar effects, to take into account the impact of known seasonal factors that have been observed in the past. For example, in the case of the production index, annual summer holidays have a negative impact on industrial production. The trend is a slow variation over a long period of years, generally associated with the structural causes of the phenomenon in question. The cycle is a quasi-periodic oscillation. It is characterised by alternating periods of higher and lower rates of change possibly, but not always, involving expansion and contraction. Generally, if this irregular component of the time series is relatively important, the trend-cycle series is a better series for the analysis of longer-term past developments. However, this advantage is less clear when analysing very recent developments. This is because trend-cycle values for recent periods may have greater revisions than the equivalent seasonally adjusted values. Hence, the latter may be more appropriate for the analysis of very recent developments; this is particularly true around turning points.

Where relevant, the Member States are encouraged to transmit seasonally adjusted data and trend-cycle indices. If they do not, Eurostat calculates the seasonal adjustment. The Member States' national statistical authorities are responsible for data collection, and the calculation of national time series. Eurostat is responsible for the euro area and EU aggregations.

NACE Rev. 2 is the latest version of the statistical classification of economic activities and has been implemented in STS during 2009. This involved not just changing data compilation practices to use NACE Rev. 2 but also recalculating or estimating a time series in NACE Rev. 2, normally back to the year 2000. Simultaneously with the introduction of NACE Rev. 2, a new base year (2005) was adopted for STS indices to better reflect the economic structure; previously indices were presented with 2000 as the base year.

Context

The profile and use of STS is expanding rapidly, as information flows have become global and the latest news release for an indicator may have significant effects on global markets, or decisions that are taken by central banks and business leaders. STS are a key resource for those who follow developments in the business cycle, or for those who wish to trace recent developments within a particular industry, construction or service.

Some of the most important STS indicators are a set of Principal European Economic Indicators (PEEIs) that are essential to the ECB for conducting monetary policy within the euro area. Six PEEIs concern industrial and construction short-term business statistics, namely indices covering: industrial production, industrial new orders, domestic industrial producer prices, industrial import prices, production in construction, and building permits.

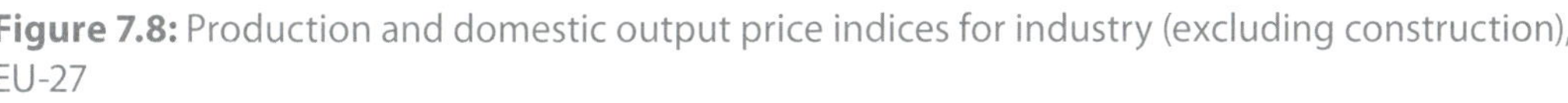

Figure 7.8: Production and domestic output price indices for industry (excluding construction), EU-27
(2005=100)

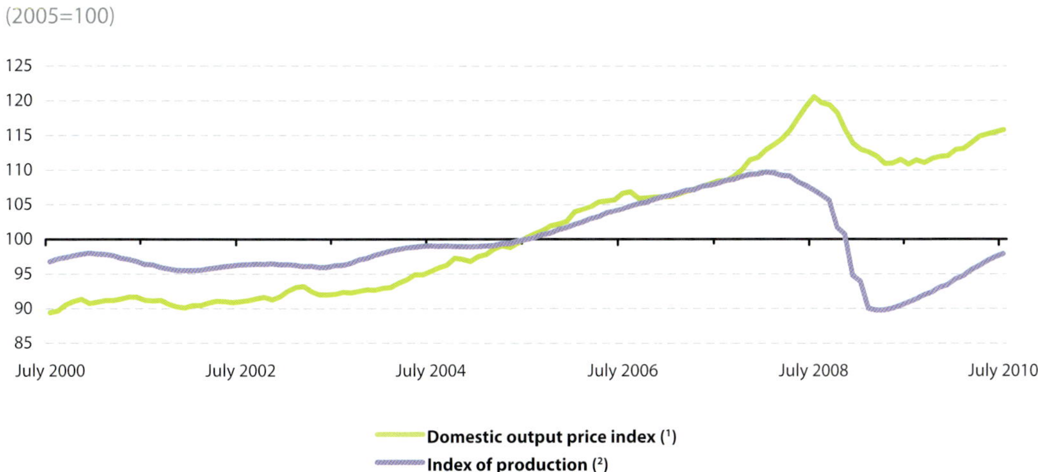

(1) Gross series; estimates, 2000-2004.
(2) Trend-cycle; estimates.

Source: Eurostat (sts_inppd_m and sts_inpr_m)

Table 7.11: Annual growth rates for industry (excluding construction)
(%)

	Index of production (1)					Domestic output price index (2)				
	2005	2006	2007	2008	2009	2005	2006	2007	2008	2009
EU-27	*1.3*	4.2	3.6	-1.8	-13.8	*5.1*	5.6	2.7	7.6	-4.4
Euro area (EA-16)	*1.4*	4.3	3.7	-1.8	-14.9	*4.1*	5.1	2.7	6.1	-5.1
Belgium	-0.9	5.0	2.9	-0.6	-13.9	5.7	5.8	2.1	9.3	-7.2
Bulgaria	7.2	6.2	9.5	0.4	-18.2	7.3	8.7	8.0	13.2	-4.3
Czech Republic	*4.3*	*8.7*	*10.6*	*-2.4*	*-13.1*	3.1	1.5	4.1	4.5	-3.2
Denmark	2.7	4.1	-2.1	-1.1	-15.1	9.2	7.9	1.6	13.2	-6.7
Germany	3.5	5.7	6.0	-0.0	-16.3	4.4	5.4	1.3	5.4	-4.1
Estonia	11.1	10.2	6.4	-4.8	-25.9	1.7	4.3	9.6	9.6	-0.3
Ireland	3.9	3.2	5.2	-2.2	-4.5	*2.3*	*3.6*	*2.4*	*6.1*	*-3.6*
Greece	-1.6	0.8	2.3	-4.2	-9.2	5.9	7.3	4.1	10.0	-5.8
Spain	0.8	3.9	2.0	-7.3	-15.8	4.7	5.4	3.6	6.6	-3.4
France	0.3	1.3	1.3	-2.8	-12.3	3.1	3.8	2.8	5.6	-6.4
Italy	-0.7	3.6	1.8	-3.5	-18.4	*4.0*	5.2	3.3	5.8	-5.4
Cyprus	1.0	0.6	4.3	3.9	-8.7	4.9	5.3	3.6	11.7	-1.8
Latvia	7.4	6.5	0.9	-3.9	-15.8	7.1	9.6	18.6	15.7	-1.8
Lithuania	7.1	6.5	2.4	5.5	-14.6	5.9	6.9	9.4	15.8	-6.7
Luxembourg	2.8	2.4	-0.6	-5.3	-15.8	3.6	12.8	4.4	15.1	-9.2
Hungary	7.3	10.6	8.0	-1.0	-17.4	6.1	8.4	6.5	11.6	1.2
Malta	:	:	:	:	:	:	17.9	-3.7	14.8	9.3
Netherlands	*0.5*	*1.5*	*2.3*	*1.4*	*-7.6*	7.0	8.6	5.3	8.9	-9.8
Austria	4.3	7.4	5.9	1.1	-11.9	3.4	2.1	4.1	4.8	*-1.8*
Poland	4.4	12.2	9.5	2.0	-3.6	*2.5*	3.4	4.0	5.4	*2.4*
Portugal	-3.5	3.2	0.1	-4.1	-8.6	:	4.4	2.9	5.2	-3.8
Romania	-2.7	9.8	10.1	2.6	-5.9	10.8	10.3	8.4	12.8	2.1
Slovenia	4.6	6.3	7.4	1.6	-17.6	2.8	2.4	5.5	5.6	-0.4
Slovakia	1.0	15.7	16.9	3.1	-13.7	3.7	6.3	1.8	6.2	-2.7
Finland	-0.6	10.1	4.8	1.0	-21.1	4.3	6.3	3.9	8.6	-6.3
Sweden	2.2	3.6	3.9	-2.9	-17.9	3.9	6.1	3.6	6.1	-0.3
United Kingdom	-1.1	0.5	0.3	-3.1	-10.0	11.1	8.6	1.7	16.0	-2.9
Norway	-0.4	-2.1	-1.3	0.3	-3.6	6.1	8.6	-0.6	15.2	-1.8
Switzerland	*2.7*	*7.8*	*9.5*	*1.2*	*-7.7*	1.6	2.7	2.5	4.2	-2.4
Croatia	5.0	4.3	5.0	0.7	-8.9	2.7	2.7	3.4	8.3	-0.5
Turkey	*5.7*	*7.3*	*6.9*	*-0.6*	*-9.8*	*7.1*	*9.8*	*6.0*	*13.0*	*1.0*
Japan	*1.4*	*4.4*	*2.8*	*-3.3*	*-21.7*	:	:	:	:	:
United States	*3.3*	*2.3*	*1.5*	*-2.3*	*-9.8*	:	:	:	:	:

(1) Working day adjusted.
(2) Gross series.

Source: Eurostat (sts_inprgr_a and sts_inppdgr_a)

Figure 7.9: Average annual growth rate for the industrial index of production, EU-27, 2004-2009 (¹)
(%)

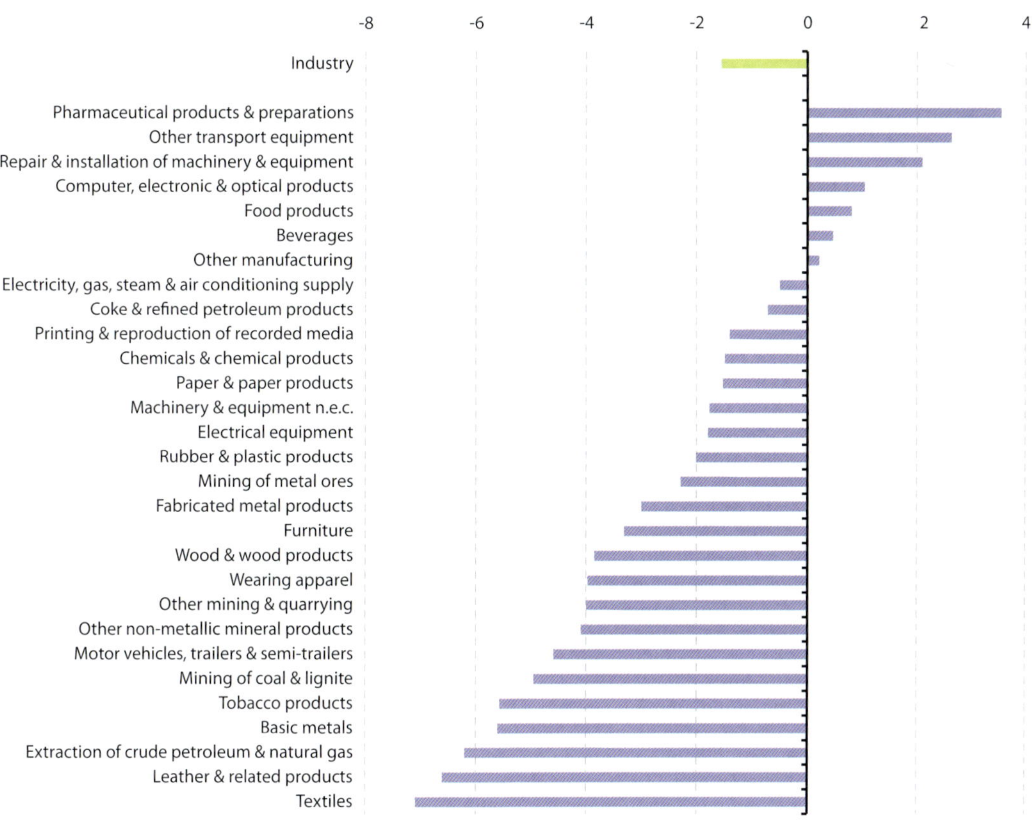

(¹) Working day adjusted; mining support service activities, not available.

Source: Eurostat (sts_inprgr_a)

Table 7.12: Annual growth rates for construction
(%)

	Index of production (¹)					Construction costs index (²)				
	2005	2006	2007	2008	2009	2005	2006	2007	2008	2009
EU-27	1.7	3.6	2.2	-3.7	-8.9	3.9	4.7	4.4	3.3	-1.5
Euro area (EA-16)	1.9	3.7	1.3	-5.3	-8.2	3.4	4.7	4.2	3.9	0.1
Belgium	*-3.4*	*3.3*	*2.3*	*-1.2*	*-6.7*	2.9	4.9	4.5	2.5	-1.1
Bulgaria	31.9	24.1	27.7	26.5	*-34.8*	8.3	5.6	7.7	*12.3*	*10.9*
Czech Republic	5.4	6.4	7.0	-0.5	-0.4	3.8	2.1	4.8	3.5	-0.3
Denmark	3.0	4.3	3.4	-5.5	-16.8	2.4	4.7	6.4	2.9	-0.4
Germany	-5.3	6.3	2.9	-0.7	0.1	1.7	2.4	3.3	3.2	0.1
Estonia	22.4	26.9	13.5	-13.3	-28.4	6.2	10.5	12.7	3.5	-8.5
Ireland	9.9	2.9	-13.2	-29.6	-36.4	8.7	9.6	1.7	-7.7	-9.9
Greece	-38.7	3.6	14.3	7.7	-20.4	3.4	4.3	4.6	5.1	-0.3
Spain	*10.1*	*2.2*	*-4.3*	*-16.3*	*-11.0*	4.6	6.9	5.0	4.7	1.0
France	2.8	4.2	2.4	-3.7	-5.9	*2.3*	*5.3*	*4.6*	*5.5*	*0.4*
Italy	1.2	3.9	6.5	-0.3	-11.5	4.0	2.8	3.7	3.8	:
Cyprus	2.9	4.1	6.8	2.3	-10.7	4.5	5.0	5.0	8.0	0.8
Latvia	15.5	13.3	13.6	-3.1	-34.9	*11.8*	*19.5*	31.6	15.6	-6.2
Lithuania	9.9	21.7	22.2	4.1	-48.5	8.3	10.7	16.1	9.5	-14.5
Luxembourg	-0.9	2.5	2.6	-1.9	1.0	3.0	2.9	2.9	3.2	1.4
Hungary	15.7	-0.7	-14.0	-5.2	-4.4	*3.3*	*6.2*	*7.2*	*7.5*	*3.0*
Malta	4.3	8.3	1.8	2.3	*-2.0*	:	:	:	:	:
Netherlands	3.4	2.6	6.3	3.7	*-5.9*	1.4	3.2	4.0	4.3	0.3
Austria	4.9	5.9	3.9	-0.9	-1.9	2.1	4.6	4.5	5.2	*0.6*
Poland	9.4	15.5	16.3	10.1	4.5	3.0	1.5	6.7	6.8	0.2
Portugal	-4.5	-6.3	-4.0	-1.2	-6.6	2.0	3.0	3.4	5.2	-0.7
Romania	6.5	15.6	33.1	26.7	-15.2	*14.3*	*11.1*	*10.2*	*16.2*	*1.5*
Slovenia	2.0	15.7	18.5	15.5	-20.9	4.5	6.5	6.3	6.4	-2.8
Slovakia	14.5	15.7	5.3	11.6	-11.2	4.9	4.0	4.1	5.8	2.1
Finland	*5.2*	*7.8*	*10.2*	*4.1*	*-13.0*	3.4	3.8	5.9	3.9	-1.1
Sweden	3.0	8.0	6.2	4.2	-3.5	3.9	5.1	6.1	4.9	2.0
United Kingdom	-0.5	1.4	2.3	-1.3	*-11.6*	5.4	4.6	4.2	0.2	*-7.5*
Norway	9.1	6.1	5.7	2.7	-0.3	3.4	3.8	7.4	5.7	2.3
Switzerland	*3.4*	*3.6*	*0.5*	*0.5*	*2.1*	:	:	:	:	:
Croatia	-0.4	9.5	2.8	12.0	-7.0	:	:	:	:	:
Turkey	:	18.4	5.5	-7.6	-16.3	*9.9*	*16.0*	*8.4*	*13.6*	*-4.3*

(¹) Working day adjusted.
(²) Gross series for new residential buildings.

Source: Eurostat (sts_coprgr_a and sts_copigr_a)

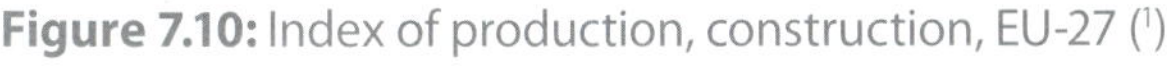

Figure 7.10: Index of production, construction, EU-27 (1)
(2005=100)

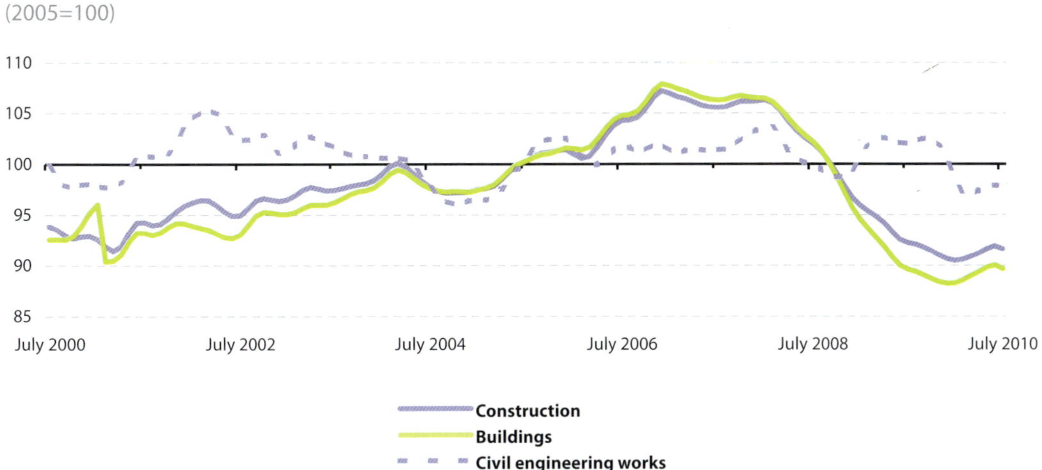

(1) Trend-cycle; estimates.

Source: Eurostat (sts_copr_m)

7.4 Services

This subchapter examines recent statistics on the developments of service activities in the European Union (EU). Short-term business statistics (STS) are provided in the form of indices that allow the rapid assessment of the economic climate within an economy. Traditionally, short-term business statistics were concentrated on industrial and construction activities, and to a lesser extent retail trade. Since the middle of the 1990s, major developments in official statistics within the EU have seen short-term data collection efforts focus increasingly on services.

Main statistical findings

The EU-27 services turnover index grew at an average rate of 2.7 % between 2004 and 2009 (see Figure 7.11). It should be noted, however, that this five-year range covers a period of relatively steady growth in turnover which came to an abrupt end in mid-2008, followed by a period of slower growth and in some cases falling turnover. In fact the services turnover index fell by 8.5 % in the EU-27 in 2009 compared with the year before. Every Member State (Belgium and Italy, not available) recorded a fall in this index in 2009, ranging from -1.2 % in Poland to in excess of -20 % in each of the Baltic Member States – with Latvia recording a fall of 30.6 %.

Among service activities (at the NACE Rev. 2 division level), the fastest rate of turnover growth in the five-year period between 2004 and 2009 was for employment activities, where sales grew at an average rate of 7.1 % per annum, followed by air transport (6.8 % per annum). In contrast, there was a negative rate of change for motor trades (-0.7 % per annum) and almost no growth for cinema, video and TV production activities (0.1 % per annum). In 2009 (compared with the year before) the EU-27 turnover index fell for all six NACE Rev. 2 service sections covered by STS, ranging from a 3.2 % reduction for information and communication to losses of nearly 10 % for distributive trades and for transport and storage.

While the turnover index shows developments in current prices, the volume of retail sales indicates developments once price changes have been removed. The decline in the volume of retail sales in 2009 reached -1.7 % in the EU-27, following on from a relatively small increase of 0.2 % in 2008 (see Table 7.14). The fall in sales in 2009 was reported across most of the EU Member States: only six countries reported year on year growth, reaching 2 % or higher in Poland, Luxembourg and Austria. In contrast, the volume of retail sales index fell by 10 % or more in seven Member States, most notably in the three Baltic Member States with Latvia recording a fall of 28.0 %. A monthly series of the index shows the volume of retail sales peaked in the EU-27 in January 2008 and fell a total of 2.1 % through to August 2009, after which the index returned to positive rates of change. Throughout this period of decline, there was no significant reduction in the volume of retail sales index for textiles, clothing, footwear and leather in specialised stores, nor for the index for medical goods, cosmetics and toiletries, although in some periods the rate of change was around zero. In contrast, the volume of sales index for retailing of household equipment fell 6.6 % between February 2008 and May 2009, while the retailing of computers and telecommunications equipment recorded a decline of 2.3 % between April 2008 and January 2010. A similar decrease was recorded for the retailing of food, beverages and tobacco between August 2007 and February 2009, however, in this activity the index remained stable through to July 2010, recording 17 consecutive months of almost unchanged sales in volume terms.

Data sources and availability

Short-term business statistics (STS) on services are compiled within the same methodological framework as short-term statistics on industry and construction. Subchapter 7.3 on short-term developments in industry and construction provides information on: the STS Regulation; the different forms of presentation of indices, namely gross, working-day adjusted, seasonally adjusted, and trend; the implementation of NACE Rev. 2; and the exercise to rebase STS indices to a new base year of 2005=100.

The turnover index and the employment index are compiled for retail trade and for other services, and it is foreseen that the labour input indices concerning wages and salaries and hours worked will be provided for all of these services starting from the new base year to be introduced in 2013. For retail trade one additional indicator is provided, namely the volume index of retail sales, which is effectively a deflated turnover index. Furthermore, service output price indices have been developed for a selection of services in recent years.

The index of turnover shows the evolution of sales in value terms. Note that prices for some services have actually been falling, perhaps due to market liberalisation and increased competition (for example, telecommunications and other technology-related activities). In such cases, the rapid growth rates observed for turnover value indices for some activities would be even greater in volume terms.

The retail trade indices have particular importance because of the role of retail trade as an interface between producers and final customers, allowing retail sales turnover and volume of sales indices to be used as short-term indicators for final domestic demand by households. The volume measure of the retail trade turnover index is more commonly referred to as the index of the volume of (retail) sales. To eliminate the price effect on turnover in retail trade, a deflator of sales is used. This deflator is an index with a similar methodology to that of an output price index, but it is adapted specifically for retail trade; it reflects price changes in the goods sold rather than those in the retail sales service provided.

Context

Some of the most important STS indicators are a set of Principal European Economic Indicators (PEEIs) that are essential to the European Central Bank (ECB) for conducting monetary policy within the euro area. Three PEEIs concern services short-term business statistics, namely indices covering: the volume of sales in retail trade, service turnover, and services producer prices.

Figure 7.11: Average annual growth rate of turnover, selected services, EU-27, 2004-2009 (1)
(%)

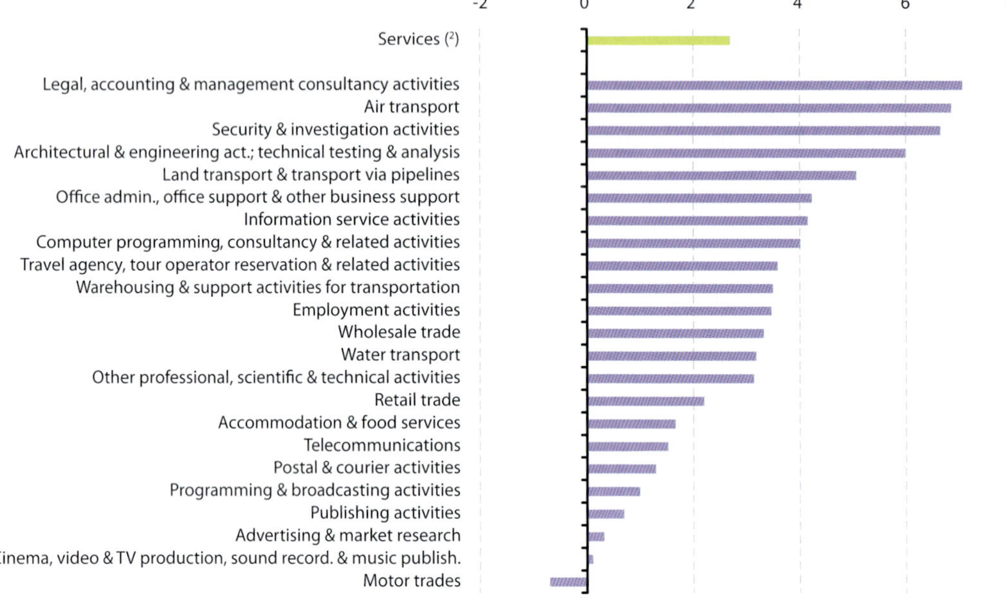

(1) Working day adjusted.
(2) As required by the STS Regulation.

Source: Eurostat (sts_setu_a and sts_trtu_a)

Table 7.13: Annual growth rates for the index of turnover, selected services (1)
(%)

	Distributive trades		Transport. & storage		Accomm. & food services		Info. & comm.		Profes., scient. & technical activities (2)		Admin. & support serv. (2)	
	2008	2009	2008	2009	2008	2009	2008	2009	2008	2009	2008	2009
EU-27	4.8	-9.4	5.7	-9.5	1.4	-5.9	2.8	-3.2	7.3	-6.2	4.4	-6.6
Euro area (EA-16)	2.5	-10.1	3.5	-10.7	0.3	-4.5	1.6	-3.5	6.6	-5.7	5.7	-7.7
Belgium	3.2	:	7.9	:	4.2	:	:	:	40.9	:	7.3	:
Bulgaria	20.0	-18.8	20.7	-25.4	13.8	-8.7	-4.8	-7.3	25.1	-18.5	18.5	-4.2
Czech Republic	3.0	-11.5	1.7	-14.0	-2.7	-9.5	4.5	-2.6	8.7	-13.7	1.0	-12.0
Denmark	0.5	-15.0	8.9	-22.1	3.4	-6.6	-1.4	-3.9	6.1	-8.4	9.5	-0.8
Germany	4.5	-10.5	3.9	-11.1	-0.5	-4.6	2.0	-3.4	7.6	-5.4	10.3	-7.3
Estonia	-4.8	-23.1	-6.2	-11.3	1.6	-20.3	12.4	-17.2	8.0	-22.8	-0.5	-17.4
Ireland	-4.9	-12.9	1.4	-7.9	-3.0	-20.0	-12.4	-15.6	-9.2	-17.1	18.4	-19.2
Greece	6.3	-9.9	5.3	-27.3	3.2	-9.0	0.1	-8.4	6.6	-16.9	8.2	2.8
Spain	-4.6	-15.2	-0.9	-13.3	-2.3	-8.6	1.1	-6.1	-4.3	-13.0	-0.3	-9.2
France	3.6	-8.1	4.0	-6.2	0.7	-0.1	4.7	-0.8	4.7	0.3	2.8	-6.7
Italy	1.0	-7.2	:	:	:	:	-1.7	-3.9	:	:	:	:
Cyprus	8.5	-11.0	4.5	-8.9	3.3	-6.2	11.1	-0.7	12.5	-0.1	-2.1	-12.1
Latvia	-4.2	-35.0	23.5	-18.2	-0.5	-32.1	5.0	-15.8	8.8	-20.2	10.0	-15.8
Lithuania	12.6	-25.2	8.1	-25.5	15.2	-19.1	10.6	-14.3	20.7	-26.1	20.5	-23.9
Luxembourg	-1.9	-4.6	9.7	-13.5	2.7	-2.4	-7.3	-1.5	10.8	-1.0	14.5	-8.0
Hungary	-0.6	-10.4	20.2	-4.7	4.8	-6.1	3.0	3.7	31.6	16.5	22.6	10.1
Malta	-0.5	-5.7	7.8	-6.3	3.1	-7.0	-1.2	2.9	-0.5	0.3	-11.9	9.8
Netherlands	5.4	-9.0	:	:	0.2	-4.8	1.9	-3.7	6.3	-3.2	6.8	-6.5
Austria	4.1	-5.4	4.3	-8.4	4.4	-0.7	0.1	-4.2	3.7	0.3	4.6	-6.9
Poland	7.9	-2.5	12.9	1.9	11.4	3.6	12.0	-1.4	30.0	5.9	22.8	10.8
Portugal	0.7	-11.5	:	:	:	:	:	:	:	:	:	:
Romania	21.3	-15.5	26.3	-18.7	-0.7	-15.4	21.4	-7.2	26.3	-8.5	20.2	-3.7
Slovenia	15.3	-19.0	-6.1	-18.8	6.3	-7.7	6.3	-6.6	6.4	-10.2	4.7	-10.2
Slovakia	12.3	-22.4	11.3	-13.1	5.9	-22.8	7.3	1.9	7.2	2.9	26.7	-8.8
Finland	6.3	-15.2	7.2	-15.4	5.8	-4.1	3.8	-3.9	8.7	-9.3	12.7	-5.9
Sweden	4.0	-6.6	2.7	-9.3	4.5	-0.9	0.7	-0.5	-0.1	-6.5	0.4	-3.1
United Kingdom	13.4	-6.7	9.0	-4.7	3.4	-9.6	5.2	-2.6	6.7	-8.1	0.7	-6.3
Norway	:	:	:	:	5.9	:	:	:	:	:	:	:
Croatia	3.5	-15.1	:	:	4.9	-2.9	:	:	:	:	:	:
Turkey	:	:	:	:	31.5	-7.8	:	:	:	:	:	:

(1) Working day adjusted.
(2) As required by the STS Regulation.

Source: Eurostat (sts_trtu_a and sts_setu_a)

Figure 7.12: Index of turnover, selected service activities, EU-27 (¹)
(2005=100)

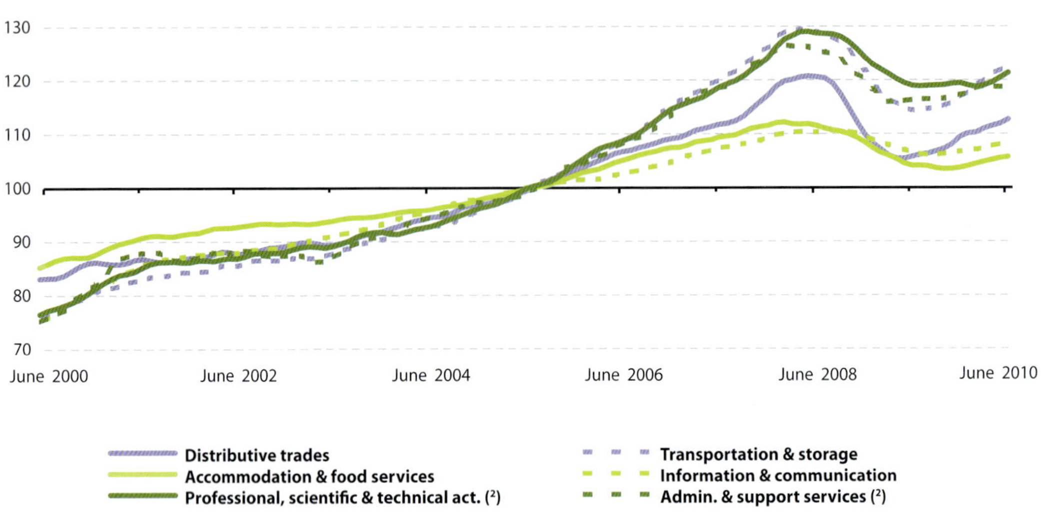

(¹) Trend-cycle; estimates.
(²) As required by the STS Regulation.

Source: Eurostat (sts_trtu_m and sts_setu_m)

Figure 7.13: Volume of sales index, selected retail trade activities, EU-27 (¹)
(2005=100)

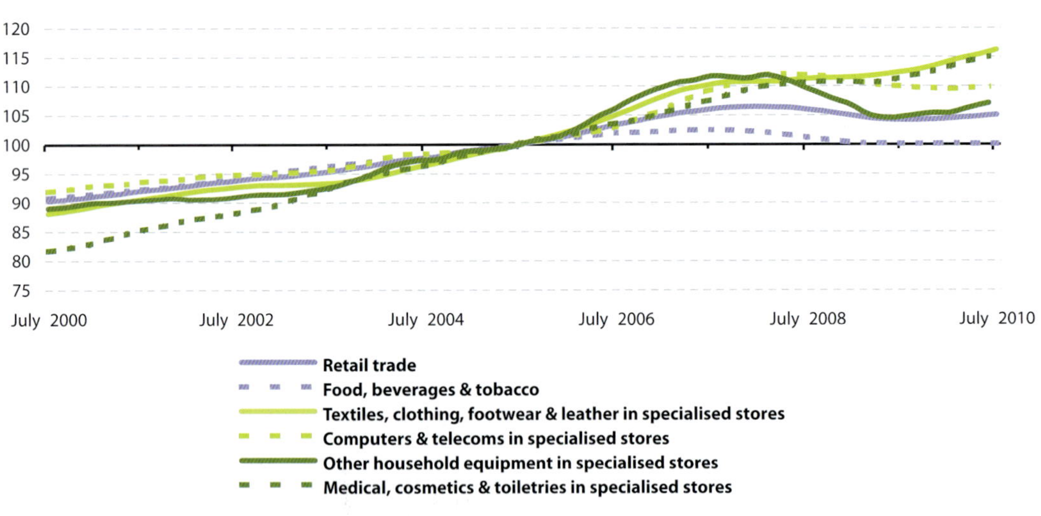

(¹) Trend-cycle.

Source: Eurostat (sts_trtu_m)

Table 7.14: Annual growth rates for the volume of sales index, retail trade (1)
(%)

	1999	2000	2001	2002	2003	2004	2005	2006	2007	2008	2009
EU-27	2.4	2.7	2.2	1.8	1.7	2.6	2.3	3.2	2.5	0.2	-1.7
Euro area (EA-16)	2.1	1.9	1.6	0.7	0.8	1.4	1.9	2.2	1.6	-0.8	-2.2
Belgium	2.2	5.3	0.2	-0.9	-0.2	1.7	1.3	1.7	1.8	1.2	0.6
Bulgaria	:	:	2.9	5.9	15.5	16.7	14.6	13.0	19.0	8.8	-8.9
Czech Republic	3.2	-2.0	7.1	1.1	8.0	3.2	6.7	8.7	7.6	3.8	-1.5
Denmark	1.1	0.8	4.2	3.4	3.3	4.6	8.8	4.6	-1.4	-3.1	-4.3
Germany	-0.2	0.8	0.2	-2.5	-1.0	1.7	1.2	0.4	-1.3	-0.2	-2.1
Estonia	2.3	14.2	12.9	13.0	-0.9	11.0	14.8	17.6	10.5	-4.5	-18.3
Ireland	:	:	9.0	3.6	3.5	5.7	6.7	8.7	8.0	-2.2	-6.2
Greece	1.8	8.9	4.3	4.9	4.3	4.5	3.0	9.0	2.2	1.3	-11.3
Spain	3.4	5.8	3.2	3.9	2.9	2.4	1.3	2.3	2.7	-5.4	-5.4
France	4.5	2.7	3.5	3.3	2.9	3.0	3.5	2.6	4.1	1.2	-0.0
Italy	0.9	-0.6	-0.6	-0.6	-0.7	-2.5	-0.6	1.3	-0.2	-2.7	-1.5
Cyprus	:	:	7.9	3.4	-0.9	3.1	4.6	6.8	7.8	5.3	-3.9
Latvia	5.9	20.1	5.5	10.7	12.7	10.1	20.0	19.9	15.3	-7.3	-28.0
Lithuania	-4.8	10.3	3.0	10.1	11.2	9.2	11.8	7.2	13.7	3.7	-21.4
Luxembourg	-2.8	10.3	4.9	5.7	7.0	3.7	1.3	3.2	4.6	1.7	2.2
Hungary	6.0	3.4	3.8	8.5	7.7	6.0	4.3	4.9	-2.0	-1.9	-5.3
Malta	:	:	-3.5	-1.8	3.4	-1.1	-4.7	-4.0	8.8	-4.1	-4.4
Netherlands	3.4	-0.9	2.9	1.2	-1.0	-0.4	1.8	4.6	2.7	-0.1	-4.4
Austria	:	2.0	-1.9	-0.5	-0.1	0.1	1.4	1.8	0.8	-0.8	2.1
Poland	:	:	1.3	0.3	5.2	5.9	-1.2	12.4	10.9	5.0	2.9
Portugal	6.3	-2.5	2.3	-0.3	-2.0	2.5	7.8	1.2	0.3	0.0	-1.8
Romania	:	:	-0.1	2.8	8.6	14.6	16.2	19.8	20.3	20.3	-10.3
Slovenia	-15.0	30.5	10.6	2.9	3.1	3.0	8.8	2.9	6.2	11.4	-10.5
Slovakia	16.7	-3.0	7.6	8.3	-2.4	8.2	10.2	8.2	5.5	9.1	-10.2
Finland	5.7	5.3	5.6	3.6	4.8	5.0	4.8	4.6	5.2	1.1	-2.5
Sweden	3.7	5.7	2.7	3.8	3.9	3.9	5.8	6.2	0.9	0.8	0.7
United Kingdom	3.5	6.1	4.2	6.0	3.3	5.6	2.2	3.9	3.7	2.0	1.3
Norway	:	:	1.8	5.2	2.7	3.2	3.4	5.6	6.6	1.5	0.9
Switzerland	:	:	2.1	-0.6	-0.2	0.8	2.2	3.4	4.2	3.0	0.6
Croatia	:	:	13.0	11.5	10.7	7.1	3.4	4.3	2.9	-0.9	-7.0

(1) Working day adjusted.

Source: Eurostat (sts_trtu_a)

7.5 Tourism

This subchapter provides information on recent statistics in relation to tourism in the European Union (EU). Tourism is important because of its economic and employment potential, as well as its social and environmental implications. Tourism statistics are not only used to monitor EU tourism policies but also its regional and sustainable development policy.

The role played by tourism, for both businesses and citizens, has grown considerably in recent decades. According to estimates from the European Commission's Directorate-General for enterprise and industry, tourism accounts for more than 5 % of the EU-27's gross domestic product (GDP). The tourist accommodation sector employs 2.3 million people in the EU-27, and total employment within the whole of the EU-27's tourism industry is estimated to be between 12 million and 14 million people (according to preliminary estimates from tourism satellite accounts).

Main statistical findings

Tourism volume – demand and supply

EU residents made more than 1 000 million holiday trips in 2009. Short trips (of one to three nights) accounted for slightly more than half (54 %) of the trips made by EU residents (see Table 7.15), while approximately three quarters (76 %) of the trips made were to domestic destinations, while 24 % were abroad.

In some Member States, over half of all holidays were spent abroad; this was the case for Luxembourg, Belgium, Denmark, the Netherlands and Ireland. However, less than 10 % of holiday trips by residents of Spain, Greece, Bulgaria and Portugal were abroad. These figures appear to be influenced by both the Member State's size and its geographical location (smaller and more northerly countries tend to report a higher propensity for their residents to take holidays abroad).

It is estimated that around 55 % of the EU-27's population took part in tourism in 2009, in other words made at least one trip of at least four overnight stays during the year. Again, large differences can be observed ranging from an 8 % tourism participation rate in Bulgaria to a rate of 78 % in Luxembourg (see Table 7.16).

From the supply perspective, over 202 000 hotels and similar establishments were active within the EU-27 in 2009. In addition, there were more than 243 000 other collective tourist accommodation establishments (such as campsites and holiday dwellings). Hotels and similar establishments provided more than 12 million bed places, of which nearly half (47 %) were in either Italy (2.2 million bed places), Germany or Spain (both 1.7 million bed places). In 2009, resident and non-resident (foreign) tourists spent over 1 512 million nights in hotels and similar establishments in the EU-27.

Over the past decade, the number of tourism nights spent in collective tourist accommodation has generally shown an upward trend. However, a decline in travel after the 2001 terrorist attacks in the United States and as a result of the recent financial and economic crisis caused short-term shocks: the number of tourism nights spent in collective tourist accommodation in the EU-27 fell by 0.2 % in 2008 and by 3.2 % in 2009 (see Figures 7.14 and 7.15).

Top destinations

Germans spent nearly 640 million nights in collective accommodation establishments outside of Germany in 2009, while residents of the United Kingdom spent 587 million nights abroad; these two Member States accounted for more than half of the total number of nights spent abroad by EU-27 residents. Extending the coverage, the ten Member States whose residents spent the most nights in tourist accommodation establishments abroad made up more than 87 % of the 2 308 million nights spent abroad in 2009 (see Table 7.17).

When taking into account a country's size in terms of population, Luxembourg was the Member State whose residents spent the most nights abroad per inhabitant (over 18 nights), followed by Cyprus and the United Kingdom. At the other end of the spectrum, Greeks and Romanians spent, on average, less than one holiday night abroad per inhabitant in 2009 (see Figure 7.16).

In 2009, Spain was the most common tourism destination for non-residents (people coming from abroad), with 201 million nights spent in collective accommodation, or 22 % of the total nights spent in the EU-27 by non-residents. The top three most popular Member States for non-residents were Spain, Italy (159 million nights) and France (99 million nights), which together represented 51 % of the nights spent by non-residents in the EU. The least common destinations were Luxembourg, Lithuania and Latvia, where the effect of the size of these Member States should not be disregarded (see Figure 7.17 and Table 7.18).

The number of nights spent (by residents and non-residents) can be put into perspective by making a comparison with the size of the country in population terms, providing an indicator of tourism intensity. In 2009, using this measure, the Mediterranean island destinations of Cyprus and Malta, as well as the alpine and city trip destination of Austria were the most popular tourist destinations in the EU (see Figure 7.18).

Financial aspects of international tourism

The economic importance of tourism can be measured by looking at the ratio of international tourism receipts relative to GDP. In 2009, this was highest in Malta (10.2 %) and Cyprus (9.2 %), confirming the importance of tourism to these island nations (see Table 7.19); an even higher ratio was observed in Croatia (15.7 %, 2008). In absolute terms, the highest international tourism receipts were recorded in Spain (EUR 38 125 million) and France (EUR 34 928 million), followed by Italy, Germany and the United Kingdom.

Germany recorded the highest level of expenditure on international tourism, totalling EUR 57 958 million in 2009, followed by the United Kingdom (EUR 35 049 million) and France (EUR 27 883 million). When analysing this expenditure relative to the size of population, Luxembourg's residents spent on average EUR 5 254 per inhabitant on travel abroad in 2009, far ahead of the second ranked country,

Ireland (EUR 1 413 per inhabitant), followed by Belgium, Denmark and Cyprus. Not surprisingly, these five Member States were also among the highest ranked in terms of the share of long (in other words four nights or more) outbound trips in the total number of holiday trips.

Data sources and availability

Tourism, in a statistical context, refers to the activity of visitors taking a trip to a destination outside their usual environment, for less than a year. It can be for any main purpose, including business, leisure or other personal reasons other than to be employed by a resident person, household or enterprise in the place visited. The statistics presented are currently limited to at least an overnight stay; the possibility of including information relating to same-day visits is being examined.

A system of tourism statistics was established in Council Directive 95/57/EC of 23 November 1995 on the collection of statistical information in the field of tourism. This legal basis requires Member States to provide a regular set of comparable tourism statistics. Amendments in 2004 and 2006 concerned the enlargement of the EU and recent changes in the world market for tourism.

Tourism statistics in the EU consist of two main components: statistics relating to capacity and occupancy in collective tourist accommodation and statistics relating to tourism demand. In most Member States, the former are collected via surveys filled in by accommodation establishments, while the latter are mainly collected via traveller surveys at border crossings or through traditional household surveys.

Statistics on the capacity of collective tourist accommodation include the number of establishments, the number of bedrooms and the number of bed places. These statistics are available by establishment type or by region, and are compiled annually.

Statistics on the occupancy of collective tourist accommodation refer to the number of arrivals (at accommodation establishments) and the number of nights spent by residents and non-residents, separated into establishment type or region; annual and monthly statistical series are available. In addition, statistics on the use of bed places (occupancy rates) are compiled.

Statistics on tourism demand refer to tourist participation, in other words, the number of people who made at least one trip of at least four overnight stays during the reference period (quarter or year). There are statistics in relation to the number of tourism trips made (and the number of nights spent on those trips), separated by:

- destination country;
- departure month;
- length of stay;
- type of trip organisation;
- transport mode;
- accommodation type;
- expenditure.

The data may also be analysed by socio-demographic explanatory variables, such as age and gender.

Data from other official sources may also be used to study tourism. These statistics include:

- data on employment in the tourism accommodation sector from the labour force survey (LFS), broken down by working time (full/part-time),

working status, age, level of education, gender, permanency and seniority of work with the same employer (annual and quarterly data);
- data on personal travel receipts and expenditure from the balance of payments;
- transport statistics (for example, air passenger transport);
- structural business statistics (SBS) may be used to provide additional information on tourism flows and on the economic performance of certain tourism-related sectors.

Context

The EU remains a major tourist destination and six Member States are among the world's top ten destinations for holidaymakers. Tourism is an important activity in the EU which has the potential to contribute towards employment and economic growth, as well as to development in rural, peripheral or less-developed areas. These characteristics drive the demand for reliable and harmonised statistics within this field, as well as within the wider context of regional policy and sustainable development policy areas.

Indeed, tourism can be a significant factor in the development of European regions. Infrastructure created for tourism purposes contributes to local development, while jobs that are created or maintained can help counteract industrial or rural decline. Sustainable tourism involves the preservation and enhancement of cultural and natural heritage, ranging from the arts to local gastronomy or the preservation of biodiversity.

In 2006, the European Commission adopted a Communication ((2006) 134) titled 'A renewed EU tourism policy: towards a stronger partnership for European tourism'. The document addressed a range of challenges that will shape tourism in the coming years, including Europe's ageing population, growing external competition, consumer demand for more specialised tourism, and the need to develop more sustainable and environmentally friendly tourism practices. It argued that more competitive tourism supply and sustainable destinations would help raise tourist satisfaction and secure Europe's position as the world's leading tourist destination. This was followed by a Communication ((2007) 621) in October 2007 titled, 'Agenda for a sustainable and competitive European tourism', which proposed actions in relation to the sustainable management of destinations, the integration of sustainability concerns by businesses, and the sustainability awareness of tourists.

A Communication ((2010) 352) titled 'Europe, the world's No. 1 tourist destination – a new political framework for tourism in Europe' was adopted in June 2010. This followed the entry into force of the Lisbon Treaty, which acknowledges the importance of tourism – outlining a specific competence for the EU in this field and allowing for decisions to be taken by qualified majority. A specific Treaty article on tourism specifies that the EU 'shall complement the action of the Member States in the tourism sector, in particular by promoting the competitiveness of Union undertakings in that sector'. With this Communication, the European Commission encouraged a coordinated approach for initiatives linked to tourism and defines a new framework for action to increase the competitiveness of tourism and its capacity for sustainable growth. It proposes a number of European or multinational initiatives – including a consolidation of the socio-economic knowledge base for tourism – aimed at achieving these objectives.

Table 7.15: Holiday trips of residents (aged 15 years or more), 2009

	Number of trips (1 000)			Breakdown of all trips by destination and duration (%)			
	All trips	Short trips (1-3 nights)	Long trips (4+ nights)	Short domestic trips (1-3 nights)	Long domestic trips (4+ nights)	Short outbound trips (1-3 nights)	Long outbound trips (4+ nights)
EU (1)	*1 038 708*	*565 132*	*473 576*	*49.2*	*27.0*	*5.2*	*18.6*
Belgium	*11 331*	*4 213*	*7 119*	*17.4*	*9.7*	*19.7*	*53.1*
Bulgaria	*7 861*	*4 868*	*2 993*	*59.0*	*31.4*	*2.9*	*6.7*
Czech Republic	32 269	17 244	15 025	49.0	25.4	4.5	21.2
Denmark (2)	10 368	4 377	5 991	32.5	15.2	9.7	42.6
Germany	224 496	118 589	105 907	46.5	21.3	6.3	25.9
Estonia	1 392	907	485	48.1	8.5	17.1	26.3
Ireland (3)	11 839	6 023	5 816	38.4	10.4	12.5	38.8
Greece (3)	13 561	5 627	7 934	40.3	50.4	1.2	8.1
Spain	122 167	82 600	39 567	65.6	27.5	2.0	4.9
France	202 284	106 999	95 285	50.6	39.2	2.3	7.9
Italy (3)	87 772	46 393	41 378	49.2	34.2	3.6	13.0
Cyprus	1 782	885	897	44.0	11.9	5.6	38.4
Latvia	4 152	3 320	832	72.8	7.7	7.1	12.4
Lithuania	3 219	2 158	1 061	54.3	13.0	12.8	20.0
Luxembourg	1 370	549	820	0.5	0.1	39.6	59.8
Hungary	18 521	12 461	6 060	59.2	19.7	8.1	13.0
Malta	:	:	:	:	:	:	:
Netherlands	29 669	10 691	18 978	24.9	22.8	11.1	41.1
Austria	17 196	7 912	9 284	33.2	19.3	12.8	34.7
Poland	*31 634*	*15 613*	*16 021*	*47.0*	*38.5*	*2.3*	*12.1*
Portugal (4)	10 265	6 423	3 842	60.5	29.6	2.1	7.9
Romania	12 164	:	:	:	:	:	:
Slovenia	4 332	2 634	1 698	40.5	11.0	20.3	28.2
Slovakia	6 062	1 715	4 347	22.4	34.1	5.9	37.6
Finland	30 201	23 016	7 185	68.0	15.6	8.2	8.2
Sweden	36 474	24 081	12 393	58.2	18.3	7.9	15.7
United Kingdom	118 493	55 835	62 657	41.1	20.3	6.0	32.6
Norway	16 830	9 980	6 850	47.7	19.5	11.6	21.2
Switzerland (3)	17 811	9 526	8 284	32.7	13.4	20.7	33.1
Croatia	6 912	3 577	3 335	38.7	31.6	13.0	16.7

(1) Estimate made for the purpose of this publication: sum/average of latest available data for the Member States, excluding Malta and Romania.
(2) 2007.
(3) 2008.
(4) 2006.

Source: Eurostat (tour_dem_ttmd)

Table 7.16: Tourism indicators

	Hotels & similar establishments (units)		Other collective accommo-dation establishments (units)		Bed places in hotels & similar establishments (1 000)		Nights spent in hotels & similar establishments (1 000) (1)		Share of the population (aged 15+) taking part in tourism (%)	
	2004 (2)	2009 (3)	2004 (2)	2009 (3)	2004 (2)	2009 (3)	2004 (2)	2009 (4)	2004	2009 (5)
EU-27	205 252	*202 070*	203 248	*243 229*	11 139	*12 057*	1 416 528	1 512 035	:	:
Euro area (EA-16)	144 728	143 678	144 721	182 511	8 664	9 365	1 129 328	1 203 019	:	:
Belgium	1 922	2 036	1 490	1 492	122	126	14 405	15 937	46.6	46.7
Bulgaria	1 016	1 784	290	466	171	249	13 562	14 054	:	8.0
Czech Republic	4 311	4 469	3 329	3 088	230	261	24 931	25 341	53.9	53.7
Denmark	485	471	618	585	70	77	9 695	9 966	62.2	:
Germany	36 839	35 814	18 439	17 365	1 609	1 694	195 047	216 228	63.7	65.8
Estonia	267	387	342	704	23	31	3 292	3 499	20.4	38.9
Ireland	4 554	3 624	4 233	4 850	145	163	25 442	23 699	:	:
Greece	8 899	9 559	331	319	668	732	51 590	64 292	35.3	42.7
Spain	17 402	18 387	15 666	22 367	1 512	1 737	234 697	250 985	32.7	41.6
France	18 598	17 723	10 731	11 128	1 241	1 248	188 524	191 741	59.0	64.9
Italy	33 518	33 967	81 009	111 391	2 000	2 228	234 020	244 385	48.9	46.2
Cyprus	803	699	132	156	92	84	14 623	12 808	:	:
Latvia	278	451	65	108	18	25	1 875	2 187	:	17.7
Lithuania	317	380	212	175	19	24	1 642	2 078	21.9	29.5
Luxembourg	297	261	263	224	14	15	1 280	1 282	62.2	77.6
Hungary	1 952	2 042	1 049	951	158	157	14 662	14 975	48.7	51.1
Malta	194	158	5	7	41	39	7 666	6 740	:	:
Netherlands	3 129	3 151	3 951	3 900	190	204	28 386	31 481	69.4	68.9
Austria	14 435	13 645	6 174	6 741	571	588	74 014	80 071	52.6	58.6
Poland	2 139	2 836	4 833	4 156	165	222	18 448	24 514	31.9	36.7
Portugal	1 954	1 988	285	311	254	274	34 141	36 457	30.2	25.4
Romania	3 301	4 566	599	513	208	247	17 190	16 514	21.2	28.6
Slovenia	350	475	371	447	30	39	4 965	5 450	56.6	58.1
Slovakia	873	1 324	1 189	1 359	56	74	6 716	6 335	:	51.7
Finland	961	867	452	454	120	120	13 812	15 127	54.9	57.6
Sweden	1 833	1 982	2 057	2 115	190	222	21 526	25 958	:	:
United Kingdom	44 625	39 024	45 133	47 857	1 223	1 176	160 377	169 930	59.8	57.7
Iceland	303	296	389	280	15	19	1 469	1 940	:	:
Liechtenstein	45	41	114	108	1	1	104	122	:	:
Norway	1 079	1 108	1 098	1 179	141	157	16 360	17 654	71.1	72.6
Switzerland	5 643	5 533	94 100	:	259	274	31 963	35 589	:	:
Croatia	940	819	525	1 269	199	150	19 972	18 607	38.2	37.8
FYR of Macedonia	150	128	175	250	16	11	616	736	:	:
Turkey	9 877	9 508	:	:	820	904	93 302	115 967	:	:

(1) Nights spent by residents and non-residents.
(2) Former Yugoslav Republic of Macedonia and Switzerland, 2002; Turkey, 2003.
(3) EU-27 estimate made for the purpose of this publication, based on latest available data; United Kingdom, former Yugoslav Republic of Macedonia and Norway, 2008; Turkey, 2006.
(4) Ireland, United Kingdom and Norway, monthly data was used to calculate the annual figures; Turkey, 2007.
(5) Belgium, Greece, Italy and the United Kingdom, 2008.

Source: Eurostat (tin00039, tin00040, tin00041, tin00043, tin00045, tour_occ_nim, tps00001 and tps00010)

Figure 7.14: Number of nights spent in collective tourist accommodation, EU-27 (1)
(1 000 million nights)

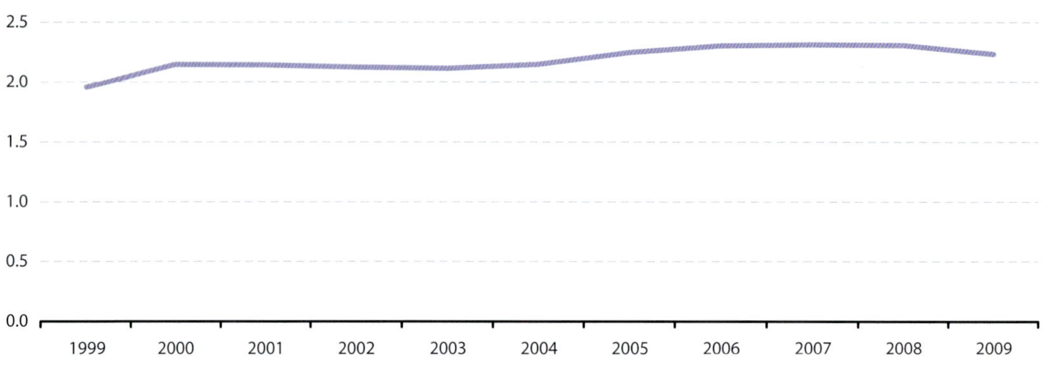

(1) Nights spent by residents and non-residents; EU-27 estimates made for the purpose of this publication.

Source: Eurostat (tour_occ_ninat and tour_occ_nim)

Figure 7.15: Annual rate of change in the total number of tourism nights spent in collective tourist accommodation, EU-27 (1)
(%)

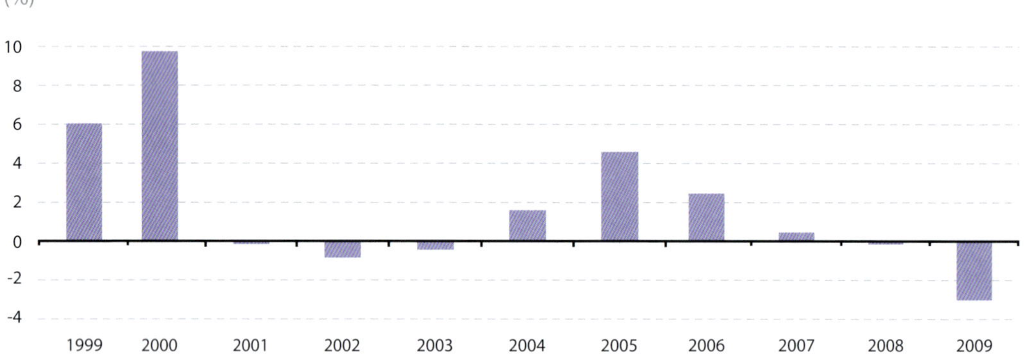

(1) Nights spent by residents and non-residents; estimates made for the purpose of this publication.

Source: Eurostat (tour_occ_ninat and tour_occ_nim)

Table 7.17: Top 10 Member States of origin for outbound holidays, 2009
(1 000 nights spent abroad by residents of the country)

		Nights abroad	Share (%)
	EU-27 (1)	2 308 004	100.0
	Top 10	2 014 146	87.3
1	Germany	636 976	27.6
2	United Kingdom	587 164	25.4
3	France	184 210	8.0
4	Netherlands	154 794	6.7
5	Italy (2)	121 811	5.3
6	Spain	80 834	3.5
7	Belgium	72 084	3.1
8	Sweden	67 961	2.9
9	Austria	62 357	2.7
10	Denmark (3)	45 954	2.0

(1) Estimate made for the purpose of this publication, based on annual and monthly data.
(2) 2008.
(3) 2007.

Source: Eurostat (tour_dem_tnw and tour_dem_tnmd)

Figure 7.16: Country of origin for outbound holidays, 2009
(average nights spent abroad per inhabitant)

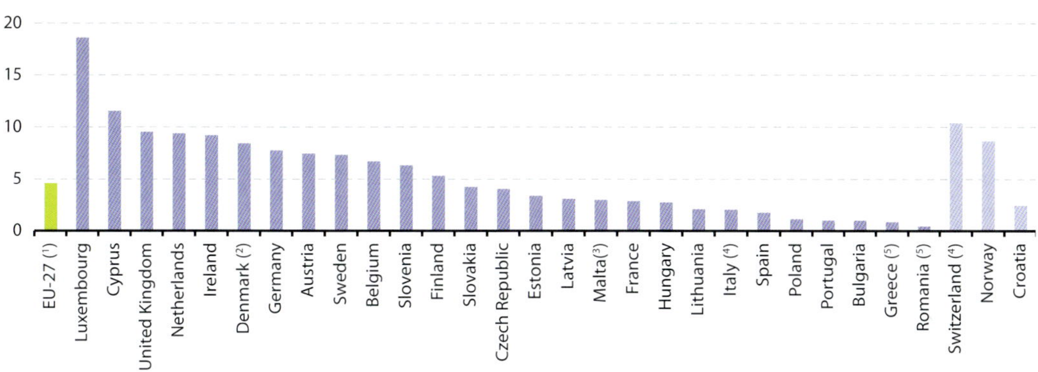

(1) Estimate made for the purpose of this publication based on latest available data for the Member States.
(2) 2007.
(3) Estimate, based on 2008 quarterly data.
(4) 2008.
(5) Estimate, based on 2009 quarterly data.

Source: Eurostat (tour_dem_tnw, tour_dem_tnmd and tps00001)

Figure 7.17: Tourism destinations - nights spent in collective tourist accommodation, 2009 (¹)
(1 000 nights spent in the country by non-residents)

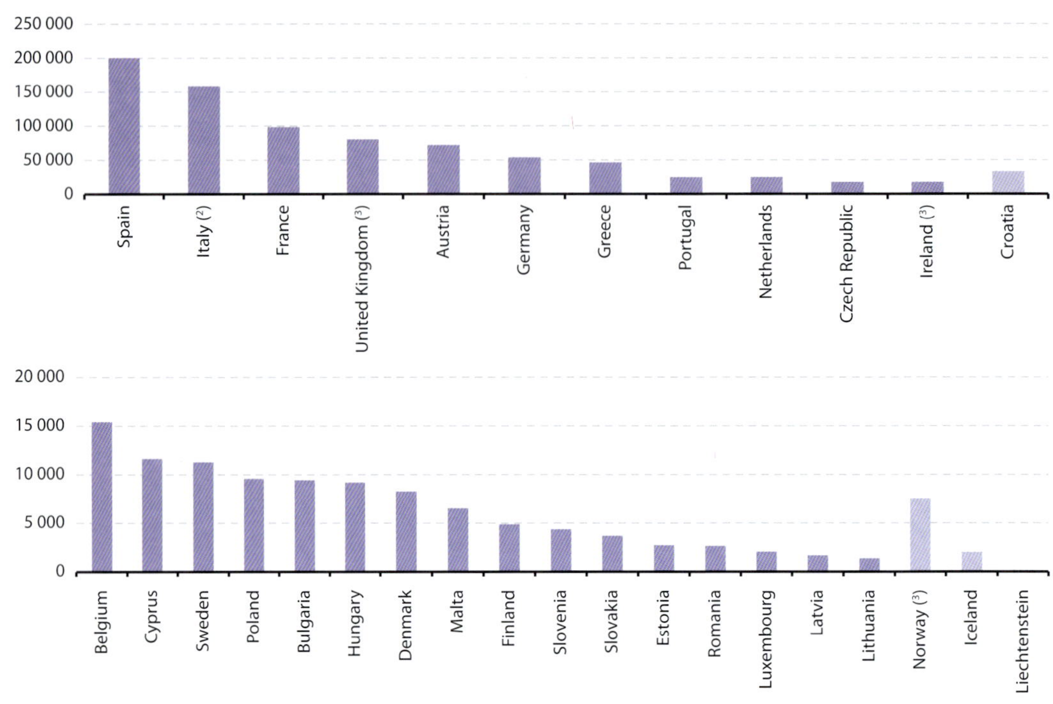

(¹) Note the differences in the scales employed between the two parts of the figure.
(²) Provisional.
(³) Estimate, based on 2009 monthly data.

Source: Eurostat (tour_occ_ni and tour_occ_nim)

Table 7.18: Top 10 tourism destinations - nights spent in collective tourist accommodation, 2009
(1 000 nights spent in the country by non-residents)

		Nights in country	Share (%)
	EU-27 (¹)	*901 880*	100.0
	Top 10	779 016	86.4
1	Spain	200 552	22.2
2	Italy	*158 527*	*17.6*
3	France	*98 700*	*10.9*
4	United Kingdom	*80 454*	*8.9*
5	Austria	72 225	8.0
6	Germany	54 097	6.0
7	Greece	*46 677*	*5.2*
8	Portugal	25 025	2.8
9	Netherlands	25 014	2.8
10	Czech Republic	17 747	2.0

(¹) Estimate made for the purpose of this publication, based on annual and monthly data.

Source: Eurostat (tour_occ_ninat and tour_occ_nim)

Figure 7.18: Tourism intensity, 2009
(nights spent by residents and non-residents in collective tourist accommodation per inhabitant)

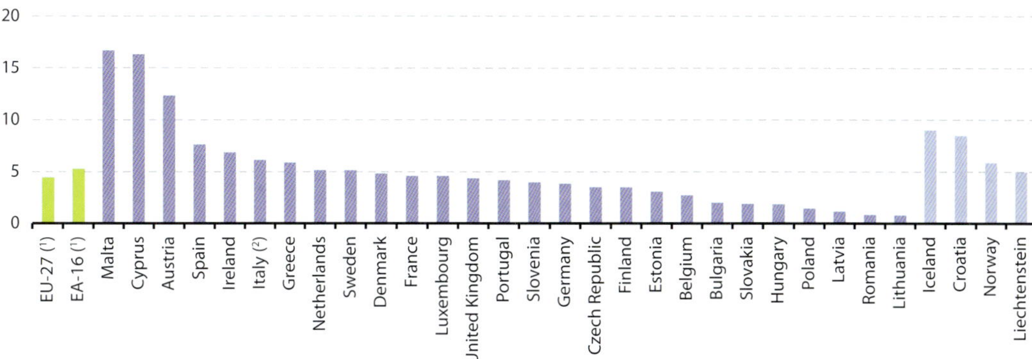

(¹) EU-27 and EA-16 estimates made for the purpose of this publication, based on annual and monthly data.
(²) Provisional.

Source: Eurostat (tour_occ_ni and tour_occ_nim)

Table 7.19: Tourism receipts and expenditure from travel

	Receipts (EUR million)			Receipts Relative to GDP, 2009 (%)	Expenditure (EUR million)			Expenditure Relative to GDP, 2009 (%)
	1999	2004	2009		1999	2004	2009	
EU-27 (1)	:	62 305	68 070	0.6	:	79 604	86 371	0.7
Euro area (EA-16) (2)	:	:	83 795	0.9	:	:	85 217	1.0
Belgium	:	7 423	7 055	2.1	:	11 274	12 808	3.8
Bulgaria	873	1 791	2 680	7.6	492	1 100	1 259	3.6
Czech Republic	2 847	3 362	4 639	3.4	1 383	1 831	2 923	2.1
Denmark	3 490	4 567	4 497	2.0	4 603	5 853	6 464	2.9
Germany	16 162	22 243	24 885	1.0	52 583	57 545	57 958	2.4
Estonia	518	717	781	5.6	202	321	433	3.1
Ireland	2 410	3 536	3 506	2.2	2 322	4 184	6 287	3.9
Greece	8 296	10 348	10 400	4.5	3 762	2 310	2 425	1.0
Spain	29 408	36 376	38 125	3.6	5 517	9 772	11 925	1.1
France	29 573	36 409	34 928	1.8	17 485	23 171	27 883	1.5
Italy	26 716	28 625	28 744	1.9	15 858	16 470	19 854	1.3
Cyprus	1 790	1 814	1 556	9.2	404	651	914	5.4
Latvia	105	217	513	2.8	251	307	572	3.1
Lithuania	516	627	778	2.9	320	513	812	3.1
Luxembourg	:	2 940	2 943	7.7	:	2 351	2 593	6.8
Hungary	3 360	3 168	4 082	4.4	1 450	1 954	2 610	2.8
Malta	637	621	589	10.2	188	205	314	5.5
Netherlands	6 565	8 306	8 887	1.6	11 324	13 211	14 830	2.6
Austria	10 085	12 203	13 912	5.1	6 332	7 473	7 744	2.8
Poland	2 977	4 646	6 439	2.1	806	3 843	5 225	1.7
Portugal	4 958	6 196	6 920	4.1	2 124	2 225	2 713	1.6
Romania	236	406	882	0.8	377	434	1 051	0.9
Slovenia	898	1 311	1 800	5.1	512	704	1 037	2.9
Slovakia	472	726	1 674	2.6	358	601	1 504	2.4
Finland	1 434	1 669	2 022	1.2	1 909	2 273	3 136	1.8
Sweden	3 892	4 994	8 704	3.0	7 521	8 182	9 087	3.1
United Kingdom	21 344	22 712	21 726	1.4	34 809	45 491	35 049	2.2
Iceland (3)	208	297	424	4.1	409	560	750	7.3
Norway (3)	2 139	2 364	3 150	1.0	4 562	6 756	10 832	3.5
Switzerland (3)	:	7 735	9 831	2.9	:	6 529	7 458	2.2
Croatia (3)	:	5 438	7 448	15.7	:	682	766	1.6
Turkey (3)	4 882	12 773	14 925	3.0	1 380	2 029	2 384	0.5
Japan (3)	3 222	9 069	7 356	0.2	30 660	30 780	18 970	0.6
United States (3)	83 882	75 655	91 724	0.9	57 288	55 974	58 044	0.6

(1) Extra EU-27 flows.
(2) Extra EA-16 flows.
(3) 2008 instead of 2009.

Source: Eurostat (bop_its_deth, bop_its_det and nama_gdp_c)

7.6 Information society

This subchapter presents recent statistical data on many different aspects of the information society in the European Union (EU). Progress in the development of the information society is regarded as critical to improve the competitiveness of EU industry and, more generally, to meet the demands of society and the EU economy.

Information and communication technologies (ICT) affect people's everyday lives in many ways, both at work and in the home, and EU policies in this area range from regulating entire sectors to trying to protect an individual's privacy.

Main statistical findings

Households and individuals

During the last decade, ICT have become widely available to the general public, both in terms of accessibility as well as cost. A boundary was crossed in 2007, when a majority (54 %) of households across the EU-27 had Internet access. This proportion has continued to increase and in 2009 reached 65 %. The highest proportion (90 %) of households with Internet access in 2009 was recorded in the Netherlands, the lowest (30 %) in Bulgaria (see Figure 7.19). Widespread and affordable broadband access is one of the means of promoting a knowledge-based and informed society. In all Member States broadband was by far the most common form of Internet access (an average of 56 % of all EU-27 households in 2009 compared with 8 % of households that used dial-up access or ISDN access).

Slightly more than two thirds (68 %) of individuals in the EU-27, aged between 16 and 74 years, used a computer in the three months before the 2009 ICT survey, while a similar proportion (65 %) used the Internet. The proportion of individuals using a computer and the Internet in the three months before the 2009 survey rose to around 90 % in Sweden and the Netherlands, but was in a minority in Bulgaria, Greece, Italy, and particularly in Romania. Furthermore, half (51 %) of the individuals in the EU-27 used the Internet for finding information on goods or services in 2009, the spread among Member States being from less than 20 % in Bulgaria and Romania to more than 70 % in the Netherlands, Sweden, Luxembourg, Denmark and Finland (see Table 7.20).

Among Internet users, in other words, those individuals within the EU-27 using the Internet in the three months before the ICT survey, a large majority (89 %) accessed the Internet from home, as shown in Table 7.21. By comparison, less than half of this subset of the population accessed the Internet at work (42 %), which in turn was around double the proportion accessing the Internet from a friend's, neighbour's or relative's house (24 %). Of the 65 % of individuals in the EU-27 that used the Internet in the three months before the 2009 ICT survey, nearly three quarters accessed the Internet on a daily or almost daily basis.

Just over one third (37 %) of individuals in the EU-27 ordered goods or services over the Internet for private use during the year prior to the 2009 survey, an increase of 5 percentage points compared with the year before (see Figure 7.22). This proportion reached close to two thirds in the United Kingdom, Denmark, the Netherlands and Sweden, whereas no more than one in ten persons made orders over the Internet in Greece, Lithuania, Bulgaria or Romania. Among persons who had not bought or ordered products over the Internet, the main reasons given for not doing so were that they preferred to shop in person or that they had no need. More than one third (35 %) had security concerns related to payment, while the next most common reasons were privacy concerns (29 %) and concerns related to trust (26 %).

Enterprises

About six in every ten enterprises (64 %) in the EU-27 had their own website in 2009, and this proportion rose to 90 % among large enterprises (see Figure 7.25). Most commonly enterprise's websites were used to provide product catalogues or price lists, this being the case for 57 % of enterprises with websites, a share that did not change greatly between enterprises of different sizes (see Figure 7.26). In contrast, around one fifth (21 %) of small enterprises with websites used them to advertise jobs or accept applications, whereas this was done by over three fifths (63 %) of large enterprises.

Some 11 % of enterprises in the EU-27 received orders on-line during 2009, which was about half the proportion of enterprises (23 %) that made purchases on-line (see Figure 7.27). The percentage of enterprises selling or purchasing on-line tends to rise with the size of the enterprise; it may be easier for large enterprises to finance investments for the introduction of e-commerce services. In total, e-commerce accounts for around 10 % of turnover among enterprises with at least ten persons employed in the EU-27, a share that ranged from 4 % for small enterprises to 17 % for large enterprises. Close to three quarters (72 %) of e-commerce turnover was generated from sales to enterprises in the seller's own country, with 8 % from sales outside of the EU.

In the EU-27 in January 2009, 3 % of enterprises with at least ten persons employed (excluding those in the financial sector) used radio frequency identification (RFID), a share that rose to 15 % for large enterprises, as shown in Figure 7.30. This technology was used for a wide variety of purposes, most commonly for person identification or access control (55 % of enterprises using RFID). The next most common purposes were for inventory tracking and tracing, for payment (such as for motorway tolls) and for product identification (see Figure 7.31).

Data sources and availability

Statisticians are well aware of the challenges posed by rapid technological change in areas related to the Internet and other new applications of ICTs. As such, there has been a considerable degree of evolution in this area, with statistical tools being adapted to satisfy new demands for data. Statistics within this domain are reassessed on an annual basis in order to meet user needs and reflect the rapid pace of technological change.

This approach is reflected in Eurostat's survey on ICT usage in households and by individuals, and Eurostat's survey on ICT usage in enterprises. These annual surveys can be used to benchmark ICT-driven developments, both by following developments for core variables over time, as well as by looking in greater depth at other aspects at a specific point in time. While the surveys initially concentrated on access and connectivity issues, their scope has subsequently been extended to cover a variety of subjects (for example, e-government and e-commerce) and socio-economic breakdowns, such as regional diversity, gender specificity, age, educational differences and the individual's employment situation in the household survey, or a breakdown by enterprise size (small, medium-sized, large) in the enterprise survey. The scope of the surveys with respect to different technologies is also adapted so as to cover new product groups and means of delivering communication technologies to end-users (enterprises and households).

Households and individuals

Included are households having at least one member in the age group 16 to 74 years old. Internet access of households refers to the percentage of households that have an Internet access, so that anyone in the household could use the Internet at home, if so desired, even simply to send an e-mail. Internet users are defined as all individuals aged 16-74 who had used the Internet in the three months prior to the survey. Regular Internet users are individuals who used the Internet, on average, at least once a week in the three months prior to the survey.

The technologies most commonly used to access the Internet are divided between broadband and dial-up access. Broadband includes digital subscriber lines (DSL) and uses technology that transports data at high speeds. Broadband lines are defined as having a capacity equal to or higher than 144 kbit/s. A dial-up access using a modem can be made over a normal or an ISDN telephone line and, due to its limited bandwidth, it is often referred to as narrowband.

A computer is defined as a personal computer powered by one of the major operating systems (Macintosh, Linux or Microsoft); handheld computers or palmtops (PDAs) are also included.

The ordering of goods and services by individuals includes confirmed reservations for accommodation, purchasing financial investments, participation in lotteries and betting, Internet auctions, as well as information services from the Internet that are directly paid for. Goods and services that are obtained via the Internet for free are excluded. Orders made by manually written e-mails are also excluded.

Enterprises

The survey on ICT usage and e-commerce in enterprises covers enterprises that have at least ten persons employed. The activity coverage is restricted to those enterprises whose principal activity is within manufacturing, electricity, gas, steam and water supply, sewerage and waste management, construction, wholesale and retail trade, repair of motor vehicles and motorcycles, transportation and storage, accommodation and food service activities, information and communication, real estate, professional, scientific and technical activities, administrative and support activities (NACE Rev. 2 Sections C to N excluding Division 75). The financial and insurance activities (Section K) are covered by the survey but are excluded from the analysis presented here. A distinction is made according to the size of enterprises in terms of persons employed into small

(10-49 persons employed), medium-sized (50-249) and large (250 or more persons employed) enterprises.

ICT usage data in tables and databases on the Eurostat website are grouped according to the year in which the survey was conducted; most data refer to the situation in January whereas some others (like e-commerce) refer to the calendar year prior to the survey year.

Radio frequency identification (RFID) is a technology which uses special tags to remotely retrieve data by radio waves. This technology is used, among other uses, to keep track of freight passing through a cargo terminal, to monitor inventory, as a payment system for motorways and bridges or to identify and control access of persons.

Context

Information and communication technologies (ICT) are considered as critical for improving the competitiveness of European industry and, more generally, to meet the demands of society and the economy. ICT affects many aspects of everyday lives, at both work and in the home, and EU policies in this area range from the regulation of entire sectors to the protection of an individual's privacy.

Broadband technologies are considered to be important when measuring access to and use of the Internet, as they offer users the possibility to rapidly transfer large volumes of data and keep access lines open. The take-up of broadband is considered to be a key indicator within the domain of ICT policy-making. Widespread access to the Internet via broadband is seen as essential for the development of advanced services on the Internet, such as e-business, e-government or e-learning. Digital subscriber lines (DSL) remain the main form of delivery for broadband technology, although alternatives, such as the use of cable, satellite, fibre optics and wireless local loops are becoming more widespread.

Since 2005 the EU policy framework for ICT has been the i2010 initiative called 'A European information society for growth and employment' (COM(2005) 229 final) which sought to boost efficiency throughout the EU economy by means of the wider use of ICT. Having undergone a mid-term review, an updated i2010 strategy was presented in April 2008, addressing key challenges for the period 2008-2010.

In May 2010 the European Commission adopted its Communication concerning a 'Digital Agenda for Europe' (COM(2010) 245 final), a strategy for a flourishing digital economy by 2020. It outlines policies and actions aimed at maximising the benefit of the digital era to all sections of society and economy. The agenda focuses on seven priority areas for action: creating a digital single market, greater interoperability, boosting Internet trust and security, providing much faster Internet access, encouraging investment in research and development, enhancing digital literacy skills and inclusion, and applying ICT to address challenges facing society like climate change and the ageing population. Examples of benefits include easier electronic payments and invoicing, rapid deployment of telemedicine and energy efficient lighting. The digital agenda for Europe was the first of seven flagship initiatives under the Europe 2020 strategy for smart, sustainable and inclusive growth.

Figure 7.19: Internet access of households
(% of all households)

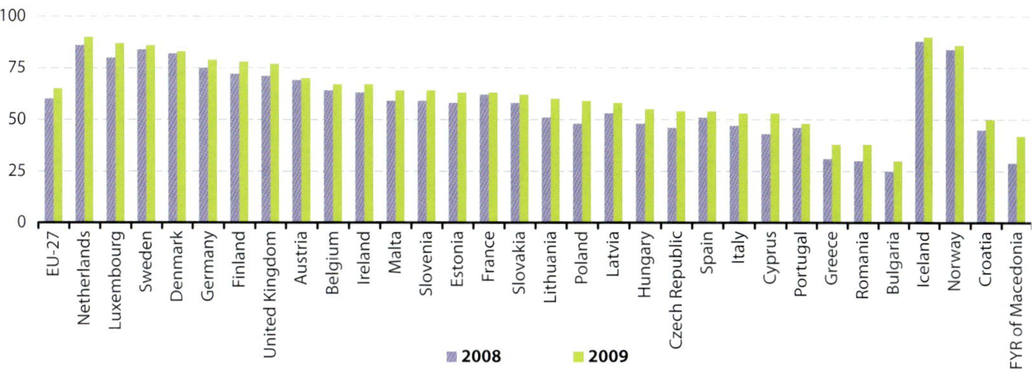

Source: Eurostat (tsiir040)

Figure 7.20: Internet access of households by type of connection, 2009
(% of all households)

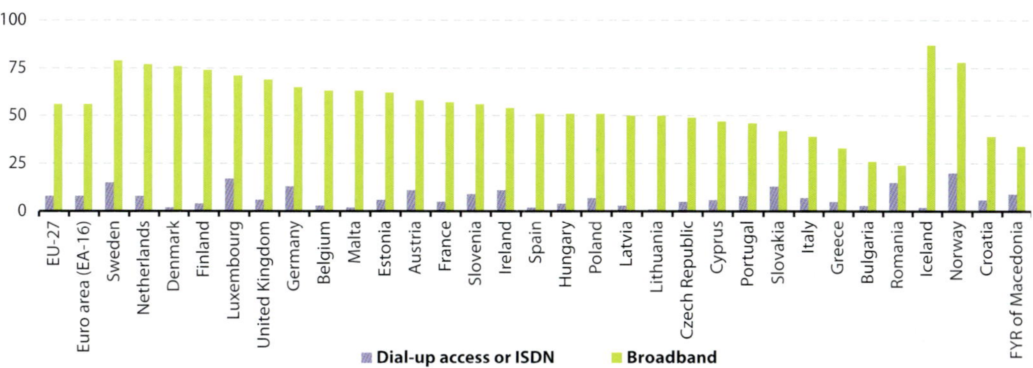

Source: Eurostat (tin00073)

Table 7.20: Use of ICTs and use of on-line services
(% of individuals aged 16 to 74)

	Computer use			Internet use			Used Internet for finding information on goods or services		
	2007	2008	2009	2007	2008	2009	2007	2008	2009
EU-27	63	66	68	57	62	65	47	50	51
Euro area (EA-16) (¹)	64	66	68	59	63	65	49	52	55
Belgium	70	71	76	67	69	75	55	58	59
Bulgaria	35	40	44	31	35	42	17	22	17
Czech Republic	55	63	64	49	58	60	37	45	50
Denmark	84	86	87	81	84	86	68	73	74
Germany	78	80	81	72	75	77	63	66	69
Estonia	65	66	71	64	66	71	48	53	54
Ireland	62	:	68	57	:	65	44	:	54
Greece	40	44	47	33	38	42	28	31	33
Spain	57	61	63	52	57	60	42	46	47
France	69	71	72	64	68	69	55	57	60
Italy	43	46	49	38	42	46	27	30	33
Cyprus	47	47	53	38	39	48	32	32	39
Latvia	58	63	65	55	61	64	39	49	50
Lithuania	52	56	60	49	53	58	36	37	44
Luxembourg	80	83	88	78	81	86	68	69	75
Hungary	58	63	63	52	59	59	43	49	48
Malta	48	51	60	45	49	58	34	42	48
Netherlands	87	88	90	84	87	89	76	76	79
Austria	73	76	75	67	71	72	47	51	54
Poland	52	55	59	44	49	56	27	33	29
Portugal	46	46	51	40	42	46	33	34	40
Romania	34	35	42	24	29	33	12	17	12
Slovenia	58	60	65	53	56	62	47	48	49
Slovakia	64	72	74	56	66	70	39	49	50
Finland	81	84	84	79	83	82	68	73	73
Sweden	88	89	91	80	88	90	70	75	77
United Kingdom	78	80	84	72	76	82	62	64	64
Iceland	91	92	93	90	91	93	78	78	80
Norway	90	90	91	85	89	91	76	80	83
Croatia	:	:	:	:	:	:	30	33	33
FYR of Macedonia	:	50	55	:	42	50	:	22	26
Turkey	30	:	:	27	:	:	11	:	:
Serbia	41	:	49	30	:	38	19	:	22

(¹) 2007 and 2008: EA-15 instead of EA-16.

Source: Eurostat (isoc_ci_cfp_cu, isoc_ci_ifp_iu and isoc_ci_ac_i)

Table 7.21: Place of Internet use, 2009
(% of individuals aged 16 to 74 who used the Internet in the three months prior to the survey)

	Home	Place of work (other than home)	Place of education	Neighbour, friend or relative's house	Other place
EU-27	89	42	13	24	13
Euro area (EA-16)	89	43	12	26	15
Belgium	92	40	12	20	7
Bulgaria	86	34	12	5	9
Czech Republic	89	39	16	14	7
Denmark	96	51	16	22	13
Germany	93	42	10	22	13
Estonia	91	40	17	15	6
Ireland	87	33	10	4	4
Greece	81	40	11	13	18
Spain	81	43	14	28	23
France	87	39	9	36	13
Italy	85	43	13	23	18
Cyprus	83	48	13	20	16
Latvia	87	34	19	31	20
Lithuania	89	35	20	22	11
Luxembourg	95	47	11	17	17
Hungary	88	36	19	20	9
Malta	94	35	6	8	4
Netherlands	98	55	14	20	6
Austria	90	46	11	12	10
Poland	89	32	16	18	8
Portugal	85	42	17	34	24
Romania	84	31	19	12	8
Slovenia	87	48	19	32	24
Slovakia	80	48	16	25	14
Finland	94	56	17	43	26
Sweden	95	54	14	25	18
United Kingdom	94	44	15	28	12
Iceland	96	59	26	46	16
Norway	96	58	13	24	18
Croatia	90	35	10	10	6
FYR of Macedonia	80	20	17	19	25
Turkey (1)	47	38	7	13	33

(1) 2007.

Source: Eurostat (isoc_pibi_pai)

Figure 7.21: Frequency of Internet use, 2009
(% of individuals aged 16 to 74)

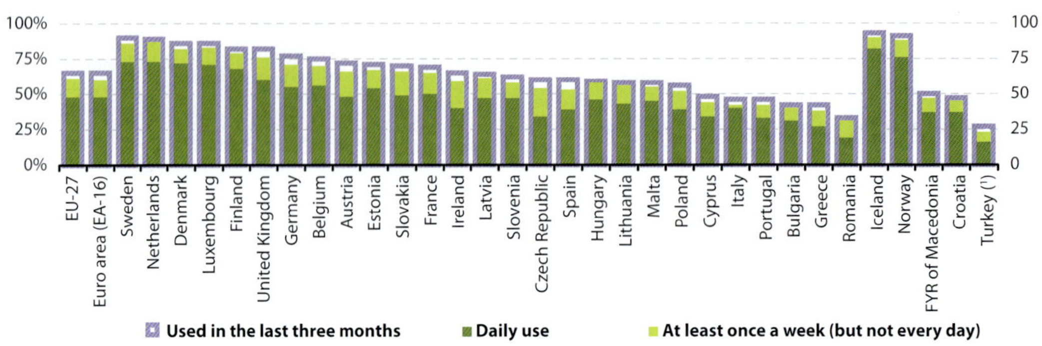

(¹) 2007.

Source: Eurostat (isoc_ci_ifp_iu and isoc_ci_ifp_fu)

Figure 7.22: Individuals who ordered goods or services over the Internet for private use in the twelve months prior to the survey
(% of individuals aged 16 to 74)

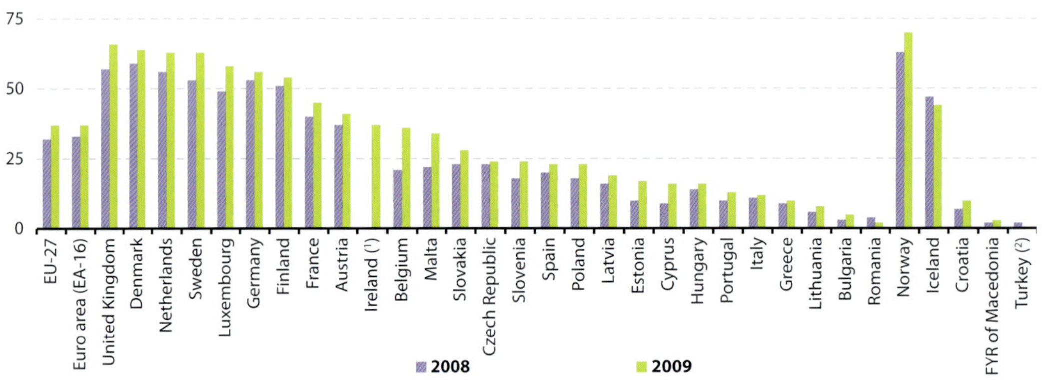

(¹) 2008, not available.
(²) 2007 instead of 2008; 2009, not available.

Source: Eurostat (isoc_ec_ibuy)

Figure 7.23: Goods or services bought or ordered over the Internet for private use, EU-27, 2009 (1)
(% of individuals buying or ordering over the Internet)

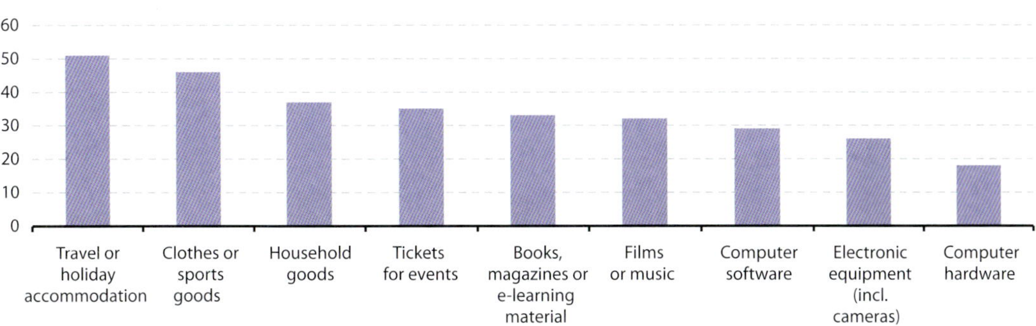

(1) During the 12 months prior to the survey.

Source: Eurostat (isoc_ec_ibuy)

Figure 7.24: Reasons for not using the Internet to buy or order goods or services, EU-27, 2009 (1)
(% of individuals not buying or ordering over the Internet)

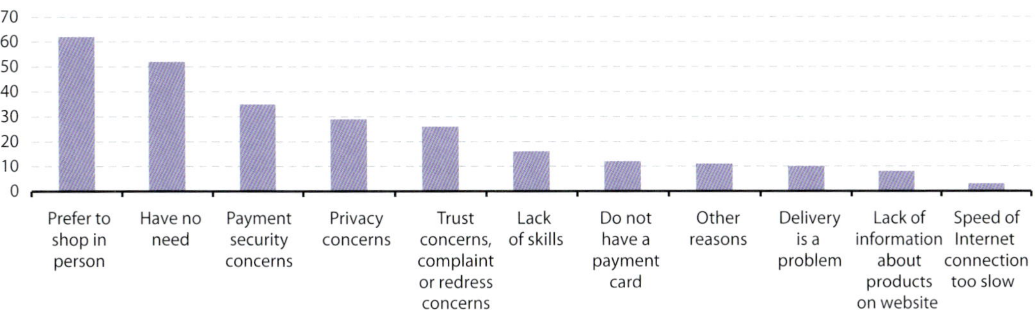

(1) During the 12 months prior to the survey.

Source: Eurostat (isoc_ec_inb)

Figure 7.25: Enterprise use of information technology, by size-class, EU-27, January 2009
(% of enterprises)

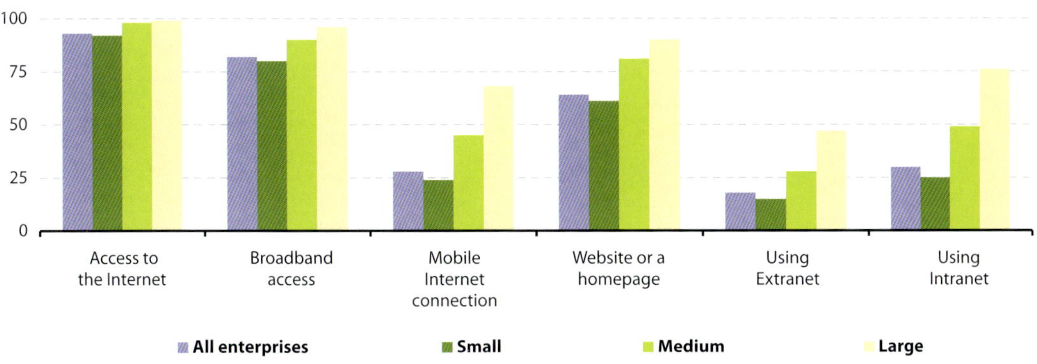

Source: Eurostat (isoc_ci_it_en2, isoc_ci_in_en2 and isoc_ci_cd_en2)

Figure 7.26: Enterprises' websites by facilities provided, EU-27, January 2009
(% of enterprises having a website)

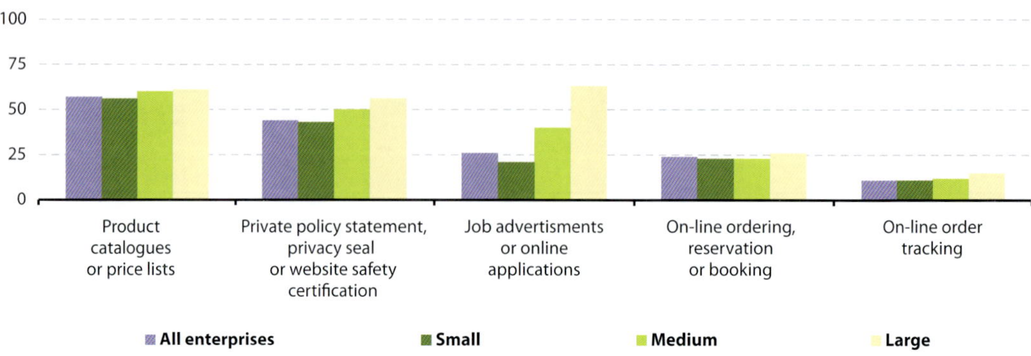

Source: Eurostat (isoc_ci_cd_en2)

Figure 7.27: E-commerce among enterprises by size-class, EU-27, 2009
(%)

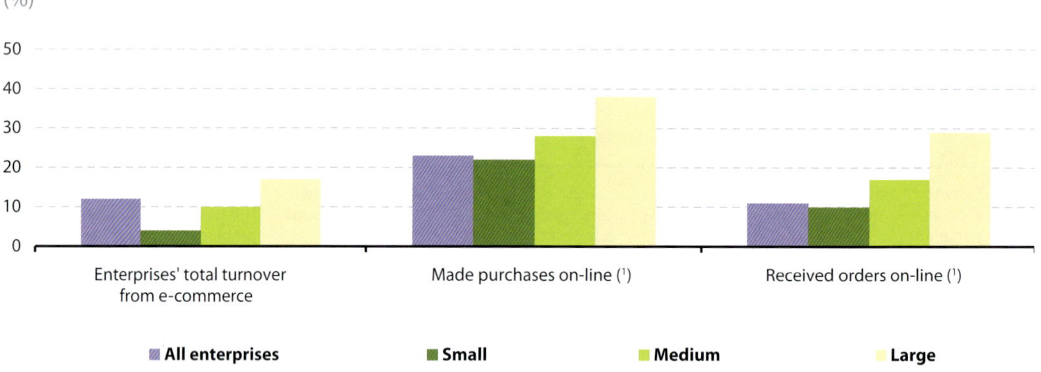

(1) Only enterprises having made purchases/received orders on-line of at least 1 % of total purchases/total turnover.

Source: Eurostat (isoc_ec_evaln2, isoc_ec_ebuyn2 and isoc_ec_eseln2)

Figure 7.28: Electronic sales by destination and size-class, EU-27, 2009
(% of turnover from e-commerce)

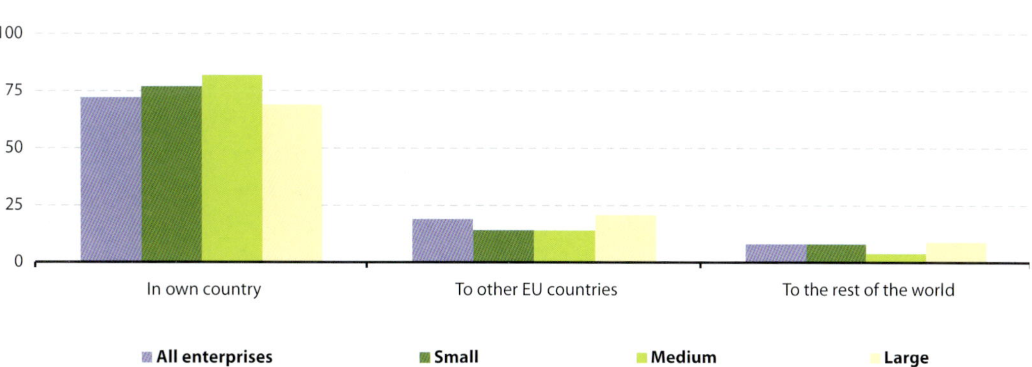

Source: Eurostat (isoc_ec_evaln2)

Figure 7.29: Enterprises regularly sending e-commerce orders, by geographical location of the supplier and size-class, EU-27, 2009
(% of enterprises sending e-commerce orders)

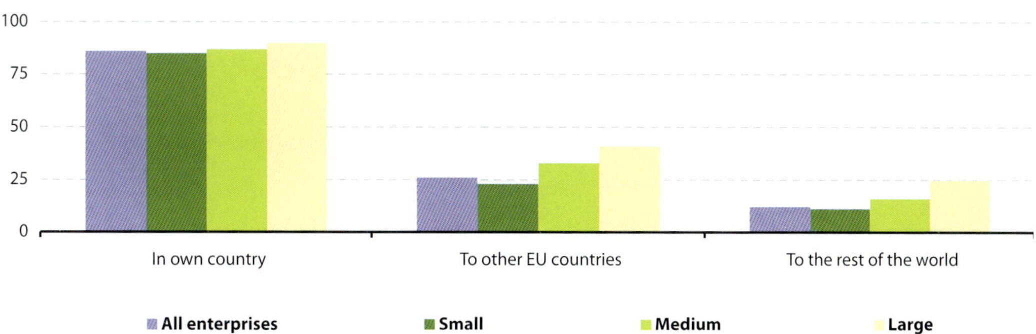

Source: Eurostat (Isoc_ec_ebuyn2)

Figure 7.30: Use of radio frequency identification (RFID) technologies by economic activity and size-class, EU-27, January 2009
(% of enterprises)

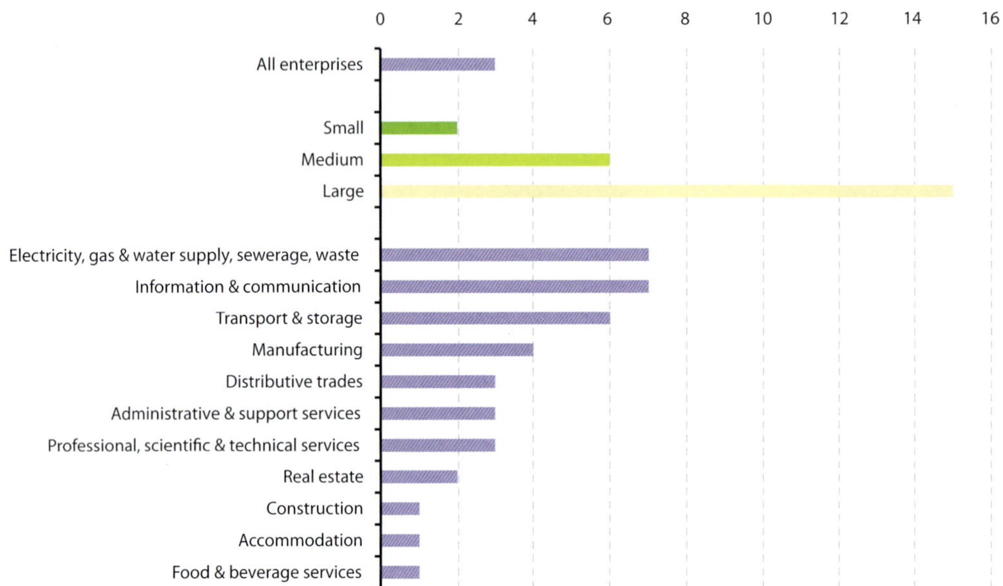

Source: Eurostat (Isoc_ci_cd_en2)

Figure 7.31: Use of radio frequency identification (RFID) technologies by purpose and size-class, EU-27, January 2009
(% of enterprises using RFID)

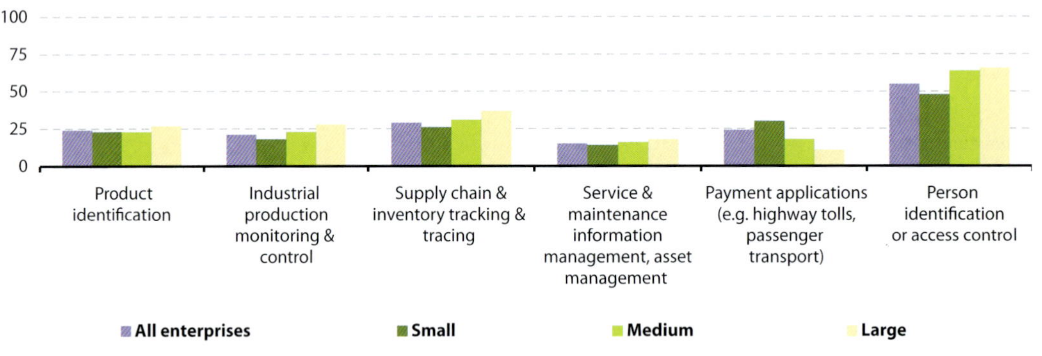

Source: Eurostat (Isoc_ci_cd_en2)

7.7 Telecommunications

Telecommunication networks and services are the backbone of Europe's developing information society (see Subchapter 7.6). Individuals, enterprises and public organisations alike rely increasingly on convenient, reliable telecommunication networks and services. This subchapter presents data on markets and prices for telecommunication services in the European Union (EU) and its Member States.

Historically, European telecommunications have been characterised by public service monopoly providers, often run in conjunction with postal services. Liberalisation of this market began in the first half of the 1980s and, at first, concerned only value added services or business users. Basic services were left in the hands of the monopoly providers. By 1998, telecommunications were, in principle, fully liberalised across the then EU Member States leading to considerable reductions in prices. For Member States joining the EU in 2004 and 2007, the liberalisation process was completed later.

Main statistical findings

Telecommunications expenditure accounted for 2.9 % of GDP in the EU-27 in 2008, compared with 3.3 % in the United States and 3.5 % in Japan (see Figure 7.32). The highest relative levels of expenditure were generally recorded in those Member States that have joined the EU since 2004 (data for Cyprus and Malta are not available), in particular in Bulgaria and Estonia.

Although overall expenditure on telephony has increased, the proportion accounted for by ex-monopoly service providers has generally fallen, as the share of the total telecommunication market accounted for by fixed-line voice operations has shrunk. Growth has been concentrated in mobile telephony markets and other data services. In 2008, the incumbent ex-monopoly service providers in fixed telecommunications markets accounted for more than two fifths of international calls across all Member States (see Table 7.22 for availability), a share that reached 85 % in Malta. The share of the leading operator in the mobile market was relatively low at 38 % in the EU-27 in 2009, varying between 21 % in the United Kingdom and 82 % in Cyprus.

The average number of mobile phone subscriptions per 100 inhabitants stood at 122 in the EU-27 in 2008 (see Figure 7.33). It surpassed parity (100) in 23 of the Member States, where there were more subscriptions than inhabitants.

Total turnover in value terms is based on sales from all telecommunication services, including leased lines, fixed network services, cellular mobile telecommunication services, interconnection services, and Internet service provision. In nearly all Member States (with data available) turnover from mobile services exceeded that from fixed network services in 2008 (see Table 7.23).

The price of telecommunications fell between 2000 and 2008 in many Member States (see Table 7.24). Price reductions were most apparent for national long-distance calls and international calls (the prices considered here are for calls to the United States). On average in the EU-27 the price of a national long-distance call almost halved between 2000 and 2008, with most of this reduction occurring by 2005, as the average price fell 13.0 % between 2005 and 2008. The price fall between 2005 and 2008 for an international call was similar, down 12.1 %, whereas the price of local calls increased by 8.6 %. Convergence of prices among local, national long-distance and international calls is notable, as well as convergence of prices among Member States for respective types of calls. The largest increase (in percentage terms) in the price of local calls between 2005 and 2008 was recorded in Finland where the price increased 63 %, while double-digit percentage increases were also recorded in four other Member States. In contrast, Romania recorded the highest decrease in the price of local calls, down 37 %.

The prices of local, national long-distance or international calls varied greatly across the Member States in 2008. Local and national long-distance calls were most expensive in Slovakia, while the price of international calls was highest in Latvia. The cheapest tariffs for local calls were in Bulgaria and Cyprus, while for national long-distance calls the cheapest were in Cyprus. For international calls, represented by calls to the United States, the cheapest call by far was from Germany, where the cost was significantly lower than for local or long-distance national calls.

Data sources and availability

Eurostat's data collection in relation to telecommunications statistics is conducted through the use of a predefined questionnaire (Telecom), which is sent on an annual basis to the national statistical institutes of the EU Member States. They collect information from their relevant regulatory authorities and send the completed questionnaires back to Eurostat.

Indicators presented in relation to market share refer to fixed-line telecommunications and mobile telephony. The incumbent service provider for fixed-line telephony is defined as the enterprise active in the market just before liberalisation. The incumbent's market share is calculated on the basis of retail revenues.

Indicators relating to the mobile market refer to the number of subscriptions to public cellular mobile telecommunication systems and also include active pre-paid cards. Note that many people have multiple mobile subscriptions, for example, for private and work use, or for use in different countries. SMS messages are short-message services, traditionally sent between mobile phones, but also between a range of other SMS-enabled devices and on-line web services.

Data on expenditure for telecommunications cover hardware, equipment, software and other services. The data are not collected by Eurostat; further meth-

odological information is available from the website of the European Information Technology Observatory (EITO).

Telecommunications prices are based on the price (including VAT) in euro of a 10-minute call at 11 a.m. on a weekday in September, based on normal rates. Three markets are presented, namely a local call (3 km), a national long-distance call (200 km) and an international call (to the United States). The data are not collected by Eurostat; further methodological information is available from the Teligen website.

Context

Telecommunication networks and services are the backbone of Europe's information society. Individuals, enterprises and public organisations alike have come to rely increasingly on convenient, reliable networks and services.

In recent years, the liberalisation of telecommunication markets has led to considerable reductions in prices and a wider range of services provided. This may, in part, reflect the introduction of competition into a number of markets that were previously the domain of incumbent monopoly suppliers. In addition, technological change has increased capacity and made it possible to communicate not only by voice, but also over the Internet. Market regulation has nonetheless continued, and the European Commission oversees this market to ensure that consumers benefit. Regulators continue to monitor the significant market power of former monopoly providers, ensure universal service provision and protect consumers. In particular, the European Commission works to ensure inclusive access to telecommunication services for all social groups.

On 30 June 2007, a new set of rules on mobile phone roaming charges entered into force. These foresee that people travelling within the EU are able to make phone calls across borders at more affordable and transparent prices than before. The so-called Roaming Regulation 717/2007 of 27 June 2007 put in place a set of maximum prices for phone calls made and received while abroad (Eurotariff). These maximum prices apply to all consumers unless they opt for special packages offered by their operator. The European Commission and national regulators have closely monitored price developments for text messages and data services. On the basis of this monitoring, in July 2009 revised rules were adopted in the Roaming Regulation 544/2009 that cut roaming prices for (voice) phone calls further and introduced new caps on the tariffs for SMS (Euro SMS tariff). In addition, as of 1 July 2010, consumers are protected by an automatic safeguard against data roaming bill shocks – for example, by providing warnings to consumers when they reach 80 % of a pre-defined limit for monthly roaming charges and automatic cut-off once the limit has been reached. The amended roaming regulation will apply until the end of June 2012 and will be a subject of a review by the end of June 2011.

Figure 7.32: Communications expenditure, 2008 (1)
(% of GDP)

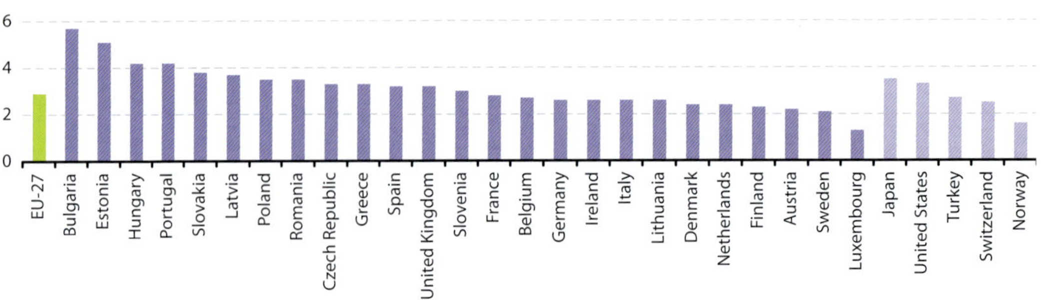

(1) Cyprus and Malta, not available.

Source: Eurostat (tsiir090), European Information Technology Observatory (EITO)

Table 7.22: Market share of incumbents in fixed telecommunications and leading operators in mobile telecommunications
(% of total market)

	Fixed telecommunications: international calls		Leading operator in mobile telecommunications		
	2007	2008	2007	2008	2009
EU-27	:	:	40	39	38
Belgium	62	62	45	43	44
Bulgaria	86	82	53	49	49
Czech Republic	50	52	42	40	39
Denmark	:	:	40	46	30
Germany	:	:	37	36	37
Estonia	:	:	45	47	47
Ireland	56	54	45	42	40
Greece	74	:	38	43	48
Spain	68	55	46	45	44
France	57	56	43	44	41
Italy	44	47	40	39	36
Cyprus	79	69	89	85	82
Latvia	65	69	35	53	46
Lithuania	77	79	41	39	40
Luxembourg	:	:	57	54	53
Hungary	:	:	44	44	45
Malta	92	85	47	53	50
Netherlands	:	:	48	38	50
Austria	58	52	40	42	43
Poland	66	63	36	33	33
Portugal	:	:	46	48	47
Romania	69	62	44	45	43
Slovenia	79	75	67	72	57
Slovakia	89	80	51	55	53
Finland	:	:	41	40	38
Sweden	43	48	43	43	42
United Kingdom	48	44	24	25	21

Source: Eurostat (tsier070 and tsier080), National Regulatory Authorities

Figure 7.33: Mobile phone subscriptions and the use of SMS, 2008

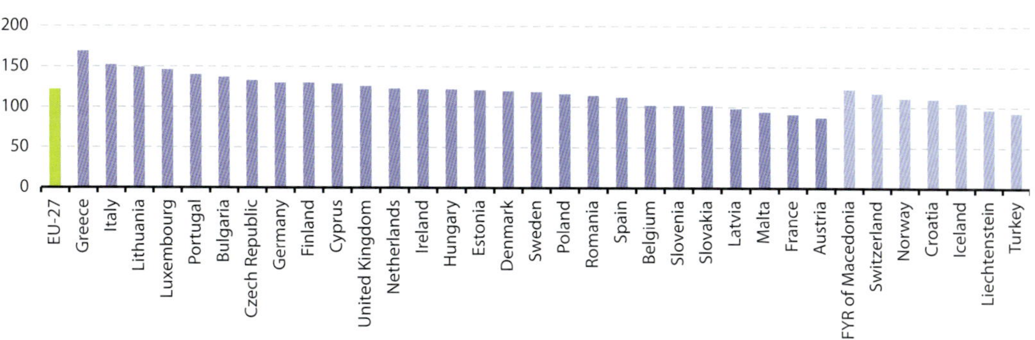

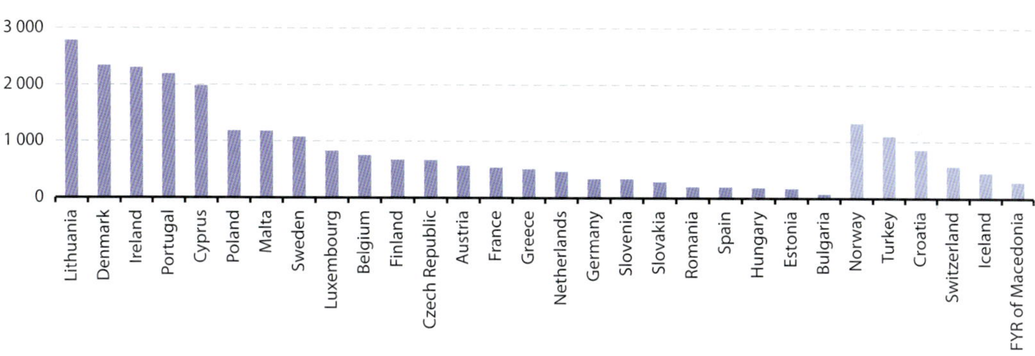

(1) Italy, Latvia and the United Kingdom, not available.

Source: Eurostat (tin00060, isoc_tc_sms and tps00001)

Table 7.23: Turnover from telecommunications, 2008 (1)
(EUR million)

	Total turnover	of which: Fixed network services	Cellular mobile services	Internet service provision
Belgium	9 658	681	4 033	:
Bulgaria	1 813	287	866	144
Czech Republic	5 684	1 895	3 424	739
Denmark	5 518	957	2 293	1 046
Germany	62 300	20 100	22 800	:
Estonia	723	290	418	89
Ireland	5 081	2 142	2 623	377
Greece (2)	8 166	3 669	4 498	152
Spain	44 186	7 105	15 068	3 882
France	49 112	10 593	18 556	5 400
Italy	:	:	:	:
Cyprus (3)	579	131	286	33
Latvia	:	:	:	:
Lithuania	905	116	395	111
Luxembourg	506	251	252	44
Hungary	3 501	591	1 613	564
Malta	261	83	132	:
Netherlands	13 018	5 228	6 659	:
Austria	5 466	1 187	3 437	641
Poland	:	:	:	:
Portugal (4)	7 781	1 601	2 112	:
Romania (5)	6 097	2 839	2 608	:
Slovenia	1 232	175	512	127
Slovakia	2 156	274	1 379	178
Finland (6)	4 263	613	2 027	:
Sweden (7)	9 098	1 970	2 016	898
United Kingdom	:	:	:	:
Iceland	296	96	117	16
Norway	3 852	816	1 919	754
Switzerland	11 053	3 223	3 178	:
Croatia	2 175	709	1 255	139
FYR of Macedonia	407	123	227	33
Turkey	11 302	4 192	6 796	945

(1) Possibility of double counting in the breakdown of total turnover.
(2) Internet services, 2007.
(3) Internet services, 2006.
(4) 2006.
(5) Cellular services, 2007.
(6) Fixed network services, 2007.
(7) 2007.

Source: Eurostat (isoc_tc_tur)

Table 7.24: Price of fixed telecommunications (¹)
(EUR per 10-minute call)

	Local calls			National long-distance calls			Calls to the United States		
	2000	2005	2008	2000	2005	2008	2000	2005	2008
EU-27	:	0.35	0.38	1.33	0.77	0.67	:	2.14	1.88
Belgium	0.49	0.57	0.60	1.74	0.57	0.60	5.95	1.98	2.06
Bulgaria	0.06	0.16	0.16	1.41	0.68	0.50	11.29	1.84	1.35
Czech Republic	0.56	0.65	0.65	1.69	1.32	0.65	:	2.40	2.36
Denmark	0.41	0.37	0.37	0.54	0.37	0.37	4.72	2.38	2.38
Germany	0.43	0.39	0.40	1.24	0.49	0.51	2.45	1.23	0.29
Estonia	0.14	0.25	0.25	0.71	0.25	0.25	10.24	2.55	1.63
Ireland	0.51	0.49	0.52	0.94	0.82	0.86	2.92	1.90	1.96
Greece	0.31	0.31	0.31	1.40	0.74	0.74	3.26	2.93	2.93
Spain	0.28	0.28	0.24	1.85	0.84	0.90	4.25	1.53	1.57
France	0.42	0.33	0.35	1.19	0.83	0.77	2.97	2.27	2.32
Italy	0.25	0.22	0.22	1.72	1.15	1.15	2.79	2.12	2.12
Cyprus	0.08	0.21	0.17	0.61	0.21	0.17	3.73	0.65	0.65
Latvia	0.34	0.34	0.34	1.00	1.00	1.00	5.74	5.75	5.75
Lithuania	0.26	0.38	0.38	1.06	0.78	0.78	11.81	4.02	4.02
Luxembourg	0.37	0.31	0.31	-	-	-	2.06	1.37	1.37
Hungary	0.38	0.44	0.39	1.33	1.17	0.40	4.62	3.19	2.51
Malta	:	0.25	0.25	-	-	-	:	1.76	1.91
Netherlands	0.30	0.33	0.45	0.42	0.49	0.45	0.78	0.85	0.69
Austria	0.69	0.49	0.49	2.30	0.59	0.59	4.32	1.90	1.99
Poland	0.39	0.39	0.56	1.63	1.42	0.56	11.78	4.16	3.26
Portugal	0.23	0.37	0.37	1.28	0.65	0.65	3.68	3.11	3.09
Romania	0.23	0.35	0.22	1.37	0.64	0.22	6.91	2.62	1.19
Slovenia	0.17	0.26	0.29	0.17	0.26	0.29	:	1.40	1.40
Slovakia	0.40	0.74	0.75	1.90	1.52	1.61	11.04	3.74	1.79
Finland	0.22	0.24	0.39	0.87	0.94	0.95	5.68	4.90	4.78
Sweden	0.28	0.28	0.28	0.28	0.28	0.28	1.04	1.01	1.01
United Kingdom	0.50	0.38	0.51	1.00	0.38	0.51	3.00	1.78	2.29
Japan	0.35	0.30	0.29	2.64	1.23	1.00	5.29	5.29	4.67
United States	0.09	0.08	0.08	0.43	1.04	0.79	-	-	-

(¹) The indicator gives the price in euro of a 10-minute call at 11 am on a weekday (including VAT) for respectively a local call (3 km), a national call (200 km) and an international call to the United States; prices refer to September; normal tariffs without special rates are used.

Source: Eurostat (tsier030), Teligen

Agriculture, forestry and fisheries

8

Agriculture

Agriculture was one of the first sectors of the economy (following coal and steel) to receive the attention of EU policymakers. Article 39 of the Treaty of Rome on the EEC (1957) set out the objectives for the first common agricultural policy (CAP); these were focused on increasing agricultural productivity as a way to ensure a fair standard of living for the agricultural community, stabilising markets, and ensuring security of supply at affordable prices to consumers.

As the primary objective of producing more food within Europe was realised, food surpluses accrued, distorting trade and raising environmental concerns. These were the principal drivers for changes in the common agricultural policy, a process that started in the early 1990s and which resulted in a change from support for production towards a market-oriented and a more environment-friendly and sustainable form of agriculture. Further reforms have taken place in recent years, most notably in 2003 and 2008. The 2003 reform introduced a new system of direct payments, known as the single payment scheme, under which aid is no longer linked to production (decoupling). The single payment scheme aims to guarantee farmers more stable incomes. Farmers can decide what to produce in the knowledge that they will receive the same amount of aid, allowing them to adjust production to suit demand. In 2008 further changes were made, building on the reform package from 2003, such that all aid to the agricultural sector will be decoupled by 2012.

The Europe 2020 strategy offers a new perspective on economic, social, environmental, climate-related and technological challenges and future agricultural reform is likely to be made in relation to the goals of developing intelligent, sustainable and inclusive growth, while taking account of the wealth and diversity of the agricultural sector within the EU Member States.

Forestry

Contrary to what is happening in many other parts of the world, forest cover in the EU-27 is slowly increasing. Forests are present in a huge variety of climatic, geographic, ecological and socio-economic conditions. Ecologically, the forests within the EU belong to numerous vegetation zones, ranging from coastal plains to Alpine zones, while socio-economic management conditions vary from small family holdings to large estates belonging to vertically integrated businesses.

Fisheries

Fish are a natural, biological, mobile (sometimes over wide distances) and renewable resource. Aside from fish farming, fish cannot be owned until they have been caught. For this reason, fish stocks continue to be regarded as a common resource, which therefore need to be managed collectively. This has led to policies that regulate the amount of fishing, as well as the types of fishing techniques and gear used to catch fish.

8.1 Agricultural output, price indices and income

One of the principal objectives of the common agricultural policy (CAP) is to provide farmers with a reasonable standard of living. Although this concept is not defined explicitly, one of the measures tracked within the policy is income development from farming activities. Economic accounts for agriculture provide information that allows an analysis of agricultural activity and the income generated by it. This subchapter gives an overview of recent changes in agricultural output, gross value added and prices in the European Union (EU), and their effect on income from agricultural activity.

Main statistical findings

The EU-27's agricultural industry generated EUR 125 400 million of gross value added at producer prices in 2009, which represented a 14.0 % reduction in relation to the previous year (see Table 8.1). There were large decreases in both the value of crop output (down 13.9 % to EUR 171 000 million in 2009) and animal output (down 10.9 % to EUR 133 000 million); these were partly compensated for by a sizeable reduction in the value of intermediate consumption of goods and services (down 10.5 %).

Changes in the value of agricultural output comprise a volume and price component: one important strand of recent changes in agricultural policy has been to move away from price support mechanisms, so that prices more accurately reflect market forces and changes in supply and demand. During the period 2005 to 2009 (see Figure 8.2) there were considerable differences between the Member States in the development of deflated agricultural output prices: such deflated prices show the extent to which agricultural prices have changed compared to consumer prices. Deflated prices rose in nine of the 26 Member States (Germany, no information available), the largest increases being recorded for the United Kingdom (average growth of 5.9 % per annum), Cyprus (3.9 % per annum between 2005 and 2008) and Romania (3.2 % per annum), while reductions were posted in 17 of the Member States, the most significant being in Latvia (-6.3 % per annum), Slovakia (-6.2 % per annum) and Estonia (-6.1 % per annum).

The development of deflated agricultural input prices showed a very different picture, as prices rose in 17 of the 25 Member States for which data are available between 2005 and 2009 (Germany and Ireland, no information). As with output prices, Cyprus (4.9 % per annum between 2005 and 2008) and the United Kingdom (4.7 % per annum) reported the highest input price increases, followed by Portugal (3.5 % per annum).

There was an overall 9.4 % increase in EU output prices for agricultural products between 2005 and 2009, with a breakdown between crop output (9.0 %) and animal output (9.8 %) showing prices increasing by a similar magnitude. The overall increase in output prices between 2005 and 2009 did not occur as a stable development, as there was a considerable reduction in prices between 2008 and 2009 when the price of agricultural products fell by 13.9 %. The largest reductions between 2008 and 2009 were recorded for cereals (-30.2 %), eggs, milk, fruits and olive oil (reductions of between 14 % and 17 %).

The real net value added at factor cost of the agricultural activity per unit of labour (expressed in annual work units – equivalent to the work performed by a person employed full-time), also termed as agricultural income indicator A, declined by 11.7 % in the EU-27 in 2009, compared with 2008. There were stark contrasts among the Member States, with decreases in income of more than 20 % in Hungary, Luxembourg, Ireland, Germany and Italy, contrasting with rapidly rising incomes in Malta (7.1 %) and Denmark (4.2 %).

Data sources and availability

Economic accounts for agriculture (EAA) provide key insights into:

- the economic viability of agriculture;
- agriculture's contribution to a Member State's wealth;
- the structure and composition of agricultural production and inputs;
- the remuneration of factors of production;
- relationships between prices and quantities of both inputs and outputs.

These accounts comprise a production account, a generation of income account, an entrepreneurial income account and some elements of a capital account. For the production items, Member States transmit to Eurostat values at basic prices, as well as their components (values at producer prices, subsidies on products, and taxes on products). The data for the production account and for gross fixed capital formation are transmitted in both current prices and the prices of the previous year.

The output of agricultural activity includes output sold (including trade in agricultural goods and services between agricultural units), changes in stocks, output for own final use (own final consumption and own-account gross fixed capital formation), output produced for further processing by agricultural producers, as well as intra-unit consumption of livestock feed products. The output of the agricultural industry is made up of the sum of the output of agricultural products and of the goods and services produced in inseparable non-agricultural secondary activities; animal and crop output are the main product categories of agricultural output.

Gross value added equals the value of output less the value of intermediate consumption, and is shown in producer prices (the producer price excludes subsidies less taxes on products). Intermediate consumption represents the value of all goods and services used as inputs in the production process, excluding fixed assets whose consumption is recorded as fixed capital consumption. The Member States transmit information on intermediate consumption to Eurostat using values at purchaser prices (basic prices).

Eurostat also collects annual agricultural prices (in principle net of VAT) to compare agricultural price levels between Member States and study sales channels. Quarterly and annual price indices for agricultural products and the means of agricultural production, on the other hand, are used principally to analyse price developments and their effect on agricultural income. Agricultural price indices are obtained by a base-weighted Laspeyres calculation (2005=100), and are expressed both in nominal terms, and deflated using an implicit HICP deflator.

Agricultural income indicators are presented in the form of:

- an index of real income of factors in agricultural activity per annual work unit (indicator A);
- the index of real net agricultural entrepreneurial income, per unpaid annual work unit (indicator B);
- net entrepreneurial income of agriculture (indicator C).

Context

Significant reforms of the common agricultural policy have taken place in recent years, most notably in 2003 and 2008, with the aim of making the agricultural sector more market-oriented. The 2003 reform introduced a new system of direct payments, known as the single payment scheme, under which aid is no longer linked to production (decoupling); the single payment scheme aims to guarantee farmers more stable incomes. Farmers can decide what to produce in the knowledge that they will receive the same amount of aid, allowing them to adjust production to suit demand. In 2008 further changes were made, building on the reform package from 2003, such that all aid to the agricultural sector will be decoupled by 2012.

The Europe 2020 strategy offers a new perspective on economic, social, environmental, climate-related and technological challenges and future agricultural reform is likely to be made in relation to the goals of developing intelligent, sustainable and inclusive growth, while taking account of the wealth and diversity of the agricultural sector within the EU Member States.

Table 8.1: Agricultural output and gross value added at producer prices
(EUR million)

	Gross value added of the agricultural industry			Crop output			Animal output		
	1999	2004	2009	1999	2004	2009	1999	2004	2009
EU-27	126 779	137 761	125 409	149 595	168 482	*171 049*	116 391	125 698	*133 009*
Belgium	2 158	2 242	1 914	2 994	2 946	*3 019*	3 190	3 618	*3 764*
Bulgaria	1 679	1 589	1 465	1 429	1 763	*1 941*	1 338	1 088	1 163
Czech Republic	731	1 126	629	1 218	1 881	*1 930*	1 292	1 467	*1 595*
Denmark	1 985	2 285	1 571	2 579	2 537	*2 988*	4 194	4 721	*4 673*
Germany	12 099	14 451	12 924	18 492	19 579	*21 204*	17 747	18 789	*19 800*
Estonia	87	180	157	111	154	*203*	136	257	*270*
Ireland	1 825	1 768	937	1 184	1 351	*1 340*	3 506	3 672	*3 393*
Greece	6 209	6 036	5 801	6 498	6 741	*6 598*	2 398	2 564	*2 792*
Spain	18 193	22 440	21 277	18 377	23 510	*22 593*	10 469	12 480	*12 976*
France	23 756	22 411	20 586	30 608	31 093	*34 109*	21 211	21 390	*22 057*
Italy	25 470	26 573	22 075	25 300	27 773	*24 236*	12 818	13 697	*14 129*
Cyprus	-256	331	302	0	313	*316*	0	306	*309*
Latvia	169	218	141	178	268	*387*	173	254	*302*
Lithuania	402	366	427	583	568	*868*	457	608	*667*
Luxembourg	114	100	87	77	85	*116*	148	153	*153*
Hungary	1 862	1 991	1 551	2 301	3 511	*3 087*	1 795	2 066	*2 085*
Malta	65	50	52	54	40	*48*	74	65	*67*
Netherlands	8 452	7 658	7 396	9 253	10 048	*11 188*	7 872	7 787	*8 659*
Austria	2 096	2 164	2 338	2 272	2 369	*2 675*	2 323	2 420	*2 726*
Poland	4 126	5 076	5 651	5 439	6 584	*7 753*	4 878	6 383	*8 137*
Portugal	2 240	2 279	1 846	3 843	3 910	*3 762*	2 052	2 311	*2 420*
Romania	4 140	7 078	5 999	4 901	9 388	*8 569*	2 683	3 368	*3 955*
Slovenia	417	413	344	435	539	*453*	485	463	*470*
Slovakia	372	388	393	551	757	*824*	643	731	*747*
Finland	798	665	699	1 360	1 404	*1 550*	1 567	1 643	*1 766*
Sweden	979	1 028	1 200	1 644	1 617	*1 677*	2 185	2 134	*2 076*
United Kingdom	6 612	6 857	7 646	7 917	7 755	7 612	10 758	11 262	*11 861*
Norway	935	905	878	1 190	1 211	1 303	1 631	1 726	*1 983*
Switzerland	2 895	2 789	2 657	3 030	3 055	*2 996*	3 093	3 341	*3 369*
FYR of Macedonia	365	474	:	563	769	:	187	201	:

Source: Eurostat (aact_eaa01)

Figure 8.1: Agricultural output and gross value added at producer prices, EU-27 (2005=100)

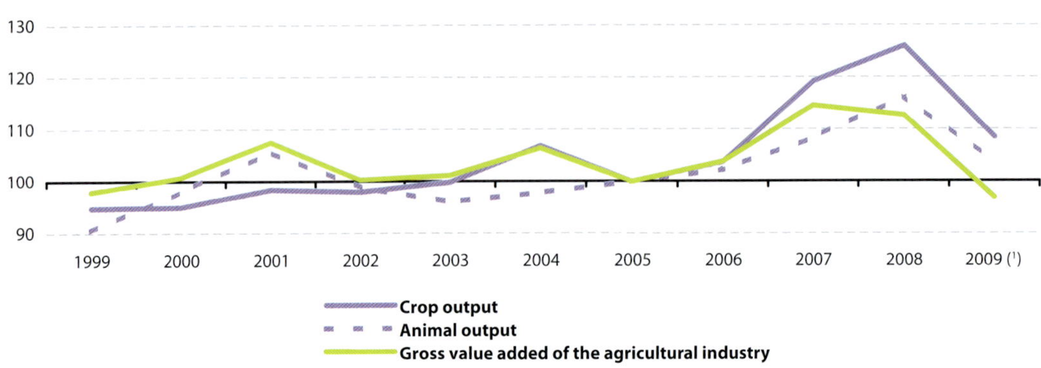

(1) Crop output and animal output, estimates.

Source: Eurostat (aact_eaa01)

Figure 8.2: Change in deflated price indices of agricultural input and output, 2005-2009 (average annual rate of change, %)

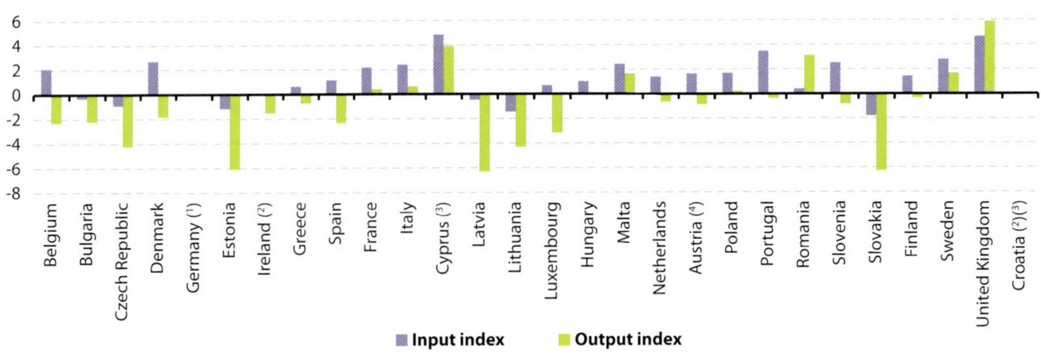

(1) Not available.
(2) Input index, not available.
(3) 2005-2008.
(4) Provisional.

Source: Eurostat (apri_pi05_ina and apri_pi05_outa)

Table 8.2: Price indices of agricultural output (nominal), EU (1)
(2005=100)

	2005	2006	2007	2008	2009
CROP OUTPUT	*100.0*	*107.0*	*123.7*	*126.7*	*109.1*
Cereals	*100.0*	*114.0*	*176.0*	*179.2*	*125.2*
Industrial crops	*100.0*	*99.3*	*113.7*	*119.3*	*106.0*
Forage plants	*100.0*	*99.6*	*118.9*	*134.7*	*131.1*
Vegetables and horticultural products	*100.0*	*102.6*	*107.1*	*107.6*	*102.9*
Potatoes	*100.0*	*154.5*	*149.5*	*133.2*	*124.7*
Fruits	*100.0*	*102.2*	*114.8*	*122.1*	*103.2*
Wine	*100.0*	*99.7*	*107.5*	*116.4*	*110.6*
Olive oil	*100.0*	*110.2*	*92.0*	*88.3*	*75.7*
Other crop products	*100.0*	*99.8*	*115.9*	*121.8*	*114.1*
ANIMAL OUTPUT	*100.0*	*102.8*	*106.0*	*116.2*	*109.5*
Animals	*100.0*	*104.5*	*102.8*	*111.6*	*110.7*
Cattle	*100.0*	*108.7*	*106.5*	*110.5*	*110.8*
Cattle (excluding calves)	*100.0*	*107.8*	*104.4*	*111.5*	*111.9*
Calves	*100.0*	*112.6*	*115.5*	*105.7*	*105.3*
Pigs	*100.0*	*104.2*	*95.6*	*107.2*	*104.6*
Equines	*100.0*	*110.9*	*113.0*	*141.7*	*144.3*
Sheep and goats	*100.0*	*100.0*	*95.6*	*103.6*	*113.8*
Poultry	*100.0*	*99.8*	*114.6*	*124.9*	*120.5*
Other animals	*100.0*	*104.7*	*95.2*	*104.8*	*109.7*
Animal products	*100.0*	*100.2*	*110.8*	*123.2*	*107.6*
Milk	*100.0*	*98.5*	*108.9*	*122.2*	*102.5*
Eggs	*100.0*	*109.3*	*128.7*	*136.6*	*147.9*
Other animal products	*100.0*	*107.8*	*96.8*	*102.7*	*95.5*
AGRICULTURAL GOODS	*100.0*	*105.0*	*115.4*	*121.8*	*109.3*

(1) EU estimates excluding Germany.

Source: Eurostat (apri_pi05_outa)

Table 8.3: Index of income from agricultural activity (indicator A)
(2005=100)

	1999	2000	2001	2002	2003	2004	2005	2006	2007	2008	2009
EU-27	:	94.7	104.0	99.5	101.5	110.1	100.0	104.2	115.4	112.8	*99.6*
Belgium	105.9	119.3	109.4	96.5	106.3	108.3	100.0	120.4	129.5	92.5	*93.0*
Bulgaria	:	101.1	113.0	91.9	86.4	84.5	100.0	96.0	98.5	152.2	*136.9*
Czech Republic	55.2	66.5	85.1	68.7	59.2	93.2	100.0	102.7	118.7	123.5	*102.5*
Denmark	81.7	105.4	127.2	90.1	88.2	99.3	100.0	105.0	104.0	54.4	*56.7*
Germany	69.5	90.0	110.9	81.7	75.4	111.9	100.0	108.6	134.5	127.6	*101.5*
Estonia	29.1	40.5	53.2	51.6	57.6	94.8	100.0	101.1	143.5	113.7	*93.9*
Ireland	73.2	95.7	90.6	79.0	75.6	80.1	100.0	84.1	94.2	87.4	*66.8*
Greece	116.6	116.7	116.4	113.1	103.4	98.3	100.0	98.3	103.8	96.6	*96.9*
Spain	99.8	104.3	112.4	108.9	123.1	113.2	100.0	95.6	107.4	103.8	*101.9*
France	112.9	111.4	112.4	108.8	106.8	105.3	100.0	111.8	124.1	110.6	*88.8*
Italy	124.4	117.9	115.4	113.5	113.8	114.6	100.0	96.4	94.2	95.5	*75.7*
Cyprus	125.4	95.1	105.9	107.3	98.7	96.6	100.0	90.4	91.3	86.7	*87.7*
Latvia	39.2	41.2	53.4	52.5	57.6	95.9	100.0	130.7	134.9	115.7	*98.6*
Lithuania	64.3	60.8	56.4	52.3	58.7	92.5	100.0	89.0	133.4	123.5	*102.2*
Luxembourg	110.2	104.3	105.5	105.5	99.2	99.1	100.0	95.8	103.9	90.3	*67.2*
Hungary	76.8	74.3	78.5	62.3	65.1	98.2	100.0	112.0	114.8	146.2	*99.2*
Malta	103.9	92.8	107.2	105.7	99.4	96.8	100.0	97.5	93.8	87.8	*94.0*
Netherlands	123.3	124.5	116.2	100.0	108.6	101.1	100.0	122.5	121.2	98.6	*89.6*
Austria	84.5	90.8	106.7	98.1	97.5	102.4	100.0	110.4	124.4	119.1	*96.2*
Poland	60.0	61.0	70.1	63.3	58.5	110.3	100.0	110.4	134.3	127.2	*126.1*
Portugal	112.2	95.2	102.1	97.4	98.4	108.8	100.0	104.3	100.0	103.8	*100.1*
Romania	80.9	66.9	114.2	106.7	121.2	175.1	100.0	99.2	76.8	112.3	*91.8*
Slovenia	63.3	71.6	62.1	81.9	64.5	99.5	100.0	97.4	109.5	98.3	*83.4*
Slovakia	85.6	82.5	93.8	88.7	82.8	107.3	100.0	122.1	128.9	143.4	*125.1*
Finland	76.4	89.6	90.4	90.3	89.2	86.2	100.0	98.6	106.0	89.3	*91.6*
Sweden	77.9	85.5	91.1	101.9	100.9	91.6	100.0	113.6	134.4	128.1	*119.8*
United Kingdom	82.8	80.0	85.0	94.6	108.4	101.1	100.0	104.7	112.0	144.7	*137.0*
Norway	141.4	124.1	120.4	126.1	122.8	121.5	100.0	93.8	104.7	99.3	*106.4*
Switzerland	99.9	103.0	95.7	102.1	94.9	105.9	100.0	97.0	102.5	107.9	*100.5*
FYR of Macedonia	83.1	77.5	51.3	74.9	87.3	121.4	100.0	112.6	97.1	:	:

Source: Eurostat (aact_eaa06)

8.2 Farm structure

The structure of agriculture in the Member States of the European Union (EU) varies as a function of differences in geology, topography, climate and natural resources, as well as the diversity of regional activities, infrastructure and social customs. The survey on the structure of agricultural holdings, also known as the farm structure survey (FSS), helps assess the agricultural situation across the EU, monitoring trends and transitions in the structure of agricultural holdings, while also modelling the impact of external developments or policy proposals.

This subchapter presents some statistics from the last farm structure survey that was conducted in 2007. The next census (2009/10) is in the process of being conducted and first results should be available in the summer of 2011.

Main statistical findings

There were 7.3 million commercial agricultural holdings in the EU-27 in 2007, with a further 6.4 million small holdings (those below a threshold of one European size unit (ESU)). Almost half (48 %) of the small holdings in the EU-27, principally being subsistence in nature, were found in Romania. A little over one third of the EU-27's commercial agricultural holdings (that were greater than one ESU) were located in Poland (15.4 %) and Italy (18.9 %), while Spain (12.9 %), Romania (11.9 %) and Greece (9.7 %) also contributed about a third of the total commercial holdings were located in 2007.

Among most Member States and across the EU-27 as a whole, there was a steady decline in the number of agricultural holdings during the period between 2003 and 2007. In this four-year period, the number of agricultural holdings in the EU-27 declined by 1.3 million (or 8.8 %), of which almost half were commercial holdings. There were particularly fast structural changes in Estonia, where the number of holdings declined by more than one third (-36.7 %), as well as in Bulgaria (-25.9 %), Portugal (-23.4 %) and Hungary (-19.0 %).

The total farm labour force in the EU-27 was the equivalent of 11.7 million full-time workers, of which 9.0 million worked on commercial holdings. Agriculture remains very much a family-oriented activity in the majority of Member States; almost four fifths (78 %) of the total agricultural labour force were farm holders or members of their family. The main exceptions were Slovakia (44 %) and the Czech Republic (27 %), where there is a different ownership structure compared with the majority of Member States. Just over one third (34 %) of the regular agricultural labour force in the EU-27 was female, although in the Baltic Member States this share was closer to half, reaching 50 % in Latvia. There were relatively few (6.1 %) agricultural holders in the EU-27 under the age of 35 years, but a relatively large proportion (34.1 %) were aged 65 years or over.

Figure 8.3 indicates the proportion of farm holdings with other gainful economic activity. Besides agricultural activity, other gainful activities were also conducted by about one in every ten

(9.9 %) of the EU's agricultural holdings in 2007, this proportion being slightly higher (13.5 %) among commercial holdings. A little over one quarter (27.6 %) of all holdings in Finland reported another gainful activity in 2007, with rates above 20 % also being recorded in Austria, Germany, Sweden, the United Kingdom, Denmark and France.

Two fifths (an estimated 40.1 %) of the total land area of the EU-27 was utilised agricultural area (UAA) in 2007. This proportion rose to two thirds (an estimated 66.3 %) of the land area of the United Kingdom, but was less than one tenth of the total in Sweden and Finland. Arable land (which includes cereals and other arable land) accounted for a little less than one quarter (24.2 %) of the total land area of the EU-27, with permanent grassland (which is composed of pasture, meadow and rough grazing) accounting for 13.2 %. During the ten years through until 2007, the make-up of land use in the EU-27 did not change very much.

Data sources and availability

A comprehensive farm structure survey is carried out by Member States every ten years (the full scope being the agricultural census) and intermediate sample surveys are carried out three times between these basic surveys. The Member States collect information from individual agricultural holdings. The information collected covers:

- land use;
- livestock numbers;
- rural development (for example, other gainful activities);
- management and farm labour input (including age, gender and relationship to the holder).

The survey data are aggregated to different geographic levels (Member States, regions, and for basic surveys also districts) and arranged by size class, area status, legal status of holding, objective zone and farm type.

The basic unit underlying the survey is the agricultural holding, a technical-economic unit under single management engaged in agricultural production. The survey covers all agricultural holdings with a utilised agricultural area (UAA) of at least one hectare (ha) and those holdings with a UAA of less than one hectare if their market production exceeds certain natural thresholds.

Other gainful activity is any activity other than that relating to farm work, including activities carried out on the holding itself (camp sites, accommodation for tourists, etc.) or that use its resources (machinery, etc.) or products (such as processing farm products, renewable energy production), and which have an economic impact on the holding. Other gainful activity is carried out by the holder, his/her family members, or one or more partners on a group holding.

The farm labour force is made-up of all individuals who have completed their compulsory education (having reached school-leaving age) and who carried out farm work on the holding under survey during the 12 months up to the survey day. The figures include the holders, even when not working on the holding, whereas their spouses are counted only if they carry out farm work on the holding. The holder is the natural person (sole holder or group of individuals) or the legal person (for example, a cooperative or other institution) on whose account and in whose name the holding is operated and who is legally and economically responsible for the holding – in other words, the entity or person that takes the economic risks of the holding. For group holdings, only the main holder (one person) is counted. The regular labour force covers the family labour force (even those who were working accidentally on the holding) and permanently employed (regular) non-family workers. The family labour force includes the holder and the members of his/her family who carried out farm work (including all persons of retiring age who continue to work on the holding). One annual work unit (AWU) corresponds to the work performed by one person who is occupied on an agricultural holding on a full-time basis. Full-time means the minimum hours required by the national provisions governing contracts of employment. If these provisions do not explicitly indicate the number of hours, then 1 800 hours are taken to be the minimum (225 working days of eight hours each).

Context

Rural development policy aims to improve: competitiveness in agriculture and forestry; the environment and countryside; the quality of life in rural areas; and the diversification of rural economies. As agriculture has modernised and the importance of industry and services within the economy has increased, so agriculture has become much less important as a source of jobs. Consequently, increasing emphasis is placed on the role farmers can play in rural development, including forestry, biodiversity, the diversification of the rural economy to create alternative jobs and environmental protection in rural areas. The farm structure survey continues to be adapted with the aim of trying to provide timely and relevant data to help analyse and follow these developments.

Table 8.4: Agricultural holdings

	Number of agricultural holdings (1 000)			Holdings with dairy cows (1 000)			Holdings with irrigable area (% of holdings)		
	2003	2005	2007	2003	2005	2007	2003	2005	2007
EU-27	15 021.0	14 482.0	13 700.4	3 199.4	2 821.4	2 486.7	:	:	:
Belgium	54.9	51.5	48.0	16.6	15.2	13.3	4.2	4.2	4.6
Bulgaria	665.6	534.6	493.1	195.0	152.6	120.8	20.5	14.3	14.8
Czech Republic	45.8	42.3	39.4	8.5	6.8	5.6	4.5	4.6	5.2
Denmark	48.6	51.7	44.6	8.0	6.6	5.4	19.4	17.9	15.0
Germany	412.3	389.9	370.5	121.8	110.4	101.1	:	:	:
Estonia	36.9	27.8	23.3	12.4	9.2	6.1	:	:	:
Ireland	135.6	132.7	128.2	28.1	23.8	21.3	0.0	0.0	0.0
Greece	824.5	833.6	860.2	11.6	9.8	8.0	64.1	64.8	62.3
Spain	1 140.7	1 079.4	1 043.9	51.0	42.4	37.3	47.5	46.1	45.3
France	614.0	567.1	527.4	113.9	103.9	93.1	17.3	17.8	18.0
Italy	1 963.8	1 728.5	1 679.4	67.5	61.0	62.8	36.2	37.6	40.4
Cyprus	45.2	45.2	40.1	0.3	0.2	0.2	74.5	76.8	78.0
Latvia	126.6	128.7	107.8	63.7	50.9	43.7	0.1	0.3	0.2
Lithuania	272.1	253.0	230.3	193.4	170.8	123.2	0.0	0.1	0.0
Luxembourg	2.5	2.5	2.3	1.0	1.0	1.1	0.0	:	0.0
Hungary	773.4	714.8	626.3	22.0	16.3	12.2	4.0	2.3	0.2
Malta	11.0	11.1	11.0	0.2	0.2	0.2	34.2	27.5	25.0
Netherlands	85.5	81.8	76.7	25.0	23.5	24.5	22.2	23.5	25.5
Austria	173.8	170.6	165.4	65.1	54.6	49.5	3.6	4.4	4.4
Poland	2 172.2	2 476.5	2 391.0	873.8	727.1	651.1	0.7	1.0	1.1
Portugal	359.3	323.9	275.1	27.1	15.9	13.5	62.1	62.0	62.0
Romania	4 484.9	4 256.2	3 931.4	1 204.9	1 134.4	1 012.4	5.6	3.4	2.6
Slovenia	77.2	77.2	75.3	17.2	19.7	19.2	1.5	2.3	2.3
Slovakia	71.7	68.5	69.0	14.2	13.5	11.5	5.9	10.2	2.2
Finland	75.0	70.6	68.2	19.4	16.9	14.4	10.6	8.1	8.5
Sweden	67.9	75.8	72.6	9.7	8.6	7.1	7.7	6.0	5.2
United Kingdom	280.6	286.8	299.8	28.2	26.3	28.1	1.7	1.4	13.5
Norway	58.2	53.0	49.9	17.5	15.9	13.7	16.5	16.7	17.4

Source: Eurostat (tag00001, ef_r_nuts and ef_ov_lusum)

Table 8.5: Farm labour force, 2007

	Total farm labour force (1 000 AWU) (1)	Regular farm labour force (% of total)	Full-time regular farm labour force (% of total)	Female regular farm labour force (% of total)	Family farm labour force (% of total)	Agric. holders being a natural person (1 000)	Agric. holders <35 years old (1 000)	Agric. holders >=65 years old (1 000)
EU-27	11 693	92	34	34	78	13 441	823	4 584
Belgium	66	95	71	29	79	44	3	9
Bulgaria	491	95	38	39	85	490	15	222
Czech Republic	137	98	68	32	27	36	4	7
Denmark	56	96	70	23	61	44	3	9
Germany	609	91	50	28	69	365	28	27
Estonia	32	98	46	46	61	22	1	7
Ireland	148	98	60	21	93	128	9	32
Greece	569	86	22	29	82	860	60	321
Spain	968	82	42	20	65	988	44	361
France	805	89	67	25	47	428	34	66
Italy	1 302	90	37	30	84	1 664	49	741
Cyprus	26	94	31	32	75	40	1	12
Latvia	105	99	30	50	84	108	8	32
Lithuania	180	98	14	48	85	230	10	93
Luxembourg	4	98	63	27	85	2	0	0
Hungary	403	97	25	37	77	619	47	172
Malta	4	99	41	14	88	11	0	3
Netherlands	165	91	56	26	61	73	3	13
Austria	163	97	53	41	88	161	16	18
Poland	2 263	97	34	42	95	2 387	294	388
Portugal	338	93	35	41	82	269	5	130
Romania	2 205	93	4	42	90	3 914	167	1 762
Slovenia	84	96	21	41	92	75	3	26
Slovakia	91	96	40	32	44	67	2	22
Finland	72	94	56	30	83	67	6	4
Sweden	65	97	42	26	76	68	4	15
United Kingdom	341	93	55	23	67	283	7	92
Norway	56	94	32	25	80	50	4	4

(1) AWU: annual work unit.

Source: Eurostat (tag00020, tag00021, ef_so_lfwtime, ef_so_lfaa, tag00029 and tag00030)

Figure 8.3: Agricultural holdings with another gainful activity, 2007
(%)

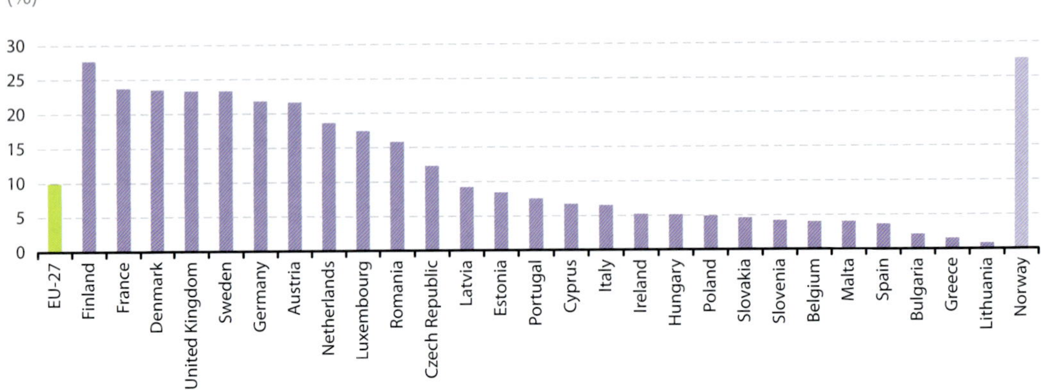

Source: Eurostat (tag00096)

Figure 8.4: Utilised agricultural area by land use, EU-27, 2007 (¹)
(% share of utilised agricultural area)

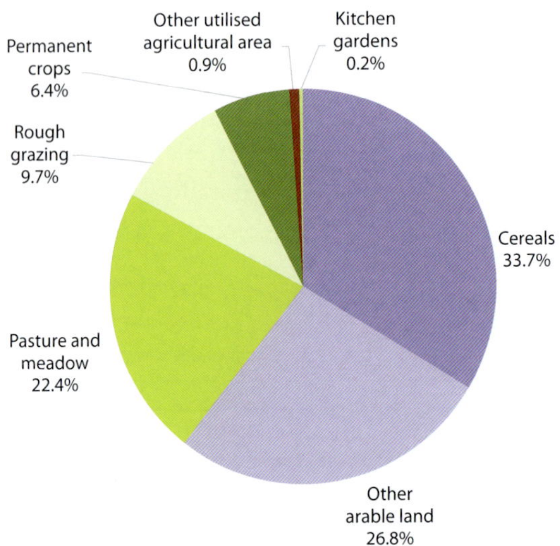

(¹) Figures do not sum to 100 % due to rounding.
Source: Eurostat (ef_lu_ovcropesu)

Table 8.6: Land use, 2007

	Total land area (km²) (¹)	Share of total land area (%) (²)							
		Utilised agricultural area	of which: Arable land	Kitchen garden	Permanent grassland & meadow	Permanent crops	Wooded area (³)	Other land (excluding wooded area) (³)
EU-27	4 303 401	40.1	24.2	0.1	13.2	2.5	7.2	2.8
Belgium	30 328	45.3	27.8	0.0	16.9	0.7	0.2	0.8
Bulgaria	111 002	27.5	24.0	0.2	2.5	0.8	8.6	0.8
Czech Republic	77 246	45.5	33.3	0.0	11.8	0.5	18.9	0.7
Denmark	43 098	61.8	56.9	0.0	4.7	0.2	4.8	2.5
Germany	357 108	47.4	33.3	0.0	13.5	0.6	3.8	1.1
Estonia	43 432	20.9	14.4	0.1	6.3	0.1	5.3	1.9
Ireland	68 394	60.5	14.7	0.0	45.8	0.0	1.9	2.1
Greece	130 822	31.2	16.2	0.1	6.3	8.6	0.5	2.0
Spain	505 987	49.2	23.5	0.0	17.1	8.6	9.6	6.7
France	632 834	43.4	28.9	0.0	12.8	1.7	1.5	0.8
Italy	295 114	43.2	23.5	0.1	11.7	7.9	12.9	4.3
Cyprus	9 250	15.8	11.7	0.0	0.2	3.9	0.2	3.4
Latvia	62 290	28.5	17.8	0.1	10.3	0.3	11.4	5.9
Lithuania	62 678	42.3	28.9	0.0	13.1	0.3	2.6	1.5
Luxembourg	2 586	50.6	23.6	0.0	26.4	0.6	2.5	0.3
Hungary	93 029	45.5	38.2	0.2	5.4	1.7	14.7	4.4
Malta	316	32.7	25.4	3.1	0.0	4.2	0.0	4.3
Netherlands	33 756	56.7	31.4	:	24.3	1.0	0.3	4.5
Austria	83 214	38.3	16.7	0.1	20.8	0.8	32.9	11.1
Poland	312 685	49.5	37.6	0.2	10.5	1.2	3.8	4.5
Portugal	92 118	37.7	11.7	0.2	19.3	6.5	7.8	2.3
Romania	229 973	59.8	37.8	0.8	19.7	1.5	4.7	1.9
Slovenia	20 141	24.3	8.6	0.1	14.3	1.3	18.8	2.7
Slovakia	49 035	39.5	27.7	0.1	11.2	0.5	21.4	1.4
Finland	304 086	7.5	7.4	0.0	0.1	0.0	10.4	2.8
Sweden	410 335	7.6	6.4	0.0	1.2	0.0	9.1	0.5
United Kingdom	243 154	66.3	24.7	0.0	41.5	0.1	2.6	1.2
Norway	304 280	3.4	2.0	0.0	1.4	0.0	7.7	9.8

(¹) EU-27, Spain, Cyprus, Luxembourg, Malta, Austria and Poland, 2006.
(²) Areas belonging to agricultural holdings.
(³) On agricultural holdings.

Source: Eurostat (demo_r_d3area and ef_lu_ovcropaa)

Map 8.1: Average UAA per holding, 2007
(ha)

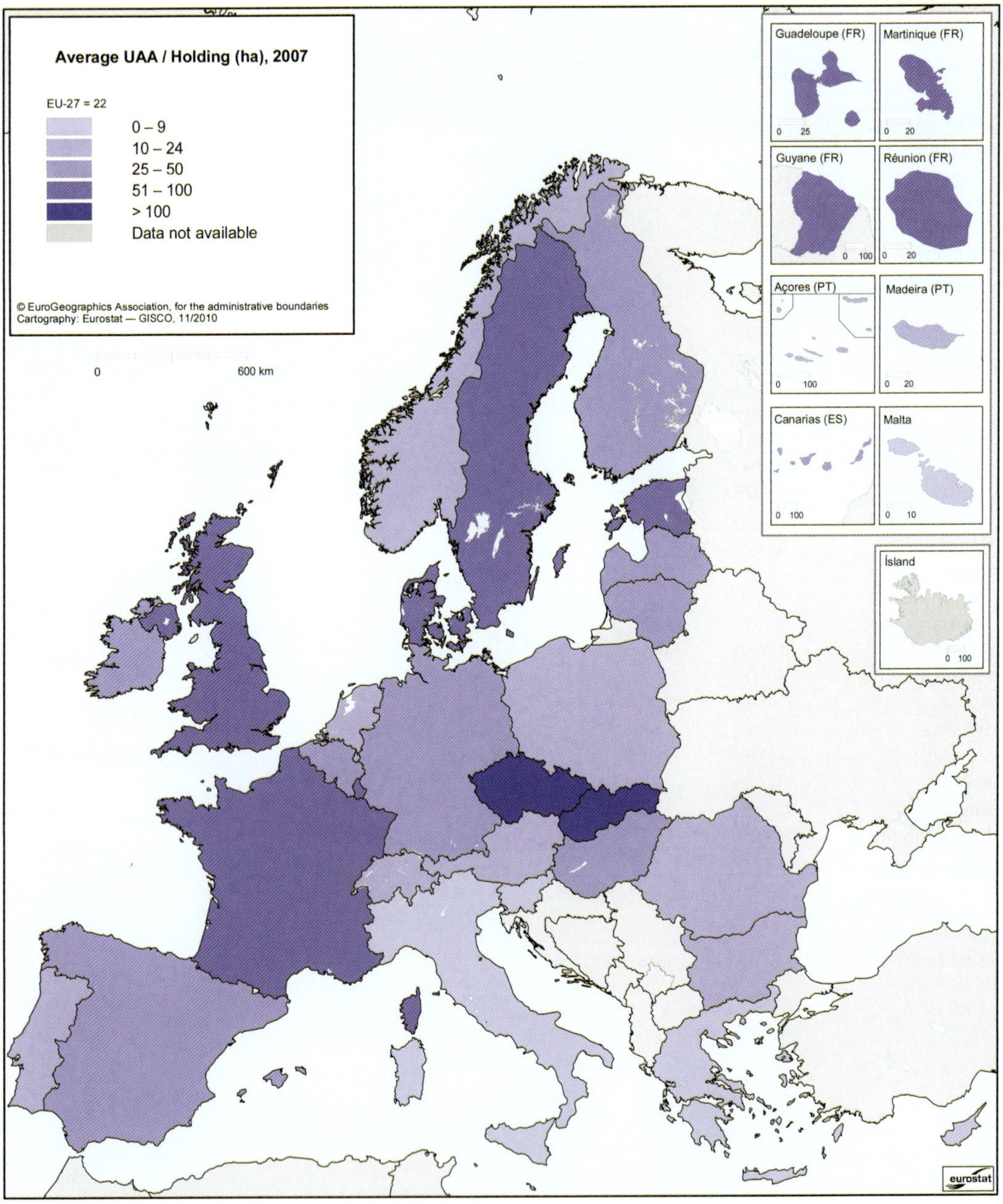

Average UAA / Holding (ha), 2007

EU-27 = 22

0 – 9
10 – 24
25 – 50
51 – 100
> 100
Data not available

© EuroGeographics Association, for the administrative boundaries
Cartography: Eurostat — GISCO, 11/2010

0 600 km

Guadeloupe (FR) 0 25
Martinique (FR) 0 20
Guyane (FR) 0 100
Réunion (FR) 0 20
Açores (PT) 0 100
Madeira (PT) 0 20
Canarias (ES) 0 100
Malta 0 10
Ísland 0 100

eurostat

Source: Eurostat (ef_ov_kvaaesu)

8.3 Agricultural products

Europe has a wide diversity in terms of natural environments, climates and farming practices that feed through into a wide array of food and drink products for human consumption and animal feed, as well as providing inputs for non-food processes. Indeed, agricultural products form a major part of the cultural identity of Europe's people and regions. With this in mind, European Union (EU) legislation has been developed to protect particular food and drink product names which are linked to a territory or to a production method, aiming to provide guarantees as to the origin and authenticity of products.

Main statistical findings

Crops

In 2009, the EU-27 produced 295.8 million tonnes of cereals (including rice). Despite the vagaries of the weather, cereal production in the EU-27 was relatively stable between 2000 and 2007 (see Figure 8.5), albeit with notably higher harvests in 2004. The production of cereals rose again sharply in 2008, to attain a level that was close to that recorded in 2004, before falling somewhat in 2009 (although the production of cereals remained 6.5 % higher than in 2000).

There was a strong rise (48.9 %) in the production of oilseeds between 2000 and 2009, which could be contrasted with a relatively steady decline in the production of potatoes (down by 24.4 % between 2000 and 2009) and a fall in the production of sugar beet (-16.7 % over the same period, with a marked reduction in 2006).

A comparison between 2008 and 2009 shows that EU-27 production of cereals fell by 6.1 %. Sugar beet and oilseed production increased by 16.5 % and 6.3 % respectively, while there was a modest increase in the production of potatoes (1.4 %).

France and Germany were by far the largest cereal, sugar beet and oilseed producers, together accounting for 40.5 % of the EU-27's cereal production in 2009, 53.0 % of its sugar beet production and 44.7 % of its oilseed production (see Table 8.7). The production of potatoes was more widely spread, with Germany recording the highest production (18.7 % of the EU-27 total in 2009), while Poland, the Netherlands, France and the United Kingdom each accounted for between 10.3 % and 15.5 % of the total. France was, by far, the leading producer of pulses and textile crops in 2009.

Figure 8.6 presents a breakdown of the production of cereals in the EU-27 in 2009. Almost half (47.0 %) of the total production of cereals was accounted for by wheat, while around one fifth of the total was composed of barley (21.0 %) and grain maize (19.5 %); rice production in the EU-27 was considerably lower (1.0 % of EU-27 cereals production).

In the EU-27, the most important vegetables in terms of production were tomatoes, onions and carrots, while the most important fruits were apples, oranges and peaches (see Figures 8.7 and 8.8 respectively). In 2009, Italy and Spain had the largest vegetable and fruit production among EU Member States. Italy produced around 11.6 million tonnes of vegetables, while Spain produced approximately 9.9 million tonnes. These two Member States jointly produced 19.9 million tonnes of dessert fruit, which equated to more than 56 % of the EU-27's production.

The bulk of fruit and fresh vegetable production was concentrated in a few Member States. For example, some 56.9 % of EU-27 apple production in 2009 was located in Poland, Italy and France, whilst more than 83 % of oranges were produced in Spain and Italy. About two thirds of all the tomatoes produced in the EU-27 originated from Italy and Spain in 2009, whilst 43.6 % of the onions produced in the EU-27 came from the Netherlands and Spain.

Meat and milk

Table 8.8 summarises agricultural production related to animals. The principal meat product in the EU-27 is pig meat (21.3 million tonnes in 2009), where the weight of production was almost three times as high as for beef/veal (7.7 million tonnes); the production of sheep meat in the EU-27 was relatively modest (0.7 million tonnes).

A quarter (24.7 %) of the EU-27's pig meat production came from Germany, the next highest contributions coming from Spain (15.5 %) and France (9.4 %), while the 7.6 % share for Poland and the 7.4 % share for Denmark were also notable. A little under one fifth (19.0 %) of the beef/veal produced in the EU-27 originated from France in 2009, with Germany and Italy the only other Member States to report production in excess of one million tonnes; Ireland reported a relatively high share of the EU-27's production of cattle meat.

Dairy production has a diverse structure across the Member States, in terms of farm and dairy herd sizes, as well as milk yields. The total collection of cows' milk in the EU-27 in 2009 amounted to 133.5 million tonnes. Figure 8.9 shows that over one third (34.8 %) of the milk utilised in the EU-27 in 2009 was converted into cheese, with butter accounting for the next highest proportion (23.7 %); approximately one eighth (12.6 %) of the milk utilised in the EU-27 was used for drinking milk.

Germany recorded the highest share (21.1 %) of EU-27 milk collected in 2009 and also accounted for the highest proportions of EU-27 butter (25.2 %) and cheese (22.8 %) production.

Data sources and availability

Annual statistics on the production of a range of specific crops are covered by Council Regulations, although the data for fresh fruit and vegetables are collected under various informal agreements with the EU Member States.

Agricultural production of crops is harvested production (excluding losses to the harvest). The harvested production includes marketed quantities, as well as quantities consumed directly on the farm, losses and waste on the holding, and losses during transport, storage and packaging. The statistics on crop production in this subchapter relate to harvested production.

Statistics on milk, eggs and meat products are compiled according to Community legislation. Milk production covers farm production of milk from cows, sheep, goats and buffaloes. A distinction is made between milk collected by dairies and milk production on the farm. Milk collection is only a part of the total use of milk production on the farm, the remainder generally includes own consumption, direct sale and cattle feed.

Meat production is based on the carcass weight of meat fit for human consumption. The concept of carcass weight is generally the weight of the slaughtered animal's cold body, although the precise definition varies according to the animal under consideration.

Context

Information on agricultural products may be used to analyse developments within agricultural markets in order to help distinguish between cycles and changing production patterns; these statistics can also be used to study how markets respond to policy actions. Agricultural product data also provides information on the supply side of agriculture, furthering understanding as regards price developments which are of particular interest to agricultural commodity traders and policy analysts.

In October 2007, the Council adopted legislation to establish a single common market organisation for agricultural products (Regulation 1234/2007). This was designed to reduce the volume of legislation in the farming sector, to improve legislative transparency, and to make agricultural policy more easily accessible. Between the start of 2008 and the start of 2009, the single common market organisation replaced 21 individual markets for a variety of different products such as fruit and vegetables, cereals, meats, eggs, dairy products, sugar or wine.

Despite reforms of the common agricultural policy (CAP) in 2003 and 2008, farm subsidies consume more than 40 % of the EU's annual spending. During the summer of 2010 a consultation process was organised in relation to the development of future agricultural policy. This identified three key areas for the stakeholders consulted, namely, food security, environmental concerns, and rural diversity. In November 2010 the European Commission released a Communication (COM(2010 672) providing a blueprint for developing agricultural policy, titled 'The CAP towards 2020: meeting the food, natural resources and territorial challenges of the future'. The document details some of the main challenges facing the EU's agricultural sector in the coming decade – for example, how to preserve the EU's food production so as to guarantee long-term food security, while supporting farming communities that provide a diverse range of quality products, and ensuring environmental, water, animal and plant health requirements are met.

Figure 8.5: Indices of the agricultural production of crops, EU-27 (1)
(2000=100)

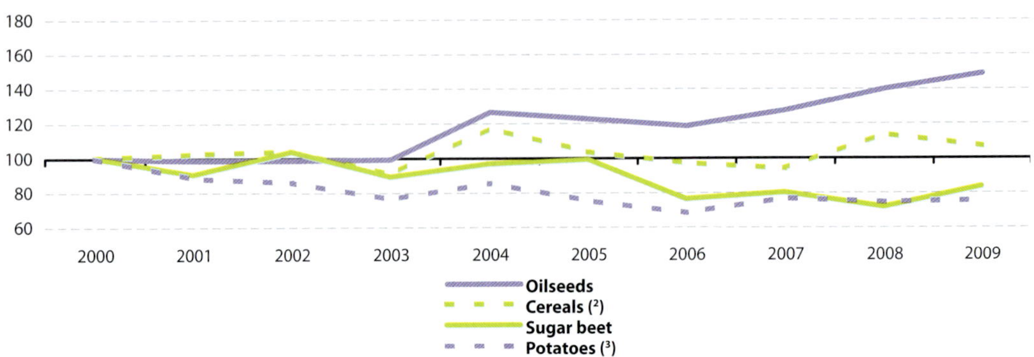

(1) Includes Eurostat estimates made for the purpose of this publication.
(2) Estimate, 2004, 2005; provisional, 2008 and 2009.
(3) Provisional, 2007-2009.

Source: Eurostat (apro_cpp_crop)

Figure 8.6: Production of cereals, EU-27, 2009 (1)
(%, based on tonnes)

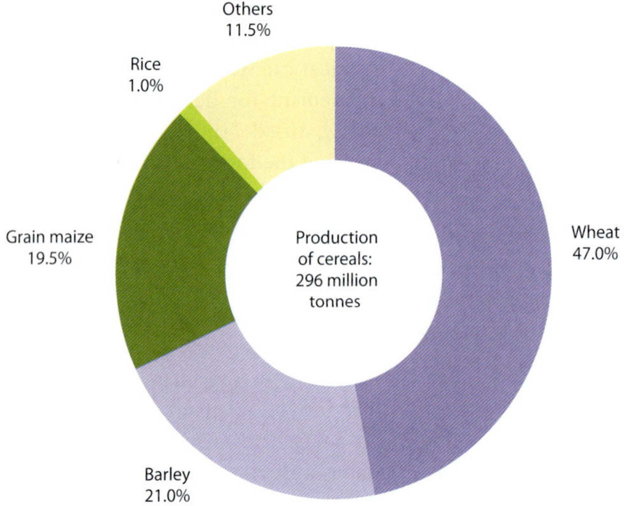

(1) Provisional; includes Eurostat estimates made for the purpose of this publication.

Source: Eurostat (apro_cpp_crop)

Table 8.7: Agricultural production of crops, 2009
(1 000 tonnes)

	Cereals	Sugar beet	Potatoes	Oilseeds	Pulses	Textile crops
EU-27 (1)	295 842	114 138	62 595	28 769	:	:
Belgium	3 324	5 185	3 296	42	8	74
Bulgaria	5 273	*0*	*353*	*1 533*	*6*	*1*
Czech Republic	7 832	3 038	753	1 280	62	1
Denmark	10 117	*2 011*	*1 417*	*596*	*19*	*0*
Germany	49 748	25 550	11 683	*5 421*	:	:
Estonia	879	:	139	136	8	*0*
Ireland	*2 384*	45	363	*23*	11	*0*
Greece	4 814	1 600	848	28	30	192
Spain	17 833	4 154	2 481	908	273	27
France	70 000	34 913	7 164	7 428	1 007	*586*
Italy	15 892	3 308	1 753	801	136	6
Cyprus	57	0	107	1	1	:
Latvia	1 663	0	525	209	5	0
Lithuania	3 807	682	656	418	86	0
Luxembourg	189	0	20	18	1	0
Hungary	13 571	708	536	*2 216*	*49*	*0*
Malta	0	0	10	0	0	0
Netherlands	2 089	5 735	7 181	15	13	21
Austria	5 144	3 083	722	327	49	:
Poland	29 827	10 849	9 703	2 528	272	6
Portugal	1 057	137	519	14	3	*0*
Romania	14 934	685	4 011	1 753	53	0
Slovenia	533	*262*	103	13	2	:
Slovakia	3 330	899	216	596	15	0
Finland	4 261	559	755	142	11	:
Sweden	5 249	2 406	854	321	*67*	:
United Kingdom	22 036	8 330	6 423	2 007	132	*37*
Croatia	3 407	1 111	230	291	6	:
FYR of Macedonia	567	:	:	:	:	:
Turkey	33 373	16 300	4 328	1 208	1 179	1 725

(1) Includes Eurostat estimates made for the purpose of this publication.

Source: Eurostat (apro_cpp_crop)

Figure 8.7: Production of vegetables, EU-27, 2009 (1)
(%, based on tonnes)

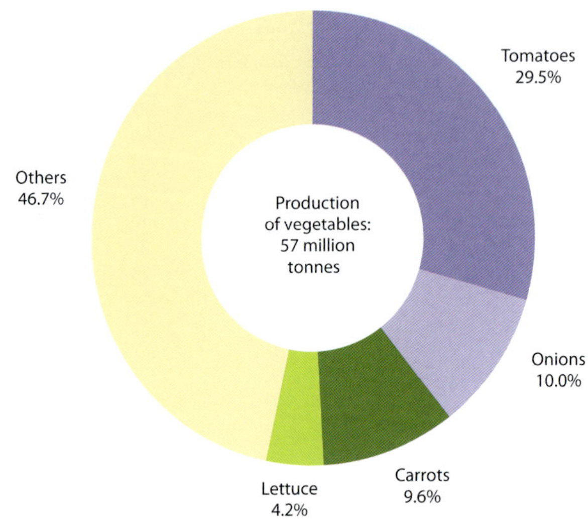

(1) Includes Eurostat estimates made for the purpose of this publication.
Source: Eurostat (apro_cpp_fruveg)

Figure 8.8: Breakdown of production of fruit, EU-27, 2009 (1)
(% of total, based on tonnes)

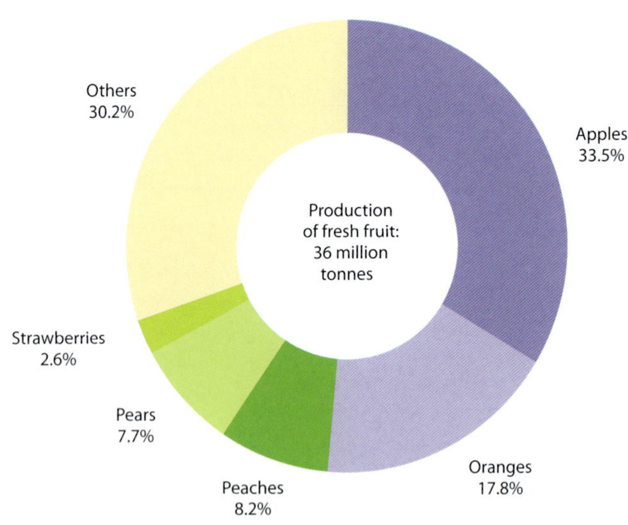

(1) Includes Eurostat estimates made for the purpose of this publication.
Source: Eurostat (apro_cpp_fruveg)

Table 8.8: Agricultural production related to animals, 2009
(1 000 tonnes)

	Collection of cows' milk	Butter	Cheese	Cattle meat	Pig meat	Sheep meat
EU-27 (1)	*133 545*	*1 623*	8 750	7 720	21 292	748
Belgium	2 954	22	72	255	1 082	1
Bulgaria	600	1	72	5	38	6
Czech Republic	2 354	27	113	77	285	0
Denmark	4 734	36	321	126	1 583	2
Germany	28 248	410	1 999	1 178	5 254	20
Estonia	612	7	37	10	31	0
Ireland	4 944	120	:	514	196	55
Greece	685	1	195	57	118	72
Spain	5 742	34	306	598	3 291	124
France	22 898	341	1 860	1 467	2 004	83
Italy	10 415	*107*	1 118	1 055	1 588	40
Cyprus	152	0	14	4	58	3
Latvia	595	4	29	19	25	0
Lithuania	1 274	12	92	44	41	0
Luxembourg	271	:	:	9	9	0
Hungary	1 407	5	75	30	389	0
Malta	:	0	:	2	7	0
Netherlands	*11 085*	*122*	*722*	402	1 275	14
Austria	2 716	29	142	224	533	7
Poland	9 140	120	634	385	1 608	1
Portugal	1 868	29	65	103	373	9
Romania	992	10	69	25	222	1
Slovenia	517	:	18	35	24	0
Slovakia	852	7	34	16	70	1
Finland	2 281	48	105	81	206	1
Sweden	2 933	24	108	150	261	5
United Kingdom	13 237	:	322	850	720	303
Switzerland (2)	3 190	6	157	:	:	:
Croatia	675	3	28	49	78	1

(1) Includes Eurostat estimates made for the purpose of this publication.
(2) 2008.

Source: Eurostat (apro_mt_pann and apro_mk_pobta)

Figure 8.9: Utilisation of milk, EU-27, 2009 (1)
(%)

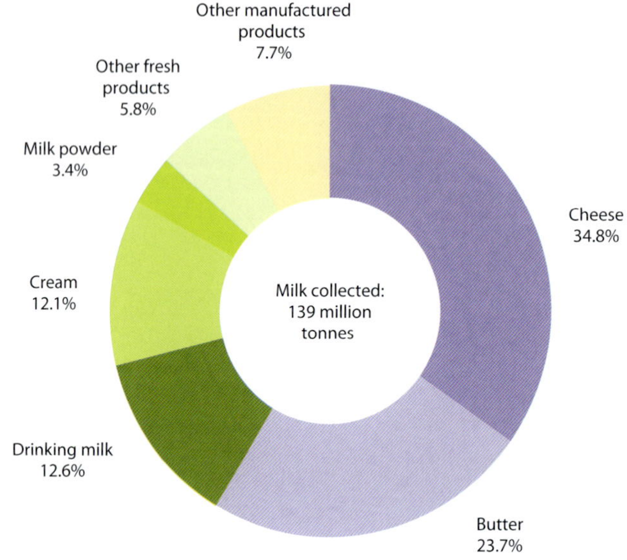

(1) Includes Eurostat estimates made for the purpose of this publication.

Source: Eurostat (apro_mk_pobta)

8.4 Agriculture and the environment

This subchapter presents data on agriculture and the environment within the European Union (EU). Around 40 % of the EU-27's land area is farmed, highlighting the importance of farming for the EU's natural environment. Links between the natural environment and farming practices are complex: farming has contributed over the centuries to creating and maintaining a variety of valuable semi-natural habitats within which a wide range of species rely for their survival; on the other hand, inappropriate agricultural practices and land use can have an adverse effect on natural resources, through the pollution of soil, water and air, or the fragmentation of habitats and a subsequent loss of wildlife.

Main statistical findings

Cropping patterns

In 2007, the total utilised agricultural area covered 172 million hectares in the EU-27, of which 60.5 % was composed of arable land, while 32.9 % of the area was accounted for by permanent grassland, and 6.4 % by permanent crops; kitchen gardens covered just 0.2 % of the utilised agricultural area in the EU-27.

Figure 8.10 shows an analysis of the main uses of agricultural land in each Member State in 2007. Several Member States (for example, Finland and Denmark) reported that almost the entirety of their utilised agricultural area was devoted to arable land, while the relative share of arable land in total utilised agricultural area was above 50 % in 20 of the Member States. Several countries (for example, Greece, Spain, Italy and Cyprus) tended to have a much higher proportion of permanent crops than the corresponding shares recorded in other Member States; this may result from favourable climatic conditions and the commercial importance of crops such as olive trees, vineyards or other fruit trees. In contrast, other Member States had considerable areas of permanent grasslands (for example, Ireland and the United Kingdom), which may be associated with relatively high numbers of grazing animals. Malta was the only Member State to report a relatively high share of its utilised agricultural area devoted to kitchen gardens.

Livestock patterns

In 2007, the total livestock population in the EU-27 amounted to 136 million livestock units (LSU), of which cattle represented 47.7 %, followed by pigs (27.6 %), poultry (13.8 %) and sheep (7.6 %).

Figure 8.11 shows the share of different livestock categories in each Member State in 2007. Cattle were particularly dominant in Luxembourg (85.0 %) and Ireland (81.0 %), and a majority of the livestock population (in LSUs) was composed of cattle in 13 of the Member States. In Denmark, pigs represented 70.6 % of the total livestock population (in LSUs): Denmark was the only Member State where pigs accounted for more than half of the livestock population, although pigs were the largest category of livestock in four other Member States (Cyprus, Hungary, Spain and Malta). More than one third (38.4 %) of the livestock in Greece was composed of sheep (while goats accounted for a further 19.0 %; goats are included within the residual category of others in Figure 8.11). Greece was the only Member State where sheep were the largest category of livestock, the next highest share being recorded in the United Kingdom (24.2 %).

Map 8.2 shows the regional distribution of livestock densities. EU-27 livestock density averaged 0.78 livestock units per hectare of utilised agricultural area in 2007 – an overall decrease of 4.9 % compared with 2003 (the first reference period for which an EU-27 figure is available). The highest livestock densities were recorded in a number of regions across the north of Belgium and the south of the Netherlands, as well as in Malta (which at the NUTS 2 level is a single region). At the other end of the range, the lowest livestock densities were registered in a range of disparate regions, such as regions with capital cities (for example, Paris and Vienna), tourist destinations (such as the Algarve), remote areas (like the Highlands and islands of the United Kingdom), or more generally the south of Italy (for example, Puglia, Basilicata and Sicily), the east of Austria (Burgenland), Estonia and Latvia.

Data sources and availability

All the data within this subchapter come from farm structure surveys, also referred to as surveys on the structure of agricultural holdings. These surveys are carried out by all EU Member States every ten years (the full scope being the agricultural census), with intermediate sample surveys being carried out three times between the main surveys.

The legal basis for the farm structure survey is Regulation 1166/2008 of 19 November 2008 on farm structure surveys and the survey on agricultural production methods.

The basic unit underlying the farm structure survey is the agricultural holding: a technical-economic unit, under single management, engaged in agricultural production. The survey covers all agricultural holdings with utilised agricultural area of at least one hectare, as well as smaller holdings of less than one hectare if their market production exceeds certain thresholds.

The Member States collect information from individual agricultural holdings; the information covers land use, livestock numbers, rural development, management and farm labour input. The survey data can be summed at different geographic levels to produce aggregates for the Member States, regions, and for main (ten-yearly) surveys also districts. The data can also be arranged by size class, area status, legal status of the holding, objective zone and farm type.

Context

The complex relationship between agriculture and the environment has resulted in environmental concerns and safeguards being integrated within the EU's common agricultural policy (CAP), with particular attention being paid to reducing the risks of environmental degradation through cross-compliance cri-

teria (as a condition for benefiting from direct payments, farmers must comply with certain requirements, some related to environmental protection), incentives and targeted agri-environmental measures, in order to enhance the sustainability of agro-ecosystems.

The importance attached to assessing the interaction between agriculture and the environment is underlined by a European Commission Communication COM(2006) 508 'Development of agri-environmental indicators for monitoring the integration of environmental concerns into the common agricultural policy', containing a list of 28 agri-environmental indicators, which are to be used to monitor the integration of environmental concerns into agricultural policy at an EU, national and regional level; the indicators relate to farming practices, agricultural production systems, pressures and risks to the environment, and the state of natural resources.

Cropping patterns provide an insight into the relationship between the environment and farming developments within the EU. Permanent grasslands (when extensively managed) are generally considered as the most important crop from a nature conservation perspective, providing habitats for many wild plants and animal species. The grazing of animals on grassland, if not too heavy, can contribute to conservation in semi-natural habitats – as plants and animals benefit from lightly or moderately grazed pastures, whereas heavy grazing is likely to reduce biodiversity. The quality (or balance between intensive and extensive farming practices) of grasslands can be roughly assessed by studying livestock densities. Higher livestock densities are likely to contribute more greenhouse gas emissions, as a result of manure production and enteric fermentation, and may also result in nutrient leaching into the water and air. In contrast, a low level of livestock density may increase the need for industrial fertilisers to be used on agricultural land or lead to the risk of land abandonment, which may also result in an elimination of environmental diversity.

Figure 8.10: Cropping pattern - utilised agricultural area (UAA) by crop type, 2007
(% of total UAA)

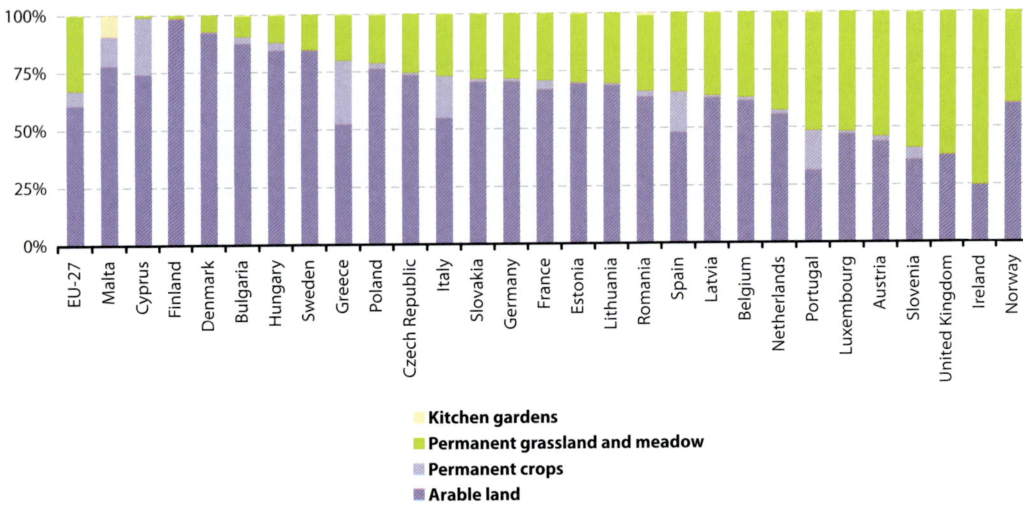

Source: Eurostat (ef_lu_ovcropaa)

Figure 8.11: Livestock pattern - number of livestock units (LSU) by type, 2007 ([1])
(% of total number of LSU)

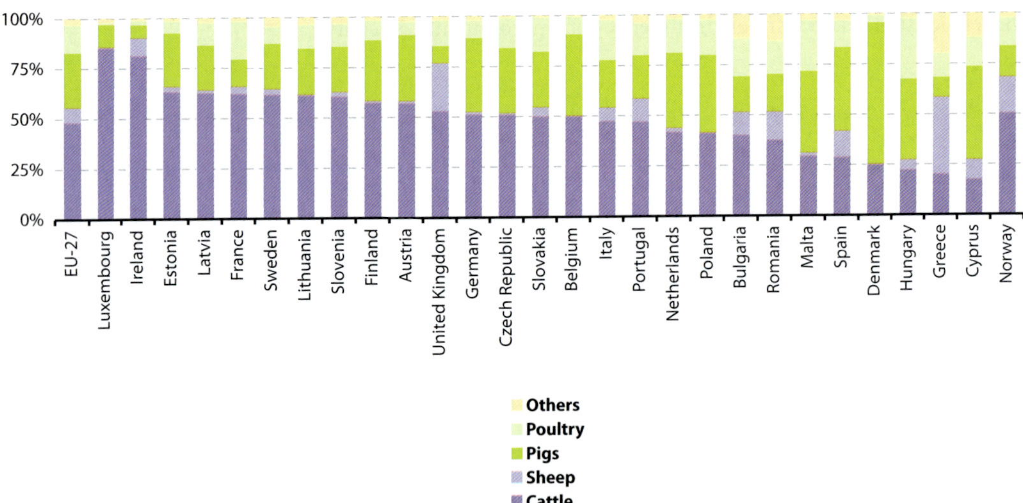

([1]) The LSU is related to the feed requirements of each individual animal category - for example, 1 LSU corresponds to one dairy cow or 10 sheep.
Source: Eurostat (ef_ov_lssum)

Map 8.2: Livestock density - livestock units per hectare of utilised agricultural area, by NUTS 2 regions, 2007
(LSU per ha)

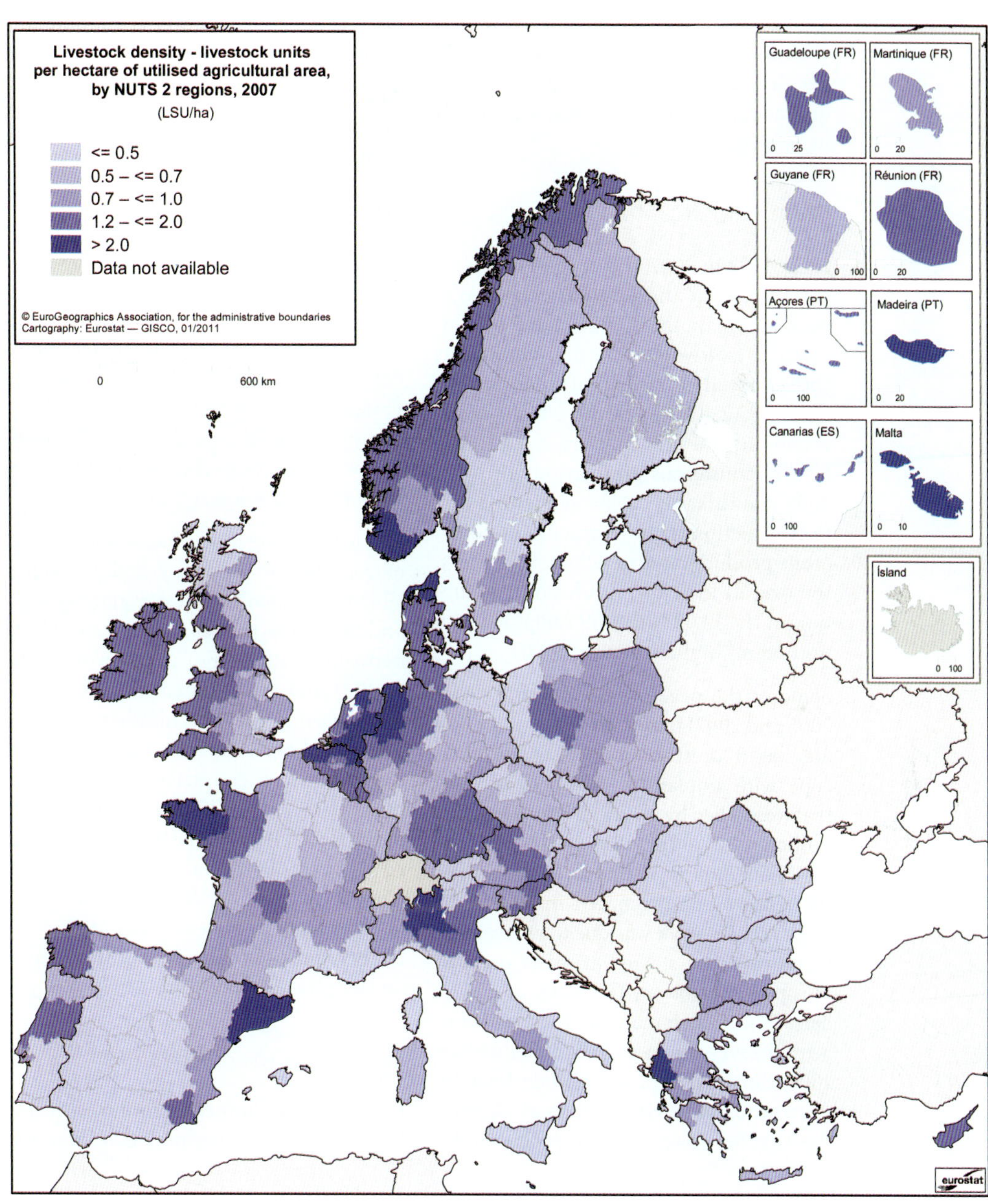

Source: Eurostat (aei_ps_ld)

8.5 Forestry

This subchapter presents statistics on forestry and logging in the European Union (EU). The EU-27 has approximately 178 million hectares of forests and other wooded land, corresponding to 42 % of its land area, and forest cover is gradually increasing.

Main statistical findings

From 1994 to 2007, there was a relatively steady rise in the level of roundwood production in the EU-27, both for coniferous (softwood) and non-coniferous (broadleaved or hardwood) species – see Figure 8.12. However, the effects of the economic and financial crisis led to the level of coniferous production falling in 2008 and this was confirmed with a further reduction in 2009, when non-coniferous production also fell. Nevertheless, the overall level of roundwood production in the EU-27 in 2009 remained 47.6 million m^3 higher than in 1994.

Some of the peaks (most recently 2000, 2005 and 2007) in roundwood production are due to forestry and logging having to cope with unplanned numbers of trees that were felled by severe storms. The 415.1 million m^3 of roundwood produced in the EU-27 in 2008 was almost 10 % less than the relative peak recorded in 2007. This latest relative peak was due to exceptional windthrows by storms in many parts of Europe – notably in Germany and Sweden – after which many more trees had to be removed from forests than planned. In 2009, roundwood production declined by a further 5.6 % to 391.9 million m^3. Among the Member States, Sweden produced the most roundwood (65.1 million m^3), followed by Germany, France and Finland (each producing between 42 million and 57 million m^3) - see Table 8.9.

Approximately 25 % of roundwood production is used as wood for fuel and 75 % is industrial roundwood that is used either for sawnwood and veneers, or for pulp and paper production.

Some 91.0 million m^3 of sawnwood were produced in the EU-27 in 2009, 40 % of which came from the two largest producing Member States namely Germany (22.7 %) and Sweden (17.8 %); Austria, Finland and France each accounted for around 9 % of the EU-27 total. The level of sawnwood production in the EU-27 in 2009 was 21.9 % lower than in 2007.

There is a strong link between the volume of roundwood produced and the value added generated by forestry and logging, and this is also the case concerning a link between the number of annual work units (AWU) and value added. However, it is worth noting that the number of AWU per area of exploited forest varies significantly between countries, ranging from more than ten AWU per 1 000 hectares in the Czech Republic to only around one AWU per 1 000 hectares in Finland and Norway (see Figure 8.14). Forestry and logging work in mountainous areas generally requires a higher labour input than on large tracts of flat land.

Data sources and availability

Eurostat, the Timber Committee of the United Nations Economic Commission for Europe (UNECE), the Forestry Section of the United Nations Food and Agriculture Organisation (FAO)and the International Tropical Timber Organisation (ITTO) collect and collate statistics on the production and trade of wood through their Joint Forest Sector Questionnaire. Each partner collects data from a different part of the world. Eurostat is responsible for data from the EU Member States and EFTA countries.

Roundwood production is a synonym for removals; it comprises all quantities of wood removed from forests and other wooded land or other felling sites during a given period; it is reported in cubic metres (m^3) underbark (in other words, excluding bark). Sawnwood production is wood that has been produced either by sawing lengthways or by a profile-chipping process and that exceeds 6 mm in thickness; it includes for example planks, beams, joists, boards, rafters, scantlings, laths, boxboards and lumber, in the following forms – unplaned, planed, and end-jointed; it is reported in cubic metres of solid volume.

Economic and employment data for forestry and logging are collected with a separate questionnaire that was developed in collaboration with Eurostat's national accountants; these statistics are part of integrated environmental and economic accounting for forests.

Context

Contrary to what is happening in many other parts of the world, forest cover in the EU-27 is slowly increasing. The area covered by forests and other wooded land increased by 0.3 % annually over the period 1990 to 2005. The EU-27's forests and other wooded land cover approximately the same proportion of land area as that used for agriculture.

Ecologically, the forests within the EU belong to many different biogeographical regions and have adapted to a variety of natural conditions, ranging from bogs to steppes and from lowland to alpine forests. Socioeconomically, they vary from small family holdings to state forests or large estates owned by companies, many as part of industrial wood supply chains; about 60 % of the EU-27's wooded land is privately owned.

In 2006 the European Commission presented an EU forest action plan (COM(2006) 302) which underpins support for sustainable forest management and the multi-functional role of forests. The plan is a framework for forest-related measures and is used to coordinate EU initiatives with the forest policies of the Member States. There are 18 key actions proposed – to be implemented jointly with the Member States during the period 2007 to 2011. The plan focuses on four main objectives:

- improving long-term competitiveness;
- improving and protecting the environment;
- contributing to the quality of life;
- fostering coordination and communication.

Table 8.9: Wood production
(1 000 m³)

	Roundwood production					Sawnwood production				
	1994	1999	2007	2008	2009	1994	1999	2007	2008	2009
EU-27	344 280	370 044	458 304	415 131	*391 897*	81 484	94 152	*116 533*	99 484	*91 011*
Belgium	:	4 400	5 015	4 700	4 395	:	1 056	1 555	1 400	1 255
Bulgaria	2 685	4 352	5 696	6 071	4 599	257	325	1 884	816	447
Czech Republic	11 950	14 203	18 508	16 187	*16 187*	3 158	3 584	5 454	4 636	*4 636*
Denmark	2 282	1 538	2 566	2 786	*2 786*	585	344	300	300	300
Germany	39 813	37 634	76 728	55 367	56 634	13 669	16 110	25 063	19 187	20 674
Estonia	3 550	6 704	4 500	4 860	4 860	305	1 200	1 584	1 120	1 150
Ireland	2 018	2 593	2 710	2 232	2 349	709	811	1 094	697	774
Greece	2 091	2 215	1 743	1 261	*1 261*	337	140	*108*	106	*106*
Spain	15 307	14 810	14 528	17 027	13 980	2 805	3 102	3 332	3 142	2 072
France	60 165	56 948	54 583	52 757	*54 108*	9 806	10 236	9 965	9 343	*7 886*
Italy	9 465	11 138	8 125	8 667	7 581	1 821	1 630	1 700	1 384	*1 220*
Cyprus	47	36	20	20	10	15	12	9	10	5
Latvia	5 700	14 008	12 173	8 806	10 409	950	3 640	3 459	2 545	2 500
Lithuania	3 992	4 924	6 195	5 594	5 460	760	1 150	1 380	1 109	1 011
Luxembourg	:	260	*291*	353	274	:	133	0	202	129
Hungary	4 527	5 231	5 640	5 276	5 244	418	308	235	207	102
Malta	0	0	0	0	0	0	0	0	0	0
Netherlands	1 043	1 044	1 022	1 117	1 016	387	362	273	243	210
Austria	14 960	14 083	21 317	21 795	16 727	7 587	9 628	11 816	10 835	8 455
Poland	18 776	24 268	35 935	34 273	34 629	5 321	4 137	4 417	3 786	3 594
Portugal	9 819	8 978	10 823	10 169	9 564	1 770	1 430	1 011	1 010	1 093
Romania	11 925	12 704	15 341	13 667	12 557	1 727	2 818	4 143	3 794	3 598
Slovenia	1 944	2 068	2 882	2 990	2 930	515	455	610	475	397
Slovakia	5 316	5 795	8 131	9 269	9 087	700	1 265	2 781	2 842	2 254
Finland	48 745	53 637	56 612	50 670	41 653	10 357	12 768	12 477	9 881	8 072
Sweden	55 900	58 700	78 200	70 800	65 100	13 842	14 858	18 738	17 601	16 200
United Kingdom	7 920	7 774	9 021	8 416	8 497	2 461	2 650	3 145	2 815	2 871
Iceland	0	:	0	:	:	0	:	0	:	:
Liechtenstein	25	:	25	28	25	:	:	10	10	4
Norway	8 744	8 424	10 465	10 324	8 884	2 417	2 336	2 402	2 228	1 850
Switzerland	4 679	4 737	5 520	4 950	4 577	1 345	1 525	1 541	1 540	1 481
Croatia	2 817	3 486	4 210	4 469	4 242	601	685	702	721	653
FRY of Macedonia	:	:	634	709	639	:	:	17	9	2
Turkey	16 845	16 608	18 319	19 420	19 430	5 163	5 039	6 599	6 175	5 853
Canada	183 224	193 890	160 792	134 947	107 266	44 687	50 412	52 284	41 548	32 820
Russia	115 670	143 600	207 000	181 400	151 400	33 750	19 100	24 258	21 618	18 974
United States	473 107	469 313	425 129	380 509	344 835	88 333	92 615	85 377	72 869	61 998

Source: Eurostat (for_remov and for_swpan)

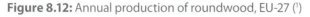

Figure 8.12: Annual production of roundwood, EU-27 (1)
(1 000 m³)

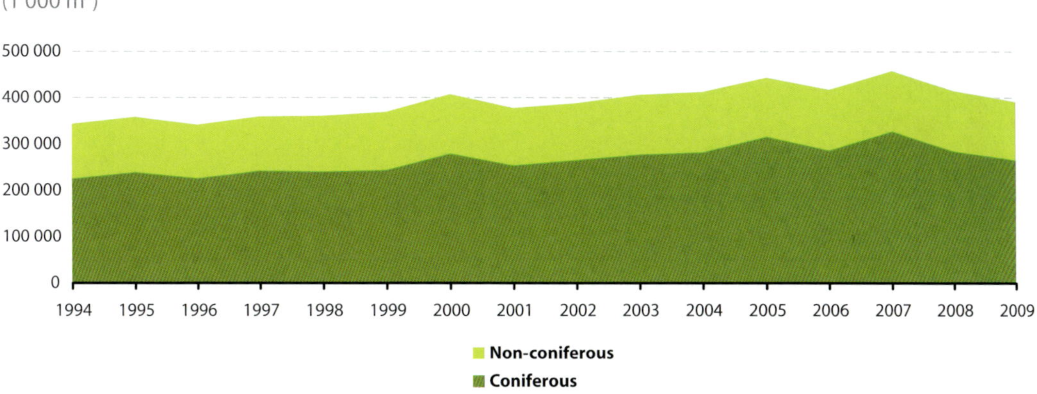

(1) 2000, 2001, 2007 and 2009, estimates.

Source: Eurostat (for_remov)

Figure 8.13: Roundwood production and gross value added of forestry and logging, 2008 (1)

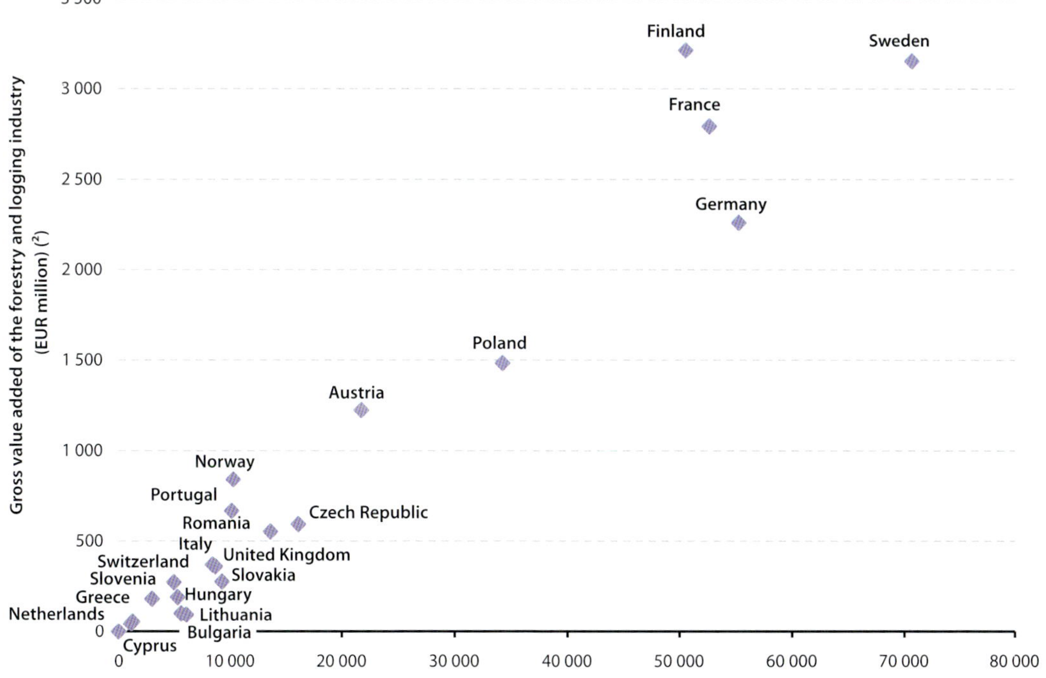

(1) Member States that are not shown, not available.
(2) France, Italy, Lithuania and Netherlands, 2006; Sweden, 2007.

Source: Eurostat (for_remov and for_ieeaf_cp)

Figure 8.14: Volume of work per area of exploited forest, 2008 (1)
(annual work units per 1 000 hectares)

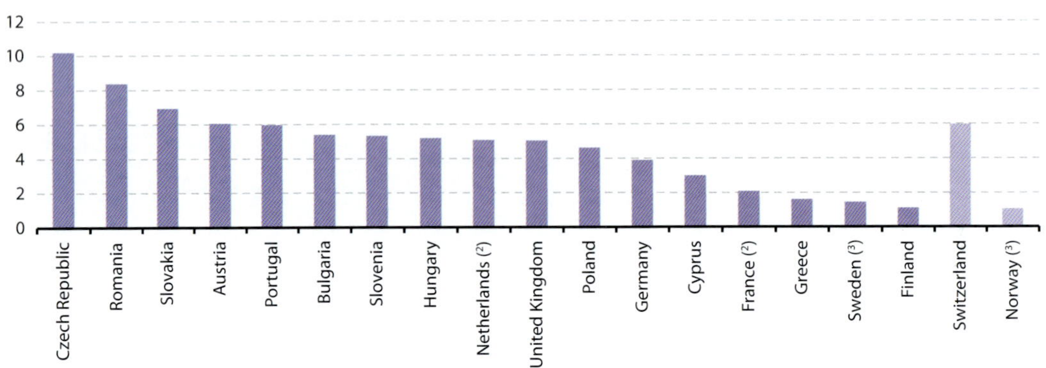

(1) Forest available for wood supply, 2005; an annual work unit is equivalent to the work performed by one person employed full-time over a year; Member States that are not shown, not available.
(2) 2006.
(3) 2007.

Source: Eurostat (for_awu and for_area), FAO Forest Resources Assessment 2005

8.6 Fisheries

Fish are a natural, biological, mobile (sometimes over wide distances) and renewable resource. Aside from fish farming, fish cannot be owned until they have been caught. For this reason, fish stocks continue to be regarded as a common resource, which needs to be managed collectively. This has led to a range of policies that regulate the amount of fishing, as well as the types of fishing techniques and gear used in fish capture. This subchapter gives an overview of recent statistics on fishing fleets, fish catches, and also on aquaculture production in the European Union (EU).

Main statistical findings

By far the largest fishing fleets among the EU Member States, in terms of power, were those from Italy, France, Spain and the United Kingdom; in 2008, the fishing fleets of each of these countries had a collective power of between 0.8 million kW and 1.1 million kW. In terms of tonnage, however, the Spanish fishing fleet was by far the largest, being about two and a half times the size of the fleets in the United Kingdom, France or Italy.

Total catches by the fishing fleets of Spain, Denmark, the United Kingdom and France accounted for more than half of all the catches made by EU-27 fishing fleets in 2008. This share has declined in recent years from about 60 % in 2000, mainly as a result of the sharp reduction in the share of the Danish catch, as well as (to a lesser degree) that of France and Spain (see Table 8.10). Since 1998, the total EU-27 catch has fallen every year with the exceptions of 2001 and 2008; the total catch by the EU-27 in 2008 was nearly 30 % less than in 1998. Around 70 % of the catches made by the EU-27 in 2008 were in the north east Atlantic, with the Mediterranean the second largest fishing area (see Figure 8.16).

The level of aquaculture production in the EU-27 remained relatively stable between 1.2 million tonnes and 1.4 million tonnes during the period 1998 to 2007. The five largest aquaculture producers among the EU Member States were Spain, France, Italy, the United Kingdom and Greece, which together accounted for around three quarters of total aquaculture production in 2007. Among the non-member countries included in Table 8.11 aquaculture production was extremely large in Norway – higher than the combined output of the three largest Member States; the aquaculture output of Turkey was also quite substantial. The development of aquaculture production between 1998 and 2007 followed different patterns across the EU Member States. Production in the Netherlands more than halved and there were also large percentage reductions in aquaculture output in Germany and Denmark, whereas, among the larger producers, aquaculture output rose by 90 % in Greece.

Data sources and availability

Fishery statistics are collected from official national sources either directly by Eurostat for the members of the European Economic Area (EEA) or indirectly through other international organisations for other countries. The data are collected using internationally agreed concepts and definitions developed by the coordinating working party on fishery statistics (CWP), comprising Eurostat and several other international organisations with responsibilities in fishery statistics. The flag of the fishing vessel is used as the primary indication of the nationality of the catch, though this concept may vary in certain circumstances.

In general, the data refer to the fishing fleet size on 31 December of the reference year. The data are derived from national registers of fishing vessels which are maintained pursuant to Regulation 26/2004 which contains information on the vessel characteristics to be recorded on the registers – the administrative file of fishing vessels maintained by the European Commission's Directorate-General for Maritime Affairs and Fisheries. There has been a transition in measuring the tonnage of the fishing fleet from gross registered tonnage (GRT) to that of gross tonnage (GT). This change, which has taken place at different speeds within the national administrations, gives rise to the possibility of non-comparability of data over time and of non-comparability between countries.

Catches of fishery products include items taken for all purposes (commercial, industrial, recreational and subsistence) by all types and classes of fishing units operating both in inland, inshore, offshore and in high-seas fishing areas. The catch is normally expressed in live weight and derived by the application of conversion factors to the landed or product weight. As such, catch statistics exclude quantities which are caught and taken from the water (that is, before processing) but which, for a variety of reasons, are not landed.

Geographical fishing areas are defined for a number of specific areas of water, including:

- the north east Atlantic, which is roughly the area to the east of 42°W longitude and north of 36°N latitude, including the waters of the Baltic Sea;
- the north west Atlantic, which is the region that is roughly the area to the west of 42°W longitude and north of 35°N latitude;
- the eastern central Atlantic, which is the region to the east of 40°W longitude between latitudes 36°N and 6°S;
- the Mediterranean and the Black Sea, which is also known as Food and Agriculture Organization (FAO) major fishing area 37, which comprises the Mediterranean Sea and the adjacent Black Sea.

Aquaculture is the farming of aquatic organisms including fish, molluscs, crustaceans and aquatic plants. Farming implies some form of intervention in the rearing process to enhance production, such as regular stocking, feeding and protection from predators. Farming also implies individual or corporate ownership of, or rights resulting from contractual arrangements to, the stock being cultivated.

Context

The first common European policy measures in the fishing sector date from 1970. They set rules for access to fishing grounds, markets and structures. All these measures became more significant when, in 1976, the Member States followed an international movement and agreed to extend their rights to marine resources from 12 to 200 miles from their coasts.

After years of difficult negotiations, the common fisheries policy (CFP), the EU's instrument for the management of fisheries and aquaculture, was born in 1983. The CFP sets maximum quantities of fish that can be safely caught every year: the total allowable catch (TAC). Each country's share is called a national quota.

The CFP was reformed in 2002 to deal with the environmental, economic and social dimensions of fishing. Common measures were agreed in four areas:

- the conservation of stocks/environmental impact – to protect fish resources by regulating the amount of fish taken from the sea, by allowing young fish to reproduce, and by ensuring that measures are respected;
- structures and fleet management (such as vessels, port facilities and fish processing plants) – to help the fishing and aquaculture sectors adapt their equipment and organisations to the constraints imposed by scarce resources and the market;
- the organisation of the market for fish in the EU – to maintain a common organisation of the market in fish products and to match supply and demand for the benefit of both producers and consumers;
- and external fisheries policy – to set-up fisheries agreements and to negotiate at an international level within regional and international fisheries organisations for common conservation measures in deep-sea fisheries.

The 2002 reform identified the need to limit fishing efforts, the level of catches, and to enforce certain technical measures. To ensure sustainable fishing, it is not only the quantity of fish taken from the sea that is important, but also their species, size, and the techniques used in catching them, as well as the areas where they are caught.

The European fisheries fund (EFF) has a budget of around EUR 3 800 million and covers the period 2007 to 2013. It aims to support the objectives of the CFP by:

- supporting sustainable exploitation of fisheries resources and a stable balance between these resources and the capacity of Community fishing fleet;
- strengthening the competitiveness and the viability of operators in the sector;
- promoting environmentally-friendly fishing and production methods;
- providing adequate support to people employed in the sector;
- fostering the sustainable development of fisheries areas.

Figure 8.15: Fishing fleet, 2008 (1)

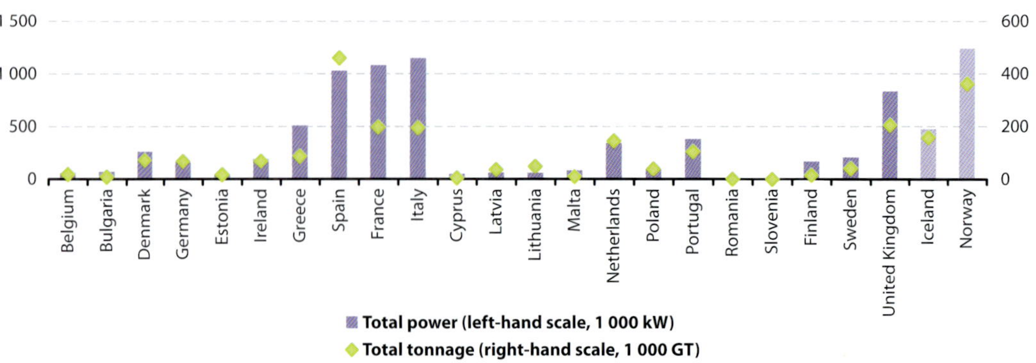

(1) The Czech Republic, Luxembourg, Hungary, Austria and Slovakia are landlocked countries without a marine fishing fleet.

Source: Eurostat (fish_fleet)

Figure 8.16: Catches by fishing region, EU-27, 2008
(%, based on tonnes)

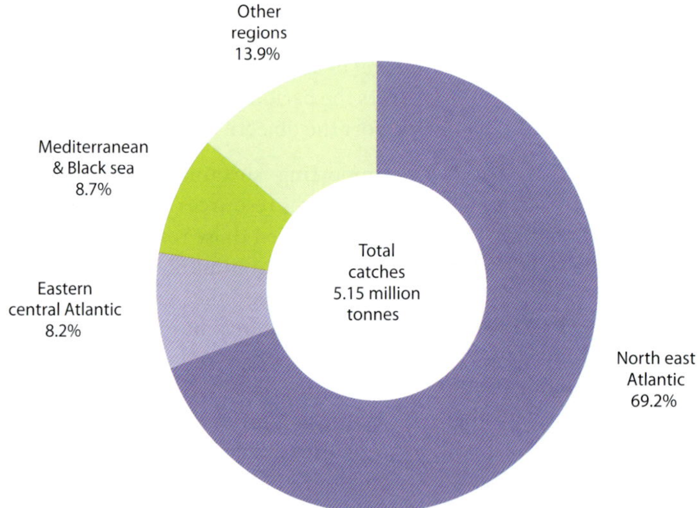

Source: Eurostat (fish_ca_main)

Table 8.10: Total catches in all fishing regions
(1 000 tonnes live weight)

	1998	1999	2000	2001	2002	2003	2004	2005	2006	2007	2008
EU-27	7 253	6 870	6 789	6 920	6 324	5 892	5 876	5 642	5 416	5 133	5 148
Belgium	31	30	30	30	29	27	27	25	23	25	23
Bulgaria	19	11	7	7	15	12	8	5	8	9	9
Czech Republic	4	4	5	5	5	5	5	4	5	4	4
Denmark	1 557	1 405	1 534	1 511	1 442	1 031	1 090	911	868	653	691
Germany	267	239	206	211	224	261	262	286	298	249	229
Estonia	119	112	113	105	101	79	88	100	87	99	101
Ireland	327	285	278	356	282	266	280	268	212	215	205
Greece	110	121	99	94	96	93	93	92	98	95	89
Spain	1 210	1 164	1 067	1 096	852	857	772	769	743	738	919
France	599	665	702	680	703	709	671	595	593	558	499
Italy	306	283	302	310	270	296	279	298	316	287	236
Cyprus	19	40	67	81	2	2	2	2	2	2	2
Latvia	102	125	136	128	114	115	125	151	140	155	158
Lithuania	67	73	79	151	150	157	162	140	155	187	183
Luxembourg	0	0	0	0	0	0	0	0	0	0	0
Hungary	7	8	7	7	7	7	7	8	8	7	7
Malta	1	1	1	1	1	1	1	1	1	1	1
Netherlands	533	511	496	518	464	526	522	549	436	414	417
Austria	0	0	0	0	0	0	0	0	0	0	0
Poland	242	236	218	225	223	180	192	155	145	152	143
Portugal	230	210	189	192	202	209	221	219	229	253	240
Romania	9	8	7	8	7	10	5	6	7	6	5
Slovenia	2	2	2	2	2	1	1	1	1	1	1
Slovakia	1	1	1	2	2	2	2	2	2	2	2
Finland	156	144	156	149	145	121	135	131	149	165	158
Sweden	411	351	339	312	295	287	270	256	269	238	231
United Kingdom	923	841	748	740	690	637	655	669	621	616	594
Iceland	1 700	1 754	2 000	2 001	2 145	2 002	1 750	1 661	1 345	1 421	1 307
Liechtenstein	0	0	0	0	0	0	0	0	0	0	0
Norway	2 861	2 628	2 700	2 687	2 740	2 549	2 525	2 393	2 256	2 378	2 436
Switzerland	2	2	2	2	2	2	2	1	1	1	2
Croatia	22	19	21	18	21	20	30	35	38	40	49
FYR of Macedonia	0	0	0	0	0	0	0	0	0	0	0
Turkey	487	574	503	528	567	508	550	426	533	632	494

Source: Eurostat (fish_ca_00)

Table 8.11: Aquaculture production
(1 000 tonnes live weight)

	1998	1999	2000	2001	2002	2003	2004	2005	2006	2007	2008
EU-27	1 376	1 429	1 399	1 386	1 272	1 343	1 311	1 261	1 283	1 307	:
Belgium	1	2	2	2	2	1	1	0	0	0	:
Bulgaria	4	8	4	3	2	4	2	3	3	4	:
Czech Republic	17	19	19	20	19	20	19	20	20	20	20
Denmark	42	43	44	42	32	38	43	39	28	31	:
Germany	73	80	66	53	50	74	57	45	38	45	44
Estonia	0	0	0	0	0	0	0	1	1	1	:
Ireland	42	44	51	61	63	63	58	60	53	53	:
Greece	60	84	95	98	88	101	97	106	113	113	115
Spain	314	318	309	309	255	268	293	219	295	285	:
France	268	265	267	252	252	240	243	245	238	237	:
Italy	209	210	217	218	184	192	118	181	174	181	:
Cyprus	1	1	2	2	2	2	2	2	4	3	:
Latvia	0	0	0	0	0	1	1	1	1	1	:
Lithuania	2	2	2	2	2	2	3	2	2	3	:
Luxembourg	0	0	0	0	0	0	0	0	0	0	0
Hungary	10	12	13	13	12	12	13	14	15	16	:
Malta	2	2	2	1	1	1	1	1	7	9	:
Netherlands	120	109	75	57	54	67	79	71	42	53	:
Austria	3	3	3	2	2	2	2	2	3	3	2
Poland	30	34	36	35	33	35	35	38	36	35	37
Portugal	8	6	8	8	8	8	7	7	8	7	6
Romania	10	9	10	11	9	9	8	7	9	10	:
Slovenia	1	1	1	1	1	1	2	1	1	1	1
Slovakia	1	1	1	1	1	1	1	1	1	1	:
Finland	16	15	15	16	15	13	13	14	13	13	:
Sweden	5	6	5	7	6	6	6	6	8	5	:
United Kingdom	137	155	152	171	179	182	207	173	172	174	:
Iceland	4	4	4	4	4	6	9	8	9	5	:
Norway	411	476	491	511	551	584	637	662	709	830	:
Switzerland	1	1	1	1	1	1	1	1	1	1	:
Croatia	6	6	7	10	9	8	10	11	14	13	:
FYR of Macedonia	1	2	2	1	1	1	1	1	1	1	:
Turkey	57	63	79	67	61	80	94	120	129	140	:

Source: Eurostat (fish_aq_q)

9 International trade

The European Union (EU) has a common trade policy (known as the common commercial policy). In other words, on trade issues, including issues related to the World Trade Organization (WTO), the EU acts as a single entity. In these cases, the European Commission negotiates trade agreements and represents Europe's interests on behalf of the EU's 27 Member States.

The EU Treaty (TEU) establishes the overall aims and objectives of the EU's trade policy: Article 3 sets out the general aims, including a highly competitive social market economy, aimed at full employment and social progress. Article 206 of the Treaty on the functioning of the Union (TFEU) explains how the common commercial policy must operate in principle: 'to contribute, in the common interest, to the harmonious development of world trade, the progressive abolition of restrictions on international trade and on foreign direct investment, and the lowering of customs and other barriers'. Article 207 of the TFEU sets out the scope, instruments and decision-making procedures. Article 218 of the TFEU establishes the current inter-institutional procedure for the conclusion of international agreements, principally by the Council.

The EU's trade policy aims to make the EU competitive in foreign markets. Being an open economy, the EU seeks to secure improved market access for its industries, services and investments, and to enforce the rules of free and fair trade. A coordinated trade policy takes on even greater importance in an era of globalisation, when economies and borders have opened up, leading to an increase in trade and capital movements, and the spread of information, knowledge and technology, often accompanied by deregulation. The economic impact of globalisation on the EU is felt through trade in goods and services, as well as through financial flows and the movement of persons linked to cross-border economic activity.

Globalisation acquires a higher profile when it is measured by actual trade flows. Within the EU, there are two main sources of trade statistics. One is international trade in goods statistics (ITGS), providing information on trade in merchandise goods, collected on the basis of customs and Intrastat declarations. This provides highly detailed information on the value and quantity (volumes) of international trade in goods as regards the type of commodity. The second main source is balance of payments statistics (BoP), which register all the transactions of an economy with the rest of the world. The current account of the BoP provides information on external trade in goods and services, as well as income (from employment and investment) and current transfers. For all these transactions, the BoP registers the value of exports (credits) and imports (debits).

Main statistical findings

In 2009 the EU-27 economy reversed its previous trend of progressively more integration with the international economy in terms of its level of credits and debits relative to GDP. The average value of EU-27 trade flows of goods corresponded to 9.7 % of GDP in 2009, down from an 11.3 % share the previous year. The level of trade integration of services also fell from 3.9 % of GDP in 2008, to 3.8 % in 2009. As can be seen from Figure 9.1 this was the first fall for goods after five years of increased integration, and for services the latest available data was the first reduction after four years of increased integration.

Data sources and availability

Subchapter 9.1 on international trade in goods gives an overview of the EU's trade in merchandise goods (within the ITGS framework) while Subchapter 9.2 on international trade in services provides an overview of its trade in services (within the BoP framework). The global financial and economic crisis which started in 2007 had a huge impact on the international exchange of goods and services and on the intensity of global financial flows and business activity. These effects are clearly evident in the data presented in these two subchapters. The upward trend of EU trade in goods and services ceased in 2009. However, as the crisis was a global economic shock, the EU-27 remains the largest global exporter and importer of goods.

Trade integration of goods and services is defined as the average value of debits and credits (summed and divided by two), presented in relation to GDP: the terms credits and debits are used for international trade in services which can roughly be considered to be equivalent to exports and imports. This indicator is calculated for both goods and services, based on balance of payments data; if the values increase over time, then the reporting territory became more integrated within the international economy. It is normal that smaller countries will display a higher degree of trade integration, as they are more likely to import a range of goods and services that are not produced within their domestic markets.

Figure 9.1: Trade integration, EU-27 (1)

(% of GDP)

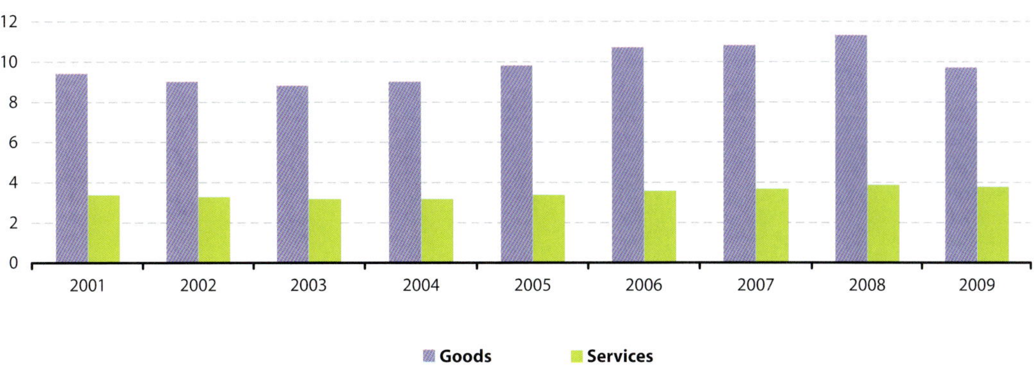

(1) EU-25 for 2001-2003.

Source: Eurostat (tsier120)

Table 9.1: Share of trade in goods and services in GDP, 2009 (1)
(% of GDP)

	Goods			Services		
	Exports	Imports	Balance	Exports	Imports	Balance
EU-27	9.4	10.1	-0.7	4.1	3.5	0.5
Euro area (EA-16)	14.4	14.0	0.5	5.2	4.9	0.3
Belgium	59.7	58.9	0.8	17.2	17.1	0.1
Bulgaria	33.6	45.3	-11.7	13.9	9.5	4.4
Czech Republic	58.8	53.8	5.0	10.6	9.9	0.7
Denmark	29.3	27.1	2.2	17.7	16.4	1.3
Germany	34.2	28.6	5.6	6.9	7.6	-0.7
Estonia	47.0	50.7	-3.8	22.8	13.2	9.5
Ireland	48.2	28.0	20.3	41.7	47.0	-5.3
Greece	*6.6*	*19.8*	*-13.2*	*11.6*	*6.2*	*5.4*
Spain	15.2	19.5	-4.3	8.4	6.0	2.4
France	17.8	20.2	-2.3	5.4	4.8	0.6
Italy	19.2	19.1	0.1	4.8	5.5	-0.7
Cyprus	8.8	33.8	-25.0	41.7	17.3	24.4
Latvia	27.7	34.3	-6.6	14.7	8.5	6.3
Lithuania	44.3	47.2	-2.9	10.2	7.9	2.2
Luxembourg	29.6	37.6	-8.0	116.5	68.6	47.8
Hungary	63.2	58.8	4.3	14.0	12.4	1.6
Malta	30.2	43.8	-13.6	42.3	26.6	15.6
Netherlands	52.7	46.6	6.1	11.7	10.7	1.0
Austria	:	:	:	13.9	9.7	4.2
Poland	32.3	33.3	-1.0	6.7	5.6	1.1
Portugal	19.0	29.5	-10.4	9.7	6.2	3.6
Romania	25.1	31.0	-5.9	6.1	6.4	-0.3
Slovenia	45.7	47.7	-2.0	12.2	9.0	3.2
Slovakia	62.7	60.8	1.9	7.1	9.1	-2.0
Finland	26.2	24.2	2.1	10.7	9.8	0.9
Sweden	32.7	29.5	3.3	15.0	11.4	3.6
United Kingdom	16.3	22.2	-5.9	10.7	7.6	3.2
Iceland	33.2	27.3	5.9	18.6	16.1	2.5
Norway	32.1	17.5	14.6	10.0	10.0	0.1
Croatia	16.9	33.3	-16.3	18.6	6.1	12.5
Turkey	17.9	21.8	-4.0	5.4	2.7	2.6
Japan (2)	15.3	14.6	0.8	3.1	3.5	-0.4
United States (2)	8.9	14.7	-5.8	3.8	2.8	1.0

(1) EU-27, extra-EU flows; euro area, extra-euro area flows; Member States and other countries, flows with the rest of the world.
(2) 2008.

Source: Eurostat (bop_q_eu, bop_q_euro, bop_q_c and tec00001)

9.1 International trade in goods

The European Union (EU) accounts for just under a fifth of the world's trade in goods. The value of external trade in goods significantly exceeds that of services, which by their nature are harder to move across borders.

This subchapter discusses the evolution in the EU's international trade in goods. It considers the EU's share in world import and export markets, intra-EU trade, the EU's main trading partners, and the most widely traded product categories.

Main statistical findings

External trade forms an increasing part of the world economy, through the influence of globalisation, as well as rapidly growing exchanges with developing economies such as China and India, and some of the countries formed out of the Soviet Union – in particular those where indigenous energy supplies are of particular importance.

The steady increase in EU-27 imports and exports between 2003 and 2008 was sharply reversed in 2009, as EU-27's total trade fell by EUR 581 157 million to EUR 2 293 607 million. Exports fell by 16.4 % to EUR 1 094 411 million, while imports fell more sharply (23.4 %) to EUR 1 199 196 million. These changes resulted in a large drop in the EU-27's trade deficit to EUR 104 785 million, less than half that recorded in 2008 and the lowest since 2004.

Looking in more detail and using monthly statistics, the marked decrease in EU-27 imports and exports gathered momentum during the second hall of 2008. Seasonally adjusted exports peaked in April 2008 and fell by 23 % to their lowest point in January 2009. The fall in imports started three months later, in July 2008, and reached their lowest value in May 2009, having fallen 32 %. After these low points both EU-27 imports and exports started to follow a slow upward trend.

Trade in goods between Member States (intra-EU trade) was valued in terms of dispatches at EUR 2 194 341 million in 2009, a little over twice the value of exports from the EU-27 to non-member countries. The importance of the internal market was underlined by the fact that for each of the Member States, intra-EU trade of goods was higher than extra-EU trade (Figure 9.6). However, the proportion of total trade in goods accounted for by intra-EU and extra-EU flows varied considerably among the Member States, reflecting to some degree historical ties and geographical location. The highest shares of intra-EU trade (about 80 %) were recorded for the Czech Republic, Slovakia and Luxembourg, with this ratio falling to less than 60 % in the United Kingdom, Italy, and Malta.

Intra-EU trade (measured by dispatches) decreased in 2009 more markedly than extra-EU exports (-19 % against -16 %). Considering arrivals and dispatches together, the biggest reductions in intra-EU trade were registered by Latvia, Lithuania, Estonia and Finland, down by about 30 %.

Germany recorded the highest trade surplus (extra and intra-EU combined) for goods in 2009, valued at EUR 134 780 million. This represented a narrowing of the German surplus by EUR 42 745 million compared with 2008. The next highest trade surplus in 2009 (EUR 39 244 million) was recorded for the Netherlands, followed by Ireland (EUR 37 753 million). In contrast, the highest trade deficit in goods (EUR 93 189 million) was recorded by the United Kingdom, although this figure represented a considerable narrowing of the deficit compared with 2008. Indeed, trade deficits for a number of Member States narrowed in 2009, none more so than Spain (from EUR 94 717 million to EUR 49 526 million).

The sharp fall in EU-27 exports in 2009 was distributed unevenly across trading partners. The United States share of EU-27 exports remained steady at just under a fifth of the total between 2008 and 2009, while China's share rose from 6.0 % to 7.5 % to become the third largest destination for EU- 27 exports after the United States and Switzerland. China was the only major destination to which EU-27 exports rose between 2008 and 2009, though by only a third of the annual rate seen over the period from 2000 to 2009.

Imports into the EU-27 were reduced from all main providers between 2008 and 2009. Imports from China, by far the largest source, fell by EUR 33 178 million, while those from the United States and Russia, the second and third largest sources, fell by EUR 27 237 million and EUR 62 510 million respectively. This fall in imports from Russia was the greatest seen in imports from any major trading partner, in both absolute and percentage terms – a decrease of over a third – and may, at least in part, be attributed to falling oil and natural gas prices.

The overall fall of EUR 215 407 million in EU-27 exports was overwhelmingly due to declines in the two largest product groups, machinery and vehicles and other manufactured goods, which fell by EUR 114 484 million and EUR 58 407 million respectively. In contrast, exports of the next largest product group, chemicals, fell by only EUR 3 279 million. Machinery and transport equipment also recorded the largest trade surplus (EUR 112 552 million) in 2009. Of the main product groups, raw materials experienced the largest fall in imports in relative terms (-37.5 %). Imports of energy products fell by EUR 166 281 million, or 36.4 %. It should be noted that comparisons over time reflect both changes in quantity and price levels.

Data sources and availability

Trade in goods statistics measure the value and quantity of goods traded between Member States of the EU (known as intra-EU trade) and goods traded by EU Member States with non-member countries (known as extra-EU trade). They are the official source of information about imports, exports and the trade balance of the EU, its Member States and the euro area.

Statistics are disseminated for each declaring country with respect to each partner country, for several product classifications. One of the most common is the Standard international trade classification (SITC Rev. 4) of the United Nations (UN); this classification allows a comparison of external trade statistics to be made on a worldwide basis.

In extra-EU trade statistics, the data shown for the EU-27 treat this entity as a single trading block and report exports from the whole of the EU to the rest of the world and imports from the rest of the world into the EU. In contrast, when reporting data for individual Member States, external trade flows are generally presented in terms of world trade flows (including both intra-EU and extra-EU partners).

The definitions of extra-EU trade are as follows:

- imports are goods which enter the statistical territory of the EU from a non-member country and are placed under the customs procedure for free circulation (as a general rule goods intended for consumption), inward processing, or processing under customs control (goods for working, processing), either immediately or after a period in a customs warehouse;
- exports are goods which leave the statistical territory of the EU for a non-member country after being placed under the customs procedure for exports (definitive export), outward processing, or re-exportation following either inward processing or processing under customs control.

Statistics on trade with non-member countries do not, therefore, include goods in transit or those placed under a customs procedure for bonded warehousing or temporary entry (for fairs, exhibitions, tests, etc.), nor do they include re-export following entry under one of these procedures.

Statistics on trade between the Member States (intra-EU trade) cover the arrivals and dispatches of goods recorded by each Member State. Arrivals and dispatches are defined as follows:

- arrivals are goods in free circulation within the EU which enter the statistical territory of a given Member State;
- dispatches are goods in free circulation within the EU which leave the statistical territory of a given Member State to enter another Member State.

Customs records are the traditional source of statistical data on trade in goods. The beginning of the single market on 1 January 1993, with its removal of customs formalities between Member States, made it necessary to adopt a new data collection system, Intrastat, as the basis for statistics on intra-EU trade. In the Intrastat system, statistical data are collected directly from trade operators, which send a monthly declaration to the relevant national statistical administration.

The statistical values of extra-EU trade and intra-EU trade are recorded at their free-on-board (FOB) value for exports/dispatches and their cost, insurance and freight (CIF) value for imports/arrivals. The values reported comprise only those subsidiary costs (freight and insurance) which relate, for exports/dispatches, to the journey within the territory of the Member State from which the goods are exported/dispatched and, for imports/arrivals, to the journey outside the territory of the Member State into which the goods are imported/enter.

Context

Trade in goods statistics are used extensively by public-body decision makers at an international, EU and national level. Businesses can use international trade data to carry out market research and define their commercial strategy. In the case of EU institutions, international trade statistics help in the preparation of multilateral and bilateral trade negotiations, in defining and implementing anti-dumping policies, for the purposes of macro-economic and monetary policies and in evaluating the progress of the single market, or the integration of European economies.

The EU has a common trade policy whereby the European Commission negotiates trade agreements and represents the EU's interests on behalf of its 27 Member States. The European Commission consults Member States through an advisory committee which discusses the full range of trade policy issues affecting the EU including multilateral, bilateral and unilateral instruments.

Globally, multilateral trade issues are dealt with under the auspices of the World Trade Organization (WTO). Its membership covers 153 countries (as of July 2008), with several candidate members in the process of joining. The WTO sets the global rules for trade, provides a forum for trade negotiations, and for settling disputes between members. The European Commission negotiates with its WTO partners and participated in the latest round of WTO multilateral trade negotiations, known as the Doha Development Agenda (DDA). However, having missed deadlines to conclude these talks in 2005 and again in 2006, the Doha round of talks broke down again at a WTO meeting in July 2008. At the time of writing, the future of the Doha round is uncertain.

Figure 9.2: Main players for external trade, 2009
(EUR 1 000 million)

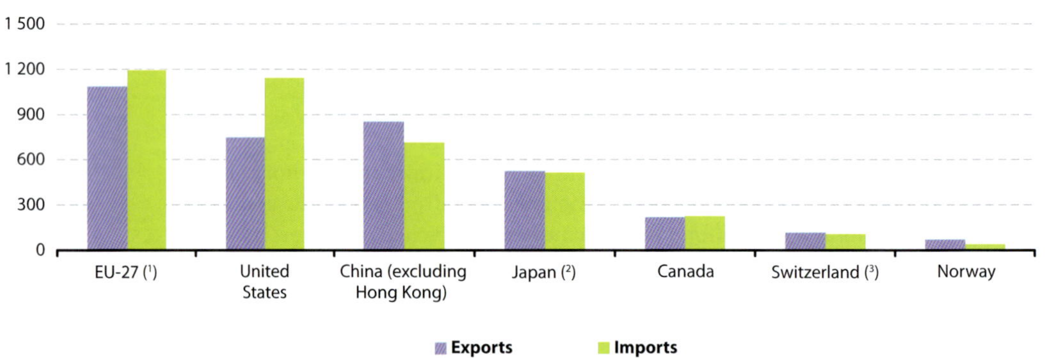

(1) External trade flows with extra EU-27.
(2) 2008 instead of 2009.
(3) Including Liechtenstein.

Source: Eurostat (ext_lt_intertrd)

Table 9.2: Main players for external trade
(EUR 1 000 million)

	Exports			Imports			Trade balance		
	1999	2004	2009	1999	2004	2009	1999	2004	2009
EU-27 (¹)	683	953	1 094	743	1 028	1 199	-60	-75	-105
Norway	43	66	78	32	39	44	11	27	34
Switzerland (²)	75	95	124	75	90	112	0	6	12
Canada	224	255	226	202	220	230	22	35	-4
China (excluding Hong Kong)	183	477	862	155	451	721	27	26	141
Japan (³)	392	455	531	291	366	518	101	89	13
United States	650	658	758	994	1 226	1 148	-344	-569	-391

(¹) External trade flows with extra EU-27.
(²) Including Liechtenstein.
(³) 2008 instead of 2009.

Source: Eurostat (ext_lt_intertrd)

Figure 9.3: Shares in the world market for exports, 2008
(% share of world exports)

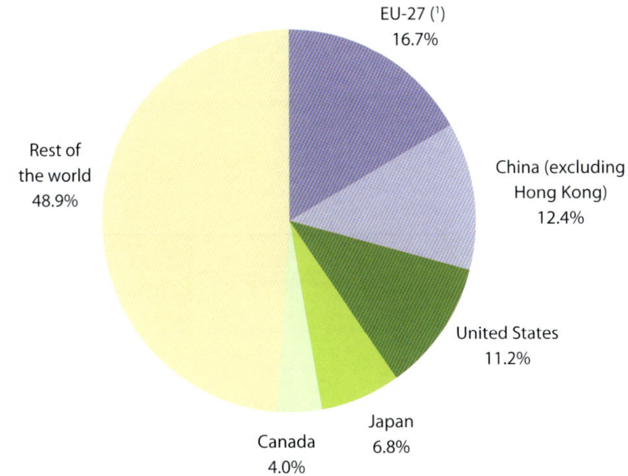

(¹) External trade flows with extra EU-27.

Source: Eurostat (ext_lt_introle)

Figure 9.4: Shares in the world market for imports, 2008
(% share of world imports)

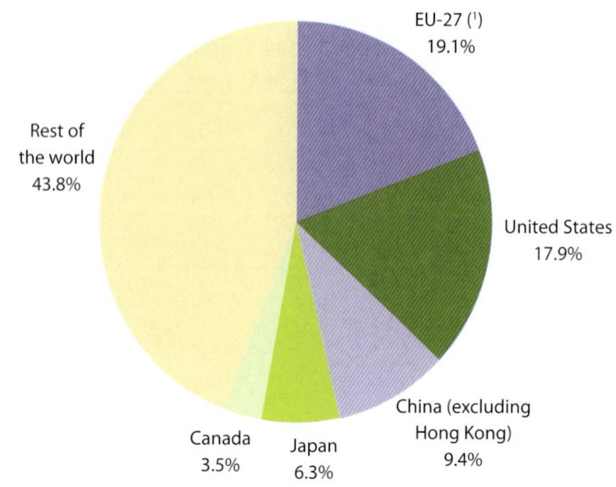

(1) External trade flows with extra EU-27.

Source: Eurostat (ext_lt_introle)

Figure 9.5: Development of external trade, EU-27 (1)
(EUR 1 000 million)

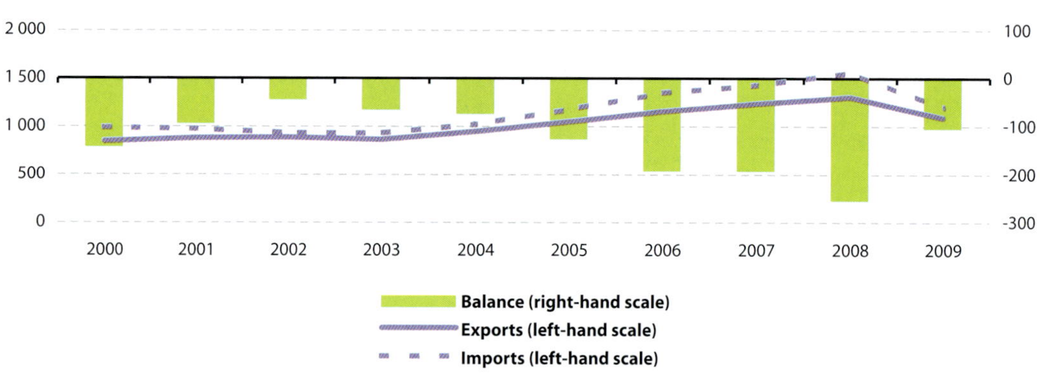

(1) External trade flows with extra EU-27.

Source: Eurostat (ext_lt_intertrd)

Table 9.3: External trade
(EUR 1 000 million)

	Exports			Imports			Balance	
	2008	2009	2008-09 growth rate (%)	2008	2009	2008-09 growth rate (%)	2008	2009
EU-27 (¹)	1 309.8	1 094.4	-16.4	1 564.9	1 199.2	-23.4	-255.1	-104.8
Belgium	320.8	265.2	-17.3	317.0	252.3	-20.4	3.8	12.8
Bulgaria	15.2	11.8	-22.5	25.1	16.7	-33.3	-9.9	-4.9
Czech Republic	99.8	81.0	-18.8	96.6	75.3	-22.0	3.2	5.7
Denmark	79.3	66.9	-15.6	74.8	59.2	-20.9	4.5	7.7
Germany	983.3	807.5	-17.9	805.7	672.7	-16.5	177.5	134.8
Estonia	8.5	6.5	-23.5	10.9	7.3	-33.4	-2.4	-0.8
Ireland	85.5	82.7	-3.2	57.1	45.0	-21.2	28.4	37.8
Greece	17.4	14.4	-17.6	61.0	42.9	-29.7	-43.5	-28.5
Spain	191.4	156.6	-18.2	286.1	206.2	-27.9	-94.7	-49.5
France	418.7	347.5	-17.0	486.5	401.4	-17.5	-67.7	-53.8
Italy	369.0	290.8	-21.2	382.1	295.9	-22.6	-13.0	-5.1
Cyprus	1.1	0.9	-18.8	7.2	5.6	-22.4	-6.1	-4.7
Latvia	6.9	5.5	-20.0	11.0	7.0	-36.0	-4.1	-1.5
Lithuania	16.1	11.8	-26.6	21.1	13.1	-37.9	-5.1	-1.3
Luxembourg	17.2	14.9	-13.4	21.5	17.5	-18.6	-4.3	-2.6
Hungary	73.8	60.0	-18.6	74.1	56.0	-24.3	-0.3	4.0
Malta	2.0	1.5	-24.9	3.3	2.6	-20.5	-1.2	-1.1
Netherlands	433.7	357.0	-17.7	395.0	317.7	-19.6	38.7	39.2
Austria	123.3	98.7	-20.0	125.3	102.8	-18.0	-2.0	-4.1
Poland	115.9	96.4	-16.8	142.0	105.1	-26.0	-26.1	-8.7
Portugal	37.9	31.1	-18.1	61.2	50.1	-18.1	-23.2	-19.0
Romania	33.7	29.1	-13.5	57.1	38.9	-31.9	-23.5	-9.8
Slovenia	23.2	18.8	-19.1	25.2	19.0	-24.5	-2.0	-0.2
Slovakia	48.4	40.1	-17.0	50.3	39.6	-21.1	-1.9	0.5
Finland	65.6	45.0	-31.3	62.4	43.6	-30.1	3.2	1.4
Sweden	124.6	94.1	-24.5	114.6	85.9	-25.0	10.1	8.2
United Kingdom	312.5	253.0	-19.1	430.4	346.2	-19.6	-117.8	-93.2
Iceland	3.7	2.9	-20.3	4.2	2.6	-38.0	-0.5	0.3
Norway	113.6	78.2	-31.2	60.4	44.4	-26.5	53.1	33.7
Switzerland (²)	136.1	124.1	-8.8	124.5	111.9	-10.1	11.6	12.2
Canada	318.2	226.1	-28.9	285.4	230.2	-19.4	32.8	-4.0
China	972.7	861.5	-11.4	770.0	720.9	-6.4	202.7	140.6
Japan	531.3	:	:	518.4	:	:	12.8	:
United States	883.8	757.6	-14.3	1 471.9	1 148.5	-22.0	-588.1	-390.9

(¹) External trade flows with extra EU-27.
(²) Including Liechtenstein.

Source: Eurostat (tet00002)

Table 9.4: Extra EU-27 trade, 2009

	Exports		Imports		Trade balance (EUR 1 000 million)
	(EUR 1 000 million)	Share of EU-27 exports (%)	(EUR 1 000 million)	Share of EU-27 imports (%)	
EU-27	1 094.4	100.0	1 199.2	100.0	-104.8
Belgium	63.9	5.8	73.0	6.1	-9.1
Bulgaria	4.2	0.4	6.6	0.6	-2.4
Czech Republic	12.4	1.1	16.6	1.4	-4.2
Denmark	21.8	2.0	17.9	1.5	3.9
Germany	299.0	27.3	234.8	19.6	64.2
Estonia	2.0	0.2	1.4	0.1	0.6
Ireland	31.9	2.9	15.5	1.3	16.4
Greece	5.4	0.5	15.3	1.3	-9.9
Spain	48.9	4.5	79.4	6.6	-30.5
France	131.6	12.0	123.7	10.3	7.8
Italy	123.8	11.3	126.5	10.6	-2.8
Cyprus	0.3	0.0	1.6	0.1	-1.3
Latvia	1.8	0.2	1.7	0.1	0.1
Lithuania	4.2	0.4	5.4	0.4	-1.2
Luxembourg	1.9	0.2	4.9	0.4	-3.1
Hungary	12.7	1.2	17.5	1.5	-4.8
Malta	0.9	0.1	0.8	0.1	0.1
Netherlands	80.7	7.4	161.9	13.5	-81.1
Austria	27.8	2.5	22.6	1.9	5.2
Poland	20.0	1.8	29.4	2.5	-9.4
Portugal	7.8	0.7	11.0	0.9	-3.2
Romania	7.5	0.7	10.4	0.9	-2.9
Slovenia	5.8	0.5	5.5	0.5	0.2
Slovakia	5.7	0.5	10.0	0.8	-4.3
Finland	20.0	1.8	15.2	1.3	4.7
Sweden	39.1	3.6	27.4	2.3	11.7
United Kingdom	113.5	10.4	163.0	13.6	-49.5

Source: Eurostat (ext_lt_intratrd)

Table 9.5: Intra EU-27 trade
(EUR 1 000 million)

	Dispatches		Arrivals		Balance	
	2004	2009	2004	2009	2004	2009
EU-27	2 071.8	2 194.3	1 993.4	2 126.3	-	-
Belgium	190.1	201.2	167.2	179.3	22.8	21.9
Bulgaria	5.0	7.6	6.6	10.1	-1.7	-2.5
Czech Republic	48.3	68.6	45.2	58.8	3.2	9.9
Denmark	43.8	45.1	38.8	41.3	4.9	3.9
Germany	472.3	508.4	377.7	437.9	94.5	70.5
Estonia	3.8	4.5	4.9	5.8	-1.1	-1.3
Ireland	53.0	50.8	32.7	29.5	20.3	21.3
Greece	7.9	9.0	25.5	27.6	-17.6	-18.6
Spain	109.2	107.8	141.1	126.7	-31.9	-19.0
France	239.8	215.9	263.6	277.6	-23.8	-61.7
Italy	175.9	167.0	177.6	169.3	-1.6	-2.3
Cyprus	0.5	0.6	3.1	4.1	-2.6	-3.5
Latvia	2.5	3.7	4.3	5.3	-1.8	-1.6
Lithuania	5.0	7.6	6.3	7.8	-1.3	-0.2
Luxembourg	11.8	13.0	12.2	12.5	-0.5	0.5
Hungary	37.1	47.3	33.3	38.6	3.8	8.8
Malta	1.0	0.6	2.1	1.8	-1.1	-1.1
Netherlands	229.5	276.2	136.6	155.8	92.9	120.4
Austria	70.0	70.8	79.8	80.2	-9.8	-9.3
Poland	48.5	76.4	54.3	75.7	-5.9	0.7
Portugal	23.1	23.3	34.1	39.1	-11.0	-15.8
Romania	14.1	21.6	17.3	28.5	-3.2	-6.9
Slovenia	8.9	13.0	11.7	13.5	-2.8	-0.5
Slovakia	19.3	34.4	18.9	29.6	0.4	4.8
Finland	28.7	25.1	27.9	28.4	0.9	-3.3
Sweden	58.5	55.0	58.3	58.5	0.2	-3.5
United Kingdom	164.2	139.5	212.0	183.2	-47.8	-43.7

Source: Eurostat (tet00039)

Figure 9.6: Intra and extra EU-27 trade, 2009
(imports plus exports, % share of total trade)

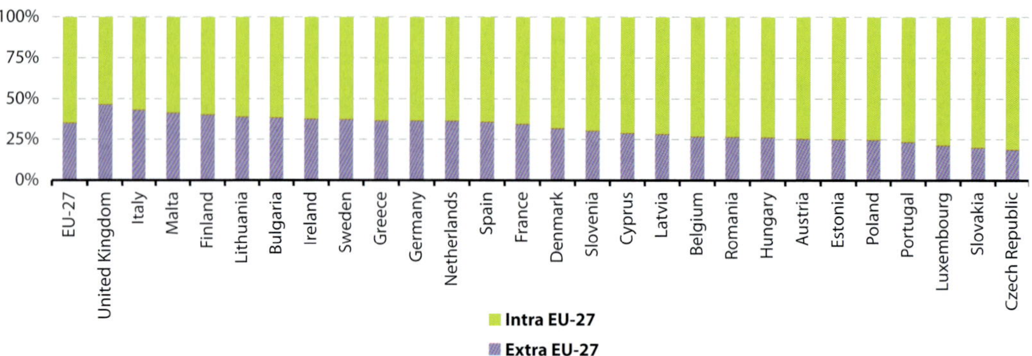

Source: Eurostat (ext_lt_intratrd)

Figure 9.7: Main trading partners for exports, EU-27, 2009
(% share of extra EU-27 exports)

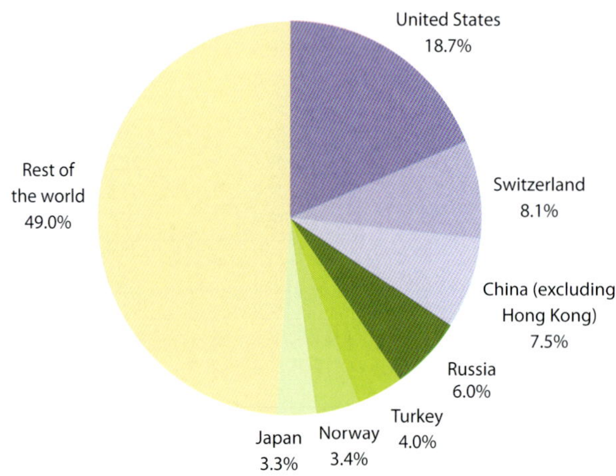

Source: Eurostat (ext_lt_maineu)

Figure 9.8: Main trading partners for imports, EU-27, 2009
(% share of extra EU-27 imports)

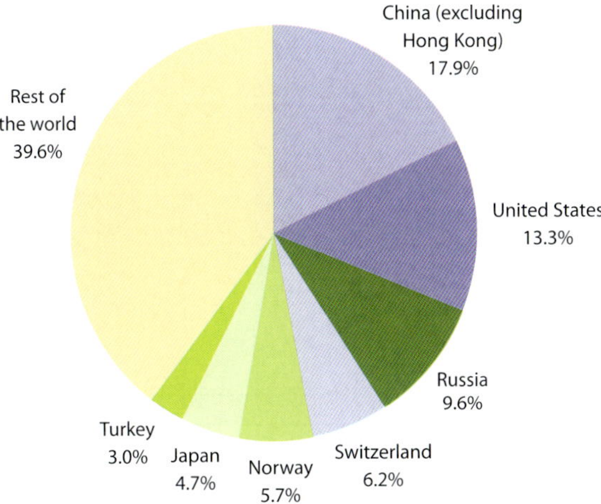

Source: Eurostat (ext_lt_maineu)

Table 9.6: Extra EU-27 trade by main trading partners, EU-27 (¹)
(EUR 1 000 million)

	2000	2001	2002	2003	2004	2005	2006	2007	2008	2009
EXPORTS										
Extra EU-27	849.7	884.7	891.9	869.2	953.0	1 052.7	1 160.1	1 240.5	1 309.8	1 094.4
United States	238.2	245.6	247.9	227.3	235.5	252.7	269.1	261.5	250.1	204.7
China (excl. Hong Kong)	25.9	30.7	35.1	41.5	48.4	51.8	63.8	71.9	78.4	81.6
Russia	22.7	31.6	34.4	37.2	46.0	56.7	72.3	89.1	105.0	65.5
Switzerland	72.5	76.5	72.8	71.4	75.2	82.6	87.8	92.8	98.0	88.3
Norway	26.4	27.2	28.2	27.7	30.8	33.8	38.5	43.6	43.8	37.5
Japan	45.5	45.5	43.5	41.0	43.4	43.7	44.8	43.7	42.3	35.9
Turkey	31.9	21.9	26.6	30.9	40.1	44.6	50.0	52.7	54.1	43.7
South Korea (Republic of)	16.7	15.8	17.7	16.4	17.9	20.2	22.9	24.8	25.6	21.5
India	13.7	13.0	14.3	14.6	17.2	21.3	24.4	29.5	31.6	27.5
Brazil	16.9	18.6	15.7	12.4	14.2	16.1	17.7	21.3	26.3	21.6
IMPORTS										
Extra EU-27	992.7	979.1	937.0	935.3	1 027.5	1 179.6	1 352.8	1 433.4	1 564.9	1 199.2
United States	206.3	203.3	182.6	158.1	159.4	163.5	175.5	181.7	186.8	159.5
China (excl. Hong Kong)	74.6	82.0	90.1	106.2	128.7	160.3	194.9	232.7	247.9	214.8
Russia	63.8	65.9	64.5	70.7	84.0	112.6	140.9	144.5	177.8	115.3
Switzerland	62.6	63.6	61.7	59.1	62.0	66.6	71.6	77.0	80.3	73.8
Norway	47.2	46.4	48.0	51.0	55.3	67.2	79.2	76.7	95.9	68.6
Japan	92.1	81.1	73.7	72.4	74.7	74.1	77.5	78.4	75.1	55.8
Turkey	18.7	22.1	24.6	27.3	32.7	36.1	41.7	47.0	46.0	36.1
South Korea (Republic of)	27.0	23.3	24.6	26.0	30.7	34.5	40.8	41.4	39.6	32.1
India	12.8	13.5	13.7	14.1	16.4	19.1	22.6	26.6	29.5	25.4
Brazil	18.7	19.6	18.4	19.1	21.7	24.1	27.2	32.8	35.9	25.7
TRADE BALANCE										
Extra EU-27	-143.0	-94.4	-45.1	-66.0	-74.6	-126.8	-192.7	-192.9	-255.1	-104.8
United States	31.9	42.3	65.3	69.2	76.1	89.2	93.6	79.7	63.4	45.2
China (excl. Hong Kong)	-48.8	-51.3	-55.1	-64.7	-80.3	-108.5	-131.1	-160.7	-169.5	-133.1
Russia	-41.0	-34.3	-30.1	-33.5	-37.9	-55.9	-68.6	-55.3	-72.7	-49.8
Switzerland	10.0	12.9	11.1	12.3	13.2	16.0	16.1	15.9	17.7	14.5
Norway	-20.8	-19.2	-19.9	-23.4	-24.5	-33.4	-40.7	-33.1	-52.2	-31.1
Japan	-46.6	-35.6	-30.2	-31.4	-31.3	-30.3	-32.7	-34.7	-32.8	-19.9
Turkey	13.2	-0.2	2.0	3.6	7.4	8.5	8.3	5.7	8.1	7.7
South Korea (Republic of)	-10.2	-7.4	-6.9	-9.6	-12.7	-14.2	-18.0	-16.6	-14.0	-10.6
India	0.8	-0.5	0.6	0.5	0.8	2.2	1.8	2.9	2.1	2.1
Brazil	-1.8	-1.0	-2.6	-6.7	-7.6	-8.1	-9.5	-11.5	-9.5	-4.1

(¹) Partners are sorted according to the sum of imports and exports in 2009.

Source: Eurostat (tet00040)

Table 9.7: Extra EU-27 trade by main products, EU-27

	1999		2004		2009	
	(EUR 1 000 million)	(%)	(EUR 1 000 million)	(%)	(EUR 1 000 million)	(%)
EXPORTS						
Total	683.1	100.0	953.0	100.0	1 094.4	100.0
Food, drinks & tobacco	41.8	6.1	48.6	5.1	62.6	5.7
Raw materials	14.5	2.1	21.0	2.2	27.8	2.5
Mineral fuels, lubricants	15.7	2.3	32.9	3.5	57.2	5.2
Chemicals & related prod.	97.4	14.3	152.6	16.0	195.5	17.9
Other manufactured goods	181.1	26.5	246.2	25.8	258.4	23.6
Machinery & transport equip.	314.5	46.1	430.1	45.1	454.7	41.5
IMPORTS						
Total	743.3	100.0	1 027.5	100.0	1 199.2	100.0
Food, drinks & tobacco	50.3	6.8	58.8	5.7	73.7	6.1
Raw materials	38.9	5.2	48.5	4.7	47.2	3.9
Mineral fuels, lubricants	84.1	11.3	183.4	17.9	290.1	24.2
Chemicals & related prod.	58.7	7.9	88.5	8.6	112.4	9.4
Other manufactured goods	200.3	26.9	262.3	25.5	295.4	24.6
Machinery & transport equip.	288.2	38.8	354.5	34.5	342.2	28.5
TRADE BALANCE						
Total	-60.2	-	-74.6	-	-104.8	-
Food, drinks & tobacco	-8.5	-	-10.3	-	-11.1	-
Raw materials	-24.4	-	-27.4	-	-19.5	-
Mineral fuels, lubricants	-68.5	-	-150.5	-	-232.9	-
Chemicals & related prod.	38.8	-	64.1	-	83.1	-
Other manufactured goods	-19.1	-	-16.1	-	-37.0	-
Machinery & transport equip.	26.4	-	75.6	-	112.6	-

Source: Eurostat (ext_lt_intertrd)

Figure 9.9: Main exports, EU-27
(% share of extra EU-27 exports)

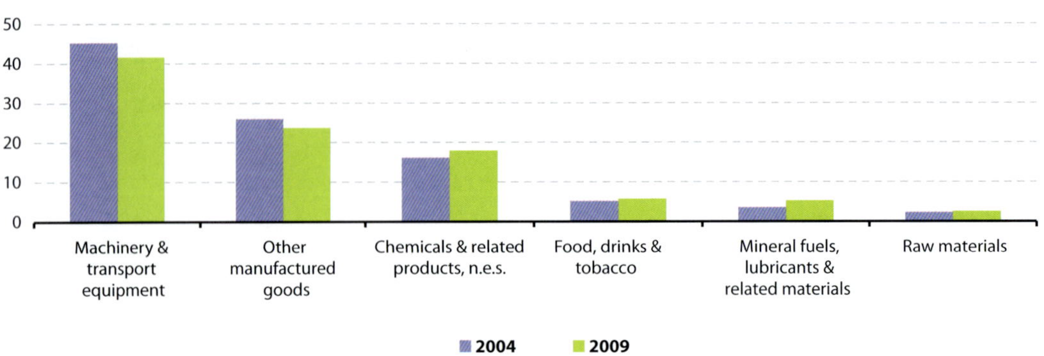

Source: Eurostat (tet00061)

Figure 9.10: Main imports, EU-27
(% share of extra EU-27 imports)

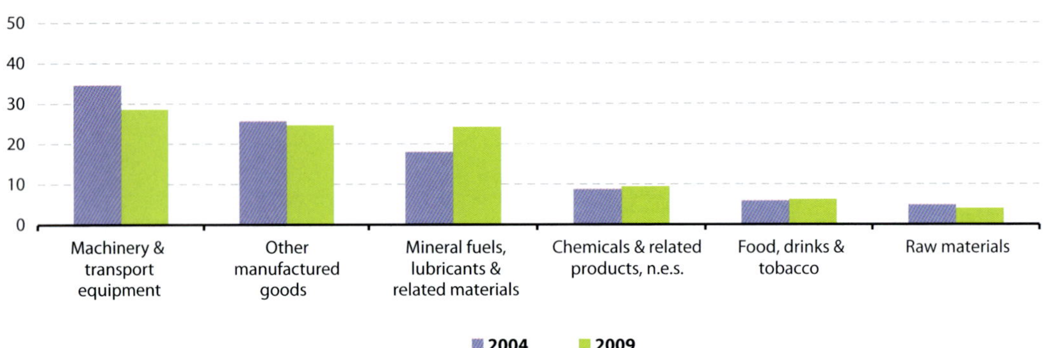

Source: Eurostat (tet00061)

9.2 International trade in services

This subchapter provides information in relation to international trade in services within individual Member States and across the European Union (EU) as a whole. It discusses the EU's main trading partners for services and the weight of different types of services in total international trade in services.

Services play a major role in all modern economies. An efficient services sector is crucial for trade and economic growth and for vibrant and resilient economies. Services provide vital support to the economy and industry as a whole, for example, through finance, logistics and communications. Increased trade in services and the widespread availability of services may boost economic growth by improving the performance of other industries, since services can provide key intermediate inputs, especially in an increasingly interlinked, globalised world.

Services differ from goods in a number of ways, most commonly in the immediacy of the relationship between supplier and consumer. Many services are non-transportable, in other words, they require the physical proximity of the service provider and consumer. This proximity requirement implies that many services transactions involve factor mobility. Thus, an important feature of services is that they are provided via various modes of supply. Many services are tailored according to the client's needs and tastes and hence tend not to be homogeneous or mass-produced. For international trade in such non-transportable services to take place, either the consumer must go to the service provider or the service provider must go to the consumer. As such, services cover a heterogeneous range of products and activities that are difficult to encapsulate within a simple definition. Services are also often difficult to separate from goods with which they may be associated or bundled.

Main statistical findings

The share of services in total exports (goods and services) was relatively stable between 27.8 % and 28.7 % from 2004 to 2008, but increased to 30.3 % in 2009. Equally the services share of imports increased in 2009, reaching 25.9 % having been at a level between 22.2 % and 23.8 % in the three previous years.

The EU-27 reported a surplus in service transactions of EUR 64 000 million with the rest of the world in 2009, reflecting credits of EUR 479 000 million and debits of EUR 415 000 million (see Table 9.8).

The United Kingdom recorded a net credit (extra and intra-EU combined) of EUR 49 500 million in service transactions in 2009, the largest value among the Member States and considerably more than the next highest that was recorded by Spain (EUR 25 300 million). In contrast, Germany recorded a net deficit in service transactions of EUR 16 700 million in 2009, the largest deficit by far among the Member States. It is important to underline that most trade in services by Member States involved intra-EU transactions, amounting to 57.2 % of credits and 59.0 % of debits.

North America was the main extra-EU trading region for the EU-27's international trade in services in 2008, accounting for 28.0 % of credits and 32.2 % of debits (see Figure 9.11). The EU-27 had negative net trade in services with North Africa, Central America and the rest of Europe (excluding EFTA countries).

More than two thirds of the EU-27's credits (67.7 %) and almost three quarters of its debits (70.2 %) in the international trade of services in 2009 were accounted for by three categories: transport, travel and other business services (see Figure 9.12). The surplus of EUR 29 800 million for other business services was the highest among services, followed by a surplus of EUR 26 200 million for financial services, EUR 21 500 million for transport and EUR 17 900 million for computer and information services. In contrast, the largest deficits were EUR 18 300 million for travel and EUR 13 900 million for royalties and license fees.

Data sources and availability

The main methodological references used for the production of statistics on international trade in services are the International Monetary Fund (IMF)'s fifth balance of payments manual (BPM5) and the United Nations' manual on statistics of international trade in services. The transmission of data on international trade in services to Eurostat is covered by Regulation (EC) No 184/2005 of the European Parliament and of the Council.

The breakdown of Eurostat statistics on international trade in services includes three main sub-items: transport, travel, and other services.

- **Transport** covers all transport services that are provided by residents of one economy for those of another and that involve the carriage of passengers, the movement of goods (freight), rentals (charters) of carriers with crew, and related supporting and auxiliary services. All modes of transport are considered including sea, air, space, rail, road, inland waterway, and pipelines, as are other supporting and auxiliary services (such as storage and warehousing).
- **Travel** covers primarily the goods and services acquired from an economy by travellers during visits of less than one year to that economy. The goods and services are purchased by, or on behalf of, the traveller or provided, without a quid pro quo (that is, are provided as a gift), for the traveller to use or give away. The transportation of travellers within the economies that they are visiting, where such transportation is provided by carriers not resident in the particular economy being visited, as well as the international carriage of travellers are excluded; both are covered in passenger services under transport. Also excluded are goods purchased by a traveller for resale in the traveller's own economy or in any other economy. Travel is divided in two subcomponents: business travel and personal travel.

- **Other services** comprise external transactions not covered under transport or travel, specifically: communications services, construction services, insurance services, financial services, computer and information services, royalties and licence fees, other business services, personal, cultural and recreational services, and government services.

International trade in services is geographically allocated according to the residence of the trading partner, distinguishing between: **intra-EU transactions** which correspond to the sum of transactions declared by EU Member States with other EU Member States; **extra-EU transactions** which correspond to the transactions declared by EU Member States with countries outside the EU. **World transactions** are equal to the sum of intra-EU transactions and extra-EU transactions.

Context

The provision of services contributes an increasing share of the economic wealth of the EU, and accounts for more than 50 % of GDP in each Member State. Nevertheless, the value of exports and imports of goods is generally two to three times higher than that of services. Part of this imbalance may be due to the nature of some services: for example, the provision of services of proximity that are difficult to provide over long distances, or alternatively professional services that are bound by distinct national legislation.

Despite the low level of international trade in services, there are a number of reasons to believe that the level of trade may grow in future years. Technological developments have increased the tradability of some services, for example facilitating web-based services such as those for finance, education, health and government amongst others. Furthermore, liberalisation efforts are likely to facilitate and therefore stimulate international trade in services. Within the EU the objective of the 'Services' Directive 2006/123/EC of 12 December 2006, on services in the internal market, is to eliminate obstacles to trade in services, thus allowing the development of cross-border operations. It is intended to improve competitiveness, not just of service enterprises but also of European industry as a whole.

Globally, the inclusion of services in the Uruguay Round of trade negotiations led to the general agreement on trade in services (GATS) that entered into force in January 1995. The GATS aims at ensuring increased transparency and predictability of relevant rules and regulations, and promoting progressive liberalisation through successive rounds of negotiation.

Table 9.8: Trade in services (1)
(EUR 1 000 million)

	Credits			Debits			Net	
	2004	2009	2008-09 growth rate (%)	2004	2009	2008-09 growth rate (%)	2004	2009
EU-27	366.7	479.0	-9.5	321.6	415.0	-6.4	45.1	64.0
Euro area (EA-16)	494.9	469.8	-9.2	445.3	439.9	-7.6	49.6	29.9
Belgium	42.4	58.3	-2.5	39.5	57.9	2.1	2.9	0.4
Bulgaria	3.3	4.9	-9.2	2.6	3.3	-17.8	0.7	1.6
Czech Republic	7.8	14.6	-1.8	7.2	13.6	11.2	0.5	1.0
Denmark	29.4	39.5	-20.0	26.8	36.7	-13.9	2.7	2.9
Germany	118.7	165.8	-6.9	158.4	182.6	-7.8	-39.7	-16.7
Estonia	2.3	3.2	-10.5	1.4	1.8	-21.5	0.9	1.3
Ireland	42.4	66.6	-1.9	52.6	75.1	-0.8	-10.2	-8.4
Greece	26.7	27.0	-20.8	11.3	14.3	-15.3	15.5	12.6
Spain	69.4	88.1	-9.6	47.6	62.7	-12.0	21.8	25.3
France	92.4	102.9	-9.5	79.2	91.4	-5.3	13.2	11.5
Italy	68.2	73.4	-9.8	67.0	83.6	-5.9	1.2	-10.1
Cyprus	5.0	7.1	-13.6	2.1	2.9	-13.6	2.9	4.1
Latvia	1.4	2.7	-11.6	1.0	1.6	-27.7	0.5	1.2
Lithuania	2.0	2.7	-18.0	1.3	2.1	-28.3	0.7	0.6
Luxembourg	27.3	43.8	-9.5	16.8	25.8	-7.9	10.5	18.0
Hungary	8.7	13.1	-5.4	8.2	11.6	-9.8	0.5	1.5
Malta	1.3	2.4	-4.3	0.8	1.5	-1.7	0.5	0.9
Netherlands	59.3	66.9	-7.0	55.9	61.3	-2.8	3.4	5.6
Austria	30.5	38.2	-9.6	22.5	26.6	-8.7	8.0	11.6
Poland	10.8	20.7	-14.7	10.8	17.2	-17.0	0.0	3.5
Portugal	11.8	16.3	-8.8	7.8	10.3	-8.5	4.1	6.0
Romania	2.9	7.0	-19.9	3.1	7.4	-8.9	-0.2	-0.4
Slovenia	2.8	4.3	-14.7	2.1	3.2	-10.2	0.7	1.1
Slovakia	3.0	4.5	-22.0	2.8	5.8	-8.0	0.2	-1.2
Finland	12.2	18.3	-15.8	11.7	16.8	-18.8	0.5	1.5
Sweden	31.4	43.8	-11.4	26.6	33.3	-10.5	4.7	10.5
United Kingdom	159.2	167.5	-14.6	120.7	118.1	-14.5	38.4	49.5
Iceland	1.3	1.6	9.1	1.5	1.4	-18.5	-0.2	0.2
Norway	25.9	27.4	-11.2	23.6	27.2	-10.6	2.3	0.1
Croatia	7.6	8.5	-16.3	2.9	2.8	-11.3	4.8	5.7
Turkey	18.5	23.6	-0.7	8.2	12.1	-0.6	10.4	11.5
Japan (2)	78.5	101.6	:	109.0	115.9	:	-30.5	-14.3
United States (2)	281.2	372.0	:	234.4	276.2	:	46.7	95.8

(1) EU-27, extra EU-27 flows; euro area, extra EA-16 flows; Member States and other countries, flows with the rest of the world.
(2) 2008 instead of 2009.

Source: Eurostat (bop_q_eu, bop_q_euro and bop_q_c)

Table 9.9: Contribution to extra EU-27 trade in services, 2008

	Credits		Debits		Net
	(EUR 1 000 million)	Share of EU-27 credits (%)	(EUR 1 000 million)	Share of EU-27 debits (%)	(EUR 1 000 million)
EU-27 (1)	521.2	100.0	442.7	100.0	78.4
Belgium	18.2	3.5	16.0	3.6	2.2
Bulgaria	1.5	0.3	1.4	0.3	0.1
Czech Republic	3.1	0.6	3.4	0.8	-0.3
Denmark	25.8	4.9	19.2	4.3	6.6
Germany	79.6	15.3	81.2	18.3	-1.6
Estonia	1.1	0.2	0.6	0.1	0.5
Ireland	24.1	4.6	38.6	8.7	-14.5
Greece	16.5	3.2	8.2	1.9	8.3
Spain	27.4	5.3	24.2	5.5	3.2
France	56.7	10.9	49.9	11.3	6.9
Italy	27.8	5.3	31.5	7.1	-3.7
Cyprus	3.1	0.6	1.1	0.2	2.1
Latvia	1.5	0.3	0.9	0.2	0.6
Lithuania	1.3	0.2	1.2	0.3	0.1
Luxembourg	12.4	2.4	8.8	2.0	3.6
Hungary	4.2	0.8	4.4	1.0	-0.2
Malta	0.6	0.1	0.5	0.1	0.1
Netherlands	35.0	6.7	35.7	8.1	-0.7
Austria	10.3	2.0	7.8	1.8	2.5
Poland	6.4	1.2	4.9	1.1	1.6
Portugal	4.6	0.9	3.2	0.7	1.4
Romania	1.8	0.4	2.1	0.5	-0.3
Slovenia	1.6	0.3	1.4	0.3	0.2
Slovakia	1.4	0.3	1.0	0.2	0.3
Finland	12.4	2.4	7.2	1.6	5.2
Sweden	26.0	5.0	14.3	3.2	11.7
United Kingdom	117.0	22.5	67.8	15.3	49.2

(1) Data for the EU institutions are included in the aggregate information presented for the EU-27.

Source: Eurostat (bop_its_det)

Table 9.10: Contribution to intra EU-27 trade in services, 2008

	Credits		Debits		Net
	(EUR 1 000 million)	Share of EU-27 credits (%)	(EUR 1 000 million)	Share of EU-27 debits (%)	(EUR 1 000 million)
EU-27 (1)	709.3	100.0	651.4	100.0	57.8
Belgium	40.7	5.7	40.0	6.1	0.7
Bulgaria	3.9	0.5	3.2	0.5	0.7
Czech Republic	12.0	1.7	8.4	1.3	3.6
Denmark	23.6	3.3	23.4	3.6	0.3
Germany	88.4	12.5	112.4	17.2	-24.0
Estonia	2.4	0.3	1.8	0.3	0.7
Ireland	45.1	6.4	35.9	5.5	9.2
Greece	17.5	2.5	8.7	1.3	8.8
Spain	70.1	9.9	47.1	7.2	23.1
France	54.9	7.7	47.3	7.3	7.6
Italy	53.7	7.6	57.3	8.8	-3.6
Cyprus	5.1	0.7	2.3	0.4	2.7
Latvia	1.6	0.2	1.3	0.2	0.3
Lithuania	2.0	0.3	1.7	0.3	0.3
Luxembourg	36.0	5.1	19.3	3.0	16.7
Hungary	9.4	1.3	8.3	1.3	1.0
Malta	1.9	0.3	1.0	0.2	0.9
Netherlands	50.9	7.2	40.8	6.3	10.2
Austria	32.0	4.5	21.3	3.3	10.7
Poland	17.8	2.5	15.8	2.4	2.0
Portugal	13.4	1.9	8.2	1.3	5.1
Romania	6.9	1.0	6.0	0.9	1.0
Slovenia	3.4	0.5	2.1	0.3	1.4
Slovakia	4.4	0.6	5.2	0.8	-0.8
Finland	9.4	1.3	12.8	2.0	-3.4
Sweden	23.6	3.3	23.1	3.5	0.6
United Kingdom	79.1	11.2	70.2	10.8	8.9

(1) Data for the EU institutions are included in the aggregate information presented for the EU-27.

Source: Eurostat (bop_its_det)

Figure 9.11: Trade in services, EU-27, 2008
(% share of extra EU-27 transactions)

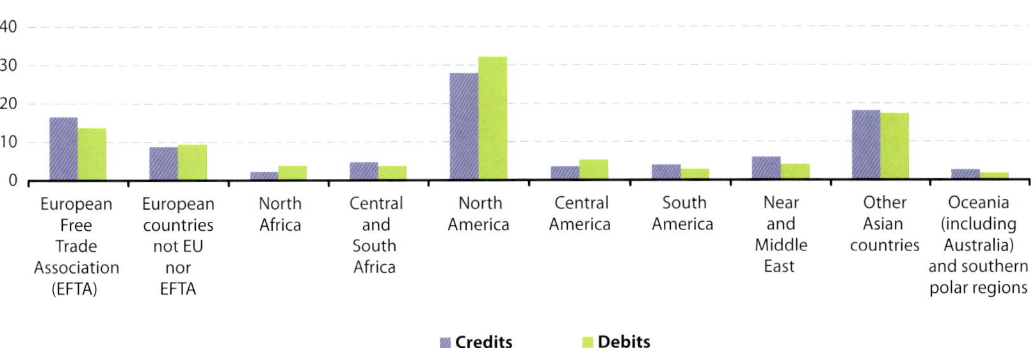

Source: Eurostat (bop_its_det)

Table 9.11: EU-27 credits for services
(%)

	2004	2005	2006	2007	2008	2009
Extra-EU	41.5	41.8	42.0	42.3	42.4	42.8
European Free Trade Association	6.9	6.8	6.7	6.9	7.0	:
Switzerland	5.3	5.2	5.0	5.2	5.4	5.7
European countries not EU nor EFTA	3.0	3.5	3.9	3.6	3.7	:
Central and Eastern Europe	0.8	0.9	0.9	0.4	0.5	:
Community of Independent States	1.5	1.8	2.0	2.3	2.4	:
Russia	1.0	1.3	1.4	1.7	1.7	1.6
Africa	2.5	2.5	2.5	2.8	3.1	:
America	16.9	16.7	16.4	15.7	15.2	:
Canada	0.9	0.9	1.0	1.0	0.9	0.9
United States	13.3	12.7	12.4	11.7	10.9	10.6
Brazil	0.4	0.5	0.5	0.6	0.7	0.8
Asia	9.3	9.8	9.9	10.4	10.3	:
China (excl. Hong Kong)	1.0	1.3	1.3	1.5	1.6	1.6
Hong Kong	0.8	0.9	0.7	0.7	0.7	0.7
India	0.4	0.6	0.7	0.8	0.7	0.8
Japan	2.1	2.0	1.8	1.6	1.6	1.5
Oceania (including Australia) and southern polar regions	1.1	1.1	1.1	1.1	1.2	:
OECD countries	83.0	81.9	81.0	79.9	79.1	:
North American Free Trade Association member countries	14.7	14.1	13.8	13.1	12.3	:
Petroleum Exporting Countries (OPEC)	2.2	2.3	2.6	3.1	3.2	:
African, Caribbean and Pacific countries, signatories of the Partnership Agreement (Cotonou agreement)	1.8	1.9	2.0	2.2	2.3	:
Association of South-East Asian Nations	1.6	1.6	1.7	1.7	1.8	:
Southern Common Market	0.6	0.7	0.7	0.8	1.0	:

Source: Eurostat (tec00080)

Table 9.12: EU-27 debits for services
(%)

	2004	2005	2006	2007	2008	2009
Extra-EU	39.9	39.9	39.9	39.8	40.5	41.0
European Free Trade Association	5.5	5.5	5.2	5.6	5.5	:
Switzerland	4.1	4.3	4.0	4.4	4.3	4.7
European countries not EU nor EFTA	4.0	4.4	4.3	3.7	3.8	:
Central and Eastern Europe	1.2	1.3	1.3	0.7	0.7	:
Community of Independent States	1.6	1.8	1.7	1.7	1.8	:
Russia	1.0	1.1	1.1	1.1	1.2	1.1
Africa	3.1	3.1	3.1	3.1	3.1	:
America	17.4	17.3	17.0	16.3	16.4	:
Canada	0.9	0.8	0.9	0.9	0.9	0.8
United States	13.5	13.4	13.0	12.4	12.1	12.5
Brazil	0.4	0.5	0.5	0.5	0.6	0.6
Asia	7.7	8.0	8.5	8.6	8.7	:
China (excl. Hong Kong)	0.9	1.1	1.3	1.3	1.4	1.3
Hong Kong	0.6	0.6	0.7	0.7	0.7	0.6
India	0.5	0.6	0.6	0.7	0.7	0.7
Japan	1.3	1.4	1.4	1.3	1.3	1.3
Oceania (including Australia) and southern polar regions	0.8	0.9	0.8	0.8	0.8	:
OECD countries	82.3	82.1	81.3	81.1	79.9	:
North American Free Trade Association member countries	14.7	14.5	14.2	13.7	13.3	:
Petroleum Exporting Countries (OPEC)	1.5	1.5	1.7	1.7	1.8	:
African, Caribbean and Pacific countries, signatories of the Partnership Agreement (Cotonou agreement)	2.1	2.1	2.0	2.0	2.0	:
Association of South-East Asian Nations	1.6	1.6	1.7	1.7	1.8	:
Southern Common Market	0.6	0.7	0.7	0.7	0.8	:

Source: Eurostat (tec00081)

Table 9.13: Development of trade in services, EU-27
(EUR 1 000 million)

Partner	2004			2008			2009		
	Credits	Debits	Net	Credits	Debits	Net	Credits	Debits	Net
Total	365.6	321.0	44.6	521.2	442.7	78.4	*480.8*	*415.5*	*65.3*
United States	117.4	108.4	9.0	134.4	132.7	1.7	*119.4*	*127.0*	*-7.6*
EFTA	60.8	44.0	16.7	86.6	60.7	26.0	:	:	:
Japan	18.4	10.7	7.7	19.2	14.6	4.7	*16.5*	*12.7*	*3.8*
Russia	9.2	8.0	1.2	21.1	13.6	7.5	*18.5*	*10.9*	*7.6*
China	9.1	7.4	1.7	20.0	15.1	4.9	*18.2*	*13.2*	*5.0*
Canada	8.3	7.0	1.3	11.6	9.7	2.0	*10.6*	*8.2*	*2.5*
India	3.8	4.1	-0.3	8.6	7.9	0.6	*8.8*	*7.5*	*1.3*
Hong Kong	7.1	5.2	1.9	8.9	7.9	0.9	*7.5*	*6.5*	*1.0*
Brazil	3.7	3.4	0.3	9.1	6.1	3.0	*8.8*	*6.4*	*2.4*
Other countries	127.9	122.8	5.1	201.6	174.4	27.2	:	:	:

Source: Eurostat (bop_its_det)

Figure 9.12: Extra-EU trade in services, by main categories, EU-27, 2009 (1)
(EUR 1 000 million)

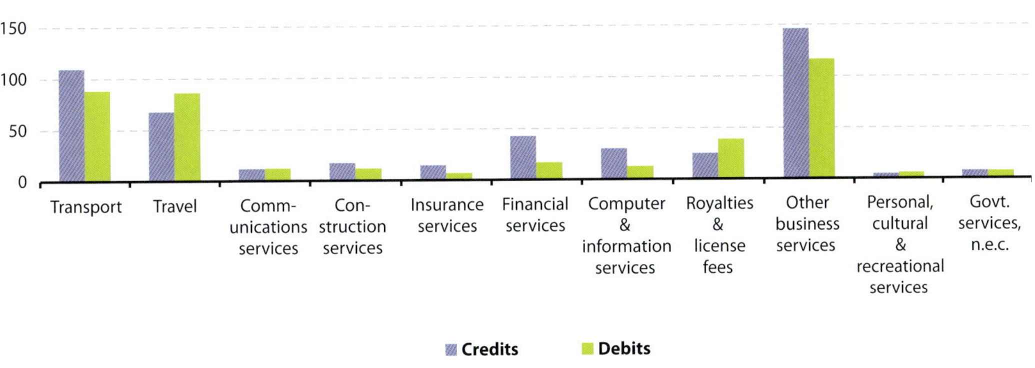

(1) Provisional.

Source: Eurostat (bop_its_det)

841053

Transport

10

An efficient and well-functioning passenger and freight transport system is vital for European Union (EU) enterprises and inhabitants. The EU's transport policy aims to foster clean, safe and efficient travel throughout Europe, underpinning the internal market for goods (transferring goods between their place of production and consumption) and the right of citizens to travel freely throughout the Union (for work or for pleasure).

No other sector of the European economy has seen its greenhouse gas emissions grow as rapidly as that of transport. This may be linked to a sizeable increase in transport volumes, as a result of (among others), trade liberalisation, globalisation, higher motorisation rates, and an increase in the number of holidays and short breaks that are taken by Europeans. Such changes have resulted in an increase in the relative share of greenhouse gas emissions accounted for by the transport sector.

On the other hand, some progress has been made in reducing air pollution within the transport sector: for example, through the application of stricter Euro emission standards. Furthermore, the energy efficiency of the transport sector has improved: for example, through the development of more efficient and hybrid vehicles, or a shift in freight transport to alternative modes such as short sea shipping. Generally, these efficiency gains have failed to outweigh the increased volume of transport. More recently, the EU has established a binding target for Member States, whereby 10 % of the fuel used within their transport sectors should be derived from sustainable and renewable energy sources by 2020.

The European Commission's Directorate-General for Mobility and Transport is responsible for developing transport policy within the EU. Its remit is to ensure mobility in a single European transport area, integrating the needs of the population, environmental policy, and competitiveness. It aims to do so by:

- completing the European internal market: so as to ensure the seamless integration of all modes of transport into a single, competitive transport system, while protecting safety and security, and improving the rights of passengers;
- developing an agenda for innovation: promoting the development of a new generation of sustainable transport technologies, in particular for integrated traffic management systems and low-carbon vehicles;
- building a trans-European network as the backbone of a multimodal, sustainable transport system capable of delivering fast, affordable and reliable transport solutions;
- projecting these mobility and transport objectives and defending EU political and industrial interests on the world stage, within international organisations, and with strategic partners.

The European Commission's White paper titled, 'European transport policy for 2010: time to decide' (COM(2001) 370 final) is the foundation of the EU's sustainable transport policy; it was supplemented in June 2006 by a mid-term review in the form of a Communication to the Council and the European Parliament, titled 'Keep Europe moving – sustainable mobility for our continent' (COM(2006) 314 final). The key conclusions of this mid-term review proposed that each transport mode should be: optimised to help ensure competitiveness and prosperity; more environmentally-friendly and energy-efficient; safe and secure; used efficiently on its own and in combination to achieve an optimal and sustainable utilisation of resources. The Communication proposed a wide range of implementing measures including:

- environmental commitments – such as those under the Kyoto Protocol, as well as air quality, noise pollution, and land use;
- a greater focus on technology – including further research and development into areas such as intelligent transport systems (such as Galileo, SESAR and ERTMS, involving communication, navigation and automation, and engine technology that could improve fuel efficiency), as well as the modernisation of air traffic systems, improvements in safety and security, urban mobility and the de-congestion of transport corridors;
- consolidation within the transport sector – especially in aviation and maritime transport, but also with the creation of large logistics enterprises with worldwide operations;
- enlargement – allowing the possibility to expand trans-European networks to corridors that are particularly suitable for rail and waterborne transport;
- changes in the international context, such as the threat of terrorism, or globalisation that have affected trade

flows and increased demand for international transport services.

The European Commission has launched a range of action plans on key transport policy issues, among which: a Green paper on urban transport (COM(2007) 551 final); a proposal for a Directive on the charging of heavy goods vehicles for the use of certain infrastructures (COM(2008) 436 final); a Communication to the European Parliament and Council titled 'Greening transport' (COM(2008) 433 final); and a freight transport logistics action plan (COM(2007) 607 final).

As the ten-year period covered by the White paper was drawing to an end, the European Commission adopted a Communication in mid-2009, titled, 'A sustainable future for transport: towards an integrated, technology-led and user friendly system' (COM(2009) 279 final); this was aimed at identifying policy options to be tested and eventually included in the next White paper. The Communication was both consultative and strategic in nature, and underlined the challenges of reducing greenhouse gas emissions, the growing demand for – but increasing scarcity of – fossil fuels, and increasing levels of congestion in many cities, airports and ports. The new transport policy White paper is, at the time of writing, under preparation and will is expected to be adopted in the spring of 2011.

Eurostat's transport statistics describe the most important features of transport, not only in terms of the quantities of freight and numbers of passengers that are moved each year, or the number of vehicles and infrastructure that are used, but also the contribution of transport services to the economy as a whole. Data collection is supported by several legal acts obliging the Member States to report statistical data, as well as voluntary agreements to supply additional data.

10.1 Transport accidents

Safety and security are of primary concern for any transport system. According to Eurostat statistics on the causes of death (see Subchapter 3.2), there were 44 355 people in the European Union (EU) in 2008 who died as a result of transport accidents, across all transport modes; this figure may be compared with 62 846 deaths in 1999 (the first year of the time series for the EU-27).

While rail, air, or sea transport incidents often receive considerable media coverage as they generally involve larger numbers of people, road accidents are often treated in a more mundane manner by the media, despite the fact that Europe's roads account for the vast majority of transport accidents and deaths.

Main statistical findings

Road accidents

The annual number of road fatalities in the EU is falling, despite the growth (prior to the economic and financial crisis) in passenger and freight transport. The reduction in road fatalities may be attributed, among others, to: improved road design; stricter enforcement of drinking and driving legislation; improved vehicle safety standards; the introduction of speed limits; stricter rules on lorry and bus driving times; and reduced lorry overloads.

Indeed, the number of road fatalities in the EU-27 fell sharply during the decade between 1999 and 2009, from 57 691 deaths to an estimated 34 500 deaths (down 40.2 % overall). Nevertheless, the number of people killed on Europe's roads still accounted for almost nine out of every ten deaths resulting from transport accidents in 2009. The use of alcohol or drugs, the failure to observe speed limits, and the refusal to wear seatbelts are involved in about half of all road fatalities in the EU. Road accidents remain the largest single cause of death among people under 45 years of age.

The road fatality rate, expressed as the number of deaths per million inhabitants, averaged 78 across the EU-27 in 2008, although there were stark contrasts between Member States (see Figure 10.1). The highest road fatality rates were recorded in Lithuania (148 deaths per million inhabitants), Poland (143), Romania (142), Bulgaria, Greece and Latvia (all 139). The rates reported by these six countries were considerably higher than in the other Member States, as the next highest figure was recorded for Slovenia (106). In contrast, road fatality rates were much lower in Sweden, the United Kingdom (both 43), the Netherlands (41), and Malta (37).

Rail accidents

Some 2 848 people were victims (seriously injured or killed) of railway accidents in the EU-27 in 2008 (see Table 10.1); this represented a slight reduction (59 victims) compared with the year before; it should be noted that the number of victims in any particular year can be greatly influenced by a small number of major accidents. Of the total number of victims seriously injured or killed in railway accidents in the EU-27 in 2008, a little over one sixth (17.4 %) were either train passengers or railway employees. Approximately two thirds (68.6 %) of the lives lost in rail accidents were from incidents involving rolling stock in motion, with almost all the others (26.6 %) from incidents at level-crossings. The highest numbers of rail fatalities within the EU in 2008 occurred in Poland (308) and Romania (208).

Air accidents

In a similar manner to rail accidents, the number of air fatalities has an irregular pattern, due to the relatively low number of accidents each year and the large variations in terms of people involved in each event. Figure 10.2 shows that there was a single, major aircraft accident within the EU-27 in 2008; this took place at Madrid's Barajas International Airport on 20 August, when a flight crashed just after takeoff, with 154 fatalities.

Data sources and availability

Road accidents

CARE is the EU's road accident database that collects information on accidents resulting in death and/or injury. The legal basis for CARE is Council Decision 93/704/EC on the creation of a database on road accidents. Its purpose is to provide information which makes it possible to: identify and quantify road safety problems; evaluate the efficiency of road safety measures; determine the relevance of EU actions; and facilitate the exchange of experiences. Accidents resulting in death or injury refer to any collision between road users involving at least one vehicle in motion on a public highway normally open to traffic and causing the death of and/or injury to one or more of the road users. The statistics include drivers and passengers of motorised vehicles, bicycles, as well as pedestrians that are involved in road accidents. Road deaths are recorded during a period of up to 30 days after the accident.

Rail accidents

The legal basis for the collection of statistics on rail accidents is Regulation 91/2003 on rail transport statistics (Annex H), amended by Regulation 1192/2003. The data collected includes information on the number of persons killed or injured (by category of persons) and the number of accidents (by type of accident). An accident involves at least one rail vehicle in motion, resulting in at least one person being killed or seriously injured, or in significant damage to stock, track, other installations, the environment, or extensive disruptions to traffic. As with road deaths, rail deaths are defined in terms of any person who is killed within 30 days as a result of a rail accident. A seriously injured person is defined as someone who is hospitalised for more than 24 hours as a result of a rail accident. Rail accident statistics are available from 2004 or 2006 onwards for all EU Member States, except for Malta and Cyprus (where there are no railways).

Air accidents

The questionnaire on air transport safety statistics is not supported by any legal acts. Rather, it is based on a gentlemen's agreement with the participating countries (EU Member States, EFTA and candidate countries). The final section of the questionnaire (part IV) deals with the topic of accidents. It contains requests for information on the number of injuries and the number of fatalities that take place as a result of aircraft accidents. Accidents are measured during the operation of an aircraft, which takes place between the time any person boards the aircraft with the intention of flight until such time as all such persons have disembarked (injuries sustained from natural causes or injuries that are self-inflicted are excluded). As with the other modes of transport, a fatal injury is one that results in death within 30 days of the accident.

Context

In a White paper titled European transport policy for 2010: time to decide (COM(2001) 370), the European Commission set an ambitious target of halving the number of road deaths in the EU by 2010. The objective to halve road casualties by 2010 has led to action being taken to reduce the number and severity of transport accidents: this has been achieved via educational programmes, stricter limits being placed on permitted blood alcohol levels and speed, the introduction of technical measures such as safety belts and air bags, as well as traffic control measures.

In June 2003, a European Commission Communication launched an action programme for European road safety (COM(2003) 311), which encouraged:

- road users to improve their behaviour in particular through greater respect of existing rules, initial and continuous training of private and professional drivers, and better law enforcement against dangerous behaviour;
- the use of technical progress to make vehicles safer through improved safety performance standards;
- the improvement of road infrastructure, in particular through the identification and diffusion of best practices and the elimination of black spots through the European Road Assessment Programme (EuroRAP) and the European Tunnel Assessment Programme (EuroTAP).

Railway, aviation and shipping accidents result in far fewer deaths than road accidents. The main reason for this is the limited size of these sectors, relative to the number of cars and goods vehicles that are on Europe's roads. However, when accidents involving trains, planes or ships do occur they have the potential to cause considerable environmental damage and often result in serious commercial and financial consequences. Major transport accidents are almost always investigated in great depth in order to find the cause of the accident, such that a reoccurrence may be prevented.

Figure 10.1: People killed in road accidents, 2008 (1)
(persons killed per million inhabitants)

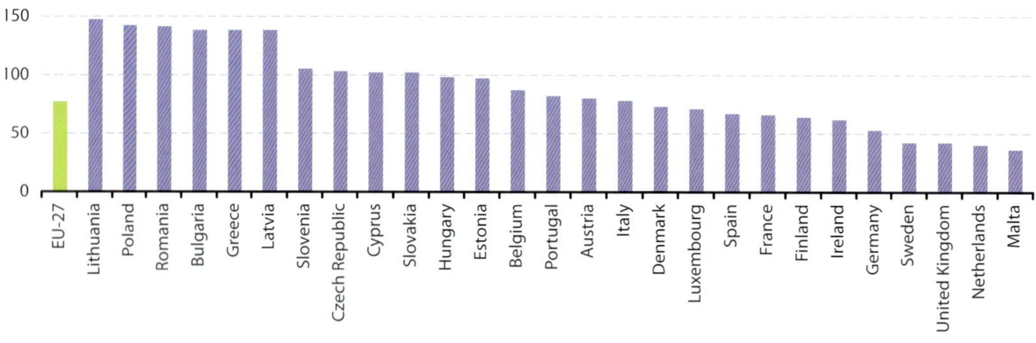

(1) Italy, 2006.

Source: Eurostat (tsdtr420), European Commission CARE database (Community Database on Road Accidents)

Table 10.1: Rail accidents by type of victim and accident, EU-27, 2008 (1)
(number of persons)

	Total		Passengers		Railway employees		Others	
	Killed	Seriously injured	Killed	Seriously injured	Killed	Seriously injured	Killed	Seriously injured
Total	1 498	1 350	89	255	40	112	1 369	983
Collisions (excluding level-crossing accidents)	23	92	12	64	6	20	5	8
Derailments	3	15	2	12	1	3	0	0
Accidents involving level-crossings	399	458	0	9	2	14	397	435
Accidents to persons caused by rolling stock in motion	1 028	684	53	115	25	48	950	521
Fire in rolling stock	9	5	9	5	0	0	0	0
Others	36	96	13	50	6	27	17	19

(1) Slightly injured persons are not included in rail accident statistics.

Source: Eurostat (rail_ac_catvict)

Figure 10.2: Air transport accidents - number of fatalities, 2008 (1)
(persons killed)

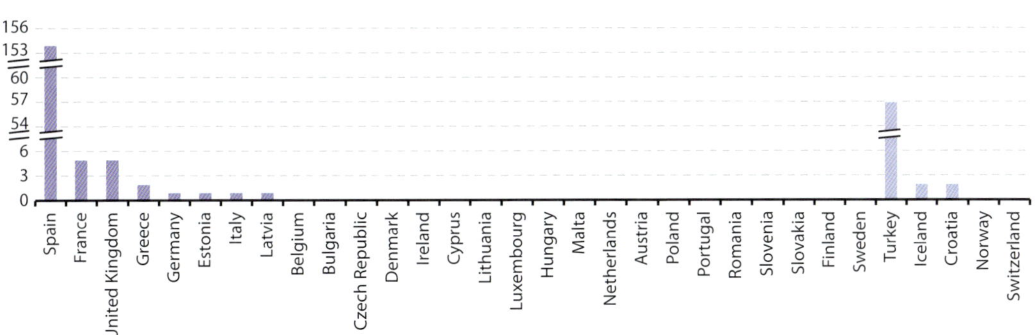

(1) Accidents on national territory regardless of the nationality of the aircraft operator; Denmark, Germany, Greece, Luxembourg, Norway, Switzerland and Turkey, 2007.

Source: Eurostat (avia_ac_fatal)

10.2 Passenger transport

This subchapter provides details relating to recent trends for passenger transport statistics. It presents information on a range of different passenger transport modes, such as road, rail, air and maritime, within the European Union (EU). Among these, the most dominant mode of passenger transport is that of the car, likely fuelled by a desire to have greater mobility and flexibility. The high reliance on the car as a means of passenger transport across the EU has resulted in increased congestion and pollution.

Main statistical findings

Passenger cars accounted for 83.3 % of inland passenger transport in the EU-27 in 2008, with buses and coaches (9.4 %) and railways, trams and metros (7.3 %) both accounting for slightly less than a tenth of the total volume of traffic (as measured by the number of inland passenger-kilometres (pkm) travelled by each mode) – see Table 10.2.

In the vast majority of EU Member States, GDP grew faster than the volume of inland passenger transport between 2000 and 2008 (see Table 10.3). Most notably GDP grew about one third faster than the rate of growth for the volume of inland passenger transport in Slovakia and Hungary. The main exceptions were Lithuania and Latvia where the rate of growth in the volume of inland passenger transport was between one quarter and one third faster than the rate of growth for GDP; other exceptions were recorded for Poland, Portugal and Greece.

It should be noted that the analysis above refers only to inland transport by car, bus or train and that a significant proportion of international passenger travel is accounted for by maritime and air transport passenger services, while in some countries national (domestic) maritime and air transport passenger services may also be of note.

Road passengers

A reliance on the car for making journeys was particularly high in Lithuania, the United Kingdom, the Netherlands and Slovenia, where it accounted for upwards of 86 % of all inland passenger-kilometres in 2008. More than a fifth of the inland passenger-kilometres travelled in Hungary and Bulgaria were by bus or coach.

Between 2000 and 2008 there was a marked increase in the use of passenger cars among many of those Member States that joined the EU in 2004 or 2007, in particular, Bulgaria and Poland. In contrast, the relative importance of cars as a mode of inland passenger transport fell in ten of the EU-15 Member States. The most sizeable reductions in the relative importance of the car between 2000 and 2008 were recorded in Italy, Spain and the United Kingdom (where the share of the car in total inland passenger transport fell 1.4 percentage points), France (-1.9 points) and Belgium (-5.0 points).

Rail passengers

There were 371 930 million passenger-kilometres travelled on national railway networks within the EU-27 in 2007; this figure was considerably higher than the 20 295 million passenger-kilometres travelled on international journeys. More than a tenth of all inland passenger-kilometres travelled in Hungary, Austria and France were made on rail networks (including trains, trams and underground railways/metros).

Approximately two thirds of all rail travel (national and international combined) was accounted for by the four largest EU Member States (note that neither Cyprus nor Malta has a railway network), with France and Germany together accounting for close to half (46.3 %) of the EU's passenger total. The number of international passenger-kilometres travelled by French passengers was, at 7 546 million passenger-kilometres, almost twice the level for Germany (3 870 million passenger-kilometres), which in turn recorded a figure that was more than double that for the United Kingdom (1 690 million passenger-kilometres).

In order to compare the relative importance of rail transport between countries, the data can be normalised by expressing passenger volumes in relation to population (see Table 10.4). France, Sweden and Denmark – all at more than 1 000 passenger-kilometres per inhabitant – registered the longest average distances travelled on national railways in 2008. In terms of international rail travel, the highest distances covered were for Luxembourg, Austria and France (the only Member States to report averages above 100 passenger-kilometres per inhabitant). These figures may reflect, among others, the proximity of international borders, the importance of international commuters within the workforce, access to high-speed rail links, and whether or not international transport corridors run through a particular country.

Note that Subchapter 10.1 on transport accidents provides more detailed information in relation to rail accidents, including breakdowns of EU-27 data according to the type of victim and accident.

Air passengers

London Heathrow was the busiest airport in the EU-27 in terms of passenger numbers in 2009 (65.9 million), followed by Paris' Charles de Gaulle airport (57.7 million), and then Frankfurt airport, Madrid's Barajas airport and Amsterdam's Schiphol airport (all with between 50.6 million and 43.5 million passengers) – see Figure 10.4.

With the exception of Barajas, the overwhelming majority (about 90 %) of passengers through the other four largest airports in the EU were on international flights. In contrast, national (domestic) flights accounted for 39.3 % of the passengers carried through Barajas in 2009. There were also relatively high proportions of passengers on national flights to and from Paris' Orly airport (54.8 %), Barcelona airport (40.6 %) and Rome's Fiumicino airport (37.6 %).

Just over 750 million passengers were carried by air in 2009 in the EU-27 (see Table 10.5); the number of air passengers had stagnated in 2008, while the number of air passengers fell by 5.9 % in 2009.

The United Kingdom reported the highest number of air passengers in 2009, with almost 199 million or 3.2 passengers per inhabitant (which was more than double the EU-27 average). Relative to population size, the importance of air travel was particularly high for the popular holiday islands of Cyprus and Malta (8.4 and 7.1 passengers carried per inhabitant).

Maritime passengers

Table 10.5 shows the number of maritime passengers, with ports in the EU-27 handling 413 million passengers in 2008; this marked a slight reduction of 0.3 % compared with 2007. Greek and Italian ports handled more passengers in 2008 than those of any other Member State (accounting for 22.1 % and 21.8 % of the EU-27 total respectively); they were followed by Danish ports (data for 2009) and then, with roughly similar numbers, ports in Sweden, the United Kingdom and Germany.

Relative to national population, the importance of maritime passenger transport was particularly high in Malta (18.9 passengers per inhabitant in 2009), followed by Greece (8.1), Denmark (7.9, 2009) and Estonia (6.9); in the remaining Member States, other than Sweden, Finland (2009) and Italy, the number of maritime passengers per inhabitant averaged less than one in 2008.

Data sources and availability

The majority of inland passenger transport statistics are based on movements of vehicles in each reporting country, regardless of the nationality of the vehicle or vessel involved (the 'territoriality principle'). For this reason, the volume measure of passenger-kilometres is generally considered as a more reliable measure, as a count of passengers entails a higher risk of double-counting, particularly for international transport. The methodology used across the Member States is not harmonised for road passenger transport. As such, the figures, especially those for the smallest reporting countries, may be somewhat unreliable.

The modal split of inland passenger transport identifies transportation by passenger car, bus and coach, and train; it generally concerns movements on the national territory, regardless of the nationality of the vehicle. The modal split of passenger transport is defined as the percentage share of each mode and is expressed in passenger-kilometres (pkm), which represent one passenger travelling a distance of one kilometre. For the purpose of this subchapter, the aggregate for inland passenger transport excludes domestic air and water transport services (inland waterways and maritime).

The volume of inland passenger transport (measured in pkm) may also be expressed in relation to gross domestic product (GDP); within this subchapter the indicator is presented in constant prices for the reference year 2000, providing information on the relationship between passenger demand and economic growth, with the series indexed on 2000=100, so that the annual intensity of passenger transport demand can be monitored relative to economic developments.

Rail passengers

A rail passenger is any person, excluding members of the train crew, who makes a journey by rail. Rail passenger data are not available for Malta and Cyprus (or Iceland) as they do not have railways.

Annual passenger statistics for national and international breakdowns generally only cover larger rail transport enterprises, although some countries use detailed reporting for all railway undertakings.

Air passengers

Air transport statistics concern national and international transport, as measured by the number of passengers carried; information is collected for arrivals and departures. Air passengers carried relate to all passengers on a particular flight (with one flight number) counted once only and not repeatedly on each individual stage of that flight. Air passengers include all revenue and non-revenue passengers whose journey begins or terminates at the reporting airport and transfer passengers joining or leaving the flight at the reporting airport; but excludes direct transit passengers. Air transport statistics are collected with monthly, quarterly and annual frequencies, although only the latter are presented in this subchapter. There are also air transport passenger statistics on the number of commercial passenger flights made, as well as information relating to individual routes and the number of seats available. Annual data are available for most of the EU Member States from 2003 onwards.

Maritime passengers

Maritime transport data are available for most of the period from 2001 onwards, although some EU Member States have provided data since 1997. Maritime transport data are not transmitted by the Czech Republic, Luxembourg, Hungary, Austria or Slovakia, as none of these has any maritime traffic. A sea passenger is defined as any person that makes a sea journey on a merchant ship; service staff are not regarded as passengers, neither are non-fare paying crew members travelling but not assigned, while infants in arms are also excluded. Double counting may arise when both the port of embarkation and the port of disembarkation reports data; this is quite common for the maritime transport of passengers, which is generally a relatively short distance activity.

More detailed definitions of the statistical terms used within transport statistics are available in the Illustrated glossary for transport statistics, 4th edition, 2010.

Context

EU transport policy seeks to ensure that passengers benefit from the same basic standards of treatment wherever they travel within the Union. The EU legislates to protect passenger rights across the different modes of transport.

Legislation for aviation (Regulation 261/2004 establishing 'common rules on compensation and assistance to passengers in the event of denied boarding and of cancellation or long delays of flights') and rail travel (Regulation 1371/2007 on 'rail passengers' rights and obligations') are already in force, while two European Commission proposals for regulations have been made concerning passenger rights in the field of bus and coach travel (2008/0237 (COD)) and sea and inland waterway passenger transport (2008/0246 (COD)).

Passengers already have a range of rights covering areas as diverse as: information about their journey; reservations and ticket prices; damages to their baggage; delays and cancellations; or difficulties encountered with package holidays. Specific provisions have also been developed in order to ensure that passengers with reduced mobility are provided with necessary facilities and not refused carriage unfairly.

A mid-term review of 'European transport policy for 2010' (COM(2001) 370) was presented in the form of a Communication to the Council and the European Parliament, titled 'Keep Europe moving – sustainable mobility for our continent' (COM(2006) 314). The review made a number of suggestions for new areas of policy development, including: intelligent transport systems to make mobility greener and more efficient; a debate on how to change the mobility of people in urban areas; an action plan to boost inland waterways, and; a programme for green power in cars.

Around 80 % of the EU's population lives in an urban area. The mid-term review therefore also suggested that local, regional and national authorities could benefit from studying best-practices in urban areas for a range of issues, including: transport infrastructure; congestion and traffic management; public transport services; infrastructure charging; urban planning; safety; security, and; cooperation with the surrounding region.

These ideas were expanded upon in September 2007 when the European Commission published a Green paper titled, 'Towards a new culture for urban mobility' (COM(2007) 551 final. The document addressed, for example, how: the quality of collective transport could be improved; the use of clean and energy efficient technologies could be increased; walking and cycling could be promoted, and; the rights of passengers on public transport could be protected. In September 2009 an 'Action plan on urban mobility' ((COM(2009) 490) was adopted by the European Commission. It proposed 20 different measures to encourage and help local, regional and national authorities to achieve their goals for sustainable urban mobility. Many of the proposals were linked to finding practical alternatives to the private use of cars, they included:

- raising the quality and accessibility of public transport services and increasing their capacity to respond flexibly to changes in transport needs;
- making walking and cycling more attractive by offering more favourable conditions;
- reducing the demand for travel, for example, by reversing the trend for housing, jobs, and schools to disperse to places which are hard to reach except by car;
- actively managing car use in congested areas;
- making transport an essential component of strategies for spatial planning, economic development and social cohesion;
- fostering new, flexible working time arrangements;
- encouraging the creation of door-to-door transport systems which people can use as an integrated network.

However, intra-urban transport is only one element of passenger transport policy and the enlargement of the EU has created additional opportunities for inter-urban passenger travel by rail, road or airplane, which may be strengthened through a range of infrastructure developments, including, among others, extensions to high-speed rail networks or increased air traffic capacity and co-ordination (the 'single European sky' policy). Furthermore, while congestion and pollution are often cited as problems linked to an excessive amount of traffic in urban areas, rural areas are more often characterised by concerns over the frequency and continuing availability of public transport services.

Table 10.2: Modal split of inland passenger transport ([1])
(% of total inland passenger-km)

	2000			2008		
	Passenger cars	Buses	Railways, trams and metros	Passenger cars	Buses	Railways, trams and metros
EU-27	*83.1*	*9.8*	*7.1*	*83.3*	*9.4*	*7.3*
Belgium	83.4	10.5	6.1	78.4	14.4	7.2
Bulgaria	*59.8*	*32.4*	*7.7*	*75.9*	*20.0*	*4.1*
Czech Republic	*73.2*	*18.5*	*8.3*	76.0	16.9	7.1
Denmark	79.8	11.6	8.6	79.4	11.1	9.4
Germany	85.2	7.1	7.7	85.1	6.3	8.6
Estonia	:	:	:	*79.4*	*18.5*	*2.1*
Ireland	*83.7*	*13.3*	*3.0*	*83.8*	*12.8*	*3.4*
Greece	*72.8*	*25.1*	*2.2*	*80.8*	*17.9*	*1.3*
Spain	81.5	13.5	5.0	80.1	14.4	5.5
France	86.1	5.3	8.6	84.2	5.7	10.1
Italy	83.8	10.8	5.4	*82.4*	11.9	*5.7*
Cyprus	:	:	-	:	:	-
Latvia	:	:	:	*80.6*	14.1	*5.3*
Lithuania	:	:	:	90.9	8.2	1.0
Luxembourg	*85.5*	*9.5*	*5.1*	*84.2*	*11.4*	*4.3*
Hungary	62.1	25.0	12.9	62.1	25.7	12.3
Malta	:	:	-	:	:	-
Netherlands	86.0	4.6	9.4	*86.5*	*3.8*	*9.7*
Austria ([2])	79.2	11.0	9.8	78.6	10.2	11.1
Poland	72.8	15.4	11.7	85.5	8.4	6.2
Portugal	*81.9*	*13.6*	*4.4*	*85.2*	*10.7*	*4.1*
Romania	*72.5*	*10.9*	*16.5*	*77.2*	*15.2*	*7.6*
Slovenia	82.9	14.3	2.9	86.2	10.9	2.9
Slovakia	67.9	23.9	8.1	74.9	18.6	6.5
Finland	83.4	11.5	5.1	84.5	10.1	5.4
Sweden	83.7	8.7	7.6	83.3	7.4	9.3
United Kingdom	88.2	6.4	5.3	86.8	6.4	6.8
Iceland	87.0	13.0	0.0	88.6	11.4	-
Norway	87.0	7.7	5.3	87.6	7.3	5.1
Croatia	*81.4*	*13.6*	*5.1*	*82.2*	*12.5*	*5.4*
FYR of Macedonia	*83.2*	*13.3*	*3.5*	*78.3*	*19.4*	*2.3*
Turkey	*45.9*	*50.7*	*3.4*	*51.0*	*46.8*	*2.2*

([1]) Excluding powered two-wheelers.
([2]) The railway in Liechtenstein is owned and operated by the Austrian ÖBB and included in their statistics.

Source: Eurostat (tsdtr210)

Table 10.3: Volume of inland passenger transport
(index of inland passenger transport volume relative to GDP (2000=100))

	1998	1999	2000	2001	2002	2003	2004	2005	2006	2007	2008
EU-27	:	:	100.0	:	99.8	:	:	96.3	95.7	94.7	93.5
Belgium	104.8	103.1	100.0	101.8	102.4	100.7	99.8	98.4	96.9	97.6	96.4
Bulgaria	101.0	103.0	100.0	99.8	100.0	92.7	88.1	84.0	82.7	82.4	81.8
Czech Republic	100.0	100.6	100.0	98.6	96.9	95.5	90.5	86.6	82.6	79.5	77.7
Denmark	104.7	103.5	100.0	98.0	97.7	98.0	95.7	93.8	92.3	92.7	93.9
Germany	104.6	104.7	100.0	100.9	101.4	101.1	101.5	99.4	97.8	95.9	93.1
Estonia	:	:	100.0	:	:	:	:	83.3	76.6	71.3	75.6
Ireland	113.0	105.2	100.0	98.1	93.4	91.5	89.1	86.3	84.8	84.3	88.8
Greece	94.5	97.8	100.0	101.5	102.7	101.0	99.9	102.1	102.2	102.8	104.0
Spain	101.6	102.3	100.0	98.4	97.2	95.8	96.0	94.5	90.9	90.2	89.1
France	103.8	103.3	100.0	101.6	101.6	101.0	98.8	96.2	94.1	92.9	92.3
Italy (¹)	96.4	95.5	100.0	97.4	96.4	96.4	96.1	92.7	97.1	98.2	93.9
Cyprus	:	:	100.0	:	:	:	:	:	:	:	:
Latvia	:	:	100.0	:	99.8	:	:	133.0	132.6	132.7	125.6
Lithuania	:	:	100.0	:	93.3	98.8	120.2	145.6	151.3	137.4	129.3
Luxembourg	105.3	97.5	100.0	101.3	99.8	98.6	95.9	94.3	91.7	88.9	91.8
Hungary	106.1	103.6	100.0	96.3	93.1	89.3	85.4	79.9	77.0	68.9	69.1
Malta	:	:	100.0	:	:	:	:	:	:	:	:
Netherlands (²)	106.0	103.8	100.0	98.5	99.8	99.5	100.8	97.3	94.1	91.5	88.8
Austria	104.1	102.3	100.0	100.0	99.6	100.0	98.5	97.3	95.7	93.3	93.7
Poland	103.8	100.3	100.0	101.5	103.1	101.3	99.6	102.2	104.5	105.6	112.5
Portugal	99.8	100.6	100.0	99.8	102.8	108.2	108.8	110.4	109.5	108.5	109.3
Romania	:	101.4	100.0	94.9	89.0	90.0	85.3	87.0	83.8	81.9	80.1
Slovenia	105.4	105.7	100.0	98.7	96.7	94.7	92.5	89.7	86.4	85.5	84.0
Slovakia	89.9	93.0	100.0	96.4	94.1	88.3	81.9	79.3	74.8	66.9	61.8
Finland	105.4	103.7	100.0	99.1	99.5	99.5	97.7	96.4	92.7	90.8	89.8
Sweden	104.4	102.8	100.0	99.6	99.6	99.5	95.8	93.1	89.5	89.8	89.6
United Kingdom	106.4	104.2	100.0	99.7	100.7	97.6	96.0	93.6	92.3	90.7	89.7
Iceland	89.9	89.8	100.0	103.7	106.5	107.0	102.5	101.9	102.7	88.3	88.9
Norway	102.9	102.1	100.0	99.8	100.2	101.1	98.4	97.3	95.8	95.2	92.7
Croatia	93.1	98.5	100.0	100.8	99.4	96.9	95.3	93.3	92.9	92.6	94.7
FYR of Macedonia	:	:	100.0	100.0	103.7	107.9	107.7	104.9	101.6	97.9	102.0
Turkey	:	108.1	100.0	100.6	97.0	94.1	93.3	93.0	92.7	93.5	96.8

(¹) Break in series, 2000.
(²) Break in series, 2003.

Source: Eurostat (tsien070)

Table 10.4: Rail passenger transport

	Rail passenger transport (million passenger-km)				Rail passenger transport (passenger-km per inhabitant) (1)				Rail accidents (number of persons)			
	National		International		National		International		Killed		Seriously injured	
	2007	2008	2007	2008	2007	2008	2007	2008	2008	2009	2008	2009
EU-27	371 930	:	20 295	:	751	:	42.9	40.8	1 498	:	1 350	:
Belgium	8 547	8 913	856	1 226	807	836	73.6	80.9	15	15	26	26
Bulgaria	2 342	2 264	62	52	305	296	5.8	8.1	44	28	38	22
Czech Republic	6 536	6 324	362	449	635	609	34.9	35.2	44	26	139	92
Denmark	5 554	5 604	425	478	1 020	1 023	66.1	78.0	12	15	9	15
Germany	79 098	81 764	3 587	3 870	961	994	42.1	43.6	182	:	180	:
Estonia	246	245	27	28	183	183	19.3	20.1	9	10	10	7
Ireland	1 898	1 872	109	104	440	425	:	25.3	3	4	1	5
Greece	1 853	1 599	77	59	166	143	5.7	6.9	17	22	29	22
Spain	19 742	21 853	223	221	444	483	16.3	13.9	49	41	24	21
France	74 473	78 970	7 488	7 546	1 170	1 234	118.7	118.6	93	76	39	61
Italy	44 707	44 708	1 278	1 059	756	750	46.4	21.6	68	82	39	71
Cyprus	-	-	-	-	-	-	-	-	-	-	-	-
Latvia	889	865	86	76	390	381	40.5	37.7	29	17	31	12
Lithuania	223	235	24	22	66	70	6.5	7.1	40	25	13	9
Luxembourg	233	246	84	99	489	508	168.4	176.4	0	0	0	0
Hungary	8 379	7 912	372	379	832	788	33.1	37.0	115	91	60	86
Malta	-	-	-	-	-	-	-	-	-	-	-	-
Netherlands	15 085	:	803	:	922	:	15.4	15.5	20	14	6	9
Austria	7 235	8 235	1 279	1 452	873	990	146.5	154.1	40	36	53	65
Poland	18 952	19 324	573	439	497	507	14.8	15.0	308	368	266	200
Portugal	3 933	4 093	55	120	371	385	5.2	5.2	42	:	39	:
Romania	7 271	6 725	146	152	337	312	7.6	6.8	208	150	233	186
Slovenia	690	713	49	53	343	355	24.0	24.4	9	11	41	14
Slovakia	1 970	2 094	195	202	365	388	31.5	36.2	56	73	38	35
Finland	3 675	3 940	103	112	696	743	17.7	19.5	21	14	6	10
Sweden	9 767	10 462	494	555	1 072	1 139	64.1	54.8	15	:	9	:
United Kingdom	48 633	51 196	1 537	1 690	800	837	24.4	25.3	59	56	21	13
Liechtenstein (2)	:	:	:	:	:	:	:	:	0	0	0	0
Norway	2 840	2 988	21	31	607	631	8.8	13.0	1	3	1	4
Switzerland	:	15 673	:	912	:	2 064	:	:	23	29	40	34
Croatia	1 508	1 703	65	66	340	384	14.6	14.6	13	50	45	65
Turkey	5 472	4 999	81	98	79	71	37.3	39.7	111	89	247	303

(1) Slovenia, break in series, 2008.
(2) The railway in Liechtenstein is owned and operated by the Austrian ÖBB and included in their statistics (other than for accidents).

Source: Eurostat (rail_pa_typepkm, tps00001 and rail_ac_catvict)

Figure 10.3: Rail passenger transport, 2008 (1)
(passenger-km per inhabitant)

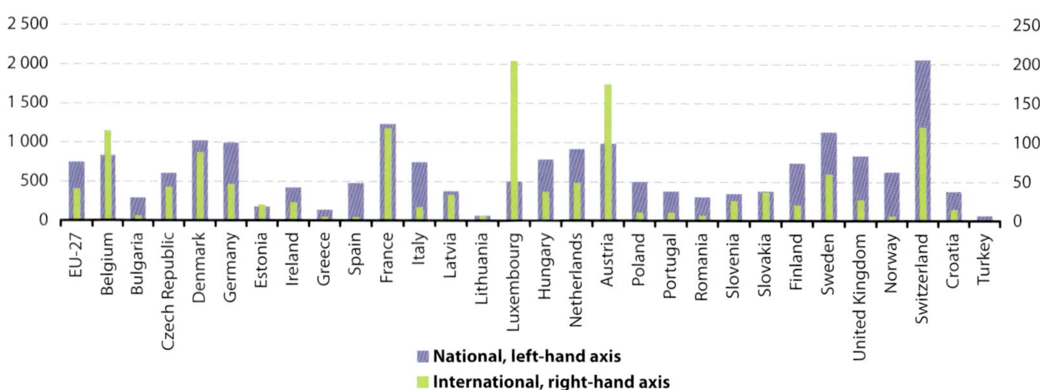

(1) EU-27 and the Netherlands, 2007; Ireland and the United Kingdom, estimates; Slovenia, break in series, 2008; Cyprus and Malta, not applicable; the railway in Liechtenstein is owned and operated by the Austrian ÖBB and included in their statistics.

Source: Eurostat (rail_pa_typepkm and tps00001)

Figure 10.4: Top 15 airports, passengers carried (embarked and disembarked), EU-27, 2009
(million passengers)

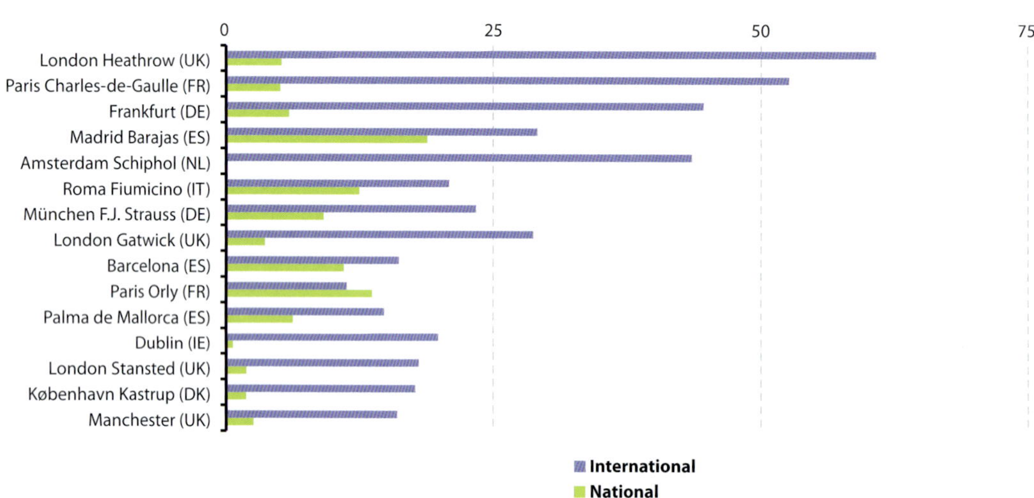

Source: Eurostat (avia_paoa)

Table 10.5: Air and sea passenger transport (1)

	Air passengers, 2009 (2)		Maritime passengers, 2008 (3)	
	(1 000)	(passengers per inhabitant)	(1 000)	(passengers per inhabitant)
EU-27	751 401	*1.5*	412 877	*0.8*
Belgium	21 314	*2.0*	799	0.1
Bulgaria	5 839	0.8	0	0.0
Czech Republic	12 367	1.2	-	-
Denmark	20 860	3.8	43 561	7.9
Germany	158 150	1.9	28 945	0.4
Estonia	1 341	1.0	9 190	6.9
Ireland	26 277	*5.9*	3 108	*0.7*
Greece	32 882	2.9	91 101	8.1
Spain	148 318	3.2	22 478	0.5
France	117 557	1.8	26 813	0.4
Italy	102 167	1.7	90 156	1.5
Cyprus	6 730	8.4	150	0.2
Latvia	4 063	1.8	437	0.2
Lithuania	1 867	0.6	205	0.1
Luxembourg	1 535	3.1	-	-
Hungary	8 081	0.8	-	-
Malta	2 919	7.1	7 799	18.9
Netherlands	46 479	2.8	1 959	0.1
Austria	21 817	2.6	-	-
Poland	17 046	0.4	2 647	0.1
Portugal	24 104	*2.3*	762	0.1
Romania	7 984	0.4	0	0.0
Slovenia	1 423	0.7	50	0.0
Slovakia	1 948	0.4	-	-
Finland	13 829	2.6	17 226	3.2
Sweden	25 219	2.7	32 745	3.6
United Kingdom	198 532	*3.2*	29 555	*0.5*
Iceland	1 837	5.8	433	1.4
Norway	27 717	5.9	6 208	1.3
Switzerland	35 928	4.7	-	-
Croatia	4 335	1.0	26 037	5.9

(1) For air: aggregates exclude the double-counting impact of passengers flying between countries belonging to the same aggregate. For maritime: figures refer to the number of passengers 'handled in ports' (i.e. the sum of passengers embarked and then disembarked in ports); if both the port of embarkation and disembarkation report data to Eurostat, then these passengers are counted twice.
(2) Total passengers carried (arrivals and departures for national and international); Norway, 2008.
(3) Bulgaria, Denmark, Lithuania, Malta, Romania, Finland and Croatia, 2009; Iceland, 2006.

Source: Eurostat (ttr00012, tps00001 and mar_pa_aa)

10.3 Freight transport

The ability to move goods safely, quickly and cost-efficiently to markets is important for international trade, national distributive trades, and economic development. This subchapter presents information on the freight transport sector in the European Union (EU), which includes the following transport modes: road, rail, air, maritime and inland waterways.

The rapid increase in global trade up to the onset of the financial and economic crisis and the deepening integration of the enlarged EU, alongside a range of economic practices (including the concentration of production in fewer sites to reap economies of scale, delocalisation, and just-in-time deliveries), may explain the relatively fast growth of freight transport within the EU. In contrast, strains on transport infrastructure (congestion and delays), coupled with constraints over technical standards, interoperability and governance issues may slow down developments within the freight transport sector.

Main statistical findings

Total inland freight transport in the EU-27 was estimated to be close to 2 400 000 million tonne-kilometres (tkm) in 2008; a little over three quarters (76.4 %) of this freight total was transported over roads in 2008 (see Table 10.6). The relative importance of road freight transport, as a share of total inland freight transport, rose by 2.7 percentage points between 2000 and 2008. The volume of inland freight transported by road was a little over four times as high as the volume transported by rail (17.8 % of inland freight transported in the EU-27 in 2008), while the remainder (5.9 %) of the freight transported in the EU-27 was carried along inland waterways. It should be noted that this analysis refers only to inland freight transport and that considerable volumes of freight may be transported by maritime freight services and for some product groups by air transport or by pipelines.

The relative ascendancy of road freight transport was common in most of the Member States, with the exception of the Baltic Member States, Austria and Sweden, where at least one third of the inland freight transported took place on the railways in 2008; in Latvia, a majority of inland freight was transported by rail (61.3 %). Between 10 % and 16 % of total inland freight was transported on the inland waterways of Belgium, Bulgaria, Germany and Romania in 2008; this share rose to over one third (34.7 %) of the total in the Netherlands.

The volume of EU-27 inland freight transport grew at a faster pace than constant price GDP during the period from 2000 to 2008 (overall 4.0 % higher) – see Table 10.7. Slovenia and Romania recorded the fastest growth in inland freight transport relative to GDP growth (50 % higher), while the volume of inland freight transport grew by at least 20 % more than GDP in Portugal, Hungary, Spain, Poland and Bulgaria. In contrast, there was lower freight transport growth than GDP growth in Estonia, Belgium and Denmark, as GDP grew at least 25 % faster.

Road freight

Relative to the size of their respective populations, the greatest volume of road freight transport was reported for Luxembourg, over 17 000 tonne-kilometres per inhabitant, almost two and a half times the next highest volume in Slovenia; in both cases, the vast majority of this road freight transportation was international, performed by vehicles registered in each of these Member States. Indeed, it is important to note that road freight statistics are generally based on movements in the registration country or abroad, of vehicles registered in the reporting country ('nationality principle').

Slightly more than two thirds of the goods transported on the EU-27's roads in 2009 related to the transportation of goods on national road networks (see Figure 10.5). However, this proportion varied considerably between the Member States: with the highest proportion of national road freight transport in the islands of Cyprus (98.1 %) and the United Kingdom (93.6 % in 2007), while the relative importance of national freight was much lower in Slovakia (19.9 %), Slovenia (15.4 %), Lithuania (14.8 %) and Luxembourg (6.3 %). For most freight hauliers registered in the EU, international road freight transport mostly relates to exchanges with other EU Member States (intra-EU partners).

Air freight

About 12.3 million tonnes of air freight (both national and international) was carried through airports within the EU-27 in 2009 (see Figure 10.6). Airports in Germany dealt with 3.3 million tonnes of air freight, considerably more than in any other EU Member State – the United Kingdom had the second highest amount of air freight at 2.2 million tonnes. Some of the smaller Member States are relatively specialised in air freight, notably all of the Benelux countries, and in particular, Luxembourg (which ranked as the seventh largest air freight transporter among the EU Member States).

Maritime freight

Maritime ports in the EU-27 handled 3 919 million tonnes of seaborne goods in 2008, which marked a modest reduction of 0.4 % when compared with 2007. Sea ports in the United Kingdom handled 562 million tonnes of goods in 2008, more than any other Member State and equivalent to 14.3 % of the EU-27 total. Among the smaller Member States, the quantity of goods handled in maritime ports of the Netherlands, Belgium and the Nordic Member States was particularly high (see Figure 10.7).

Data sources and availability

The development of freight transport statistics is based upon a raft of framework legislation and implementing legislation, generally broken down according to the mode of transport under consideration.

Information on inland freight transport is available with an annual frequency and the time series generally begin in the early 1990s. The majority of inland freight transport statistics are based on movements in each reporting country, regardless of the nationality of the vehicle or vessel involved (the 'territoriality principle'). For this reason, the volume measure of tonne-kilometres is generally considered as a more reliable measure, as the use of tonnes entails a higher risk of double-counting, particularly for international transport. The methodology used across the EU Member States is not completely harmonised, for example, road freight statistics are generally based on all movements (in the registration country or abroad) of vehicles registered in the reporting country (the 'nationality principle'). Therefore, the statistics presented, especially those for the smallest reporting countries, may be somewhat unrepresentative.

The modal split of inland freight transport is based on transportation by road, rail and inland waterways, and therefore excludes air, maritime and pipeline transport. It measures the share of each transport mode in total inland freight transport and is based on the volume of goods transported in tonne-kilometres, in other words, one tonne of goods travelling a distance of one kilometre.

The volume of inland freight transport may also be expressed in relation to gross domestic product (GDP); within this subchapter the indicator is presented in constant prices for the reference year 2000, providing information on the relationship between the demand for freight transport and economic growth, with the series indexed on 2000=100, so that the annual intensity of freight transport demand can be monitored relative to economic developments.

Goods loaded are those goods placed on a road vehicle, a railway vehicle or a merchant ship for dispatch by road, rail or sea. The weight of goods transported by rail and inland waterways is the gross-gross weight. This includes the total weight of the goods, all packaging, and the tare-weight of the container, swap-body and pallets containing goods; in the case of rail freight transport, it also includes road goods vehicles that are carried by rail. In contrast, the weight measured for maritime and road freight transport is the gross weight (in other words, excluding the tare-weight).

Road freight

Road freight transport statistics are collected under the framework provided by Regulation 1172/98 on statistical returns in respect of the carriage of goods by road, amended by Regulation 399/2009 which details implementing powers conferred on the European Commission. The data are based on sample surveys carried out in the reporting countries and record the transport of goods by road, as undertaken by vehicles registered in each of the Member States. It is important to note that almost all of the Member States apply a cut-off point for carrying capacity under which vehicles are not surveyed; this should not be greater than 3.5 tonnes carrying capacity, or 6 tonnes in terms of gross vehicle weight; some of the Member States also apply a limit on the age of the vehicles surveyed.

Rail freight

Rail freight data are collected under the framework provided by Regulation

91/2003 on rail transport statistics. The data are collected for a quarterly frequency (usually limited to larger enterprises) and for an annual frequency (which covers enterprises of all sizes). Rail freight data are not available for Malta and Cyprus (or Iceland) as they do not have a railway infrastructure. Rail statistics are also collected every five years in relation to a regional breakdown (NUTS 2 level).

Aside from the mandatory collection of data based on legal acts, Eurostat also collects rail transport statistics through a voluntary data collection exercise. The questionnaire used for this exercise provides information in relation to railway transport infrastructures, equipment, enterprises, traffic and train movements.

Maritime freight

The legal framework for the collection of statistics on maritime freight transport is Directive 2009/42/EC on statistical returns in respect of carriage of goods and passengers by sea (Recast). Maritime transport data are available for most of the period from 2001 onwards, although some EU Member States have provided data since 1997. Maritime freight statistics are not transmitted to Eurostat by the Czech Republic, Luxembourg, Hungary, Austria and Slovakia as they have no maritime ports.

Inland waterways freight

The legal framework for the collection of statistics on inland waterway freight transport is Regulation 1365/2006 on statistics of goods transport by inland waterways. Data on inland waterways are only required for those Member States with an annual quantity of goods transported that exceeds one million tonnes, namely Belgium, Bulgaria, the Czech Republic, Germany, France, Luxembourg, Hungary, the Netherlands, Austria, Poland, Romania, Slovakia and the United Kingdom; Croatia also provides data. Data collection is based on an exhaustive survey of all inland waterway undertakings for all goods that are loaded or unloaded. In the case of transit, some countries make use of sampling methods in order to estimate the quantity of goods.

Air freight

The legal framework for air transport statistics is provided by Regulation 437/2003 on statistical returns in respect of the carriage of passengers, freight and mail by air. Air freight statistics are collected for freight and mail loaded and unloaded in relation to commercial air flights. The information is broken down to cover national and international freight transport, with the latter being split between intra-EU and extra-EU partners.

Air transport statistics are collected at the airport level by the EU Member States, Norway, Iceland, Switzerland and the candidate countries. Annual data are available for most of the EU Member States for the period from 2003 onwards, while some countries have provided data back to 1993. The statistics that are collected are also available for a monthly and a quarterly frequency. Air freight statistics are also collected for a regional breakdown (NUTS 2 level).

More detailed definitions of the statistical terms used within transport statistics are available in the Illustrated Glossary for Transport Statistics - 4th edition, 2010.

Context

One of the main challenges identified by the 2001 White paper, titled 'European transport policy for 2010: time to decide' (COM(2001) 370) was to address the imbalance in the development of different transport modes. Specific actions looking to boost rail and maritime connections were foreseen, including the establishment of the Marco Polo programme which aims to free Europe's roads through the promotion of alternative forms of freight transport that may be greener, cleaner and (in the long-run) cheaper. Part of the Marco Polo programme concentrates on making better use of existing infrastructures, by encouraging the integration of short-sea shipping, rail transport and inland waterways into the logistics chain, through the recognition that each transport mode has its own advantages either in terms of potential capacity, levels of safety, flexibility, energy consumption, or environmental impact.

A mid-term review of the White paper, titled 'Keep Europe moving – sustainable mobility for our continent' (COM(2006) 314) made a number of suggestions for new policy developments, which have been subsequently expanded upon in the form of a series of European Commission Communications and internal working documents, these include:

- The EU's freight transport agenda: boosting the efficiency, integration and sustainability of freight transport in Europe (COM(2007) 606), which proposed a series of measures to: promote freight transport logistics; make rail freight more competitive; create a framework to allow European ports to attract investment for their modernisation; put maritime freight transport on an equal footing with other transport modes, and; review progress made in developing so-called 'motorways of the sea'.
- A freight transport logistics action plan (COM(2007) 607), which covered, among others, e-freight and intelligent transport systems, the promotion of interoperability across transport modes, single transport documents, and the removal of regulatory obstacles.
- A move towards a rail network giving priority to freight COM(2007) 608), which proposed improvements to the infrastructure of existing freight corridors, measures to improve service quality, the introduction of harmonised rules for the allocation of train paths, and the improvement of terminal and marshalling yard capacities.
- A European ports policy (COM (2007) 616) including proposals for modernisation with respect to the simplification of procedures for short-sea shipping, an e-maritime approach to administration and improved port equipment, and the expansion of capacity whilst respecting the environment.
- A document reporting on the motorways of the sea (SEC(2007) 1367) which discussed the progress made in relation to trans-European networks and the Marco Polo programme, as

well as opportunities to reduce bureaucracy, improve promotion and marketing, ensure the availability of suitable vessels, provide adequate training, ensure the availability of connections, and establish integrated information systems.

- A 'Greening transport' package (COM(2008) 433) which included a three-pronged strategy that sought to: ensure that the price of transport better reflects its real cost to society in terms of environmental damage and congestion; develop more efficient and greener road tolls for lorries, and; reduce noise pollution from rail freight.
- A set of strategic goals and recommendations for the EU's maritime transport policy until 2018 (COM(2009) 8) presented the main strategic objectives for the EU's maritime transport system, including the ability of the maritime transport sector to provide cost-efficient maritime transport services adapted to the needs of sustainable economic growth, and the long-term competitiveness of the EU's shipping sector.
- A European maritime transport space without barriers (COM(2009) 10) which presented ideas designed to help boost short-sea services, through a reduction in administrative formalities, in particular the removal of customs formalities that do not apply to similar road transport services.

Table 10.6: Modal split of inland freight transport ([1])
(% of total inland tkm)

	2000			2008		
	Roads	Railways	Inland waterways	Roads	Railways	Inland waterways
EU-27	*73.7*	*19.7*	*6.6*	*76.4*	*17.8*	*5.9*
Belgium	77.4	11.6	10.9	69.1	15.1	15.8
Bulgaria	52.3	45.2	2.6	66.9	20.5	12.6
Czech Republic	68.0	31.9	0.2	76.7	23.3	:
Denmark	92.1	7.9	-	91.3	8.7	:
Germany	65.3	19.2	15.5	65.5	22.2	12.3
Estonia	37.3	62.7	0.0	55.3	44.7	:
Ireland	96.2	3.8	-	99.4	0.6	:
Greece	:	:	-	97.3	2.7	:
Spain	92.8	7.2	-	95.9	4.1	:
France	76.0	20.6	3.4	80.6	15.9	3.5
Italy	89.0	11.0	0.1	*88.3*	*11.7*	:
Cyprus	100.0	-	-	100.0	-	:
Latvia	26.5	73.5	0.0	38.7	61.3	0.0
Lithuania	46.6	53.4	0.0	58.0	41.9	0.1
Luxembourg	87.8	7.9	4.4	94.2	2.5	3.3
Hungary	68.1	28.8	3.1	74.7	20.6	4.7
Malta	100.0	-	-	100.0	-	:
Netherlands	63.4	3.7	32.9	59.9	5.4	34.7
Austria ([2])	64.8	30.6	4.5	58.6	37.4	4.0
Poland	56.9	42.2	0.9	75.9	24.0	0.1
Portugal	92.5	7.5	-	93.9	6.1	:
Romania	42.9	49.1	7.9	70.2	19.0	10.8
Slovenia	*71.9*	*28.1*	-	82.2	17.8	:
Slovakia	53.0	41.7	5.3	73.8	23.4	2.8
Finland	75.8	24.0	0.3	73.3	26.5	0.2
Sweden	63.9	36.1	-	64.7	35.3	:
United Kingdom	90.0	9.8	0.1	*88.5*	*11.5*	:
Iceland	100.0	-	-	100.0	-	:
Norway	83.5	16.5	-	85.0	15.0	:
Croatia	:	:	:	72.7	21.8	5.5
FYR of Macedonia	86.9	13.1	-	:	:	:
Turkey	94.3	5.7	-	:	:	:

([1]) Excluding pipelines.
([2]) The railway in Liechtenstein is owned and operated by the Austrian ÖBB and included in their statistics.

Source: Eurostat (tsdtr220)

Table 10.7: Volume of inland freight transport (¹)
(index of inland freight transport volume relative to GDP, 2000=100)

	1998	1999	2000	2001	2002	2003	2004	2005	2006	2007	2008
EU-27	*101.1*	*100.1*	100.0	*99.0*	*100.2*	*99.3*	*105.4*	*105.4*	*106.0*	*106.5*	*104.0*
Belgium	89.1	80.2	100.0	102.2	101.3	97.3	91.3	84.9	*82.5*	*80.0*	*72.8*
Bulgaria	63.6	49.9	100.0	104.8	105.0	109.9	119.7	128.0	118.3	116.6	120.7
Czech Republic	100.9	101.5	100.0	99.6	103.9	105.2	98.6	88.5	94.0	86.2	86.6
Denmark	95.6	100.1	100.0	91.9	92.7	94.4	93.9	91.1	80.7	77.9	73.8
Germany	97.0	100.4	100.0	99.9	98.9	100.0	104.5	106.1	109.7	111.7	110.0
Estonia	76.6	91.7	100.0	89.5	92.7	84.6	90.1	87.0	76.7	66.5	61.8
Ireland	82.2	92.0	100.0	95.1	102.3	107.0	111.8	109.3	100.6	102.9	97.0
Greece	:	:	100.0	:	:	:	:	:	:	:	:
Spain	*93.6*	95.5	100.0	104.0	114.9	116.1	*128.1*	130.1	129.4	133.1	123.9
France	100.2	103.0	100.0	96.9	94.9	92.4	92.7	87.2	87.6	88.7	83.4
Italy	*105.1*	99.4	100.0	98.8	100.4	91.6	101.7	108.2	*95.5*	*91.2*	*92.0*
Cyprus	*104.7*	*101.6*	100.0	99.3	101.2	105.2	80.6	96.6	77.6	76.1	80.0
Latvia	104.3	96.7	100.0	99.9	101.9	111.0	107.2	105.0	91.6	95.2	101.0
Lithuania	85.0	96.5	100.0	89.9	107.6	109.2	106.2	116.8	118.5	120.5	119.0
Luxembourg	*80.9*	91.6	100.0	109.2	109.4	111.6	107.1	92.2	88.2	87.7	96.1
Hungary	110.4	101.9	100.0	93.9	89.5	85.8	93.6	105.1	118.4	132.4	131.1
Malta	:	:	100.0	:	:	:	:	:	:	:	:
Netherlands	106.7	106.9	100.0	97.4	97.8	96.2	105.6	98.7	95.2	91.4	89.1
Austria	93.4	98.1	100.0	104.7	105.7	105.2	104.3	98.5	102.2	97.7	91.4
Poland	112.0	103.0	100.0	97.6	98.4	98.4	108.2	108.9	115.2	121.6	122.5
Portugal	101.7	101.2	100.0	108.4	107.0	99.7	143.5	148.6	153.8	155.9	133.0
Romania	:	95.2	100.0	106.3	119.6	127.1	145.1	174.2	171.4	165.6	148.5
Slovenia	*106.5*	*102.4*	100.0	101.3	95.5	98.8	114.5	128.7	132.0	138.4	152.5
Slovakia	116.3	112.9	100.0	92.3	87.0	88.1	88.2	93.7	86.9	92.0	90.9
Finland	98.9	98.7	100.0	93.7	95.0	91.6	91.1	86.7	81.4	76.7	76.4
Sweden	*102.9*	*98.0*	100.0	95.4	96.9	96.7	94.4	95.3	94.4	94.4	97.1
United Kingdom	110.8	104.3	100.0	97.0	95.1	94.1	*93.6*	*91.3*	*93.3*	*90.2*	*87.0*
Iceland	102.1	103.8	100.0	*105.5*	*108.3*	*108.8*	*109.6*	*113.1*	*119.2*	:	:
Norway	102.6	101.5	100.0	97.8	96.6	101.4	103.1	105.9	109.9	107.6	111.9
FYR of Macedonia	:	:	100.0	93.5	*111.8*	146.1	139.0	141.5	198.5	141.2	:
Turkey	96.7	99.2	100.0	98.4	92.2	89.1	84.2	82.2	81.7	79.8	:

(¹) Excluding pipelines; breaks in series: Bulgaria, Hungary and Slovakia, 2000; Bulgaria, 2001; EU-27, Portugal and Romania, 2004.

Source: Eurostat (tsien060)

Table 10.8: Inland freight transport, 2009

	(million tkm)			(tkm per inhabitant)			National air freight and mail transport (tonnes) (4)
	Road (1)	Rail (2)	Inland water-ways (3)	Road (1)	Rail (2)	Inland water-ways (3)	
EU-27	:	442 738	144 953	:	*889.6*	*291.3*	591 286
Belgium	36 174	8 572	8 746	*3 365.0*	803.6	819.9	326
Bulgaria	17 742	4 693	5 436	2 332.5	614.2	714.6	26
Czech Republic	44 955	15 437	33	4 294.7	1 487.0	3.2	2 157
Denmark	16 876	1 866	-	3 065.3	340.8	-	1 975
Germany	307 547	115 652	55 652	3 750.5	1 406.7	678.7	119 942
Estonia	5 340	5 943	:	3 983.8	4 432.0	:	0
Ireland	12 668	103	-	*2 846.7*	23.4	-	9 267
Greece	28 850	786	-	2 572.7	70.1	-	12 670
Spain	211 895	10 475	-	4 623.7	231.3	-	81 290
France	173 621	40 627	8 673	2 697.4	634.8	134.7	136 255
Italy	179 411	23 831	:	3 034.1	399.7	:	54 895
Cyprus	963	-	-	1 208.5	-	-	178
Latvia	8 115	19 581	:	3 588.7	8 622.6	:	0
Lithuania	17 757	14 748	:	5 300.8	4 381.0	:	0
Luxembourg	8 400	279	279	17 021.3	576.7	565.3	0
Hungary	35 373	9 874	1 831	3 526.4	982.9	182.5	0
Malta	:	-	-	:	-	-	0
Netherlands	71 566	6 984	35 656	4 341.1	425.7	2 162.8	2
Austria	29 075	21 915	2 003	3 479.8	2 634.5	239.7	782
Poland	180 742	52 043	202	4 739.4	1 365.4	5.3	6 859
Portugal	35 808	2 549	-	*3 369.5*	240.1	-	20 049
Romania	34 269	15 236	11 765	1 594.0	707.7	547.2	217
Slovenia	14 762	3 520	:	7 263.5	1 751.0	:	0
Slovakia	27 705	9 299	899	5 118.9	1 721.7	166.1	1
Finland	27 805	10 777	:	5 220.3	2 033.2	:	3 921
Sweden	35 047	23 116	-	3 786.3	2 517.3	-	15 732
United Kingdom	171 477	24 831	:	2 821.2	405.9	:	124 741
Liechtenstein	263	17	:	7 389.9	480.8	:	:
Norway	18 447	3 621	-	3 843.7	764.4	-	17 095
Switzerland	11 882	12 265	:	1 542.7	1 615.2	:	4 092
Croatia	9 426	3 312	727	2 125.3	746.6	163.9	1 163
Turkey	:	10 552	-	:	149.5	-	:

(1) Greece, 2008; Italy and the United Kingdom, 2007; road transport is based on movements all over the world of vehicles registered in the reporting country.
(2) 2008.
(3) EU-27 and Belgium, 2008.
(4) Data based on departures; France underestimated as freight transport at Paris Charles-de-Gaulle and Paris Orly is incomplete.

Source: Eurostat (road_go_ta_tott, rail_go_typeall, ttr00007, tps00001 and avia_gooc) and Directorate-General for Mobility and Transport

Figure 10.5: National and international road transport of goods, 2009 (1)
(% based on million tkm of laden transport)

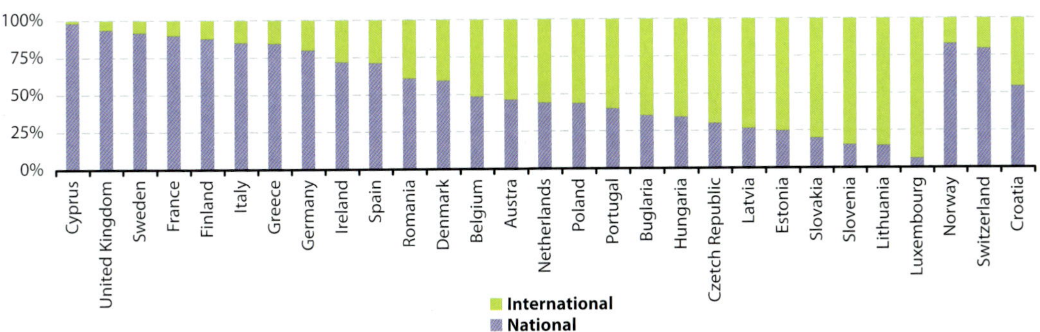

(1) Greece, 2008; Italy and the United Kingdom, 2007; Malta, not available.

Source: Eurostat (road_go_ta_tott)

Figure 10.6: Air freight transport, 2009
(1 000 tonnes)

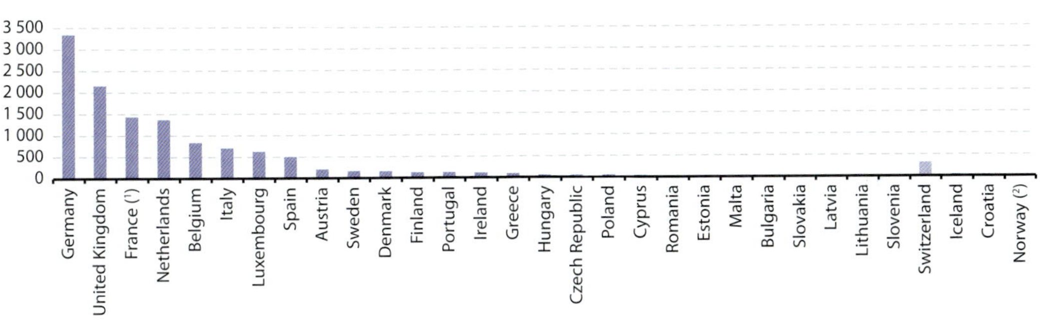

(1) Underestimated: freight transport at Paris Charles-de-Gaulle and Paris Orly is incomplete.
(2) 2008.

Source: Eurostat (ttr00011)

Figure 10.7: Gross weight of seaborne goods handled in ports, 2008 (1)
(million tonnes)

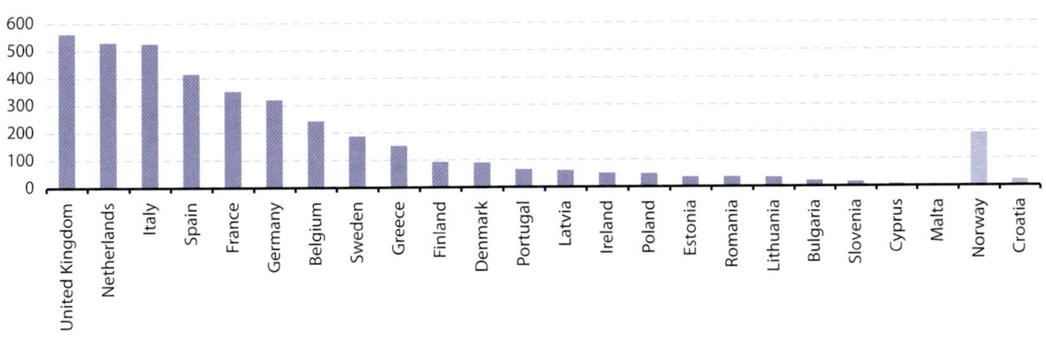

(1) Bulgaria, Denmark, Lithuania, Malta, Romania, Finland and Croatia, 2009; the Czech Republic, Luxembourg, Hungary, Austria and Slovakia, not applicable.

Source: Eurostat (mar_go_aa)

11 Environment

Eurostat, in close partnership with the European Environment Agency (EEA), provides statistics and further information on environmental pressures and the state of the environment. This data supports the implementation and monitoring of the European Union's (EU's) environmental legislation, including its sixth environment action programme (EAP). The action programme, laid down by the European Parliament and Council of Ministers Decision 1600/2002/EC of 22 July 2002 is a ten-year (2002-2012) policy programme for the environment. It identifies four key priorities:

- tackling climate change;
- nature and biodiversity;
- environment and health;
- sustainable use of natural resources and the management of waste.

Climate change: the action programme foresees an 8 % cut in greenhouse gas emissions in the period 2008-2012 compared with 1990 levels. Furthermore, the EU adopted a climate action and renewable energy package in December 2008, obliging it to cut emissions to at least 20 % below 1990 levels by 2020.

Nature and biodiversity: although the original goal of halting biodiversity loss by 2010 was not reached, a new target was adopted in March 2010: to halt the loss of biodiversity and the degradation of ecosystem services in the EU by 2020, and to restore them insofar as feasible – while stepping up the EU's contribution to averting global biodiversity loss. Policies include completion of the Natura 2000 network, which is the largest network of protected areas in the world. Other actions concern developing new sectoral biodiversity action plans; paying greater attention to protecting landscapes, the marine environment and soils; and establishing measures to prevent industrial and mining accidents.

Environment and health: the EU strives to engender closer cooperation between health, environment and research areas. Its policies in this domain include a complete overhaul of the EU's risk-management system for chemicals, developing a strategy for reducing risks from pesticides, protection of water quality in the EU, noise abatement, and a thematic strategy for air quality.

Sustainable use of natural resources and the management of waste: the EU's policies in this area include increasing resource efficiency and decoupling resource use from economic growth, increasing recycling and waste prevention with the aid of an integrated product policy and measures targeting specific waste streams, such as hazardous waste, sludges and biodegradable waste.

In order to implement the sixth environment action programme, the European Commission adopted seven thematic strategies: air pollution (adopted in September 2005); marine environment (October 2005); the prevention and recycling of waste (December 2005); the sustainable use of natural resources (December 2005); urban environment (January 2006); soil (September 2006); and the sustainable use of pesticides (July 2006). The data required to monitor the action programme are collected in ten environmental data centres. Eurostat manages the data centres on waste, natural resources and products, while the EEA is responsible for air, climate change and water, biodiversity and land use, and the Joint Research Centre (JRC) is responsible for soil and forestry. Each strategy follows an in-depth review of existing policy and wide-ranging stakeholder consultation. The aim is to create positive synergies between the seven strategies, as well as to integrate them with existing sectoral policies and the sustainable development strategy. At the European Council meeting of 26 March 2010, EU leaders set out their plans for a Europe 2020 strategy for smart, sustainable and inclusive growth. As part of the sustainable growth priority one of the flagship initiatives concerns a resource-efficient Europe. The aims are to help decouple economic growth from the use of resources, support the shift towards a low-carbon economy, increase the use of renewable energy sources, modernise the transport sector, and promote energy efficiency. The integrated economic and employment guidelines, first combined in 2008, were also revised as part of the Europe 2020 strategy. Guideline 5 concerns improving resource efficiency and reducing greenhouse gases.

11.1 Air emissions accounts

Air emissions accounts record emissions of greenhouse gases and air pollutants in the European Union (EU) by the economic activities responsible for their production (in line with the 'polluter pays' principle), following the same economic activity classification that is used within the national accounts, namely NACE. Air emissions accounts are thus different from emissions inventories, for example, those used for official reporting under international obligations (for example, under the Kyoto Protocol).

Air emissions accounts are a statistical information system that combines air emissions data and economic data from national accounts. The main purpose of these accounts is to provide data for integrated environmental-economic analyses and modelling, by supplementing traditional economic data with environmental indicators.

Main statistical findings

Examining environmental variables together with economic ones can help identify which economic activity contributes to which environmental pressure and thus be helpful in devising specific policy measures where most needed. When considering the six economic activities presented in Figure 11.1, there were only modest changes in the economic weight of each activity in EU-25 gross monetary output during the period from 1996 to 2006.

The largest activity was the grouping of construction and other services (both private and public) which comprises construction, retail and wholesale trade, real estate, renting, financial services, hotels and restaurants, as well as public administration, education, health and social work, that accounted for 56.8 % of the EU-25's gross monetary output in 2006. Manufacturing activities accounted for 30.2 % of output in 2006, followed by transport, storage and communication with 8.1 %. The shares of electricity, gas and water supply (2.9 %) and the primary activities of agriculture, hunting, forestry and fisheries (1.5 %) and mining and quarrying (0.5 %) were relatively small.

When looking at the air emissions that stem from economic activity across the EU economy, the image has a very different structure to that of economic output – as shown in Figures 11.2 to 11.4. This was particularly the case for the construction and other services grouping, as these activities were responsible for 11.3 % of EU-27 direct greenhouse gas (GHG) emissions, for 4.9 % of acidifying emissions, and for 12.8 % of ground ozone precursors in 2006. In the same year, manufacturing industries accounted for 25.9 % of GHG emissions, 15.5 % of acidifying substances and 27.0 % of ground ozone precursors. These shares for construction and other services and for manufacturing represented a reduction when compared with data for 1996; the biggest reduction being recorded for ground ozone precursors from construction and other services which fell by 2.8 percentage points from 1996 to 2006.

The main emitting activities in the EU-27 in 2006 were agriculture, hunting, forestry and fishing, electricity, gas and water supply, and transport services (which are reported together with storage and communications but exclude the use of private cars, reported under households). These three activity groupings together contributed the majority of the EU-27's greenhouse gas emissions (59.9 %), acidifying emissions (78.7 %), and ground ozone precursors (58.4 %), while their share of EU-25 monetary output was 12.5 %. Note that the EU increasingly imports metals and industrial minerals, whose production potentially generates pressures on the environment in non-member countries (see Subchapter 11.4 on material flow accounts).

There was a rapid increase in the relative importance of emissions from transport, storage and communication activities between 1996 and 2006, its share of acidifying emissions rising by 8.2 percentage points (mainly due to increased sulphur dioxide and nitrous oxide emissions resulting from the combustion of fossil fuels in vehicle engines, in particular from road freight transport). The share of transport, storage and communication activities in EU-27 ground ozone precursors rose by 4.7 points between 1996 and 2006, and its share of greenhouse gases rose by 3.2 points (note that the figures presented do not include greenhouse gas emissions from private transport, principally passenger cars as these emissions are produced by households).

In contrast, the relative importance of emissions from manufacturing fell between 1996 and 2006 for each of the three types of emissions covered in Figures 11.2 to 11.4. Furthermore, the share of manufacturing in EU-25 output was higher than manufacturing's share of any of the three types of emissions covered – indicating that its relative contribution to emissions was lower than the average across all economic activities.

Among the economic activities covered, electricity, gas and water supply was the largest contributor of greenhouse gas emissions in the EU-27 in 2006 (35.1 %); these activities also had the highest greenhouse gas emissions intensity (as measured by the volume of carbon dioxide equivalent emissions per unit of monetary output). Indeed, the relatively small contribution of electricity, gas and water supply to economic output was in stark contrast to providing the biggest share of EU-27 greenhouse gas emissions.

Electricity, gas and water supply was also the largest contributor of acidifying emissions in the EU-27 in 1996 (37.2 %), mainly due to sulphur dioxide emissions from fossil fuel combustion. It was followed by agriculture, hunting, forestry and fishing (27.3 %), mainly due to ammonia emissions. The picture was quite different in 2006, as agriculture, hunting, forestry and fishing contributed the largest share (32.3 %), principally due to emissions of ammonia. The share of electricity, gas and water supply fell to 26.4 %, followed by transport, storage and communication services (20.0 %); this reduction may reflect a change in the energy mix and a switch from traditional fossil fuels to cleaner fuels and technologies.

More than one quarter (28.6 %) of the EU-27's ground level ozone precursors came from transport, storage and communication services in 2006 (mainly non-methane volatile organic compounds and nitrous oxides).

Data sources and availability

The compilation of air emissions accounts is based on information that is already available; it does not require any new statistical surveys. The two main sources of data are two international conventions that govern efforts to reduce the release of polluting substances into the air, namely: the Kyoto Protocol for the United Nations Framework Convention on Climate Change (UNFCCC) concerning greenhouse gases; and the Gothenburg Protocol to the Convention on Long-Range Transboundary Air Pollution (CLRTAP) concerning acidifying substances. The core data from these emissions inventories is published and distributed by the European Environment Agency (EEA). In order to produce air emissions accounts, this emissions data are re-organised according to a breakdown by economic activity, as used within national accounts (based on the statistical classification of economic activities, NACE).

The activity headings that are used in this subchapter are constructed as follows:

- Agriculture, hunting, forestry and fishing - NACE Rev. 1.1 Sections A and B;
- Mining and quarrying - NACE Rev. 1.1 Section C;
- Manufacturing - NACE Rev. 1.1 Section D;
- Electricity, gas and water supply - NACE Rev. 1.1 Section E;
- Transport, storage and communication - NACE Rev. 1.1 Section I;
- Other services and construction - NACE Rev. 1.1 Sections F, G, H, J, K, L, M, N, O and Q.

The scope for air emissions accounts encompasses all nationally registered businesses (including those operating in other countries – the residence principle). Emissions are allocated to the economic activity responsible for producing them; unlike national emissions inventories, where the boundary for measuring the extent of emissions is the territorial border. As such, the accounting methodology used within air emissions accounts is not suited for monitoring progress towards internationally agreed emissions reduction targets, such as under the Kyoto Protocol.

Emissions of individual greenhouse gases and air pollutants may be aggregated to provide information on three environmental pressures: greenhouse gas emissions are typically reported in terms of carbon dioxide equivalents, acidifying emissions in terms of sulphur dioxide equivalents, and ground level ozone precursors in terms of non-methane volatile organic compound equivalents. The use of these units allows the relative effect of different gases to be accounted for in a single, aggregated value – for example, a single kilogram of methane has 21 times the global warming effect of a kilogram of carbon dioxide.

Air emissions accounts present information for three of the six Kyoto Protocol greenhouse gases – carbon dioxide, methane and nitrous oxide; at the time of writing, no information is available for perfluorocarbons (PFCs), hydrofluorocarbons (HFCs) or sulphur hexafluoride, as most EU Member States are unable to provide a breakdown for these gases by economic activity (NACE).

Eurostat is working on the establishment of a legal base for the compilation of environmental accounts and the European Commission has put forward a proposal for a Regulation on European environmental economic accounts COM(2010) 132. The proposal provides a framework for the development of various types of accounts, initially based on three modules with a view of adding other modules as they reach methodological maturity. Air emissions accounts are one of the three modules, alongside modules for material flow accounts (see Subchapter 11.4) and environmentally related taxes by economic activity (see Subchapter 11.7). It is expected that this proposed legal base will strengthen the coherence and availability of environmental accounts across the EU by providing a legal framework for their compilation, including methodology, common standards, definitions, classifications and accounting rules.

Context

Environmental accounts are one statistical means to try to measure the interplay between the economy and the environment in order to see whether current production and consumption activities are on a sustainable path of development. Measuring sustainable development is a complex undertaking as it has to incorporate economic, social and environmental indicators without contradiction. The data obtained may subsequently feed into political decision-making, underpinning policies that target both continued economic growth and sustainable development, for example, initiatives such as the Europe 2020 strategy, which aims to achieve a resource-efficient, low-carbon economy for the EU by 2020. Note that a reduction in one type of environmental pressure can result in an increase in another type of pressure. For example, passenger cars with diesel engines are typically more fuel efficient and therefore tend to produce less carbon dioxide emissions per kilometre travelled. However, if consumers switch to driving diesel cars then (with current engine technology) it is likely that such a switch would be accompanied by an increase in acidifying emissions and ground level ozone precursors.

In order to have such a holistic view of the various aspects of sustainable development, the already existing frameworks of measuring the economy – in other words, the system of national accounts – is supplemented by satellite systems representing environmental or social indicators. These satellite accounts are developed using the same concepts, definitions, classifications and accounting rules as the national accounts, bringing environmental or social data together with economic data in a coherent and comparable framework. Thus, environmental accounts serve to enhance the understanding of pressures exerted by the economy on the environment – for example, accounting for the subsequent release of substances (such as air emissions or waste) into the environment as a result of economic activities. If carried out at an unsustainable rate, there will, in the long-run, be a detrimental effect not only on the environment but also on the economy – as the fundamental resources for production and consumption activities would be irreversibly depleted.

The need to supplement existing information on the economy with environmental indicators has been recognised in a European Commission Communication titled 'GDP and beyond' (COM(2009) 433). Furthermore, similar recommendations have been made within the so-called Stiglitz report, released by the Commission on the Measurement of Economic Performance and Social Progress. The recommendations made support the expansion of the statistical understanding of human well-being by supplementing economic indicators such as GDP with additional information, including physical indicators on the environment.

Table 11.1: Differences between inventories and accounts

	National emissions inventories (territory principle)	Air emissions accounts (residence principle)
Scope of national emissions reported	Direct emissions within the geographical national territory and: - emissions from international bunkers allocated to countries where the fuel is sold and not to the nationality of the purchasing unit; - emissions/removals induced by land use change and forestry are accounted for.	Emissions within the economic territory of the country covered, for example: - emissions of entities registered in the country (e. g. ships operating abroad, residents); - CO_2 from biomass is included since these emissions arise when using these energy carriers)

Figure 11.1: Gross monetary output, analysis by activity, EU-25
(% of total, based on EUR million in constant prices from 2000)

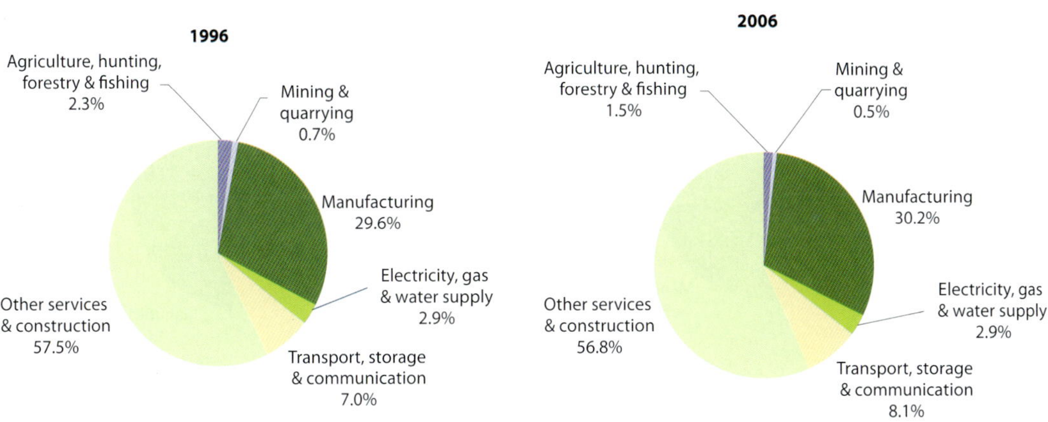

Source: Eurostat (EUKLEMS, http://www.euklems.net/data/09I/eu25_output_09I.xls)

Figure 11.2: Greenhouse gas emissions, analysis by activity (excluding households), EU-27 (1)
(% of total, based on CO_2 equivalents of CO_2, CH_4 and N_2O)

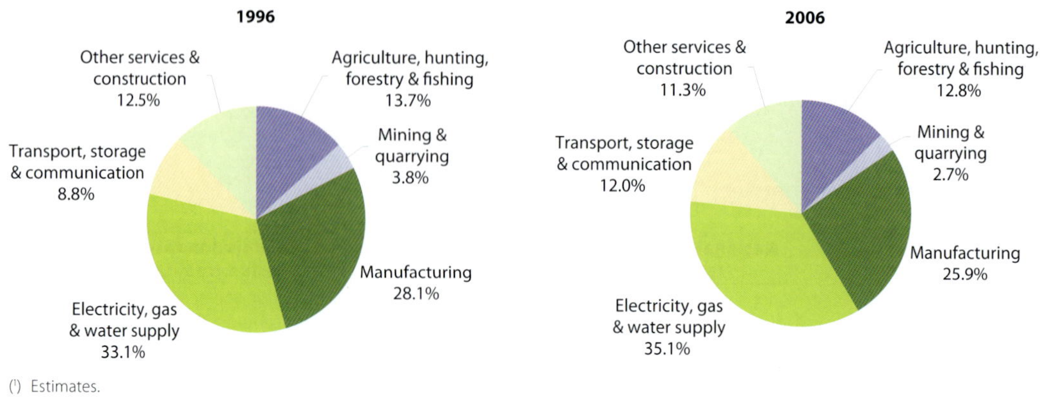

(1) Estimates.

Source: Eurostat (env_ac_ainacehh)

Figure 11.3: Emissions of acidifying substances, analysis by activity (excluding households), EU-27 (1)
(% of total, based on acid equivalents of SO_x, NH_3 and NO_x)

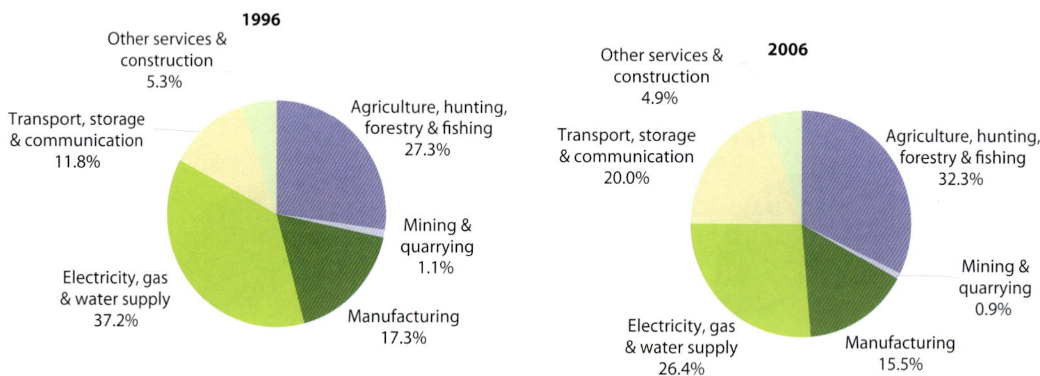

(1) Estimates.

Source: Eurostat (env_ac_ainacehh)

Figure 11.4: Emissions of ground level ozone precursors, analysis by activity (excluding households), EU-27 (1)
(% of total)

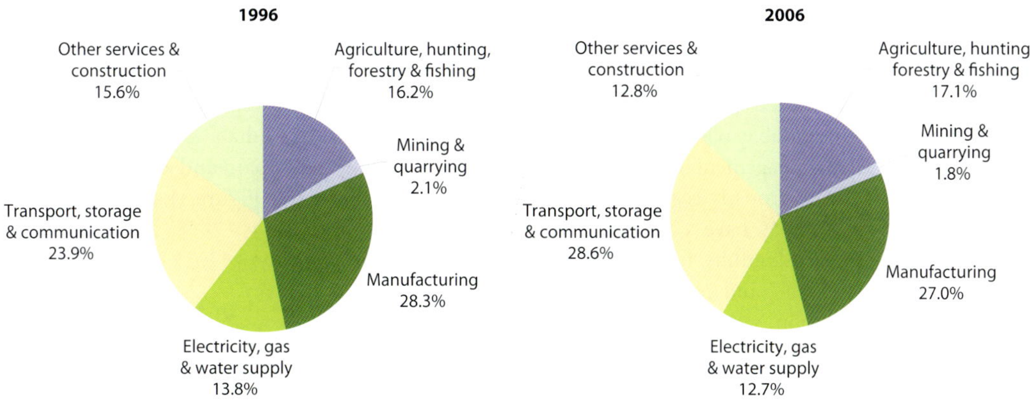

(1) Estimates; values are based on tropospheric ozone formation potential equivalents of NO_x, NMVOC, CO, CH_4.

Source: Eurostat (env_ac_ainacehh)

Table 11.2: Calculation of aggregated environmental pressures

Theme	Unit	Substance	Weighting factors	Pressure
Greenhouse gases	CO_2-equivalents	Carbon dioxide (CO_2)	1	Aggregated greenhouse gas emissions - using Global Warming Potential weighting factors for 100 years
		Methane (CH_4)	21	
		Nitrous oxide (N_2O)	310	
Acidification	SO_2-equivalents	Sulphur dioxide (SO_2)	1	Aggregated acidification emissions
		Nitrogen oxides (NO_x)	0.7	
		Ammonia (NH_3)	1.9	
Tropospheric ozone formation	NMVOC-equivalents	Non-methane volatile organic compounds (NMVOC)	1	Aggregated emissions of tropospheric ozone forming precursors
		Nitrogen oxides (NO_x)	1.22	
		Carbon monoxide (CO)	0.11	
		Methane (CH_4)	0.014	

11.2 Waste

Waste refers to materials for which the generator has no further use for its own purpose of production, transformation or consumption. The large majority of waste in the European Union (EU) is landfilled, incinerated or recycled. There have been considerable efforts in waste prevention and management in the EU in recent years. Unless properly regulated, the disposal of waste may have a serious environmental impact: landfills, for example, can take up land space and may cause air, water and soil pollution, while incineration might result in emissions of dangerous air pollutants.

Main statistical findings

In 2008, about 2 600 million tonnes of waste was generated in the EU-27 (see Table 11.3), of which some 98 million tonnes constituted hazardous waste. Relative to the size of the population, the waste generated in the EU-27 averaged 5 300 kg per inhabitant (see Figure 11.3).

EU-27 waste generation was 240 million tonnes lower in 2008 than it had been in 2006. However, this decrease may be linked more to the application of the statistical classification on waste rather than any real difference in the amount of waste generated. For example, the substantial decrease in agricultural waste may well have resulted from manure no longer being considered as a waste stream (if used for soil improvement in agriculture).

Waste generated by households

Households in the EU-27 generated an average of 444 kg of waste per inhabitant in 2008. The quantity of household waste generated ranged between 300 kg and 500 kg per inhabitant in most of the EU Member States in 2008, with Poland (180 kg per inhabitant) and Latvia notably below this range, and the Netherlands (578 kg per inhabitant), Luxembourg, Cyprus, Italy, Spain and the United Kingdom above (see Figure 11.4).

Waste generated by businesses

In 2008, more than half (54.6 %) of the waste generated in the EU-27 by businesses could be attributed to industrial activities(manufacturing, mining and quarrying), while a little over one third (35.8 %) was from the construction sector. Mining and quarrying produced more than half of the waste generated by industry, although it should be noted that this activity, and as a consequence its waste, is unevenly spread across the EU. Services accounted for 6.7 % of the waste generated by business within the EU-27 in 2008, while the share for agriculture was 1.9 % (see Figure 11.5).

Lithuania reported a substantial proportion of its business waste from agriculture (23.5 %), whereas Bulgaria and Sweden reported most of their business waste from industry (98.6 % and 92.9 % respectively). Luxembourg and Malta reported high shares from construction (88.9 % and 82.6 %) and Portugal reported 34.1 % of its business waste from services. These differences between countries in the structure of the source of waste may be partly explained by differences in the structure of their economies.

Hazardous waste

Some 3.7 % of the waste generated in the EU-27 in 2008 was hazardous – meaning it was harmful for health or the environment (see Figure 11.6). This share ranged from less than 1 % in Greece and Romania to 9.2 % in Portugal and 9.9 % in Belgium; the very high share of hazardous waste in Estonia (38.5 %) is due to energy production from shale oil.

Waste treatment

Figure 11.7 summarises the quantity of waste treated by the three main treatment types: disposal, incineration (including energy recovery) and recovery (including all treatment of biodegradable matter, for example composting). In the EU-27, 5.4 % of waste was incinerated in 2008, 45.7 % was recovered and 48.9 % was disposed. Bulgaria and Malta disposed of more than 96 % of their waste, much of which came from mining and quarrying or construction (including demolition) activities; Denmark and Belgium incinerated a high percentage of their waste, as did Norway.

Composition of waste by treatment

The characteristics of different sorts of waste determine their suitability for various types of treatment. Table 11.4 shows the composition of EU-27 waste by treatment type for 2008. Both recovery and disposal were dominated by mineral waste (for example glass, or waste from construction). The largest category of incinerated waste was household and similar waste, but in general the composition of waste for incineration was more diverse than for the other treatment types. About 8 % of the waste treated by incineration was hazardous, whereas for recovery and disposal this share was roughly 3 %.

Treatment of municipal waste

A time series for municipal waste is available from 1999 to 2009. The quantity of municipal waste generated per inhabitant in the EU-27 grew by 0.4 % overall between 1999 and 2009 to reach 513 kg. There was a significant change in the way municipal waste was treated during this period. Landfilling was the most common option at the start of the period under consideration, with a 59 % share of municipal waste treatment within the EU-27 in 1999; in 2004 the share of landfilling fell below 50 %, and by 2009 it had fallen still further to 38 %. Some 16 % of municipal waste was incinerated in 1999 and this share rose to 20 % by 2009, while the share of waste that was recycled or composted rose from 25 % to 42 % during the same period. Note that the amount of municipal waste indicated as not allocated in Figure 11.8 is the quantity that was generated but not reported in any treatment operation. This is due to incomplete coverage of the population by municipal waste collection schemes in some countries, but also results from weight losses in (pre-)treatment operations.

Data sources and availability

Reliable statistics on the production and management of waste from businesses and private households are used to monitor the implementation of waste policy – in particular, compliance with the principles of recovery and safe disposal. In 2002, Regulation (EC) 2150/2002 on waste statistics was adopted, creating a framework for harmonised Community statistics on waste. Member States are required to provide data on the generation, recovery and disposal of waste every two years; the first reference period for the data collection exercise was 2004. As such, the Regulation on waste statistics has replaced a voluntary Eurostat/OECD joint questionnaire as the main source of waste data for the EU.

Care should be taken when comparing waste levels between Member States. In some countries, households are considered as sources of discarded vehicles, or sources of mineral waste from construction activities, or as a source of sewage sludge; in other countries, specialised services take care of these waste streams. Waste is attributed to the household or business that hands over the waste to the waste collection system. Differences in household waste levels may be partly explained by the problems some countries face to distinguish between waste generated by households and municipal waste.

The implementation of the Regulation replaced the concept of municipal waste with the category of waste generated by households. However, data on municipal waste is still collected annually as part of the structural indicators database. Municipal waste is defined as waste collected by or on behalf of municipalities and includes waste produced by households; it may also include similar waste from offices, small businesses and so on, depending on the arrangements in the municipality. For areas not covered by a municipal waste scheme, estimates have been made as to the amount of waste generated. The treatment of municipal waste can be classified into its principal categories:

- landfill, which is defined as the depositing of waste into or onto land, including specially engineered landfills, and temporary storage of over one year on permanent sites;
- incineration, which refers to the thermal treatment of waste in a specifically designed plant;
- recycling, which refers to any reprocessing of material in a production process that diverts it from the waste stream, except reuse as fuel;
- composting, which is defined as a biological process that submits biodegradable waste to anaerobic or aerobic decomposition, and that results in a product that is recovered.

Context

The EU's sustainable development strategy and its sixth environment action programme (EAP)identify waste prevention and management as one of four top priorities. The objective of these policies is to decouple the use of resources and the generation of waste from economic growth, while ensuring that sustainable consumption does not exceed environmental capacity.

The EU's approach to waste management is based on three principles: waste prevention, recycling and reuse, and improving final disposal and monitoring. Waste prevention can be achieved through cleaner technologies, eco-design, or more eco-efficient production and consumption patterns. Waste prevention and recycling, focused on materials technology, can also reduce the environmental impact of resources that are used through limiting raw materials extraction and transformation during production processes. EU policy promotes the incineration of waste that cannot be recycled or reused, with landfills only used as a last resort. Both of these latter two methods of waste treatment often require close monitoring because of their potential for causing environmental damage.

The European Commission has defined several specific waste streams for priority attention, the aim being to reduce their overall environmental impact. These include packaging waste, end-of-life vehicles, batteries, and electrical and electronic waste. EU Directives require Member States to legislate for waste collection, reuse, recycling and disposal of these waste streams.

Table 11.3: Generation of waste, total arising and by selected activities
(1 000 tonnes)

	Total waste from economic activities and households		Manufacturing		Mining & quarrying		Construction		Services (1)	
	2006	2008	2006	2008	2006	2008	2006	2008	2006	2008
EU-27	2 864 450	2 626 450	360 130	342 700	740 670	727 050	969 730	870 420	155 800	137 700
Belgium	59 352	59 542	15 308	10 090	*159*	503	*13 090*	26 362	*7 039*	*4 402*
Bulgaria	242 489	286 093	4 316	3 447	225 338	267 559	1 023	1 829	1 473	1 462
Czech Republic	24 746	25 420	5 932	5 293	472	167	8 380	10 651	1 025	881
Denmark	14 703	15 155	1 643	1 454	2	2	5 802	5 674	1 486	1 680
Germany	363 786	372 796	31 705	52 322	47 222	28 288	196 536	197 207	15 107	10 067
Estonia	18 933	19 584	3 981	3 772	5 961	7 198	717	1 099	*1 601*	706
Ireland	*29 599*	*23 637*	4 067	4 026	*4 766*	*2 061*	16 599	*0*	1 327	*0*
Greece	51 325	68 644	5 285	5 703	14 888	*38 152*	6 829	*6 828*	1 518	*1 796*
Spain	160 947	149 254	22 427	19 369	26 015	25 716	47 323	44 926	15 376	12 742
France	445 865	345 002	22 973	21 640	1 040	1 195	358 878	252 980	*24 158*	24 083
Italy	155 025	*179 034*	39 997	43 086	1 005	*1 263*	52 316	*69 732*	5 534	*5 550*
Cyprus	1 249	1 843	174	138	28	505	298	431	247	191
Latvia	1 859	1 495	570	501	0	3	19	12	239	166
Lithuania	7 665	6 835	2 948	2 758	6	3	349	412	586	625
Luxembourg	9 586	9 592	604	673	56	10	6 775	8 282	243	184
Hungary	*22 287*	*20 385*	5 528	4 789	*27*	*578*	*3 045*	*5 240*	*2 445*	*1 232*
Malta	2 861	*1 499*	2	13	0	0	2 493	1 099	195	*210*
Netherlands	93 808	99 591	15 562	15 824	213	270	56 610	59 477	5 349	5 784
Austria	54 287	56 309	11 470	13 077	1 043	678	31 322	31 390	3 458	3 396
Poland	170 230	140 340	61 131	56 746	38 671	33 666	14 141	6 930	3 512	4 977
Portugal	*34 953*	36 480	10 929	9 001	*3 563*	1 891	*3 607*	8 085	*10 353*	10 344
Romania	344 425	189 323	9 161	11 064	199 127	140 677	34	330	5 593	4 139
Slovenia	6 036	5 038	2 385	1 735	377	55	995	1 376	429	547
Slovakia	14 501	11 472	5 527	4 469	332	151	916	1 302	3 236	829
Finland	72 205	81 793	17 977	16 948	21 501	31 796	23 146	24 455	1 668	799
Sweden	115 583	86 169	30 363	11 927	62 084	58 702	8 943	3 310	1 517	1 320
United Kingdom	346 144	334 127	28 161	22 837	86 779	85 963	109 546	100 999	41 088	39 584
Liechtenstein	:	348	:	33	:	11	:	0	:	0
Norway	9 051	10 427	3 519	3 689	136	113	1 248	1 498	1 472	1 675
Croatia	:	4 172	:	1 727	:	34	:	129	:	87
FYR of Macedonia	:	1 362	:	1 362	:	0	:	0	:	0
Turkey	46 092	64 770	0	10 741	:	:	:	:	:	:

(1) Except wholesaling of waste and scrap.

Source: Eurostat (env_wasgen)

Figure 11.5: Waste generated, 2008
(kg per inhabitant)

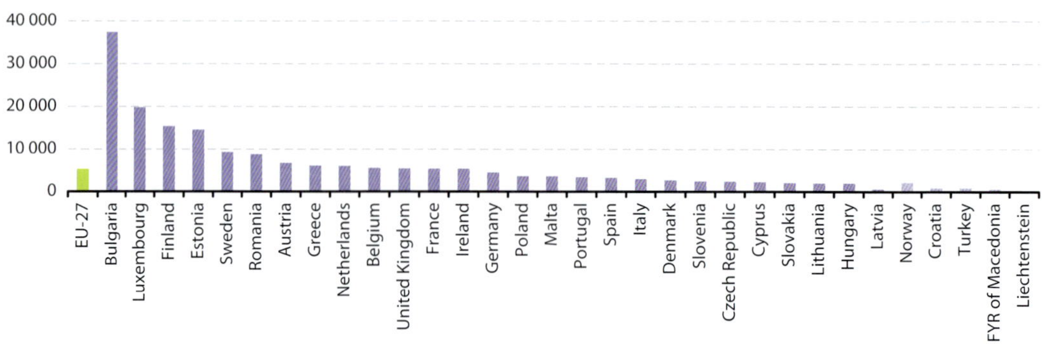

Source: Eurostat (env_wasgen and tps00001)

Figure 11.6: Waste generated by households, 2008
(kg per inhabitant)

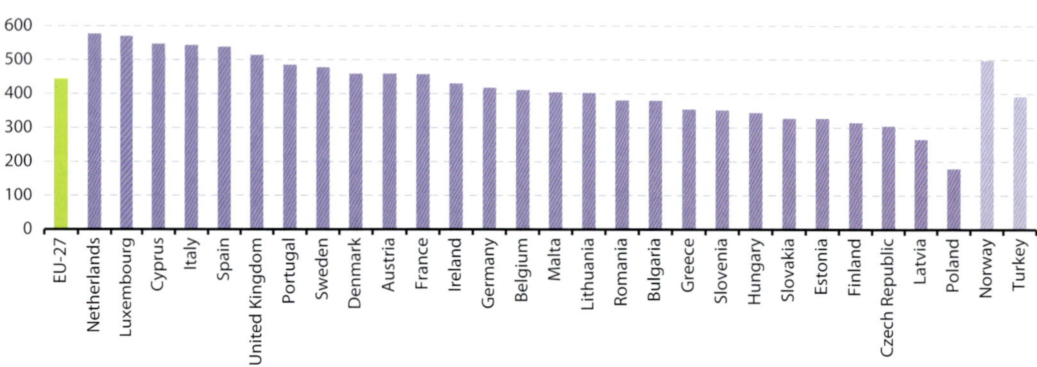

Source: Eurostat (env_wasgen and tps00001)

Figure 11.7: Waste generated by activity, 2008
(% of total)

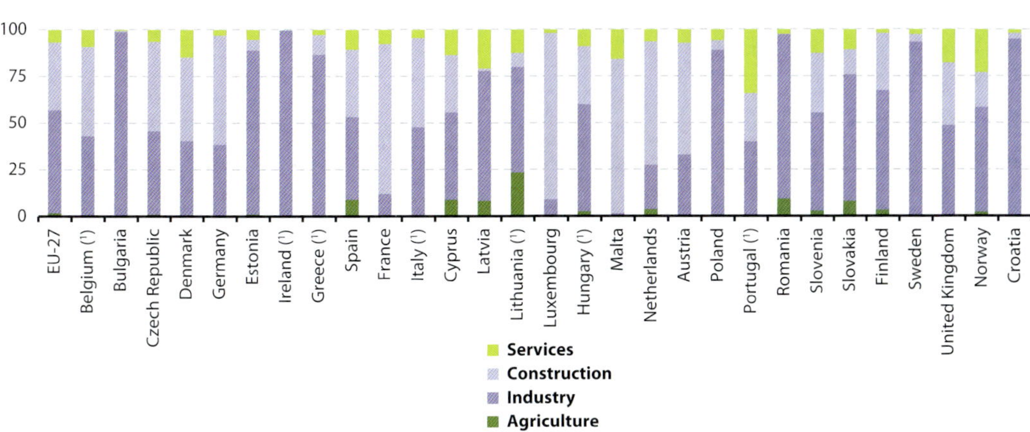

(¹) Including estimates or provisional data.

Source: Eurostat (env_wasgen)

Figure 11.8: Hazardous waste generated, 2008
(% of total waste generated)

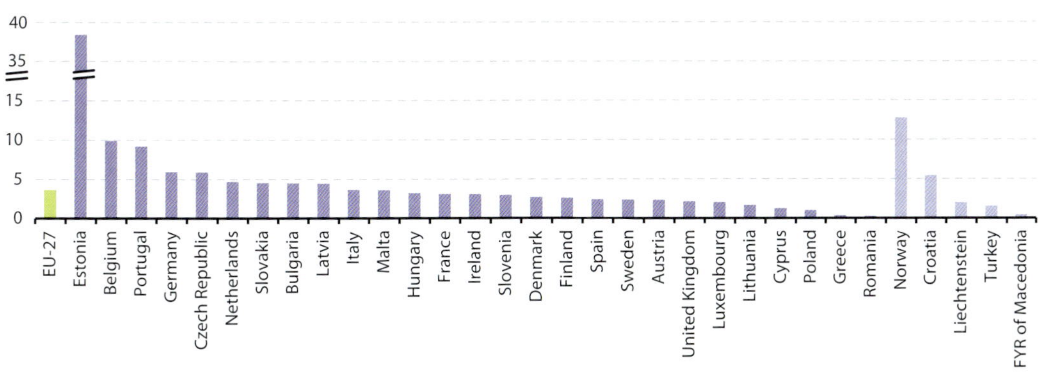

Source: Eurostat (env_wasgen)

Figure 11.9: Types of waste treatment, 2008
(% of total waste treated)

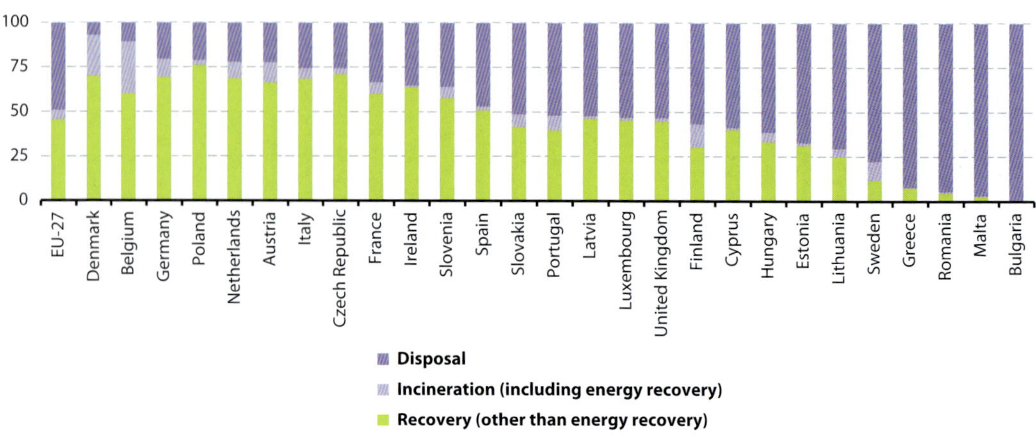

Source: Eurostat (env_wastrt)

Table 11.4: Composition of waste by treatment type, EU-27, 2008

	(million tonnes)	(% of treatment type)
Recovery (other than energy recovery)	1 092.4	-
Mineral wastes	764.7	70
Metallic wastes	76.5	7
Animal and vegetal wastes	65.5	6
Paper and cardboard wastes	43.7	4
Incineration (including energy recovery)	129.1	-
Household and similar wastes	50.4	39
Sorting residues	12.9	10
Chemical wastes	9.8	8
Mixed and undifferentiated materials	3.3	3
Disposal	1 168.9	-
Mineral wastes	970.2	83
Household and similar wastes	97.7	8
Common sludges	39.6	3
Sorting residues	27.4	2

Source: Eurostat (env_wastrt)

Table 11.5: Waste treatment (non-hazardous), recovery other than energy recovery, 2008
(1 000 tonnes)

	Metallic waste	Glass waste	Paper and cardboard waste	Rubber waste	Plastic waste	Wood waste	Textile waste
EU-27	73 980	12 680	38 260	1 480	7 150	24 970	1 210
Belgium	2 673	377	574	13	99	565	11
Bulgaria	1 085	66	196	50	22	19	1
Czech Republic	1 406	38	246	36	108	113	15
Denmark	781	107	782	51	73	891	0
Germany	9 612	2 855	5 908	234	1 387	2 642	99
Estonia	272	11	35	1	7	319	0
Ireland	10	21	6	19	29	159	3
Greece	2 386	24	440	35	30	88	2
Spain	4 082	1 184	5 060	286	1 709	1 737	52
France	9 143	1 902	5 659	179	183	4 583	370
Italy	11 159	2 009	4 450	134	1 357	1 790	233
Cyprus	17	5	23	0	7	2	0
Latvia	15	0	19	0	13	0	0
Lithuania	32	36	146	12	36	60	1
Luxembourg	3 086	31	18	0	35	69	0
Hungary	940	42	354	18	58	135	1
Malta	1	0	3	2	1	0	0
Netherlands	2 576	672	2 268	118	321	1 422	86
Austria	943	273	1 401	30	67	3 565	35
Poland	6 751	609	1 326	108	1 091	2 194	34
Portugal	1 649	811	303	79	107	981	81
Romania	1 131	97	325	1	30	761	4
Slovenia	719	15	380	12	26	165	1
Slovakia	597	30	102	7	41	151	2
Finland	57	52	468	22	6	115	39
Sweden	1 613	98	2 339	4	51	178	0
United Kingdom	11 251	1 320	5 430	32	257	2 272	142
Norway	879	118	683	49	40	418	15
Croatia	124	5	7	0	8	19	0
FYR of Macedonia	302	0	16	0	0	0	0
Turkey	1 522	273	1 040	169	401	117	96

Source: Eurostat (env_wastrt)

Table 11.6: Municipal waste
(kg per inhabitant)

	Municipal waste generated (1)			Municipal waste landfilled (2)			Municipal waste incinerated (3)		
	1999	2004	2009	1999	2004	2009	1999	2004	2009
EU-27	511	514	514	287	240	192	76	89	102
Belgium	463	487	491	91	35	25	147	163	168
Bulgaria	503	490	468	388	396	450	0	0	0
Czech Republic	327	278	316	277	222	228	30	39	33
Denmark	627	696	822	68	31	29	315	379	420
Germany	638	587	587	180	104	2	125	144	189
Estonia	413	449	346	412	283	214	0	0	0
Ireland	581	745	742	517	452	449	0	0	19
Greece	393	433	478	358	389	389	0	0	0
Spain	615	608	547	331	309	285	36	32	48
France	509	521	536	224	189	173	169	181	182
Italy	498	538	541	382	306	267	37	61	69
Cyprus	670	739	778	605	659	671	0	0	0
Latvia	256	311	333	236	259	307	0	6	0
Lithuania	650	366	360	350	334	326	0	0	0
Luxembourg	650	683	707	140	132	122	311	269	254
Hungary	482	454	430	404	381	320	34	15	41
Malta	477	625	647	410	540	617	0	0	0
Netherlands	599	625	616	40	11	4	203	202	204
Austria	563	620	591	195	46	4	57	154	174
Poland	319	256	316	312	241	206	0	1	3
Portugal	442	436	488	303	291	301	62	95	90
Romania	314	345	396	255	273	304	0	0	0
Slovenia	551	417	449	455	313	309	0	8	7
Slovakia	261	274	339	185	222	256	32	34	30
Finland	485	470	481	208	273	222	38	55	87
Sweden	428	464	485	108	42	7	163	217	235
United Kingdom	570	605	529	469	419	260	40	49	59
Iceland	457	506	554	345	365	379	62	45	56
Norway	596	416	473	328	82	67	92	128	196
Switzerland	637	662	706	66	3	0	298	337	344
Turkey	463	421	392	354	345	332	0	0	*0*

(1) Breaks in series: between 1999 and 2004 for Bulgaria, Estonia, Spain, Latvia, Hungary, Portugal, Slovenia, Slovakia, Norway, Switzerland and Turkey; between 2004 and 2009 for the Netherlands.
(2) Breaks in series: between 1999 and 2004 for Estonia, Latvia, Hungary, the Netherlands, Austria, Portugal, Norway and Turkey.
(3) Breaks in series: between 1999 and 2004 for Italy, Austria, Portugal and Switzerland.

Source: Eurostat (tsien120 and tsien130)

Figure 11.10: Municipal waste, EU-27
(kg per inhabitant)

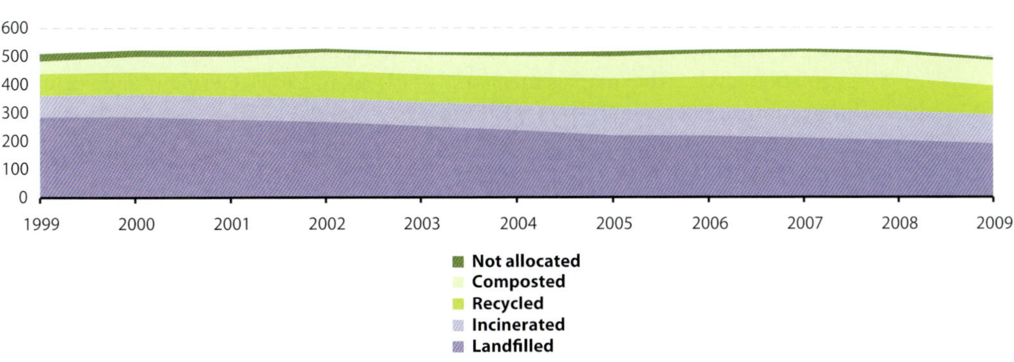

Source: Eurostat (tsien120 and tsien130)

11.3 Water

Water is essential for life, it is an indispensable resource for the economy, and also plays a fundamental role in the climate regulation cycle. The management and protection of water resources, of fresh and salt water ecosystems, and of the water we drink and bathe in is therefore one of the cornerstones of environmental protection. This subchapter on water statistics presents data on freshwater resources and the human use of water in the European Union (EU), and includes information on water abstraction, water use and wastewater treatment and disposal.

Main statistical findings

Freshwater resources

The three main users of water are agriculture, industry and the domestic sector (households and services). The overall abstraction and use of water resources can be considered to be sustainable in the long-term in most of Europe. However, specific regions may face problems associated with water scarcity; this is especially the case in southern Europe, where it is likely that efficiency gains in relation to agricultural water use will need to be achieved in order to prevent seasonal water shortages. Regions associated with low rainfall, high population density, or intensive industrial activity may also face sustainability issues in the coming years, which may be exacerbated by natural resource endowments, geographical characteristics and freshwater management systems. A number of Member States receive a significant proportion of their water resources as inflows from upstream rivers: this is particularly the case in the Danube basin and for the Netherlands, and is also the case, to a lesser extent, in Latvia, Germany and Portugal.

One measure of sustainability in water management is the water exploitation index (WEI), calculated as water abstraction divided by long-term annual resources (Cosgrove and Rijsberman, 2000). A WEI above 20 % typically indicates water scarcity problems in a country or region, and the European Environment Agency (EEA) uses this value as a warning threshold, while WEI values of more than 40 % indicate severe stress on resources and unsustainable water use. Using this measure and subject to data availability, a relatively high pressure exists on water resources in Cyprus, Belgium, Spain, Italy and Malta, with Cyprus being the only Member State to record a ratio of more than 40 %.

In absolute terms (see Table 11.7), total freshwater resources were broadly similar in Germany, France, Sweden, the United Kingdom and Italy, as each of these Member States reported a long-term average of annual freshwater resources of between 188 000 million m^3 and 175 000 million m^3. When expressed in relation to population size (see Figure 11.11), Finland and Sweden recorded the highest freshwater annual resources per capita (20 000 m^3 per inhabitant or more). In contrast, relatively low levels (below 3 000 m^3 per capita) were recorded in the six largest Member States (Germany, Spain, France, Italy, Poland and the United Kingdom), as well as Belgium, Denmark and the Czech Republic, with the lowest level in Cyprus (410 m^3 per inhabitant).

Water abstraction

There are considerable differences in the per capita amounts of freshwater abstracted within each of the Member States, in part reflecting the resources available, but also abstraction practices for public water supply, industrial and agricultural purposes, as well as land drainage and land sealing. These differences are also apparent when looking at the breakdown of water abstraction between groundwater and surface water resources (see Table 11.8). In Bulgaria, Lithuania and Romania surface water abstraction accounted for ten or more times the volume of water abstracted from groundwater resources. At the other end of the range, larger volumes of water were abstracted from groundwater resources in Latvia, Slovakia, Cyprus, the United Kingdom (England and Wales only) and Malta.

The United Kingdom (England and Wales only), Spain and France recorded the highest amounts of groundwater extracted in 2006 (subject to data availability), all with in excess of 6 000 million m³. Looking at the development of groundwater abstraction during the ten-year period to 2007, the volume of groundwater extracted generally fell, although Greece and Slovenia recorded abstraction levels that were between 15 % and 20 % higher, and Spain reported an increase of over 40 %.

Spain, France and Germany headed the ranking of Member States in relation to surface water abstraction, with more than 25 000 million m³ in 2006 or 2007. Developments in surface water abstraction levels were somewhat more pronounced than for groundwater, with Cyprus reporting an increase of 89 % in the nine-year period to 2007, and the Netherlands an increase of 63 % in the ten-year period to 2006; the volume of surface water abstracted in Latvia, Lithuania and Slovakia in 2007 was around half the level recorded some ten years earlier.

Public water supply

While the share of the public water supply sector in total water abstraction depends on the economic structure of a given country and can be relatively small, it is nevertheless often the focus of public interest, as it comprises the water volumes that are directly used by the population. Most EU Member States calculate annual rates of freshwater abstraction of between 50 m³ and 100 m³ per capita (see Figure 11.12), although extremes reflect specific conditions: for example, in Ireland (141 m³ per capita) – where the use of water from the public supply is free; or Bulgaria (134 m³ per capita) – where there are particularly high losses from the public network. Abstraction rates were also rather high in some Nordic and Alpine non-member countries, notably Iceland, Norway and Switzerland, where water resources are abundant and supply is hardly restricted. At the other end of the scale, Estonia and Lithuania reported low abstraction rates, in part resulting from below-average connection rates to the public supply, while Malta has partially replaced groundwater by desalinated seawater.

An analysis of the development of abstraction rates over time is shown for selected Member States in Figure 11.13. There was a marked decrease in abstraction in a few Member States (the example of Bulgaria is shown in the figure), while there was an increase in abstraction for other Member States (for example, Portugal). Abstraction rates were relatively stable in the majority of the Member States (see the example of Belgium), with a pattern of gradually decreasing abstraction rates commonly observed (see the example of Sweden). It is likely that the reduction in abstraction is a result of various factors, including the introduction of water-saving household appliances, and an increasing level of consciousness concerning the value of water and the environmental consequences of wasting it.

Wastewater treatment

The proportion of the population connected to urban wastewater treatment covers those households that are connected to any kind of sewage treatment (see Table 11.9). This share was above 80 % in approximately half of the Member States for which data are available (mixed reference years), rising to 99 % in the Netherlands, 95 % in Germany and 94 % in Italy, while Switzerland (97 %) also recorded a very high connection rate. At the other end of the range, less than one in two households were connected to urban wastewater treatment in Bulgaria, Malta, Cyprus and Romania; new treatment plants are under construction in Malta and it is expected that this will lead to a 100 % connection rate by 2011.

In terms of treatment levels (see Figure 11.14), tertiary wastewater treatment was most common (again mixed reference periods) in the Netherlands, Germany, Austria, Italy and Sweden, where more than four in every five persons were connected to this type of wastewater treatment, and in Greece the share was just below this level. In contrast, less than one in ten persons was connected to tertiary wastewater treatment in Romania, Bulgaria and Malta (no data reported for seven of the Member States).

The residual of wastewater treatment is sewage sludge. While the amount of sludge generated per capita depends on many factors and hence is quite variable across countries, the nature of this sludge – rich in nutrients, but also often loaded with high concentrations of pollutants such as heavy metals – has led countries to seek different pathways for its disposal, as is illustrated by Figure 11.15. Typically, four different types of disposal make up a considerable share of the total volume of sewage sludge treated: more than two thirds of the total was used as fertiliser in agriculture in Cyprus, Ireland and the United Kingdom, while another five Member States (Spain, Lithuania, Luxembourg, France and Latvia) reported agricultural use for between one and two thirds of the total mass disposed. In contrast, more than 40 % of sewage sludge was composted in Finland, Slovakia, Hungary and the Czech Republic. Alternatives that reduce or eliminate the spread of pollutants on agricultural or gardening land include incineration and landfill. While the Netherlands, Germany, Austria and Switzerland reported incineration as their primary pathway for disposal, its discharge into controlled landfills was practised as the primary pathway in Italy and Bulgaria, and was used almost exclusively in Malta, Greece and Iceland.

Data sources and availability

Water statistics are collected through the inland waters section of a joint OECD/Eurostat questionnaire which is frequently adapted to the relevant policy frameworks. It currently reports on the following:

- freshwater resources in groundwater and surface water – these can be re-

plenished by precipitation and external inflow (water flowing into a country from other territories);

- water abstraction – a major pressure on resources, although a large part of the water abstracted for domestic, industrial (including energy production) or agricultural use is returned to the environment and its water bodies, but often as wastewater with impaired quality;
- water use – analysed by supply category and by industrial activities;
- treatment capacities of urban wastewater treatment plants and the share of the population connected to them – gives an overview of the development status of the infrastructure, in terms of quantity and quality, that is available for the protection of the environment from pollution by wastewater;
- sewage sludge production and disposal – an inevitable product of wastewater treatment processes, its impact on the environment depends on the methods chosen for its processing and disposal;
- generation and discharge of wastewater – pollutants present in wastewater have different source profiles and, similarly, the efficiency of treatment of any pollutant varies according to the method applied.

A large amount of data and other information on water is accessible via WISE, the water information system for Europe, which is hosted by the European Environment Agency (EEA) in Copenhagen.

Context

Many of the water statistics produced by Eurostat have been used in the context of the development of EU legislation relating to water, as well as for environmental assessments, which in turn can give rise to new data needs.

The central element of European water policy is a Directive for Community action in the field of water policy (2000/60/EC) - often referred to as the Water Framework Directive (WFD) - which aims to achieve a good ecological and chemical status of European waters by 2015. In this respect, the Directive focuses on water management at the level of (in most cases transboundary) hydrological catchments, the river basins. An important step in the course of its implementation is the establishment of river basin management plans in 2010.

A study on water saving potential conducted for the European Commission estimates that water use efficiency could be increased by nearly 40 % through technological improvements alone and that changes in human behaviour or production patterns could lead to further savings. In a scenario without changes in practices, it was estimated that water use by the public, industry and agriculture would increase by 16 % by 2030. Conversely, the use of water saving technologies and irrigation management in the industrial and agricultural sectors could reduce excesses by as much as 43 %, while water efficiency measures could decrease water wastage by up to a third.

In a Communication addressing water scarcity and droughts (COM(2007) 414), the European Commission identified an initial set of policy options to be taken at European, national and regional levels to address water scarcity within the EU. This set of proposed policies aims to move the EU towards a water-efficient and water-saving economy, as both the quality and availability of water are of major concern in many regions.

A major step forward in efforts to reduce pollutants discharged into the environment with wastewater was achieved by implementing legislation on urban wastewater treatment (Directive 1991/271/EC). The pollution of rivers, lakes and groundwater and water quality is affected by human activities such as industrial production, household discharges, or arable farming a report (COM(2007) 120) on the protection of waters against pollution by nitrates from agricultural sources was issued in March 2007.

Another aspect of water quality relates to coastal bathing waters. The European Commission and the EEA present an annual bathing water report – the latest of these covers information for 2009 and shows that 95.6 % of Europe's coastal bathing waters and 89.4 % of its inland bathing waters met the minimum water quality standards. Legislation concerning the management of bathing water quality (Directive 2006/7/EC) will provide for a more proactive approach to informing the public about water quality; it was transposed into national law in 2008 but Member States have until December 2014 to implement it.

An increase of variability in weather patterns and catastrophic floods (such as the those along the Danube and Elbe in 2002) prompted a review of flood risk management. This process culminated in a Directive (2007/60/EC) of the European Parliament and Council on the assessment and management of flood risks, which aims to reduce and manage risks to human health, the environment, cultural heritage, and economic activity.

Figure 11.11: Freshwater resources per capita - long-term average (1)
(1 000 m^3 per inhabitant)

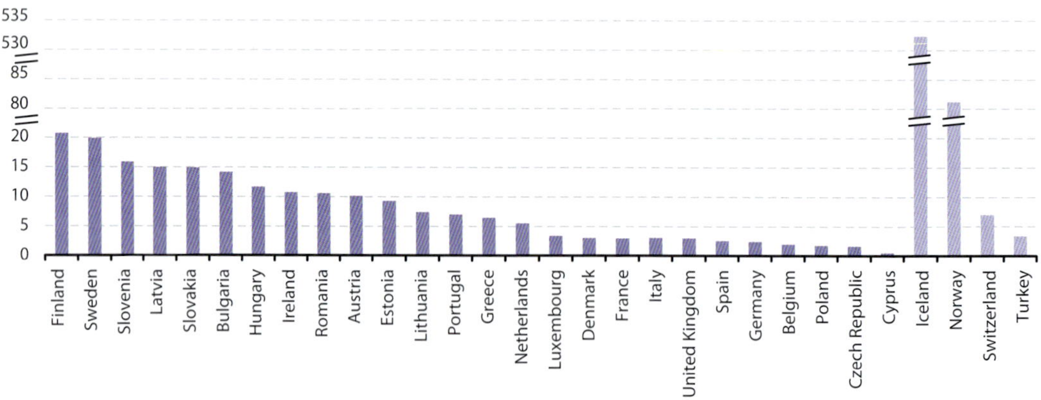

(1) The minimum period taken into account for the calculation of long term annual averages is 20 years; population data are as of 1 January 2009; Malta, not available.

Source: Eurostat (env_watq1a)

Table 11.7: Water resources - long-term annual average (1)
(1 000 million m³)

	Precipitation	Evapotrans-piration	Internal flow	External inflow	Outflow	Freshwater resources
Belgium	28.9	16.6	12.3	7.6	15.3	19.9
Bulgaria	68.6	50.5	18.1	89.1	108.5	107.2
Czech Republic	54.7	39.4	15.2	0.7	16.0	16.0
Denmark	38.5	22.1	16.3	0.0	1.9	16.3
Germany	307.0	190.0	117.0	75.0	182.0	188.0
Estonia	29.0	:	:	:	12.3	12.3
Ireland	80.0	32.5	47.5	:	:	47.5
Greece	115.0	55.0	60.0	12.0	:	72.0
Spain	346.5	235.4	111.1	0.0	111.1	111.1
France	485.7	310.4	175.3	11.0	168.0	186.3
Italy	296.0	129.0	167.0	8.0	155.0	175.0
Cyprus	3.1	2.7	0.3	0.0	0.1	0.3
Latvia	42.7	25.8	16.9	16.8	32.9	33.7
Lithuania	44.0	28.5	15.5	9.0	25.9	24.5
Luxembourg	2.0	1.1	0.9	0.7	1.6	1.6
Hungary	55.7	48.2	7.5	108.9	115.7	116.4
Malta	:	:	:	:	:	:
Netherlands	29.8	21.3	8.5	81.2	86.3	89.7
Austria	98.0	43.0	55.0	29.0	84.0	84.0
Poland	193.1	138.3	54.8	8.3	63.1	63.1
Portugal	82.2	43.6	38.6	35.0	34.0	73.6
Romania	154.0	114.6	39.4	186.3	245.6	225.7
Slovenia	31.7	13.2	18.6	13.5	32.3	32.1
Slovakia	37.4	24.3	13.1	67.3	81.7	80.3
Finland	222.0	115.0	107.0	3.2	110.0	110.0
Sweden	313.9	141.2	172.7	11.8	194.6	183.4
United Kingdom	283.7	111.2	172.5	2.8	175.3	175.3
Iceland	200.0	30.0	170.0	-	170.0	170.0
Norway	470.7	112.0	377.3	12.2	389.4	389.4
Switzerland	61.6	21.6	40.7	12.8	53.5	53.5
Croatia	63.1	40.1	23.0	:	:	:
FYR of Macedonia	19.5	:	:	1.0	6.3	:
Turkey	501.0	273.6	227.4	6.9	178.0	234.3

(1) The minimum period taken into account for the calculation of long term annual averages is 20 years.

Source: Eurostat (env_watq1a)

Table 11.8: Groundwater and surface water abstraction
(million m³)

	Groundwater abstraction			Surface water abstraction		
	1997	2002	2007	1997	2002	2007
Belgium	646	662	:	6 929	6 076	:
Bulgaria	798	493	473	6 735	6 096	5 708
Czech Republic	587	540	381	1 906	1 368	1 589
Denmark	917	650	:	16	18	:
Germany (1)	6 710	6 204	5 825	33 880	31 802	26 476
Estonia	322	236	:	1 306	1 177	:
Ireland	:	:	213	:	:	517
Greece (2)	3 119	3 188	3 651	4 603	6 072	5 821
Spain (3)	4 250	5 310	6 022	30 353	32 210	27 738
France (3)	:	6 240	6 184	:	26 923	26 368
Italy	:	:	:	:	:	:
Cyprus (4)	143	145	145	34	62	64
Latvia	167	115	108	196	142	104
Lithuania	234	158	175	4 552	2 966	2 094
Luxembourg	:	:	:	:	:	:
Hungary (3)	851	730	541	:	:	:
Malta	20	16	14	0	0	0
Netherlands (5)	1 153	977	1 059	5 354	7 938	8 720
Austria	1 148	:	:	2 496	:	:
Poland	2 871	:	:	9 928	:	:
Portugal	:	:	:	:	:	:
Romania	1 260	860	508	8 000	6 379	5 426
Slovenia	159	208	191	:	691	745
Slovakia	498	410	358	812	684	330
Finland	:	*285*	:	:	:	:
Sweden	654	628	346	2 057	2 048	2 285
United Kingdom (6)	10 524	7 503	7 005	2 383	2 379	2 266
Iceland	154	160	:	6	5	:
Norway	:	:	:	:	:	:
Switzerland (3)	880	854	788	1 678	1 674	:
Croatia	:	:	1 162	:	:	:
FYR of Macedonia	:	48	116	:	585	435
Turkey (7)	9 330	10 990	12 096	*26 222*	*33 780*	:

(1) 1998 instead of 1997; 2001 instead of 2002.
(2) 1996 instead of 1997.
(3) 2006 instead of 2007.
(4) 1998 instead of 1997.
(5) 1996 instead of 1997; 2001 instead of 2002; 2006 instead of 2007.
(6) England and Wales only; 2006 instead of 2007.
(7) 2001 instead of 2002 for surface water abstraction.

Source: Eurostat (env_watq2_1)

Figure 11.12: Total freshwater abstraction by public water supply, 2007 (1)
(m³ per inhabitant)

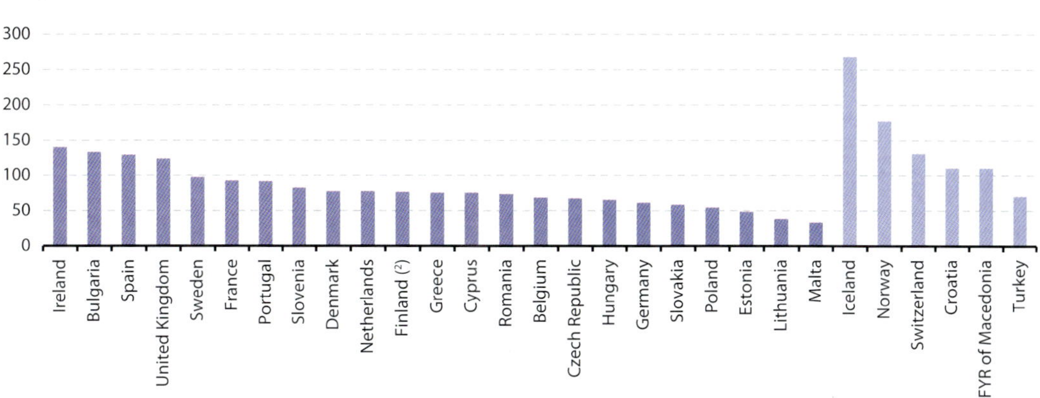

(1) Spain, France, Hungary, the Netherlands, Switzerland and Turkey, 2006; Finland and Iceland, 2005; Denmark, Estonia and the United Kingdom, 2004; Austria, Italy, Latvia and Luxembourg, not available.
(2) Estimate.

Source: Eurostat (env_watq2_1)

Figure 11.13: Total freshwater abstraction for public water supply, selected countries
(million m³)

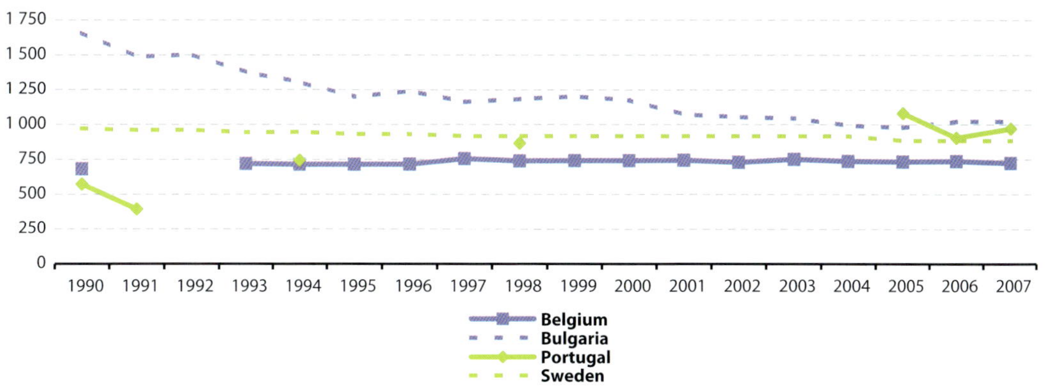

Source: Eurostat (env_watq2_1)

Table 11.9: Population connected to urban wastewater treatment
(% of total)

	1997	1998	1999	2000	2001	2002	2003	2004	2005	2006	2007
Belgium	35	38	39	41	46	48	52	53	55	56	60
Bulgaria	36	36	36	37	38	39	40	40	41	41	42
Czech Republic	59	62	62	64	65	70	71	71	73	74	75
Denmark	88	89	:	:	:	:	:	:	:	:	:
Germany	:	91	:	:	93	:	:	94	:	:	95
Estonia	72	69	69	69	69	70	70	72	74	74	74
Ireland	:	:	66	:	70	:	:	:	84	:	:
Greece	56	:	:	:	:	:	:	:	:	:	85
Spain	:	:	:	:	:	:	:	:	:	:	:
France	:	77	:	:	79	:	:	80	:	:	:
Italy	:	:	69	:	:	:	:	:	94	:	:
Cyprus	12	13	13	14	16	18	23	28	30	:	:
Latvia	:	:	:	:	:	65	70	66	66	65	65
Lithuania	:	:	:	:	:	57	59	:	69	69	69
Luxembourg	:	:	93	:	:	:	95	:	:	:	:
Hungary	24	26	29	46	50	57	:	:	54	57	:
Malta	13	13	13	36	36	36	36	36	36	36	35
Netherlands	98	98	98	98	98	99	99	99	99	99	:
Austria	:	81	:	85	86	86	89	89	:	92	:
Poland	47	50	52	54	55	57	58	59	60	61	62
Portugal (1)	:	42	:	:	:	57	60	:	65	72	68
Romania	:	:	:	:	:	:	:	27	27	28	28
Slovenia	:	19	21	23	25	25	26	34	37	52	51
Slovakia	49	49	50	51	51	52	53	54	55	55	57
Finland	78	79	80	80	81	81	:	:	:	:	:
Sweden	:	93	:	86	:	85	:	86	:	86	:
United Kingdom (2)	86	91	92	95	99	98	96	97	97	99	99
Iceland	4	8	16	33	33	50	50	50	57	:	:
Norway	70	73	73	73	74	74	75	76	77	78	78
Switzerland	95	96	96	96	96	96	:	:	97	:	:
Croatia	:	:	:	9	:	:	:	15	28	28	29
FYR of Macedonia	:	:	:	5	6	6	6	6	7	7	7
Turkey	14	17	*23*	*26*	27	28	30	36	36	42	:

(1) The totals for urban wastewater treatment also contain values for preliminary treatment and for undefined treatment. These values refer to the public urban wastewater treatment, including collective septic tanks.
(2) England and Wales only.

Source: Eurostat (env_watq4)

Figure 11.14: Population connected to wastewater treatment, 2007 (¹)
(% of total)

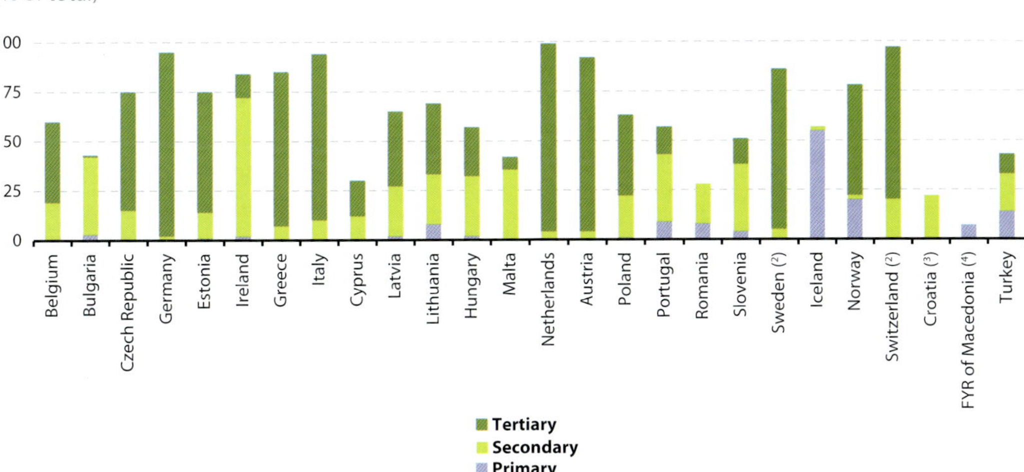

(¹) Malta, 2008; Hungary, the Netherlands, Austria, Sweden and Turkey, 2006; Ireland, Italy, Cyprus, Romania (only tertiary treatment), Iceland and Switzerland, 2005; Denmark, Spain, France, Luxembourg, Slovakia, Finland and the United Kingdom, not available.
(²) Primary, not available.
(³) Primary and tertiary, not available.
(⁴) Secondary and tertiary, not available.

Source: Eurostat (env_watq4)

Figure 11.15: Sewage sludge disposal from urban wastewater treatment, by type of treatment, 2007 (¹)
(% of total mass)

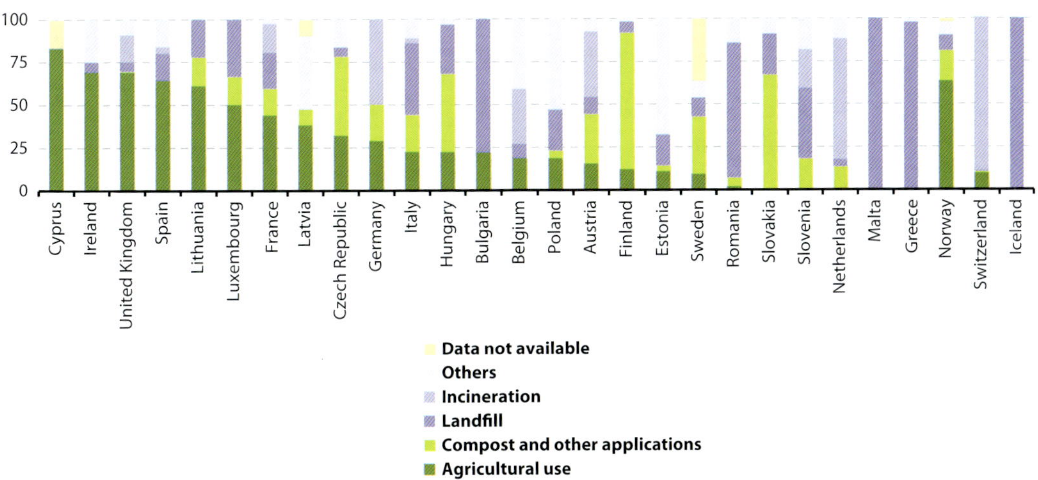

(¹) Malta, 2008; Greece, Spain, Netherlands, Austria and Switzerland, 2006; Italy, Cyprus and the United Kingdom, 2005; Belgium, France and Hungary, 2004; Luxembourg and Iceland, 2003; Sweden, 2002; Finland, 2000; Denmark and Portugal, not available.

Source: Eurostat (env_watq6)

11.4 Material flow accounts

Economy-wide material flow accounts provide information about the physical flows of materials through economies. The accounts provide an aggregate overview of the annual extraction of raw materials as well as of the physical amounts of imports and exports.

Typically as economies grow, more materials such as fossil fuels, biomass, construction materials and metals are needed, but the rate of increase is less than that of GDP, a phenomenon known as 'decoupling' which can also be observed for the EU-27.

A 'resource-efficient Europe' is an initiative the European Commission launched as part of the Europe 2020 strategy aiming to deliver smart, sustainable and inclusive growth. The initiative aims at decoupling economic growth from the use of resources.

In the EU-27, the average material consumption per inhabitant was 16.5 tonnes in 2007, an increase of 5 % since 2000.

Main statistical findings

Resource productivity and direct material inputs

Resource productivity is the total amount of materials used by an economy in relation to economic activity. The development of resource productivity over time provides insights into whether decoupling between the use of natural resources and economic growth is taking place.

Resource use is measured as domestic material consumption (DMC). Resource productivity of the EU is expressed by the amount of gross domestic product (GDP) generated per unit of material consumed, in other words GDP / DMC in euro per kg.

Resource productivity in the EU-27 rose 7 % from 2000 to 2003, decreased in 2004 by 2 %, and then increased gradually during the next three years to reach a level in 2007 that was slightly above that recorded in 2003 (Figure 11.16). Over the entire period from 2000 to 2007 resource productivity in the EU-27 increased by almost 8 %. While the EU-27's GDP continuously increased during the 2000 to 2007 period, DMC declined until 2003. When an economy grows at the same time as DMC is decreasing, this is called 'absolute decoupling' of resource use from economic growth. This situation was observed for the period from 2000 to 2003. From 2003 to 2007, however, DMC increased together with GDP at nearly the same rate (11 %).

The level of DMC increased by about 8 % from 2000 to 2007, while on a per capita basis DMC increased somewhat less, by about 5 %.

Another indicator often used is direct material input (DMI) which measures the direct input of materials for use into the economy, in other words all materials which are of economic value and are used in production and consumption activities (excluding water flows). The relation of DMC to DMI indicates to what extent material resources inputs are used for own domestic consumption or are exported for consumption in other economies. The

difference between DMC and DMI (the two bars shown for each country in Figure 11.17) is exports.

Ten of the countries (nine EU Member States and Switzerland) had direct material inputs (DMI), between 6 and 20 tonnes per capita in 2007. Their share of direct material inputs (DMI) that was used for own domestic consumption (DMC) ranged from two thirds for Slovakia to 90 % for Greece and Malta.

A second group of 11 EU Member States had a DMI between 20 and 30 tonnes per capita. Their share of direct material inputs used for own domestic consumption ranged from 38 % for the Netherlands to 95 % for Romania. Another group of seven EU Member States and Norway had a DMI higher than 30 tonnes per capita.

By making a comparison of these concepts, different types of economies can be characterised, namely:

(a) through-transport countries with both high imports and exports;
(b) countries where domestic extraction is used mostly at home;
(c) extraction exporting countries.

Belgium, the Netherlands and Luxembourg are economies with high DMI but significantly lower DMC due to a high level of imports that are again exported. In contrast, the economy of Ireland is characterised by high resource requirements (its DMI was the second highest per capita) which are predominantly for domestic use. Finland shows a similar pattern also due to a high use of extracted natural resources in its own economy. In contrast, Norway shows a unique pattern with the highest DMI per capita of all European countries studied, calculated at 82 tonnes in 2007. Norway has a high resource extraction based economy with the majority of the material being largely exported. This is seen with DMC being only 45 % of DMI. Norway was the largest net exporter of natural resources among the EU and EFTA Member States.

Due to limited data availability only the DMC can be derived for the EU-27, which was 16.5 tonnes per capita in 2007.

Domestic material consumption

Domestic material consumption is composed of two elements, namely the domestic extraction and the physical trade balance (equal to imports less exports). From 2000 to 2003, the EU-27's domestic material consumption – the total amount of materials directly used within the economy – declined from 7 600 million tonnes to 7 400 million tonnes, before rising again to 8 200 million tonnes by 2007, an overall increase of nearly 8 % when compared with 2000 (see Figure 11.18).

Domestic extraction accounted for an estimated 84 % of the EU-27's domestic material consumption in 2007, with the physical trade balance accounting for the remainder, thereby confirming the EU-27 as a net importer. From 2000 to 2003, the domestic extraction decreased from 6 600 million tonnes to 6 300 million tonnes but then increased to 6 900 million tonnes by 2007, which was 5 % higher than in 2000. In contrast, the physical trade balance rose almost constantly during the period 2000-2007, rising from 1 000 million tonnes to 1 300 million tonnes, an overall increase of 27 %.

Figure 11.19 shows the main components of the EU-27's domestic extraction in 2007. The main materials extracted from the national territories of the EU-27 Member States were non-metallic minerals including sand and gravel (61 %), fossil energy materials/carriers (13 %), other biomass (13 %), grazed biomass and crop residues (11 %) and metal ores (2 %). From this breakdown, the importance of the construction activity – which uses much of the sand, gravel and other non-metallic minerals – can be seen. Thus, when there are large construction projects (such as building new tunnels, repairing dykes, dredging harbours, building highways, etc.) there can be a noticeable impact on the figures. Note that water flows are excluded from economy-wide material flow analyses as they would be so large that they would dominate all other materials.

Domestic extraction and external trade

The material requirements of most economies are dominated by domestic extraction of raw materials, but the EU is no longer self-sufficient for all of the materials that it needs. Materials that are not available or whose domestic production is not competitive are typically obtained through external trade. Most EU Member States are net importers of materials, in other words, they require more resources from the rest of the world than they provide to the rest of the world.

From 2000 to 2007 the domestic extraction in the EU-27 increased moderately, rising overall by 5 % (see Figure 11.20). In contrast, the EU-27's external trade rose substantially, with imports increasing by 21 % and exports by 18 %.

Within the EU Member States, only Sweden was a net exporter of materials in 2007, while Latvia had almost equal exports and imports of materials (see Figure 11.21). The largest net importers of materials among the EU Member States were Italy, Germany, Spain and France. Among the EU and EFTA countries, Norway was the only significant net exporter of materials as it has a natural resource-based economy with high levels of extraction and exports of oil and gas, as well as other resources such as fish or timber.

Data sources and availability

Economy-wide material flow accounts are provided to Eurostat by all EU Member States, Norway, Switzerland and the candidate countries based on a gentleman's agreement. The data sources used for the compilation of these accounts may differ in scope and quality between countries.

Eurostat is working on the establishment of a legal base for the compilation of environmental accounts. The European Commission has put forward a proposal for a Regulation on European environmental economic accounts (COM(2010) 132) which provides a framework for the development of various types of accounts. The current proposal includes three modules with a view of adding other modules as these subject areas reach methodological maturity. Material flow accounts are one of the first three modules being proposed, alongside modules for air emissions accounts (see Subchapter 11.1) and environmentally related taxes (see Subchapter 11.7) by economic activities. It is expected that this proposed legal base will strengthen the coherence and availability of environmental accounts across the EU by providing a legal framework for their compilation, including methodology, common standards, definitions, classifications and accounting rules.

Context

Environmental accounts are one statistical means to try to measure the interplay between the economy and the environment in order to see whether current production and consumption activities are on a sustainable path of development. Measuring sustainable development is a complex undertaking as it has to incorporate economic, social and environmental indicators without contradiction. The data obtained may subsequently feed into political decision-making, underpinning policies that target both continued economic growth and sustainable development, for example, initiatives such as the Europe 2020 strategy, which aims to achieve a resource-efficient, low-carbon economy for the EU by 2020.

In order to have such a holistic view of the various aspects of sustainable development, the existing framework for measuring the economy – in other words, the system of national accounts – is supplemented by satellite systems representing environmental or social indicators. These satellite accounts are largely developed using the same concepts, definitions, classifications and accounting rules as the national accounts, bringing environmental or social data together with economic data in a coherent and comparable framework. Thus, environmental accounts serve to enhance the understanding of pressures exerted by the economy on the environment.

The need to supplement existing information on the economy with environmental indicators has been recognised in a European Commission Communication titled 'GDP and beyond' (COM(2009) 433). Furthermore, similar recommendations have been made within a report by the Commission on the measurement of economic performance and social progress, an initiative of the French government. The recommendations made support the expansion of the statistical understanding of human well-being by supplementing economic indicators such as GDP with additional information, including physical indicators on the environment.

Figure 11.16: Index of resource productivity, EU-27 (1)
(2000=100)

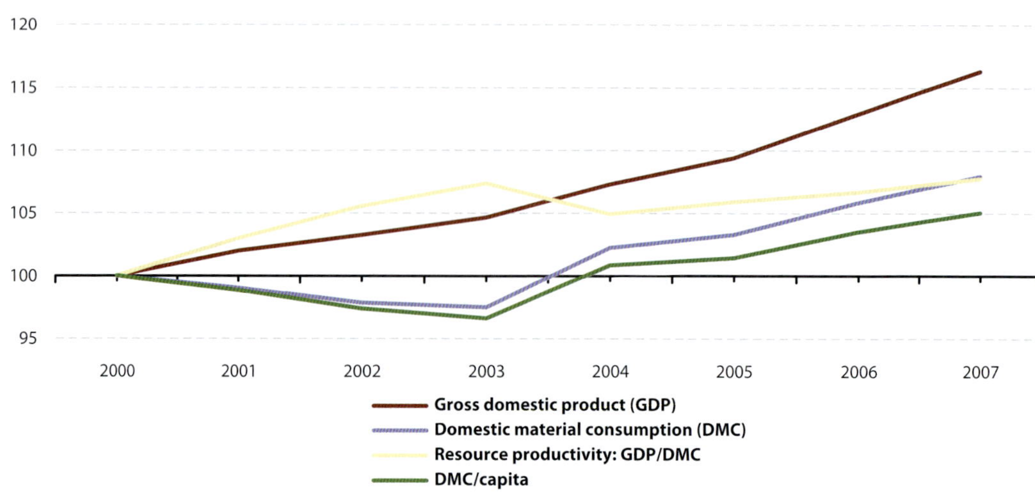

(1) Estimates..

Source: Eurostat (tsieb020 and env_ac_mfa)

Figure 11.17: Domestic material consumption and inputs, 2007
(tonnes per inhabitant)

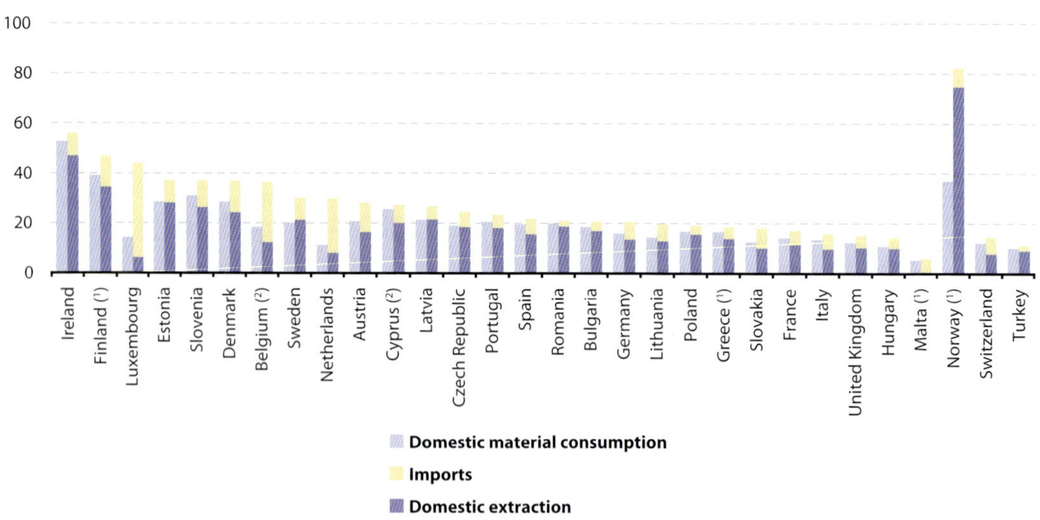

(1) Trade data are estimated using external trade statistics.
(2) Estimates.

Source: Eurostat (env_ac_mfa and demo_gind)

Figure 11.18: Domestic material consumption by components, EU-27 (1)
(million tonnes)

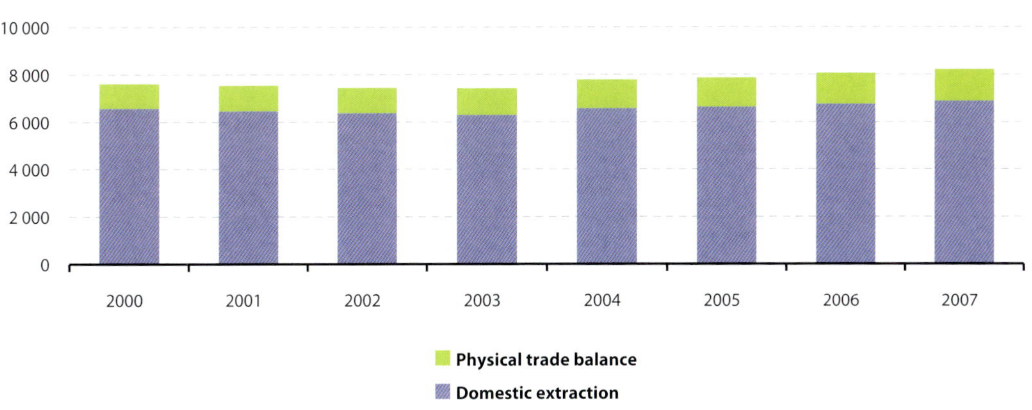

(1) Estimates.

Source: Eurostat (env_ac_mfa)

Figure 11.19: Domestic extraction by materials, EU-27, 2007 (1)
(% of total)

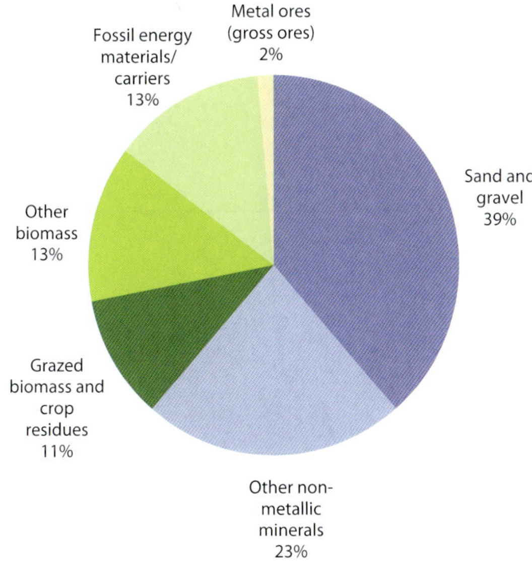

(1) Estimates; figures do not sum to 100 % due to rounding.

Source: Eurostat (env_ac_mfa)

Figure 11.20: Indices of domestic extraction, imports and exports, EU-27 (1)
(2000=100)

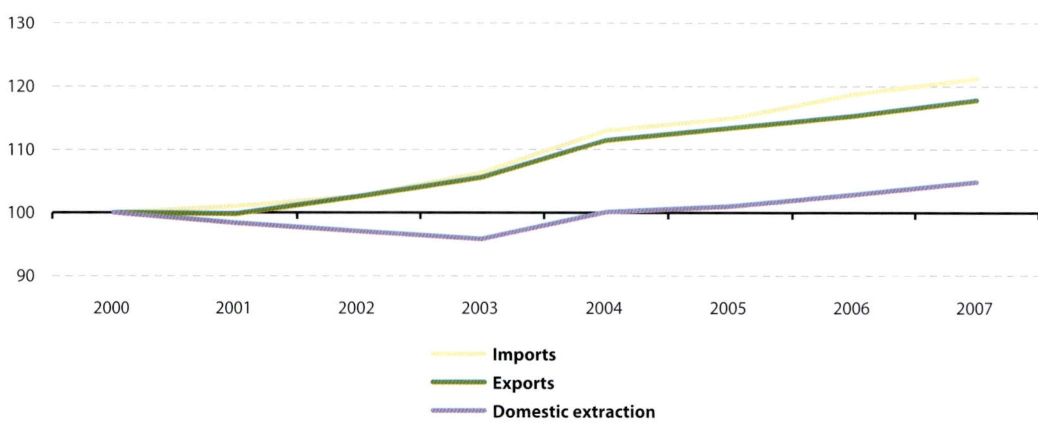

(1) Estimates.

Source: Eurostat (env_ac_mfa)

Figure 11.21: Physical trade balances, 2007 (1)
(million tonnes)

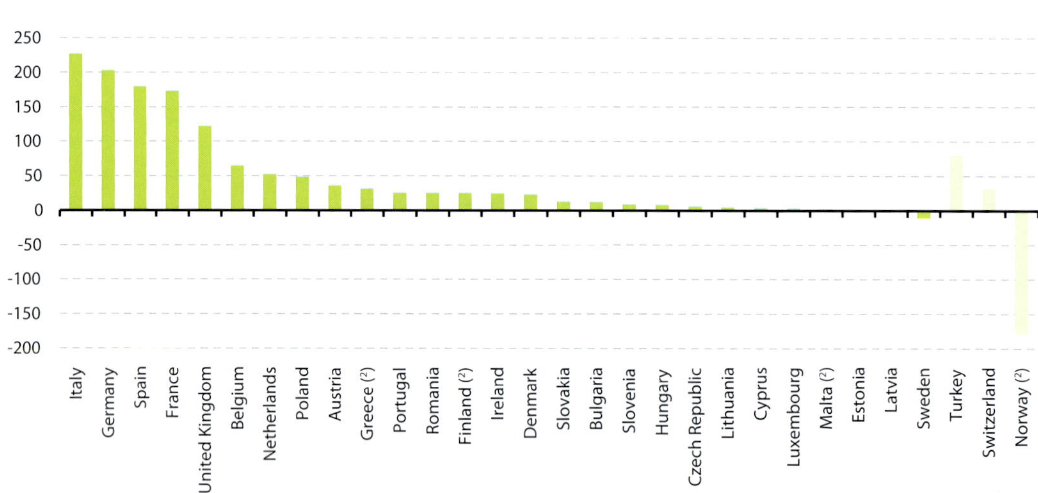

(1) Negative values indicate net exporters, positive values indicate net importers.
(2) Trade data are estimated using external trade statistics.

Source: Eurostat (env_ac_mfa)

11.5 Chemicals management

Work on European Union (EU) statistics concerning hazardous substances started in the mid-1990s when some environmental pressure indicators (EPIs) related to chemicals were developed. More recently, a set of indicators to monitor the effectiveness of the Regulation on the registration, evaluation, authorisation and restriction of chemicals (REACH) were developed. This subchapter presents two indicators developed and compiled by Eurostat that cover the production of some of these chemicals.

Main statistical findings

Total production of chemicals

Figure 11.22 shows the development of EU-27 and EU-15 chemical production in terms of the level (or quantity) of output. The production of chemicals is largely concentrated in western Europe: Germany is the largest producer in the EU, followed by France, Italy and the United Kingdom and these four Member States collectively generated two thirds of the EU-27's chemical production in 2009; adding Spain, the Netherlands, Belgium and Ireland, the overall share was raised to 88 %.

In the EU-15, between 1995 and 2007, the total production of chemicals increased by 65 million tonnes (26.2 %) to reach a total of 313 million tonnes. In 2008, production decreased by 27 million tonnes (-8.7 %) and in 2009 by a further 34 million tonnes (-11.8 %) to reach a level of 252 million tonnes.

A shorter time series is available for the EU-27 which shows that the total production of chemicals increased continuously between 2002 and 2007, rising overall by 9.6 % to reach a peak of 362 million tonnes. During the financial and economic crisis, the EU-27's production of chemicals fell by 25 million tonnes (-6.9 %) in 2008 and by another 46 million tonnes (-13.6 %) in 2009 to reach a level of 291 million tonnes.

Production of environmentally harmful chemicals

Figure 11.23 presents the development of production of environmentally harmful chemicals. Aggregated production of these environmentally harmful chemicals in the EU-27 grew from 2002 to 2007 by 10.1 % overall to a peak of 194 million tonnes. Production fell by 31 million tonnes (-16.5 %) over the next two years to a level of 162 million tonnes, which was 8.1 % lower than in 2002.

EU-15 production of environmentally harmful chemicals increased from 1996 to 2005 by 15.9 % overall to record a peak in production of 168 million tonnes. However, by 2009 the EU-15's output stood at 138 million tonnes and was 4.7 % lower than in 1996.

The share of environmentally harmful chemicals in total EU-27 chemical output was 53.3 % in 2002 and 55.7 % in 2009. The 12 Member States that joined the EU in 2004 and 2007 produced 24.0 million tonnes of environmentally harmful chemicals, equivalent to 14.8 % of the EU-27 total.

Production of toxic chemicals

Figure 11.24 presents the development of production quantities of toxic chemicals, broken down into five toxicity classes. The EU-27's production of toxic chemicals (all five toxicity classes aggregated) increased by 6.8 % overall between 2002 and 2007 to reach a peak of 218 million tonnes. Production fell by 17 million tonnes in 2008 (-7.9 %) and by a further 21 million tonnes (-10.4 %) in 2009 to reach a level of 180 million tonnes.

The overall share of chemicals classified as toxic (all five classes) in total EU-27 chemicals production was 62 % in 2009 – which was the same ratio that had been recorded in 2002. EU-27 production of the most toxic carcinogenic, mutagenic and reprotoxic (CMR) chemicals reached 38 million tonnes in 2004. The level of production in 2007 was just below this recent peak, at 37 million tonnes, but output fell substantially in 2008 to 32 million tonnes and remained at that level in 2009. The relative share of CMRs in total EU-27 chemical production fell from 10.8 % in 2004 to 9.4 % in 2008 before increasing to 11.0 % in 2009. A more detailed analysis shows that most CMRs were produced in lower volumes in 2009; however, a higher production of chlorine compounds, such as vinyl chloride, compensated for these reductions to produce a stable overall quantity of CMR production.

The 12 Member States that joined the EU in 2004 or 2007 produced 15.0 % (27 million tonnes) of the EU-27's toxic chemicals in 2009, compared with an 11.0 % share of total production of all industrial chemicals. The development of toxic chemicals production followed a similar path to that recorded for the production of all chemicals. The time series from 2002 to 2009 provides little indication that EU-27 production of chemicals that are toxic to human health and/or harmful to eco-systems is being significantly decoupled from the overall production level for chemicals.

Data sources and availability

The indicators presented in this subchapter are derived from annual statistics on the production of manufactured goods (Prodcom). EU-15 statistics on toxic chemicals cover the years from 1995 to 2008, while statistics on environmentally harmful substances start in 1996. EU-27 data are available for the years 2002 to 2009 for both of these indicators.

The information presented on the production of environmentally harmful chemicals and the production of toxic chemicals has been aggregated, in both cases, to five impact classes: these classes of environmental impacts and toxicity to human health follow official classifications in EU legislation and scientific expert judgement. It should be noted that the indicators do not describe the actual risks associated with the use of chemicals, but instead their level of production in quantity terms. Indeed, production and consumption are not synonymous with exposure, as some chemicals are handled in closed systems, or as intermediate goods in controlled supply chains.

The production of environmentally harmful chemicals is divided into five classes based on their environmental impact.

The impacts, beginning with the most harmful, are:

- severe chronic environmental impacts;
- significant chronic environmental impacts;
- moderate chronic environmental impacts;
- chronic environmental impacts;
- significant acute environmental impacts.

The indicator monitors progress in shifting production from more environmentally harmful to less harmful chemicals; the indicator focuses on aquatic toxicity. It seeks to take into account the inherent eco-toxicity of chemical substances, their potential for bioaccumulation and their persistence in the environment. For this purpose, substance specific data on eco-toxicity, biodegradability and bioaccumulation potential have been used. The production of environmentally harmful chemicals is primarily based on the official environmental classification of substances; certain risk-phrases related to chronic human toxicity are also included.

The indicator on toxic chemicals is also published as a sustainable development indicator within the theme for public health. Aggregated production quantities of toxic chemicals may be broken down into five toxicity classes. The classes, beginning with the most dangerous, are:

- carcinogenic, mutagenic and reprotoxic (CMR) chemicals;
- chronic toxic chemicals;
- very toxic chemicals;
- toxic chemicals;
- chemicals classified as harmful.

This indicator monitors progress in shifting production from more toxic to less toxic chemicals and addresses an important objective of REACH: to reduce risks by substitution of hazardous by less hazardous substances.

Eurostat has recently, in collaboration with the Directorate-Generals of the European Commission responsible for industry and for the environment, published a baseline study providing a set of indicators to monitor the effectiveness of the REACH Regulation.

Context

The sixth environment action programme (EAP), which runs from 2002 to 2012, requires a complete overhaul of EU policies on chemicals management. It is intended that REACH shall ensure a high level of protection for human health and the environment, including the promotion of alternative methods to assess the hazards of substances, the free circulation of substances on the internal market, and the enhancement of competitiveness and innovation in the EU's chemical manufacturing sector. Through increasing knowledge about the hazardous properties of chemicals, REACH is expected to enhance conditions for their safe use in supply chains and contribute towards the substitution of dangerous substances by less dangerous ones, such that there are fewer risks to human health and the environment.

For this purpose, statistical indicators that provide information on the production of toxic chemicals and chemicals that are harmful to the environment may be used to measure progress towards a number of objectives. These include the headline objective for public health established under the EU's sustainable development strategy, alongside the aim of ensuring a high level of protection for human health and the environment – an objective of the EU's sixth environment action programme (EAP).

Figure 11.22: Total production of chemicals
(million tonnes)

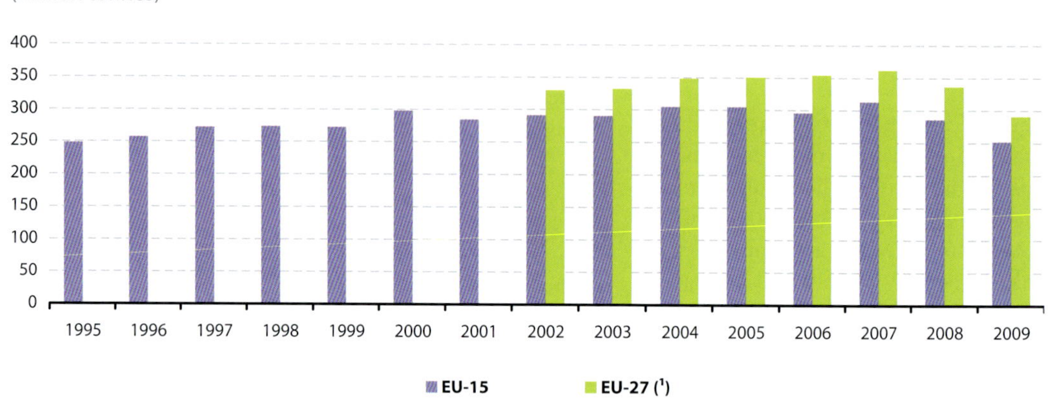

(1) Not available, 1995 to 2001.

Source: Eurostat (tsdph320)

Figure 11.23: Production of environmentally harmful chemicals
(million tonnes)

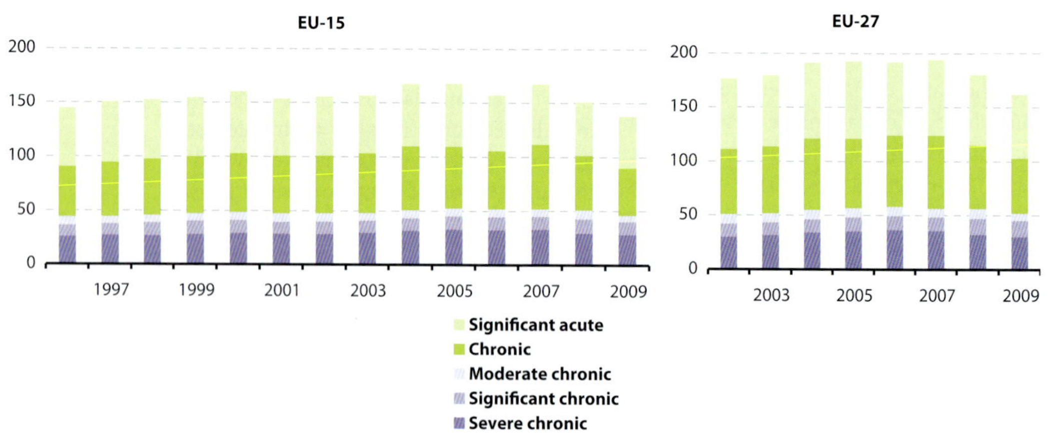

Source: Eurostat (tsdph330)

Figure 11.24: Production of toxic chemicals
(million tonnes)

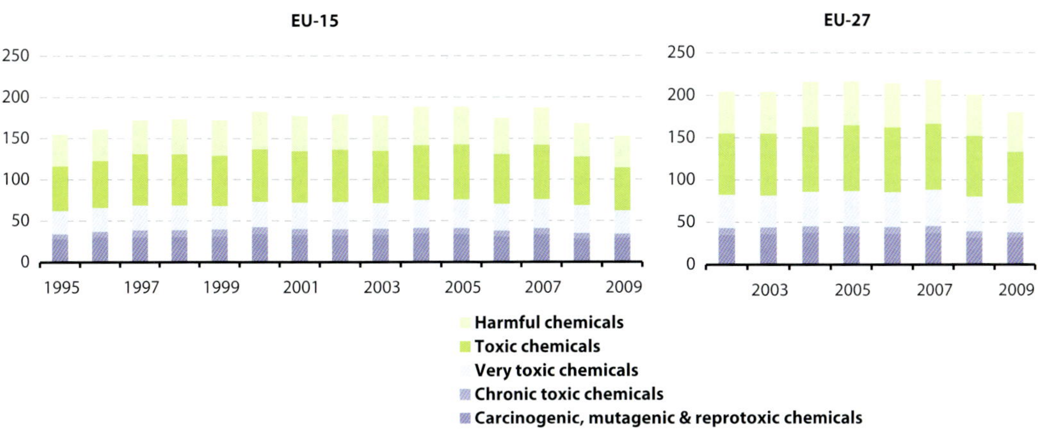

Source: Eurostat (tsdph320)

11.6 Environmental protection expenditure

The protection of the environment is integrated within all European Union (EU) policy fields with the general aim of attaining sustainable development. Clean air, water and soils, healthy ecosystems, and rich biodiversity are vital for human life, and thus it is not surprising that societies devote large amounts of money to curbing pollution and preserving a healthy environment.

This subchapter provides details on expenditure carried out with the purpose of protecting the environment (total environmental protection investment and current expenditure). It refers to the money spent by the public sector, private and public specialised producers, and industry on activities directly aimed at the prevention, reduction, and elimination of pollution resulting from the production or consumption of goods and services.

Main statistical findings

Figure 11.25 shows that in 2006, private and public specialised producers (providing environmental protection services) had the highest environmental protection expenditure within the EU-25. Their expenditure accounted for 0.86 % of gross domestic product (GDP), which was equal to EUR 214 per inhabitant. The public sector and industry spent roughly similar amounts on environmental protection (0.47 % and 0.44 % of GDP respectively), or EUR 116 and EUR 109 per inhabitant respectively. Combining the expenditure of these three activities gives a total of 1.76 % of the EU-25's GDP allocated to protecting the environment in 2006.

Between 2000 and 2006, environmental protection expenditure by private and public specialised producers, industry and the public sector grew in absolute and per inhabitant terms, but decreased relative to GDP for the public sector and for industry. For private and public specialised producers, environmental protection expenditure grew relative to GDP (see Figure 11.26). This increase and the corresponding decrease for the public sector could, in part, be due to outsourcing or the (semi-) privatisation of some environmental activities such as waste collection and wastewater treatment.

Public sector's expenditure

In 2006, some 42.4 % of public sector environmental protection expenditure in the EU-25 was devoted to non-core domains, 39.6 % to waste management activities, and 16.8 % to wastewater management (see Figure 11.27). Only a fraction (1.1 %) of public sector environmental protection expenditure was destined for air protection activities (these activities are almost exclusively conducted by industry).

In most EU Member States public sector environmental protection expenditure ranged between 0.3 % and 0.7 % of GDP (see Figure 11.28). The Netherlands (2005 data) devoted 1.4 % of its GDP to such expenditure and Denmark 1.1 % (2007 data), while Latvia (2005 data) and Estonia allocated less than 0.2 %.

Current expenditure generally accounted for the majority of the public sector's environmental protection expenditure. Most of the Member States that joined the

EU in 2004 or 2007 recorded investment shares in public sector environmental protection expenditure that were above the EU average (see Figure 11.29), Cyprus and Slovakia being notable exceptions. These relatively high shares of investment may, in part, be attributed to higher levels of expenditure in fixed assets that could have been needed to start a variety of activities in order to comply with more stringent EU environmental legislation. For EFTA countries and Turkey, the investment share of public sector environmental protection expenditure was generally close to the average across the EU Member States, although in Croatia it reached 96.7 % in 2007 (much higher than in previous years).

Public sector environmental protection expenditure is mainly focused on waste management and wastewater treatment (see Figure 11.30). However, in several EU Member States a substantial share is devoted to other domains. This was notably the case in Spain (for the protection of biodiversity and other environmental domains, 2005 data), as well as in Cyprus (2004 data), France, Italy and Finland (where the 'others' category had a relatively important role; this category includes general environmental administration and management, education, training and information for the environment, as well as activities leading to indivisible expenditure and activities not elsewhere classified). The analysis of public sector environmental protection expenditure by domain also highlights the particular case of Croatia where more than 95 % of expenditure in 2007 was devoted to soil and groundwater protection.

Private and public specialised producers' expenditure

In 2006, the environmental protection expenditure of private and public specialised producers represented 0.86 % of the EU-25's GDP; when compared with 2000 this ratio increased by almost 8 %. Slovakia (2004 data) and Finland were the only Member States where the environmental protection expenditure of private and public specialised producers was less than 0.2 % of GDP (see Figure 11.31). Conversely, in Austria (2007 data) and Romania (2004 data), the share rose to more than 1.7 % of GDP. This large range may reflect the degree of internalisation by industry of some environmental activities, such as waste and wastewater management. This could particularly be the case for industrial activities with in-house waste management services aiming to recycle part of the discarded materials for reintroduction into their production process. In 15 of the 19 countries for which data are available (see Figure 11.32), expenditure for waste management and wastewater management together accounted for close to or more than 90 % of private and public specialised producers' environmental protection expenditure. The remaining expenditure was for soil and groundwater protection (for example, soil decontamination activities) or was classified in the 'other' domain.

On average, approximately 60 % of the environmental protection expenditure of private and public specialised producers in 2007 was estimated to be directed towards waste management, with wastewater treatment the second most common domain. In Latvia (2005 data), Finland and Portugal (both 2006 data) wastewater treatment was the majority beneficiary of environmental protection expenditure among private and public specialised producers. Spain recorded an atypical structure, as around 40 % of its expenditure was devoted to domains other than waste and wastewater.

Industry's expenditure

Industrial environmental protection expenditure depends, to some extent, on the industrial structure of each country. It was generally equivalent to 0.25 % or more of GDP, with only France (2004 data), Latvia (2005 data) and Cyprus below this level – among those Member States for which data are available. This proportion rose to more than 0.8 % of GDP for six of the EU Member States, with the highest share being recorded in Bulgaria (1.0 %, 2007 data).

In most of the EU Member States, current expenditure represented a higher share of industrial environmental protection expenditure than investment. For example, in Italy, Belgium, and the Netherlands more than 80 % of the total took the form of current expenditure. The main exception was Portugal, where current expenditure accounted for only 35 % of industrial environmental protection expenditure.

As well as differences in the levels and types of industrial environmental protection expenditure, differences also emerge when analysing expenditure by subsector (see Figure 11.33). The manufacturing subsector accounted for the largest share of industrial expenditure in all but one of the EU Member States: in Slovakia the highest level of expenditure was accounted for by electricity, gas and water supply. The manufacturing subsector accounted for more than 90 % of industrial environmental protection expenditure in Belgium (2004 data), the highest proportion among the EU Member States.

Some Member States that joined the EU in 2004 or 2007 recorded relative high proportions of their environmental protection expenditure being accounted for by the electricity, gas and water supply subsector; this may, in part, be due to efforts made to reduce emissions from electricity generation. The share of the electricity, gas, and water supply subsector was lowest in Belgium (9.0 %, 2004 data) and Hungary (10.4 %, 2007 data). Romania, Poland and the Czech Republic (all 2007) accounted for the highest shares of industrial environmental protection expenditure contributed by the mining and quarrying subsector and these were the only Member States where the share of this activity rose into double-digits, peaking at 24.6 % in Romania (compared with an EU-27 average of 3.8 %).

Data sources and availability

Eurostat works towards systematically collecting environmental statistics for all economic sectors within the EU. These statistics are used to assess the effectiveness of new legislation and policies and to analyse the links between environmental pressures and the structure of the economy.

For many years, European statistical services have collected data on air pollution, energy, water consumption, wastewater, solid waste, and their management. The links between these data and environmental data of an economic nature, such as environmental expenditure enable policymakers to consider the environmental impacts of economic activities, for example on resource consumption, air or water pollution, and waste production, and to assess actions (such as investment and current expenditure) that may be carried out to limit the causes and risks of pollution.

Data on environmental expenditure are collected through a joint OECD/Eurostat questionnaire on environmental protection expenditure and revenues (EPER). The Member States are free to decide on the data collection methods used, and the main options are: surveys, administrative sources, statistical estimations, the use of already existing sources, or a combination of methods.

Traditionally, data availability has been better for the public sector as many countries have collected data in this area for a number of years. However, problems concerning data comparability across countries exist; these are often related to the structure of expenditure. For industrial activities (mining and quarrying, manufacturing, electricity, gas and water supply) most countries provide data, while the comparability of the information is considered to be good. For private and public specialised producers (mainly NACE Rev. 1.1 Divisions 37 and 90), while overall data availability is considered to be satisfactory, there are a number of countries that have so far not provided any data.

The data currently published on Eurostat's website covers:

- four economic sectors, namely the public sector, industry, private and public specialised producers and households;
- several economic variables concerning current expenditure, investment, fees and purchases, receipts from by-products, subsidies/transfers and revenues;
- nine environmental domains according to the classification of environmental protection activities (CEPA 2000) – protection of ambient air and climate; wastewater management; waste management; protection and remediation of soil, groundwater and surface water; noise and vibration abatement; protection of biodiversity and landscape; protection against radiation; research and development; and other environmental protection activities.

Total environmental protection expenditure is the sum of investment (with the distinction between pollution treatment and pollution prevention) and current expenditure for industry and private and public specialised production sectors, while for the public sector it equates to the sum of investment, current expenditure, and subsidies/transfers. As such, environmental protection expenditure is an indicator of the total resources used by a particular sector to protect the environment.

Investment expenditure includes all outlays in a given year (purchases and own-account production) for machinery, equipment and land used for environmental protection purposes and is the sum of two categories: end-of-pipe (pollution treatment) investment and investment in integrated technologies (pollution prevention investment). Current expenditure is the sum of internal current expenditure and fees/purchases. Subsidies/transfers (given or received) include all types of transfers financing environmental protection activities in other sectors, including transfers to or from other countries: these constitute expenditure for the paying sector (public sector), and revenue for the receiving sector (industry sector and private and public specialised producers sector).

In order to compare expenditure between countries as well as over time, environmental protection expenditure can be expressed in EUR per inhabitant and as a percentage of gross domestic product (GDP), or as a percentage of gross value added when analysing environmental protection expenditure within industrial subsectors.

Context

Businesses and households both pay to safely dispose of waste; businesses spend money to mitigate the polluting effects of production processes; governments pay to provide environmental public goods, such as the basic levels of sanitation required to safeguard health. Governments subsidise environmentally beneficial activities and use public funds to make it easier to borrow money on financial markets for environmental projects.

The analysis of spending on environmental protection has a strategic interest and allows an evaluation of environmental policies already in place. A low level of expenditure does not necessarily mean that a country is not effectively protecting its environment. Indeed, information on expenditure tends to emphasise clean-up costs at the expense of cost reductions which may have resulted from lower emissions or more effective protection measures.

Figure 11.25: Environmental protection expenditure, EU-25, 2006 (1)
(% of GDP)

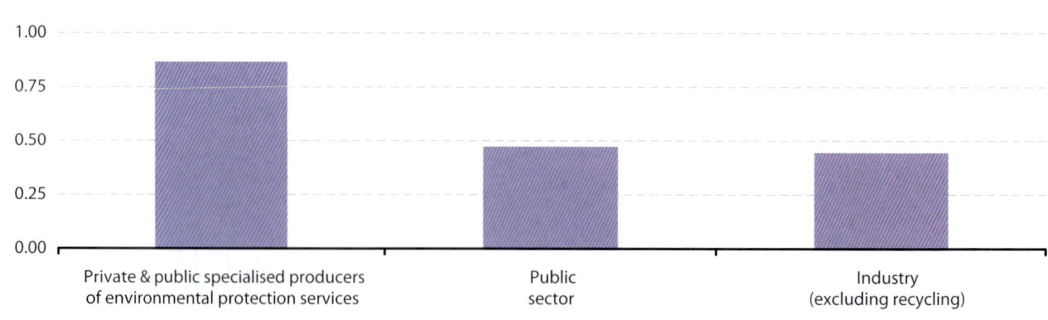

(1) Including estimates made for the purpose of this publication.

Source: Eurostat (env_ac_exp1 and env_ac_exp2)

Figure 11.26: Environmental protection expenditure, rate of change between 2000 and 2006, EU-25 (¹)
(%)

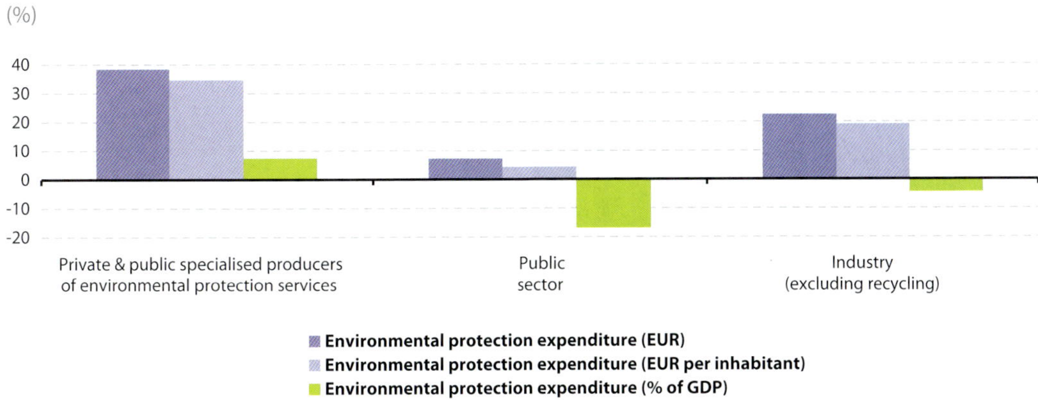

Environmental protection expenditure (EUR)
Environmental protection expenditure (EUR per inhabitant)
Environmental protection expenditure (% of GDP)

(¹) Including estimates made for the purpose of this publication.

Source: Eurostat (env_ac_exp1 and env_ac_exp2)

Figure 11.27: Public sector environmental protection expenditure by environmental domain, EU-25, 2006 (¹)
(%)

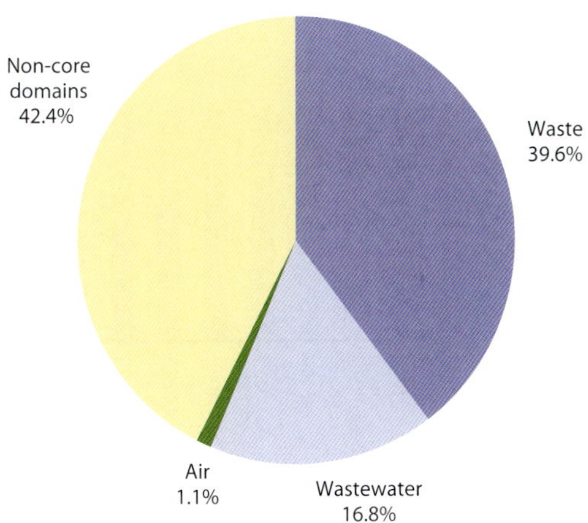

(¹) Including estimates made for the purpose of this publication.

Source: Eurostat (env_ac_exp1)

Figure 11.28: Public sector environmental protection expenditure, 2006 (¹)
(% of GDP)

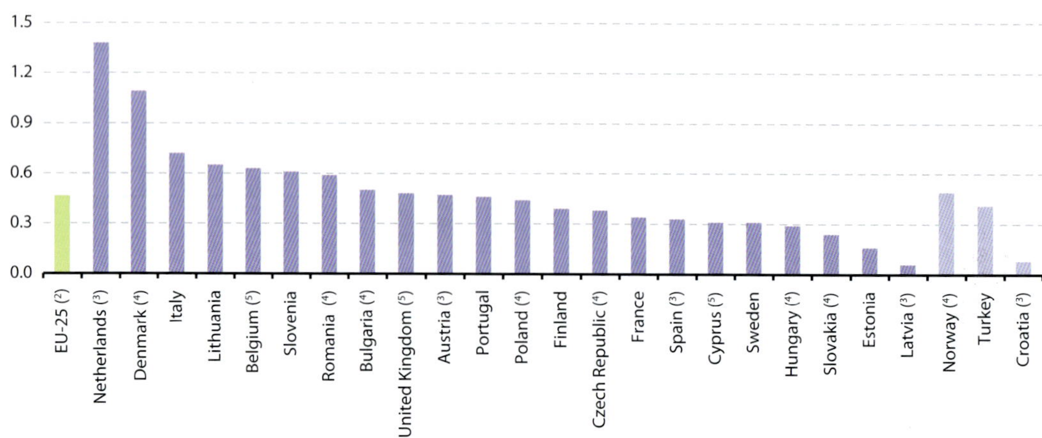

(¹) Germany, Greece, Ireland, Luxembourg and Malta, not available.
(²) Estimate made for the purpose of this publication.
(³) 2005.
(⁴) 2007.
(⁵) 2004.

Source: Eurostat (env_ac_exp1 and tec00001)

Figure 11.29: Public sector environmental protection expenditure by type of expenditure, 2006 (¹)
(% of total)

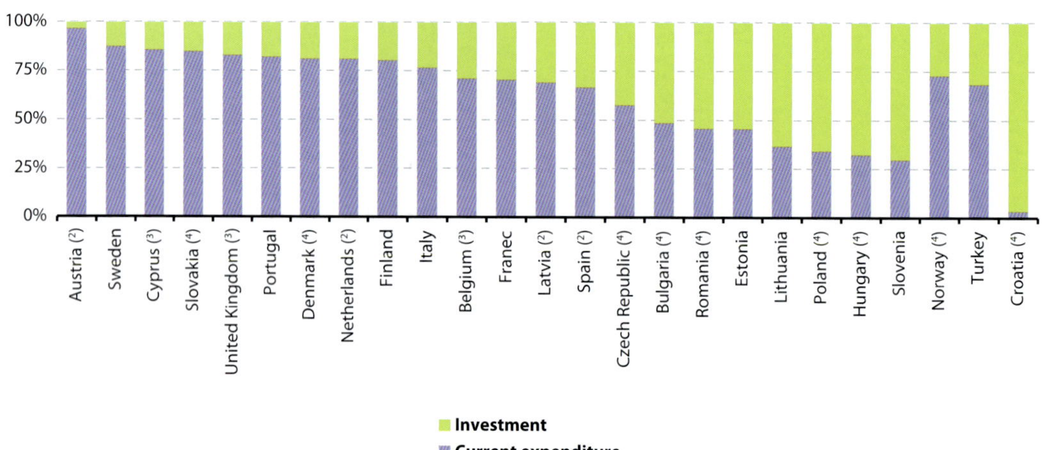

(¹) Germany, Greece, Ireland, Luxembourg and Malta, not available.
(²) 2005.
(³) 2004.
(⁴) 2007.

Source: Eurostat (env_ac_exp1)

Figure 11.30: Public sector environmental protection expenditure by environmental domain, 2006 (1)
(% of total)

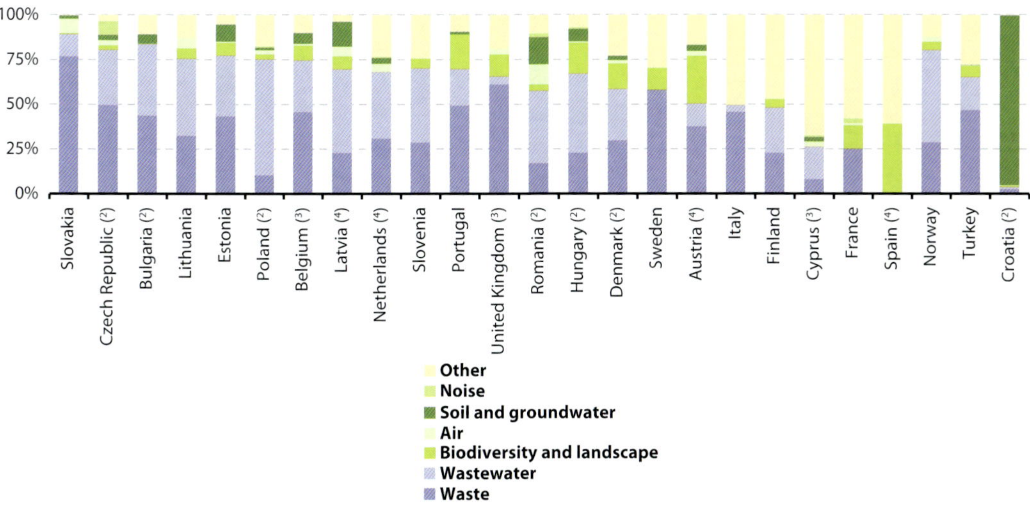

(1) Germany, Greece, Ireland, Luxembourg and Malta, not available.
(2) 2007.
(3) 2004.
(4) 2005.

Source: Eurostat (env_ac_exp1)

Figure 11.31: Public and private specialised producers environmental protection expenditure, 2006 (1)
(% of GDP)

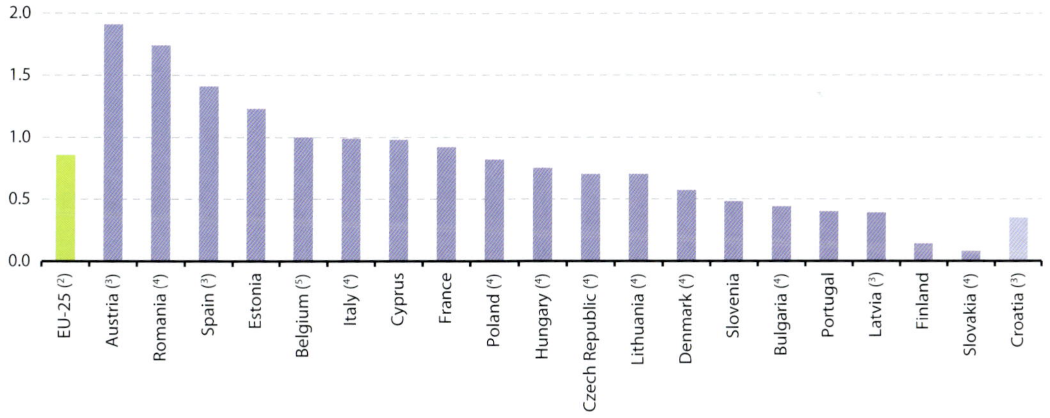

(1) Germany, Greece, Ireland, Luxembourg, Malta, Netherlands, Sweden and the United Kingdom, not available.
(2) Estimate made for the purpose of this publication.
(3) 2005.
(4) 2007.
(5) 2004.

Source: Eurostat (env_ac_exp1 and tec00001)

Figure 11.32: Public and private specialised producers environmental protection expenditure by environmental domain, 2007 (¹)
(% of total)

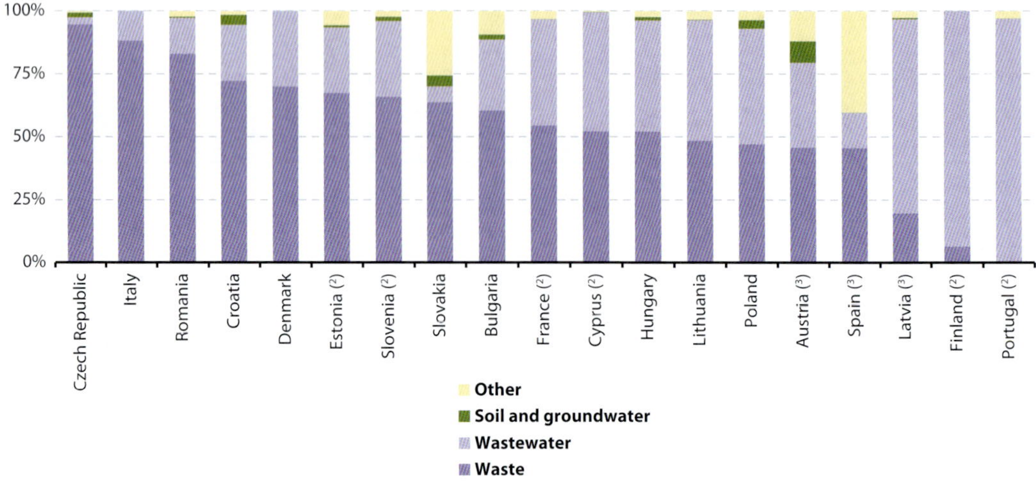

(¹) Belgium, Germany, Greece, Ireland, Luxembourg, Malta, Netherlands, Sweden and the United Kingdom, not available.
(²) 2006.
(³) 2005.

Source: Eurostat (env_ac_exp1)

Figure 11.33: Industrial environmental protection expenditure, 2006 (¹)
(% of GDP)

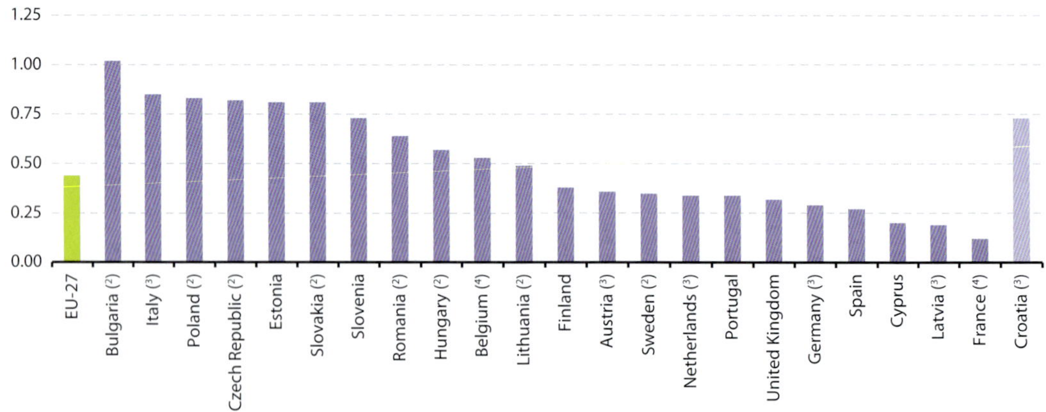

(¹) Denmark, Greece, Ireland, Luxembourg and Malta, not available.
(²) 2007.
(³) 2005.
(⁴) 2004.

Source: Eurostat (env_ac_exp1 and tec00001)

Figure 11.34: Industrial environmental protection expenditure by subsector, 2006 (1)
(% of total)

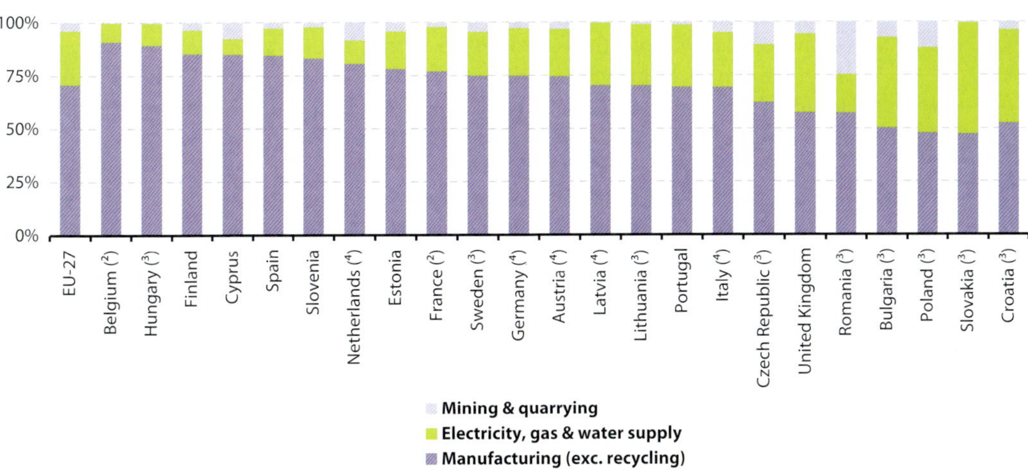

(1) Denmark, Greece, Ireland, Luxembourg and Malta, not available.
(2) 2004.
(3) 2007.
(4) 2005.

Source: Eurostat (env_ac_exp1)

11.7 Environmental taxes

Environmentally related taxes can be used as an economic instrument to discourage behaviour that is potentially harmful to the environment, by integrating the cost of adverse environmental impacts into prices, thereby lessening the impact of polluting substances on the environment. Taxes may be used as a tool for implementing the 'polluter pays' principle, as they allow the pricing-in of environmental externalities. By applying environmental taxes, governments within the European Union (EU) seek to influence the behaviour of consumers and producers, by encouraging them to use natural resources more responsibly and to limit or avoid pollution they might produce. Environmental taxes on polluters may provide incentives for them to innovate, thereby improving the performance of products and processes.

An environmental tax is a tax whose tax base is a physical unit that has a proven, specific, negative impact on the environment; for example, emissions of polluting substances such as carbon dioxide, nitrous oxide, or sulphur dioxide. It may be difficult and expensive to measure emissions directly; so many taxes are based on proxies for emissions, for example volumes of petrol, diesel, or other fuel oils that are used within various activities.

Main statistical findings

Environmental taxes in the EU

Figure 11.35 shows that environmental tax revenues in the EU-27 increased during the period between 1999 and 2007, to reach a relative peak of EUR 304.3 thousand million. However, the effects of the financial and economic crisis were apparent in 2008, with the tax base being reduced and revenues falling to EUR 299.0 thousand million. Increasing revenues from environmental taxes may be related to a range of issues, including: the introduction of new taxes; an increase in tax rates; an expansion of the tax base (for example, a lower emissions ceiling); or greater use of products and processes that have a negative impact on the environment.

The revenue from environmental taxes may be compared with total economic activity by expressing environmental taxes relative to gross domestic product (GDP); alternatively, environmental taxes may be expressed as a share of the total revenue from all taxes and social contributions (see Figure 11.36). In the first case, the comparison provides an insight into the tax burden on products and processes which damage the environment. In the second case, the comparison allows an assessment of tax reforms, and in particular whether or not 'green taxes' account for an increasing share of the tax burden. In 2008, the revenue from environmental taxes in the EU-27 accounted for 2.4 % of GDP and 6.1 % of all taxes and social contributions.

While the value of EU-27 environmental taxes rose by 22.8 % between 1999 and 2008, there was a decrease of 16.1 % in the ratio of environmental taxes to GDP and of 13.0 % in these taxes share of all taxes and social contributions over the same period. The decrease in environmental tax revenue relative to GDP may be explained by several factors, including a reduction in the nominal value of environmental taxation; environmental taxes are generally levied in the form of a specific duty, a tax based on a physical unit (for example, per tonne of carbon dioxide) measured in quantity terms, irrespective of price. As such, revenues from environmental taxes in relation to GDP are likely to fall over time, unless they are adjusted for inflation or increased at regular intervals.

The level of environmental taxation across EU Member States is shown in Map 11.1. Environmental taxes were equivalent to 2 % to 3 % of GDP in 2007 in 20 of the Member States. There were two Member States with environmental tax revenue equivalent to less than 2 % of GDP, namely Spain and Lithuania (both 1.8 %). At the other end of the range, the Netherlands, Malta, Bulgaria and Cyprus had environmental tax revenues that were over 3.4 %, while in Denmark environmental taxation reached 5.9 % of GDP.

The map also shows the relative importance of environmental taxes as a share of total revenue from taxes and social contributions. The same five Member States (as for the ratio of environmental taxes to GDP) were at the head of the ranking in 2007; with environmental taxation accounting for 12.0 % of total taxes and social contributions revenue in Denmark, followed by Malta (10.9 %), Bulgaria (10.1 %), the Netherlands (9.8 %) and Cyprus (8.2 %).

Environmental taxes by tax category

Energy taxes represented almost three quarters (72.1 %) of environmental taxes within the EU-27 in 2008 (see Figure 11.37); this share was above 50 % in the vast majority of European countries. The decrease in the magnitude of environmental taxes relative to GDP or total revenue from taxes and social contributions may be largely attributed to a decline in the total value of energy taxes between 1999 and 2008.

EU-27 transport taxes accounted for 23.0 % of environmental taxes in 2008. There was a wide variation in the contribution of transport taxes across the Member States, with Malta, Cyprus and Ireland reporting that more than 40 % of their environmental taxes were raised from transport taxes, as did Norway.

Resource and pollution taxes represent a small share of total environmental tax revenue in most European countries, although their share rose to more than 10 % of the total environmental tax revenue in Estonia, Slovakia, the Netherlands and Denmark, as well as in Norway; the EU-27 average was 4.9 %.

Environmental taxes by economic activity

On the basis of a limited set of information for 2007 – which covers 15 of the Member States and Norway – businesses (NACE Rev. 1.1 Sections A to K and N and Divisions 90, 92 and 93) generally contributed the highest proportion of energy tax revenues, their share equal to at least 50 % of the total in the Baltic Member States, Bulgaria, Austria, Belgium, Malta and Italy, as well as in Norway.

Households were generally the second most important contributor to energy tax revenues, although the governments of the Netherlands, Denmark, Germany and the

United Kingdom raised more revenues from energy taxes among households than they did from businesses.

Luxembourg and Malta were somewhat atypical insofar as public administration, education, and similar activities (NACE Rev. 1.1 Sections L, M, P and Q and Division 91) were responsible for 40 % of energy tax revenues in Luxembourg, while 31 % of revenues in Malta were attributed to non-residents.

Data sources and availability

Eurostat collects data on environmental tax revenues and on environmental taxes broken down by economic activity. The data are collected using a questionnaire which is sent to the EU-EFTA countries every year. The questionnaire consists of a cross-classification of the main environmental tax categories (total environmental taxes, energy taxes, transport taxes, pollution taxes, and resources taxes) with a breakdown using the NACE Rev. 1.1 classification – generally at the Section level; information is also available for households and non-residents. The European Commission's Directorate-General for Taxation and Customs Union also publishes environmental tax revenue statistics that are based on annual updates of information reported to Eurostat through the national accounts transmission programme.

Among the four main categories of environmental taxes, energy taxes include taxes on energy products used for both transport (for example, petrol and diesel) and stationary purposes (for example, fuel oil, natural gas, coal and electricity); carbon dioxide taxes are included under energy taxes rather than under pollution taxes. Transport taxes include taxes relating to the ownership and use of motor vehicles; these taxes may be one-off purchase taxes (for example, related to the engine size or the emissions of a particular vehicle) or recurrent taxes (such as an annual road tax). Pollution taxes include taxes for: emissions into the air (except for carbon dioxide taxes) and water; the management of waste; and noise. Taxes on resources cover taxes on the extraction of raw materials (with the exception of oil and gas).

Environmental tax revenues can also be allocated according to the different actors who pay them – which may be classified by economic activity (NACE). The European strategy on environmental accounts, approved in 2003 and revised in 2008, regards the collection of data and the implementation of estimates for environmental taxes by economic activity as a priority.

Environmental taxes – a statistical guide constitutes the methodological guidelines for filling-in the questionnaire. Taxes are defined as compulsory and unrequited payments to general government. Eurostat and OECD members have agreed on a definition for environmental taxes that is based on all taxes with environmental relevance, regardless of the explicit motives behind their introduction. This means that the purpose of the tax can be something other than environmental protection, while still being classified as an environmental tax (for example, an annual vehicle tax). The main categories of environmentally relevant tax bases are shown in Table 11.10.

Eurostat is working on the establishment of a legal base for the compilation of environmental accounts and the European Commission has put forward a proposal for a Regulation on European environmental economic accounts (COM(2010) 132). The proposal provides a framework for the development of various types of accounts, initially based on three modules with a view of adding other modules as they reach methodological maturity. Environmental taxes by economic activity are one of the three modules, alongside modules for air emissions accounts (see Subchapter 11.1) and material flow accounts (see Subchapter 11.4). It is expected that this proposed legal base will strengthen the coherence and availability of environmental accounts across the EU by providing a legal framework for their compilation, including methodology, common standards, definitions, classifications and accounting rules.

Context

Policymakers seek economic instruments that are capable of producing behavioural changes that will limit the damage that is done on the environment. A variety of tools may be used to help the EU achieve its environmental and sustainable development goals; these include fines, charges and taxes, tradable permits, and deposit-refund systems. Generally, such systems are used to penalise those who pollute or misuse the environment – through imposing the costs of use on the user. These systems may also be used to provide incentives to users, so that they adopt more environmentally-friendly behaviour.

The economic rationale for incentive-based tools for the environment (also called market-based instruments) comes from their ability to correct market failures in a cost-effective way, unlike regulatory or administrative approaches which tackle environmental problems only as technical issues to be resolved by setting emissions limits, banning specific substances, or enforcing the use of specific abatement technologies. Environmental taxes (and to a lesser extent, charges) have been used increasingly to influence behaviour, since they also generate revenue that can be used for environmental protection, which is not the case with tradable permit schemes, for instance. The use of EU-wide market-based tools has been increasing, for example, through the introduction of instruments such as the EU's emissions trading scheme (EU ETS), the energy taxation Directive (2003/96/EC), or, in the field of transport, the Eurovignette Directive (2006/38/EC).

Figure 11.35: Total environmental tax revenue, EU-27
(EUR 1 000 million)

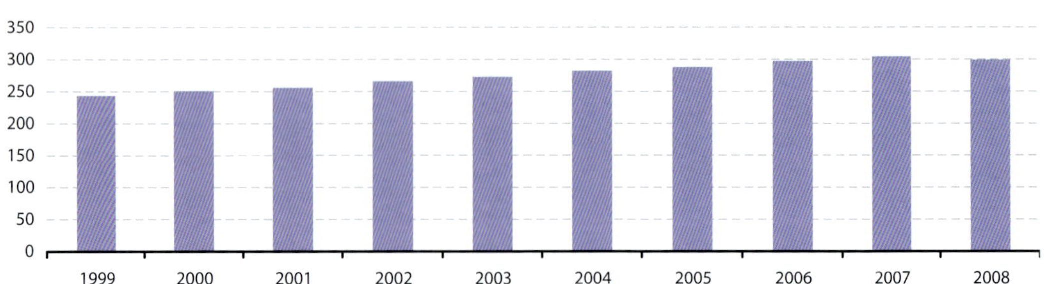

Source: Eurostat (env_ac_tax)

Figure 11.36: Total environmental tax revenue, EU-27
(%)

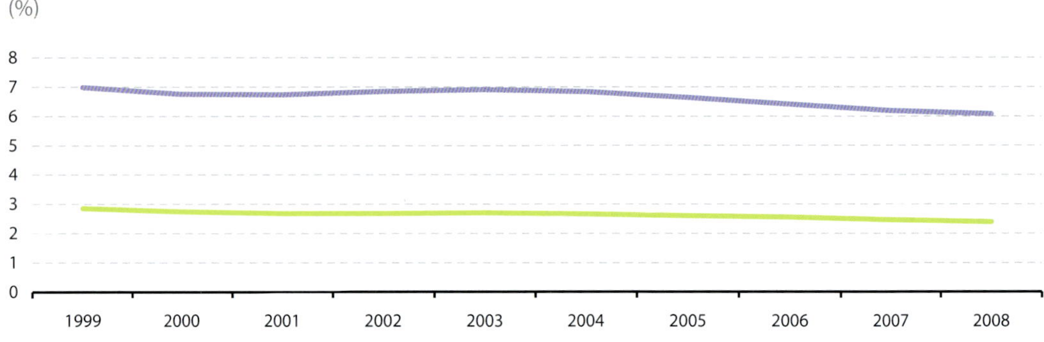

Source: Eurostat (env_ac_tax)

Map 11.1: Total environmental tax revenue, 2007
(%)

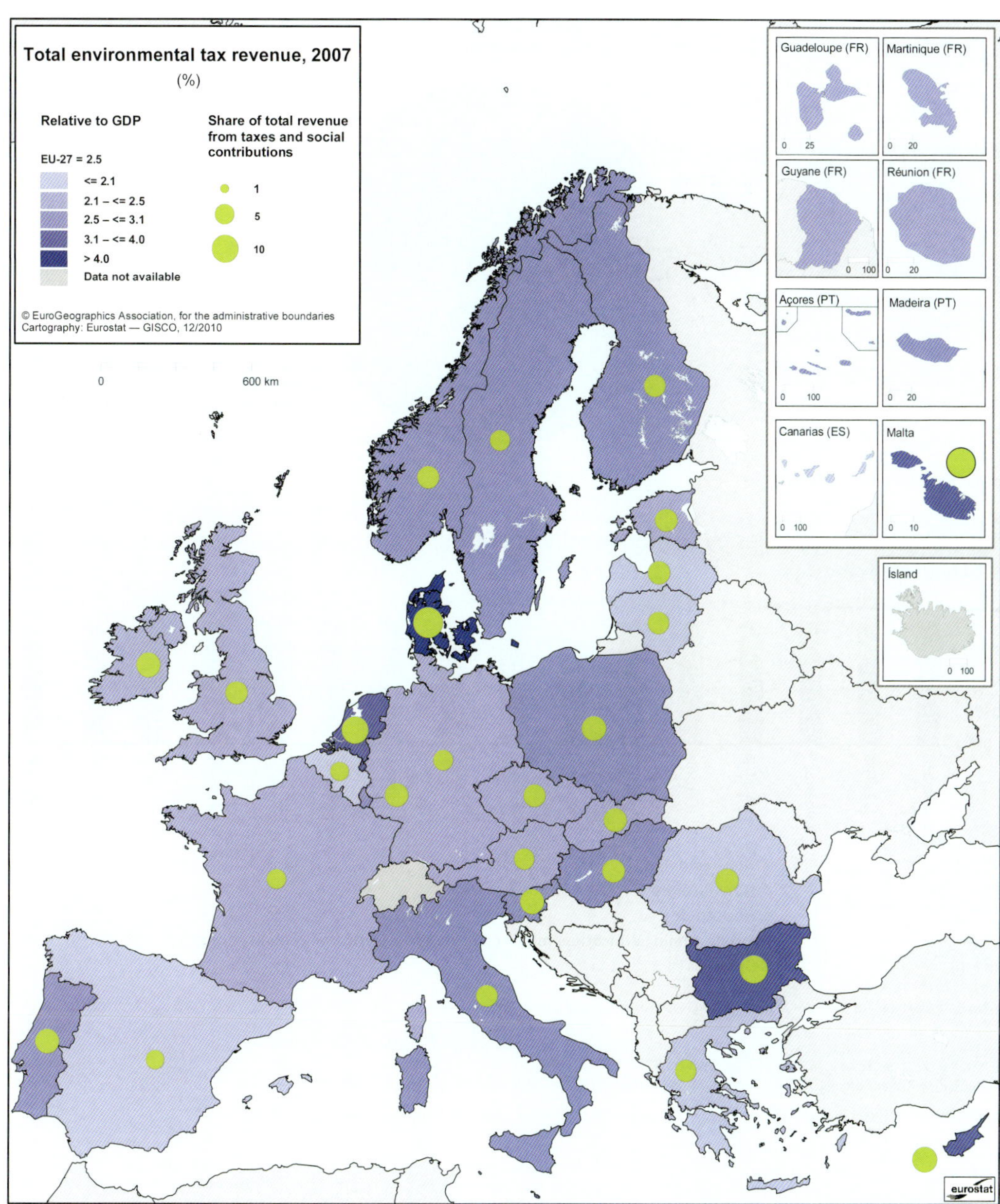

Source: Eurostat (env_ac_tax)

Figure 11.37: Environmental taxes by tax category, EU-27, 2008
(% of total)

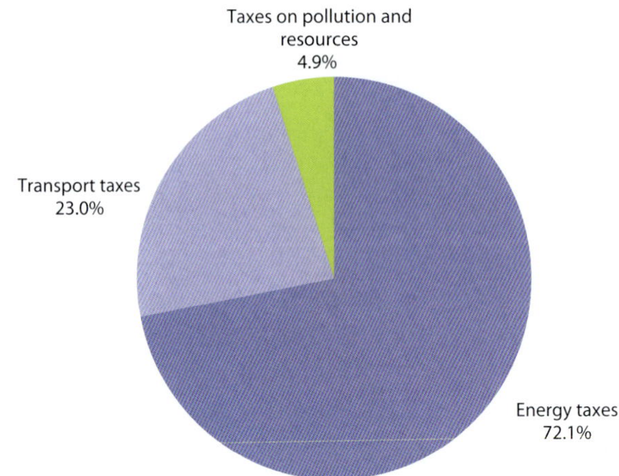

Source: Eurostat (env_ac_tax)

Figure 11.38: Energy taxes by economic activity, 2007 (1)
(% of energy tax revenue)

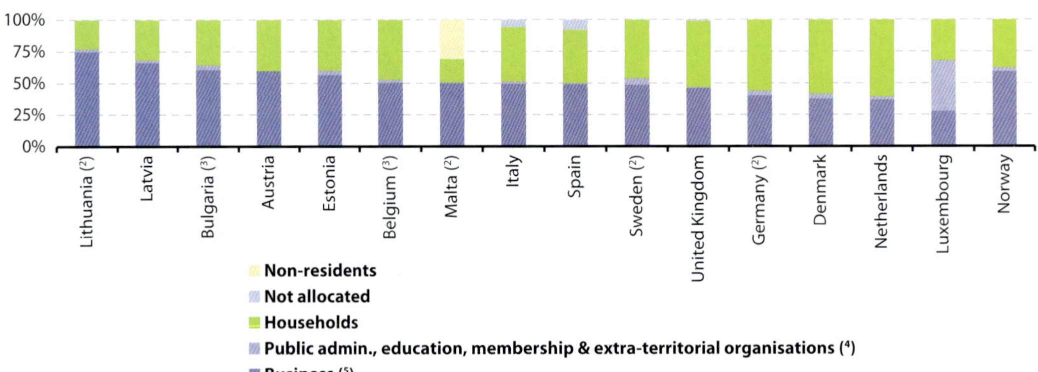

(1) No data available for Member States that are not shown.
(2) 2006.
(3) 2005.
(4) NACE Rev. 1.1 Sections L, M, P and Q and Division 91.
(5) NACE Rev. 1.1 Sections A to K and N and Divisions 90, 92 and 93.

Source: Eurostat (env_ac_taxind)

Table 11.10: Tax bases for environmental taxes

Tax base
Measured or estimated emissions to air
Measured or estimated NO_x emissions
SO_2 content of fossil fuels
Other measured or estimated emissions to air
Ozone depleting substances (e.g. CFC or halon)
Measured or estimated effluents to water
Measured or estimated effluents of oxydizeable matters (BOD, COD)
Other measured or estimated effluents to water
Effluent collection and treatment, fixed annual taxes
Certain non-point sources of water pollution
Pesticides (based on e.g. chemical content, price or volume)
Artificial fertilisers (based e.g. on phosphorus or nitrogen content or price)
Manure
Waste management
Waste management in general (e.g. collection or treatment taxes)
Waste management, individual products (e.g. packaging, beverage containers)
Noise (e.g. aircraft take-off and landings)
Energy products
Energy products used for transport purposes
Unleaded petrol
Leaded petrol
Diesel
Other energy products for transport purposes (e.g. LPG or natural gas)
Energy products used for stationary purposes (mostly CO_2 taxes)
Light fuel oil
Heavy fuel oil
Natural gas
Coal
Coke
Biofuels
Other fuels for stationary use
Electricity consumption
Electricity production
District heat consumption
District heat production
Transport
Motor vehicles, one-off import or sales taxes
Registration or use of motor vehicles, recurrent (e.g. yearly) taxes
Resources
Water abstraction
Extraction of raw materials (except oil and gas)
Other resources (e.g. forests)

11.8 Biodiversity

Biodiversity – a contraction of biological diversity – encompasses the number, variety and variability of living organisms, including mankind. Preventing a loss of biodiversity is important for mankind, given that humans depend on the natural richness of our planet for the food, energy, raw materials, clean air and clean water that make life possible and drive our economies and societies. As such, a reduction or loss of biodiversity may not only undermine the natural environment but also economic and social goals. The challenges associated with preserving biodiversity have made this topic an international issue. This subchapter presents some of the main indicators of biodiversity, such as the number of protected areas and bird populations, and examines the trends for these indicators in the European Union (EU).

Main statistical findings

Habitats

Areas protected for the preservation of biodiversity are proposed by the Member States under the EU's Habitats Directive; they are indicated as a percentage of the total area of each country. About 14 % of the EU-27's territory was proposed for protection under the Habitats Directive as of 2008. Additional areas were proposed for protection under the Birds Directive. Since there is some overlap between the two types of protected areas, the joint area for both Directives was estimated to amount to approximately 18% of the EU-27's terrestrial area in mid-2010. This number will be reviewed using a geographical information system and published shortly. Figures for the Member States show that protected areas range between 31 % of the total area of Slovenia to less than 10 % in six other Member States. In general, these protected areas adequately cover the biogeographical regions present in the Member States, with an EU-27 average of 84 % of sufficiently covered species and habitats in 2008; only Poland and Cyprus reported less than 50 % sufficiency.

Birds

Since 1990 there has been a general downward trend in the abundance of both common farmland and forest species of birds, as measured by common bird indices. Part of the relatively steep decline (-17 % between 1990 and 2008) in numbers of common farmland birds may be attributed to changes in land use and agricultural practices. There was a more rapid reduction in numbers of common forest birds between 1990 and 2000 across the EU (-26 % between 1990 and 2000). However, recent years have seen a recovery in forest bird numbers, with the index rising from a relative low of 75 to reach 86 by 2008. The index of all common bird species has been relatively stable since 1995, some 10 % below its 1990 level, and stood at 92 in 2008.

Data sources and availability

Habitats

Annual data are available on areas protected under the Habitats Directive. The data are presented as the percentage of compliance with the obligation to protect habitats and species that are typical for the wider biogeographical regions of the EU. The indicator is based on the extent of the area proposed by countries for the protection of natural and semi-natural habitats, wild fauna and flora according to annexes I and II of the Habitats Directive. The index of sufficiency measures the extent to which sites of Community importance proposed by the Member States adequately cover the species and habitats listed in those annexes, in proportion to the share of the biogeographical region that falls within the territory of the country.

Birds

Birds are considered good proxies for measuring the diversity and integrity of ecosystems as they tend to be near the top of the food chain, have large ranges and the ability to move elsewhere when their environment becomes unsuitable; they are therefore responsive to changes in their habitats and ecosystems. The bird indicators presented in this subchapter measure trends of bird populations.

The indicators are designed to capture the overall, average changes in population levels of common birds to reflect the health and functioning of the ecosystems they inhabit. The population index of common birds is an aggregated index (with base year 1990 or the first year the Member State entered the scheme) of population trend estimates of a selected group of common bird species. Indices are calculated for each species independently and then combined to create a multi-species EU indicator by averaging the indices with an equal weight using a geometric average. Indices rather than bird abundance are averaged in order to give each species an equal weight in the resulting indicator. The EU index is based on trend data from 20 Member States, derived from annually operated national breeding bird surveys collated by the Pan-European Common Bird Monitoring Scheme (PECBMS); these data are considered as a good proxy for the whole of the EU.

Three different indices are presented:

- common farmland birds (36 species);
- common forest birds (29 species);
- all common birds (136 species).

For the first two categories, the bird species have a high dependence on agricultural or on forest habitats in the nesting season and for feeding. Both groups comprise both year-round residents and migratory species. The aggregated index comprises farmland and forest species together with 71 other common species that are generalists, meaning that they occur in many different habitats or are particularly adapted to life in cities.

Context

People depend on natural resources and the variety of species found on the planet for tangible goods that make life possible and drive economic development, such as food, energy, wood, raw materials, clean air and water. Many aspects of our natural environment are public goods, in other words they have no market value or price. As such, the loss of biodiversity can often go undetected by economic systems. However, the natural environment also provides a range of intangibles, such as the aesthetic pleasure derived from viewing landscapes and wildlife, or recreational opportunities. In order to protect this legacy for future generations, the EU seeks to promote policies in a range of areas to ensure that biodiversity is protected through the sustainable development of, among others, agriculture, rural and urban landscapes, energy provision and transport. Many of these issues were touched upon by G8 environment ministers in Potsdam in March 2007, where an extensive study of the economics of ecosystems and biodiversity (TEEB) was commissioned.

Biodiversity strategy is based on the implementation of two landmark Directives, the Habitats Directive (92/43/EEC) of 21 May 1992 and the Birds Directive (79/409/EEC) of 2 April 1979. Implementation of these Directives has involved the establishment of a coherent European ecological network of sites under the title Natura 2000. The EU wants to expand Natura 2000, which currently counts around 26 000 sites (and an area of almost 930 000 km^2 including marine sites) where plant and animal species and their habitats are protected. Establishing the Natura 2000 network may be seen as the first pillar of action relating to the conservation of natural habitats. However, EU legislation also foresees measures to establish a second pillar through strict protection regimes for certain animal species (for example, the Arctic fox and the Iberian lynx, both under serious threat of extinction).

In 1998, the EU adopted a biodiversity strategy. Four action plans covering the conservation of natural resources, agriculture, fisheries, and economic and development cooperation were subsequently agreed as part of this strategy in 2001. The European Commission released a Communication ((2006) 216) on 'halting the loss of biodiversity by 2010 – and beyond'; this underlined the importance of biodiversity protection as a pre-requisite for sustainable development and set out an action plan which addresses the challenge of integrating biodiversity concerns into other policy areas. The Communication also contained indicators to monitor progress and a timetable for evaluations, whereby the European Commission has undertaken to report annually. In March 2010, the Council of the environment ministers of the EU acknowledged that the 2010 targets had not been met and agreed to set a new target, namely, to halt the loss of biodiversity and the degradation of ecosystem services in the EU by 2020, restoring them insofar as feasible, while stepping up the EU's contribution to averting global biodiversity loss.

Figure 11.39: Protected areas for biodiversity - sufficiency of sites, 2008
(%)

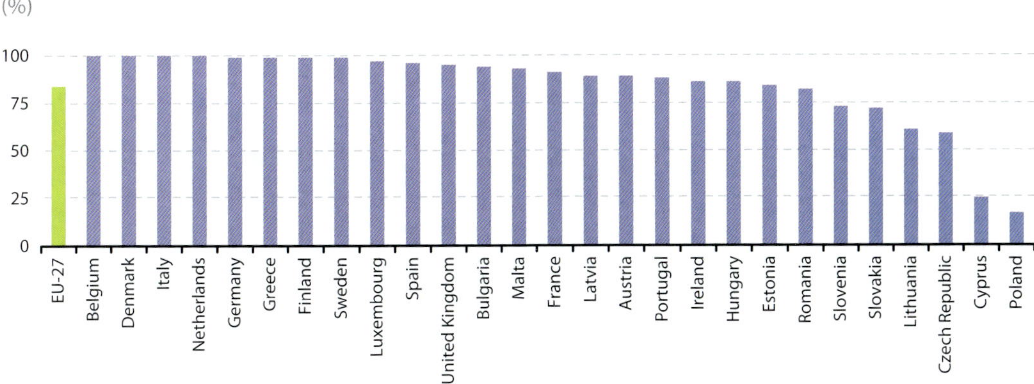

Source: EEA/European topic centre on biodiversity, Eurostat (env_bio1)

Figure 11.40: Common bird indices, EU (1)
(aggregated index of population estimates of selected groups of breeding bird species, 1990=100)

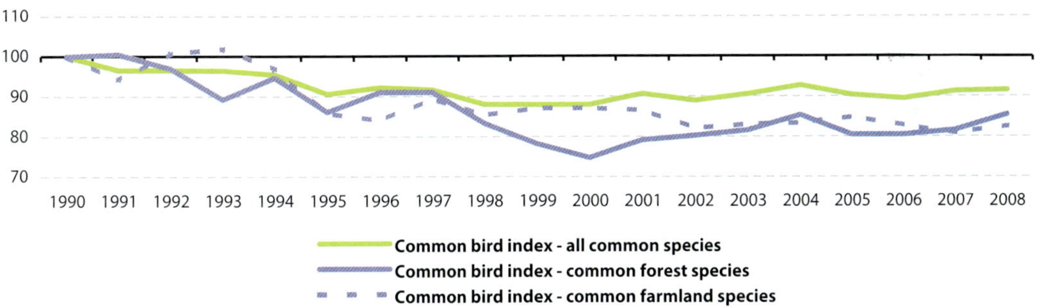

(1) Estimates; 'all common species' covers information on 135 different bird species; 'common farmland species' covers 36 bird species; 'common forest species' covers 29 bird species.

Source: EBCC/RSPB/BirdLife/Statistics Netherlands, Eurostat (env_bio2)

Energy

12

A competitive, reliable and sustainable energy sector is essential for all advanced economies. The energy sector has been under the spotlight in recent years due to a number of issues that have pushed energy to the top of national and European Union (EU) political agendas, these include:

- the volatility of oil prices;
- interruptions to energy supply from non-member countries;
- blackouts aggravated by inefficient connections between national electricity networks;
- the difficulties of market access for suppliers in relation to gas and electricity markets;
- increased attention to anthropogenic (human-induced) effects on climate change, in particular, increased greenhouse gas emissions.

The use of renewable energy sources is seen as a key element of European energy policy and should help to: reduce dependence on fuel from non-member countries; reduce emissions from carbon-based energy sources, and; decouple energy costs from oil prices. Another key aspect of the EU's energy policy is to constrain consumption by promoting energy efficiency, both within the energy sector itself and among end-users. Indeed, the EU is putting in place an ambitious energy policy – covering a broad range of energy sources from fossil fuels (oil, gas and coal) to nuclear energy and renewables (solar, wind, biomass, geothermal, hydroelectric and tidal). This policy is designed to bring about a new industrial revolution that will result in a low-energy economy, whilst making the energy consumed more secure, competitive and sustainable, with the goal of the EU becoming a world leader in renewable energy and low-carbon technologies.

In January 2007, the European Commission adopted a Communication (COM(2007) 1) proposing a new energy policy for Europe, with the goal of combating climate change and boosting the EU's energy security and competitiveness through the development of a more sustainable and low-carbon economy. Based on the European Commission's proposal, the European Council endorsed the following targets in March 2007, namely, to:

- reduce greenhouse gas emissions by at least 20 % (compared with 1990 levels) by 2020;
- improve energy efficiency by 20 % by 2020;
- increase the share of renewable energy in final energy consumption to 20 % by 2020;
- increase the share of renewable energy sources in the fuel used by the transport sector to 10 % by 2020.

In a Communication titled 'Towards a low carbon future' (COM(2007) 723 final), the European Commission put forward a strategic energy technology plan (SET-plan) in November 2007. This aims to support decarbonised energy technologies, such as off-shore wind, by accelerating their development and implementation.

In January 2008, the European Commission proposed a package of measures relating to energy and the climate in order to supplement existing initiatives. The European Council, on 11 and 12 December 2008, reached an agreement on an energy/climate change package that was endorsed by the European Parliament at the end of 2008. This breakthrough should help the EU to honour its commitments and to maintain its leading role in the search for an ambitious and comprehensive post-Kyoto global agreement.

In November 2008, the European Commission put forward its second strategic energy review (COM(2008) 781) that contained plans designed to achieve the objectives of sustainability, competitiveness and security of supply. These included a new strategy for building energy security and solidarity between EU Member States, as well as a package of energy efficiency proposals to make energy efficiency savings in areas such as buildings and energy-using products.

In July 2009, new rules to improve the security of gas supplies were introduced through Regulation 715/2009, designed to strengthen the existing system and ensure that all Member States and their gas market participants take effective action to prevent and mitigate the consequences of potential disruptions to gas supplies.

In order to meet the increasing requirements of policymakers for energy monitoring, the legislation relating to energy statistics has in recent years undergone a period of renewal. The new legal basis is Regulation 844/2010 on energy statistics. The data collection exercise covers all EU Member States, Iceland, Norway, Switzerland, Croatia, the former Yugoslav Republic of Macedonia and Turkey. Time series for energy statistics go back to 1985 for some countries, but are more generally available from 1990 onwards; monthly data are also available for certain indicators.

12.1 Energy production and imports

The dependency of the European Union (EU) on energy imports, particularly of oil and more recently of gas, forms the backdrop for policy concerns relating to the security of energy supplies. This subchapter looks at the production of primary energy in the EU and, as a result of the shortfall between production and consumption, the EU's increasing dependency on energy imports from non-member countries. Indeed, more than half (54.8 %) of the EU's gross inland energy consumption in 2008 came from imported sources.

Main statistical findings

Primary production

Production of primary energy in the EU-27 totalled 842.7 million tonnes of oil equivalent in 2008. This continued the generally downward trend of EU-27 production, as supplies of raw materials become exhausted and/or producers considered the exploitation of limited resources uneconomical. Production was dominated by the United Kingdom with a 19.5 % share of the EU-27 total, although this marked a considerable reduction when compared with a decade earlier (28.6 % of the EU-27 total in 1998). Indeed, the United Kingdom experienced by far the largest reduction in its output of primary energy, with production falling by 104.8 million tonnes of oil equivalent (toe) over the period from 1998 to 2008; the next largest decline was recorded in Poland (16.3 million toe). Germany, in contrast, maintained its level of production broadly in line with the 1998 level, while there was an expansion in the production of primary energy in France (up 11.0 million toe during the period under consideration); alongside the United Kingdom, Germany and France were the only other Member States to report that their production of primary energy was in excess of 100 million toe in 2008 (see Table 12.1).

Primary energy production in the EU-27 in 2008 was spread across a range of different energy sources, the most important of which was nuclear energy (28.7 % of the total); the significance of nuclear fuel was particularly high in Belgium, Spain, France, Lithuania, Slovakia and Sweden – where it accounted for more than half of the national production of primary energy. Around one fifth of the EU-27's total production of primary energy was accounted for by solid fuels (largely coal) and by natural gas, with shares of 21.0 % and 19.9 % respectively, while renewable energy sources (17.6 %) and crude oil (12.7 %) made up the remainder of the total (see Figure 12.1).

The growth of primary production from renewable energy sources exceeded that of all the other energy types, with particularly strong growth since 2002 (see Figure 12.2). Indeed, there appears to be something of a watershed since this date, as the production of renewables accelerated, rising by 48.8 % overall between 2002 and 2008 (and by 5.5 % between 2007 and 2008). In contrast, the production levels for the other sources of energy generally fell between 1998 and 2008 – aside from a modest increase of 2.2 % for nuclear energy. The largest reductions in the production of primary energy were recorded for crude oil (-37.4 %), solid fuels (-25.3 %) and natural gas (-15.9 %).

Imports

The downturn in the primary production of hard coal, lignite, crude oil and natural gas has led to a situation where the EU is increasingly reliant on primary energy imports in order to satisfy demand. The EU-27's imports of primary energy exceeded exports by some 1 015.0 million toe in 2008. The largest net importers of primary energy were generally the most populous Member States, with the exception of the United Kingdom and Poland (where some indigenous reserves of oil/natural gas and coal remain). Since 2004 the only net exporter of primary energy among the EU Member States has been Denmark (see Table 12.2).

The origin of EU-27 energy imports has changed rapidly in recent years, as Russia has emerged as the leading supplier (see Table 12.3). In 2008, some 29.0 % of the EU-27's imports of crude oil were from Russia; this was slightly down on the peak of 30.4 % recorded in both 2006 and 2007. Russia was also the principal supplier of hard coal, its share of EU-27 imports rising from 7.9 % in 2000 to 23.7 % by 2008, well ahead of the next highest share recorded by South Africa (15.3 %). In contrast, Russia's share of EU-27 imports of natural gas declined from 40.4 % to 31.5 % between 2000 and 2008; note, however, that during this period the volume of natural gas imports from Russia remained relatively unchanged, while there was an increase in the share of natural gas imports from Norway (rising to 24.1 % of the total by 2008).

The security of the EU's primary energy supplies may be threatened if a high proportion of imports are concentrated among relatively few partners. More than two thirds (68.0 %) of EU-27 imports of natural gas in 2008 came from Russia, Norway or Algeria. A similar analysis shows that 52.4 % of EU-27 crude oil imports came from Russia, Norway and Libya, while 51.4 % of hard coal imports were from Russia, South Africa and the United States. Although their import volumes remain relatively small, there was some evidence of new partner countries emerging between 2000 and 2008. This was notably the case for hard coal imports from Indonesia, crude oil imports from Kazakhstan and Azerbaijan, or natural gas imports from Libya, Nigeria and Egypt.

EU-27 dependency on energy imports increased from less than 40 % of gross energy consumption in the 1980s to 54.8 % by 2008 (see Table 12.4), with the highest energy dependency rates recorded for crude oil (84.2 %) and for natural gas (62.3 %). The dependency on non-member countries for supplies of solid fuels and natural gas grew at a faster pace in the last decade than the dependency on crude oil (which was already at a high level). Since 2004, the EU-27's net imports of energy have been greater than its primary production; in other words, more than half of the EU-27's gross inland energy consumption was supplied by net imports.

As it was a net exporter, Denmark was the only EU-27 Member State in 2008 with a negative dependency rate (see Figure 12.3). Among the other Member States, the lowest dependency rates were recorded by Estonia, the United Kingdom the Czech Republic and Romania (the only other countries to report dependency rates below 30 %); meanwhile, Malta, Luxembourg and Cyprus were almost entirely dependent on primary energy imports.

Data sources and availability

Energy commodities extracted or captured directly from natural resources are called primary energy sources, while energy commodities which are produced from primary energy sources in transformation plants are called derived products. Primary energy production covers the national production of primary energy sources and takes place when natural resources are exploited, for example, in coal mines, crude oil fields, hydropower plants, or in the fabrication of biofuels. Whenever consumption exceeds primary production, the shortfall needs to be accounted for by imports of primary or derived products.

The heat produced in a reactor as a result of nuclear fission is regarded as primary production of nuclear heat, alternatively referred to as, nuclear energy. It is calculated either on the basis of the actual heat produced or on the basis of reported gross electricity generation and the thermal efficiency of the nuclear plant. Primary production of coal and lignite consists of quantities of fuels extracted or produced, calculated after any operation for the removal of inert matter.

Transformation of energy from one form to another, such as electricity or heat generation from thermal power plants, or coke production from coke ovens is not considered as primary production. Net imports are calculated as the quantity of imports minus the equivalent quantity of exports. Imports represent all entries into the national territory excluding transit quantities (notably via gas and oil pipelines); exports similarly cover all quantities exported from the national territory.

Context

More than half of the EU-27's energy comes from countries outside the Union – and this proportion is rising. Much of this energy comes from Russia, whose disputes with transit countries have disrupted supplies in recent years – for example, between 6 and 20 January 2009, gas flows from Russia via Ukraine were interrupted.

The European Commission adopted its second strategic energy review in November 2008. This addressed how the EU could reduce its dependency on imported energy, thereby improving its security of supply, as well as reducing its emissions of greenhouse gases. The review encouraged energy solidarity among Member States, proposed an action plan to secure sustainable energy supplies, and adopted a package of energy efficiency proposals aimed at making energy savings in key areas, such as buildings and energy-using products.

The European Commission made a proposal at the end of 2008 to repeal Directive 2004/67/EC concerning measures to safeguard security of natural gas supply. In response to the Russian-Ukrainian gas crisis of January 2009, the European Parliament and Council called for an accelerated revision of the Directive, arguing that the crisis demonstrated the need to define more clearly the roles of the gas industry, Member States and EU institutions to deal with potential supply disruptions. As a result, the European Council adopted a Directive (2009/119/EC) in September 2009 imposing an obligation on Member States to maintain minimum stocks of crude oil and/or petroleum products. These new measures for oil and gas markets are designed to ensure that all parties take effective action to prevent and mitigate the consequences of potential disruptions to supplies, while also creating mechanisms for Member States to work together to deal effectively with any major oil or gas disruptions which might arise; a coordination mechanism has been set-up so that Member States can react uniformly and immediately in emergency cases.

There are a number of on-going initiatives to develop gas pipelines between Europe and its eastern and southern neighbours. These include the north stream (between Russia and the EU via the Baltic Sea), the south stream (between Russia and the EU via the Black Sea) and Nabucco (connecting the Caspian region and Middle East to the EU); all three are scheduled to be in operation (at the latest) by the end of 2015.

Table 12.1: Energy production
(million tonnes of oil equivalent)

	Total production of primary energy		Share of total production 2008 (%)				
	1998	2008	Nuclear energy	Solid fuels	Natural gas	Crude oil	Renewable energy
EU-27	940.0	842.7	28.7	21.0	19.9	12.7	17.6
Euro area (EA-16)	439.3	456.8	41.9	14.5	17.8	2.8	22.9
Belgium	12.1	13.6	86.7	0.0	0.0	-	13.3
Bulgaria	10.2	10.1	40.4	47.9	1.6	0.2	9.9
Czech Republic	30.5	32.5	21.1	70.1	0.5	0.8	7.6
Denmark	20.3	26.5	-	-	34.0	54.1	11.9
Germany	131.7	132.5	28.9	37.8	8.5	2.3	22.4
Estonia	3.2	4.2	-	82.1	-	-	17.9
Ireland	2.4	1.5	-	42.4	23.3	-	34.3
Greece	10.0	10.0	-	83.3	0.1	0.6	15.9
Spain	32.0	30.3	50.3	13.9	0.1	0.4	35.4
France	124.0	135.0	84.0	0.0	0.6	0.8	14.7
Italy	30.1	26.4	0.0	0.3	28.7	20.1	51.0
Cyprus	0.0	0.1	-	-	-	-	100.0
Latvia	1.8	1.8	-	0.2	-	-	99.9
Lithuania	4.4	3.6	71.2	0.5	-	3.6	24.6
Luxembourg	0.1	0.1	-	-	-	-	100.0
Hungary	11.9	10.4	36.7	16.3	19.3	11.8	15.9
Malta	-	-	-	-	-	-	-
Netherlands	63.6	66.3	1.6	-	90.3	3.3	4.7
Austria	8.7	10.6	-	0.0	12.4	9.4	78.2
Poland	86.8	70.4	-	85.9	5.2	1.1	7.7
Portugal	3.7	4.4	-	0.0	-	-	100.0
Romania	29.2	29.1	10.0	24.0	30.9	16.5	18.6
Slovenia	3.0	3.6	44.4	32.5	0.1	0.0	22.9
Slovakia	4.7	6.1	70.7	10.2	1.4	0.3	17.3
Finland	13.1	16.3	36.4	7.1	-	-	56.4
Sweden	33.0	32.8	50.3	0.8	-	0.0	49.0
United Kingdom	269.3	164.5	8.2	6.4	38.1	44.4	2.9
Iceland	1.8	:	:	:	:	:	:
Norway	206.6	219.3	:	1.0	39.7	53.2	6.1
Switzerland	10.6	12.3	57.9	:	0.0	:	42.1
Croatia	4.0	3.9	:	0.0	55.8	22.2	22.0
Turkey	29.1	29.1	:	57.4	2.9	7.5	32.2

Source: Eurostat (ten00076, ten00080, ten00077, ten00079, ten00078 and ten00081)

Figure 12.1: Production of primary energy, EU-27, 2008
(% of total, based on tonnes of oil equivalent)

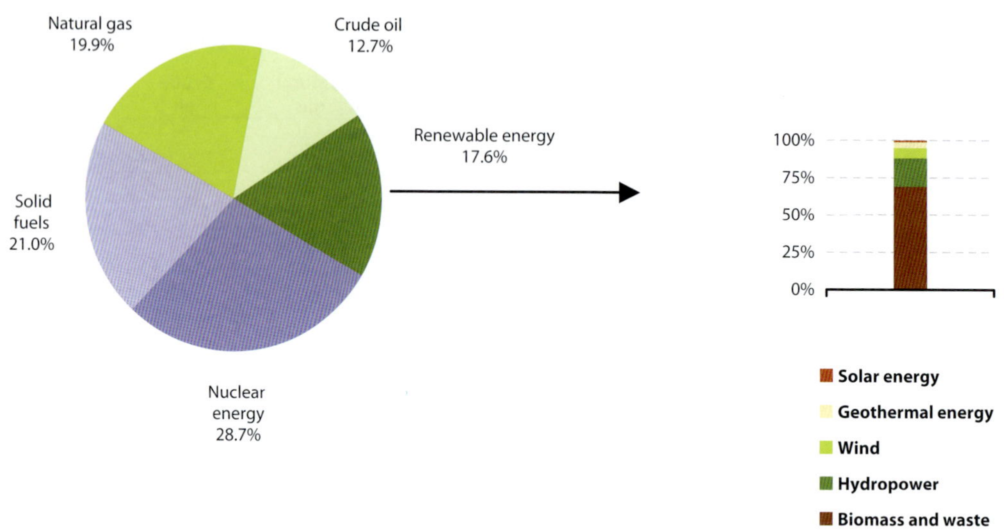

Source: Eurostat (ten00080, ten00077, ten00079, ten00078, ten00081 and ten00082)

Figure 12.2: Development of the production of primary energy (by fuel type), EU-27
(1998=100, based on tonnes of oil equivalent)

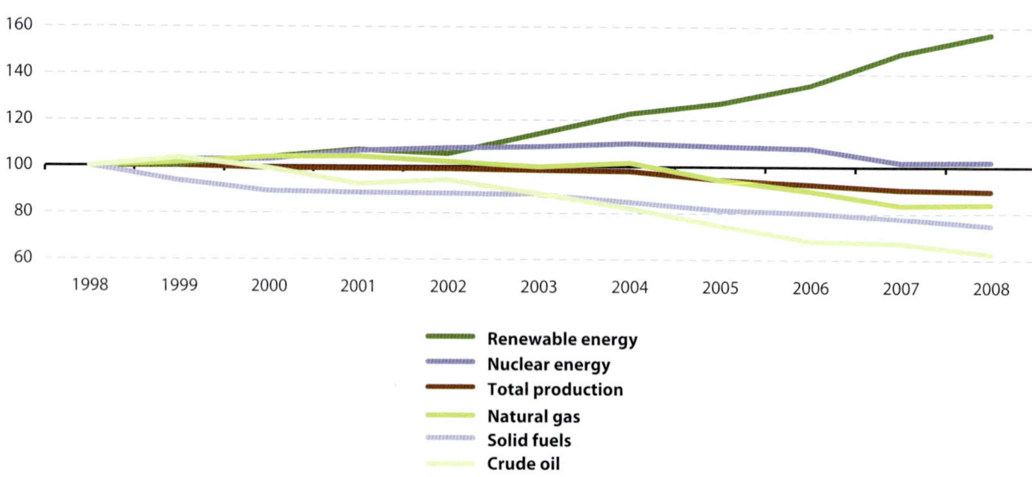

Source: Eurostat (ten00076, ten00081, ten00080, ten00079, ten00078 and ten00077)

Table 12.2: Net imports of primary energy

	(1 000 tonnes of oil equivalent)					(tonnes of oil equivalent per inhabitant)				
	2000	2002	2004	2006	2008	2000	2002	2004	2006	2008
EU-27	826 732	858 657	941 376	1 010 880	1 014 961	1.71	1.77	1.93	2.05	*2.04*
Euro area (EA-16)	795 294	813 614	848 185	868 166	850 889	2.54	2.58	2.65	2.69	*2.60*
Belgium	50 812	49 341	53 940	53 486	53 896	4.96	4.79	5.19	5.09	5.05
Bulgaria	8 718	8 936	9 241	9 540	10 543	1.06	1.13	1.18	1.24	1.38
Czech Republic	9 475	11 358	11 742	12 921	12 462	0.92	1.11	1.15	1.26	1.20
Denmark	-7 255	-8 610	-9 946	-7 930	-4 638	-1.36	-1.60	-1.84	-1.46	-0.85
Germany	205 682	209 252	215 533	215 558	211 181	2.50	2.54	2.61	2.61	2.57
Estonia	1 656	1 448	1 653	1 614	1 449	1.21	1.06	1.22	1.20	1.08
Ireland	12 270	13 742	13 865	14 221	14 261	3.25	3.52	3.44	3.38	*3.24*
Greece	22 065	23 308	24 708	24 857	25 484	2.02	2.12	2.24	2.23	2.27
Spain	99 334	108 012	115 282	124 054	122 500	2.48	2.64	2.72	2.83	2.71
France	134 196	137 477	141 485	141 895	141 472	2.22	2.24	2.27	2.25	2.21
Italy	153 527	153 542	159 548	164 570	157 064	2.70	2.69	2.76	2.80	2.63
Cyprus	2 547	2 586	2 417	2 971	3 032	3.69	3.67	3.31	3.88	3.84
Latvia	2 246	2 455	3 173	3 170	2 781	0.94	1.05	1.37	1.38	1.22
Lithuania	4 343	3 739	4 439	5 481	5 507	1.24	1.08	1.29	1.61	1.64
Luxembourg	3 630	3 950	4 535	4 662	4 498	8.37	8.90	9.97	9.94	9.30
Hungary	14 032	14 777	16 095	17 408	17 049	1.37	1.45	1.59	1.73	1.70
Malta	1 466	1 565	1 902	1 648	1 857	3.86	3.97	4.76	4.07	4.53
Netherlands	35 239	32 279	31 062	36 962	34 215	2.22	2.00	1.91	2.26	2.09
Austria	19 112	21 181	23 383	24 973	23 628	2.39	2.63	2.87	3.03	2.84
Poland	10 161	10 100	13 345	19 485	30 095	0.26	0.26	0.35	0.51	0.79
Portugal	21 881	22 519	22 653	21 569	21 263	2.15	2.18	2.16	2.04	2.00
Romania	8 129	9 165	12 000	11 901	11 289	0.36	0.42	0.55	0.55	0.52
Slovenia (1)	3 366	3 440	3 709	3 827	4 289	1.69	1.73	1.86	1.91	2.13
Slovakia	11 581	12 576	13 204	12 046	12 066	2.15	2.34	2.45	2.24	2.23
Finland	18 587	18 844	20 958	20 866	20 181	3.59	3.63	4.02	3.97	3.81
Sweden	19 182	19 913	20 373	19 797	19 752	2.16	2.24	2.27	2.19	2.15
United Kingdom	-39 249	-28 239	11 076	49 327	57 783	-0.67	-0.48	0.19	0.82	*0.94*
Iceland	1 036	969	1 072	*1 099*	:	3.71	3.38	3.69	*3.66*	:
Norway	-198 280	-208 707	-202 897	-188 231	-188 612	-44.27	-46.13	-44.33	-40.57	-39.82
Switzerland	14 079	15 047	15 168	16 111	15 419	1.97	2.07	2.06	2.16	2.03
Croatia	4 181	4 977	5 105	4 878	5 507	0.93	1.12	1.15	1.10	1.24
Turkey	51 062	51 107	58 705	69 293	72 872	0.76	0.74	0.83	0.96	1.03

(1) Tonnes of oil equivalent per inhabitant, break in series, 2008.

Source: Eurostat (ten00083 and tps00001)

Table 12.3: Main origin of primary energy imports, EU-27
(% of extra EU-27 imports)

	Hard coal								
	2000	2001	2002	2003	2004	2005	2006	2007	2008
Russia	7.9	9.8	11.4	12.6	17.6	21.2	22.5	22.6	23.7
South Africa	21.2	23.2	26.8	27.1	23.4	22.7	21.5	18.5	15.3
United States	10.8	9.5	7.0	6.0	6.7	6.9	7.0	8.4	12.8
Colombia	12.3	10.7	10.6	10.9	10.7	10.6	10.6	11.7	11.1
Australia	15.1	13.9	14.6	14.7	13.4	11.9	11.0	12.0	10.8
Indonesia	4.8	4.8	5.7	6.1	6.1	6.5	8.5	7.1	6.7
Canada	3.4	3.3	2.7	1.8	1.9	2.9	2.5	2.9	2.4
Ukraine	1.1	1.4	1.7	1.1	1.9	1.8	1.3	1.5	1.9
Venezuela	1.8	1.4	1.7	2.4	1.0	0.9	0.8	1.0	0.9
Others	21.6	22.1	17.9	17.2	17.1	14.6	14.2	14.5	14.5
	Crude oil								
	2000	2001	2002	2003	2004	2005	2006	2007	2008
Russia	18.7	22.7	26.1	28.1	30.0	29.9	30.4	30.4	29.0
Norway	19.3	17.9	17.4	17.5	17.3	15.5	14.3	13.8	14.0
Libya	7.6	7.3	6.6	7.6	7.9	8.1	8.5	9.1	9.3
Saudi Arabia	10.8	9.5	9.0	10.1	10.2	9.7	8.2	6.6	6.3
Iran	5.9	5.2	4.4	5.7	5.7	5.6	5.8	5.6	5.0
Kazakhstan	1.6	1.5	2.3	2.6	3.5	4.2	4.3	4.4	4.6
Nigeria	3.7	4.3	3.1	3.8	2.4	3.0	3.2	2.5	3.7
Iraq	5.2	3.4	2.7	1.4	2.0	2.0	2.7	3.1	3.1
Azerbaijan	0.6	0.8	0.9	0.9	0.8	1.1	1.9	2.6	2.7
Others	26.6	27.4	27.5	22.3	20.1	21.0	20.7	22.0	22.2
	Natural gas								
	2000	2001	2002	2003	2004	2005	2006	2007	2008
Russia	40.4	38.5	36.7	37.2	35.9	34.5	33.0	31.7	31.5
Norway	17.4	18.6	21.3	21.0	20.3	20.7	21.4	23.2	24.1
Algeria	19.6	17.0	17.2	16.4	14.8	15.3	13.8	12.7	12.4
Nigeria	1.5	1.9	1.8	2.6	3.0	3.0	3.6	3.9	3.3
Libya	0.3	0.3	0.2	0.2	0.3	1.4	2.1	2.5	2.5
Egypt	0.1	0.2	0.7	0.6	1.2	1.3	1.5	1.8	1.8
Qatar	0.0	0.0	0.0	0.0	0.0	1.4	2.1	1.5	1.4
Trinidad and Tobago	0.3	0.2	0.2	0.0	0.0	0.2	1.1	0.7	1.4
Croatia	0.0	0.0	0.0	0.0	0.0	0.0	0.3	0.2	0.2
Others	20.4	23.3	22.1	21.9	24.4	22.2	21.2	21.8	21.4

Source: Eurostat (nrg_122a, nrg_123a and nrg_124a)

Table 12.4: Energy dependency rate, EU-27
(% of net imports in gross inland consumption and bunkers, based on tonnes of oil equivalent)

	1998	1999	2000	2001	2002	2003	2004	2005	2006	2007	2008
All products	46.1	45.2	46.8	*47.5*	*47.6*	49.0	50.3	52.6	53.8	53.1	54.8
Solid fuels	26.6	27.8	30.7	33.8	33.1	34.9	38.1	39.9	41.1	41.5	44.9
Crude oil	76.0	73.0	74.5	76.7	75.4	77.7	80.0	81.6	83.2	82.9	84.2
Natural gas	45.6	47.9	48.9	47.3	51.2	52.5	54.0	57.7	60.8	60.3	62.3

Source: Eurostat (nrg_100a, nrg_101a, nrg_102a and nrg_103a)

Figure 12.3: Energy dependency rate - all products, 2008
(% of net imports in gross inland consumption and bunkers, based on tonnes of oil equivalent)

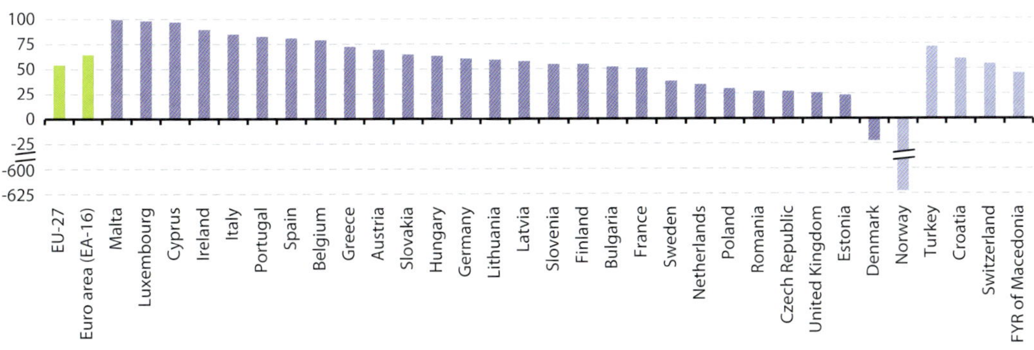

Source: Eurostat (tsdcc310 and nrg_100a)

12.2 Consumption of energy

The European Union (EU) has pledged to cut its energy consumption by 20 % (compared with projected levels) by 2020. This subchapter explains how the consumption of energy in the EU has evolved, highlighting a gradual shift from fossil fuels to renewable energy sources, such as solar energy, wind power, and biofuels; it also looks at the evolution of energy use within the transport sector.

In tandem with supply-side policies, the EU has launched a number of initiatives which aim to reduce energy demand and attempt to decouple it from economic growth. Several instruments and implementing measures exist in this field, including the promotion of co-generation, the energy performance of buildings (whether private or public buildings), and energy labelling of domestic appliances.

Main statistical findings

Consumption

Gross inland energy consumption of primary energy within the EU-27 in 2008 was 1 799 million tonnes of oil equivalent (toe). As such, gross inland consumption remained relatively unchanged throughout the period from 2003 to 2008, in contrast to a rising trend prior to this period (see Table 12.5).

The gross inland consumption of each Member State depends, to a large degree, on the structure of its energy system, the availability of natural resources for primary energy production, and the structure and development of each economy (general trends in economic growth); this is true not only for conventional fuels and nuclear power, but also for renewable energy sources. Gross inland consumption of primary energy rose at a fast pace in Spain throughout the period from 1998 to 2008. There was also a rapid expansion in energy consumption in Poland between 2003 and 2008, as witnessed by the second highest growth rate, behind Spain; the largest reductions in gross inland consumption of primary energy (during the same five-year period) were recorded in the United Kingdom and Germany.

Over the period 1998 to 2008 there was a gradual decline in the share of crude oil and petroleum products, solid fuels, and nuclear energy in total gross inland consumption, while an increasing share of EU-27 consumption was accounted for by natural gas and renewable energy sources (see Figure 12.4). The combined share of crude oil, petroleum products and solid fuels fell from 59.0 % of total consumption to 53.5 %, reflecting changes in the EU-27's energy mix and a move away from the most polluting fossil fuels. During the same period, the relative importance of natural gas and of renewable energy sources rose by 2.9 percentage points, reaching 24.5 % and 8.4 % of the EU-27's gross inland consumption by 2008; the relative importance of renewable energy sources rose to almost one third of the total in Sweden and Latvia, and was close to one quarter of the total in Austria and Finland.

Final energy consumption (in other words, excluding energy used by power producers) in the EU-27, was equivalent to just under two thirds (64.9 %) of gross inland consumption, at 1 169 million toe in 2008. Almost one fifth (19.2 %) of the EU-27's final energy consumption was accounted for by Germany (see Table 12.6).

The lowest levels of energy intensity – a measure of an economy's energy efficiency – were recorded for Denmark and Ireland in 2008, while the most energy-intensive Member States were Bulgaria and Romania (see Figure 12.5). It should be noted that the economic structure of an economy plays an important role in determining energy intensity, as post-industrial economies with large service sectors will, a priori, have considerably lower energy use than economies characterised by heavy, traditional industries. Between 1998 and 2008, substantial energy savings were made in the Bulgarian and Romanian economies, as well as in the Baltic Member States, as the amount of energy required to produce a unit of economic output (as measured by the gross domestic product (GDP)) was almost halved (reductions of between 40 and 46 %).

End-users

An analysis of the final end use of energy shows three dominant categories: as transport, industry and households each accounted for at least one quarter of the EU-27's final energy consumption in 2008. The total energy consumption of all transport modes amounted to 374.3 million toe in 2008, almost one third (32.0 %) of the total (see Figure 12.6). There were, however, considerable differences in the development of energy consumption across transport modes in the EU-27, with the most rapid growth recorded for aviation (33.4 % between 1998 and 2008) and an upward trend for road transport (11.6 %), while the energy consumption of rail was relatively unchanged (-2.7 %) – see Figure 12.7. The largest increase in energy consumption among the different transport modes, in absolute terms, was recorded for road transport, where EU-27 consumption rose by 31.5 million toe between 1998 and 2008, compared with a 13.6 million toe increase for aviation. These changes in energy consumption reflect the popularity of each transport mode, but can also be influenced by technological changes, especially when these relate to fuel-efficiency gains.

Data sources and availability

Gross inland energy consumption represents the quantity of energy necessary to satisfy inland consumption of the geographical entity under consideration. It may be defined as primary production plus imports, recovered products and stock changes, less exports and fuel supply to maritime bunkers (for seagoing ships of all flags). It describes the total energy needs of a country (or entity), covering: consumption by the energy sector itself; distribution and transformation losses; final energy consumption by end-users; and statistical differences

Final energy consumption includes the consumption of energy by all users except the energy sector itself (whether for deliveries, for transformation, and/or its own use), and includes, for example, energy consumption by agriculture, industry, services and households, as well as energy consumption for transport. It should be noted that fuel quantities transformed in the electrical power stations of industrial auto-producers and the quantities of coke transformed into blast-furnace gas are not part of overall industrial energy consumption but of the transformation sector.

Energy intensity is measured as the ratio between gross inland consumption of energy and GDP; this indicator is a key indicator for measuring progress under the Europe 2020 strategy for smart, sustainable and inclusive growth. The ratio is expressed in kilograms of oil equivalent (kgoe) per EUR 1 000, and to facilitate analysis over time the calculations are based on GDP at constant prices (currently chain-linked 2000 prices). If an economy becomes more efficient in its use of energy and its GDP remains constant, then the ratio for this indicator should fall. The economic structure of an economy plays an important role in determining energy intensity, as post-industrial economies with large service sectors will, a priori, display relatively low energy intensity rates, while developing economies may have a considerable proportion of their economic activity within industrial sectors, thus leading to higher energy intensity.

Context

As well as supply-side policies to influence the production of energy, there is a growing trend for policy initiatives to focus on improving energy efficiency in an attempt to reduce energy demand and decouple it from economic growth. This process was given impetus by the integrated energy and climate change strategy that committed the EU to cut its energy consumption by 20 % by 2020 (in relation to projected levels) and, in so doing, simultaneously address the issues of import dependency, energy-related emissions, and energy costs.

To achieve these goals, the EU seeks to engage public opinion, decision-makers and market operators, while setting minimum energy efficiency standards and rules on labelling for products, services and infrastructure, in order to encourage significant reductions in consumption – for example, through the promotion of co-generation, improving the energy performance of buildings, or improving the information given to consumers with respect to the energy consumption of domestic appliances. Indeed, daily life is becoming increasingly dependent on energy-consuming devices. Without compromising standards of living, there are a range of actions that could be employed to reduce energy consumption across many European households. Aside from making efficiency savings, these measures could also cut average fuel bills, for example, by: turning the thermostat down; using thermostatic radiator valves; not leaving televisions, music systems, DVD players or similar devices on stand-by; defrosting fridges and freezers regularly; turning off lights when leaving rooms; using low-energy light bulbs; insulating hot-water tanks and heating pipes; or using loft insulation and cavity wall insulation.

The EU harmonises national measures relating to the publication of information on the consumption of energy by household appliances, thereby allowing consumers to choose appliances on the basis of their energy efficiency – a range of different products (for example, light bulbs, refrigerators, washing machines) carry the EU's energy label that details the energy efficiency of products, rating them according to a scale that ranges from A to G, with 'A' as the most energy efficient products and 'G' for the least efficient products.

The transport sector is the fastest growing consumer of energy and producer of greenhouse gases, even if advances in transport technology and fuel have resulted in marked decreases in emissions of certain pollutants. There are many factors that impact on energy use within the transport sector, for example, overall economic growth, the efficiency of individual transport modes, the take-up of alternative fuels, and lifestyle choices. The globalised nature of the economy has fuelled demand for international freight movements (principally by ship), while within the Single Market there has been a considerable expansion in the use of road freight transport. The growth in demand for energy from the EU's transport sector is not confined to business, as it has been accompanied by an expansion in personal travel. The growth of low-cost airlines, an increase in motorisation rates (the average number of motor vehicles per inhabitant), a trend for living in suburban areas, or the expansion of tourism (more frequent breaks, and more long-haul destinations) are among some of the factors that have contributed to increased demand for energy as a result of personal travel.

Table 12.5: Gross inland consumption of primary energy
(million tonnes of oil equivalent)

	1998	1999	2000	2001	2002	2003	2004	2005	2006	2007	2008	Share in EU-27 2008 (%)
EU-27	1 723	1 711	1 724	*1 763*	*1 759*	1 803	1 825	1 825	1 826	1 808	1 799	100.0
Euro area (EA-16)	1 177	1 181	1 198	*1 228*	*1 228*	1 257	1 277	1 277	1 273	1 265	1 260	70.0
Belgium	60.1	61.1	61.5	60.3	58.4	61.6	61.5	61.1	60.4	57.3	58.3	3.2
Bulgaria	20.2	18.2	18.7	19.4	19.0	19.6	19.0	20.0	20.6	20.3	20.0	1.1
Czech Republic	41.2	38.5	40.5	41.5	42.0	45.6	45.9	44.4	46.4	46.3	45.1	2.5
Denmark	20.8	20.1	19.5	20.2	19.8	20.8	20.2	19.7	21.0	20.5	19.9	1.1
Germany	346.7	340.8	342.4	353.3	345.6	348.3	350.3	347.1	348.9	341.3	343.7	19.1
Estonia	5.4	5.0	5.0	5.1	5.0	5.5	5.7	5.6	5.4	6.1	5.9	0.3
Ireland	13.0	13.7	14.4	15.0	15.3	15.0	15.8	15.1	15.5	15.9	15.8	0.9
Greece	27.0	26.9	28.2	29.1	29.9	30.3	30.8	31.4	31.5	31.5	31.9	1.8
Spain	112.6	118.4	123.6	126.5	130.8	135.3	141.5	144.6	144.1	146.6	141.9	7.9
France	255.2	254.7	258.2	266.3	266.5	271.0	275.6	276.2	273.1	270.3	273.7	15.2
Italy	169.9	172.5	174.6	175.4	175.9	184.2	186.2	188.5	187.1	185.3	181.4	10.1
Cyprus	2.2	2.3	2.4	2.4	2.4	2.7	2.5	2.5	2.6	2.7	2.9	0.2
Latvia	4.3	4.0	3.7	4.1	4.0	4.3	4.4	4.5	4.6	4.8	4.6	0.3
Lithuania	9.3	7.9	7.1	8.1	8.6	9.0	9.1	8.6	8.4	9.1	9.2	0.5
Luxembourg	3.3	3.4	3.6	3.8	4.0	4.2	4.6	4.7	4.7	4.7	4.6	0.3
Hungary	25.6	25.5	25.0	25.5	25.9	27.1	26.6	28.0	27.8	27.0	26.8	1.5
Malta	0.8	0.9	0.8	0.9	0.8	0.9	0.9	0.9	0.9	0.9	0.9	0.1
Netherlands	76.6	75.8	77.2	*79.5*	*79.7*	81.9	83.8	82.5	80.6	85.5	83.7	4.7
Austria	29.2	29.3	29.1	30.8	31.1	32.7	33.3	34.6	34.3	33.9	33.9	1.9
Poland	96.2	93.8	90.8	90.9	89.5	91.8	92.2	93.4	98.1	97.8	98.8	5.5
Portugal	23.2	24.9	25.1	25.2	26.3	25.7	26.4	27.0	25.3	26.0	24.9	1.4
Romania	41.5	36.9	37.1	36.9	38.5	40.2	39.6	39.2	40.7	40.5	40.6	2.3
Slovenia	6.4	6.4	6.4	6.7	6.8	6.9	7.1	7.3	7.3	7.3	7.7	0.4
Slovakia	17.5	17.4	17.5	19.3	19.3	19.2	19.1	19.1	18.8	18.1	18.5	1.0
Finland	33.4	32.9	32.5	33.2	35.3	37.3	37.6	34.8	37.9	37.6	36.3	2.0
Sweden	50.6	50.2	47.6	50.6	51.7	50.7	52.7	51.7	50.4	50.2	50.0	2.8
United Kingdom	230.6	229.2	231.6	232.7	226.8	231.2	232.3	232.7	229.2	220.3	218.5	12.1
Iceland	2.7	3.1	3.2	3.4	3.4	3.4	3.5	3.6	4.3	:	:	-
Norway	25.5	26.8	26.1	26.5	24.1	27.3	28.2	26.7	27.2	27.3	29.8	-
Switzerland	26.1	26.1	25.9	27.4	26.5	26.6	26.9	26.9	28.1	26.9	28.0	-
Croatia	8.1	8.0	7.8	8.0	8.3	8.8	8.9	8.9	9.0	9.4	9.1	-
Turkey	72.5	71.2	77.6	71.6	75.5	79.4	82.0	85.4	94.7	101.5	100.3	-

Source: Eurostat (ten00086)

Figure 12.4: Gross inland consumption, EU-27
(% of total consumption)

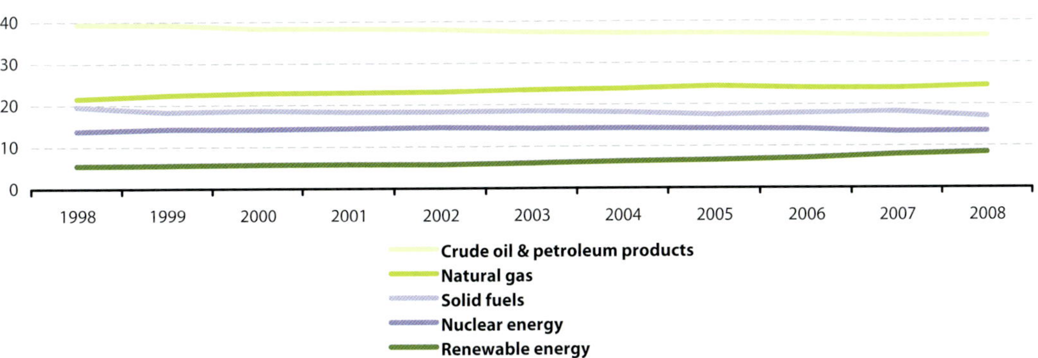

Source: Eurostat (nrg_102a, nrg_103a, nrg_101a, nrg_104a and nrg_1071a)

Figure 12.5: Energy intensity of the economy
(kg of oil equivalent per EUR 1 000 of GDP)

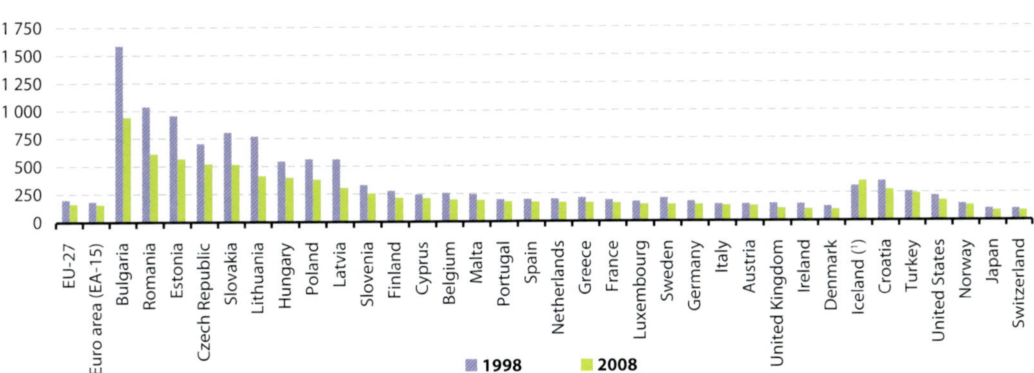

(¹) 2006 instead of 2008.

Source: Eurostat (tsien020)

Table 12.6: Final energy consumption
(million tonnes of oil equivalent)

	1998	1999	2000	2001	2002	2003	2004	2005	2006	2007	2008	Share in EU-27, 2008 (%)
EU-27	1 116	1 113	*1 117*	1 143	1 129	1 166	1 181	1 182	*1 186*	*1 165*	*1 169*	100.0
Euro area (EA-16)	767	770	*778*	800	793	821	832	832	*833*	*816*	*821*	70.2
Belgium	39.0	39.0	39.1	39.4	37.7	40.0	39.4	38.4	38.1	34.9	37.6	3.2
Bulgaria	9.9	8.8	8.6	8.6	8.7	9.4	9.2	9.7	10.1	9.9	9.6	0.8
Czech Republic	24.5	23.8	23.9	24.1	23.7	25.7	26.3	26.0	26.5	25.9	25.4	2.2
Denmark	15.0	15.0	14.6	15.0	14.7	15.1	15.3	15.4	15.6	15.7	15.5	1.3
Germany	223.5	218.7	218.1	223.9	219.2	226.2	225.3	222.0	226.2	216.0	224.0	19.2
Estonia	2.7	2.4	2.4	2.6	2.5	2.7	2.8	2.9	2.9	3.1	3.0	0.3
Ireland	9.3	9.9	10.7	11.1	11.2	11.5	11.8	12.5	13.1	12.2	13.2	1.1
Greece	18.2	18.2	18.6	19.2	19.5	20.5	20.3	20.8	21.4	21.9	21.2	1.8
Spain	71.9	74.5	79.6	83.4	84.8	90.4	94.4	97.5	96.1	98.8	95.4	8.2
France	151.6	151.3	151.1	157.4	153.0	157.1	158.7	158.0	157.1	154.1	156.3	13.4
Italy	120.3	124.8	124.9	126.2	125.6	131.1	134.9	136.7	135.4	133.9	128.2	11.0
Cyprus	1.5	1.6	1.6	1.7	1.7	1.8	1.8	1.8	1.8	1.9	2.0	0.2
Latvia	3.6	3.4	3.2	3.6	3.6	3.8	3.9	4.0	4.2	4.4	4.2	0.4
Lithuania	4.5	4.0	3.7	3.9	4.0	4.1	4.3	4.5	4.7	5.0	4.9	0.4
Luxembourg	3.2	3.4	3.6	3.7	3.7	4.0	4.4	4.4	4.4	4.4	4.3	0.4
Hungary	15.7	15.9	15.7	16.5	17.0	17.6	17.5	18.1	18.0	16.9	17.0	1.5
Malta	0.3	0.3	0.3	0.4	0.4	0.5	0.5	0.5	0.4	0.4	0.5	0.0
Netherlands	50.3	49.6	50.5	51.3	51.4	52.1	52.9	51.6	50.9	49.7	51.2	4.4
Austria	22.9	23.0	23.2	24.9	25.1	26.4	26.6	27.9	27.1	26.9	27.0	2.3
Poland	60.0	58.8	55.3	55.9	54.2	56.1	57.5	57.8	60.8	61.2	61.8	5.3
Portugal	16.2	16.7	17.7	18.1	18.4	18.4	18.7	18.7	18.5	18.7	18.3	1.6
Romania	26.2	22.4	22.5	23.0	23.1	24.2	25.5	24.7	24.8	24.0	24.9	2.1
Slovenia	4.3	4.3	4.4	4.6	4.5	4.7	4.8	4.9	4.9	4.9	5.2	0.4
Slovakia	10.5	10.3	10.3	10.9	11.1	10.7	10.8	10.6	10.7	10.5	10.7	0.9
Finland	24.3	24.7	24.2	24.2	25.2	25.7	26.2	25.4	26.9	26.7	25.9	2.2
Sweden	35.5	35.1	34.9	34.4	34.1	33.9	33.9	33.7	33.1	33.2	32.8	2.8
United Kingdom	150.8	153.6	154.3	155.2	150.6	152.2	153.5	153.9	152.3	149.7	148.6	12.7
Iceland	1.9	2.0	2.1	2.1	2.2	2.2	2.2	2.2	2.4	:	:	-
Norway	18.3	18.7	18.1	18.3	18.1	18.0	18.4	18.5	18.4	18.8	18.9	-
Switzerland	20.3	20.5	20.3	20.8	20.2	20.8	21.1	21.6	21.5	21.0	21.8	-
Croatia	5.2	5.4	5.3	5.5	5.6	6.0	6.1	6.3	6.4	6.5	6.6	-
Turkey	49.9	49.2	55.5	50.2	54.7	58.7	60.4	63.2	69.1	73.0	71.9	-

Source: Eurostat (ten00095)

Figure 12.6: Final energy consumption, EU-27, 2008 (1)
(% of total, based on tonnes of oil equivalent)

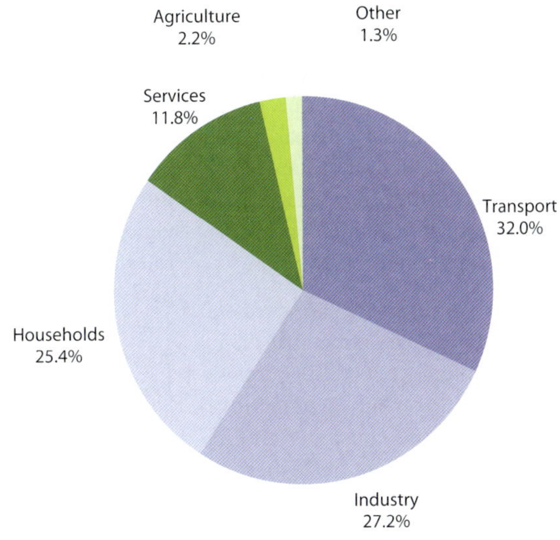

(1) Provisional.

Source: Eurostat (tsdpc320)

Figure 12.7: Energy consumption by transport mode, EU-27 (1)
(1998=100, based on tonnes of oil equivalent)

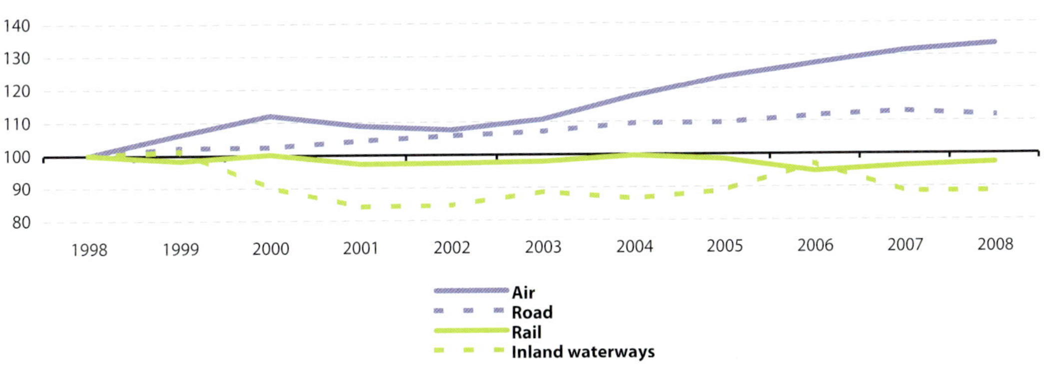

(1) Provisional for road transport, 2006 to 2008.

Source: Eurostat (tsdtr250)

12.3 Electricity production

This subchapter describes the electricity market in the European Union (EU) with information on the breakdown of electricity generation according to a range of different fuels used within power stations. It also provides statistics on the level of market liberalisation (as measured by the share of the largest generator) within electricity markets and concludes with details concerning electricity consumption by households.

The European Commission launched its third legislative package to liberalise energy markets in September 2007. The proposals were designed to: create a competitive energy market; expand consumer choice; promote fairer prices; result in cleaner energy; and promote the security of supply. In order to reach these goals, the proposals sought to: separate production and supply from transmission networks; facilitate cross-border collaboration, investment and trade in energy; introduce more effective regulation; encourage greater market transparency; and increase solidarity between Member States.

Main statistical findings

Electricity generation

Total gross electricity generation in the EU-27 was 3.4 million gigawatt hours (GWh) in 2008 – which marked an increase of 0.2 % compared with the year before, but an increase of 15.9 % when compared with the volume of electricity generated in 1998. As such, electricity generation in the EU-27 grew, on average, by 1.5 % per annum between 1998 and 2008. Over the same ten-year period, the most rapid growth in electricity generation among the Member States was recorded in Luxembourg, at more than 10 % per annum (largely due to a significant increase in generating output in 2002 as new gas-fired capacity was introduced). Cyprus, Spain, Ireland and Greece recorded the next highest growth rates (expansions of between 3 and 5 % per annum). Lithuania, Denmark and Sweden were the only Member States to generate less electricity in 2008 than in 1998 (see Table 12.7).

Around one quarter of the total electricity generated in the EU-27 in 2008 came from nuclear power plants (27.8 %) and from natural gas-fired power stations (23.0 %); while coal-fired, lignite-fired and oil-fired power stations accounted for 16.1 %, 10.6 % and 3.1 % respectively of the total electricity generated. Among renewable energy sources, the highest share of total electricity generation in 2008 was from hydropower plants (10.6 %), followed by wind turbines and biomass-fired power stations, which generated 3.5 % and 3.2 % of the total respectively (see Figure 12.8).

The relative importance of natural gas increased at the expense of coal, lignite and oil, probably as a result of lower emissions from gas; its share of total electricity generation rose from 13.5 % in 1998 to 23.0 % by 2008. Over the same period, there was also an increase in the use of renewables, particularly wind turbines and biomass, although their contribution remained relatively small.

Market shares

Germany and France were the principal electricity generators in the EU-27 in 2008, with shares of 18.9 % and 17.1 % respectively, while the United Kingdom was the only other Member State to report a share in double-digits (11.5 %). The relative weight of Spain in EU-27 electricity generation rose quickly between 1998 and 2008, gaining 2.8 percentage points to reach 9.5 % (see Table 12.7).

One measure that is used to monitor the extent of electricity market liberalisation is the market share of the largest generator in each country (see Figure 12.9). The small island nations of Cyprus and Malta were both characterised by a complete monopoly in 2008, with 100 % of their electricity being generated by the largest (sole) generator. Two other Member States - Estonia and Greece - reported shares for the largest generator of more than 90 %. In 11 of the 23 Member States for which data are available, the largest generator provided less than 50 % of the total electricity generated, with the lowest shares (below 20 %) in the United Kingdom and Poland.

Household electricity consumption

During the ten-year period from 1998 to 2008, the consumption of electricity by households rose in the EU-27 by 17.2 % overall (see Figure 12.10). There was much faster growth in a number of Member States, in particular the southern Mediterranean countries of Cyprus, Spain and Greece, as well as Portugal, all three of the Baltic Member States, and Ireland. At the other end of the range, household electricity consumption fell in four of the Member States (Belgium, Bulgaria, Slovakia and Sweden). These figures on overall household electricity consumption are likely to be influenced, among others, by the average number of persons living in each household and by the total number of households - both of which are linked to demographic events.

Data sources and availability

Gross electricity generation at the plant level is defined as the electricity measured at the outlet of the main transformers. In other words, it includes the consumption of electricity in plant auxiliaries and in other transformers. Gross national electricity consumption comprises total gross national electricity generation from all fuels (including auto-production), plus electricity imports, minus exports. Final consumption of electricity covers the electricity delivered to the consumer's door (industry, transport, households and other sectors). It excludes deliveries for transformation and/or own use of energy producing activities, as well as network losses. The market share of electricity generators is based on their net electricity production, and as such the electricity used by generators for their own consumption is not taken into account.

Context

Since July 2004, small business consumers in the EU have been free to switch their gas or electricity supplier, and in July 2007 this right was extended to all consumers. Independent national regulatory authorities have been established across the Member Sates to ensure that suppliers and network companies operate correctly. However, a number of shortcomings were identified in the opening-up of markets, and it was therefore decided to embark upon a third legislative package of measures with the aim of ensuring that all users could take advantage of the benefits provided by a truly competitive energy market. The European Commission launched its third legislative package to liberalise energy markets in September 2007. These proposals were designed to: create a competitive energy market; expand consumer choice; promote fairer prices; result in cleaner energy; and promote the security of supply. During 2009, a number of these proposals were adopted by the European Parliament and the Council. This draft of legislation will come into effect as of March 2011:

- Regulation 713/2009 of 13 July 2009 establishing an agency for the cooperation of energy regulators;
- Regulation 714/2009 of 13 July 2009 on conditions for access to the network for cross-border exchanges in electricity and repealing Regulation 1228/2003;
- Directive 2009/72/EC of 13 July 2009 concerning common rules for the internal market in electricity and repealing Directive 2003/54/EC.

The use of nuclear power for electricity generation has received renewed attention amid concerns about an increasing dependency on imported primary energy, rising oil and gas prices, and commitments to reduce greenhouse gas emissions. These have been balanced against long-standing concerns about safety and waste from nuclear power plants. Some Member States have recently started construction or have planned new nuclear reactors. On 25 June 2009, a European Council Directive (2009/71) was adopted concerning a framework for the nuclear safety of nuclear installations.

Figure 12.8: Electricity generation by fuel used in power stations, EU-27, 2008
(% of total, based on GWh)

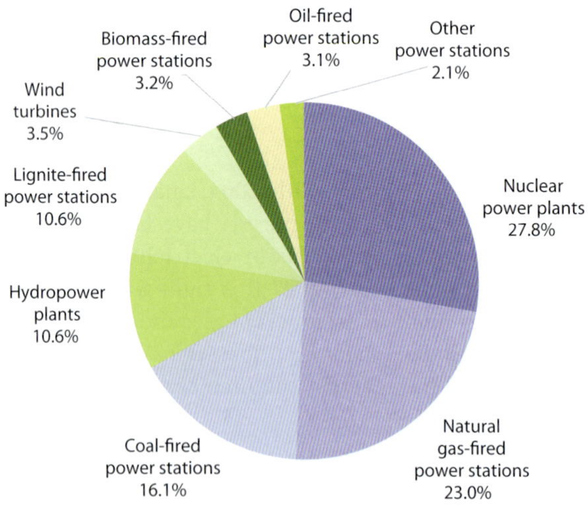

Source: Eurostat (nrg_105a)

Table 12.7: Gross electricity generation
(1 000 GWh)

	1998	1999	2000	2001	2002	2003	2004	2005	2006	2007	2008	Share in EU-27 2008 (%)
EU-27	2 911	2 940	3 021	3 108	3 117	3 216	3 289	3 310	3 354	3 368	3 374	100.0
Euro area (EA-16)	1 976	2 018	2 091	2 142	2 159	2 234	2 299	2 308	2 350	2 359	2 379	70.5
Belgium	83.2	84.5	83.9	79.7	82.1	84.6	85.4	87.0	85.5	88.8	84.9	2.5
Bulgaria	41.7	38.2	40.9	44.0	42.7	42.6	41.6	44.4	45.8	43.3	45.0	1.3
Czech Republic	65.1	64.7	73.5	74.6	76.3	83.2	84.3	82.6	84.4	88.2	83.5	2.5
Denmark	41.1	38.9	36.1	37.7	39.3	46.2	40.4	36.2	45.6	39.2	36.4	1.1
Germany	556.7	555.5	571.6	586.3	571.6	599.5	616.8	620.3	636.6	637.1	637.2	18.9
Estonia	8.5	8.3	8.5	8.5	8.5	10.2	10.3	10.2	9.7	12.2	10.6	0.3
Ireland	21.2	22.0	24.0	25.0	25.2	25.2	25.6	26.0	27.5	28.2	29.7	0.9
Greece	46.3	49.9	53.8	53.7	54.6	58.5	59.3	60.0	60.8	63.5	63.7	1.9
Spain	195.2	209.1	225.2	238.0	246.1	262.9	280.0	294.0	299.5	305.1	313.7	9.3
France	511.0	524.0	540.7	549.8	559.2	566.9	574.3	576.2	574.6	569.8	576.0	17.1
Italy	259.8	265.6	276.6	279.0	284.4	293.9	303.3	303.7	314.1	313.9	319.1	9.5
Cyprus	3.0	3.1	3.4	3.6	3.8	4.1	4.2	4.4	4.7	4.9	5.1	0.2
Latvia	5.8	4.1	4.1	4.3	4.0	4.0	4.7	4.9	4.9	4.8	5.3	0.2
Lithuania	17.6	13.5	11.4	14.7	17.7	19.5	19.3	14.8	12.5	14.0	13.9	0.4
Luxembourg	1.3	1.0	1.2	1.2	3.7	3.6	4.1	4.1	4.3	4.0	3.6	0.1
Hungary	37.2	37.7	35.2	36.4	36.2	34.1	33.7	35.8	35.9	40.0	40.0	1.2
Malta	1.7	1.8	1.9	2.0	2.1	2.2	2.2	2.2	2.3	2.3	2.3	0.1
Netherlands	91.1	86.7	89.6	93.7	95.9	96.8	102.4	100.2	98.4	105.2	107.6	3.2
Austria	57.5	60.9	61.5	62.4	62.5	60.2	64.1	66.6	63.5	64.8	67.1	2.0
Poland	142.8	142.1	145.2	145.6	144.1	151.6	154.2	156.9	161.7	159.3	156.2	4.6
Portugal	39.0	43.3	43.8	46.5	46.1	46.9	45.1	46.6	49.0	47.3	46.0	1.4
Romania	53.5	50.7	51.9	53.9	54.9	56.6	56.5	59.4	62.7	61.7	65.0	1.9
Slovenia	13.7	13.3	13.6	14.5	14.6	13.8	15.3	15.1	15.1	15.0	16.4	0.5
Slovakia	25.5	27.7	30.7	32.1	32.4	31.2	30.6	31.5	31.4	28.1	29.0	0.9
Finland	70.2	69.4	70.0	74.5	74.9	84.2	85.8	70.6	82.3	81.2	77.4	2.3
Sweden	158.3	155.2	145.6	161.6	146.7	135.4	151.7	158.4	143.4	148.9	150.0	4.4
United Kingdom	362.7	368.2	377.1	384.8	387.2	398.2	393.9	398.3	397.3	397.0	389.4	11.5
Iceland	6.3	7.2	7.7	8.0	8.4	8.5	8.6	8.7	9.9	:	:	-
Norway	117.0	122.7	140.1	119.7	130.7	107.4	110.7	138.0	121.6	137.2	142.7	-
Switzerland	63.5	69.7	67.5	72.4	67.2	67.4	65.6	59.6	64.0	68.0	69.0	-
Croatia	10.9	12.2	10.7	12.2	12.3	12.7	13.3	12.5	12.4	12.2	12.3	-
Turkey	111.0	116.4	124.9	122.7	129.4	140.6	150.7	162.0	176.3	191.6	198.4	-

Source: Eurostat (ten00087)

Figure 12.9: Market share of the largest generator in the electricity market, 2008 (¹)
(% of total generation)

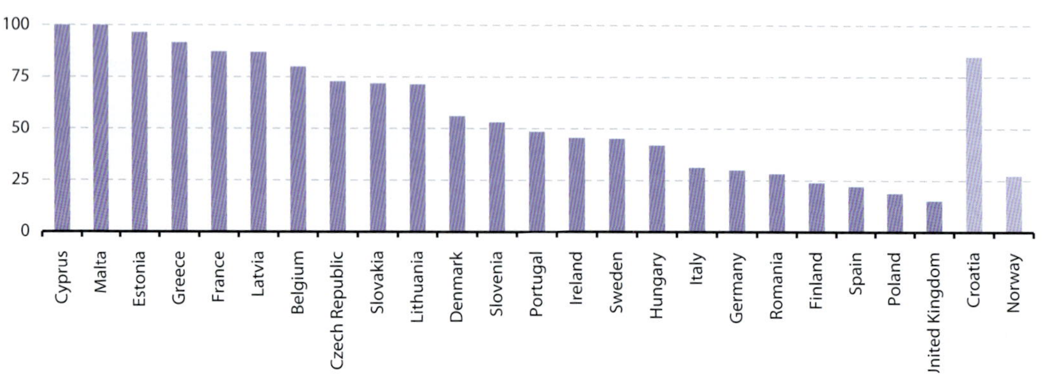

(¹) Bulgaria, Luxembourg, the Netherlands and Austria, not available.

Source: Eurostat (tsier060)

Figure 12.10: Electricity consumption by households, 2008
(1998=100)

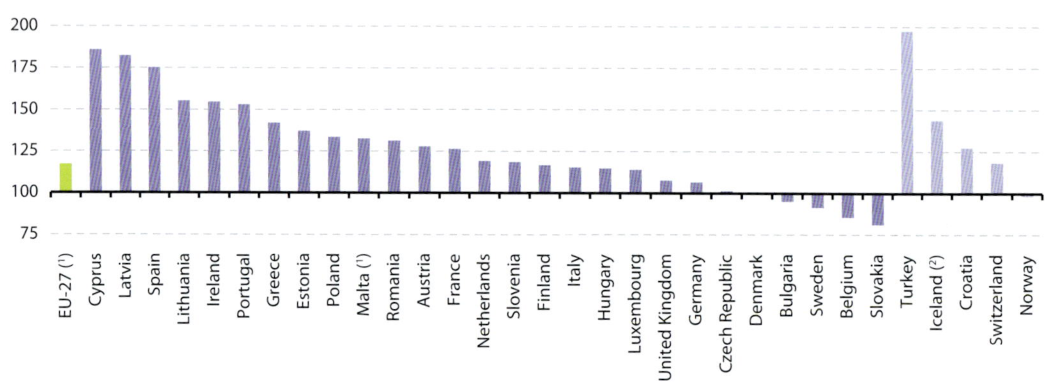

(¹) Provisional.
(²) 2006.

Source: Eurostat (tsdpc310)

12.4 Renewable energy

This subchapter provides information in relation to recent statistics on renewable energy sources in the European Union (EU). Renewable energy sources include wind power, solar power (thermal, photovoltaic and concentrated), hydroelectric power, tidal power, geothermal energy and biomass.

The use of renewable energy has many potential benefits, including a reduction in greenhouse gas emissions, the diversification of energy supplies and a reduced dependency on fossil fuel markets (in particular, oil and gas). The growth of renewable energy sources may also have the potential to stimulate employment in Europe, through the creation of jobs in new 'green' technologies.

Main statistical findings

Primary production

The primary production of renewable energy within the EU in 2008 was 148.1 million tonnes of oil equivalent (toe) – a 17.6 % share of total primary energy production (see Table 12.8). The volume of renewable energy produced within the EU-27 increased overall by 57.0 % between 1998 and 2008, equivalent to an average increase of 4.6 % per year.

Among renewable energies, the most important source in the EU was biomass and waste, accounting for 69.1 % of primary renewables production in 2008. Hydropower was the other main contributor to the renewable energy mix (19.0 % of the total). Although its level of production remains relatively low, there was a particularly rapid expansion in the output of wind energy, which accounted for 6.9 % of the EU's renewable energy produced in 2008.

The largest producer of renewable energy within the EU in 2008 was Germany, with a 20.1 % share of the EU total; France (13.4 %) and Sweden (10.8 %) were the only other countries to record a double-digit share. There were considerable differences in the renewable energy mix across the Member States, which reflected to a large degree natural endowments and climatic conditions. For example, more than three quarters (75.7 %) of the renewable energy produced in Cyprus was from solar energy, while more than a third of the renewable energy in the relatively mountainous countries of Austria, Slovenia and Sweden was from hydropower (much higher shares were recorded in Norway and Switzerland). More than one third of the renewable energy production in Italy was from geothermal energy sources (where active volcanic processes still exist); this share rose to more than 80 % in Iceland.

The output of renewable energy in Germany grew at an average rate of 13.6 % per year between 1998 and 2008, as such its share of the EU-27 total rose by 11.2 percentage points from an 8.8 % share in 1998. There were also average growth rates in excess of 10 % per year recorded for Belgium, Hungary and the Czech Republic, where the fastest growth in renewable energy production was recorded, averaging 14.2 % per year between 1998 and 2008.

Consumption

Renewable energy sources accounted for 8.4 % of the EU's gross inland energy consumption in 2008 (see Table 12.9).

Almost one third (32.1 %) of the energy consumed in Sweden was derived from renewables in 2008, while Latvia, Austria and Finland reported that more than a quarter of their energy consumption was accounted for by renewables.

The EU seeks to have a 20 % share of its energy consumption from renewable sources by 2020; this target is broken down between the Member States with national action plans designed to plot a pathway for renewable energies in each country. Figure 12.11 shows the latest data available for the share of renewable energies in gross final energy consumption and the indicative targets that have been set for each country by 2020. The share of renewables in gross final energy consumption stood at 10.3 % in the EU in 2008, almost half the target that has been set for 2020.

Among the Member States, the highest share of renewables in gross final energy consumption in 2008 was recorded in Sweden (44.4 %), while Finland, Latvia and Austria each reported more than a quarter of their final energy consumption derived from renewables. Compared with the most recent data available for 2008, the indicative targets for Denmark, Ireland, Greece, France, Italy, Latvia, the Netherlands and the United Kingdom require each of these countries to increase their share of renewables in final energy consumption by at least 10 percentage points.

Electricity

Directive 2001/77/EC set indicative targets for the production of electricity from renewable energy sources: according to these, 21 % of the EU's gross electricity consumption should be sourced from renewables by 2010. The latest information available for 2008 (see Figure 12.12) shows that electricity generated from renewable energy sources contributed 16.7 % of the EU-27's gross electricity consumption. In Austria (62.0 %) and Sweden (55.5 %) more than half of all the electricity consumed was generated from renewable energy sources, largely as a result of hydropower and biomass. Across the Member States, only Germany and Hungary had already surpassed their indicative targets for 2010 by 2008; Belgium, Denmark, the Netherlands and Finland were each within a single percentage point of attaining their targets.

The growth in electricity generated from renewable energy sources during the period 1998 to 2008 largely reflects an expansion in two renewable energy sources; namely, wind turbines and biomass. Although hydropower remained the single largest source for renewable electricity generation in the EU in 2008, the amount of electricity generated was somewhat lower than a decade earlier (-2.6 %). In contrast, the volume of electricity generated from biomass increased by 244 %, while that from wind turbines rose by 953 %.

Transport

At the end of 2008, the EU agreed to set a target for each Member State, such that renewable energy sources (including biofuels, hydrogen or 'green' electricity) should account for at least 10 % of all fuel used within the transport sector by 2020. The average share of renewable energy sources across the EU was 3.5 % in 2008, ranging from a high of 7.1 % in Austria, and more than 6 % in Sweden, Slovakia and Germany, to less than 1 % in Latvia,

Denmark, Bulgaria, the Czech Republic, Estonia and Malta (see Figure 12.14).

Data sources and availability

The share of renewable energy in gross final energy consumption is identified as a key indicator for measuring progress under the Europe 2020 strategy for smart, sustainable and inclusive growth.

The share of renewables in gross final energy consumption may be considered as an estimate for the purpose of monitoring Directive 2009/28/EC on the promotion of the use of energy from renewable sources; note, the statistical system for some renewable energy technologies is not yet fully developed to meet the requirements of this Directive.

Electricity from renewable energy sources is defined as the ratio between electricity produced from renewable energy sources and gross national electricity consumption. Electricity produced from renewable energy sources comprises electricity generation from hydropower plants (excluding pumping), as well as electricity generated from biomass/wastes, wind, solar and geothermal installations.

The share of renewable energies in the fuel consumed by the transport sector is calculated on the basis of energy statistics, according to the methodology as described in Directive 2009/28/EC. Note, the contribution of all biofuels is currently included within the calculation for this indicator and that the data are not restricted to biofuels satisfying the sustainability criteria.

Context

The EU has set out plans for a new energy strategy based on a more secure, sustainable and low-carbon economy. Aside from combating climate change through a reduction in greenhouse gas emissions, the use of renewable energy sources is likely to result in more secure energy supplies, greater diversity in energy supply, less air pollution, as well as the possibility for job creation in environmental and renewable energy sectors.

The integrated energy and climate change strategy adopted in December 2008 provided a further stimulus for increasing the use of renewables to 20 % of total energy consumption by 2020, while calling for energy consumption and greenhouse gas emissions to both be cut by 20 %. Directive 2009/28/EC of the European Parliament and Council on the promotion of the use of energy from renewable sources set an overall goal across the EU-27 for a 20 % share of energy consumption to be derived from renewable sources by 2020, while renewables should also account for a 10 % share of the fuel used in the transport sector by the same date. The Directive changes the legal framework for promoting renewable electricity, requires national action plans to show how renewable energies will be developed in each Member State, creates cooperation mechanisms, and establishes sustainability criteria for biofuels (following concerns over their potential adverse effects on crop prices, food supply, forest protection, biodiversity, water and soil resources).

Table 12.8: Primary production of renewable energy

	Primary production (1 000 toe)		Share of total 2008 (%)				
	1998	2008	Solar energy	Biomass & waste	Geothermal energy	Hydropower energy	Wind energy
EU-27	94 343	148 134	1.2	69.1	3.9	19.0	6.9
Euro area (EA-16)	62 824	104 788	1.6	66.4	5.3	18.5	8.2
Belgium	678	1 806	0.5	94.4	0.2	1.9	3.1
Bulgaria	678	997	-	71.3	3.3	24.4	1.0
Czech Republic	650	2 456	0.2	91.9	-	7.1	0.9
Denmark	1 814	3 159	0.4	80.0	0.7	0.1	18.9
Germany	8 337	29 743	2.5	78.9	0.8	6.1	11.7
Estonia	512	755	-	98.3	-	0.3	1.5
Ireland	231	521	0.6	43.0	0.8	15.9	39.7
Greece	1 329	1 594	10.9	60.9	1.1	17.9	9.3
Spain	6 875	10 717	3.3	51.9	0.1	18.9	25.8
France	16 783	19 825	0.2	68.9	0.6	27.9	2.5
Italy	8 813	13 491	0.6	33.0	36.8	26.5	3.1
Cyprus	43	74	75.7	23.0	0.0	-	-
Latvia	1 756	1 782	-	84.7	-	15.0	0.3
Lithuania	612	883	-	94.8	0.1	4.0	1.2
Luxembourg	50	84	2.4	78.6	-	13.1	6.0
Hungary	483	1 656	0.2	91.8	5.8	1.1	1.1
Malta	:	:	:	:	:	:	:
Netherlands	1 691	3 135	0.8	87.2	0.1	0.3	11.7
Austria	6 030	8 292	1.4	56.7	0.5	39.4	2.1
Poland	3 883	5 457	0.0	95.0	0.2	3.4	1.3
Portugal	3 734	4 441	0.8	70.8	4.2	13.2	11.1
Romania	4 640	5 418	0.0	72.2	0.5	27.3	0.0
Slovenia	528	835	-	58.7	-	41.3	-
Slovakia	444	1 056	0.0	66.0	1.0	32.9	0.1
Finland	7 257	9 172	0.0	83.7	-	16.0	0.2
Sweden	14 206	16 051	0.1	61.9	-	37.0	1.1
United Kingdom	2 286	4 733	1.2	76.5	0.0	9.4	12.9
Iceland (1)	1 814	3 259	-	0.1	80.7	19.2	0.0
Norway	11 202	13 384	0.0	9.8	-	89.7	0.6
Switzerland	3 969	5 190	0.6	35.9	3.7	59.7	0.0
Croatia	845	864	0.5	46.9	0.3	51.9	0.3
Turkey	11 481	9 360	4.5	51.9	12.3	30.6	0.8

(1) 2006 instead of 2008.

Source: Eurostat (ten00081 and ten00082)

Table 12.9: Share of renewables in gross inland energy consumption, 2008
(%)

	Total	Biomass	Hydro	Geothermal	Wind	Solar
EU-27	8.39	5.85	1.56	0.32	0.56	0.10
Euro area (EA-16)	8.49	5.69	1.54	0.44	0.69	0.13
Belgium	3.73	3.55	0.06	0.01	0.09	0.02
Bulgaria	4.86	3.43	1.21	0.16	0.05	:
Czech Republic	5.02	4.57	0.39	:	0.05	0.01
Denmark	18.11	14.93	0.01	0.11	3.00	0.06
Germany	8.62	6.79	0.52	0.07	1.02	0.21
Estonia	11.04	10.80	0.03	:	0.19	:
Ireland	3.58	1.70	0.53	0.03	1.31	0.02
Greece	5.02	3.06	0.89	0.05	0.47	0.55
Spain	7.72	4.09	1.42	0.01	1.95	0.25
France	7.37	5.11	2.02	0.04	0.18	0.02
Italy	7.82	2.84	1.97	2.73	0.23	0.05
Cyprus	3.04	1.05	:	0.00	:	1.96
Latvia	30.08	24.16	5.81	:	0.11	:
Lithuania	9.27	8.76	0.38	0.01	0.12	:
Luxembourg	2.65	2.24	0.24	:	0.11	0.04
Hungary	6.10	5.60	0.07	0.36	0.07	0.01
Malta	:	:	:	:	:	:
Netherlands	4.17	3.69	0.01	0.00	0.44	0.03
Austria	25.29	14.69	9.63	0.12	0.51	0.35
Poland	5.69	5.41	0.19	0.01	0.07	0.00
Portugal	17.76	12.55	2.35	0.74	1.99	0.14
Romania	13.50	9.80	3.64	0.06	0.00	0.00
Slovenia	10.99	6.53	4.46	:	:	:
Slovakia	5.47	3.54	1.87	0.06	0.01	0.00
Finland	25.19	21.08	4.05	:	0.06	0.00
Sweden	32.10	19.86	11.88	:	0.34	0.02
United Kingdom	2.56	2.05	0.20	0.00	0.28	0.03
Iceland (1)	74.94	0.05	14.42	:	0.00	:
Norway	45.23	4.75	40.22	:	0.26	0.00
Switzerland	18.59	6.70	11.08	0.69	0.01	0.12
Croatia	8.63	3.58	4.92	0.03	0.03	0.04
Turkey	9.33	4.84	2.85	1.15	0.07	0.42

(1) 2006.

Source: Eurostat (nrg_100a, nrg_1071a and nrg_1072a)

Figure 12.11: Share of renewables in gross final energy consumption
(%)

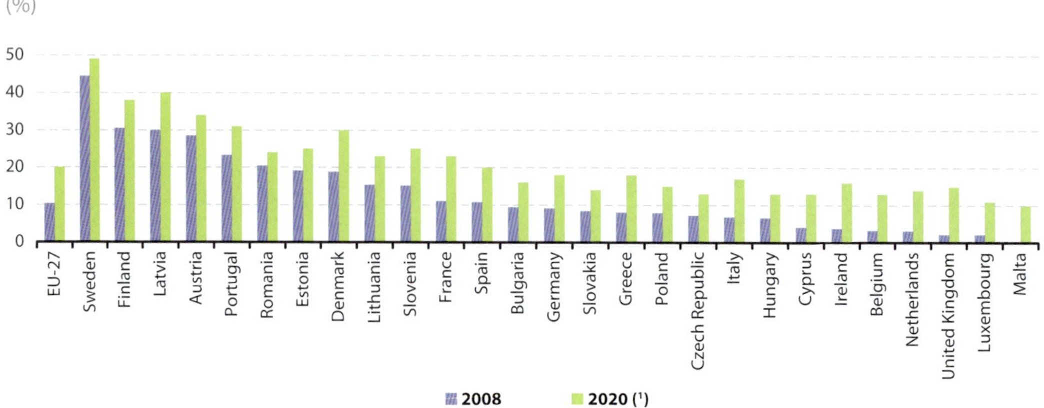

(1) Indicative targets for 2020.

Source: Eurostat (tsdcc110)

Figure 12.12: Proportion of electricity generated from renewable energy sources
(% of gross electricity consumption)

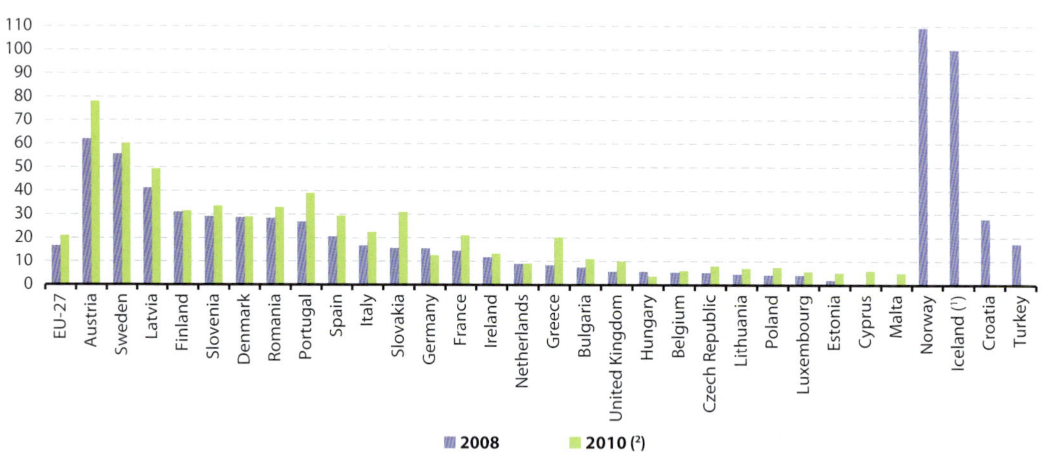

(1) 2006 instead of 2008.
(2) Indicative targets for 2010 are not available for Iceland, Norway, Croatia and Turkey.

Source: Eurostat (tsien050)

Figure 12.13: Electricity generated from renewable energy sources, EU-27

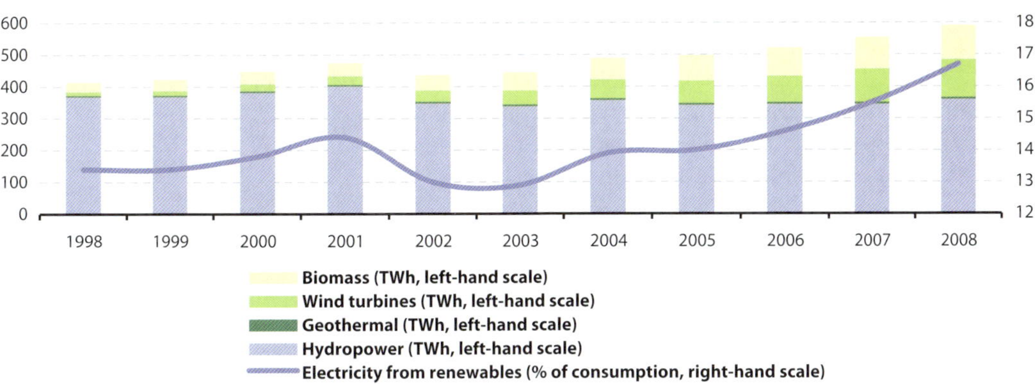

Source: Eurostat (nrg_105a and tsdcc330)

Figure 12.14: Share of renewable energy in fuel consumption of transport, 2008
(%)

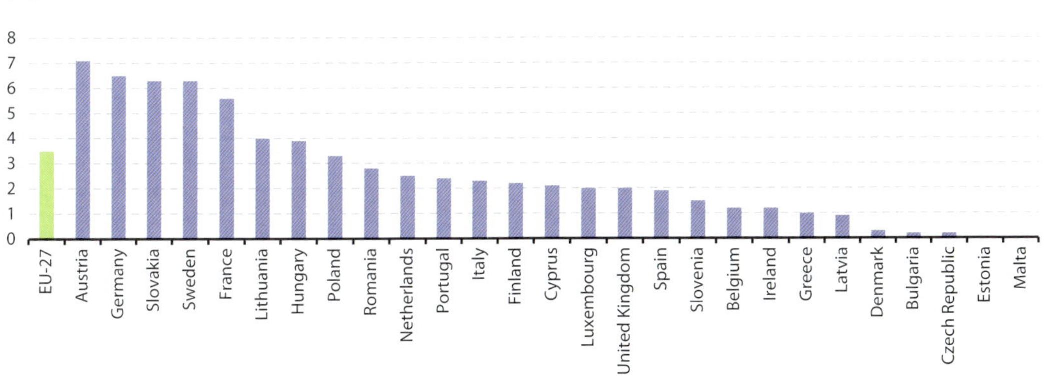

Source: Eurostat (tsdcc340)

12.5 Energy prices

This subchapter highlights the evolution of electricity and gas prices for both industrial and household users within the European Union (EU). The price of energy in the EU depends on a range of different supply and demand conditions, including the geopolitical situation, import diversification, distribution costs, environmental protection costs, severe weather conditions, or levels of excise and taxation; note that all of the prices presented in this subchapter include taxes and VAT for household consumers but exclude refundable taxes and VAT for industrial/business users.

Main statistical findings

Between the first half of 2009 and the first half of 2010, electricity prices for households increased in 16 of the EU Member States (see Table 12.10) while in nine of the Member States prices went down; Hungary and Malta did not report any price data. During the same period, prices of electricity for industrial/business users decreased in 13 of the Member States, rose in ten others and remained stable in Bulgaria. On average, the price of electricity for households in the EU-27 rose by 2.0 %, while it went down by 2.5 % for industrial users. There were a few notable exceptions to these trends among the EU Member States, as electricity prices fell by in excess of 10 % for household users in Ireland and in the Netherlands. For industrial users, the only countries to report double-digit price increase were Cyprus and Sweden, with increases in excess of 20 % for both of these Member States (while prices in Norway went up by more than 30 % and in Turkey by 14.5 %).

The price of electricity for households was more than three times higher in the most expensive Member State, Denmark (EUR 0.27 per kilowatt hour (kWh)), compared with the cheapest Member State, Bulgaria (EUR 0.08 per kWh). For industrial/business users, the price of electricity in Cyprus (EUR 0.15 per kWh) was slightly more than double the price in Bulgaria (EUR 0.065 per kWh). Some of the price differences between Member States may be attributed to taxes (for household users).

During the period from the first half of 2009 to the first half of 2010, natural gas prices for household consumers went down in 19 of the EU Member States, while they rose in three (Denmark, Poland and Sweden). For industrial/business users of natural gas, prices decreased in 17 of the Member States, but rose in five (Estonia and Lithuania joining the three Member States that also reported rising natural gas prices for household consumers). On average, the EU-27 price of natural gas for households fell by 10.4 % during the period considered, and by 15.5 % for industrial users. There was a significant price increase for industrial users of natural gas in Sweden (up 11.9 %), contrary to the general trend observed, while Swedish natural gas prices for households rose by 15.9 % between the first half of 2009 and the first half of 2010.

Indeed, the highest prices for household consumers of natural gas were registered in Sweden (EUR 28.71 per gigajoule (GJ) and in Denmark (EUR 29.70 per GJ), at nearly four times the lowest price which was recorded in Romania (EUR 7.64 per GJ). Among industrial users, the highest prices for natural gas were recorded in Denmark (EUR 15.81 per GJ), while the lowest prices were registered in the United Kingdom (EUR 5.94 per GJ). Due to the limited penetration of the natural gas markets in Greece, Cyprus, Malta and Finland (household sector only) gas prices for these countries are not presented.

Data sources and availability

Due to a change in methodology from 2007 onwards, there is a break in series and hence a relatively short time series available. Nevertheless, even in this relatively short timeframe, electricity and gas prices have fluctuated considerably - in particular, gas prices.

The transparency of energy prices is guaranteed within the EU through the obligation for EU Member States to send Eurostat information relating to prices for different categories of industrial and business users (prices for the household sector are provided on a voluntary basis), as well as data relating to market shares, conditions of sale, and pricing systems.

Electricity and gas tariffs or price schemes vary from one supplier to another. They may result from negotiated contracts, especially for large industrial users. For smaller consumers, they are generally set according to the amount of electricity or gas consumed along with a number of other characteristics; most tariffs also include some form of fixed charge. There is, therefore, no single price for electricity or gas. In order to compare prices over time and between countries, this subchapter shows information for consumption bands from the household sector and for industrial/business users. There are in total five different types of households for which electricity prices are collected following different annual consumption bands, while for natural gas statistics information is collated for three different types of household. Across industrial/business users, electricity prices are collected for a total of seven different types of users, while for natural gas prices there are six different types of users distinguished.

Statistics on electricity and natural gas prices charged to industrial/business users are collected under the legal basis of a European Commission Decision (2007/394/EC) of 7 June 2007 amending Council Directive (90/377/EEC) with regard to the methodology to be applied for the collection of gas and electricity prices. Directive 2008/92/EC of the European Parliament and Council of 22 October 2008 concerns procedures to improve the transparency of gas and electricity prices charged to industrial end-users. As noted above, gas and electricity prices for households are collected on a voluntary basis.

The prices presented cover average prices over a period of six months (semester) from January to June (semester 1 or S1) and from July to December (semester 2 or S2) of each year. Prices include the basic price of the electricity/gas, transmission and distribution charges, meter rental, and other services. Electricity prices for household consumers are presented in this subchapter including taxes and value added tax (VAT) as this generally reflects the end price paid by consumers in the domestic sector. As industrial/business users are usually able to recover VAT and some other taxes, prices for these enterprises are shown without VAT in this subchapter. The unit for electricity prices in this subchapter is that of euro per kilowatt hour (EUR per kWh); a similar set of criteria are used for gas prices, except the unit changes to euro per gigajoule (EUR per GJ).

Context

The price and reliability of energy supplies, electricity in particular, are key elements in a country's energy supply strategy. Electricity prices are of particular importance for international competitiveness, as electricity usually represents a significant proportion of total energy costs for industrial and service-providing businesses. In contrast to the price of fossil fuels, which are usually traded on global markets with relatively uniform prices, there is a wider range of prices within the EU Member States for electricity or gas. The price of electricity and gas is, to some degree, influenced by the price of primary fuels and, more recently, by the cost of carbon dioxide (CO_2) emission certificates.

These issues were touched upon in a Communication from the European Commission titled, 'Facing the challenge of higher oil prices' (COM(2008) 384), which called on the EU to become more efficient in its use of energy, and less dependent on fossil fuels - in particular, by following the approach laid out in the climate change and renewable energy package.

The EU has acted to liberalise electricity and gas markets since the second half of the 1990s. Directives adopted in 2003 established common rules for internal markets for electricity and natural gas. Deadlines were set for opening markets and allowing customers to choose their supplier: as of 1 July 2004 for business customers and as of 1 July 2007 for all consumers (including households). Certain countries anticipated the liberalisation process, while others were much slower in adopting the necessary measures. Indeed, significant barriers to entry remain in many electricity and natural gas markets as seen through the number of markets that are still dominated by (near) monopoly suppliers. In July 2009, the European Parliament and Council adopted a third package of legislative proposals aimed at ensuring a real and effective choice of suppliers, as well as benefits for customers. It is thought that increased transparency for gas and electricity prices should help promote fair competition, by encouraging consumers to choose between different energy sources (oil, coal, natural gas and renewable energy sources) and different suppliers. Energy price transparency can be made more effective by publishing and broadcasting as widely as possible prices and pricing systems.

Table 12.10: Half-yearly electricity and gas prices
(EUR)

	Electricity prices (per kWh)						Gas prices (per GJ)					
	Households (1)			Industry (2)			Households (3)			Industry (4)		
	2008s1	2009s1	2010s1	2008s1	2009s1	2010s1	2008s1	2009s1	2010s1	2008s1	2009s1	2010s1
EU-27	0.16	0.16	0.17	0.10	0.11	0.10	15.09	16.23	14.54	9.42	9.99	8.44
Euro area (EA-16)	0.16	0.17	0.18	0.10	0.11	0.11	17.05	18.41	15.98	9.93	10.55	8.90
Belgium	0.20	0.19	0.20	0.11	0.11	0.11	16.26	16.82	14.70	9.15	9.04	7.93
Bulgaria	0.07	0.08	0.08	0.06	0.06	0.06	9.85	13.14	10.21	5.72	8.74	6.66
Czech Republic	0.13	0.13	0.13	0.11	0.11	0.10	12.20	13.75	13.04	8.87	9.29	8.56
Denmark	0.26	0.27	0.27	0.09	0.09	0.09	:	25.55	29.70	:	15.43	15.81
Germany	0.21	0.23	0.24	0.11	0.11	0.11	17.81	18.00	15.70	12.40	11.98	10.10
Estonia	0.08	0.09	0.10	0.06	0.06	0.07	9.30	10.96	10.07	6.97	7.50	8.00
Ireland	0.18	0.20	0.18	0.13	0.12	0.11	15.09	17.89	13.79	11.05	9.30	7.83
Greece	0.10	0.12	0.12	0.09	0.09	0.09	:	:	:	:	:	:
Spain	0.14	0.16	0.17	0.10	0.12	0.12	15.98	16.98	14.83	7.64	8.70	7.70
France	0.12	0.12	0.13	0.07	0.07	0.07	14.46	15.29	14.46	9.23	10.01	9.19
Italy	0.20	0.21	0.20	0.14	0.15	0.14	17.47	21.04	17.15	9.34	11.08	8.24
Cyprus	0.18	0.16	0.19	0.14	0.12	0.15	:	:	:	:	:	:
Latvia	0.08	0.11	0.10	0.07	0.09	0.09	8.70	14.54	8.73	7.92	10.87	7.17
Lithuania	0.09	0.10	0.12	0.08	0.09	0.10	9.15	11.80	10.43	8.79	8.73	8.91
Luxembourg	0.16	0.19	0.17	0.10	0.12	0.10	15.48	13.68	12.07	10.49	11.21	10.26
Hungary	0.15	0.15	:	0.11	0.12	:	11.24	13.38	:	9.69	10.31	:
Malta	0.10	0.17	:	0.12	0.15	:	:	:	:	:	:	:
Netherlands	0.17	0.19	0.17	0.10	0.11	0.10	19.37	23.13	19.46	9.61	10.64	8.96
Austria	0.18	0.19	0.20	0.11	:	:	16.27	18.03	17.29	:	:	:
Poland	0.13	0.11	0.13	0.09	0.09	0.10	11.56	10.80	11.81	8.36	7.73	8.40
Portugal	0.15	0.15	0.16	0.09	0.09	0.09	17.37	16.78	16.49	8.69	9.81	7.62
Romania	0.11	0.10	0.10	0.09	0.08	0.09	9.21	8.11	7.64	7.79	6.52	6.19
Slovenia	0.11	0.13	0.14	0.09	0.10	0.10	15.51	18.28	16.00	10.12	12.13	10.53
Slovakia	0.14	0.15	0.15	0.12	0.14	0.12	11.42	12.83	12.11	8.92	11.30	9.11
Finland	0.12	0.13	0.13	0.06	0.07	0.07	:	:	:	7.90	8.50	8.40
Sweden	0.17	0.16	0.18	0.07	0.07	0.08	26.53	24.77	28.71	14.37	10.96	12.26
United Kingdom	0.15	0.15	0.14	0.10	0.11	0.10	10.99	11.84	11.26	7.73	8.35	5.94
Norway	0.16	0.16	0.20	0.08	0.08	0.10	:	:	:	:	:	:
Croatia	0.10	0.12	0.12	0.08	0.09	0.09	7.59	8.86	10.63	6.37	7.32	9.45
Turkey	0.10	0.11	0.13	0.07	0.08	0.09	9.04	10.84	8.98	7.04	7.99	6.66

(1) Annual consumption: 2 500 kWh < consumption < 5 000 kWh.
(2) Annual consumption: 500 MWh < consumption < 2 000 MWh.
(3) Annual consumption: 20 GJ < consumption < 200 GJ.
(4) Annual consumption: 10 000 GJ < consumption < 100 000 GJ.

Source: Eurostat (nrg_pc_204, nrg_pc_205, nrg_pc_202 and nrg_pc_203)

13 Science and technology

Science is part of almost every aspect of our lives: at the flick of a switch, we have light; when we are ill, medicines help us get better; when we want to talk to a friend we just pick up the telephone or send a text message or e-mail. Europe has a long tradition of excellence in research and innovation, having been the birthplace of the industrial revolution. Today, the European Union (EU) is a world leader in a range of cutting-edge industrial sectors – for example, biotechnology, pharmaceuticals, telecommunications or aerospace.

Research and development (R & D) is often considered as one of the driving forces behind growth and job creation. However, its influence extends well beyond the economic sphere, as it can potentially resolve environmental or international security threats, ensure safer food, or lead to the development of new medicines to fight illness and disease.

Since their launch in 1984, the EU's framework programmes for research have played a leading role in multidisciplinary research activities. The seventh framework programme for research and technological development (FP7) is the EU's main instrument for funding research in Europe; it runs from 2007 to 2013 and has a total budget of EUR 50 521 million, with an additional EUR 2 751 for 2007-2011 for nuclear research and training activities to be carried out under the Euratom treaty. This money is generally intended to finance grants to research actors all over Europe, usually through co-financing research, technological development and demonstration projects. FP7 is made up of four broad programmes – cooperation (collaborative research), ideas (the European Research Council), people (human potential) and capacities (research capacity). Through these programmes, FP7 aims to create European 'poles of excellence' across a wide array of scientific themes, such as information technologies, energy and climate change, health, food, and social sciences. FP7 also foresees direct research at the European Commission's own research institute (the Joint Research Centre (JRC)), whose activities are divided into 17 policy agendas, with an emphasis on understanding the relationship between the environment and health, internal and external security, and support for Europe's 2020 economic strategy.

The European Research Area (ERA) was launched at the Lisbon European Council in March 2000. ERA aims to ensure open and transparent trade in scientific and technical skills, ideas and know-how. Europe's research efforts are often described as being fragmented along national and institutional lines. Indeed, entire Member States may find it difficult to play a leading role in important areas of scientific and technological advance as research is increasingly complex, interdisciplinary and expensive.

ERA was given new impetus in April 2007 with the European Commission's Green paper on the European research area: new perspectives. In May 2008 the ERA was re-launched as part of what has become known as the Ljubljana process, including specific initiatives for five different areas: researchers' careers and mobility; research infrastructures; knowledge sharing; research programmes; and international science and technology cooperation. As a result, in the years through to 2020 the ERA will aim to establish a single European labour market for researchers, as well as single markets for knowledge and for innovative goods and services. Furthermore, the ERA should: encourage trust and dialogue between society and the scientific and technological community; benefit from a strong publicly-supported research and technology base and world-class research infrastructures and capacities across Europe; provide for the joint design of research, education and innovation policies; address major challenges through strategic partnerships; and enable Europe to speak with one voice to its main international partners.

International cooperation forms an integral part of the EU's scientific policy, which includes programmes to enhance Europe's access to worldwide scientific expertise, attract top scientists to work in Europe, contribute to international responses to shared problems, and put research at the service of EU external and development policies. In December 2008, the competitiveness Council adopted a 2020 vision for the ERA, which foresees the introduction of a 'fifth freedom' for the EU's internal market – namely, the free circulation of researchers, knowledge and technology.

In October 2010, the European Commission launched a Europe 2020 flagship initiative, titled 'innovation union' (COM(2010) 546 final) which sets out a strategic approach to a range of challenges like climate change, energy and food security, health and an ageing population. The proposals seek to use public sector intervention to stimulate the private sector and to remove bottlenecks which stop ideas reaching the market (such as access to finance, fragmented research systems and markets, under-use of public procurement for innovation, and speeding-up harmonised standards and technical specifications).

Official European statistics on science and technology provide a leading example of cooperation activities between international statistical organisations. In the domain of R & D statistics a joint survey produced by the OECD and Eurostat has been introduced, which is based on the collection of information following guidelines laid out in the Frascati manual. As regards human capital, the OECD, UNESCO and Eurostat are working towards developing internationally comparable indicators on the careers and mobility of doctorate (PhD) holders. Within the domain of innovation statistics, Eurostat conducts a Community innovation survey, which is based on the guidelines laid out within the Oslo manual (jointly produced with other European Commission services and the OECD). Together with the European Patent Office (EPO), the United States Patent and Trademark Office (USPTO) and the OECD, Eurostat has worked towards the improvement of PATSTAT, a harmonised database covering EPO patent applications and USPTO patents granted.

13.1 R & D expenditure

Most European research is funded at the national level, by private and/or public sources. This subchapter presents data on R & D spending within the European Union (EU), according to the sector performing the research and according to the source of funds.

Framework programmes are the main instrument for funding R & D within the EU. The 7th framework programme (FP7) started in 2007 and is due to continue for a total of seven years. The European Research Area (ERA) is composed of all research and development activities, programmes and policies in Europe which involve a transnational perspective. In December 2008, the Competitiveness Council adopted a 2020 vision for the ERA, which foresees the introduction of a 'fifth freedom' - namely, the free circulation of researchers, knowledge and technology.

Main statistical findings

Gross domestic expenditure on R & D (GERD) stood at EUR 237 001 million in the EU-27 in 2008, which marked a 3.5 % increase on the level of GERD in 2007. The level of expenditure on R & D in the EU-27 was 87.6 % of that recorded by the United States, although slightly more than double the level of expenditure in Japan (in 2007) and considerably above R & D expenditre levels in the emerging economies - for example, EU-27 expenditure was 6.4 times as high as in China in 2007.

In order to make figures more comparable, GERD is often expressed relative to gross domestic product (GDP) - see Figure 13.1 - or in relation to population. The ratio of GERD to GDP increased marginally in the EU-27 during the period up to 2002 reaching a high of 1.87 %, before gradually declining through to 2005 (1.82 %), and climbing again to 1.90 % by 2008. Nevertheless, the EU-27's R & D expenditure relative to GDP remains well below the corresponding shares recorded in Japan (3.44 % in 2007) and the United States (2.76 % in 2008); this pattern has existed for a lengthy period. There was a far higher increase in the relative importance of GERD in the Japanese economy, as its share of GDP rose by 0.44 percentage points during the period 1998 to 2007; note however that Japanese economic growth was also subdued during this period.

One of the key objectives of the EU during the last decade has been to encourage increasing levels of investment, in order to provide a stimulus to the EU's competitiveness. At the Barcelona Council in 2002, the EU agreed to a target of spending at least 3 % of gross domestic product (GDP) on research by 2010, of which two thirds was to be financed by the business sector; most of the EU Member States specified their own targets in national reform programmes. Using this measure, the highest R & D intensity was recorded in Sweden (3.75 % in 2008) and Finland (3.73 %) – see Table 13.1. While none of the other Member States reported GERD rising above 3 % of GDP at a national level, R & D intensity also rose to relatively high levels in a number of regions clustered in southern Germany (motor vehicles), through Switzerland into France (chemicals and pharmaceuticals) and on towards the Pyrenees (aerospace); regions containing capital cities also tended to report relatively high levels of R & D intensity. In contrast, there were nine Member States that reported R & D expenditure accounting for less than 1 % of their GDP in 2008 (Greece, data for 2007), with Bulgaria, Cyprus and Slovakia below 0.5 %. The regions with the lowest R & D intensity were generally those found in southern and eastern Europe.

The differences in the relative importance of R & D expenditure between countries are often explained by referring to levels of expenditure within the business enterprise sector. Table 13.2 shows that the share of R & D conducted within the business enterprise sector was equivalent to 1.21 % of the EU-27's GDP in 2008, compared with 2.68 % in Japan (2007) and 2.00 % in the United States, while the relative importance of R & D expenditure in the government and higher education sector was broadly similar across all three members of the Triad. An evaluation of the data for the Member States also confirms that those countries – namely, Sweden, Finland, Denmark, Austria and Germany – with relatively high shares of business enterprise R & D also reported relatively high levels of total GERD. These countries also tended to feature near the top-end of the rankings of expenditure by government and higher education sectors, where they were joined by the Czech Republic and France, as well as Slovenia for expenditure within the government sector.

A breakdown of R & D expenditure by source of funds shows that more than half (55.0 %) of the total expenditure in 2008 within the EU-27 came from business enterprises, while just over one third (33.5 %) was from government, and a further 8.9 % from abroad; business-funded R & D accounted for 77.7 % of total R & D expenditure in Japan (2007) and 67.3 % in the United States (2007). Table 13.3 confirms the relatively important role played by the business enterprise sector as a source of R & D funding in Luxembourg, Finland, Germany, Denmark and Sweden. In contrast, a majority of the gross expenditure on R & D made in 2008 in Romania, Cyprus (2007), Poland, Bulgaria (2007), Lithuania, Slovakia and Estonia was funded by the government sector. There were also considerable differences in the source of R & D funding from abroad, with relatively high shares (in excess of 15 % of total GERD) reported in the Baltic Member States, Ireland, Malta, Austria and the United Kingdom.

Data sources and availability

Statistics on science, technology and innovation (STI statistics) are based on Decision 1608/2003/ECconcerning the production and development of Community statistics on science and technology. In close cooperation with the Member States, this Decision was implemented by Eurostat in the form of legislative measures and through additional work. Regulation 753/2004 was adopted in 2004 implementing Decision 1608/2003/EC.

Eurostat's statistics on R & D expenditure are compiled using guidelines laid out in the Frascati manual, published in 2002 by the OECD. R & D expenditure is a basic measure that covers intramural expenditure, in other words, all expenditures for R & D that are performed within a statistical unit or sector of the economy.

The main breakdown of R & D statistics is by four institutional sectors of performance. These four sectors are the business enterprise sector, the government sector, the higher education sector, and the private non-profit sector (the latter is not shown in this subchapter). Gross domestic expenditure on R & D (GERD) is composed of expenditure from each of these four sectors. Expenditure data considers the research spend on the national territory, regardless of the source of funds; data are usually expressed in relation to GDP, otherwise known as R & D intensity. Additional breakdowns of R & D expenditure are available by: source of funds; field of science; type of costs; economic activity (NACE); enterprise size class; type of R & D; socio-economic objectives; and regions (NUTS).

The European Commission develops three levels of indicators to support research and innovation policymaking. These indicators are generally grouped together as: headline indicators; core indicators; and comprehensive indicators. Within the headline indicators – also referred to as Europe 2020 strategy indicators – is the measure of research intensity (with a 3 % target for investment in research across the EU). The core indicators are designed to monitor research and innovation for the Competitiveness Council, while the comprehensive indicators are for analytical purposes and Commission services to produce a science, technology and competitiveness report.

Context

The European Commission has through its Europe 2020 flagship initiative, titled 'innovation union', placed renewed emphasis on the conversion of Europe's scientific expertise into marketable products and services, through seeking to use public sector intervention to stimulate the private sector and to remove bottlenecks which stop such ideas reaching the market. Furthermore, the latest revision of the integrated economic and employment guidelines (revised as part of the Europe 2020 strategy for smart, sustainable and inclusive growth) includes a guideline to optimise support for R & D and innovation, strengthening the knowledge triangle and unleashing the potential of the digital economy. Additional information about the Europe 2020 strategy can be found on the Europe 2020 website.

One area that has received considerable attention in recent years is the structural difference in R & D funding between Europe and its main competitors. Policymakers in Europe have tried to increase R & D business expenditure so that it is more in line with relative contributions observed in Japan or the United States. The European Research Area (ERA) is designed to overcome some of these barriers that are thought to have hampered European research efforts, for example, by addressing geographical, institutional, disciplinary and sectoral boundaries.

One specific area where studies have already been conducted in respect to business enterprises' investment is a November 2009 report, titled the EU's industrial R & D investment scoreboard. This presents information on the top 1 000 research investors whose registered offices are in the EU and the top 1 000 investors registered elsewhere. The report shows that R & D investment by these EU investors grew by 8.1 % in 2008 despite the economic crisis that took hold in the second half of the year. This rate of growth was faster than that recorded for investors from either Japan or the United States, although higher R & D investment growth was registered by investors based in the emerging economies of China and India. Volkswagen and Nokia were among the global top ten, which was led by Toyota Motors (Japan) and Microsoft (the United States).

In December 2008, the Competitiveness Council adopted a 2020 vision for the ERA. According to the opening statement of this vision, all players should benefit from: the 'fifth freedom', introducing the free circulation of researchers, knowledge and technology across the ERA; attractive conditions for carrying out research and investing in R & D intensive sectors; Europe-wide scientific competition, together with the appropriate level of cooperation and coordination. The 2020 vision for the ERA is part of the wider picture of Europe's 2020 strategy for smart, sustainable and inclusive growth. As part of the Europe 2020 strategy, the European Commission announced in July 2010 nearly EUR 6 400 million of investment in research and innovation, with the aim of providing an economic stimulus expected to create more than 165 000 jobs.

Figure 13.1: Gross domestic expenditure on R&D in the Triad
(% share of GDP)

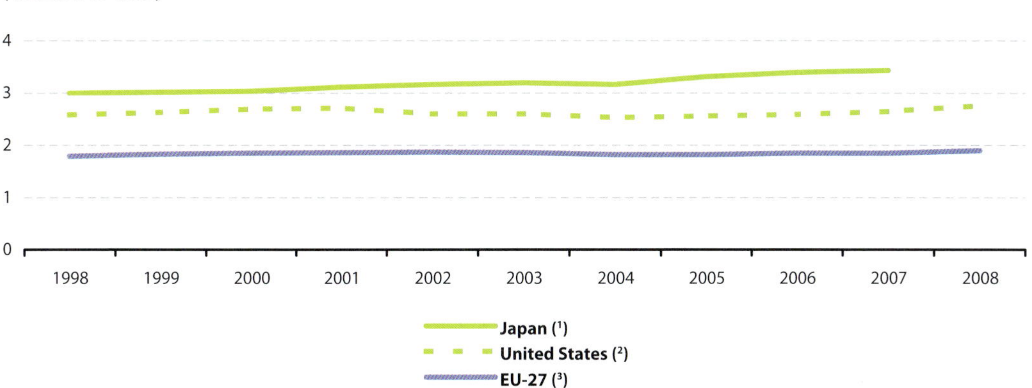

(¹) Not available, 2008.
(²) Excludes most or all capital expenditure.
(³) Estimates.

Source: Eurostat (tsc00001), OECD

Table 13.1: Gross domestic expenditure on R&D
(% share of GDP)

	1998	1999	2000	2001	2002	2003	2004	2005	2006	2007	2008
EU-27	*1.79*	*1.83*	*1.85*	*1.86*	*1.87*	*1.86*	*1.82*	*1.82*	*1.85*	*1.85*	*1.90*
Euro area (EA-16)	:	*1.82*	*1.84*	*1.85*	*1.87*	*1.86*	*1.84*	*1.84*	*1.86*	*1.87*	*1.91*
Belgium	1.86	1.94	1.97	2.07	1.94	1.88	1.86	1.83	1.86	1.90	*1.92*
Bulgaria (1)	0.57	0.57	0.52	0.47	0.49	0.50	0.50	0.49	0.48	0.48	*0.49*
Czech Republic	1.15	1.14	1.21	1.20	1.20	1.25	1.25	1.41	1.55	1.54	1.47
Denmark (2)	2.04	2.18	2.24	2.39	2.51	2.58	2.48	2.46	2.48	2.55	*2.72*
Germany	2.27	2.40	2.45	2.46	2.49	2.52	2.49	2.49	2.53	2.53	*2.63*
Estonia	0.57	0.68	0.60	0.70	0.72	0.77	0.85	0.93	1.14	1.11	*1.29*
Ireland	1.24	*1.18*	1.12	1.10	1.10	1.17	1.23	1.25	1.25	*1.28*	*1.43*
Greece	:	0.60	:	0.58	:	0.57	*0.55*	0.59	*0.58*	*0.58*	:
Spain	0.87	0.86	0.91	0.91	0.99	1.05	1.06	1.12	1.20	1.27	1.35
France (3)	2.14	2.16	2.15	2.20	2.23	2.17	2.15	2.10	2.10	*2.04*	*2.02*
Italy	1.05	1.02	1.05	1.09	1.13	1.11	1.10	1.09	1.13	1.18	*1.18*
Cyprus	0.22	0.23	0.24	0.25	0.30	0.35	0.37	0.40	0.43	0.44	*0.46*
Latvia	0.40	0.36	0.44	0.41	0.42	0.38	0.42	0.56	0.70	0.59	0.61
Lithuania	0.54	0.50	0.59	0.67	0.66	0.67	0.75	0.75	0.79	0.81	0.80
Luxembourg	:	:	1.65	:	:	1.65	1.63	1.56	1.65	1.58	*1.62*
Hungary (4)	0.66	0.67	0.79	0.92	1.00	0.93	0.87	0.94	1.00	0.97	1.00
Malta (4)	:	:	:	:	0.26	0.26	0.53	0.57	0.61	*0.58*	*0.54*
Netherlands (1)	1.90	1.96	1.82	1.80	1.72	1.76	1.81	*1.79*	*1.78*	*1.71*	*1.63*
Austria	1.78	*1.90*	*1.94*	*2.07*	2.14	*2.26*	2.26	*2.45*	2.47	2.54	*2.67*
Poland	0.67	0.69	0.64	0.62	0.56	0.54	0.56	0.57	0.56	0.57	*0.61*
Portugal	0.65	0.71	*0.76*	0.80	*0.76*	0.74	*0.77*	0.81	*1.02*	1.21	*1.51*
Romania	0.49	0.40	0.37	0.39	0.38	0.39	0.39	0.41	0.45	0.52	0.58
Slovenia	1.34	1.37	1.39	1.50	1.47	1.27	1.40	1.44	1.56	1.45	1.66
Slovakia	0.78	0.66	0.65	0.63	0.57	0.57	0.51	0.51	0.49	0.46	0.47
Finland	2.88	3.17	3.35	3.32	3.37	3.44	3.45	3.48	3.48	3.48	3.73
Sweden (5)	:	3.61	:	4.17	:	3.85	3.62	3.60	3.74	3.61	*3.75*
United Kingdom	1.76	1.82	1.81	1.79	1.79	1.75	1.68	1.73	1.75	1.82	*1.88*
Iceland	2.00	2.30	*2.67*	2.95	*2.95*	2.82	:	2.77	2.99	2.70	2.65
Norway	:	1.64	:	1.59	1.66	1.71	1.59	1.52	1.52	1.65	*1.62*
Switzerland	:	:	2.53	:	:	:	2.90	:	:	:	:
Croatia	:	:	:	:	0.96	0.97	1.05	0.87	0.76	0.81	0.90
Turkey	0.37	0.47	0.48	0.54	0.53	0.48	0.52	0.59	0.58	0.72	:
Japan	3.00	3.02	3.04	3.12	3.17	3.20	3.17	3.32	3.40	3.44	:
United States	2.58	2.63	2.69	2.71	2.60	2.60	2.53	2.56	2.59	2.65	*2.76*

(1) Break in series, 1999.
(2) Break in series, 2007.
(3) Break in series, 2000 and 2004.
(4) Break in series, 2004.
(5) Break in series, 2005.

Source: Eurostat (tsiir020), OECD

Table 13.2: Gross domestic expenditure on R&D by sector
(% share of GDP)

	Business enterprise sector		Government sector		Higher education sector	
	2003	2008	2003	2008	2003	2008
EU-27	*1.19*	*1.21*	*0.24*	*0.24*	*0.41*	*0.43*
Euro area (EA-16)	*1.18*	*1.22*	*0.26*	*0.26*	*0.40*	*0.41*
Belgium	1.31	*1.32*	0.13	*0.17*	0.42	*0.41*
Bulgaria	0.10	*0.15*	0.35	*0.28*	0.05	*0.05*
Czech Republic	0.76	0.91	0.29	0.31	0.19	0.25
Denmark (1)	1.78	*1.91*	0.18	*0.09*	0.60	*0.71*
Germany	1.76	*1.84*	0.34	*0.36*	0.43	*0.43*
Estonia	0.26	*0.56*	0.12	0.15	0.36	0.56
Ireland	0.79	*0.93*	0.09	*0.11*	0.29	*0.39*
Greece	0.18	:	0.12	:	0.26	:
Spain	0.57	0.74	0.16	0.25	0.32	0.36
France (2)(3)	1.36	*1.27*	0.36	*0.32*	0.42	*0.40*
Italy (4)	0.52	*0.60*	0.19	0.16	0.37	0.39
Cyprus	0.07	*0.10*	0.13	*0.10*	0.11	*0.21*
Latvia	0.13	0.15	0.09	0.17	0.16	0.29
Lithuania	0.14	0.19	0.18	0.19	0.35	0.43
Luxembourg	1.47	*1.32*	0.17	*0.25*	*0.01*	*0.05*
Hungary (5)	0.34	*0.53*	0.29	0.23	0.25	0.22
Malta (6)	0.08	*0.35*	0.02	*0.01*	0.16	*0.17*
Netherlands (3)	1.01	*0.89*	0.26	*0.21*	0.49	*0.52*
Austria	:	*1.88*	:	*0.14*	:	*0.64*
Poland	0.15	*0.19*	0.22	*0.21*	0.17	*0.20*
Portugal	0.24	*0.76*	0.12	*0.12*	0.28	*0.51*
Romania	0.22	0.17	0.12	0.24	0.04	0.17
Slovenia	0.81	1.07	0.28	0.36	0.17	0.22
Slovakia	0.32	0.20	0.18	0.15	0.08	0.11
Finland	2.43	2.77	0.33	0.30	0.66	0.64
Sweden (7)	2.86	*2.78*	0.13	*0.17*	0.84	*0.80*
United Kingdom	1.11	*1.21*	0.18	*0.16*	0.42	*0.47*
Iceland	1.46	1.45	0.70	0.47	0.60	*0.67*
Norway (8)	0.98	*0.87*	0.26	*0.24*	0.47	*0.51*
Switzerland	:	:	:	0.02	:	:
Croatia	0.38	0.40	0.21	0.23	0.38	0.27
Turkey	0.11	:	0.05	:	0.32	:
Japan	2.40	:	0.30	:	0.44	:
United States	1.80	2.00	0.32	*0.29*	0.36	*0.35*

(1) Break in series, 2007.
(2) Break in series, business enterprise sector, 2006.
(3) Break in series, higher education sector, 2004.
(4) Break in series, higher education sector, 2005.
(5) Break in series, government sector, 2004.
(6) Break in series, business enterprise sector, 2004.
(7) Break in series, business enterprise sector and government sector, 2005.
(8) Break in series, government sector and higher education sector, 2007.

Source: Eurostat (tsc00001), OECD

Table 13.3: Gross domestic expenditure on R&D by source of funds
(% of total gross expenditure on R&D)

	Business enterprises		Government		Abroad	
	2003	2008	2003	2008	2003	2008
EU-27	*54.1*	*55.0*	*35.1*	*33.5*	*8.6*	*8.9*
Euro area (EA-16)	*55.9*	*56.3*	*36.4*	*34.7*	*6.3*	*7.2*
Belgium (¹)	60.3	61.4	23.5	22.2	12.9	13.0
Bulgaria (¹)	26.8	34.2	66.9	56.7	5.8	7.6
Czech Republic	51.4	52.2	41.8	41.3	4.6	5.3
Denmark (²)	59.9	*61.1*	27.1	*25.3*	10.3	*9.7*
Germany (¹)	66.3	67.9	31.2	27.7	2.3	4.0
Estonia	32.9	*33.6*	48.6	*50.0*	15.2	*15.5*
Ireland	60.3	*49.6*	29.8	*32.2*	8.3	*15.9*
Greece	28.2	:	46.4	:	21.6	:
Spain (¹)	48.4	45.5	40.1	43.7	5.7	7.0
France (³)	50.8	50.5	39.0	39.4	8.4	8.0
Italy (¹)(⁴)	39.7	42.0	50.7	44.3	8.0	9.5
Cyprus (¹)	19.9	16.4	60.1	64.6	13.9	14.5
Latvia	33.2	27.0	46.4	47.3	20.4	23.1
Lithuania	16.7	21.4	64.6	55.6	13.8	15.5
Luxembourg (¹)	80.4	76.0	11.2	18.2	8.3	5.7
Hungary	30.7	48.3	58.0	41.8	10.7	9.3
Malta (⁵)	21.6	*50.8*	59.8	*28.1*	18.6	*21.0*
Netherlands	51.1	:	36.2	:	11.3	:
Austria	*45.1*	*46.3*	*34.4*	*37.2*	*20.0*	*16.1*
Poland	30.3	*30.5*	62.7	*59.8*	4.6	*5.4*
Portugal (¹)	31.7	47.0	60.1	44.6	5.0	5.4
Romania	45.4	23.3	47.6	70.1	5.5	4.0
Slovenia	52.2	62.8	37.5	31.3	9.9	5.6
Slovakia	45.1	34.7	50.8	52.3	3.3	12.3
Finland (⁶)	70.0	70.3	25.7	21.8	3.1	6.6
Sweden (¹)(⁶)	65.1	64.0	24.3	22.2	7.3	9.3
United Kingdom	42.2	*47.2*	31.7	*29.5*	20.3	*17.6*
Iceland	43.9	50.4	40.1	38.8	14.5	10.0
Norway (¹)	49.2	45.3	41.9	44.9	7.4	8.3
Croatia	42.0	40.8	55.9	49.3	2.2	7.9
Turkey (¹)	36.2	48.4	57.0	47.1	1.6	0.5
Japan (¹)	74.6	77.7	18.0	15.6	0.3	0.3
United States	64.3	*67.3*	30.0	*27.0*	:	:

(¹) 2007 instead of 2008.
(²) Break in series, 2007.
(³) Break in series, 2004.
(⁴) 2005 instead of 2003.
(⁵) 2002 instead of 2003.
(⁶) Break in series, 2005.

Source: Eurostat (tsiir030), OECD

13.2 R & D personnel

This subchapter analyses data on research and development (R & D) personnel and human resources in science and technology in the European Union (EU). Statistics on human resources in science and technology are a key indicator for measuring the knowledge-based economy and how it is developing. They show the supply of, and demand for highly qualified science and technology specialists.

Main statistical findings

R & D personnel

The number of researchers in the EU-27 has increased in recent years. There were 1.5 million researchers (full-time equivalents (FTE)) employed in the EU-27 in 2008 (see Table 13.4), which marked an increase of almost 386 000 (or 34.5 %) when compared with 2000.

A breakdown of R & D personnel in the EU-27 by institutional sector in 2008 shows that close to half (46 %) were concentrated in the business enterprise sector, while two fifths (40 %) were in the higher education sector and 13 % in the government sector. The relative importance of the different institutional sectors varied considerably across the Member States, with business enterprises accounting for more two thirds of all researchers in Sweden and Luxembourg. Bulgaria was the only country to report a majority (56 %) of its researchers employed within the government sector, while more than three fifths of all researchers working in Latvia, Lithuania, Poland and Slovakia were employed within the higher education sector.

R & D personnel from all sectors together made up more than 2 % of the labour force in Luxembourg and Finland in 2008. Aside from these two Member States, this share ranged from less than 0.5 % in Romania, Cyprus, Poland and Bulgaria to just over 1.5 % in Denmark and Sweden, with the EU-27 average estimated around 1.0 %. A gender breakdown shows that men accounted for 71 % of the EU-27's workforce of researchers in 2007; there was almost no change in the relative balance between male and female researchers during the period 2000-2007.

Human resources in science and technology

Human resources in science and technology (HRST) provide a broad measure of the supply of, and demand for, people highly qualified in science and technology. Some 65.1 million people were employed in the EU-27 within science and technology occupations in 2007; this amounted to 29.8 % of total employment. Between 2005 and 2007 there was a modest increase in the relative importance of HRST within the EU-27 workforce, as their share rose by 0.6 percentage points. The HRST 'core' – made up of people within science and technology occupations with a tertiary level education (for example, university graduates) – amounted to 37.4 million persons in 2007 (or 17.1 % of the total number of persons employed).

Persons in HRST occupations accounted for just over 40 % of the workforce in Luxembourg in 2008 and close to this share in Denmark and Sweden (2007). The lowest shares were recorded in Portugal and Romania which were below half this level; in other words persons in HRST occupations accounted for less than one fifth of total employment. Concerning core HRST, in other words persons simultaneously in HRST occupations and having completed a tertiary level of education, the range between countries was greater still: in Portugal some 11.5 % of total employment was core HRST in 2008, while at the other end of the scale the share rose to 27.9 % in Luxembourg (see Table 13.5).

Within the EU-27 there were 13.9 graduates in mathematics, science and technology fields of education per 1 000 persons aged 20 to 29 years in 2008, with particularly high ratios in Finland, Portugal, France and Ireland. This ratio should be interpreted with care as some graduates may be foreigners who return home following their studies and so push up the ratio in the country where they studied and pull down the ratio in their country of origin; this may explain to a large extent the very low ratios recorded in the three smallest Member States.

A similar but more specific measure of a country's potential research capability is provided by the number of doctoral students. There were 525 800 doctoral students in the EU-27 in 2007, compared with levels of 460 800 in the United States and 75 000 in Japan (both 2008 data). In relative terms, the broad subject group of science, mathematics, computing, engineering, manufacturing and construction-related studies accounted for more than one third (36.4 %) of the doctoral students in the EU-27 in 2007, a proportion that was somewhat higher than in Japan (32.2 %) but lower than in the United States (38.2 %).

Women accounted for 47.8 % of doctoral students in the EU-27 in 2007 (see Table 13.7), a share that was not too dissimilar from that recorded in the United States, where women were in a slight majority (50.1 %) in 2008; in contrast, men accounted for a much higher share of doctoral students in Japan (69.2 %) in 2008. The gender split of doctoral students across the Member States was typically quite balanced in 2008: women accounted for more than half of all the doctoral students in the Baltic Member States, Portugal, Italy, Finland, Spain, Poland and Bulgaria, and at least 40 % of all doctoral students in the remaining Member States for which data are available, with the exception of Luxembourg and Malta.

Data sources and availability

Statistics on science, technology and innovation (STI statistics) are based on Decision 1608/2003/EC concerning the production and development of Community statistics on science and technology. In close cooperation with the Member States, this Decision was implemented by Eurostat in the form of legislative measures and through additional work. Regulation 753/2004 was adopted in 2004 implementing Decision 1608/2003/EC.

Statistics on R & D personnel are compiled using guidelines laid out in the Frascati manual, published in 2002 by the OECD. R & D personnel include all persons employed directly on R & D, as well as persons supplying direct services to R & D, such as managers, administrative staff and clerical staff. For statistical purposes, indicators on R & D personnel who are mainly or partly employed on R & D are compiled as head counts (HC) and as full-time equivalents (FTEs). Researchers are a sub-category of R & D personnel and are professionals engaged in the conception or creation of new knowledge, products, processes, methods and systems, and in the management of the projects concerned.

Statistics on HRST are compiled using guidelines laid out in the Canberra manual, prepared in cooperation between the OECD, European Commission, UNESCO and the International Labour Organization, and published in 1995. Human resources in science and technology (HRST) are defined on the basis of education and/or occupation. HRST based on education are persons having successfully completed tertiary education in one or more of seven broad fields: natural sciences, engineering and technology, medical sciences, agricultural sciences, social sciences, humanities, and other fields. HRST based on occupation are persons who are employed in science and technology occupations as professionals or technicians. Persons who fulfil both education and occupation criteria are classified as the HRST 'core'. Tertiary education is defined as levels 5a, 5b or 6 of the 1997 version of the International standard classification of education (ISCED). Science and technology occupations are covered by major groups 2 and 3 of the International standard classification of occupations (ISCO-88). HRST data can be broken down by gender, age, region, sector of activity, occupation, educational attainment and fields of education (although it should be noted that not all combinations are possible). Data relating to stocks of HRST provide information on the characteristics of the current labour force.

Information on HRST flows from education are obtained from a UNESCO/OECD/Eurostat questionnaire on education and this can be used to provide a measure of the current and future supply of HRST from the education system, in terms of actual inflows (graduates from the reference period) and potential inflows (students participating in higher education during the reference period). Science and technology graduates are defined as the number of new graduates from all public and private institutions completing science and technology-related graduate and post-graduate studies in the reference year; it is expressed relative to the total number of persons aged 20-29 years.

Indicators based on the number of doctoral students give an idea of the extent to which countries will have researchers at the highest level of education in the future. The data relate to the number of students in the reference year not to the number of new graduates nor to the total number (stock) of graduates in the labour market that year. The number of doctoral students is measured as students enrolled in ISCED level 6: this level concerns tertiary programmes which lead to the award of an advanced research degree, for example, a doctorate in economics. These programmes should be devoted to advanced study and original research and are not based on course-work alone; studies at the doctoral level usually require 3-5 years.

Context

The European Research Area (ERA) is composed of all research and development activities, programmes and policies in Europe which involve a transnational perspective. In May 2008, the European Commission adopted a Communication to launch an initiative titled, 'better careers and more mobility: a European partnership for researchers'. The goal of this initiative is to improve the mobility of researchers and to enhance the diffusion of knowledge throughout Europe, by: balancing demand and supply for researchers at a European level; helping create centres of excellence; and improving the skills of researchers in Europe.

In December 2008, the competitiveness Council adopted a 2020 vision for the ERA. According to the opening statement of the vision, all players should benefit from: the 'fifth freedom', introducing the free circulation of researchers, knowledge and technology across the ERA; attractive conditions for carrying out research and investing in R & D intensive sectors; Europe-wide scientific competition, together with the appropriate level of cooperation and coordination. The 2020 vision for the ERA is part of the wider picture of Europe's 2020 strategy for smart, sustainable and inclusive growth. As part of the Europe 2020 strategy, the European Commission announced in July 2010 nearly EUR 6 400 million of investment in research and innovation, with the aim of providing an economic stimulus expected to create more than 165 000 jobs.

In the seventh framework programme for research and technological development (FP7) the Marie Curie actions have been regrouped and reinforced within the specific programme titled people. Entirely dedicated to human resources in research, this programme has an overall budget of more than EUR 4 700 million over a seven-year period until 2013. Within this programme, efforts will also be made to increase participation by women researchers, by encouraging equal opportunities in all Marie Curie actions, by designing the actions to ensure that researchers can achieve an appropriate work/life balance and by facilitating resuming a research career after a break. A number of groups are actively promoting greater gender equality. Among others these include the European association for women in science, engineering and technology (WiTEC), and the European platform of women scientists (EPWS).

Table 13.4: Researchers, by institutional sector, 2008 (1)

	Total - all sectors	Business enterprise sector		Government sector		Higher education sector	
	(1 000 FTE)	(1 000 FTE)	(% of total)	(1 000 FTE)	(% of total)	(1 000 FTE)	(% of total)
EU-27	1 504.6	689.9	46	188.4	13	608.6	40
Euro area (EA-16)	1 006.3	501.8	50	137.2	14	354.4	35
Belgium	36.4	17.8	49	2.7	7	15.6	43
Bulgaria	11.4	1.5	13	6.0	53	3.8	33
Czech Republic	29.8	13.3	44	7.1	24	9.4	31
Denmark	30.9	19.6	63	1.2	4	9.9	32
Germany	299.0	178.0	60	44.0	15	77.0	26
Estonia	4.0	1.2	31	0.5	13	2.1	53
Ireland	13.7	7.4	54	0.6	5	5.7	41
Greece (2)	20.8	6.1	29	2.2	11	12.4	59
Spain	131.0	46.4	35	22.6	17	61.7	47
France (2)	215.8	118.6	55	26.5	12	67.4	31
Italy	96.3	36.1	37	16.3	17	39.8	41
Cyprus	0.9	0.2	23	0.1	11	0.5	59
Latvia	4.4	0.5	11	0.9	19	3.0	69
Lithuania	8.5	1.2	14	1.7	20	5.6	66
Luxembourg	2.3	1.5	67	0.6	24	0.2	8
Hungary	18.5	7.9	43	4.7	26	5.9	32
Malta	0.5	0.2	48	0.0	4	0.3	49
Netherlands	51.1	26.6	52	6.9	14	17.5	34
Austria	34.4	21.8	63	1.5	4	11.0	32
Poland	61.8	8.9	14	12.9	21	39.9	65
Portugal	40.6	10.6	26	3.3	8	22.5	56
Romania	19.4	6.3	33	6.2	32	6.8	35
Slovenia	7.0	3.1	43	2.2	31	1.8	26
Slovakia	12.6	1.6	13	2.9	23	8.1	64
Finland	40.9	24.1	59	4.5	11	11.8	29
Sweden	48.2	33.4	69	1.8	4	12.9	27
United Kingdom	261.4	94.3	36	8.2	3	154.9	59
Iceland	2.3	1.1	48	0.5	21	0.6	28
Norway (2)	24.8	12.4	50	3.9	16	8.5	34
Switzerland	:	:	:	0.5	:	:	:
Croatia	6.7	1.1	16	1.9	28	3.7	55
Turkey (2)	49.7	15.3	31	4.8	10	29.5	59
Japan (2)	710.0	483.7	68	32.7	5	185.2	26
United States (3)	1 430.0	1 140.0	80	:	:	:	:

(1) Shares do not sum to 100 % due to estimates, the exclusion of private non-profit sector data from the table and the conversion of data to a count in terms of FTE.

(2) 2007.

(3) 2006.

Source: Eurostat (tsc00004), OECD

Figure 13.2: Proportion of research and development personnel by sector, 2008 (1)
(% of labour force)

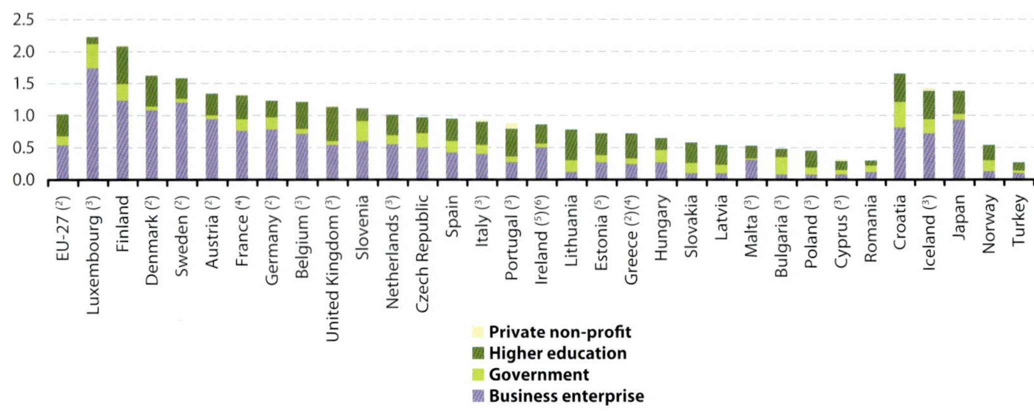

(1) Germany, Ireland, Latvia, Lithuania, Luxembourg, Hungary, the Netherlands, Norway and Turkey, higher education, not available.
(2) Estimates.
(3) Provisional.
(4) 2007.
(5) Business enterprises, provisional.
(6) Higher education, estimate.

Source: Eurostat (tsc00002)

Figure 13.3: Gender breakdown of researchers in all institutional sectors, 2007 (1)
(% of total researchers, based on FTEs)

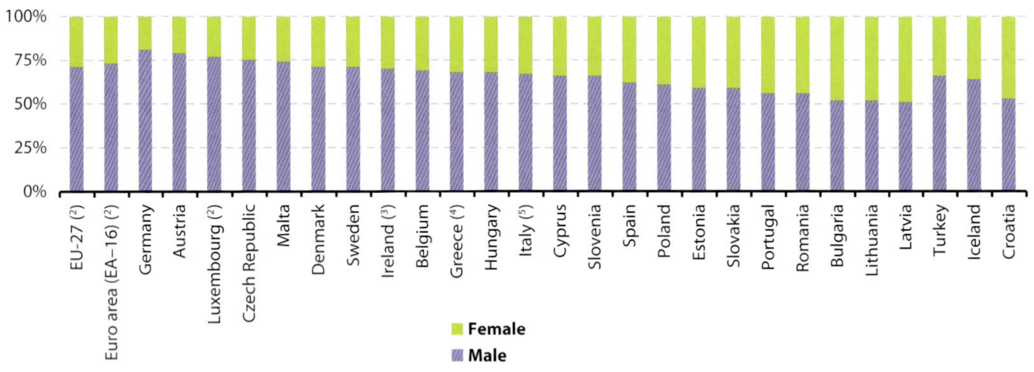

(1) France, the Netherlands, Finland and the United Kingdom, not available.
(2) Estimates.
(3) Provisional.
(4) 2005.
(5) 2006.

Source: Eurostat (tsc00006)

Table 13.5: Human resources in science and technology (1)

	People working in an S&T occupation					People who have a tertiary education and work in an S&T occupation				
	(1 000)	(% of total employment)				(1 000)	(% of total employment)			
	2008	2005	2006	2007	2008	2008	2005	2006	2007	2008
EU-27 (2)	65 120	29.2	29.7	29.8	:	37 378	16.6	17.0	17.1	:
Belgium	1 441	32.7	32.9	33.0	32.5	1 018	22.6	23.1	23.6	22.9
Bulgaria (2)	710	23.2	21.5	21.9	:	531	16.8	16.2	16.3	:
Czech Republic	1 687	32.6	32.6	33.3	33.8	591	11.3	11.6	11.5	11.8
Denmark (3)	1 117	36.6	36.8	36.0	39.1	699	24.2	24.6	21.9	24.5
Germany	14 181	36.1	36.5	36.3	36.5	7 130	17.9	17.7	17.9	18.4
Estonia	175	27.4	26.9	27.2	26.7	117	18.3	18.3	18.0	17.9
Ireland	494	23.2	22.4	23.3	23.5	384	17.1	17.0	17.7	18.3
Greece	1 061	21.9	22.8	23.1	23.3	829	16.7	17.5	17.9	18.2
Spain	5 119	23.8	23.9	24.2	25.3	3 966	18.2	18.8	18.7	19.6
France	8 338	31.2	31.8	31.8	32.0	5 225	19.0	19.7	19.6	20.1
Italy	7 347	29.5	31.1	31.9	31.5	3 050	11.4	11.9	12.5	13.1
Cyprus	104	25.7	26.1	27.0	27.2	83	19.1	19.9	21.3	21.8
Latvia	350	24.5	27.0	29.7	31.1	194	13.9	14.8	15.7	17.2
Lithuania	443	26.1	25.7	26.9	29.2	311	17.7	17.8	19.0	20.5
Luxembourg	84	38.4	39.0	39.5	41.5	56	25.5	23.9	26.3	27.9
Hungary	1 078	26.1	26.6	26.5	27.8	634	14.8	15.1	15.4	16.3
Malta	45	25.6	26.7	27.3	28.2	23	11.9	13.1	13.6	14.5
Netherlands	3 187	37.1	36.0	37.2	37.4	1 895	21.8	21.1	21.8	22.3
Austria	1 218	30.6	30.5	29.7	29.9	480	12.0	11.7	11.5	11.8
Poland (2)	3 988	25.9	26.2	26.2	:	2 429	15.3	15.8	16.0	:
Portugal	943	17.4	17.7	17.6	18.5	588	10.4	10.8	10.9	11.5
Romania	1 813	17.8	18.6	18.6	19.3	1 094	9.7	10.4	10.8	11.7
Slovenia (2)	300	30.7	31.6	30.6	:	172	16.3	17.4	17.6	:
Slovakia	707	29.5	29.7	29.3	29.0	298	12.0	12.5	12.1	12.2
Finland	882	33.5	34.1	34.5	34.8	621	22.4	22.8	23.1	24.5
Sweden (2)	1 780	39.2	39.1	39.2	:	1 083	23.2	23.5	23.9	:
United Kingdom	7 847	26.1	26.9	26.8	26.8	5 281	17.5	18.0	18.0	18.0
Iceland	64	31.2	32.7	33.4	36.2	36	17.9	13.8	18.9	20.5
Norway	940	36.2	36.4	36.9	37.4	661	24.6	25.2	25.9	26.3
Switzerland	1 704	38.3	38.9	39.4	40.5	909	19.1	19.5	20.3	21.6
Croatia (3)	406	23.8	24.4	24.0	24.9	248	14.5	14.7	14.6	15.3
FYR of Macedonia (2)	122	:	21.1	20.7	:	77	:	13.0	13.1	:
Turkey	2 748	:	12.5	12.5	12.8	1 768	:	7.4	7.7	8.2

(1) Break in series, 2006, with the exception of Belgium and Luxembourg.
(2) 2007 instead of 2008 for the number of people.
(3) Break in series, 2007.

Source: Eurostat (hrst_st_nocc)

Table 13.6: Science and technology graduates
(tertiary graduates in science and technology per 1 000 persons aged 20-29 years)

	Total		Male		Female	
	2003	2008	2003	2008	2003	2008
EU-27	*12.3*	13.9	*16.5*	18.4	*7.9*	9.2
Belgium	11.0	11.6	16.4	17.1	5.6	6.0
Bulgaria	8.3	9.1	9.4	11.2	7.2	6.9
Czech Republic	6.4	15.0	8.8	20.3	3.8	9.3
Denmark	12.5	15.5	17.3	19.5	7.6	11.4
Germany	8.4	12.5	12.7	17.0	4.0	7.9
Estonia	8.8	11.4	10.0	13.1	7.6	9.8
Ireland	24.2	19.5	31.5	27.1	16.8	11.8
Greece (1)	8.0	11.2	9.2	12.5	6.8	9.8
Spain	12.6	11.6	17.1	15.8	7.8	7.2
France	22.0	20.1	30.4	28.9	13.4	11.4
Italy (2)	9.1	12.1	11.6	14.8	6.6	9.4
Cyprus	3.6	4.0	4.2	5.1	3.0	3.0
Latvia	8.6	8.8	10.5	11.7	6.6	5.7
Lithuania	16.3	17.8	20.8	23.2	11.8	12.1
Luxembourg	:	1.8	:	1.8	:	1.7
Hungary	4.8	6.1	6.9	8.8	2.6	3.2
Malta	3.6	6.0	4.8	8.3	2.3	3.5
Netherlands	7.3	8.8	11.7	14.2	2.7	3.4
Austria	8.2	11.8	12.8	17.7	3.5	5.8
Poland	9.0	14.1	11.8	16.6	6.1	11.5
Portugal	8.2	20.7	9.5	26.8	6.9	14.3
Romania	9.4	15.2	11.1	16.9	7.5	13.4
Slovenia	8.7	10.7	12.5	15.3	4.6	5.9
Slovakia	8.3	15.0	10.7	18.6	5.8	11.3
Finland	17.4	24.3	24.0	31.8	10.4	16.5
Sweden	13.9	13.2	17.9	17.2	9.7	9.0
United Kingdom	21.0	17.6	27.5	23.7	14.5	11.2
Iceland	9.5	10.4	12.0	13.0	6.9	7.5
Liechtenstein	5.6	7.0	7.2	10.3	4.1	3.7
Norway	9.3	9.2	13.4	12.8	5.1	5.5
Switzerland	14.1	17.4	24.0	28.0	4.1	6.8
Croatia	5.6	10.1	6.4	13.3	3.5	6.8
FYR of Macedonia	3.3	6.1	3.8	6.7	2.8	5.3
Turkey	5.2	7.6	7.0	10.4	3.3	4.8
Japan	13.2	14.3	22.1	23.9	3.9	4.1
United States	10.9	10.1	14.6	13.5	7.1	6.4

(1) 2004 instead of 2003.
(2) 2007 instead of 2008.

Source: Eurostat (tsiir050)

Table 13.7: PhD students (ISCED level 6), 2008
(% of total PhD students)

	Total number of PhD students (1 000)	Male	Female	Social science, business & law	Teacher training & educ.; humanities & arts	Science maths & comput.; engin. manuf. & construc.	Agriculture & veterinary	Health & welfare; services	Others (1)
EU-27 (2)	*525.8*	*52.2*	*47.8*	*21.8*	*21.0*	*36.4*	*2.9*	*14.5*	*2.0*
Belgium	9.8	56.3	43.7	19.5	12.9	:	6.5	:	:
Bulgaria	4.4	49.9	50.1	23.3	20.3	39.9	2.9	13.6	0.0
Czech Republic	24.3	60.4	39.6	17.0	16.3	49.8	4.1	12.7	0.0
Denmark	6.1	53.5	46.5	14.4	14.1	38.5	5.8	27.2	0.0
Germany	:	:	:	:	:	:	:	:	:
Estonia	2.4	44.4	55.6	21.8	22.5	:	4.6	:	:
Ireland	6.1	51.6	48.4	15.7	22.8	47.1	2.6	11.5	0.3
Greece	21.6	56.2	43.8	22.6	20.4	33.1	2.6	21.3	0.0
Spain	67.0	47.7	52.3	22.1	22.1	21.4	2.2	19.9	12.2
France	70.0	53.5	46.5	28.5	24.7	44.0	0.1	2.7	0.0
Italy	39.3	47.4	52.6	:	:	:	:	:	100.0
Cyprus	0.4	53.0	47.0	15.9	30.5	:	0.5	:	:
Latvia	2.0	40.2	59.8	35.0	21.6	30.3	2.0	11.2	0.0
Lithuania	2.9	41.5	58.5	31.2	:	39.7	4.8	:	:
Luxembourg	0.2	60.8	39.2	:	:	:	:	:	100.0
Hungary	7.2	51.3	48.7	22.5	27.1	30.6	5.7	14.1	0.0
Malta	0.1	67.2	32.8	20.9	35.8	29.9	0.0	13.4	0.0
Netherlands	7.4	57.6	42.4	:	:	:	:	:	100.0
Austria	17.3	54.2	45.8	33.8	21.2	:	3.3	:	3.1
Poland	31.8	48.9	51.1	20.8	32.9	31.1	5.3	9.9	0.0
Portugal	16.0	43.3	56.7	25.8	22.7	33.2	2.0	16.3	0.0
Romania	28.6	54.0	46.0	16.0	:	41.1	6.9	19.2	:
Slovenia	1.6	50.6	49.4	13.5	15.7	41.1	3.0	26.7	0.0
Slovakia	10.7	54.0	46.0	20.0	18.9	36.7	3.6	20.9	0.0
Finland	21.6	47.4	52.6	22.3	24.5	39.7	2.1	11.4	0.0
Sweden	20.1	50.8	49.2	11.8	11.7	41.5	2.0	33.0	0.0
United Kingdom	80.9	53.6	46.4	21.2	21.3	39.8	1.1	16.6	0.1
Iceland	0.3	43.2	56.8	14.8	24.2	37.9	0.0	23.1	0.0
Liechtenstein	0.1	71.7	28.3	22.6	15.1	0.0	0.0	62.3	0.0
Norway	6.2	51.6	48.4	20.5	10.8	40.4	2.2	26.1	0.0
Switzerland	18.2	57.6	42.4	26.4	16.3	38.7	2.4	15.8	0.4
Croatia	3.1	49.2	50.8	12.5	23.9	41.3	3.7	18.7	0.0
FYR of Macedonia	0.2	46.5	53.5	28.9	22.0	36.5	0.0	12.6	0.0
Turkey	35.1	57.1	42.9	23.4	23.5	33.6	7.9	11.7	0.0
Japan	75.0	69.2	30.8	13.0	13.9	32.2	5.7	32.3	2.8
United States	460.8	49.9	50.1	20.8	24.9	38.2	0.6	15.6	0.0

(1) Unknown or not specified.
(2) 2007.

Source: Eurostat (educ_enrl5)

13.3 Innovation

Europe has a long-standing tradition of producing inventions. However, commentators often focus on an entrepreneurial gap in order to explain why some ideas for new products or services do not become a success in the marketplace, or why other ideas relating to new processes do not get implemented, thereby surrendering the opportunity to make efficiency gains on production lines or within industrial organisations. This subchapter looks at the state of innovation in the European Union (EU) by presenting data on where innovation takes place and how many enterprises are involved.

Main statistical findings

Among the EU Member States the highest propensity to innovate in 2008 (see Figure 13.4) was recorded in Germany (79.9 %), followed by Luxembourg (64.7 %) – these were the only Member States where more than 60 % of all enterprises were innovative - the EU-27 average (excluding Greece) was 51.6 %. The lowest propensity to innovate was recorded in Latvia (24.3 %), Poland (27.9 %) and Hungary (28.9 %) - the only Member States where the proportion of innovative enterprises was below 30 %. Estonia, Cyprus and the Czech Republic were the only Member States that joined the EU in 2004 to report a propensity to innovate above the EU average. Note that large enterprises tend to innovate more than small and medium-sized enterprises (SMEs) and as such these figures for the Member States may, at least to some degree, reflect the enterprise structure of each domestic economy.

New or significantly improved products contributed a relatively small proportion of total turnover among innovative enterprises in 2008, some 6.4 % for the EU-27 (excluding Greece) in 2008, with 19 of the 26 Member States for which data are available reporting single-digit shares (see Figure 13.5). These products did however account for a higher proportion of sales in Malta (23.4 %), Hungary (14.8 %), Bulgaria (13.9 %) and the Czech Republic (13.1 %).

Large enterprises (with 250 or more employees) were more likely to have brought product innovations to market in 2008 than either medium-sized enterprises (50 to 249 employees) or small enterprises (10 to 49 employees); this pattern held for all of the Member States for which data are available – as shown in Table 13.8. Lithuania was the only Member State where the proportion of small enterprises with process innovations was above the overall proportion for all enterprises.

A similar size class breakdown for process innovations that are developed within the enterprise also showed that large innovative enterprises were more likely to introduce processes innovations: the main exception to this was Cyprus where such process innovations were much less likely to have been introduced in large enterprises than in small or medium-sized enterprises.

Data sources and availability

The Community innovation survey (CIS) collects information about product and process innovation, as well as organisational and marketing innovations. The legal basis for the collection of these statistics is Regulation 1450/2004 of 13 August 2004 implementing Decision 1608/2003/EC concerning the production and development of Community statistics on innovation.

Innovations are based on the results of new technological developments, new combinations of existing technology, or the use of other knowledge acquired (by the enterprise). For the purpose of the Community innovation survey an innovation is defined as a new or significantly improved product (good or service) introduced to the market, or the introduction within an enterprise of a new or significantly improved process, as well as organisational and marketing innovations, including new logistics or distribution methods. Such innovations may be developed by the innovating enterprise or by another enterprise. However, purely selling innovations wholly produced and developed by other enterprises is not included as an innovation activity, nor is introducing products with purely aesthetic changes. Innovations should therefore be new to the enterprise concerned: for product innovations they do not necessarily have to be new to the market, and for process innovations the enterprise does not necessarily have to be the first one to have introduced the process.

Enterprises with innovation activity include all types of innovator, namely product and process innovators, as well as enterprises with only on-going and/or abandoned innovation activities. Enterprises may cooperate with other parties (for example suppliers, competitors, customers, educational/research establishments) when engaging in an innovative activity. The proportion of enterprises with innovation activity is also referred to as the propensity to innovate.

Context

While Europe is good at producing initial ideas (inventions), it is regarded by some as not being so good at bringing them to market; as such, EU policy in this field increasingly aims to provide more focus to industry-driven, applied research and development (R & D).

Education is another area seen as key to developing an innovation-orientated society, through the acquisition of entrepreneurial, managerial, scientific, mathematical and foreign-language skills, as well as digital literacy. Policymakers express concern at the numbers of science and technology graduates who directly apply their education once they move into the labour market, while a lack of job mobility between universities and business may potentially hinder the transfer of ideas, thereby reducing the EU's innovation performance (see Subchapter 13.2 on R & D personnel).

In October 2006, the European Parliament and the Council adopted a Decision 1639/2006/EC establishing a competitiveness and innovation framework programme (CIP) for the period 2007-2013. With SMEs as its main target, the competitiveness and innovation framework programme aims to support innovation activities (including eco-innovation), provide better access to finance and deliver business support services in the regions. It encourages the take-up and use of information and communication technologies and aims to help to develop the information society. Furthermore, it also promotes the increased use of renewable energies and energy efficiency.

The European Council called for a plan on innovation in December 2008, which provided the basis for a period of public consultation and business debate on the EU's future innovation policy. In September 2009, the European Commission adopted a Communication ((2009) 442) 'reviewing Community innovation policy in a changing world'. In October 2010, as one of the seven flagship initiatives of the Europe 2020: a strategy for smart, sustainable and inclusive growth, the European Commission adopted a Communication ((2010) 546) on an innovation union. This sets outs a comprehensive innovation strategy for Europe, focusing on major areas of concern for citizens such as climate change, energy efficiency and healthy living. It pursues a broad concept of innovation, not only technological, but also in business models, design, branding and services that add value for users. It includes public sector and social innovation as well as commercial innovation. It aims to involve all actors and all regions in the innovation cycle. The policies in the innovation union aim to do three things:

- make Europe into a world-class science performer;
- revolutionise the way public and private sectors work together, notably through innovation partnerships;
- remove bottlenecks like expensive patenting, market fragmentation, slow standard setting and skill shortages, that currently prevent ideas getting quickly to market.

Figure 13.4: Proportion of innovative enterprises, 2008 (1)
(% of all enterprises)

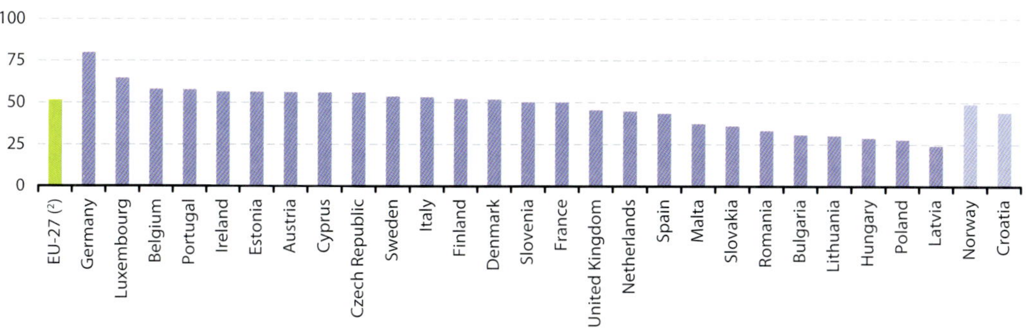

(1) Greece, not available.
(2) Excluding Greece.

Source: Eurostat (inn_cis6_type)

Figure 13.5: Turnover from new or significantly improved products new to the market, 2008 (1)
(% of total turnover of innovative enterprises)

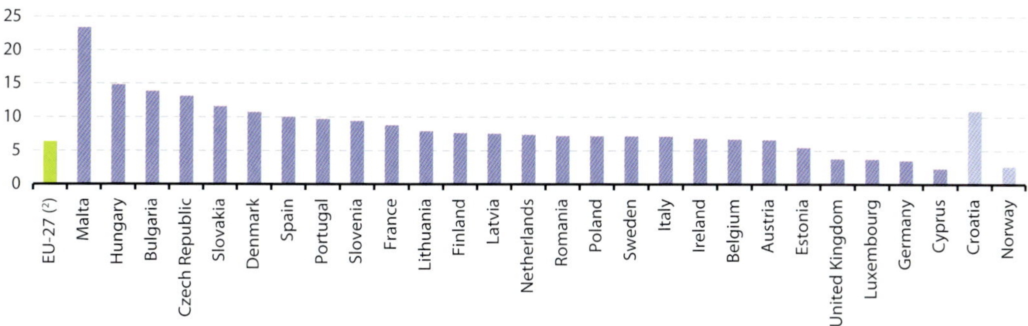

(1) Greece, not available.
(2) Excluding Greece.

Source: Eurostat (inn_cis6_prod)

Table 13.8: Proportion of innovative enterprises which introduced products new to the market or own-developed process innovations, 2008
(% of enterprises within size class or total)

	Process innovations: developed by the enterprise or group				Product innovations: new to market			
	Total	With 10 to 49 employees	With 50 to 249 employees	With ≥ 250 employees	Total	With 10 to 49 employees	With 50 to 249 employees	With ≥ 250 employees
Belgium	42.2	42.7	39.3	47.5	47.5	47.1	45.5	59.3
Bulgaria	41.3	40.7	43.8	38.1	25.9	23.3	30.8	30.8
Czech Republic	39.0	40.1	35.4	41.2	39.1	34.0	47.0	54.1
Denmark	:	:	:	:	44.4	44.1	42.3	54.1
Germany	30.1	27.1	35.6	42.0	26.0	23.2	29.5	43.7
Estonia	40.5	37.9	44.3	56.0	25.8	24.2	28.0	36.1
Ireland	:	:	:	:	:	:	:	:
Greece	:	:	:	:	:	:	:	:
Spain	50.7	50.6	49.4	57.4	21.5	18.0	28.1	43.6
France	50.8	50.8	49.1	55.0	43.2	39.9	46.3	60.0
Italy	44.9	44.0	48.7	47.9	47.7	45.5	55.5	61.4
Cyprus	50.9	53.5	47.3	22.7	26.8	24.0	33.6	40.9
Latvia	33.9	31.3	36.1	50.6	23.4	22.7	21.5	35.6
Lithuania	51.8	55.0	47.3	46.4	37.2	40.2	28.8	47.1
Luxembourg	51.7	48.0	53.2	69.7	40.6	35.3	47.6	55.8
Hungary	24.8	25.0	21.0	32.6	33.1	31.2	32.0	45.2
Malta	47.7	46.9	46.9	55.0	39.1	38.3	32.7	60.0
Netherlands	23.4	22.0	25.7	29.4	49.2	48.1	51.3	53.6
Austria	37.6	34.9	41.7	45.8	49.5	46.3	52.1	66.4
Poland	43.7	45.8	40.7	42.7	41.5	40.1	41.6	47.5
Portugal	52.0	52.4	50.7	52.2	35.6	33.1	41.7	53.7
Romania	66.0	67.0	64.4	63.7	24.8	23.0	26.8	31.4
Slovenia	37.2	36.2	38.8	38.7	51.3	51.3	48.1	59.5
Slovakia	34.2	34.6	31.3	39.7	35.7	34.2	33.4	48.0
Finland	39.2	40.4	35.1	40.0	37.3	35.5	35.9	57.7
Sweden	33.5	33.1	33.0	39.5	50.4	48.3	53.6	62.8
United Kingdom	:	:	:	:	:	:	:	:
Norway	27.4	28.0	25.1	29.0	34.5	36.8	28.5	34.6
Croatia	37.4	36.9	39.3	36.0	37.4	36.7	38.5	39.1

Source: Eurostat (inn_cis6_prod)

13.4 Patents

Intellectual property rights and in particular patents provide a link between innovation, inventions and the marketplace. Applying for a patent makes an invention public, but at the same time gives it protection. A count of patents is one measure of a country's inventive activity and also shows its capacity to exploit knowledge and translate it into potential economic gains. In this context, indicators based on patent statistics are widely used to assess the inventive and innovative performance of a country. This subchapter provides information on patent applications in the European Union (EU).

Main statistical findings

With the exception of the years 2000 to 2002, the number of EU-27 patent applications filed with the European Patent Office (EPO) increased at a relatively fast pace from 1997 to the latest period for which data are available (2007), with annual growth averaging 8.2 % per annum between 1997 and 2000, and 2.7 % between 2002 and 2007; over the whole period under consideration, the number of patents increased from 40 576 to 57 725. Among the Member States, Germany had by far the highest number of patent applications to the EPO, some 23 929 in 2007 (41.5 % of the EU-27 total). In relative terms, Sweden reported the highest number of patent applications per million inhabitants (298.4), followed by Germany (290.7), Finland (250.8) and Luxembourg (230.2).

EU-27 high-technology patent applications to the EPO represented an increasing share of total patent applications up until 2001 when they accounted for 23.1 % of all applications. Their relative importance declined somewhat after this, as did their absolute number – from 11 763 high-tech patent applications in 2001, there was a relatively slow reduction through to 2006 (including growth in 2004). This was followed by a collapse in the number of high-tech applications in 2007, with the total falling to 5 684. This pattern of a sharp fall between 2001 and 2007 was observed across the majority of the Member States and particularly for the larger countries or those countries with traditionally the highest propensity to make patent applications.

Finland and Sweden registered the highest number of high-technology patent applications per million inhabitants in 2007, the figures for both countries being over 35, while Belgium, Denmark, Germany France, the Netherlands and Austria were the only other Member States to record double-digit ratios. The considerable reduction in high-technology patent applications filed with the EPO may reflect the length of patent procedures. Given the increasing speed of technological change and the rapid pace at which imitators are able to bring new technologies to market, it is perhaps not surprising that many enterprises increasingly choose to invest in continued innovation rather than spend time and resources to protect goods or services that may soon become copied or obsolete.

Data sources and availability

From 2007 onwards, Eurostat's production of European Patent Office (EPO) data has been based almost exclusively on the EPO's worldwide statistical patent database (PATSTAT). The EPO grants European patents for the contracting states to the European Patent Convention (EPC), of which there are currently 32 – the EU Member States, Iceland, Liechtenstein, Switzerland, Monaco and Turkey.

European patent applications refer to applications filed directly under the EPC or to applications filed under the Patent Co-operation Treaty (PCT) and designated to the EPO (Euro-PCT). Patent applications are counted according to the year in which they are filed and are assigned to a country according to the inventor's place of residence, using fractional counting if there are multiple inventors.

In contrast, the United States Patent and Trademark Office (USPTO) data refer to patents granted; data are recorded by year of publication as opposed to the year of filing. This methodological difference implies that any comparison between EPO and USPTO patent data should be interpreted with caution.

High-technology patents are counted following criteria established by the trilateral statistical report (drafted by the EPO, USPTO and the Japan Patent Office (JPO)), where the following technical fields are defined as high-technology groups in accordance with the international patent classification (IPC): computer and automated business equipment; micro-organism and genetic engineering; aviation; communication technology; semiconductors; and lasers.

Context

Intellectual property law establishes protection over intangibles – for example, when a manufactured product is sold, the product itself becomes the property of the purchaser, however, intellectual property rights allow intangible elements to remain in the ownership of the creator; these intangibles include (among others) the idea itself, or the name or sign/logo used to distinguish the product from others.

Patents and trademarks are common ways to protect industrial property. Patents are a limited term exclusive right granted to an inventor, maintained through the payment of fees. While patents are generally used to protect research and development (R & D) results, they are also a source of technical information, which can potentially prevent re-inventing and re-developing ideas. A count of patents shows a country's capacity to exploit knowledge and translate it into potential economic gains; in this context, patent statistics are widely used to assess the inventive and innovative performance of countries. Most studies show that innovative enterprises tend to make more use of intellectual property protection than enterprises that do not innovate. Enterprise size and the economic sector in which an enterprise operates are also likely to play an important role in determining whether an enterprise chooses to protect its intellectual property.

The use of patents is relatively restricted within the EU – this may be due to a range of influences: their relative cost; the overlap between national and European procedures; or the need for translation into foreign languages. Furthermore, the increasing number and complexity of patent applications worldwide has resulted in a backlog of pending applications, while the constant expansion of the human knowledge base makes it increasingly difficult for patent offices to keep abreast of technological developments.

The European Council held in Lisbon in March 2000 called for the creation of a Community patent system to address shortcomings in the legal protection of inventions, while providing an incentive for investments in R & D. In July of the same year the European Commission made a first proposal for the creation of a Community patent: this was discussed at various levels and despite a number of proposals and amendments for a Council Regulation during 2003 and 2004 no legal basis was forthcoming. In April 2007 the European Commission released a Communication (COM(2007) 165) titled 'Enhancing the patent system in Europe', stating that European patent systems were more expensive, uncertain and unattractive than those in non-member countries.

In July 2008 the European Commission adopted a Communication (COM(2008) 465) titled 'An industrial property rights strategy for Europe' foreseeing the development of legislation, arguing that the harmonisation of patent law could make it easier for European enterprises to patent their inventions both within and outside the EU.

On 4 December 2009, the European Council unanimously adopted conclusions on an enhanced patent system in the EU. The package agreed covers two main areas: firstly, agreement on the approach to be adopted in order to move towards an EU patent regulation; secondly, an agreement on establishing a new patent court in the EU. It is hoped that these measures will together make it less costly for businesses to protect innovative technology and make litigation more accessible and predictable. However, the creation of the EU patent depends on a solution being found for translation arrangements which were the subject of European Commission proposal (COM(2010) 350) for a 'Council Regulation on the translation arrangements for the European Union patent' in July 2010.

Table 13.9: Patent applications to the EPO and patents granted by the USPTO

	Patent applications to the EPO			High technology patent applications to the EPO			Patents granted by the US Patent & Trademark Office		
	(number of patent applications)		(per million inhab.)	(number of patent applications)		(per million inhab.)	(number of patents granted)		(per million inhab.)
	2002	2007	2007	2002	2007	2007	1999	2004	2004
EU-27	50 462	57 725	116.5	10 964	5 684	11.5	31 172	15 775	32.3
Belgium	1 287	1 472	139.0	333	231	21.8	794	395	38.0
Bulgaria	15	29	3.8	2	:	:	10	48	6.2
Czech Republic	88	162	15.8	6	9	0.9	37	49	4.8
Denmark	935	1 057	194.1	230	110	20.2	564	246	45.5
Germany	21 503	23 929	290.7	3 823	2 098	25.5	12 799	6 874	83.3
Estonia	6	23	17.4	1	7	5.2	5	4	2.8
Ireland	224	288	66.8	65	38	8.8	214	156	38.8
Greece	74	109	9.8	18	6	0.6	18	20	1.8
Spain	938	1 451	32.6	148	96	2.2	381	210	5.0
France	7 321	8 421	132.4	1 821	1 128	17.7	4 616	2 344	37.6
Italy	4 168	5 107	86.4	489	253	4.3	1 938	1 049	18.1
Cyprus	7	9	11.5	2	5	6.0	4	1	1.6
Latvia	6	19	8.4	2	2	1.0	2	2	0.9
Lithuania	3	8	2.4	0	2	0.7	7	19	5.5
Luxembourg	61	110	230.2	4	5	9.9	39	38	83.5
Hungary	120	173	17.2	17	19	1.9	76	39	3.9
Malta	4	8	20.5	1	:	:	3	:	:
Netherlands	3 442	3 656	223.5	1 160	348	21.3	1 535	938	57.7
Austria	1 269	1 797	217.0	216	149	18.0	640	366	44.9
Poland	81	146	3.8	12	24	0.6	31	40	1.0
Portugal	41	121	11.4	5	29	2.7	15	14	1.4
Romania	11	21	1.0	3	7	0.3	8	13	0.6
Slovenia	76	103	51.5	12	14	7.0	15	8	4.2
Slovakia	24	42	7.8	7	4	0.7	7	6	1.1
Finland	1 257	1 323	250.8	598	209	39.7	1 169	544	104.3
Sweden	2 002	2 719	298.4	463	331	36.4	1 796	509	56.8
United Kingdom	5 500	5 422	89.2	1 527	558	9.2	4 451	1 936	32.4
Iceland	35	28	90.6	10	3	9.8	33	25	85.2
Liechtenstein	26	31	895.4	2	1	28.4	15	13	377.2
Norway	377	515	110.0	81	16	3.5	300	149	32.7
Switzerland	2 641	3 224	429.3	404	222	29.6	1 520	762	103.5
Croatia	37	32	7.2	4	2	0.5	9	10	2.3
Turkey	60	220	3.2	:	:	:	16	9	0.1
Japan	20 218	20 657	161.7	7 111	3 615	28.3	39 467	29 149	228.1
United States	31 171	31 908	105.8	10 919	3 686	12.2	103 966	80 322	273.8

Source: Eurostat (tsc00009, tsiir060, pat_ep_ntec, tsc00010, pat_us_ntot and tsiir070)

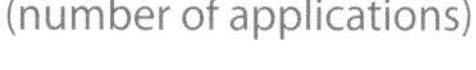

Figure 13.6: Patent applications to the EPO, EU-27
(number of applications)

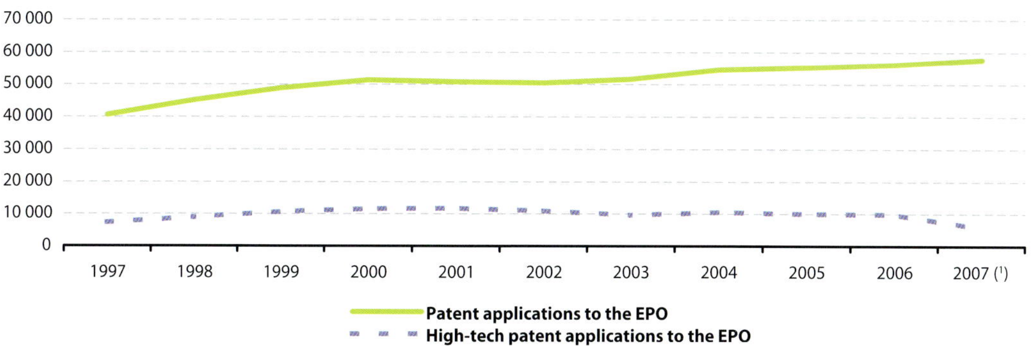

(1) Estimate for total patent applications; provisional for high-tech patent applications.

Source: Euostat (pat_ep_ntot and pat_ep_ntec)

Figure 13.7: Co-patenting at the EPO according to inventors' country of residence, 2007 (1)
(% of total)

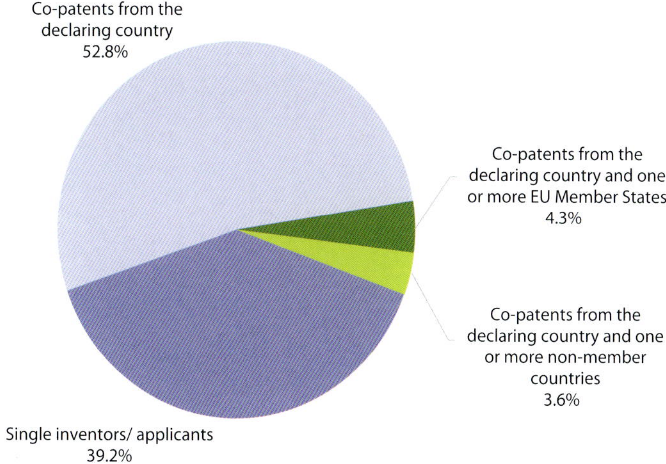

(1) Figures do not sum to 100 % due to rounding.

Source: Eurostat (pat_ep_cpi)

Figure 13.8: EU patent citations (EPO) according to inventors' country of residence (number)

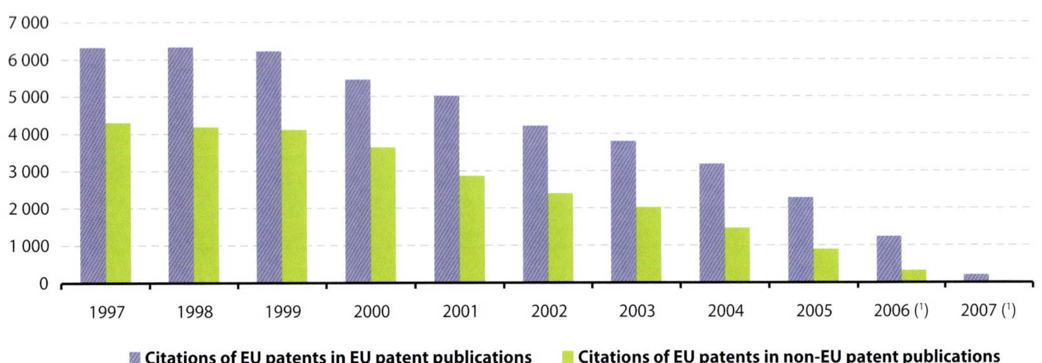

(1) Provisional.

Source: Eurostat (pat_ep_cti)

Annexes

NUTS (classification of territorial units for statistics)

European Union: NUTS 2 regions

Belgium

BE10 Région de Bruxelles-Capitale/ Brussels Hoofdstedelijk Gewest
BE21 Prov. Antwerpen
BE22 Prov. Limburg (B)
BE23 Prov. Oost-Vlaanderen
BE24 Prov. Vlaams-Brabant
BE25 Prov. West-Vlaanderen
BE31 Prov. Brabant Wallon
BE32 Prov. Hainaut
BE33 Prov. Liège
BE34 Prov. Luxembourg (B)
BE35 Prov. Namur

Bulgaria

BG31 Severozapaden
BG32 Severen tsentralen
BG33 Severoiztochen
BG34 Yugoiztochen
BG41 Yugozapaden
BG42 Yuzhen tsentralen

Czech Republic

CZ01 Praha
CZ02 Střední Čechy
CZ03 Jihozápad
CZ04 Severozápad
CZ05 Severovýchod
CZ06 Jihovýchod
CZ07 Střední Morava
CZ08 Moravskoslezsko

Denmark

DK01 Hovedstaden
DK02 Sjælland
DK03 Syddanmark
DK04 Midtjylland
DK05 Nordjylland

Germany

DE11 Stuttgart
DE12 Karlsruhe
DE13 Freiburg
DE14 Tübingen
DE21 Oberbayern
DE22 Niederbayern
DE23 Oberpfalz
DE24 Oberfranken
DE25 Mittelfranken
DE26 Unterfranken
DE27 Schwaben
DE30 Berlin
DE41 Brandenburg – Nordost
DE42 Brandenburg – Südwest
DE50 Bremen
DE60 Hamburg
DE71 Darmstadt
DE72 Gießen
DE73 Kassel
DE80 Mecklenburg-Vorpommern
DE91 Braunschweig
DE92 Hannover
DE93 Lüneburg
DE94 Weser-Ems
DEA1 Düsseldorf
DEA2 Köln
DEA3 Münster
DEA4 Detmold
DEA5 Arnsberg
DEB1 Koblenz
DEB2 Trier
DEB3 Rheinhessen-Pfalz

DEC0 Saarland
DED1 Chemnitz
DED2 Dresden
DED3 Leipzig
DEE0 Sachsen-Anhalt
DEF0 Schleswig-Holstein
DEG0 Thüringen

Estonia

EE00 Eesti

Ireland

IE01 Border, Midland and Western
IE02 Southern and Eastern

Greece

GR11 Anatoliki Makedonia, Thraki
GR12 Kentriki Makedonia
GR13 Dytiki Makedonia
GR14 Thessalia
GR21 Ipeiros
GR22 Ionia Nisia
GR23 Dytiki Ellada
GR24 Sterea Ellada
GR25 Peloponnisos
GR30 Attiki
GR41 Voreio Aigaio
GR42 Notio Aigaio
GR43 Kriti

Spain

ES11 Galicia
ES12 Principado de Asturias
ES13 Cantabria
ES21 País Vasco
ES22 Comunidad Foral de Navarra
ES23 La Rioja
ES24 Aragón
ES30 Comunidad de Madrid
ES41 Castilla y León
ES42 Castilla-La Mancha
ES43 Extremadura
ES51 Cataluña
ES52 Comunidad Valenciana
ES53 Illes Balears
ES61 Andalucía
ES62 Región de Murcia
ES63 Ciudad Autónoma de Ceuta
ES64 Ciudad Autónoma de Melilla
ES70 Canarias

France

FR10 Île-de-France
FR21 Champagne-Ardenne
FR22 Picardie
FR23 Haute-Normandie
FR24 Centre
FR25 Basse-Normandie
FR26 Bourgogne
FR30 Nord – Pas-de-Calais
FR41 Lorraine
FR42 Alsace
FR43 Franche-Comté
FR51 Pays de la Loire
FR52 Bretagne
FR53 Poitou-Charentes
FR61 Aquitaine
FR62 Midi-Pyrénées
FR63 Limousin
FR71 Rhône-Alpes
FR72 Auvergne
FR81 Languedoc-Roussillon
FR82 Provence-Alpes-Côte d'Azur
FR83 Corse
FR91 Guadeloupe
FR92 Martinique
FR93 Guyane
FR94 Réunion

Italy

ITC1 Piemonte
ITC2 Valle d'Aosta/Vallée d'Aoste
ITC3 Liguria
ITC4 Lombardia
ITD1 Provincia Autonoma Bolzano/Bozen

ITD2 Provincia Autonoma Trento
ITD3 Veneto
ITD4 Friuli-Venezia Giulia
ITD5 Emilia-Romagna
ITE1 Toscana
ITE2 Umbria
ITE3 Marche
ITE4 Lazio
ITF1 Abruzzo
ITF2 Molise
ITF3 Campania
ITF4 Puglia
ITF5 Basilicata
ITF6 Calabria
ITG1 Sicilia
ITG2 Sardegna

Cyprus

CY00 Kýpros/Kıbrıs

Latvia

LV00 Latvija

Lithuania

LT00 Lietuva

Luxembourg

LU00 Luxembourg (Grand-Duché)

Hungary

HU10 Közép-Magyarország
HU21 Közép-Dunántúl
HU22 Nyugat-Dunántúl
HU23 Dél-Dunántúl
HU31 Észak-Magyarország
HU32 Észak-Alföld
HU33 Dél-Alföld

Malta

MT00 Malta

Netherlands

NL11 Groningen
NL12 Friesland (NL)
NL13 Drenthe
NL21 Overijssel
NL22 Gelderland
NL23 Flevoland
NL31 Utrecht
NL32 Noord-Holland
NL33 Zuid-Holland
NL34 Zeeland
NL41 Noord-Brabant
NL42 Limburg (NL)

Austria

AT11 Burgenland (A)
AT12 Niederösterreich
AT13 Wien
AT21 Kärnten
AT22 Steiermark
AT31 Oberösterreich
AT32 Salzburg
AT33 Tirol
AT34 Vorarlberg

Poland

PL11 Łódzkie
PL12 Mazowieckie
PL21 Małopolskie
PL22 Śląskie
PL31 Lubelskie
PL32 Podkarpackie
PL33 Świętokrzyskie
PL34 Podlaskie
PL41 Wielkopolskie
PL42 Zachodniopomorskie
PL43 Lubuskie
PL51 Dolnośląskie
PL52 Opolskie
PL61 Kujawsko-Pomorskie
PL62 Warmińsko-Mazurskie
PL63 Pomorskie

Portugal

PT11 Norte
PT15 Algarve
PT16 Centro (P)
PT17 Lisboa

PT18 Alentejo
PT20 Região Autónoma dos Açores
PT30 Região Autónoma da Madeira

Romania

RO11 Nord-Vest
RO12 Centru
RO21 Nord-Est
RO22 Sud-Est
RO31 Sud - Muntenia
RO32 Bucureşti - Ilfov
RO41 Sud-Vest Oltenia
RO42 Vest

Slovenia

SI01 Vzhodna Slovenija
SI02 Zahodna Slovenija

Slovakia

SK01 Bratislavský kraj
SK02 Západné Slovensko
SK03 Stredné Slovensko
SK04 Východné Slovensko

Finland

FI13 Itä-Suomi
FI18 Etelä-Suomi
FI19 Länsi-Suomi
FI1A Pohjois-Suomi
FI20 Åland

Sweden

SE11 Stockholm
SE12 Östra Mellansverige
SE21 Småland med öarna
SE22 Sydsverige
SE23 Västsverige
SE31 Norra Mellansverige
SE32 Mellersta Norrland
SE33 Övre Norrland

United Kingdom

UKC1 Tees Valley and Durham
UKC2 Northumberland and Tyne and Wear
UKD1 Cumbria
UKD2 Cheshire
UKD3 Greater Manchester
UKD4 Lancashire
UKD5 Merseyside
UKE1 East Yorkshire and Northern Lincolnshire
UKE2 North Yorkshire
UKE3 South Yorkshire
UKE4 West Yorkshire
UKF1 Derbyshire and Nottinghamshire
UKF2 Leicestershire, Rutland and Northamptonshire
UKF3 Lincolnshire
UKG1 Herefordshire, Worcestershire and Warwickshire
UKG2 Shropshire and Staffordshire
UKG3 West Midlands
UKH1 East Anglia
UKH2 Bedfordshire and Hertfordshire
UKH3 Essex
UKI1 Inner London
UKI2 Outer London
UKJ1 Berkshire, Buckinghamshire and Oxfordshire
UKJ2 Surrey, East and West Sussex
UKJ3 Hampshire and Isle of Wight
UKJ4 Kent
UKK1 Gloucestershire, Wiltshire and Bristol/Bath area
UKK2 Dorset and Somerset
UKK3 Cornwall and Isles of Scilly
UKK4 Devon
UKL1 West Wales and the Valleys
UKL2 East Wales
UKM2 Eastern Scotland
UKM3 South Western Scotland
UKM5 North Eastern Scotland
UKM6 Highlands and Islands
UKN0 Northern Ireland

EFTA countries: statistical regions at level 2

Iceland

IS00	Ísland

Liechtenstein

LI00	Liechtenstein

Norway

NO01	Oslo og Akershus
NO02	Hedmark og Oppland
NO03	Sør-Østlandet
NO04	Agder og Rogaland
NO05	Vestlandet
NO06	Trøndelag
NO07	Nord-Norge

Switzerland

CH01	Région lémanique
CH02	Espace Mittelland
CH03	Nordwestschweiz
CH04	Zürich
CH05	Ostschweiz
CH06	Zentralschweiz
CH07	Ticino

Candidate countries: statistical regions at level 2

Croatia

HR01	Sjeverozapadna Hrvatska
HR02	Središnja i Istocna (Panonska) Hrvatska
HR03	Jadranska Hrvatska

The former Yugoslav Republic of Macedonia

MK00	Poranešna jugoslovenska Republika Makedonija

Turkey

TR10	Istanbul
TR21	Tekirdağ
TR22	Balikesir
TR31	Izmir
TR32	Aydin
TR33	Manisa
TR41	Bursa
TR42	Kocaeli
TR51	Ankara
TR52	Konya
TR61	Antalya
TR62	Adana
TR63	Hatay
TR71	Kirikkale
TR72	Kayseri
TR81	Zonguldak
TR82	Kastamonu
TR83	Samsun
TR90	Trabzon
TRA1	Erzurum
TRA2	Ağri
TRB1	Malatya
TRB2	Van
TRC1	Gaziantep
TRC2	Şanliurfa
TRC3	Mardin

There is currently no implementation of the NUTS classification within Montenegro.

A full listing of the classification is accessible on the Eurostat website (http://ec.europa.eu/eurostat/ramon/nomenclatures/index.cfm?TargetUrl=LST_CLS_DLD&StrNom=NUTS_33&StrLanguageCode=EN#).

NACE Rev. 1.1 (statistical classification of economic activities in the European Community)

- A Agriculture, hunting and forestry
- B Fishing
- C Mining and quarrying
- D Manufacturing
- E Electricity, gas and water supply
- F Construction
- G Wholesale and retail trade; repair of motor vehicles, motorcycles and personal and household goods
- H Hotels and restaurants
- I Transport, storage and communication
- J Financial intermediation
- K Real estate, renting and business activities
- L Public administration and defence; compulsory social security
- M Education
- N Health and social work
- O Other community, social and personal service activities
- P Activities of households
- Q Extra-territorial organisations and bodies

A full listing of the NACE Rev. 1.1 classification is accessible on the Eurostat website (http://ec.europa.eu/eurostat/ramon/nomenclatures/index.cfm?TargetUrl=LST_NOM_DTL&StrNom=NACE_1_1&StrLanguageCode=EN&IntPcKey=&StrLayoutCode=HIERARCHIC).

NACE Rev. 2 (statistical classification of economic activities in the European Community)

- A Agriculture, forestry and fishing
- B Mining and quarrying
- C Manufacturing
- D Electricity, gas, steam and air conditioning supply
- E Water supply; sewerage, waste management and remediation activities
- F Construction
- G Wholesale and retail trade; repair of motor vehicles and motorcycles
- H Transportation and storage
- I Accommodation and food service activities
- J Information and communication
- K Financial and insurance activities
- L Real estate activities
- M Professional, scientific and technical activities
- N Administrative and support service activities
- O Public administration and defence; compulsory social security
- P Education
- Q Human health and social work activities
- R Arts, entertainment and recreation
- S Other service activities
- T Activities of households as employers; undifferentiated goods- and services-producing activities of households for own use
- U Activities of extraterritorial organisations and bodies

A full listing of the NACE Rev. 2 classification is accessible on the Eurostat website (http://ec.europa.eu/eurostat/ramon/nomenclatures/index.cfm?TargetUrl=LST_NOM_DTL&StrNom=NACE_REV2&StrLanguageCode=EN).

SITC Rev. 4 (standard international trade classification)

0 Food and live animals
1 Beverages and tobacco
2 Crude materials, inedible, except fuels
3 Mineral fuels, lubricants and related materials
4 Animal and vegetable oils, fats and waxes
5 Chemicals and related products, n.e.s.
6 Manufactured goods classified chiefly by material
7 Machinery and transport equipment
8 Miscellaneous manufactured articles
9 Commodities and transactions not classified elsewhere in the SITC

A full listing of the classification is accessible on the UN website (http://unstats.un.org/unsd/trade/sitcrev4.htm).

ISCED (international standard classification of education)

The classification comprises 25 fields of education (at two-digit level) which can be further refined into three-digit level. For the purpose of this publication only, the following nine broad groups (at one-digit level) are distinguished:

0 General programmes
1 Education
2 Humanities and arts
3 Social sciences, business and law
4 Science
5 Engineering, manufacturing and construction
6 Agriculture
7 Health and welfare
8 Services

Empirically, ISCED assumes that several criteria exist which can help allocate education programmes to levels of education. The following ISCED 1997 levels can be distinguished:

0 Pre-primary education
1 Primary education (first stage of basic education)
2 Lower secondary education (second stage of basic education)
3 Upper secondary education
4 Post-secondary non-tertiary education
5 Tertiary education (first stage)
6 Tertiary education (second stage)

A full listing of the classification and more details are accessible on the UNESCO website: http://www.uis.unesco.org/ev.php?ID=3813_201&ID2=DO_TOPIC.

Statistical symbols, abbreviations and acronyms

Statistical symbols

Statistical data are often accompanied by additional information in the form of statistical symbols (also called 'flags') to indicate missing information or some other meta-data. In this yearbook, the use of statistical symbols has been restricted to a minimum. The following symbols are included where necessary:

Italic Value is a forecast, provisional or an estimate and is therefore likely to change

:	Not available, confidential or unreliable value
–	Not applicable or zero by default
0	Less than half the final digit shown and greater than real zero

Breaks in series are indicated in the footnotes provided with each table and graph.

In the case of the EU Member States, even when data are not available, these countries have been included in tables and graphs systematically (with appropriate footnotes for graphs indicating that data are not available, while in tables use has been made of the colon (:) to indicate that data are not available). For non-member countries outside the EU, when data are not available for a particular indicator the country has been removed from the table or graph in question.

Geographical aggregates and names

EU	European Union
EU-27	European Union of 27 Member States including Belgium, Bulgaria, the Czech Republic, Denmark, Germany, Estonia, Ireland, Greece, Spain, France, Italy, Cyprus, Latvia, Lithuania, Luxembourg, Hungary, Malta, the Netherlands, Austria, Poland, Portugal, Romania, Slovenia, Slovakia, Finland, Sweden and the United Kingdom. Note that unless otherwise stated, the EU aggregate in this publication refers to 27 countries, as if all 27 of these had been part of the EU in periods prior to 1 January 2007
EU-25	EU-27 other than Bulgaria and Romania (from 1 May 2004 to 31 December 2006)
EU-15	Belgium, Denmark, Germany, Ireland, Greece, Spain, France, Italy, Luxembourg, the Netherlands, Austria, Portugal, Finland, Sweden and the United Kingdom (from 1 January 1995 to 30 April 2004)
Euro area	Note that unless otherwise stated, the euro area (EA) aggregate in this publication refers to 16 countries, as if all 16 of these had been part of the EA in periods prior to 1 January 2009 Estonia joined the euro area on 1 January 2011, after this publication was drafted, and Estonia is not included in the data for the euro area presented here

EA-16 Belgium, Germany, Ireland, Greece, Spain, France, Italy, Cyprus, Luxembourg, Malta, the Netherlands, Austria, Portugal, Slovenia, Slovakia and Finland

FYR of Macedonia [1] former Yugoslav Republic of Macedonia

Other abbreviations and acronyms

AA	agricultural area
AES	adult education survey
AIDS	acquired immune deficiency syndrome or acquired immunodeficiency syndrome
Benelux	Belgium, Luxembourg and the Netherlands
bioETBE	ethyltertio-butyl-ether
bioMTBE	methyl-tertio-butyl-ether
BoP	balance of payments
BPM5	fifth balance of payments manual
CAP	common agricultural policy
CARE	EU's road accident database of accidents resulting in death and/or injury
CEPA	classification of environmental protection activities
CEPOL	European Police College
CFC	consumption of fixed capital
CFP	common fisheries policy
CH_4	methane
CHP	combined heat and power
CIF	cost, insurance and freight
CIP	competitiveness and innovation framework programme
CIS	1. Commonwealth of Independent States 2. Community innovation survey
CLRTAP	convention on long-range transboundary air pollution
CMR	carcinogenic, mutagenic and reprotoxic (chemicals)
CN	combined nomenclature
CO_2	carbon dioxide
COD	codification
COFOG	classification of the functions of government
COICOP	classification of individual consumption by purpose
COM	Communication
CPA	classification of products by activity
CPI	consumer price index
DDA	Doha Development Agenda
DMC	domestic material consumption
DMI	direct material input
DSL	digital subscriber line
EAA	economic accounts for agriculture
EAP	environment action programme
EAEC	European Atomic Energy Community (also know as Euratom)
EC	1. European Commission 2. European Community
ECB	European Central Bank
EDI	electronic data interchange
EDP	excessive deficit procedure
EEA	1. European Economic Area 2. European Environment Agency
EEAICP	European Economic Area index of consumer prices
EEC	European Economic Community
EES	European employment strategy
EFF	European Fisheries Fund

[1] The name of the former Yugoslav Republic of Macedonia is shown in tables as FYR of Macedonia – this does not prejudge in any way the definitive nomenclature for this country, which is to be agreed following the conclusion of negotiations currently taking place on this subject at the United Nations.

EFTA	European Free Trade Association
EHEA	European higher education area
EICP	European index of consumer prices
EIT	European Institute of Innovation and Technology
EITO	European Information Technology Observatory
EMU	economic and monetary union
EODS	European occupational diseases statistics
EP	European Parliament
EPER	European pollutant emission register
EPO	European Patent Office
EPC	European Patent Convention
EPI	environmental pressure indicators
EPWS	European platform of women scientists
EQF	European qualifications framework for lifelong learning
ERA	European research area
ERM	exchange rate mechanism
ERTMS	European rail traffic management system
ESA	European system of national and regional accounts (ESA 95)
ESAC	European statistical advisory committee
ESAW	European statistics on accidents at work
ESGAB	European statistical governance advisory board
ESS	European statistical system
ESSC	European statistical system committee
ESSPROS	European system of integrated social protection statistics
ESU	European size unit
eTEN	trans-European telecommunications networks
ETS	Emissions trading system *or* scheme
EU	European Union
EURES	European jobs and mobility portal
EU-SILC	European Union statistics on income and living conditions
Europol	European Police Office
EUROPOP 2008	Eurostat's 2008-based national population projections
EuroRAP	European road assessment programme
EuroTAP	European tunnel assessment programme
Eurotariff	(Regulation on) roaming charges
EUROSTAT	statistical office of the European Union
FAO	Food and Agriculture Organisation (UN)
FATS	statistics on foreign affiliates
FDI	foreign direct investment
FOB	free on board
FP7	seventh framework programme (for research and technological development)
Frontex	European agency for the management of operational cooperation at the external borders of the Member States of the EU
FSS	farm structure survey
FTE	full-time equivalents

G8	the group of eight (Germany, France, Italy, the United Kingdom, Canada, Japan, Russia, and the United States; the European Union is not a G8 nation but has all the privileges and obligations of membership except the right to host and chair a Summit)
GATS	general agreement on trade in services
GBAORD	government budget appropriation or outlays on R & D
GDP	gross domestic product
GERD	gross domestic expenditure on R & D
GFCF	gross fixed capital formation
GNI	gross national income
GOS	gross operating surplus
GPG	gender pay gap
GVA	gross value added
HBS	household budget survey
HDI	human development index
HFCE	household final consumption expenditure
HICP	harmonised index of consumer prices
HIV	human immunodeficiency virus
HLY	healthy life years
HRST	human resources in science and technology
ICD	international statistical classification of diseases and related health problems
ICHA	international classification for health accounts
ICT	information and communication technology
ILO	International Labour Organisation
IMF	International Monetary Fund
IPC	international patent classification
IPRs	intellectual property rights
IRIS	interactive coding system for causes of death
ISCED	international standard classification of education
ISCO	international standard classification of occupations
ISDN	integrated services digital network
IT	information technology
ITGS	international trade in goods statistics
ITTO	International Tropical Timber Organisation
IWT	inland waterways transport
JFSQ	joint forest sector questionnaire
JHA	justice and home affairs
JRC	Joint Research Centre
JVR	job vacancy rate
LCI	labour cost index
LCS	labour cost survey
LFS	labour force survey
LLP	lifelong learning programme
LMP	labour market policy
LUCAS	land use/cover area frame survey
MEETS	modernisation of European enterprise and trade statistics
MTO	medium-term budgetary objective
MUICP	monetary union index of consumer prices
N	north

NACE	statistical classification of economic activities within the European Community
NDP	net domestic product
n.e.s.	not elsewhere specified
NOS	net operating surplus
NPISH	non-profit institutions serving households
NUTS	hierarchical classification/ nomenclature of territorial units for statistics (Eurostat) (NUTS 1, 2 and 3)
OECD	Organisation for Economic Co-operation and Development
OEEC	Organization for European Economic Co-operation and Development
PCT	Patent Cooperation Treaty
PDA	personal digital assistant
PECBMS	pan-European common bird monitoring scheme
PEEI	principal European economic indicator
PFCs	perfluorocarbons
PLI	price level index
PPP	purchasing power parity
Prodcom	EU's industrial production statistics
PROGRESS	EU's employment and social solidarity programme
PTB	physical trade balance
R & D	research and development
REACH	(Regulation on the) registration, evaluation, authorisation and restriction of chemicals
RES	renewable energy sources
RFID	radio frequency identification
R-phrase	risk-phrase
S	south
SBS	structural business statistics
SDI	sustainable development indicator
SDR	standardised death rate
SEATS	signal extraction in ARIMA (autoregressive integrated moving average) time-series
SEC	Secretariat-General document; SEC documents are internal documents of the European Commission, typically staff working documents
SES	structure of earnings survey
SESAR	single European sky ATM (air traffic management) research programme
SET-plan	strategic energy technology plan
SET	strategic energy technology
SF6	sulphur hexafluoride
SGP	stability and growth pact
SHA	system of health accounts
SI	structural indicators
SITC	standard international trade classification
SME	small and medium-sized enterprise
SMS	short message service
SNA	system of national accounts
SPE	special purpose entities
STS	short-term (business) statistics
TAC	total allowable catch
TEEB	the economics of ecosystems and biodiversity
TEN-E	trans-European energy networks
TENs	trans-European networks

TEN-T	trans-European transport networks
TEU	EU Treaty
TFEU	Treaty on the functioning of the European Union
TRAMO	time-series regression with ARIMA noise, missing observations, and outliers
UAA	utilised agricultural area
UCI	ultimate controlling institutional unit
UIS	UNESCO institute for statistics
UN	United Nations
UNECE	United Nations economic commission for Europe
UNESCO	United Nations educational, scientific and cultural organisation
UNFCCC	United Nations framework convention on climate change
UIS	UNESCO institute for statistics
UNSCR	United Nations Security Council Resolution
UNSD	United Nations Statistical Division
UOE	United Nations/OECD/Eurostat
USPTO	United States Patent and Trademark Office
VAT	value added tax
VIS	visa information system
W	west
VET	vocational education and training
WHO	World Health Organisation
WiTEC	European association for women in science, engineering and technology
WTO	World Trade Organisation
xDSL	variations of digital subscriber line

Units of measurement

%	per cent
AWU	annual work unit
BMI	body mass index
CHF	Swiss franc
cm^3	cubic centimetre
CO_2 equivalent	carbon dioxide equivalent
ESU	economic size unit
EUR	euro
FTE	full-time equivalent
GJ	gigajoule
GRT	gross registered tonnage
GT	gross tonnage
GWh	gigawatt-hour
ha	hectare (1 ha = 10 000 m^2)
HC	head count
JPY	Japanese yen
kbit/s	kilobit per second
kg	kilogram
kgoe	kilogram of oil equivalent
km	kilometre
km^2	square kilometre
km/h	kilometre per hour
kW	kilowatt
kWh	kilowatt hour
l	litre
LU or LSU	livestock unit
m	metre
mm	millimetre
m^2	square metre
m^3	cubic metre
MWh	megawatt-hour
p/st	piece/unit
pkm	passenger-kilometre
PPS	purchasing power standard
t	tonne
tkm	tonne-kilometre
toe	tonne of oil equivalent
TWh	terawatt hour
USD	United States dollar

Glossary

Accident at work

An **accident at work** is a discrete occurrence during the course of work which leads to physical or mental harm. The phrase 'in the course of work' means whilst engaged in an occupational activity or during the time spent at work. This includes cases of road traffic accidents in the course of work but excludes accidents during the journey between home and the workplace.

Adult education survey (AES)

The **adult education survey**, abbreviated as **AES**, is a survey carried out by 29 European Union (EU), EFTA and candidate countries between 2005-2008, collecting information on education and lifelong learning activities by individuals aged 25-64 living in private households. The AES, which uses 2007 as a reference year, was a pilot exercise, and there are plans to conduct additional surveys every 5 years. The survey allows for international comparisons of education, occupation and economic activity.

Agricultural area (AA)

Agricultural area, abbreviated to **AA**, (or **utilised agricultural area**, abbreviated to **UAA**) describes the area used for farming. It includes the land categories: arable land; permanent grassland; permanent crops; other agricultural land such as kitchen gardens (even if they only represent small areas of total UAA).

The term does not include unused agricultural land, woodland and land occupied for example by buildings, farmyards, tracks or ponds.

Agricultural holding

An **agricultural holding** is a single unit, in both technical and economic terms, operating under a single management, which produces agricultural products. Other supplementary (non-agricultural) products and services may also be provided by the holding.

Agricultural income

The main indicator for **agricultural income** is the factor income per labour input expressed in annual work units (AWU).

Animal output

Animal output comprises the sales, changes in stock levels, and the products used for processing and own final use by the producers.

Annual work unit (AWU)

One **annual work unit**, abbreviated as **AWU**, corresponds to the work performed by one person who is occupied on an agricultural holding on a full-time basis. Full-time means the minimum

hours required by the relevant national provisions governing contracts of employment. If the national provisions do not indicate the number of hours, then 1 800 hours are taken to be the minimum annual working hours: equivalent to 225 working days of eight hours each.

Aquaculture

Aquaculture, also known as **aquafarming**, refers to the farming of aquatic (freshwater or saltwater) organisms, such as fish, molluscs, crustaceans and plants for human use or consumption, under controlled conditions. Aquaculture implies some form of intervention in the natural rearing process to enhance production, including regular stocking, feeding and protection from predators. Farming also implies individual or corporate ownership of, or contractual rights to, the stock being cultivated.

Arable land

Arable land, in agricultural statistics, is land worked (ploughed or tilled) regularly, generally under a system of crop rotation.

Asset

Assets are economic resources that have some value or usefulness (usually convertible in cash) and that are owned by enterprises or individuals, for example a piece of machinery or a house. According to the International Accounting Standards Board, assets are a result of past events and are expected to provide future economic benefits.

In the context of national accounts, economic assets can be defined as entities functioning as stores of value and over which ownership rights are enforced by institutional units, individually or collectively, and from which economic benefits may be derived by their owners by holding them, or using them, over a period of time (the economic benefits consist of primary incomes derived from the use of the asset and the value, including possible holding gains/losses, that could be realised by disposing of the asset or terminating it).

At-risk-of-poverty rate

The **at-risk-of-poverty rate** is the share of persons with an equivalised disposable income (after social transfers) below the **at-risk-of-poverty threshold**, which is set at 60 % of the national median equivalised disposable income after social transfers. This indicator does not measure wealth or poverty, but low income in comparison to other residents in that country, which does not necessarily imply a low standard of living.

The **at-risk-of-poverty rate before social transfers** is calculated as the share of persons having an equivalised disposable income before social transfers that is below the at-risk-of-poverty threshold calculated after social transfers. Pensions, such as old-age and survivors' (widows' and widowers') benefits, are counted as income (before social transfers) and not as social transfers. This indicator examines the hypothetical non-existence of social transfers.

The **persistent at-risk-of-poverty rate** shows the percentage of the population living in households where the equivalised disposable income was below the at-risk-of-poverty threshold for the current year and at least two out of the preceding three years. Its calculation requires a longitudinal instrument, through which the individuals are followed over four years.

Balance of payments

The **balance of payments** is a statistical summary of the transactions of a given economy with the rest of the world. It comprises three elements:

- the **current account** covers international transactions in goods, services, income, and current transfers;
- the **financial account** deals with transactions involving financial claims on, or liabilities to, the rest of the world, including international purchases of securities, such as stocks and bonds;
- the **capital account** covers international capital transfers (for example debt forgiveness) and the acquisition/disposal of non-produced, non-financial assets (such as patents).

Baseline study

A **baseline study** is an analysis of the current situation to identify the starting points for a programme or project. It looks at what information must be considered and analysed to establish a **baseline** or starting point, the benchmark against which future progress can be assessed or comparisons made.

Bed places

The number of **bed places** in an establishment or dwelling is determined by the number of persons who can stay overnight in beds set up in that establishment, ignoring any extra beds that may be set up following a specific customer request. The term 'bed place' applies to a single bed. A double bed is counted as two bed places. This unit serves to measure the capacity of any type of accommodation. A bed place is also defined to cover a pitch or, in a boat, a mooring that can accommodate one person. A pitch for a tent (if counted), caravan, mobile home and similar shelter, or a boat on a mooring, is usually counted as four bed places if the actual number is not known.

Biodiversity

Biodiversity, a contraction of biological diversity, refers to the number, variety and variability of living organisms, including mankind, within a given area. A reduction or loss of biodiversity undermines not only the natural environment, but also the economic and social goals of human societies, as mankind depends on natural resources for the food, energy, raw materials, clean air and clean water making life possible. The importance of preserving biodiversity, and the possible consequences of not doing so, has made it an international issue.

Biofuels

Biofuels are liquid fuels from a non-fossil biological origin and a renewable energy source, to be distinguished from fossil fuels. Biofuels can be split up into two categories, biogasoline and biodiesel.

Biomass

Biomass is organic, non-fossil material of biological origin that can be used for heat production or electricity generation. It includes: wood and wood waste; biogas; municipal solid waste; biofuels.

Births

A **birth** is defined as the start of life when a child emerges from the body of its mother. The total number of births includes both live births and stillbirths.

Live births are defined as the birth of children who showed any sign of life; they refer to the number of births excluding stillbirths.

Stillbirths are defined as the expulsion or extraction from the mother of a dead foetus after the time at which it would normally be presumed capable of independent extra-uterine existence (outside the uterus or womb). This is commonly taken to be after 24 or 28 weeks of **gestation** (the time from a child's conception to its birth).

Live births outside marriage are defined as births where the mother's marital status at the time of birth is other than married.

The **crude birth rate** is the ratio of the number of births during the year to the average population in that year; the value is expressed per 1 000 inhabitants.

Broadband

Broadband refers to telecommunications in which a wide band of frequencies is available to send data. Broadband telecommunication lines or connections are defined as those transporting data at high speeds, with a speed of data transfer for uploading and downloading data (also called capacity) equal to or higher than 144 kbit/s (kilobits per second or kbps).

The technologies most widely used for broadband Internet access are digital subscriber line (DSL) and its variations (xDSL), or cable modem (connects a computer to a local television line).

Budget deficit

A **budget deficit** occurs when a government's spending is greater than its revenues.

In the European Union, Member States which are part of the euro area are required to keep their budget deficits below 3 % of gross domestic product to promote economic stability and sustainable public finances.

Bunkers

Bunkers include all dutiable petroleum products loaded aboard a vessel for consumption by that vessel.

International maritime bunkers describe the quantities of fuel oil delivered to ships of all flags that are engaged in international navigation. It is the fuel used to power these ships. International navigation may take place at sea, on inland lakes and waterways, and in coastal waters.

International maritime bunkers do not include fuel oil consumption by:

- ships engaged in domestic navigation; whether a vessel is engaged in domestic or international navigation is determined only by the ship's port of departure and port of arrival - not by the flag or nationality of the ship;
- fishing vessels;
- military forces.

Business cycle

A **business cycle** describes the expansions and contractions of economic activity in an economy over a period of time.

The economy considered may be a country, or a geographical aggregate such as the euro area or the European Union. The development of economic activity is expressed as a percentage change of an economic indicator, for example production, hours worked, employment, gross domestic product. The business cycle is usually represented in a graph showing the ups and downs of the economy over time.

Business investment rate

The **business investment rate** is defined as gross investment (fixed capital formation) divided by gross value added.

Carcass weight

The definition of **carcass weight** depends on the animal species under consideration.

For pigs it is the weight of the slaughtered pig's cold body, either whole or divided in half along the mid-line, after being bled and eviscerated and after removal of the tongue, bristles, hooves, genitalia, flare fat, kidneys and diaphragm.

For cattle it is the weight of the slaughtered animal's cold body after being skinned, bled and eviscerated, and after removal of the external genitalia, the limbs, the head, the tail, the kidneys and kidney fats, and the udder.

For sheep and goats it is the weight of the slaughtered animal's cold body after having been bled, skinned and eviscerated, and after removal of the head, feet, tail and genital organs. Kidneys and kidney fats are included in the carcass weight.

For poultry it is the weight of the cold body of the slaughtered farmyard poultry after being bled, plucked and eviscerated. The weight includes poultry offal, with the exception of *foie gras*.

For other species, the carcass weight is considered to be the weight of the slaughtered animal's cold body.

Carcinogenic, mutagenic and reprotoxic (CMR)

Carcinogenic, mutagenic and reprotoxic chemicals, abbreviated as **CMR** chemicals, make up the first and most toxic category of the toxicity classes into which hazardous chemicals can be subdivided, according to EU legislation.

Carcinogenic chemicals can cause or promote cancers. Mutagenic chemicals can cause genetic mutations. Reprotoxic chemicals can damage the reproductive process.

Cattle

Cattle or **bovines** refers to domestic animals of the species *Bos taurus* or *Bubalus bubalis*, including hybrids like *Beefalo*.

A distinction can be made by the age of the animal (less than one year old, aged between one and two years, and two years and over), with a further division between male and female bovines. Female bovines aged two years and over are divided into **heifers** (female bovines that have not yet calved) and cows. The latter are further divided into dairy cows and others.

Central government

Central government consists of all administrative departments of the state and other central agencies whose responsibilities cover the whole economic territory of a country, except for the administration of social security funds.

Cereal

Cereal includes wheat (common wheat and spelt and durum wheat), rye, maslin, barley, oats, mixed grain other than maslin, grain maize, sorghum, triticale, and other cereal crops such as buckwheat, millet, canary seed and rice.

Classification of territorial units for statistics (NUTS)

The **classification of territorial units for statistics**, abbreviated as **NUTS** (from the French *Nomenclature des Unités territoriales statistiques*) is a geographical classification subdividing the territory of the European Union (EU) into regions at three different levels (NUTS 1, 2 and 3, respectively, moving from larger to smaller territorial units). Above NUTS 1 is the 'national' level of the Member State.

Classification of individual consumption by purpose (COICOP)

The **classification of individual consumption by purpose**, abbreviated as **COICOP**, is a classification developed by the United Nations Statistics Division to classify and analyse individual consumption expenditures incurred by households, non-profit institutions serving households and general government according to their purpose. It includes categories such as clothing and footwear, housing, water, electricity, and gas and other fuels.

Classification of the functions of government (COFOG)

The **classification of the functions of government**, abbreviated as **COFOG**, was developed in its current version in 1999 by the Organisation for Economic Co-operation and Development and published by the United Nations Statistical Division as a standard classifying the purposes of government activities.

The classification has three levels of detail: divisions; groups; classes.

Divisions describe the broad objectives of government, while groups and classes both define the means by which these broad objectives are achieved.

Co-generation

Co-generation, also known as **combined heat and power** (**CHP**), describes the simultaneous production of both useful heat (that can be used, for example, in industrial processes or district heating schemes) and electricity in a single process or unit. Co-generation enables much greater plant efficiencies to be obtained in terms of energy conversion with overall efficiencies as high as 80 %-90 %. The energy savings potential of co-generation is important with regard to reducing emissions and improving energy efficiency.

COICOP/HICP

The **COICOP/HICP** is the United Nations classification of individual consumption by purpose, adapted to the compilation of the harmonised index of consumer prices of the European Union and the euro area. Adapting COICOP to the HICP calculation involved a number of changes:

- some sub-indices of the COICOP, such as narcotics and owner-occupied housing, had to be excluded because they are not within the HICP coverage;
- certain sub-classes (those with 4 digits) have been combined to ensure their weight was above one part per thousand in most of the Member States.

Collective tourist accommodation

A **collective tourist accommodation** establishment provides overnight lodging for the traveller in a room or some other unit, but the number of places it provides must be greater than a specified minimum for groups of persons exceeding a single family unit and all the places in the establishment must come under a common commercial-type management, even if it is non-profit-making.

Combined nomenclature (CN)

The **combined nomenclature**, abbreviated as **CN**, is a classification of goods, designed to meet the needs of:

- the Common customs tariff (setting import duties for products imported into the European Union and the Integrated tariff of the European Communities (Taric), incorporating all European Union and trade measures applied to goods imported into and exported out of the EU;
- the external trade statistics of the EU.

The CN provides the means of collecting, exchanging and publishing data on EU external trade statistics. It is also used for the collection and publication of external trade statistics in intra-EU trade.

Commodity

A **commodity**, also called **primary good** or **primary product**, is a good sold for production or consumption as it was found in nature or in a standardised form. Commodities include crude oil, coal, copper or iron ore, rough diamonds, and agricultural products such as wheat, coffee beans or cotton; they are often traded on commodity exchanges.

The Standard international trade classification (SITC) distinguishes five main

categories (sections) of commodities or primary goods:

- Food and live animals (SITC Section 0);
- Beverages and tobacco (SITC Section 1);
- Crude materials, excluding fuels (SITC Section 2);
- Mineral fuels (SITC Section 3);
- Animal and vegetable oils, fats and waxes (SITC Section 4).

Sections 0 and 1 can be grouped together as 'food and drink', 2 and 4 as '**raw materials**'.

Community innovation survey (CIS)

The **Community innovation survey**, abbreviated as **CIS**, is conducted in every European Union Member State to collect data on innovation activities in enterprises, in other words on product innovation (goods or services) and process innovation (organisational and marketing).

The CIS is based on the Eurostat/OECD Oslo Manual 1997. The legal basis for CIS is Commission Regulation (EC) 1450/2004 of 13 August 2004 carrying out Decision No 1608/2003/EC of the European Parliament and of the Council on the production and development of Community statistics on innovation.

Community survey on ICT usage in enterprises

The **Community survey on ICT usage and e-commerce in enterprises** collects data on the use of information and communication technology, the Internet, e-government and e-commerce in enterprises.

Community survey on ICT usage in households and by individuals

The **Community survey on ICT usage in households and by individuals** collects data on the use of information and communication technologies (ICT), the Internet, e-government and electronic skills in households and by individuals.

Comparative price level

Comparative price levels are defined as the ratios of purchasing power parities (PPPs) to market exchange rates in each country. They give a measure of the difference in cross-border price levels by indicating for a given product the number of units of the common currency needed to buy the same volume of the product group in each country.

Competitiveness

Competitiveness is a measure of the comparative advantage or disadvantage of enterprises, industries, regions, countries or supranational economies like the European Union in selling its products in international markets. It refers to the ability to generate relatively high income and employment levels on a sustainable basis while competing internationally.

Computer

A **computer**, in the surveys on ICT usage in enterprises and households, is defined as a personal computer powered by one of

the major operating systems (Macintosh, Linux or Microsoft); handheld computers or palmtops (PDAs) are also included.

Consumer price index (CPI)

The **consumer price index**, abbreviated as CPI, measures the change over time in the prices of consumer goods and services acquired, used or paid for by households. It is an important measure of inflation in the European Union.

Convergence criteria

The **convergence criteria**, sometimes also called **Maastricht criteria**, are conditions that Member States of the European Union must fulfil to join the economic and monetary union and to use the euro as their official currency. There are four conditions, all aimed at increasing convergence of EMU participants:

- **price stability**: Member States should have a price performance that is sustainable and an average rate of inflation that does not exceed by more than 1.5 percentage points that of the three best-performing Member States in terms of price stability for a period of one year before the examination;
- **government budgetary position**: Member States are to avoid situations of excessive government deficits, that is their ratio of planned or actual government deficit to gross domestic product should be no more than 3 %, and their ratio of (general) government debt to GDP should be no more than 60 %, unless the excess over the reference value is only exceptional or temporary or the ratios have declined substantially and continuously;
- **exchange rates**: Member States should have respected the normal fluctuation margins of the exchange rate mechanism without severe tensions for at least the two years before the examination. In particular, the Member State shall not have devalued its currency's bilateral central rate against any other Member State's currency on its own initiative over the same period;
- **long-term interest rates**: Member States should have had an average nominal long-term interest rate over a period of one year before the examination that does not exceed by more than 2 percentage points that of the three best-performing Member States in terms of price stability.

Cow

A **cow** is a female bovine that has calved (including any aged less than 2 years). A **dairy cow** is a cow kept exclusively or principally for the production of milk for human consumption and/or other dairy produce, including cows for slaughter (whether fattened or not between last lactation and slaughter).

Credit

Credit is an amount for which there is a specific obligation of repayment. Credits include loans, trade credits, bonds, bills and other agreements that give rise to specific obligations to repay over a period of time usually, but not always, with interest. Credit is extended to finance consumption and investment expenditures, and financial transactions.

Crop output

Crop output comprises sales, changes in stock levels, and crop products used as animal feedstuffs, or for processing and own final use by the producers.

Deaths

A **death**, according to the United Nations definition, is the permanent disappearance of all vital functions without possibility of resuscitation at any time after a live birth has taken place; this definition therefore excludes foetal deaths (stillbirths).

The **crude death rate** represents the ratio of the number of deaths during the year to the average population in that year. The value is expressed per 1 000 inhabitants.

The **infant mortality rate** represents the ratio of the number of deaths of children under one year of age to the number of live births in the reference year. The value is expressed per 1 000 live births.

Debit

A **debit** is the opposite to a **credit** and is an expression of a debt owed in the form of a loan that must be repaid, trade credits, bonds, bills and other agreements that give rise to specific obligations to repay over a period of time usually, but not always, with interest.

Deficit

Deficit means in general that the sum or balance of positive and negative amounts is negative, or that the total of negatives is larger than the total of positives.

Deficit can be used in different statistical areas:

- in balance of payments statistics, it refers to the balance of credit (negative) and debit (positive) transactions of a given economy with the rest of the world, organised in two different accounts: the current account; and the capital and financial account;
- in external trade statistics, it refers to the trade balance of imports (negative, as they have to be paid for) and exports (positive, because they yield revenue), which may result in a trade deficit.
- in government finances statistics, it refers to the public balance between government revenue and expenditure, a budget deficit when negative, and the resulting government debt, in the case of cumulated deficits.

Deflator

A **deflator** is a figure expressing the change in prices over a period of time for a product or a basket of products, which is used to deflate a measure of value changes for the same period (for example the sales or new orders of the product or basket of products), thus removing the price increases or decreases and leaving only volume changes.

A deflator can be expressed either as an indicator or a percentage change.

Dial-up

A **dial-up** Internet connection provides access to the Internet using a modem over a normal or an Integrated services digital network (ISDN) telephone line. Due to its limited bandwidth, it is often called **narrow band**.

Digital literacy

Digital literacy refers to the skills required to achieve digital competence, the confident and critical use of ICT for work, leisure, learning and communication.

Digital subscriber line (DSL)

Digital subscriber line, abbreviated as **DSL**, is a family of technologies that allows for digital data transmission over the wires of a local telephone network. DSL can be used at the same time and on the same telephone line as normal telephone calls since DSL operates at high-frequency bands while the telephone call uses low frequencies. The most common form of DSL technology is **ADSL**, or **asymmetric digital subscriber line**, where the bandwidth used in either direction is different.

Direct material input (DMI)

Direct material input, abbreviated as **DMI**, measures the direct input of materials for use in an economy, in other words, all materials which are of economic value and are used in production and consumption activities (excluding water flows). DMI can be calculated as domestic (used) extraction plus imports. The relation of domestic material consumption (DMC) to DMI indicates to what extent inputs of material resources are used for own domestic consumption or are exported to be consumed in other economies.

Discharge

A **discharge** from hospital is the formal release of a patient from a hospital after a procedure or course of treatment. A discharge occurs whenever a patient leaves hospital upon completion of treatment, signing out against medical advice, transferring to another healthcare institution, or on death. A discharge includes inpatients or day cases and healthy newborn babies should also be included. Discharges should exclude transfers to another department within the same institution.

Distributive trade

Distributive trades refer to the wholesale and retail trades and the repair of motor vehicles and motorcycles (NACE Rev. 2 Section G).

Divorces

A **divorce** is defined as the final legal dissolution (ending) of a marriage. A divorce is the type of separation of husband and wife that confers on the parties the right to remarry under civil, religious or other provisions, according to the laws of each country. Divorce is possible in all European Union Member States, except Malta. In almost all countries, divorces are registered at a court.

The **crude divorce rate** is the ratio of the number of divorces during the year to the average population in that year. The value is expressed per 1 000 inhabitants.

Domestic extraction used

Domestic extraction used, abbreviated as DEU, is the input from the natural environment to be used in the economy. DEU is the annual amount of raw material

(except for water and air) extracted from the natural environment.

Domestic material consumption (DMC)

Domestic material consumption, abbreviated as **DMC**, measures the total amount of materials directly used by an economy and is defined as the annual quantity of raw materials extracted from the domestic territory, plus all physical imports minus all physical exports.

Dwelling

A **dwelling** is a room or suite of rooms - including its accessories, lobbies and corridors - in a permanent building or a structurally separated part thereof which, by the way it has been built, rebuilt or converted, is designed for habitation by one private household all year round. A dwelling can be either a one-family dwelling in a stand-alone building or detached edifice, or an apartment in a block of flats. Dwellings include garages for residential use, even when apart from the habitation or belonging to different owners.

Early leavers from education and training

Early leavers from education and training (previously named 'early school leavers') refers to the percentage of the population aged 18 to 24 who have received no more than a secondary education and are not engaged in further education or training.

Earnings

Earnings are the wage or salary paid to an employee. There are two main types:

- **Gross earnings** are paid in cash directly to an employee before any deductions for income tax and social security contributions paid by the employee. All bonuses, whether or not regularly paid, are included (for example 13th or 14th month, holiday bonuses, profit-sharing, allowances for leave not taken, and occasional commissions).
- **Net earnings** represent the part of remuneration that employees can actually spend and are calculated by deducting social security contributions and income taxes payable by employees from gross earnings and by adding family allowances if there are children in the family.

E-commerce

E-commerce can be defined generally as the sale or purchase of goods or services, whether between businesses, households, individuals or private organisations, through electronic transactions conducted via the Internet or other computer-mediated (online communication) networks.

The term covers the ordering of goods and services which are sent over computer networks, but the payment and the ultimate delivery of the goods or service may be conducted either on- or off-line.

For the Community survey on ICT usage in households and by individuals, e-commerce by individuals or households via the Internet is defined more specifically as the placing of orders for goods or services via the Internet. Also included in the definition are: buying financial investments - such as shares; confirming reservations for accommodation and travel; participating in lotteries and betting; paying for information services from the Internet; buying via online auctions.

Orders via manually typed e-mails, however, are excluded.

For the Community survey on ICT usage and e-commerce in enterprises, e-commerce is defined more specifically as purchasing or selling goods and services over computer networks. It comprises orders made in web pages, extranet or EDI and excludes orders made by a phone call, facsimile, or manually typed e-mail. The indicator on enterprises having received orders or made purchases on-line covers enterprises purchasing/selling on-line for at least 1 % of total purchases/turnover.

Delivery or payment via electronic means is not a requirement for an e-commerce transaction.

Economic accounts for agriculture (EAA)

The **economic accounts for agriculture**, abbreviated as EAA, are a satellite account of the European system of national and regional accounts, adapted to the specific nature of the agricultural industry, providing complementary information and concepts. Although the structure of EAA matches very closely that of national accounts, their compilation requires the formulation of appropriate rules and methods.

The EAA analyse the production processes of the agricultural industry and the primary income generated by these activities. The accounts are therefore based on the industry concept. The agricultural industry, as described in the EAA, corresponds to Division 01 in NACE Rev. 1, namely agriculture, hunting and related service activities.

The EAA measure the total output of the agricultural activity which includes: output sold (including trade in agricultural goods and services between agricultural units); changes in stocks; output for own final consumption and own-account gross-fixed capital formation; output produced for further processing by other agricultural producers; intra-unit consumption of livestock feed products.

The agricultural industry's output equals the sum of the output of agricultural products plus goods and services produced in non-agricultural secondary activities.

Education

Broadly speaking, **education** refers to any act or experience that has a formative effect on an individual's mind, character, or physical ability.

In its technical sense, **education** is the formal process by which society, through schools, colleges, universities and other institutions, deliberately transmits its cultural heritage and its accumulated knowledge, values and skills to the next generation.

E-government

E-government refers to the use of information and communication technology

in public administration procedures. One aspect of e-government, on its demand side, concerns the interaction of individuals or enterprises with public administrations through ICT.

For both individuals and enterprises this interaction can consist of: obtaining information; downloading forms; returning filled-in forms; going through an administrative procedure completely electronically.

For enterprises, in addition, it can also involve submitting a proposal in an electronic tender system.

E-learning

E-learning, or **electronic learning**, also referred to as **web-based learning**, encompasses a broad range of knowledge transferred through digital technologies, sometimes as a complement to traditional education channels. The use of information and communication technology (ICT) tools is especially powerful for reaching individuals with no access to traditional education and training, either because they live in remote areas or because of their socioeconomic situation or special needs.

Emissions trading system

An **emissions trading system**, abbreviated as ETS, is a market mechanism that allows those bodies (such as countries, companies or manufacturing plants) which release greenhouse gases into the atmosphere (emissions) to buy and sell these emissions (as permits or allowances) amongst themselves.

Emissions mean the release of greenhouse gases and/or their precursors into the atmosphere over a set area and period of time. The European Union emissions trading system (EU ETS) is based on the idea that creating a price for carbon offers the most cost-effective way to achieve the significant cuts in global greenhouse gas emissions that are needed to prevent climate change from reaching dangerous levels.

Employee

An **employee** is a person who has a contract to carry out work for an employer and receives compensation in the form of wages, salaries, fees, gratuities, piecework pay or remuneration in kind.

Employee - LFS

The labour force survey defines an **employee** as an individual who works for a public or private employer and who in return receives compensation in the form of wages, salaries, fees, gratuities, payment by results or payment in kind. Professional military staff are also included.

Employment

Employment is defined as the number of persons engaged in productive activities in an economy. The concept includes both employees and the self-employed. The two main measures used for employment are the number of persons employed or the number of employees.

More complex measures of employment are sometimes produced by measuring the number of hours worked or by converting the number of hours into full-time equivalent units. In addition, some particular categories of employment are measured, such as part-time employment, female employment, self-employment, apprenticeships, homeworkers and unpaid employment (unpaid family workers and working proprietors).

Employment rate

The **employment rate** is the percentage of employed persons in relation to the comparable total population. For the overall employment rate, the comparison is made with the population of working-age; but employment rates can also be calculated for a particular age group and/or gender in a specific geographical area (for example the males of age 15-24 employed versus total in one European Union Member State).

Energy dependency rate

The **energy dependency rate** shows the proportion of energy that an economy must import. It is defined as net energy imports divided by gross inland energy consumption plus fuel supplied to international maritime bunkers, expressed as a percentage. A negative dependency rate indicates a net exporter of energy while a dependency rate in excess of 100 % indicates that energy products have been stocked.

Energy intensity

Energy intensity measures the energy consumption of an economy relative to its output, and gives an indication of its energy efficiency. It is the ratio between gross inland consumption of energy and gross domestic product (GDP).

Enterprise

The **enterprise** is the smallest combination of legal units that is an organisational unit producing goods or services, which benefits from a certain degree of autonomy in decision-making, especially for the allocation of its current resources. An enterprise carries out one or more activities at one or more locations. An enterprise may be a sole legal unit.

Entrepreneurial income account

The purpose of the **entrepreneurial income account** is to determine a balancing item corresponding to the concept of current profit before distribution and income tax, as normally used in business accounting. Entrepreneurial income corresponds to the operating surplus or mixed income (on the resources side): plus property income receivable in connection with financial and other assets belonging to the enterprise (on the resources side); minus interest on debts payable by the enterprise and rents payable on land and other non-produced tangible assets rented by the enterprise (on the uses side). Property income payable in the form of dividends or reinvested earnings on direct foreign investment is not deducted from entrepreneurial income.

Equivalised disposable income

The **equivalised disposable income** is the total income of a household, after tax and other deductions, that is available for spending or saving, divided by the number of household members converted into equivalent adults; household

members are made equivalent by weighting each according to their age, using the so-called modified OECD equivalence scale.

EU statistics on income and living conditions (EU-SILC)

The **EU statistics on income and living conditions**, abbreviated as **EU-SILC**, is the reference source for comparative statistics on income distribution and social inclusion in the European Union (EU). It is used for policy monitoring within the open method of coordination (OMC).

European size unit (ESU)

European size unit, abbreviated as **ESU**, is a standard gross margin of EUR 1 200 that is used to express the economic size of an agricultural holding or farm.

For each activity (or enterprise) on a farm (for example wheat production, dairy cows or the output from a vineyard), the standard gross margin (SGM) is estimated based on the area used for the particular activity (or the number of heads of livestock) and a regional coefficient. The sum of all such margins derived from activities on a particular farm is its **economic size**, which is then expressed in European size units (by dividing the total SGM in euro by 1 200).

European system of integrated social protection statistics (ESSPROS)

The **European system of integrated social protection statistics**, abbreviated as **ESSPROS**, is a common framework developed in the late 1970's by Eurostat and the European Union Member States providing a coherent comparison between European countries of social benefits to households and their financing, thus making an international comparison of the administrative national data on social protection possible.

ESSPROS is built on the concept of social protection, or the coverage of precisely defined risks and needs including health, disability, old age, family and unemployment; it records the receipts and the expenditure of the organisations or schemes involved in social protection interventions.

ESSPROS is composed of the *core system* and of *modules*. The core system contains annual data (collected by Eurostat from 1990 on):

- quantitative data: social protection receipts and expenditures by schemes (a distinct body of rules, supported by one or more institutional units, governing the provision of social protection benefits and their financing).
- qualitative data: metadata by scheme and detailed benefit.

Social protection benefits are transfers to households, in cash or in kind, intended to relieve them from the financial burden of a number of risks or needs. The risks or needs of social protection included in ESSPROS are disability, sickness/healthcare, old age, survivors, family/children, unemployment, housing and social exclusion not elsewhere classified.

The modules contain supplementary statistical information on particular aspects of social protection: they relate to pensions' beneficiaries and to net social benefits.

European system of national and regional accounts (ESA95)

The **European system of national and regional accounts**, abbreviated as **ESA95** or sometimes **1995 ESA**, collects comparable, up-to-date and reliable information on the structure and developments of the economy of the Member States of the European Union and their respective regions. By providing an internationally compatible accounting framework, ESA95 makes it possible to describe the total economy of a region, country or group of countries, its components and its relation to other total economies.

The ESA95 prescribes the structure and layout of supply and use tables, symmetric input-output tables and tables linking supply and use tables to the sector accounts. These requirements refer to definitions of transactions and to concepts of classification and valuation.

ESA95 is broadly consistent with the system of national accounts of the United Nations (1993 SNA) with regards to definitions, accounting rules and classifications. But due to greater accuracy requirements for definitions and the accounting rules, it also has some specificities, particularly in its presentation, which are more in line with EU practices.

Excessive deficit procedure (EDP)

The **excessive deficit procedure**, abbreviated as **EDP**, is an action launched by the European Commission against any European Union Member State that exceeds the budgetary deficit ceiling imposed by the EU's Stability and growth pact legislation. The procedure entails several steps, potentially culminating in sanctions, to encourage a Member State to get its budget deficit under control, a requirement for the smooth functioning of economic and monetary union.

According to the Protocol on the Excessive deficit procedure, annexed to the Maastricht Treaty on economic and monetary union, Member States in the euro area and euro area candidate countries must demonstrate sound public finances. There are two criteria:

- the budget deficit must not exceed 3 % of gross domestic product;
- public debt must not exceed 60 % of GDP.

Exchange rate

The exchange rate is the price of one currency in relation to another.

Exchange rates are classified by the International Monetary Fund (IMF) into three broad categories, reflecting the role of the authorities in determining the exchange rates and/or the multiplicity of exchange rates in a country:

1. the **market rate** is used to describe exchange rates set largely by market forces;
2. the **official rate** is used to describe the exchange rate determined by authorities;
3. for countries maintaining multiple exchange arrangements, the rates may be labelled **principle rate**, **secondary rate** and **tertiary rate.**

A **nominal effective exchange rate** is the exchange rate of the domestic currency vis-à-vis (as compared with) other currencies weighted by their share in either the country's international trade or payments.

Real effective exchange rates take account of price level differences between trading partners. Movements in real effective exchange rates give an indication of the development of a country's aggregate (total) external price competitiveness.

Expenditure approach

The **expenditure approach** of GDP is defined as private final consumption expenditure + government final consumption expenditure + gross capital formation + exports - imports.

In the system of national accounts, only households, NPISH and government have final consumption, whereas corporations have intermediate consumption. Private final consumption expenditure is defined as expenditure on goods and services for the direct satisfaction of individual needs, whereas government consumption expenditure includes goods and services produced by government, as well as purchases of goods and services by government that are supplied to households as social transfers in kind. Gross capital formation is the sum of gross fixed capital formation and the change in inventories (stocks). The external balance is the difference between exports and imports of goods and services. Depending on the size of exports and imports, it can be positive (a surplus) or negative (a deficit).

Expenditure on pensions

Expenditure on pensions comprises the following social benefits: disability pension, early retirement due to reduced capacity to work, old-age pension, anticipated old-age pension, partial pension, survivors' pension and early retirement due for labour market reasons.

Exports - national accounts

Extra-EU exports of goods are goods which leave the statistical territory of the European Union for a non-member country after being placed under the customs procedure for exports (for definitive export) or outward processing (goods for working, further processing) or repair or following inward processing. **Intra-EU exports of goods** are goods which leave a Member State of the EU for another Member State for definitive export, outward processing or repair or following inward processing.

In **national accounts** exports consist of transactions in goods and services (sales, barter, gifts or grants) from residents to non-residents:

- An export of a good occurs when there is a change of ownership from a resident to a non-resident; this does not necessarily imply that the good in question physically crosses the frontier. If goods cross the border due to *financial leasing*, as *deliveries between affiliates of the same enterprise* or for *significant processing to order or repair* national accounts impute a change of ownership even though in legal terms no change of ownership takes place. According to the European system of accounts (ESA95) also smuggled goods must be included in exports.

- Exports of services consist of all services rendered by residents to non-residents. In national accounts any direct purchases by non-residents in the economic territory of a country are recorded as exports of services; therefore all expenditure by foreign tourists in the economic territory of a country is considered as part of the exports of services of that country. Also international flows of illegal services must be included.

Analogously, the national accounts' transactions in goods and services from non-residents to residents are **imports**.

Extensive farming

Extensive farming, the opposite of intensive farming, is characterised by a low use of capital and labour (for example fertilisers, pesticides, machinery) relative to land area. The crop yields per unit of land are lower than in intensive agriculture.

Extensive farming in general is more beneficial to the environment. Due to a lower use of fertilisers and pesticides, the risks of nutrient and pesticide run-off into surface and groundwater are lower. However, the actual effect of the use of inputs on the environment is not only depending on the amount of inputs used, but also on how they are applied. Inputs like fertilisers are also needed to sustain soil fertility, when crops are harvested. Too little use of fertilisers may therefore also lead to environmental degradation.

External inflow

External inflow is the volume of water flowing into rivers and groundwater that originates in neighbouring territories.

Farm structure survey (FSS)

The basic **farm structure survey**, abbreviated as **FSS**, also known as **survey on the structure of agricultural holdings** is carried out by all European Union Member States every 10 years (the full scope being the agricultural census) with intermediate sample surveys being carried out three times between the basic surveys.

The Member States collect information from individual agricultural holdings and, observing strict rules of confidentiality, data are forwarded to Eurostat. The information collected in the FSS covers land use, livestock numbers, rural development, management and farm labour input (including the age, gender and relationship to the holder of the agricultural holding). The survey data can then be aggregated by different geographic levels (Member States, regions, and for basic surveys also district level). The data can also be arranged by size class, area status, legal status of the holding, objective zone and farm type.

The basic unit underlying the FSS is the agricultural holding: a technical-economic unit, under single management, engaged in agricultural production. The FSS covers all agricultural holdings with a utilised agricultural area of at least 1 hectare (ha) and also those holdings with a UAA of less than 1 ha where their market production exceeds certain natural thresholds.

The legal basis for the FSS is Regulation 1166/2008 of 19 November 2008 on farm structure surveys and the survey on agricultural production methods, which repealed Council Regulation 571/88.

Fatal accident at work

A **fatal accident at work** is a physical or mental injury that occurs during work activities, leading to death within one year. It excludes accidents on the way to or from work, occurrences of a strictly medical origin and occupational diseases.

Feed

Feed (or **feedingstuff**) is any substance or product, including additives, whether processed, partially processed or unprocessed, intended to be used for oral feeding to animals.

Fertility

Fertility is the ability to conceive (become pregnant) and give birth to children.

The **total fertility rate** is defined as the mean number of children who would be born to a woman during her lifetime, if she were to spend her childbearing years conforming to the age-specific fertility rates that have been measured in a given year.

The **age-specific fertility rate** or the **fertility rate by age of mother** is the number of births to mothers of age *x* proportional to the average female population of age *x*.

Final consumption expenditure

Final consumption expenditure consists of expenditure by resident institutional units on goods or services that are used for the direct satisfaction of individual needs or wants or the collective needs of members of the community.

Final energy consumption

Final energy consumption is the total energy consumed by end users, such as households, industry and agriculture. It is the energy which reaches the final consumer's door and excludes that which is used by the energy sector itself.

Final energy consumption excludes energy used by the energy sector, including for deliveries, and transformation. It also excludes fuel transformed in the electrical power stations of industrial auto-producers and coke transformed into blast-furnace gas where this is not part of overall industrial consumption but of the transformation sector.

Final energy consumption in the category 'households, services, etc.' covers quantities consumed by private households, commerce, public administration, services, agriculture and fisheries.

Fish catch

Fish catch (or simply **catch**) refers to catches of fishery products including fish, molluscs, crustaceans and other aquatic animals, residues and aquatic plants, that are taken:

- for all purposes (commercial, industrial, recreational and subsistence);

- by all types and classes of fishing units (including for example fishermen, vessels, gear); that are
- operating in inland, fresh and brackish water areas, and in inshore, offshore and high-seas fishing areas.

Production from aquaculture is excluded. Catch is normally expressed in live weight and derived by the application of conversion factors to the actual landed or product weight. As such, the catch statistics exclude quantities of fishery products which are caught but which, for a variety of reasons, are not landed.

Fishery products

In the context of external trade statistics, **fishery products** consist of:

- edible fishery products, including
- fresh, chilled, frozen, salted, smoked and dried fish,
- fish preserves and conserves,
- fresh, chilled, frozen, dried and smoked crustaceans and molluscs,
- preparations and conserves of crustaceans and molluscs;
- inedible products, including
- meals and solubles,
- oils and fats,
- sponges, corals, and so on;
- aquatic plants

Fishing area

Geographical **fishing areas** in the European Union common fisheries policy are defined for a number of specific areas of water:

- the *north-east Atlantic*, which is roughly the area to the east of 42°W longitude and north of 36°N latitude, including the waters of the Baltic Sea;
- the *north-west Atlantic*, which is the region that is roughly the area to the west of 42°W longitude and north of 35°N latitude;
- the *eastern central Atlantic*, which is the region to the east of 40°W longitude between latitudes 36°N and 6°S;
- the *Mediterranean*, which is also known as the Food and Agriculture Organization Major Fishing Area 37, comprises the Mediterranean Sea and the adjacent Black Sea.

Fishing fleet

The data on the number of fishing vessels, the **fishing fleet**, in general refer to the fleet size as recorded on 31 December of the specified reference year. The data are derived from the national registers of fishing vessels which are maintained according to Council Regulation 26/2004 which specifies the information on vessel characteristics to be recorded in the registers.

Foreign direct investment (FDI)

Foreign direct investment, abbreviated as **FDI**, is an international investment within the balance of payment accounts. Essentially, a resident entity in one economy seeks to obtain a lasting interest in an enterprise resident in another economy. A lasting interest implies the existence of a long-term relationship between the direct investor and the enterprise, and an investor's significant influence on the management of the enterprise.

A direct investment enterprise is one in which a direct investor owns 10 % or

more of the ordinary shares or voting rights (for an incorporated enterprise) or the equivalent (for an unincorporated enterprise).

FDI flows and positions: through direct investment flows, an investor builds up a FDI position that has an impact on an economy's international investment position. This FDI position (or FDI stock) differs from the accumulated flows because of revaluation (changes in prices or exchange rates), and other adjustments like rescheduling or cancellation of loans or debt-equity swaps.

Forest

Forest is defined as land with tree crown cover (meaning all parts of the tree above ground level including for example its leaves and branches), or equivalent stocking level, of more than 10 % and with an area of more than 0.5 hectares (ha). The trees should be able to reach a minimum height of 5 metres at maturity *in situ*.

Fossil fuel

Fossil fuel is a generic term for non-renewable natural energy sources such as coal, natural gas and oil that were formed from plants and animals (biomass) that existed in the geological past (for example, hundreds of million of years ago). Fossil fuels are carbon-based and currently supply most human energy requirements.

Freshwater resources

Freshwater resources refers to the total volume of water available in a territory, resulting from internal flow (water from precipitation minus evapotranspiration in a territory) as well as external inflow (water inflow from neighbouring territories).

Fruit

For the purposes of Eurostat's statistics on food and agriculture, **fruit** includes apples, pears, stoned fruits (for example peaches or apricots), nuts (for example walnuts or hazelnuts), other top fruits (for example figs or kiwi - top fruit are fruit that grow on trees), other soft fruit (including fruit that grow on bushes such as berries, currants), citrus fruits, grapes, olives, and wild fruits.

Full-time equivalent (FTE)

A **full-time equivalent**, sometimes abbreviated as **FTE**, is a unit to measure employment or students in a way that makes them comparable although they may work or study a different number of hours per week.

The unit is obtained by comparing the number of hours worked or studied by a person to the average number of hours of a full-time worker or student. A full-time person is therefore counted as one FTE, while a part-time person gets a score in proportion to the hours he or she works or studies. For example, a part-time worker employed for 20 hours a week where full-time work consists of 40 hours, is counted as 0.5 FTE.

The workforce of an enterprise, activity, or country for example can then be added up and expressed as the number of full-

time equivalents. In the context of education the FTE unit attempts to standardise a student's actual course load in comparison with the normal course load.

Galileo

The **Galileo** programme is Europe's initiative for a global satellite navigation system, providing an accurate, guaranteed global positioning service under civilian control.

Gender gap

Gender gap may refer to any statistical disparities between men and women. Usually, however, it refers to differences in labour market statistics, such as the gender pay gap, employment and unemployment.

Gender pay gap (GPG)

The **gender pay gap**, abbreviated as **GPG**, refers to the difference in average wages between men and women. The unadjusted gender pay gap is calculated as the difference between the average gross hourly earnings of male and female paid employees as a percentage of average gross hourly earnings of male paid employees.

General government sector

The **general government sector** by convention includes all the public corporations that are not able to cover at least 50 % of their costs by sales, and, therefore, are considered non-market producers. It has four subsectors: central government; state government; local government; social security funds.

In the European system of accounts (ESA95), paragraph 2.68), the general government sector has been defined as containing 'all institutional units which are other non-market producers whose output is intended for individual and collective consumption, and mainly financed by compulsory payments made by units belonging to other sectors, and/or all institutional units principally engaged in the redistribution of national income and wealth'.

Generation of income account

The **generation of income account** of the national accounts shows the types of primary incomes and the sectors, sub-sectors or industries in which the primary incomes originate, as distinct from the sectors or sub-sectors destined to receive such incomes. It includes as uses the compensation of employees and the taxes less subsidies on production and imports and as resources the gross value added (GVA) and net value added (NVA) for sectors and industries and the gross domestic product (GDP) and net domestic product (NDP) for the total economy, which are the balancing items of the production account. It analyses the extent to which value added and domestic product can cover compensation of employees and taxes on production and imports less subsidies. The balancing items of the generation of income account are the gross operating surplus (GOS), net operating surplus (NOS), gross mixed income and net mixed income, which are the surpluses/

deficits on production activities before account has been taken of paid or received interest, rents or charges on financial or tangible non-produced assets.

Goods loaded

Goods placed on a railway vehicle and dispatched by rail. Unlike in road and inland waterway transport, transshipments from one railway vehicle directly to another and change of tractive vehicle are not regarded as unloading/loading. However, if the goods are unloaded from a railway vehicle, loaded on another mode of transport and, again loaded on another railway vehicle, this is considered as unloading from the first railway vehicle followed by loading on the second railway vehicle.

Goods placed on a road vehicle and dispatched by road. Transshipment from one goods road vehicle to another or change of the road tractor are regarded as loading after unloading.

Goods placed on an inland waterways transport (IWT) vessel and dispatched by inland waterways. Transshipment from one IWT vessel to another is regarded as loading after unloading. The same applies to changes of pusher tugs or tugs.

Goods placed on a merchant ship for transport by sea. Transshipment from one merchant ship to another is regarded as loading after unloading. Goods loaded include national goods, transshipment goods (national or foreign goods arriving in port by sea) and land transit goods (foreign goods arriving in port by road, rail, air or inland waterway).

Government

Government consists of all departments and agencies responsible for the administration of an economic territory (usually a country). According to the level, it can be further subdivided into: central government; state government; local government.

Greenhouse gas (GHG)

Greenhouse gases are a group of gases which are believed to contribute to global warming and climate change.

There are six **greenhouse gases** covered by the Kyoto Protocol, an environmental agreement adopted by many of the parties to the United Nations Framework Convention on Climate Change (UNFCCC) in 1997 to curb global warming.

- The non-fluorinated gases: carbon dioxide (CO_2); methane (CH_4); nitrous oxide (N_2O).
- The fluorinated gases: hydrofluorocarbons (HFCs); perfluorocarbons (PFCs); sulphur hexafluoride (SF_6).

Converting them to carbon dioxide (or CO_2) equivalents makes it possible to compare them and to determine their individual and total contributions to global warming.

Gross capital formation

Gross capital formation in the national accounts is measured by the total value of the gross fixed capital formation, changes in inventories and acquisitions less disposals of valuables for a unit or sector.

Net capital formation is reached by deducting the consumption of fixed capital.

Gross domestic expenditure on R & D (GERD)

Gross domestic expenditure on R & D (GERD) includes expenditure on research and development by business enterprises, higher education institutions, as well as government and private non-profit organisations.

Gross domestic product (GDP)

Gross domestic product, abbreviated as **GDP**, is a basic measure of a country's overall economic health.

As an aggregate measure of production, GDP is equal to the sum of the gross value-added of all resident institutional units (in other words industries) engaged in production, plus any taxes, and minus any subsidies, on products not included in the value of their outputs. Gross value-added is the difference between output and intermediate consumption.

GDP is also equal to:

- the sum of the final uses of goods and services (all uses except intermediate consumption) measured in purchasers' prices, minus the value of imports of goods and services;
- the sum of primary incomes distributed by resident producer units.

Gross electricity generation

Gross electricity generation or **gross electricity production** refers to the process of producing electrical energy. It is the total amount of electrical energy produced by transforming other forms of energy, for example nuclear or wind power. It is commonly expressed in gigawatt-hours (GWh) in other words 1 thousand million (10^9) watt-hours.

Total gross electricity generation covers gross electricity generation in all types of power plants. The **gross electricity generation at plant level** is defined as the electricity measured at the outlet of the main transformers, in other words including the amount of electricity used in the plant auxiliaries and in the transformers.

Gross fixed capital formation (GFCF)

Gross fixed capital formation (GFCF) consists of resident producers' investments, deducting disposals, in fixed assets during a given period. It also includes certain additions to the value of non-produced assets realised by producers or institutional units. Fixed assets are tangible or intangible assets produced as outputs from production processes that are used repeatedly, or continuously, for more than one year.

Gross inland energy consumption

Gross inland energy consumption, sometimes abbreviated as **gross inland consumption**, is the total energy demand of a country or region. It represents the quantity of energy necessary to satisfy inland consumption of the geographical entity under consideration.

Gross inland energy consumption covers: consumption by the energy sector itself; distribution and transformation losses; final energy consumption by end users; statistical differences (not already captured in the figures on primary energy consumption and final energy consumption).

Gross inland consumption does not include energy (fuel oil) provided to international maritime bunkers. It is calculated as follows:

primary production + recovered products + net imports + variations of stocks - bunkers.

The difference between gross inland energy consumption and **gross (energy) consumption** is that in gross energy consumption the transformation output (electricity or heat produced from other energy sources) is included. Therefore, gross energy consumption is a product-specific consumption and does not reflect the demand for primary energy.

Gross national electricity consumption

Gross national electricity consumption includes the total gross national electricity generation from all fuels (including auto-production), plus electricity imports, minus exports. Auto-production is defined as a natural or legal person generating electricity essentially for his/her own use. Gross electricity generation is measured at the outlet of the main transformers, in other words it includes consumption in the plant auxiliaries and in transformers.

Gross national income (GNI)

Gross national income, abbreviated as **GNI**, is the sum of incomes of residents of an economy in a given period. It is equal to GDP minus primary income payable by resident units to non-resident units, plus primary income receivable from the rest of the world.

It is conceptually identical to gross national product (GNP, the concept in ESA 79), though GNP was calculated differently in ESA 79.

Gross operating rate - structural business statistics

The **gross operating rate** is the ratio of the gross operating surplus to turnover, expressed as a percentage.

Gross operating surplus – structural business statistics

Gross operating surplus or **gross operating profits** is defined, in the context of structural business statistics, as value added minus personnel costs. It is the surplus generated by operating activities after the labour factor input has been recompensed.

Gross operating surplus can be calculated from value added at factor cost. It is the balance available to a unit which allows it to recompense the providers of own funds and debt, to pay taxes and eventually to finance all or a part of its investment.

Income and expenditure classified as financial or extraordinary in company accounts is excluded from gross operating surplus.

Gross operating surplus (GOS) - national accounts

Gross operating surplus, abbreviated as **GOS**, can be defined in the context of national accounts as a balancing item in the generation of income account representing the excess amount of money generated by incorporated enterprises' operating activities after paying labour input costs. In other words, it is the capital available to financial and non-financial corporations which allows them to repay their creditors, to pay taxes and eventually to finance all or part of their investment.

GOS differs from profits shown in company accounts for several reasons. Only a subset of total costs are subtracted from gross output to calculate the GOS. Essentially GOS is gross output *less* the cost of intermediate goods and services to give gross value added, and *less* compensation of employees. It is *gross* because it makes no allowance for consumption of fixed capital (CFC). By deducting CFC from GOS one calculates **net operating surplus (NOS)**.

A similar concept for unincorporated enterprises (for example small family businesses like farms and retail shops or self-employed taxi drivers, lawyers and health professionals) is **gross mixed income**. Since in most such cases it is difficult to distinguish between income from labour and income from capital, the balancing item in the generation of income account is mixed by including both, the remuneration of the capital and labour (of the family members and self-employed) used in production. By deducting CFC from gross mixed income one obtains **net mixed income**.

Gross value added at market prices

Gross value added (GVA) at market prices is output at market prices minus intermediate consumption at purchaser prices; it is a balancing item of the national accounts' production account:

- **GVA at producer prices** is output at producer prices minus intermediate consumption at purchaser prices. The producer price is the amount receivable by the producer from the purchaser for a unit of a product minus *value added tax (VAT)*, or similar deductible tax, invoiced to the purchaser.
- **GVA at basic prices** is output at basic prices minus intermediate consumption at purchaser prices. The basic price is the amount receivable by the producer from the purchaser for a unit of a product minus any *tax on the product* plus any *subsidy on the product.*

GVA at factor costs is not a concept explicitly used in national accounts. It can be derived by subtracting *other taxes on production* from GVA at basic prices and adding *other subsidies on production.*

GVA can be broken down by industry. The sum of GVA at basic prices over all industries plus taxes on products minus subsidies on products gives gross domestic product. Gross value added of the total economy usually accounts for more than 90 % of GDP.

By subtracting consumption of fixed capital from GVA the corresponding **net value added (NVA)** is obtained. NVA can also be measured at producer prices or basic prices or factor costs.

Gross-gross weight

The **gross-gross weight** includes the total weight of the goods, all packaging, and tare-weight of the transport unit (for example containers, swap bodies and pallets for containing goods as well as road goods vehicles carrying goods and transported by rail).

The **gross weight** is the total weight of goods carried, including packaging but excluding the tare weight of the transport unit.

The **tare weight** is the weight of a transport unit before any cargo is loaded.

Groundwater

Groundwater is freshwater found beneath the earth's surface - specifically in the cracks and spaces in soil, sand and rock - that supplies wells and springs. The definition applies to all permanent and temporary water deposits, formed both artificially and naturally, of sufficient quality for at least seasonal use. Groundwater supplies are replenished, or recharged, by rain and melting snow, depending on climate conditions. They can usually be recovered from, or via, an underground formation.

Harmonised index of consumer prices (HICP)

The **harmonised index of consumer prices**, abbreviated as **HICP**, is the consumer price index as it is calculated in the European Union, according to a harmonised approach and a single set of definitions. It is mainly used to measure inflation.

There are several types of HICP depending on the geographic area under consideration. The most important ones are:

- the **Monetary Union index of consumer prices (MUICP)** — an aggregate index covering the countries in the euro area;
- the **European index of consumer prices (EICP)** — for the whole European Union (the euro area plus the other Member States);
- the national HICPs — for each of the EU Member States.

In addition to the EU HICPs, an additional HICP aggregate index for the European Economic Area is calculated:

- the **European Economic Area index of consumer prices (EEAICP)**, which in addition to the EU also covers Iceland and Norway.

Healthcare

Healthcare in a country comprises the sum of activities performed either by institutions or individuals pursuing, through the application of medical, paramedical and nursing knowledge and technology, the purposes/core functions of:

- promoting health and preventing disease;
- curing illness and reducing premature mortality;
- caring for persons affected by chronic illness who require nursing care;
- caring for persons with health-related impairment, disability, and handicaps who require nursing care;
- assisting patients to die with dignity;
- providing and administering public health;

- providing and administering health programs, health insurance and other funding arrangements.

Health-related functions such as the education and training of the health workforce, research and development in health, and environmental health should be distinguished from the core functions; as far as possible they should be excluded when measuring activities belonging to core healthcare functions.

Healthy life years (HLY)

The number of **healthy life years**, abbreviated as **HLY** and also called **disability-free life expectancy** (**DFLE**), is defined as the number of years that a person is expected to continue to live in a healthy condition.

This statistical indicator is compiled separately for men and women, both at birth and at age 65. It is based on age-specific prevalence (proportions) of the population in healthy and unhealthy condition and age-specific mortality information. A healthy condition is defined as one without limitation in functioning and without disability.

The indicator is calculated following the widely used Sullivan method. It is based on measures of the age-specific proportion of population with and without disability and on mortality data. Its interest lies in its simplicity, the availability of its basic data, and its independence of the size and age structure of the population. However, cultural differences in reporting disability can influence the HLY indicator.

High-speed rail

High-speed rail is a rail passenger service running at much higher speeds than normal passenger trains.

The network of the trans-European high-speed rail system includes:

- specially built high-speed lines equipped for speeds generally equal to or greater than 250 km/h;
- specially upgraded high-speed lines equipped for speeds of the order of 200 km/h;
- specially upgraded high-speed lines which have special features as a result of topographical, relief or town-planning constraints, on which the speed must be adapted to each case.

Hospital

Hospitals include licensed establishments primarily engaged in providing medical, diagnostic and treatment services that include physician, nursing, and other health services to in-patients and the specialised accommodation services needed by in-patients.

Hospital bed

Hospital bed numbers provide information on healthcare capacities, in other words on the maximum number of patients who can be treated by hospitals. Hospital beds are those which are regularly maintained and staffed and immediately available for the care of admitted patients. They cover beds accommodating patients who are formally admitted (or hospitalised) to an institution for treatment and/or care and who stay for

a minimum of one night. These include: beds in all hospitals, including general hospitals, mental health and substance abuse hospitals, and other specialty hospitals, irrespective of whether the bed is occupied or not. The statistics presented exclude surgical tables, recovery trolleys, emergency stretchers, beds for same-day care, cots for healthy infants, beds in wards which were closed for any reason, provisional and temporary beds, or beds in nursing and residential care facilities.

A **curative care bed** or **acute care bed** is a hospital bed available for curative care; these form a subgroup of total hospital beds.

Hotels and similar establishments

Hotels and similar establishments are tourist accommodation establishments offering overnight lodgings for the traveller which share common characteristics:

- the accommodation is arranged in rooms;
- the total number of rooms exceeds a specified minimum;
- the establishment comes under a common management;
- certain services are provided, including room service, daily bed-making and cleaning of sanitary facilities;
- establishments are grouped in classes and categories according to the facilities and services provided;
- the accommodation does not fall in the category of specialised establishments.

The category 'hotels and similar establishments' consists of

- hotels, comprising of: hotels, apartment hotels, motels, roadside inns, beach hotels, residential clubs and similar establishments providing hotel services including more than daily bed-making and cleaning of the room and sanitary facilities;
- similar establishments, comprising of: rooming and boarding houses, tourist residence and similar accommodation arranged in rooms and providing limited hotel services including daily bed-making and cleaning of the room and sanitary facilities; this group also includes guest houses, bed & breakfast and farmhouse accommodation.

Hours worked

Hours worked is the number of hours actually worked, defined as the sum of all periods spent on direct and ancillary activities to produce goods and services.

Household

The term **household** is used in different statistical contexts:

- household in national accounts (NA);
- household in social statistics.

Household - social statistics

A **household**, in the context of surveys on social conditions or income such as EU-SILC or household budget surveys, is defined as a housekeeping unit or, operationally, as a social unit that: has common arrangements; shares household expenses or daily needs; lives in a shared common residence.

A household includes either one person living alone or a group of people, not necessarily related, living at the same address with common housekeeping, in other words sharing at least one meal per day or sharing a living or sitting room.

Collective households or **institutional households** (as opposed to **private households**) are, for instance: hospitals, old people's homes, residential homes, prisons, military barracks, religious institutions, boarding houses and workers' hostels.

Household budget survey (HBS)

The **household budget survey** (HBS) is a national survey which focuses on households' expenditure on goods and services, giving a picture of living conditions in the European Union. It is carried out by each Member State and is used to compile weightings for important macro-economic indicators, such as consumer price indices (which are measures of inflation) and national accounts.

Household debt-to-income ratio

The **household debt-to-income ratio** combines non-financial and financial accounts data. It is defined as the ratio of households' debt arising from loans, recorded at the end of a calendar year, to the gross disposable income earned by households in the course of that year. It thereby constitutes a measure of the indebtedness of households, in relation with their ability to pay back their debt's principal sum. The debt-to-income ratio is calculated on the basis of gross debt – that is without taking account of any assets held by households.

Household final consumption expenditure (HFCE)

Household final consumption expenditure, abbreviated as **HCFE**, consists of the total outlay on individual goods and services by resident households, including those sold at below-market prices. HCFE includes imputed expenditures or transactions which do not occur in monetary terms and can therefore not be measured directly.

Household investment rate

The **household investment rate** is defined as gross investment (gross fixed capital formation; mainly dwellings) divided by gross disposable income of the household sector in national accounts. Consumer durables (which include passenger cars) are not considered as part of household investment.

Household net financial assets-to-income ratio

The **household net financial assets-to-income ratio** combines non-financial and financial accounts data. It is defined as the ratio of households' net financial assets – which refers to all financial assets minus all financial liabilities – at the end of a calendar year, to the gross disposable income earned by households in the course of that year. It therefore represents the accumulation of financial assets, after deduction of liabilities, of households as a proportion of their annual income. However, this ratio does not account for non-financial assets such as dwellings.

Household saving

Household saving, total savings of the household sector in national accounts, may be estimated by subtracting consumption expenditure and the adjustment for the change in net equity of households in pension funds reserves from disposable income. The latter consists essentially of income from employment and from the operation of unincorporated enterprises, plus receipts of interest, dividends and social benefits minus payments of income taxes, interest and social security contributions.

Household saving rate

The **household saving rate** is defined as gross household saving divided by gross disposable income, with the latter being adjusted for the change in the net equity of households in pension funds reserves. Saving rates can be measured on either a gross or net basis. Net saving rates are measured after deducting consumption of fixed capital (depreciation).

Household sector

The **household sector** in national accounts encompasses all households and non-profit institutions serving households.

Housing cost overburden rate

The **housing cost overburden rate** is the percentage of the population living in households where the total housing costs (net of housing allowances) represent more than 40 % of disposable income (net of housing allowances).

Human development index (HDI)

The **human development index**, abbreviated as **HDI**, is a summary composite index incorporating statistical measures of life expectancy, literacy, educational attainment and GDP per capita, calculated by the United Nations (UN) under the UN Development Programme. It measures a country's average achievements in three basic aspects of human development: health, knowledge, and a decent standard of living.

Eurostat uses the 2006 HDI classification as the basis for grouping countries by level of development.

The HDI provides an alternative to the common practice of evaluating a country's progress in development only based on per-capita GDP.

Import

Imports are goods which enter the statistical territory of the European Union from a non-member country and are placed under the customs procedure for free circulation within the EU (as a general rule goods intended for consumption), inward processing or processing under customs control (goods for working, processing or repair) immediately or after bonded warehousing.

Inactive

A person is economically **inactive**, according to the International Labour Organization definition, if he or she is not part of the labour force. So inactive persons are neither employed nor unemployed. The inactive population can include pre-school children, school children, students, pensioners and homemakers, for example, provided that they are not working at all and not available or looking for work either; some of these may be of working-age.

Incineration

Incineration is a method of waste disposal that involves the combustion of waste. It may refer to incineration on land or at sea. Incineration with energy recovery refers to incineration processes where the energy created in the combustion process is harnessed for re-use, for example for power generation. Incineration without energy recovery means the heat generated by combustion is dissipated in the environment.

Income approach

The **income approach** to calculate GDP sums the compensation of employees, net taxes on production and imports, gross operating surplus and mixed income. The income-side approach shows how GDP is distributed among different participants in the production process, as the sum of:

- **compensation of employees**: the total remuneration, in cash or in kind, payable by an employer to an employee in return for work done by the latter during the accounting period; the compensation of employees is broken down into: wages and salaries (in cash and in kind); employers' social contributions (employers' actual social contributions and employers' imputed social contributions);
- **gross operating surplus**: this is the surplus (or deficit) on production activities before account has been taken of the interest, rents or charges paid or received for the use of assets;
- **mixed income**: this is the remuneration for the work carried out by the owner (or by members of his/her family) of an unincorporated enterprise; this is referred to as 'mixed income' since it cannot be distinguished from the entrepreneurial profit of the owner;
- **taxes on production and imports less subsidies**: these consist of compulsory (in the case of taxes) unrequited payments to or from general government or institutions of the EU, in respect of the production or import of goods and services, the employment of labour, and the ownership or use of land, buildings or other assets used in production.

Incumbent (in fixed telecommunications)

In telecommunications, the **incumbent** is the company (often a regulated monopoly) active on the market just before it was liberalised, or opened to competition.

Indicator A

Indicator A of the income from agricultural activity corresponds to the deflated (real) net value added at factor cost of agriculture, per total annual work unit; the implicit price index of GDP is used as deflator.

Inequality of income distribution

Inequality of income distribution is the ratio of total income received by the 20 % of the population having the highest income (top quintile) to the total income of the 20 % of the population having the lowest income (bottom quintile). Income is based on equivalised disposable income.

Inflation

Inflation is an increase in the general price level of goods and services. When there is inflation in an economy, the value of money decreases because a given amount will buy fewer goods and services than before. Inflation in an economy is often calculated by examining a basket of goods and services and comparing the changes in the prices of that basket over time.

The **inflation rate** is the percentage change in the price index for a given period compared to that recorded in a previous period. It is usually calculated on a year-on-year or annual basis. For an index value of 183.1 for January of this year, and an index value of 178.4 recorded in January last year, the annual rate of inflation of January this year would be: (183.1 / 178.4 – 1) * 100 = 2.6 %

Similarly, one may compile month-on-month rates of change or average annual rates of change.

Deflation is the opposite of inflation. It is a decrease in the general price level of goods and services and represents an increase in the value of money, where an amount of money can be exchanged for more goods and services.

Information and communication technology (ICT)

Information and communication technology, abbreviated as **ICT**, covers all technical means used to handle information and aid communication. This includes both computer and network hardware, as well as their software.

Innovation

Innovation is the use of new ideas, products or methods where they have not been used before.

For the Community innovation survey (CIS), an innovation is defined as a new or significantly improved product (good or service) introduced to the market, or the introduction within an enterprise of a new or significantly improved process. Innovations are based on the results of new technological developments, new technology combinations, or the use of other knowledge, acquired by the enterprise. The innovations may be developed by the innovating enterprise or by another enterprise. However, purely selling innovations wholly produced and developed by other enterprises is not included as an innovation activity, nor is introducing products with purely aesthetic changes. Innovations should be new to the enterprise concerned: for product innovations they do not necessarily have to be new to the market and for process innovations the enterprise does not necessarily have to be the first one to have introduced the process.

Enterprises carrying out innovation activities cover all types of innovators including

product and process innovators, as well as those enterprises with only ongoing and/or abandoned innovation activities. The proportion of enterprises undertaking innovation activities is also called the propensity (tendency) to innovate.

A **product innovation** is the market introduction of a new or a significantly improved good or service. A **process innovation** is the implementation of a new or significantly improved production process, distribution method or support activity for goods or services.

Intellectual property right

Intellectual property rights, abbreviated as IPRs, refers to the general term for the assignment of property rights through patents, copyrights and trademarks. These property rights allow the holder to exercise a monopoly on the use of the item for a set period. By restricting imitation and duplication IPRs confer monopoly power, but the social costs of monopoly power may be offset by the social benefits of higher levels of creative activity encouraged by the monopoly earnings. Ownership of ideas includes literary and artistic works (protected by copyright), inventions (protected by patents), signs for distinguishing goods of an enterprise (protected by trademarks) and other elements of industrial property.

Interest rate

An **interest rate** is the cost of borrowing or the gain from lending, normally expressed as an annual percentage amount.

Intermediate consumption

Intermediate consumption is an accounting concept which measures the value of the goods and services consumed as inputs by a process of production. It excludes fixed assets whose consumption is recorded as consumption of fixed capital. The goods and services may be either transformed or used up by the production process.

International classification for health accounts (ICHA)

The **international classification for health accounts**, abbreviated as **ICHA**, is a classification managed by the OECD. Its purpose is to define, within the context of the system of national accounts:

- healthcare **financing agents**: who is paying?
- healthcare by **function**: for which services and goods?
- healthcare **service provider industries**: who provides the services?

International classification of diseases (ICD)

The **international classification of diseases**, abbreviated as ICD, is used to classify diseases and other health problems on many types of health and vital (essential to life) records, as well as death certificates. As well as enabling the storage and retrieval of diagnostic information for clinical, epidemiological (which deals with the study of the causes, distribution, and control of disease in populations) and quality purposes, ICD records

also form the basis for compiling national mortality and morbidity statistics by WHO Member States.

International standard classification of education (ISCED)

The International standard classification of education (ISCED) is used to describe different education levels and fields to allow international comparisons to be made.

There are seven ISCED levels of education:

0 **pre-primary education** - for example nursery school education for children up to 3 years old;
1 **primary education** - usually the first stage of compulsory education;
2 **lower secondary education** - building on primary education with a stronger subject focus;
3 **upper secondary education** - generally non-compulsory and with entry requirements;
4 **post-secondary non-tertiary education** - for example vocational training for specific labour markets;
5 **tertiary education (first stage)** - generally university-level, academic and vocational education;
6 **tertiary education (second stage)** - further university-level studies usually leading to doctoral qualifications (PhD).

Fields of education

The ISCED classification comprises 25 fields of education in all (at two-digit level), which can be further refined into the three-digit level. Empirically, ISCED assumes that several criteria exist which can help allocate education programmes to levels of education. Depending on the level and type of education concerned, there is a need to establish a hierarchical ranking system between main and subsidiary criteria (for example typical entrance qualification, minimum entrance requirement, minimum age, and staff qualification) The full classification comprises 25 fields of education (at two-digit level) which can be further refined into the three-digit level. At the highest one-digit level the following nine broad groups of fields of education are distinguished:

0 general programmes;
1 education;
2 humanities and arts;
3 social sciences, business and law;
4 science;
5 engineering, manufacturing and construction;
6 agriculture;
7 health and welfare;
8 services.

Internet access

In the context of the survey on Internet use within households, **Internet access** refers to the possibility for anyone in a household to access the Internet from home. It does not mean connectivity, in other words whether connections can be made in the household's area or street.

Internet users

This covers any **use of the Internet** - whether at home, at work or from anywhere else, whether for private or professional purposes, and regardless of the device or type of connection used.

Invention

An **invention** is a new solution to a technical problem which satisfies the criteria of:

- novelty: the solution must be novel (new);
- inventiveness: it must involve a (non-obvious) inventive step;
- industrial applicability: it must be capable of industrial use.

Job vacancy rate (JVR)

A **job vacancy** is a post, either newly created, unoccupied or about to become vacant, which the employer:

- actively seeks to fill with a suitable candidate from outside the enterprise, including any further necessary steps;
- immediately or in the near future.

Although the definition states that a job vacancy should be open to candidates from outside the enterprise, this does not exclude the possibility of appointing an internal candidate to the post. A post that is open to internal candidates only, however, is not considered a job vacancy.

The **job vacancy rate**, abbreviated as **JVR**, measures the percentage of vacant posts, as defined above, compared with the total number of occupied and unoccupied posts; it is calculated as follows:

JVR = number of job vacancies/(number of occupied posts + number of job vacancies) * 100.

An **occupied post** is a post within an organisation to which an employee has been assigned.

Data on job vacancies and occupied posts are broken down by economic activity, occupation, size of enterprise and region.

Joint forest sector questionnaire (JFSQ)

The **joint forest sector questionnaire (JFSQ)** is an initiative of the International Tropical Timber Organization (ITTO), the United Nations Economic Commission for Europe (UNECE), the Food and Agriculture Organization of the United Nations (FAO) and Eurostat to collect statistics on the world timber situation. Each agency collects data from the countries for which it is responsible, with Eurostat compiling information from EU Member States and EFTA Member States.

Kitchen gardens

Kitchen gardens are areas of an agricultural holding devoted to the cultivation of agricultural products not intended for selling but for consumption by the farm holder and his/her household.

Labour cost

Labour cost or **total labour cost** is the total expenditure borne by employers for employing staff.

Labour cost includes employee compensation (including wages, salaries in cash and in kind, employers' social security contributions), vocational training costs, other expenditure such as recruitment costs, spending on working clothes and employment taxes regarded as labour costs minus any subsidies received.

The Eurostat definition closely follows the international one laid down by the International Conference of Labour Statisticians (Geneva, 1966) in its resolution on the statistics of labour cost.

The labour cost includes both direct and indirect costs.

Direct costs (compensation of employees):

- gross wages and salaries paid in cash;
- direct remuneration (pay) and bonuses;
- wages and salaries in kind (for example company products, housing, company cars, meal vouchers, crèches).

Direct costs are dominated by wages and salaries paid in cash.

Indirect costs:

- employers' actual social contributions (in other words statutory, collectively agreed, contractual and voluntary social security contributions);
- employers' imputed social contributions (mostly guaranteed pay in the event of sickness or short-time working, plus severance pay and compensation instead of notice);
- vocational training costs;
- recruitment costs and work clothes given by the employer;
- taxes paid by the employer (based on their wages and salaries bill or on the numbers they employ) **minus** subsidies received by the employer (intended to refund part or all of the cost of direct pay).

Indirect costs are dominated by employers' actual social contributions, in particular by employers' statutory social security contributions.

Labour force

The **labour force** or the **economically active population**, also shortened to the **active population**, includes both employed and unemployed persons, but not the economically inactive, such as pre-school children, school children, students and pensioners.

Labour force survey (LFS)

A **labour force survey**, abbreviated as **LFS**, is an inquiry directed to households, designed to obtain information on the labour market and related issues through a series of personal interviews.

The European Union (EU) LFS covers all citizens living in private households and excludes those in collective households, such as boarding houses, residence halls and hospitals. The definitions used are common to all EU Member States and are based on international recommendations by the International Labour Organization (ILO).

Labour market

The **labour market** is the real or virtual meeting point, within an economy or market place, where people selling their labour (employees) negotiate and may reach an agreement with those who buy it (employers). Labour markets provide the structure through which workers and employers interact about jobs, working conditions and pay. Other actors are the institutions and processes of collective bargaining, including the roles played by employers' organisations and trade unions. The labour market concept also covers issues such as employment, unemployment, participation rates and wages.

Labour market policy (LMP)

The **labour market policy (LMP)** database covers all labour market measures which can be described as public interventions in the labour market aimed at reaching its efficient functioning and to correct disequilibria and which can be distinguished from other general employment policy measures in that they act selectively to favour particular groups in the labour market.

Public interventions refer to measures taken by general government in this respect which involve expenditure, either in the form of actual disbursements or of forgone revenue (reductions in taxes, social contributions or other charges normally payable). The scope of the database is also limited to labour market measures which are explicitly targeted in some way at groups of persons with difficulties in the labour market – referred to here as target groups. In broad terms, this covers persons who are unemployed, persons in employment but at risk of involuntary job loss, and inactive persons who are currently not part of the labour force (in the sense that they are not employed or unemployed according to the ILO definitions) but who would like to enter the labour market and are disadvantaged in some way.

Labour productivity

Labour productivity measures the amount of goods and services produced by each member of the labour force or the output per input of labour. It can be measured in a variety of ways.

For structural indicators, it may be measured by gross domestic product (GDP), expressed in terms of the purchasing power standard (PPS), either relative to the number of employed persons or to the number of hours worked. In both cases, it is then expressed as an index.

Within national accounts and structural business statistics, labour productivity is often defined as the value added per employed person.

Lagging indicator

A **lagging indicator** is an economic statistical indicator that changes after macro-economic conditions have already changed. Typical examples of lagging indicators are unemployment figures, profits or interest rates. Within short-term statistics the number of persons employed is a typical lagging indicator. The lagging indicator is contrasted with the coincident indicator which changes simultaneously with economic conditions, and the leading indicator which changes in advance of expected economic developments. Lagging indicators are used to confirm economic trends that have already been predicted by leading indicators or shown by coincident indicators. Although they change after the change in the general economic conditions, they are still useful since they are available before complete national accounts data.

Land use/cover area frame survey (LUCAS)

The **land use/cover area frame statistical survey**, abbreviated as **LUCAS**, is a Eu-

ropean field survey program funded and executed by Eurostat. Its objective is to set up area frame surveys for the provision of coherent and harmonised statistics on land use and land cover in the European Union. In addition, it is to provide information on agriculture, the environment, landscapes and sustainable development, ground evidence for calibration of satellite images and a register of points for specific surveys (such as soil and biodiversity) and for the core European in situ data collection network. Land cover and land use are of high importance in the definition and evaluation of common agricultural and environment policies. LUCAS was launched as a pilot in 2001 following Decision 1445/2000/EC of 22 May 2000 on the application of aerial-survey and remote-sensing techniques to the agricultural statistics.

Landfill

Landfill is the deposit of waste into or onto land. It includes specially engineered landfill sites and temporary storage of over one year on permanent sites. The definition covers both landfill in internal sites, in other words where a generator of waste is carrying out its own waste disposal at the place of generation, and in external sites. Landfill is often simply referred to as deposit.

Large enterprises

For statistical purposes, **large enterprises** are those employing 250 persons or more. Enterprises employing fewer than 250 persons are known as small and medium-sized enterprises.

Liability

A **liability** is a present obligation arising from past events, in some cases specified in a written contract. A company's liabilities may include bank loans, short-term debts for goods and services received, as well as the company's loan capital and capital subscribed by shareholders. According to basic accounting principles, a company's equity is equal to assets plus liabilities.

Life expectancy

Life expectancy at a specified age represents the mean number of years still to be lived by a person who has reached the specified age, if subjected throughout the rest of his or her life to the current mortality conditions (age-specific probabilities of dying).

Lifelong learning

Lifelong learning is the lifelong, voluntary and self-motivated pursuit of knowledge for personal or professional reasons. The overall aim of learning is to improve knowledge, skills and competences. The intention to learn distinguishes learning activities from non-learning activities such as cultural activities or sports activities.

Within the domain of lifelong learning statistics, formal education covers education and training in the regular system of schools, universities and colleges. Non-formal education and training includes all taught learning activities which are not part of a formal education programme.

The information collected relates to all education or training regardless of whether it is relevant to the respondent's current or possible future job. Lifelong learning statistics collected by Eurostat do not cover informal learning.

In contrast to lifelong learning as a concept, lifelong learning statistics do not cover informal learning, which corresponds to self-learning (for example through the use of printed material, computer-based learning/training, online Internet-based web education, or visiting libraries).

Livestock density index

The **livestock density index** measures the stock of animals per hectare (ha). It is the ratio of the number of livestock units (LSUs) (converted from the number of animals using standard coefficients) per hectare of utilised agricultural area (UAA). The livestock density index is an indicator for the pressure of livestock farming on the environment. Livestock, through manure production, contributes to climate change (greenhouse gas emissions) and nutrient leaching into water and air. A higher livestock density means that a higher amount of manure is available per ha of UAA, which increases the risk of nutrient leaching. The actual impact on the environment of livestock farming depends not only on the amount of livestock, but also on farming practices. Therefore, an increase in the livestock index does not necessarily lead to environmental degradation.

Livestock unit (LSU)

The **livestock unit**, abbreviated as **LSU** (or sometimes as **LU**), is a reference unit which facilitates the aggregation of livestock from various species and age via the use of specific coefficients established initially on the basis of the nutritional or feed requirement of each type of animal (see table below for an overview of the most commonly used coefficients). The reference unit used for the calculation of livestock units (=1 LSU) is the grazing equivalent of one adult dairy cow producing 3 000 kg of milk annually, without additional concentrated foodstuffs.

Livestock unit coefficients

Bovine animals	
Under 1 year old	0.400
1 but less than 2 years old	0.700
Male, 2 years old and over	1.000
Heifers, 2 years old and over	0.800
Dairy cows	1.000
Other cows, 2 years old and over	0.800
Sheep and goats	0.100
Equidae	0.800
Pigs	
Piglets having a live weight of under 20 kg	0.027
Breeding sows weighing 50 kg and over	0.500
Other pigs	0.300
Poultry	
Broilers	0.007
Laying hens	0.014
Ostriches	0.350
Other poultry	0.030
Rabbits, breeding females	0.020

Local government

Local government consists of all types of public administration whose responsibility covers only a local part of the economic territory, apart from local agencies of social security funds.

Long-distance call

A **long-distance call** is a telephone call made from one local calling area or network to another.

Marriages

A **marriage** is the act, ceremony or process by which the legal relationship between two persons is formed. The legality of the union may be established by civil, religious or other means as recognised by the laws of each country.

In all European Union and other European countries, contracting a **civil marriage** (before official authorities and on a legal basis) is possible. However, the relation between a civil marriage and a **religious marriage** (before religious representative only) is not the same in all countries. In 15 countries (Denmark, Estonia, Ireland, Greece, Spain, Italy, Cyprus, Latvia, Lithuania, Poland, Slovak, Finland, Sweden and the United Kingdom as well as Norway,) a religious marriage has consequences for the civil marriage in the sense that a religious marriage is recognised by the state as equivalent to a civil marriage. France states that a religious marriage has no consequences for marital status, unless it has been contracted abroad.

The **crude marriage rate** is the ratio of the number of marriages during the year to the average population in that year. The value is expressed per 1 000 inhabitants.

Material deprivation

Material deprivation refers to a state of economic strain and durables strain, defined as the enforced inability (rather than the *choice* not to do so) to pay unexpected expenses, afford a one-week annual holiday away from home, a meal involving meat, chicken or fish every second day, the adequate heating of a dwelling, durable goods like a washing machine, colour television, telephone or car, being confronted with payment arrears (mortgage or rent, utility bills, hire purchase instalments or other loan payments).

The **material deprivation rate** is an indicator in EU-SILC that expresses the inability to afford some items considered by most people to be desirable or even necessary to lead an adequate life. The indicator distinguishes between individuals who cannot afford a certain good or service, and those who do not have this good or service for another reason, for example because they do not want or do not need it.

The indicator adopted by the Social Protection Committee measures the percentage of the population that cannot afford at least three of the following nine items: 1. to pay their rent, mortgage or utility bills; 2. to keep their home adequately warm; 3. to face unexpected expenses; 4. to eat meat or proteins regularly; 5. to go on holiday; 6. a television set; 7. a refrigerator; 8. a car; 9. a telephone.

Severe material deprivation rate is defined as the enforced inability to pay for at least four of the above-mentioned items.

Maturity

Maturity date (final) The date on which a debt obligation is contracted to be extinguished.

Migration

Migration refers to the number of **migrants**, persons changing their residence to or from a given area (usually a country) during a given time period (usually one year).

Immigrants are persons arriving or returning from abroad to take up residence in a country for a certain period, having previously been resident elsewhere. According to the 1998 United Nations recommendations on the statistics of international migration (Revision 1), an individual is a **long-term immigrant** if *he/she stays in his/her country of destination for a period of 12 months or more, having previously been resident elsewhere for 12 months or more*. **Immigration** is the number of immigrants for a given area during the year.

Emigrants are persons leaving the country where they usually reside and effectively taking up residence in another country. According to the 1998 UN recommendations on the statistics of international migration (Revision 1), an individual is a **long-term emigrant** if *he/she leaves his/her country of previous usual residence for a period of 12 months or more*. **Emigration** is the number of emigrants for a given area during the year.

Net migration is the difference between immigration to and emigration from a given area during the year (net migration is positive when there are more immigrants than emigrants and negative when there are more emigrants than immigrants). Since many countries either do not have accurate figures on immigration and emigration, or have no figures at all, net migration has to be estimated. It is usually estimated as the difference between the total population change and the natural increase during the year. Net migration gives no indication of the relative scale of the separate immigration and emigration flows to and from a country; a country may report low net migration but experience high immigration and emigration flows.

A **recognised non-citizen** is a person who is not a citizen of the reporting country nor of any other country, but who has established links to that country which include some but not all rights and obligations of full citizenship. Recognised non-citizens are not included in the number of European Union (EU) citizens.

Minimum wage

The **minimum wage** is the lowest wage that employers are legally obliged to pay their employees. The basic national minimum wage can be fixed at an hourly, weekly or monthly rate, and this minimum wage is enforced by law (the government), often after consultation with the social partners, or directly by national intersectoral agreement (in the European Union (EU) this is the case for Belgium and Greece).

The national minimum wage usually applies to all employees, or at least to a large majority of employees in the country. Some countries have exceptions, for example for younger workers, apprentices or workers with disabilities. Gross amounts are reported, that is, before income tax and social security deductions, which vary between countries.

Mobile phone subscription

A **mobile phone subscription** refers to the use of public mobile telecommunication systems (also called mobiles or cell phones) using cellular technology. In the context of the Telecom survey on telecommunications services:

- active pre-paid cards (where you pay for your calls as you make them) are treated as subscriptions (where you make an advance payment);
- a person may have more than one subscription.

Morbidity

Morbidity is the condition of being diseased. The morbidity rate is the rate or prevalence of a disease.

National accounts

National accounts, often called **macro-economic accounts**, are statistics focusing on the structure and development of economies. They describe and analyse, in an accessible and reliable way, the economic interactions (transactions) within an economy. There are an almost unimaginable large number of these transactions.

The **national accounts sector** refers to the whole economy (a country, the European Union or the euro area) as a sector. All institutional units operating within an economy are classified in a particular **institutional sector**. Breakdowns by institutional sector are given by the sector accounts.

The institutional sectors group institutional units with broadly similar characteristics and behaviour: households and non-profit institutions serving households; non-financial corporations; financial corporations; government.

Transactions with non-residents and the financial claims of residents on non-residents, or vice versa, are recorded in the 'rest of the world' account.

Macro-economic developments, such as economic growth and inflation, are driven by the actions of the individual economic subjects in an economy. Grouping economic subjects with similar behaviour into institutional sectors helps significantly in understanding the functioning of the economy.

Natural population change

Natural population change is the difference between the number of live births and deaths during a given time period (usually one year). It can be either positive or negative. **Natural population increase** is a positive natural change, when the number of live births is larger than the number of deaths during the time period considered. **Natural population decrease** is the opposite, a negative natural change, when number of deaths exceeds the number of births.

Navigable inland waterway

A **navigable inland waterway** is a stretch of water, not part of the sea, which by natural or man-made features is suitable for navigation, primarily by inland waterway vessels. This term covers navigable rivers, lakes, canals and estuaries.

The length of rivers and canals is measured in mid-channel. The length of lakes and lagoons is measured along the shortest navigable route between the most distant points to and from which transport operations are performed. A waterway forming a common frontier between two countries is reported by both.

Waterways also include river estuaries, the boundary (with the sea) being that point nearest the sea where the width of the river is both less than 3 kilometres (km) at low water and less then 5 km at high water.

Nights spent

Nights spent in hotels and similar establishments (also called **tourist nights**) by a resident or non-resident person (an overnight stay), is the number of nights that the person actually spends (sleeps or stays) or is registered (his or her physical presence there is not necessary) in a hotel or similar establishment.

Non-financial business economy

The **non-financial business economy** includes the sectors of industry, construction and distributive trades and services.

This refers to economic activities covered by Sections C to J and L to N and Division 95 of NACE Rev. 2 and the enterprises or its legal units that carry out those activities.

Non-financial services

The **non-financial services** sector includes economic activities, such as computer services, real estate, research and development, legal services and accounting. For European Union statistical purposes, it refers to activities covered by Sections G to I and K of the European Union's classification system NACE Rev. 1.1 and the enterprises or parts of enterprises that carry out those activities. Based on NACE Rev. 2 it covers Sections G to J and L to N and Division 95.

Non-profit institutions serving households (NPISH)

Non-profit institutions serving households, abbreviated as **NPISH**, make up an institutional sector in the context of national accounts consisting of non-profit institutions which are not mainly financed and controlled by government and which provide goods or services to households for free or at prices that are not economically significant. Examples include churches and religious societies, sports and other clubs, trade unions and political parties.

NPISH are private, non-market producers which are separate legal entities. Their main resources, apart from those derived from occasional sales, are derived from voluntary contributions in cash or in kind from households in their capacity as consumers, from payments made by general governments, and from property income.

Occupancy rate

The **occupancy rate** at hotels and similar establishments is calculated as a percentage as follows:

- (total number of nights for residents and non-residents at hotels and similar establishments) * 100 / (total number of bed places at hotels and similar establishments * 365).

Output approach

The **output approach** to calculate GDP sums the gross value added of various sectors, plus taxes and less subsidies on products. The output of the economy is measured using gross value added. Gross value added is defined as the value of all newly generated goods and services less the value of all goods and services consumed in their creation; the depreciation of fixed assets is not included. When calculating value added, output is valued at basic prices and intermediate consumption at purchasers' prices. Taxes less subsidies on products have to be added to value added to obtain GDP at market prices.

Overcrowding rate

The **overcrowding rate** is defined as the percentage of the population living in an overcrowded household.

A person is considered as living in an **overcrowded** household if the household does not have at its disposal a minimum number of rooms equal to:

- one room for the household;
- one room per couple in the household;
- one room for each single person aged 18 or more;
- one room per pair of single people of the same gender between 12 and 17 years of age;
- one room for each single person between 12 and 17 years of age and not included in the previous category;
- one room per pair of children under 12 years of age.

Passenger car

A **passenger car** is a road motor vehicle, other than a moped or a motor cycle, intended for the carriage of passengers and designed to seat no more than nine persons (including the driver). The term passenger car also covers **microcar**s (small cars which, depending on individual Member State legislation, may need no permit to be driven and/ or benefit from lower vehicle taxation), taxis and passenger hire cars, provided that they have fewer than 10 seats. This category also includes vans designed and used primarily for transport of passengers, as well as ambulances and motor homes. Excluded are light goods road vehicles, as well as motor coaches and buses and mini-buses/mini-coaches.

Passenger-kilometre

A **passenger-kilometre**, abbreviated as **pkm**, is the unit of measurement representing the transport of one passenger by a defined mode of transport (for example road, rail, air, sea, or inland waterways) over a distance of one kilometre.

Patent

A **patent** is an intellectual property right, a public title of industrial property that gives its owner the exclusive right to use his/her invention in the technical field for a limited number of years.

A **patent application**, the application for a patent, needs to be for an invention, in

other words a new solution to a technical problem which satisfies the criteria of:

- novelty: the solution must be novel;
- inventiveness: it must involve a non-obvious inventive step;
- industrial applicability: it must be capable of industrial use.

A patent may be granted to a firm, an individual or a public body by a patent office. It remains valid in a given country or area for a limited period of time.

Per capita

When used in conjunction with a statistical indicator, such as GDP or income, **per capita** (Latin, meaning per head) indicates the average per person in a group. The group referred to can be based upon many criteria (gender, age, socio-economic status, or any combination), but it usually is the entire population of a country, region, or the European Union.

Permanent crops

Permanent crops are ligneous crops not grown in rotation, but occupying the soil and yielding harvests for several (usually more than five) consecutive years. Permanent crops mainly consist of fruit and berry trees, bushes, vines and olive trees. Permanent crops are usually intended for human consumption and generally yield a higher added value per hectare than annual crops. They also play an important role in shaping the rural landscape (through orchards, vineyards and olive tree plantations) and helping to balance agriculture within the environment.

Permanent grassland

Permanent grassland and meadow is land used permanently (for several, usually more than five, consecutive years): to grow herbaceous forage crops, through cultivation (sown) or naturally (self-seeded); not included in the crop rotation scheme on the agricultural holding. Permanent grassland and meadow can be either used for grazing by livestock, or mowed for hay or silage (stocking in a silo).

Personnel costs - structural business statistics

In the context of structural business statistics (SBS), **personnel costs** can be defined as the total remuneration, in cash or in kind, payable by an employer to an employee (regular and temporary employees, as well as home-workers) in return for work done by the latter during the reference period. **Personnel costs** are made up of wages, salaries and employers' social security costs. They include taxes and employees' social security contributions retained by the employer, as well as the employer's compulsory and voluntary social contributions.

Persons living in households with low work intensity

The indicator **persons living in households with low work intensity** is defined as the share of persons with the work intensity of the household below the threshold set at 0.20.

The work intensity of the household refers to the ratio between on the one hand the number of months that all working age

household members have been working during the income reference year and on the other hand the total number of months that could theoretically have been worked by the same household members. A working age person is defined as a person aged 18-59, not being a student aged between 18 and 24. Households composed only of children, of students aged less then 25 and/or people aged 60 or more are totally excluded from the indicator computation.

Physical trade balance

Physical trade balance, abbreviated as PTB is calculated by taking the amount of imports in physical units minus exports in physical units.

Physician

A **physician** or (medical) doctor has a degree in medicine. Physicians may be described as practising, professionally active or licensed.

A **practising physician** provides services directly to patients as consumers of healthcare. These services include:

- conducting medical examinations and making diagnoses;
- prescribing medication and treating diagnosed illnesses, disorders or injuries;
- giving specialised medical or surgical treatment for particular illnesses, disorders or injuries;
- giving advice on and applying preventive medical methods and treatments.

A **professionally active physician** is a practising physician or any other physician for whom medical education is a prerequisite for the execution of the job (practising medicine as defined above or, for example, verifying medical absences from work, drug testing, or medical research).

A **licensed physician** is a physician who is licensed to practise; this category includes practising physicians, professionally active physicians, as well as all registered physicians who are entitled to practise as healthcare professionals.

Pig

A **pig** is a domesticated animal of the species *Sus*. A distinction is made between pigs, piglets, fattening pigs and breeding pigs.

Police officer

Police officers generally include all ranks of police officers including criminal police, traffic police, border police, gendarmerie, uniformed police, city guard, and municipal police. They exclude civilian staff, customs officers, tax police, military police, secret service police, part-time officers, special duty police reserves, cadets, and court police.

Population change

Population change is defined as the difference between the size of the population at the end and the beginning of a given time period (usually one year). There are two components of population change: natural population change; net migration.

Population change is equal to the sum of the natural population change (number of births minus number of deaths) and net migration (number of immigrants minus number of emigrants), including corrections. A negative population change occurs when both population change and net migration are negative or when one is negative and has a higher absolute value than the other positive one.

Poultry

Poultry, in the context of EU statistics, refers to domestic birds of the species: *Gallus gallus* (hens and chickens); *Meleagris spp.* (turkeys); *Anas spp.* and *Cairina moschata* (ducks); *Anser anser dom.* (geese); *Coturnix spp.* (quails); *Phasianus spp.* (pheasants); *Numida meleagris dom.* (guineafowl); *Columbinae spp.* (pigeons); *Struthio camelus* (ostriches). It excludes, however, birds raised in confinement for hunting purposes and not for meat production.

Precipitation

Precipitation is defined as the total volume of atmospheric wet precipitation (mainly rain, snow and hail) and is usually measured by meteorological or hydrological institutes.

Price level index (PLI)

The **price level index**, abbreviated as **PLI**, expresses the price level of a given country relative to another (or relative to a group of countries like the EU), by dividing the purchasing power parities by the current nominal exchange rate.

If the price level index of a country is higher than 100, the country concerned is relatively expensive compared to the one to which it is compared (for example the EU), while if the price level index is lower than 100 the country is relatively cheap compared to the other country.

Price level indices are not intended to rank countries strictly. In fact, they only provide an indication of the order of magnitude of the price level in one country in relation to others, particularly when countries are clustered around a very narrow range of outcomes. The degree of uncertainty associated with the basic price data and the methods used for compiling PPPs, may affect in such a case the minor differences between the PLIs and result in differences in ranking which are not statistically or economically significant.

Primary production of energy

Primary production of energy is any extraction of energy products in a useable form from natural sources. This occurs either when natural sources are exploited (for example, in coal mines, crude oil fields, hydro power plants) or in the fabrication of biofuels.

Transforming energy from one form into another, such as electricity or heat generation in thermal power plants (where primary energy sources are burned), or coke production in coke ovens, is not primary production.

Principal European Economic Indicators (PEEI)

Principal European Economic Indicators, abbreviated as **PEEI**, constitute a set of economic indicators for the European Union and its Member States which also are essential for monitoring the euro area. In 2002, Eurostat produced an initial list

of 19 principal indicators, which has since been expanded to 26 (of which 22 are currently available); they are published regularly and posted on a specific PEEI page on the Eurostat website.

Since 2002, PEEIs have been regularly monitored and improved, in terms of coverage as well as timeliness. The list of indicators include gross domestic product, private final consumption, external trade balance and three-month interest rates.

Prison population

For statistical purposes, the **prison population** is defined as the total number of adult and juvenile prisoners (including pre-trial detainees) at 1 September of a given year. The definition includes offenders held in prison administration facilities, other facilities, juvenile offenders institutions, drug addicts institutions and psychiatric or other hospitals. It excludes, however, non-criminal prisoners held for administrative purposes (for example, people held pending an investigation into their immigration status).

Prodcom

Prodcom is a survey, with an annual frequency at the least, for the collection of statistics on the production of industrial (mainly manufactured) goods, both in value and quantity terms, in the European Union (EU). It is abbreviated from the French term '**Prod***uction* **Com***munautaire*'.

The Prodcom survey is based on a list of products called the **Prodcom list** which comprises about 4 500 headings relating to industrial products. These products are detailed at an eight-digit level. The first four digits refer to the equivalent class within the statistical classification of economic activities in the European Community (NACE), and the next two digits refer to subcategories within the statistical classification of products by activity (CPA). Most Prodcom headings correspond to one or more combined nomenclature (CN) codes.

Producer price index (PPI)

The **producer price index**, abbreviated as **PPI** and also called **output price index**, is a business-cycle indicator whose objective is to measure the monthly development of transaction prices of economic activities.

The PPI is not only an early indicator of inflationary pressures in the economy before it reaches the consumer, but it can also record the development of prices over longer time periods.

The domestic output price index for an economic activity measures the average price development of all goods and related services resulting from that activity and sold on the domestic market. The non-domestic price index shows the average price development (converted to local currency) of all goods and related services resulting from that activity and sold outside of the domestic market. When combined, these two indices show the average price development of all goods and related services resulting from an activity.

The following rules apply for the definition of prices:

- The appropriate price is the basic price that excludes VAT and similar deductible taxes directly linked to turnover

as well as all duties and taxes on the goods and services invoiced by the unit, whereas subsidies on products received by the producer, if there are any, should be added.

- If transport costs are included, this should be part of the product specification,
- In order to show the true development of price movements, it should be an actual transaction price, and not a list price.
- The output price index should take into account quality changes in products.
- The price collected in period t should refer to orders booked during period t (moment of order), not the moment when the commodities leave the factory gates.
- For output prices of the non-domestic market, the price should be calculated at national frontiers, fob (free on board).

The index should in principle reflect the average price during the reference period. In practice the information actually collected may refer to a particular day in the middle of the reference period that should be determined as a representative figure for the reference period. For products with a significant impact on the national economy that are known to have, at least occasionally, a volatile price development, it is important that the index does indeed reflect average prices.

Production account

The **production account** records the activity of producing goods and services as defined within national accounts; it is drawn up for institutional sectors and for industries. Its resources include gross output and taxes on products less subsidies on products and its uses include intermediate consumption. The production account is used to obtain one of the most important balancing items in the system – gross value added, or the value generated by any unit engaged in a production activity – and gross domestic product. Value added is economically significant for both the institutional sectors and the industries.

Productivity

Productivity is the output produced from each unit of input, for example, the number of cars assembled by one worker in a year. In statistical analysis, productivity may refer to capital productivity, labour productivity, resource productivity (of which energy productivity is a specific case), depending on the input considered.

Profit share of non-financial corporations

The **profit share of non-financial corporations** is defined as gross operating surplus divided by gross value added. Profits/gross operating surplus are the complement of wages costs that remunerate labour, plus net taxes on production that (partially) finance government services.

Profitability

Profitability refers to the degree to which an enterprise makes a financial gain from bringing goods and services to market af-

ter all expenses of doing so have been taken into consideration. Profitability may be defined as the proportion between revenues obtained from output and expenses associated with the consumption of inputs.

Public expenditure on education

Public expenditure on education generally refers to:

- direct expenditure on educational institutions: bearing directly the current and capital expenses of educational institutions;
- transfers to private households and firms: supporting students and their families with scholarships and public loans, as well as transferring public subsidies for educational activities to private firms or non-profit organisations.

Both types of transactions constitute total public expenditure on education.

Purchasing power parities (PPPs)

Purchasing power parities (PPPs) indicate how many currency units a given quantity of goods and services costs in different countries. Using PPPs to convert expenditure expressed in national currencies into an artificial common currency, the purchasing power standard (PPS), eliminates the effect of price level differences across countries created by fluctuations in currency exchange rates.

Purchasing power parities are obtained by comparing price levels for a basket of comparable goods and services that are selected to be representative of consumption patterns in the various countries. PPPs make it possible to produce meaningful indicators (based on either price or volume) required for cross-country comparisons, truly reflecting the differences in the purchasing power of, for example, households. Monetary exchange rates cannot be used to compare the volumes of income or expenditure because they usually reflect more elements than just price differences, for example, volumes of financial transactions between currencies and expectations in the foreign exchange markets.

Purchasing power standard (PPS)

The **purchasing power standard**, abbreviated as **PPS**, is an artificial currency unit. Theoretically, one PPS can buy the same amount of goods and services in each country. However, price differences across borders mean that different amounts of national currency units are needed for the same goods and services depending on the country. PPS are derived by dividing any economic aggregate of a country in national currency by its respective purchasing power parities. PPS is the technical term used by Eurostat for the common currency in which national accounts aggregates are expressed when adjusted for price level differences using PPPs. Thus, PPPs can be interpreted as the exchange rate of the PPS against the euro.

R & D intensity

R & D (Research and Development) intensity for a country is defined as the R & D expenditure as a percentage of gross domestic product (GDP). For an

enterprise, R & D intensity is the ratio of an enterprise's R & D expenditure to its revenue (the percentage of revenue that is spent on R & D). R & D is the main driver of innovation, and R & D expenditure and intensity are two of the key indicators used to monitor resources devoted to science and technology worldwide. Governments are increasingly referring to international benchmarks when defining their science polices and allocating resources.

The European Union is currently lagging behind both the USA and Japan in terms of expenditure on R & D as a proportion of GDP, primarily due to slow relative growth in business R & D expenditure. The European Council set an overall target for R & D intensity of 3 % of GDP by the year 2010, with industry asked to contribute two thirds of this objective.

Radio frequency identification (RFID)

Radio frequency identification (RFID) is an automatic identification method, relying on storing and remotely retrieving data using devices called RFID tags or transponders. A RFID tag is an object that can be applied to or incorporated into a product for the purposes of identification using radio waves.

Railway

A **railway line** is a line of communication made up by rail exclusively for the use of railway vehicles. **Lines** are one or more adjacent running tracks forming a route between two points. Where a section of network comprises two or more lines running alongside one another, there are as many lines as routes to which tracks are allotted exclusively. A **running track** is a track providing end-to-end line continuity designed for trains between stations or places indicated in tariffs as independent points of departure or arrival for the conveyance of passengers or goods. A **track** is a pair of rails over which rail borne vehicles can run.

Relative median at-risk-of-poverty gap

The **relative median at-risk-of-poverty gap** is calculated as the difference between the median equivalised disposable income of persons below the at-risk-of-poverty threshold and the at-risk-of-poverty threshold, expressed as a percentage of the at-risk-of-poverty threshold (cut-off point: 60 % of national median equivalised disposable income).

Relative median income ratio

The **relative median income ratio** is defined as the ratio of the median equivalised disposable income of persons aged 65 and over to the median equivalised disposable income of those aged below 65.

Renewable energy sources (RES)

Renewable energy sources (RES), also called **renewables**, are energy sources that replenish (or renew) themselves naturally, such as solar, wind, and tidal energy. Renewable energy sources include the following:

- **biomass and wastes**: organic, non-fossil material of biological origin,

which may be used for heat production or electricity generation; comprises wood and wood waste, biogas, municipal solid waste and biofuels; includes the renewable part of industrial waste;

- **hydropower**: the electricity generated from the potential and kinetic energy of water in hydroelectric plants (the electricity generated in pumped storage plants is not included);
- **geothermal energy**: the energy available as heat from within the earth's crust, usually in the form of hot water or steam;
- **wind energy**: the kinetic energy of wind converted into electricity in wind turbines;
- **solar energy**: solar radiation exploited for solar heat (hot water) and electricity production.

Research and development (R & D)

Research and development, abbreviated as **R & D**, includes creative work carried out on a systematic basis in order to increase the stock of knowledge of man, culture and society, and the use of this knowledge to devise new applications.

Intramural research and development (R & D) expenditure is all the expenditure on R & D within a statistical unit or economic sector, whatever the source of funds. Also included is money spent outside the unit or sector but in support of intramural R & D (for example, purchase of supplies for R & D). Both current and capital expenditures are included.

Research and development (R & D) personnel and researchers

Research and development (R & D) personnel consists of all individuals employed directly in the field of research and development, including persons providing direct services, such as managers, administrators, and clerical staff.

R & D researchers can be employed in the public or the private sector - including academia - to create new knowledge, products, processes and methods, as well as to manage the projects concerned.

Researcher

A **researcher** is a professional engaged in the conception or creation of new knowledge, products, processes, methods and systems, as well as in the management of the projects concerned.

Reserve currency

A **reserve currency** is a foreign currency held by a government or central bank as part of a country's reserves. The United States dollar is the most common global reserve currency, but the euro is increasingly widely used. **Foreign official reserves** form part of the financial assets which a country holds with respect to the rest of the world. The main parts are holdings of foreign exchange and gold.

Resident institutional unit

A **resident institutional unit** is an institutional unit that is resident because it has a centre of economic interest in

the economic territory of a country (or a grouping like the European Union (EU) or the euro area).

The sectors of an economy are composed of two main types of institutional units:

- households and individuals who make up a household;
- legal and social entities, such as corporations and quasi-corporations (for example branches of foreign direct investors), non-profit institutions, and the government of that economy.

These institutional units must meet certain criteria to be considered resident units of the economy. Residence is a particularly important attribute of an institutional unit in the balance of payments because the identification of transactions between residents and non-residents underpins the system. Residence is also important in the European system of national and regional accounts (ESA95) because the residency status of producers determines the limits of domestic production and effects the measurements of gross domestic product (GDP) and many important flows. The concept of residence is based on a sectoral transactor's centre of economic interest. It is necessary to recognise the economic territory of a country as the relevant geographical area to which the concept of residence is applied. An institutional unit is a resident unit when it has a centre of economic interest in the economic territory of a country.

The institutional unit is an elementary economic decision-making centre characterised by similarity of behaviour and decision-making autonomy in the exercise of its main function. A resident unit is regarded as constituting an institutional unit if it has decision-making autonomy for its main function and either keeps a complete set of accounts or it would be possible and meaningful, from both an economic and legal viewpoint, to make a complete set of accounts if they were needed.

Retail trade

Retail trade is defined as a form of trade in which goods are mainly purchased (bought) and resold to the consumer or end-user, generally in small quantities and in the state in which they were purchased by the retailer (or following minor transformations).

Risk-phrase

Risk-phrase, sometimes abbreviated as **R-phrase**, refers to the labelling, via a phrase or sentence, of dangerous substances according to the risks they present. Dangerous substances can be classified according to the type of risk and each category has a code with an associated risk-phrase, a label with a standardised meaning in different languages. The list of risk-phrases for the European Union (EU), which is also widely used outside Europe, was first published in Directive 67/548/EEC and later updated and consolidated in Annex III of Directive 59/2001 of 6 August 2001.

Road transport type

There may be different **types of transport**:

- **Transport for hire or reward**: the carriage for remuneration of persons or goods (on behalf of third parties).
- **Transport on own account**: transport which is not for hire or reward.

Roaming charge

A **roaming charge** refers to the cost of using mobile communications (typically with a mobile phone) to automatically make and receive voice calls, send and receive data, or access other services when travelling outside the geographical area of the user's home network by using a different network in the location they are visiting.

Roundwood production

Roundwood production (the term is also used as a synonym for **removals** in the context of forestry) comprises all quantities of wood removed from the forest and other wooded land, or other tree felling site during a defined period of time.

Sawnwood

Sawnwood is wood that has been produced either by sawing lengthways or by a profile-chipping process and, with a few exceptions, is greater than 6 millimetres (mm) in thickness.

Seasonal adjustment

Seasonal adjustment (or the adjustment of seasonal changes) is a statistical method for removing the effects of recurring seasonal influences which have been observed in the past from an economic time series, thus showing non-seasonal trends more clearly.

The level and direction of the seasonal effects depend on several factors such as the economic activity (for example the turnover of hotels typically increases during holidays, while the industrial production index develops more weakly during the summer). Seasonal effects vary between economies and countries (for example depending on which industries are particularly important in the economic structure) and between indicators.

Seasonal effects are one of the four main components that determine the development of economic indicators (apart from the general trend, cyclical effects and irregular component) and seasonal adjustment are a central element of time series analysis.

Self-employed

A **self-employed** person is the sole or joint owner of the unincorporated enterprise (one that has not been incorporated in other words formed into a legal corporation) in which he/she works, **unless** they are also in paid employment which is their main activity (in that case, they are considered to be employees).

Self-employed persons also include:

- unpaid family workers;
- outworkers (who work outside the usual workplace, such as at home);
- workers engaged in production done entirely for their own final use or own capital formation, either individually or collectively.

SESAR

The **SESAR** project is the European air traffic control infrastructure modernisation programme. SESAR aims at developing the new generation air traffic management system capable of ensuring the safety and fluidity of air transport worldwide over the next 30 years.

Severe housing deprivation rate

Severe housing deprivation rate is defined as the percentage of population living in the dwelling which is considered as overcrowded, while also exhibiting at least one of the housing deprivation measures. Housing deprivation is a measure of poor amenities and is calculated by referring to those households with a leaking roof, no bath/shower and no indoor toilet, or a dwelling considered too dark.

Sewage sludge

Sewage sludge refers to the accumulated settled solids separated from various types of waste water, and which are either moist or partly liquefied as a result of natural or artificial processes.

Sheep

Sheep are domesticated animals of the species *Ovis aries* kept in flocks mainly for their wool or meat.

Sheep (of all ages) are divided into:

- **Breeding females** – which are female sheep (called **ewes**). These include: ewes that have lambed (been bred from); ewes and ewe lambs (kept) for breeding; cull ewes (unproductive ewes sent for slaughter).
- **Other sheep** - all sheep other than breeding females.

Short-term business statistics (STS)

Short-term business statistics, or simply **short-term statistics** , abbreviated as **STS**, are a set of indicators, usually with a monthly or quarterly frequency, used for closely tracking the business cycle of an economy (a single country, the European Union or the euro area). In order to be relevant, they have to reflect current developments with the shortest possible delays.

STS indicators are important tools for formulating and monitoring economic and monetary policies. They are in great demand by policymakers (national and regional governments, the European Commission, central banks (particularly the European Central Bank), private enterprises, professional organisations and financial markets.

The indicators covered by STS are for example the production index, turnover, new orders, hours worked, number of persons employed, gross wages and output prices. They are collected for the all major sectors of the non-financial business economy (industry, construction, trade and services).

Single market

The **single market**, or **internal market** as it is often called, is one of the cornerstones of the European Union. It refers to the free movement of people, goods, services and capital within the EU, the so-called 'four freedoms' laid down in the Treaty of Rome. This has been achieved by eliminating barriers and simplifying existing rules so that everyone in the EU can make the most of the opportunities offered to them as a result of direct access to 27 countries and 500 million people.

The enabling instrument for the single market was the Single European

act, which came into force in July 1987. Among other things it called for:

- extending the powers of the Community in some policy areas (social policy, research, environment);
- gradually establishing the single market over a period up to the end of 1992, by means of a vast legislative programme involving the adoption of hundreds of directives and regulations; and
- making more frequent use of majority voting in the Council of Ministers.

EU policies in the areas of transport, competition, financial services and consumer protection underpin the single market.

Small and medium-sized enterprises (SMEs)

Small and medium-sized enterprises are enterprises employing fewer than 250 persons. According to European Commission Recommendation 2003/361/EC of 6 May 2003, enterprises are defined with regard to their number of employees, annual turnover, and their independence.

For statistical purposes, small and medium-sized enterprises may be further subdivided into:

- **micro enterprises** (fewer than 10 employees);
- **small enterprises** (10 to 49 employees);
- **medium-sized enterprises** (50 to 249 employees).
- **Large enterprises** are defined as those with 250 or more employees.

Social benefits

Social benefits other than social transfers in kind are transfers made in cash to households to relieve them of the financial burden of certain risks or needs, for example, pensions, family and child allowances, and disabled persons' allowances.

Social benefits are paid out by social security funds, other government units, non-profit institutions serving households (NPISHs), employers administering unfunded social insurance schemes, insurance enterprises or other institutional units administering privately funded social insurance schemes.

Social contributions

Social contributions are paid on a compulsory or voluntary basis by employers, employees and self- and non-employed persons. There are two types of social contributions, actual and imputed, paid by the employer for the benefit of their employees:

- **Actual social contributions** or actual payments consist of payments made by employers for the benefit of their employees to insurers (social security funds and private funded schemes). These payments cover statutory, conventional, contractual and voluntary contributions in respect of insurance against social risks or needs.
- Employers' **imputed social contributions** represent the counterpart to unfunded social benefits paid directly by employers to their employees or former employees and other eligible persons without involving an insurance enterprise or autonomous pension fund, and without creating a special fund or segregated reserve for the purpose.

Social protection

Social protection can be defined as the coverage of precisely defined risks and needs associated with: sickness/healthcare and invalidism; disability; old age; parental responsibilities; the loss of a spouse or parent; unemployment; housing; social exclusion.

Social protection benefits

Social protection benefits are transfers to households, in cash or in kind, intended to relieve them of the financial burden of several risks and needs as defined in ESSPROS. These include disability, sickness/healthcare, old age, survivors, family/children, unemployment, housing and social exclusion not covered elsewhere.

Social protection expenditure

Social protection expenditure is the outlay for social protection interventions. It consists mainly of:

- social benefits, or transfers in cash or in kind, to households and individuals with the aim to relieve them of the burden of a defined set of risks or needs;
- administration costs, or costs of managing or administering the social protection scheme; and
- other miscellaneous expenditure by social protection schemes (payment of property income and other).

Social security fund

A **social security fund** is a central, state or local institutional unit whose main activity is to provide social benefits. It fulfils the two following criteria:

- by law or regulation (except those about government employees), certain population groups must take part in the scheme and have to pay contributions;
- general government is responsible for the management of the institutional unit, for the payment or approval of the level of the contributions and of the benefits, independent of its role as a supervisory body or employer.

Social transfers

Social transfers cover the social help given by central, state or local institutional units. They include: old-age (retirement) and survivors' (widows' and widowers') pensions; unemployment benefits; family-related benefits; sickness and invalidity benefits; education-related benefits; housing allowances; social assistance; other benefits.

Sourcing

Sourcing refers to the total or partial movement of core or support business functions of a resident enterprise currently performed in-house to either non-affiliated (external suppliers) or affiliated enterprises located either domestically or abroad.

International sourcing is sourcing to affiliated or non-affiliated enterprises located abroad. This definition excludes, however, the movement of core or support business functions abroad without a reduction of activity and/or jobs in the enterprise concerned - for example, if a new production line is set up abroad without reductions, even if the line also could have been set up in the country for which statistics are compiled, then this

does not constitute international sourcing. International sourcing is sometimes also called **off-shoring**, **near-shoring**, **delocalisation** or **outsourcing**.

Stability and growth pact (SGP)

The **Stability and growth pact**, abbreviated as **SGP**, is a rule-based framework for the coordination of national fiscal policies under economic and monetary union and the creation of the euro area with its single currency, the euro. It was established to safeguard sound public finances, an important requirement for EMU to function properly. The SGP consists of a preventive and a dissuasive arm.

The SGP has to be seen against the background of Stage III of economic and monetary union, which began on 1 January 1999. Its aim is to ensure that the Member States continue their budgetary discipline efforts once the euro has been introduced.

The pact stems from a European Council resolution (adopted at Amsterdam on 17 June 1997) and two Council regulations of 7 July 1997 laying down detailed technical arrangements, one on the surveillance of budgetary positions and coordination of economic policies and the other on implementing the Excessive deficit procedure.

In the medium term, the euro area Member States undertake to achieve a balanced or nearly balanced budget and to give the Council and the European Commission a stability programme every year. Along the same lines, Member States outside the euro area are required to submit a convergence programme.

The Stability and growth pact opens the way for the Council to penalise any euro area Member State that fails to take appropriate measures to end an excessive deficit. Initially, the penalty takes the form of a non-interest bearing deposit with the EU, but it could be converted into a fine if the excessive deficit is not corrected within two years.

Standard international trade classification (SITC)

The **standard international trade classification**, abbreviated as **SITC**, is a product classification of the United Nations used for external trade statistics (export and import values and volumes of goods), allowing for international comparisons of commodities and manufactured goods.

The groupings of SITC reflect: the production materials; the processing stage; market practices and uses of the products; the importance of the goods in world trade; technological changes.

The **main categories** are:

- *food, drinks and tobacco* (Sections 0 and 1 - including live animals);
- *raw materials* (Sections 2 and 4);
- *energy products* (Section 3);
- *chemicals* (Section 5);
- *machinery and transport equipment* (Section 7);
- *other manufactured goods* (Sections 6 and 8).

SITC, Revision 4 was accepted by the United Nations Statistical Commission at its 37th session in 2006 and it is currently being implemented.

Standardised death rate (SDR)

The **standardised death rate**, abbreviated as **SDR**, is the death rate of a population adjusted to a standard age distribution. It is calculated as a weighted average of the age-specific death rates of a given population; the weights are the age distribution of that population. As most causes of death vary significantly with people's age and sex, the use of standardised death rates improves comparability over time and between countries. The reason for this is that death rates can be measured independently of the age structure of populations in different times and countries (sex ratios usually are more stable).

Standardised death rates are calculated on the basis of a standard European population defined by the World Health Organization (WHO).

State government

State government is defined as the separate institutional units that exercise some government functions below those units at central government level and above those units at local government level, excluding the administration of social security funds.

Statistical classification of economic activities in the European Community (NACE)

The **statistical classification of economic activities in the European Community**, abbreviated as **NACE**, designates the classification of economic activities in the European Union. Various NACE versions have been developed since 1970. The term NACE is derived from the French N*omenclature statistique des activités économiques dans la Communauté européenne*.

NACE is a four-digit classification providing the framework for collecting and presenting a large range of statistical data according to economic activity in the fields of economic statistics (for example production, employment and national accounts) and in other statistical domains developed within the European statistical system (ESS).

NACE Rev. 2, a revised classification, was adopted at the end of 2006 and, in 2007, its implementation began. The first reference year for NACE Rev. 2 compatible statistics is 2008, after which NACE Rev. 2 will be consistently applied to all relevant statistical domains.

Previous versions of NACE have been:

- **NACE (1970)**, the original version of NACE (succeeding and integrating the narrower classifications NICE for industry, NCE for trade and commerce, and other specific classifications for agriculture and for services);
- **NACE Rev. 1**, the first revision of NACE (1970);
- **NACE Rev. 1.1**, a minor revision of NACE Rev. 1.

Statistical classification of products by activity (CPA)

The **statistical classification of products by activity**, abbreviated as **CPA**, is the classification of products (goods as well as services) at the level of the European Union. Product classifications are

designed to categorise products that have common characteristics. They provide the basis for collecting and calculating statistics on the production, distributive trade, consumption, foreign trade and transport of such products.

CPA product categories are related to activities as defined by the statistical classification of economic activities in the European Community. Each CPA product - whether a transportable or non-transportable good or a service - is assigned to one single NACE activity. This linkage to NACE activities gives the CPA a structure parallel to that of NACE at all levels.

The CPA is part of an integrated system of statistical classifications, developed mainly under the auspices of the United Nations Statistical Division. This system makes it possible to compare statistics across countries and in different statistical domains.

Structural business statistics (SBS)

Structural business statistics, sometimes abbreviated as **SBS**, describe the structure, activity, competitiveness and performance of economic activities in the European Union, down to the detailed level of several hundred sectors.

Structural business statistics measure the economy through the observation of units engaged in economic activity, which generally are the enterprises. These data are collected within the framework of Council Regulation 58/97 on structural business statistics, recast in Regulation 295/2008. SBS cover the business economy, which includes industry, construction and services (NACE Rev. 1.1 Sections C to K; NACE Rev. 2 Sections B to N and Division 95). Financial services (NACE Rev. 1.1 Section J; NACE Rev. 2 Section K) are included, but because of their specific nature and the limited availability of most types of standard business statistics in this area, are treated separately within SBS. SBS do not cover agriculture, forestry and fishing, nor public administration and (to a large extent) non-market services such as education and health.

Structure of earnings survey (SES)

The **structure of earnings survey**, abbreviated as **SES**, is conducted every four years in the Member States of the European Union (EU) and provides comparable information at EU level on relationships between the level of earnings, individual characteristics of employees (sex, age, occupation, length of service, educational level) and their employer (for example the economic activity or size of the enterprise) for reference years 2002 and 2006 (next survey with reference year 2010).

Surface water

Fresh surface water flows over, or rests on the surface of a land mass, natural waterway (rivers, streams, brooks and lakes) or artificial waterway, including irrigation, industrial and navigation canals, drainage systems and artificial reservoirs.

Surface water abstraction

Surface water abstraction is the removal of water from natural or artificial waterways containing freshwater, including lakes, rivers, streams and canals.

Surplus

Surplus means in general that the sum or balance of positive and negative amounts is positive, or that the total of positives is larger than the total of negatives. Surplus can be used in different statistical areas:

- in balance of payments statistics, it refers to the balance of credit (positive) and debit (negative) transactions of a given economy with the rest of the world, organised in two different accounts: the current account; and the capital and financial account;
- in external trade statistics, it refers to the trade balance of imports (negative, as they have to be paid for) and exports (positive, because they yield revenue), which may result in a trade surplus;
- in government finance statistics, it refers to the public balance between government revenue and expenditure.

Sustainable development

Sustainable development is economic growth and social progress which is sustainable in the future, not only for the present but also the coming generations. It combines economic development with protection of the environment and social justice.

Sustainable development indicator (SDI)

Sustainable development indicators, abbreviated as **SDI**, aim to measure sustainable development over longer periods of time. Indicators are grouped into 10 subject categories: socioeconomic development; sustainable consumption and production; social inclusion; demographic changes; public health; climate change and energy; sustainable transport; natural resources; global partnership; good governance.

System of health accounts (SHA)

The **system of health accounts**, abbreviated as **SHA**, provides for health accounting in the European Union Member States, an economic framework, and accounting rules which are methodologically compatible with the system of national accounts.

The SHA provides a standard framework for producing a set of comprehensive, consistent and internationally comparable accounts to meet the needs of public and private sector health analysts and policymakers. At present, national health accounts are at different stages of development and may not only differ in the boundaries drawn between health and other social and economic activities but also in the classifications used, the level of detail provided, and in the accounting rules. The SHA provides a framework for a family of interrelated tables for standard reporting for expenditure (spending) on health and for its financing. It has been written with the dual aim of providing this framework for international data collections and as a possible model for redesigning and complementing national health accounts to aid policymakers.

The demand for improved health accounts is driven by an increasing complexity of healthcare systems in many countries and the rapid development in medical technology. Policymakers and observ-

ers of healthcare systems and recent reforms have questioned the adequacy of accounting practices and the ability of health accounts to monitor fast-changing healthcare systems that are becoming increasingly complex. Raising consumers' expectations of healthcare contributes to the demand for up-to-date information on healthcare systems.

Tax revenue

Total **tax revenue** is the income a government generates through the taxation of the people. It includes taxes on production and imports, current tax on income and wealth, capital gains tax, and social contributions. Total tax revenue is an aggregate comprising:

- **taxes on production and imports**, such as value added tax (VAT), import duties, excise duties and consumption taxes, stamp taxes, payroll taxes, taxes on pollution, and others;
- **current taxes on income, wealth, etc.**, such as corporate and personal income taxes, taxes on holding gains, payments by households for licences to own or use cars, hunt or fish, current taxes on capital that are paid periodically, and others;
- **capital taxes**, such as inheritance taxes, death duties and taxes on gifts and capital levies that are occasional or exceptional;
- **actual social contributions** paid on a compulsory or voluntary basis by employers or employees or the self- or non-employed to insure against social risks (sickness, invalidity, disability, old age, survivors, family and maternity);
- **imputed or implicit social contributions** payable under unfunded social insurance schemes (in which employers pay social benefits to their employees, ex-employees or their dependants out of their own resources without creating special reserve for the purpose).

The calculation of total tax revenue must be reduced by the amount of **taxes and social contributions assessed as unlikely to be collected**.

Tax wedge

The **tax wedge** is the difference between the employer's labour costs and the employee's net take-home pay, including any cash benefits from government welfare programmes.

Taxes on production and imports

Taxes on production and imports are compulsory, unrequited (not made for a consideration) payments, in cash or in kind, levied (charged) generally by a government or a European Union institution.

The payments are called unrequited because the government or institution provides nothing directly in return for the payment. The taxes are paid on the production and import of goods and services; the employment of labour; the ownership or use of land, buildings or other assets used in production.

Time series

A **time series** is a sequence of data which shows the value of a variable over time.

Normally such data are collected on a regular periodic basis.

Tonnes of oil equivalent (toe)

Tonne(s) of oil equivalent, abbreviated as **toe**, is a normalised unit of energy. By convention it is equivalent to the approximate amount of energy that can be extracted from one tonne of crude oil. It is a standardised unit, assigned a net calorific value of 41 868 kilojoules/kg and may be used to compare the energy from different sources.

Other energy carriers can be converted into tonnes of oil equivalent using the following conversion factors:

- 1 tonne (t) diesel = 1.01 toe
- 1 cubic metre (m^3) diesel = 0.98 toe
- 1 t petrol = 1.05 toe
- 1 m^3 petrol = 0.86 toe
- 1 t biodiesel = 0.86 toe
- 1 m^3 biodiesel = 0.78 toe
- 1 t bioethanol = 0.64 toe
- 1 m^3 bioethanol = 0.51 toe

Total general government expenditure

Total general government expenditure is all the money that a government spends.

Total general government expenditure is defined according to Commission Regulation (EC) No 1500/2000 of 10 July 2000 on general government expenditure and revenue. It comprises the following categories of the European system of accounts 1995 (ESA 95): intermediate consumption; gross capital formation; compensation of employees; other taxes on production; subsidies payable; property income; current taxes on income, wealth, etc.; social benefits other than social transfers in kind; social transfers in kind related to expenditure on products supplied to households via market producers; other current transfers; adjustment for the change in net equity of households in pension fund reserves; capital transfers payable; acquisitions less disposals of non-financial non-produced assets.

Tourism intensity

Tourism intensity, also called **carrying capacity**, is the ratio of nights spent in hotels and similar establishments relative to the total permanent resident population of the area.

Trade balance

The **trade balance** is the difference between the value of the goods that a country (or another geographic or economic area such as the European Union or the euro area) exports and the value of the goods that it imports. If exports exceed imports then the country has a **trade surplus** and the trade balance is said to be positive. If imports exceed exports, the country or area has a **trade deficit** and its trade balance is said to be negative. However, the words 'positive' and 'negative' have only a numerical meaning and do not necessarily reflect whether the economy of a country or area is performing well or not. A trade deficit may for instance reflect an increase in domestic demand for goods destined for consumption and/or production. The total trade balance, including all goods exported and imported, is one of the major components of the balance of payments. A big surplus or deficit for a single product or product category can show a particular national competitive

advantage or disadvantage in the world market for goods.

Trans-European networks (TENs)

The function of **trans-European networks**, abbreviated as **TENs**, is to create a modern and effective infrastructure for transport, energy and telecommunications that link European countries and regions. In the European Union they are essential to the proper operation of the single market, since they ensure free movement of goods, people and services. TENs exist in three sectors of activity:

- **Trans-European transport networks (TEN-T)** cover road and intermodal transport, waterways and seaports, and the European high-speed railway network. Intelligent transport management systems also fall into this category, as does Galileo, Europe's satellite radio navigation system.
- **Trans-European energy networks (TEN-E)** cover the electricity and natural gas sectors. They help to create a single energy market and contribute to security of energy supply.
- **Trans-European telecommunications networks (eTEN)** have as their aim the deployment of telecommunication network-based services.

The construction of trans-European networks is also an important element for economic growth and the creation of employment.

Transport mode

The **transport mode** is the method of transport used for the carriage of goods and passengers.

Transport modes for *both passengers and goods* may include: rail; maritime (sea); road; inland waterways air.

Transport modes for *goods only* include: pipelines.

Passenger road and rail transport include for example passenger cars, powered two wheelers (moped and motor cycles), buses, coaches, trolley-buses, trams (also known as street cars), light railways and metros (also known as subway, metropolitan railway, underground).

The **modal split** of transport describes the relative share of each mode of transport, for example by road, rail or sea. It is based on passenger-kilometres (p-km) for passenger transport and tonne-kilometres (t-km) for freight or goods transport. The modal split is usually defined for a specific geographic area and/or time period.

In practice, an analysis of the modal split may exclude certain modes of transport. For example, the analysis may be limited to inland transport and therefore exclude sea transport.

Unemployment

An **unemployed** person is defined by Eurostat, according to the guidelines of the International Labour Organization, as:

- someone aged 15 to 74 (in Italy, Spain, the United Kingdom, Iceland, Norway: 16 to 74);
- without work during the reference week;
- available to start work within the next two weeks (or has already found a job to start within the next three months);

- actively having sought employment at some time during the last four weeks.

The **unemployment rate** is the number of unemployed persons as a percentage of the labour force.

Urban wastewater treatment

Urban wastewater treatment is all treatment of wastewater in urban wastewater treatment plants, which are usually operated by public authorities or by private companies working by order of public authorities.

Value added tax (VAT)

The **value added tax**, abbreviated as **VAT**, in the European Union is a general, broadly based consumption tax assessed on the value added to goods and services. It applies more or less to all goods and services bought and sold for use or consumption in the EU; goods sold for export or services sold to customers abroad are normally not subject to value added tax. VAT is charged as a percentage of the price, meaning that the actual tax burden is visible at each stage in the production and distribution chain.

EU Directive 2006/112/EC, in effect since 1 January 2007, is the main piece of EU legislation relating to VAT. It guarantees that the VAT contributed by each Member State to the Community's own resources can be calculated, while allowing Member States many possible exceptions and derogations from standard VAT coverage. Rates vary between 15 % and 25 % in Member States. There are also several temporary derogations, for example zero VAT rates for some products in Belgium, Denmark, Ireland, Italy, Malta, Finland, Sweden and the United Kingdom.

Vegetable

For Eurostat purposes **vegetables** include: brassicas (for example cabbage, cauliflower and broccoli); other leafy or stalked vegetables (for example celery, leeks, lettuce, spinach and asparagus); vegetables cultivated for fruit (for example tomatoes, cucumbers, gherkins, melons, aubergine (egg-plant), pumpkins and red pepper); root and tuber vegetables (for example turnips, carrots, onions, garlic, beetroot and radishes); pulses (for example peas and beans); cultivated mushrooms; wild products; and other fresh vegetables.

Vocational education and training (VET)

Vocational education and training, abbreviated as **VET**, sometimes simply called **vocational training**, is the training in skills and teaching of knowledge related to a specific trade, occupation or vocation in which the student or employee wishes to participate. Vocational education may be undertaken at an educational institution, as part of secondary or tertiary education, or may be part of initial training during employment, for example as an apprentice, or as a combination of formal education and workplace learning.

Waste

Waste means any substance or object which the holder disposes of or is required to dispose of pursuant to the provisions of national law in force.

Disposal of waste means:

- the collection, sorting, transport and treatment of waste as well as its storage and tipping above or under ground;
- the transformation operations necessary for its re-use, recovery or recycling.

Wastewater

Wastewater is water that is of no further immediate value to the purpose for which it was used or in the pursuit of which it was produced because of its quality, quantity or time of occurrence. However, wastewater from one user can be a potential supply to another user elsewhere.

Water abstraction

Water abstraction is the process of taking water from a source. For European Union (EU) statistical purposes, it is the groundwater and surface water collected for use by households and enterprises.

Water use

Water use refers to water actually used by end users (for example households, services, agriculture, industry) within a territory for a specific purpose such as domestic use, irrigation or industrial processing.

Water supply, in contrast, is the delivery of water to end users including abstraction for own final use.

Weight

A **weight** in statistical terms is defined as a coefficient assigned to a number in a computation, for example when determining an average, to make the number's effect on the computation reflect its importance.

An illustration of weights and weighting is the calculation of the harmonised index of consumer prices (HICP) performed by Eurostat. The HICP is composed of prices for a selection (referred to as a basket) of items regularly purchased by consumers. However, some items are purchased more frequently than others, while the unit value of items also varies greatly. To account for these issues, the various items in the basket are assigned a weight to reflect the total consumer expenditure on these items.

Working-day adjustment

Working-day adjustment is a statistical method for removing the calendar effect from an economic time series. The **calendar effect** is the variation caused by the changing number of working days in different months or other time periods (quarters, years). Working day adjustment is mainly used in the calculation of short-term statistics (STS), for converting gross figures or indices into their working-day adjusted equivalent. In order to adjust a figure or an index, the calendar nature of a given month is taken into account and calendar effects are removed, whatever their nature. The number of working days for a given month may depend on:

- the timing of certain public holidays (Easter can fall in March or in April, depending on the year);
- the possible overlap of certain public holidays and non-working days (1 May can fall on a Sunday);
- the occurrence of a leap year.

Youth unemployment

Youth unemployment includes all the youth (in other words persons between the ages of 15 and 24, inclusive) who are unemployed.

Youth unemployment rate is the percentage of the unemployed in the age group 15 to 24 years old compared to the total labour force (both employed and unemployed) in that age group. However, it should be remembered that a large share of persons between these ages are outside the labour market (since many youths are studying full time and thus are not available for work), which explains why youth unemployment rates are generally higher than overall unemployment rates, or those of other age groups.

Subject index

A

B

C

D

E

F

G

H

I

J

K

L

M

N

O

P

U

V

W

Y

A selection of Eurostat publications

Eurostat offers various types of publications on a wide range of statistical topics. Below there is a list of references for further reading, relating to some of Eurostat's most recent publications.

All publications are available in PDF format and can be downloaded free of charge from Eurostat's website at http://ec.europa.eu/eurostat. Moreover, the latest publications include a new feature – as access to on-line tables and databases is just one click away from the published table or graph, by means of hyperlinks that are inserted as part of each source.

Paper copies of publications can be ordered via the EU Bookshop at http://bookshop.europa.eu. Both websites allow searches to be made using the catalogue number (for example KS-CD-10-220-EN-C) and offer guidance on how paper copies can be ordered.

News-oriented publications

Three collections are dedicated to the rapid release of key data: news releases, 'Statistics in focus' and 'Data in focus'. They are web-based publications that are freely available on the Eurostat website.

Statistical books

This collection contains publications which provide in-depth analysis, tables, graphs or maps for one or more statistical domains.

Eurostat regional yearbook 2010

Eurostat regional yearbook 2010 gives a detailed picture of a large number of statistical fields in the 27 Member States of the European Union, as well as in candidate and EFTA countries. If you would like to take a closer look at social and economic trends in Europe's regions, this publication is for you! The texts are written by specialists in statistics and are accompanied by maps, figures and tables on each subject. There is a broad set of regional indicators for the following 15 subjects: population, European cities, labour market, gross domestic product, household accounts, structural business statistics, information society, science, technology and innovation, education, transport, tourism, health, agriculture, costal regions, and last but not least, a study on a new urban-rural typology.

Available languages:
DE, EN, FR
KS-HA-10-001-EN-C
Paper version: EUR 20

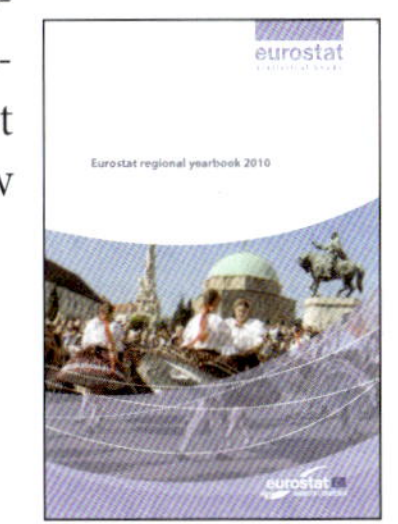

European economic statistics

This flagship publication on European economic statistics gives a wide-ranging overview of economic developments over recent years in the European Union, its Member States and selected partner countries. The publication covers key economic indicators available at Eurostat, including national accounts, government finances, balance of payments, foreign trade, prices, monetary and financial accounts, and the labour market. In addition, editorial and methodological sections provide commentary on topical issues and on the data presented. The statistical annex includes data covering the above mentioned areas.

Available language: EN
KS-GK-10-001-EN-C
Paper version: EUR 20

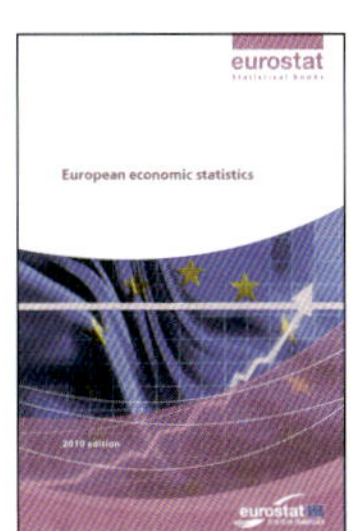

Environmental statistics and accounts in Europe

Environmental statistics and accounts in Europe presents a selection of environmental statistics and accounts available at Eurostat and its partner institutions, such as the Directorate-General for the Environment of the European Commission and the European Environment Agency with its Topic Centres. It is an attempt to provide information on various aspects of the environment to the general public.

Available language: EN
KS-32-10-283-EN-C
Paper version: EUR 20

Income and living conditions in Europe

This publication is about the incomes and living standards of the people of Europe. It treats employment, income inequality and poverty, housing, health, education, deprivation and social exclusion. The reader will learn about many of the social issues confronting Europe. How much income poverty is there in Europe? Is inequality increasing? Does a job guarantee escape from income poverty? How is Europe's welfare state coping with the economic crisis? The book is a timely contribution to the Europe 2020 Agenda as it explores 'the new landscape of EU targets' and the implications for monitoring at EU and national levels.

Available language: EN
KS-31-10-555-EN-C
Paper version: EUR 20

Pocketbooks and brochures

This series of publications (pocketbooks and brochures) are available free of charge. They present essential statistical information from one or more domains and are generally around 100 pages in length. The flagship pocketbook *Key figures on Europe* is also translated into German and French.

Key figures on Europe

KS-EI-11-001-EN-C

Energy, transport and environment indicators

KS-DK-10-001-EN-C

The EU in the world – A statistical portrait

KS-31-10-901-EN-C

Key figures on European business with a special feature on SMEs

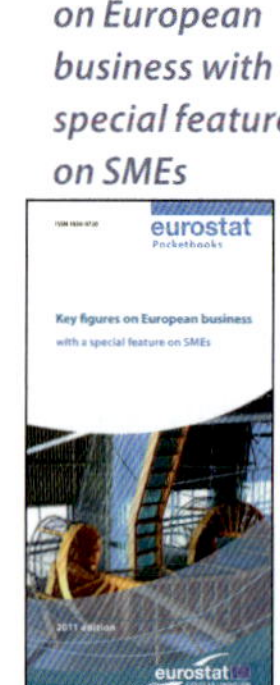

KS-ET-11-001-EN-C

Pocketbook on Euro-Mediterranean statistics

KS-32-10-359-EN-C

Pocketbook on candidate and potential candidate countries

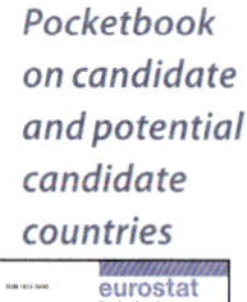

KS-PF-10-001-EN-C

Methodologies & Working papers

Statistical manuals, classifications or nomenclatures are published under the collection 'Methodologies & Working papers'. Intended for specialists, these publications are also only released through the Internet, they are freely available on the Eurostat website.

Please consult the Eurostat website for a full list of publications, at:

http://epp.eurostat.ec.europa.eu/portal/page/portal/publications/collections

European Commission

Europe in figures — Eurostat yearbook 2011

Luxembourg: Publications Office of the European Union

2011 — 692 pp. — 17.6 x 25 cm

Theme: General and regional statistics
Collection: Statistical books

ISBN 978-92-79-18414-7
ISSN 1681-4789
doi:10.2785/12017
Cat. No KS-CD-11-001-EN-C

Price (excluding VAT) in Luxembourg: EUR 30